©Ekaphon maneechot/Shutterstock

Essentials of
Business
Communication 11e

MARY ELLEN GUFFEY & **DANA LOEWY**

Emerita Professor of Business
Los Angeles Pierce College
m.e.guffey@cox.net

Emerita Lecturer, Business Communication
California State University, Fullerton
dloewy@fullerton.edu

 CENGAGE

Australia • Brazil • Mexico • Singapore • United Kingdom • United States

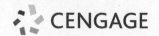

Essentials of Business Communication, **11E**
Mary Ellen Guffey
Dana Loewy

SVP, Higher Ed Product, Content, and Market Development: Erin Joyner

VP, Product Management: Mike Schenk

Product Director: Bryan Gambrel

Product Manager: Heather Mooney

Content Developer Manager: John Rich

Content Developer: Bethany Sexton

Product Assistant: Tawny H. Schaad

Marketing Manager: Eric Wagner

Sr. Content Project Manager: Kim Kusnerak

Production Service: SPi Global

Sr. Art Director: Bethany Bourgeois

Internal Design: Ted & Trish Knapke/Knapke Design

Cover Design: Ted & Trish Knapke/Knapke Design

Cover Image: Ekaphon maneechot/ Shutterstock.com

Internal Images: Writing Plan: REDPIXEL.PL/ Shutterstock.com; Office Insider: Rawpixel .com/Shutterstock.com; Workplace in Focus: Nomad_Soul/Shutterstock.com

Intellectual Property

   Analyst: Diane Garrity

   Project Manager: Sarah Shainwald

For product information and technology assistance, contact us at
Cengage Customer & Sales Support, 1-800-354-9706 or **support.cengage.com.**

For permission to use material from this text or product, submit all requests online at **www.cengage.com/permissions**.

Library of Congress Control Number: 2017952176

Student Edition:
ISBN: 978-1-337-38649-4
Loose Leaf Edition:
ISBN: 978-1-337-38661-6

Cengage
200 Pier 4 Boulevard
Boston, MA 02210
USA

Cengage is a leading provider of customized learning solutions with employees residing in nearly 40 different countries and sales in more than 125 countries around the world. Find your local representative at **www.cengage.com.**

Cengage products are represented in Canada by Nelson Education, Ltd.

To learn more about Cengage platforms and services, register or access your online learning solution, or purchase materials for your course, visit **www.cengage.com.**

Printed at CLDPC, USA, 10-19

Essentials of Business Communication 11e

Dear Business Communication Student:

Chances are that you are no longer holding a textbook in your hands but access the **Eleventh Edition** of *Essentials of Business Communication* via MindTap on your laptop, tablet, or your smartphone. MindTap is a multimedia learning experience that makes studying business communication and sharpening important career skills easier and more fun.

Our well-researched, market-leading e-text saves you money while helping you sharpen important job skills. Whether you access *Essentials of Business Communication*, 11e on mobile devices or own a print copy of this award-winning text, you are on your way to developing essential communication skills that will not only serve you well in college but will also stay with you in your chosen career.

Mary Ellen Guffey and Dana Loewy

Here are a few of the major features you can expect from the No. 1 business communication book in this country and abroad:

- **Workplace readiness.** The marketplace today is challenging. One way to outshine the competition is by offering superior communication skills to future employers. Your business communication course and this book are the ideal tools for making yourself job ready.

- **Communication technology and best practices.** Obviously, the workplace is relying on technology and digital media. It is social and mobile. You may be tech savvy, but are you familiar with workplace-appropriate best practices? Even if you know your way around mobile devices and social media, you still need to be able to write well and make a positive impression. This book not only covers the latest workplace technology but above all it stresses solid writing skills and good grammar.

- **Latest trends in job searching.** Chapter 13 presents the most current trends, technologies, and practices affecting the job search, résumés, and cover letters that will help you stand out. You will learn how to build a personal brand, how to network, and how to write customized résumés and create an effective LinkedIn profile.

- **Hottest trends in job interviewing.** Chapter 14 provides countless tips on how to interview in today's highly competitive job market, including one-way and two-way video interviewing.

The many contemporary examples and model documents, along with writing plans providing step-by-step instructions, will get you started quickly and help you stay focused on the writing process. We wish you well in your course!

Cordially,

Mary Ellen Guffey & Dana Loewy

Dr. Mary Ellen Guffey
Emerita Professor of Business
Los Angeles Pierce College
m.e.guffey@cox.net

Dr. Dana Loewy
Emerita Lecturer, Business Communication
California State University, Fullerton
dloewy@fullerton.edu

What Is MindTap?

MindTap is your personal, customized learning environment. It presents engaging course content along with videos, activities, apps, and other interesting features making learning fun and easy. With MindTap, you can create a unique learning path that will help you understand key concepts in depth and fast, so that you can produce your best work.

The following activities will help you shape and pace your own learning:

- **Aplia homework assignments.** Aplia™ is an online application that improves comprehension and performance by motivating you to stay interested and increase your effort. Aplia provides automatically graded assignments that contain detailed explanations on every question over multiple question sets. In short, you get results without needing your instructor's feedback. These assignments cover chapter content as well as grammar and mechanics.

- **YouSeeU activities.** Learning is easier with visuals. YouSeeU helps you stay on track with videos that draw you in and reinforce what you learn in and out of the classroom. The YouSeeU MindApp allows you to complete oral communication activities for various assignment types that include creating individual videos, responding to question and answer tasks, viewing visual aids, and making group presentations.

- **Write Experience activities.** Write Experience assignments help improve your writing skills. They evaluate the voice, style, format, content, and originality of what you write. Find out how you are doing without needing your instructor's feedback.

- **How-To Videos.** Understand fully how it's done before you write a business document. How-to videos show you expert writing techniques.

- **Writing Plan Reviews.** The writing plans in your textbook structure your writing assignments step by step. The writing plan reviews illustrate the popular *Essentials* writing plans with before-and-after treatments.

- **Writing Workshops.** Helping you learn without an instructor, Writing Workshops bring *Essentials* writing assignments to life with interactive quizzing and in-depth feedback.

- **Narrated PowerPoint slides.** To review important concepts and definitions, you can watch the narrated PowerPoint slides—perfect for traditional and distance learners.

Brief Contents

Contents

Unit 1 Business Communication in the Digital Age

Unit 2 The Writing Process in the Information Age

4 Revising Business Messages 87

Unit 3 Workplace Communication

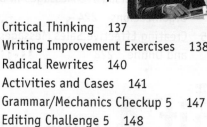

Rawpixel.com/Shutterstock.com

5 Short Workplace Messages and Digital Media 114

6 Positive and Neutral Messages 150

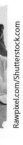

Unit 4 Business Reports and Proposals—Best Practices

GaudiLab/Shutterstock.com

9 Informal Reports 252

Unit 5 Professionalism, Teamwork, Meetings, and Speaking Skills

LuckyImages/Shutterstock.com

Unit 6 Employment Communication

Monkey Business Images/Shutterstock.com

13 The Job Search, Résumés, and Cover Messages 398

14 Interviewing and Following Up 444

Appendixes

End Matter

Are You Job-Ready?

Employers today often complain that many new graduates are simply not job-ready. As a matter of fact, writing, communication, and other so-called soft skills consistently rank high on recruiters' wish lists. Most students realize this and chose this class to develop these necessary workplace skills as efficiently and effectively as possible. *Essentials of Business Communication* is the tool to make this happen.

This time-honored, tried-and-true text will guide you in developing the job-readiness you need for the twenty-first century. *Essentials* highlights best practices and strategies backed by leading-edge research to help you develop professionalism, expert writing techniques, workplace digital savvy, and the latest job-search and résumé-building skills.

Yes, you must be literate in all current communication technologies. The good news is that *Essentials* effectively addresses best practices for social media as well as for mobile technology. You will learn how to build credibility online as well as offline, and understand that writing is central to business success, regardless of the communication channel. It is a foundational skill. Employers want good writers and communicators. This is why *Essentials* continues to provide grammar exercises and documents for editing and grammar practice that our competitors have abandoned. You need a diversity of skills beyond tech savvy alone—now more than ever!

Guided by traditional rigor, *Essentials of Business Communication* addresses both contemporary student needs as well as those of instructors.

Perfecting Professionalism

The Eleventh Edition emphasizes positive workplace behavior and clearly demonstrates the importance of professionalism. Today's businesses desire workers who exhibit strong communication skills and project positive attitudes. Employers seek team members who can effectively work together to deliver positive results that ultimately boost profits and bolster the company's image. Graduates who possess these highly desirable soft skills excel in today's challenging job market. In this edition you will discover how to perfect those traits most valued in today's competitive, mobile, and social workplace.

> "I picked this text with its excellent resources for our new Business Communication class that was added as a core class in the College of Business. All instructors who teach that class use this text. This is the only course in the university that emphasizes professionalism."
> **Dr. Mary Kiker,** *Auburn University, Montgomery*

Unprofessional		Professional
Uptalk, a singsong speech pattern, making sentences sound like questions; *like* used as a filler; *go for said;* slang; poor grammar and profanity.	Speech habits	Recognizing that your credibility can be seriously damaged by sounding uneducated, crude, or adolescent.
Sloppy messages with incomplete sentences, misspelled words, exclamation points, IM slang, and mindless chatter. E-mail addresses such as partyanimal@gmail.com, snugglykitty@icloud.com, or hotmama@outlook.com.	E-mail	Messages with subjects, verbs, and punctuation, free from IM abbreviations; messages that are concise and spelled correctly even when brief. E-mail addresses that include a name or a positive, businesslike expression.
Suggestive Twitter handles and user names that point to an immature, unhealthy lifestyle. Posts that reveal political, religious, and other personal leanings.	Internet, social media	Real name Twitter handles and user names that don't sound cute or like chatroom nicknames. Posts in good taste, fit for public consumption.
An outgoing message with strident background music, weird sounds, or a joke message.	Voice mail	An outgoing message that states your name or phone number and provides instructions for leaving a message.
Soap operas, thunderous music, or a TV football game playing noisily in the background when you answer the phone.	Telephone presence	A quiet background when you answer the telephone, especially if you are expecting a prospective employer's call.
Using electronics during business meetings for unrelated purposes or during conversations with fellow employees; raising your voice (cell yell); forcing others to overhear your calls.	Cell phones, tablets	Turning off phone and message notification, both audible and vibrate, during meetings; using your smart devices only for meeting-related purposes.
Sending and receiving text messages during meetings, allowing texting to interrupt face-to-face conversations, or texting when driving.	Texting	Sending appropriate business text messages only when necessary (perhaps when a cell phone call would disturb others).

Developing Expert Writing Techniques for a Digital Workplace

Abundant before-and-after documents with descriptive callouts create a clear road map to perfecting the writing process. These documents demonstrate how to apply expert writing techniques, as well as highlight the critical significance of the revision process.

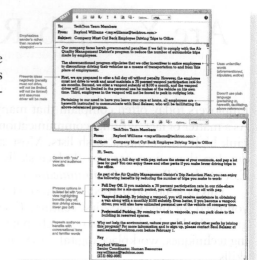

Applying Strategic Writing Plans

Original business message writing plans, initially created by author Mary Ellen Guffey and expanded in this edition, provide efficient step-by-step instructions that enable you to overcome fear and start writing quickly and confidently. The Eleventh Edition now offers ten sets of writing plans that cover a variety of business situations. This signature feature of *Essentials* is especially important for novice writers who lack business experience and composition training.

Direct Claims

OPENING: Describe clearly the desired action.

BODY: Explain the claim, tell why it is justified, and provide details describing the desired action.

CLOSING: End pleasantly with a goodwill statement, and include an end date and action request, if appropriate.

WRITING PLAN

Emphasizing Grammar and Writing Fundamentals

Throughout the text, proven learning features help you review and rebuild vital basic grammar skills. In every chapter *Grammar/Mechanics Checkups* systematically review the fundamentals and are keyed to an authoritative and streamlined Grammar/Mechanics Handbook. *Editing Challenge* and *Radical Rewrite* exercises also provide innumerable opportunities for you to sharpen your grammar, punctuation, spelling, capitalization, and writing skills by editing typical business documents.

> "I really love *Essentials of Business Communication* for my students. I'm always alarmed at how poor their grammar and writing skills are, and this is one of the few books that addresses those skills effectively."
> **Shawnna Patterson,** *Chemeketa Community College, Salem Oregon*

Grammar/Mechanics Checkup 4

Adjectives and Adverbs

Review Sections 1.16 and 1.17 of the Grammar/Mechanics Handbook. Then select the correct form to complete each of the following statements. Record the appropriate G/M section and letter to illustrate the principle involved. When you finish, compare your responses with those provided at the bottom of the page. If your answers differ, study carefully the principles shown in parentheses.

b (1.17e)		EXAMPLE	Surprisingly, most of the (a) *twenty year old*, (b) *twenty-year-old* equipment is still working.
_____	1.		The newly opened restaurant offered many (a) *tried and true*, (b) *tried-and-true* menu items.
_____	2.		Although purchased twenty years ago, the equipment still looked (a) *brightly*, (b) *bright*.
_____	3.		The committee sought a (a) *cost-effective*, (b) *cost effective* solution to the continuing problem.
_____	4.		How is the Shazam app able to process a song so (a) *quick*, (b) *quickly*?
_____	5.		Of the two plans, which is (a) *more*, (b) *most* comprehensive?
_____	6.		Employees may submit only (a) *work-related*, (b) *work related* expenses to be reimbursed.
_____	7.		Amy and Marusia said that they're planning to open (a) *there*, (b) *their* own business next year.
_____	8.		Haven't you ever made a (a) *spur of the moment*, (b) *spur-of-the-moment* decision?
_____	9.		Not all decisions that are made on the (a) *spur of the moment*, (b) *spur-of-the-moment* turn out badly.
_____	10.		The committee offered a (a) *well-thought-out*, (b) *well thought out* plan to revamp online registration.
_____	11.		You must complete a (a) *change of address*, (b) *change-of-address* form when you move.
_____	12.		Employment figures may get (a) *worse*, (b) *worst* before they get better.
_____	13.		I could be more efficient if my printer were (a) *more nearer*, (b) *nearer* my computer.
_____	14.		Naturally, our team members felt (a) *bad*, (b) *badly* when our project was canceled.
_____	15.		The truck's engine is certainly running (a) *smooth*, (b) *smoothly* after its tune-up.

1. b (1.17l) 2. b (1.17c) 3. a (1.17c) 4. b (1.17d) 5. a (1.16) 6. a (1.16) 7. b (1.17g) 8. b (1.17c) 9. a (1.17e) 10. a (1.17e) 11. b (1.17e) 12. a (1.16)
13. b (1.17c) 14. a (1.17c) 15. b (1.17d)

Learning Workplace Best Practices

Most students arrive in the classroom with some work experience and technology skills, but many are not aware of what businesses expect of them when they use digital tools. The Eleventh Edition provides comprehensive guidance in the professional use of e-mail, texting, instant messaging, blogging, and social media. You will master best practices that clearly demonstrate how to avoid damaging your career or hurting your employers' reputation with careless online behavior.

Developing Digital Skills

Regardless of the communication channel, writing proficiency is a must in a workplace dominated by mobile technology and social media. Technology and writing skills go hand in hand in today's professional environment of success. For this reason, *Essentials* provides how-to instructions and best practices for today's digital workplace while also emphasizing good writing and professionalism. This focus is rooted in the belief that today's communicators and their skills are on display 24/7. Credibility takes significant time to build but is easy to lose in an instant.

Writing a Captivating Blog

Using Digital Media Like a Pro: Dos and Don'ts

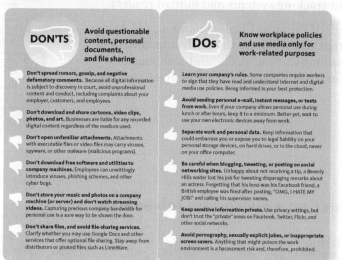

Establish your credibility.

- Zero in on your objective and make your comment as concise as possible.
- Focus only on the facts and be able to support them.

Check posting rules.

- Understand what's allowed by reading the terms and conditions on the site.
- Keep your complaint clean, polite, and to the point.

Provide balanced reviews.

- To be fair, offset criticism with positives to show that you are a legitimate consumer.
- Suggest improvements even in glowing reviews; all-out gushing is suspicious and not helpful.

Consider the reach and permanence of posts.

- Know that your review may be posted indefinitely, even if you change your mind and modify a post later.
- Be open; even anonymous comments can be tracked down. Privacy policies do not protect writers from subpoenas.

Accept offers to help.

- Reply if a business offers to help or discuss the problem; update your original post as necessary.

Refuse payment for favorable critiques.

- Never accept payment to change your opinion or your account of the facts.
- Comply with requests for a review if you are a satisfied customer.

Writing Online Reviews and Complaints

Social media posts have a way of ending up in the wrong hands, making vicious complainers seem irrational. In this edition you learn to write well-considered private social media messages as well as professional responses that increase the credibility and reputation of employers.

Finding a Job in Today's Challenging Job Market

One of the most important chapters in the book, Chapter 13 updates you on the latest trends, technologies, and practices affecting today's job search, résumés, and cover letters. Thorough revisions will prepare you for a labor market that is more competitive, more social, more mobile, and more dependent on technology than ever before. You will learn how to network, employ current technologies, build your own brand, and prepare an effective LinkedIn profile. Many annotated résumé models will guide you in creating and sending customized résumés that appeal to both applicant tracking systems and human readers.

Essentials of Business Communication, 11E helps ensure that you will have the finely honed writing and communication skills and contemporary digital understanding for exceptional job success.

"I was blown away by the exceptional personal service from the author. All of the Guffey supplementary materials are unbelievably helpful. This is one author who works hard to make me look good in my classes."
Staci Groeschell, *South Puget Sound Community College, Olympia, Washington*

Mobile technologies are on the rise.
Candidates use apps to apply for jobs, and recruiters use mobile devices to post jobs, contact candidates, and forward résumés to colleagues.

Networking— it's whom you know.
Recruiters say their best job candidates come from referrals. Now, more than ever, you need to be proactive in making professional connections.

Communication and interpersonal skills are in high demand.
Sales and marketing careers are booming, and these careers demand writing, speaking, and team skills.

Social media presence is a must.
Those who haven't developed a social media presence may be left in the dust.

It's all digital.
Today candidates e-mail their résumés, post them to Internet job boards, or publish them on their own Web pages.

Résumés must please scanners and skimmers.
Overwhelmed with candidates, recruiters hurriedly skim résumés preselected by scanning devices.

Conducting a Successful Job Search

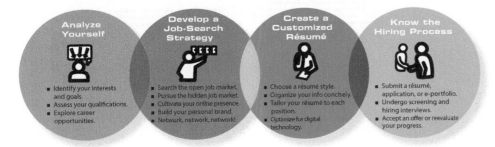

Analyze Yourself
- Identify your interests and goals.
- Assess your qualifications.
- Explore career opportunities.

Develop a Job-Search Strategy
- Search the open job market.
- Pursue the hidden job market.
- Cultivate your online presence.
- Build your personal brand.
- Network, network, network!

Create a Customized Résumé
- Choose a résumé style.
- Organize your info concisely.
- Tailor your résumé to each position.
- Optimize for digital technology.

Know the Hiring Process
- Submit a résumé, application, or e-portfolio.
- Undergo screening and hiring interviews.
- Accept an offer or reevaluate your progress.

Developing Your Own Brand

John Smith Design/Shutterstock.com

Using LinkedIn to Land a Job

Monkey Business Images/Shutterstock.com;
Courtesy of LinkedIn

Making a Career E-Portfolio

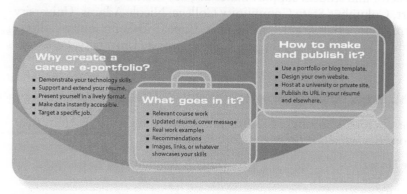

Why Are Instructors Such Great Fans of *Essentials of Business Communication?*

In Their Words...

"As an experienced instructor teaching business communication for the first time, I want to praise the layout and clear instructions provided for *Essentials of Business Communication*. Getting to know a textbook usually takes a lot of time, but I read the Instructor's Manual, and it helped me prepare quickly for my class and get me up to speed—without having to spend valuable time learning how to present the material. The 'how-to' instructions for *Essentials of Business Communication* gave me a comfort level that would otherwise have taken several semesters."

Danielle Shaker, *Naugatuck Valley Community College and Post University, Waterbury, CT*

"One year I decided to try a business communication textbook from another publisher, but I immediately returned to the Guffey text this year. The quality of the content and support resources for *Essentials of Business Communication* just can't be matched."

Laurie Johnson, *Manhattan Area Technical College, Manhattan, Kansas*

"I am astounded at the resources for the instructor. Last quarter, I had to create the examples and documents for revision and business scenarios for document creation. Thanks for allowing me to spend time on planning and instruction rather than on creating quizzes, tests, worksheets, and PowerPoint presentations."

Beverly Miller, *Miller-Motte Technical College, Lynchburg, VA*

Appreciation for Support

No successful textbook reaches a No. 1 position without a great deal of help. We are exceedingly grateful to the reviewers and other experts who contributed their pedagogic and academic expertise in shaping the many editions of *Essentials of Business Communication*.

We extend sincere thanks to outstanding professionals at Cengage Learning, including Erin Joyner, senior vice president, Higher Education; Michael Schenk, vice president, Product Management; Heather Mooney, product manager, Business Communication; John Rich, content development manager; Eric Wagner, marketing manager; Bethany Bourgeois, senior art director; and Kim Kusnerak, senior content project manager. We are also grateful to Crystal Bullen, DPS Associates, who ensured premier quality and excellent accuracy throughout the publishing process. Our very special thanks go to Bethany Sexton, content developer, for her meticulous planning, project management, and always-helpful assistance.

For their expertise in creating superior instructor and student support materials, our thanks go to Jane Flesher, Chippewa Valley Technical College; Carol Hart, Columbus State Community College; Nicole Adams, University of Dayton; Janet Mizrahi, University of California, Santa Barbara; Kathleen Bent, Cape Cod Community College; Susan Schanne, Eastern Michigan University; and Thanakorn Kooptaporn, California State University, Fullerton.

Heartfelt Thanks to Recent Reviewers

We are especially grateful to the following instructors who offered significant relevant suggestions from their hands-on classroom experience in teaching from *Essentials of Business Communication*:

Penny A. Braboy
Thomas More College

Westelle Florez
Harris-Stowe State University

Judy A. Reiman
Columbia College

Susan M. Campbell
Arkansas Tech University

Laurie J. Johnson
Manhattan Area Technical College

Daniel Schlittner
Phoenix Community College

Alma Cervantes
Skyline College

Diana Macdonald
Uintah Basin Applied Technology College

Amy Weaver
Potomac State College

Debbie Cook
Utah State University

Patti McMann
Klamath Community College

Sincere Appreciation to Previous Reviewers

We continue to celebrate and remember the following reviewers who over the years have contributed their expertise in helping create a remarkably successful textbook:

Faridah Awang
Eastern Kentucky University

Karen Bounds
Boise State University

Therese Butler
Long Beach City College

Joyce M. Barnes
Texas A & M University, Corpus Christi

Daniel Brown
University of South Florida

Derrick Cameron
Vance-Granville Community College

Patricia Beagle
Bryant & Stratton Business Institute

Cheryl S. Byrne
Washtenaw Community College

Brennan Carr
Long Beach City College

Nancy C. Bell
Wayne Community College

Jean Bush-Bacelis
Eastern Michigan University

Steven V. Cates
Averett University

Ray D. Bernardi
Morehead State University

Mary Y. Bowers
Northern Arizona University

Irene Z. Church
Muskegon Community College

Lise H. Diez-Arguelles
Florida State University

Dee Anne Dill
Dekalb Technical Institute

Dawn Dittman
Dakota State University

Elizabeth Donnelly-Johnson
Muskegon Community College

Jeanette Dostourian
Cypress College

Nancy J. Dubino
Greenfield Community College

Donna N. Dunn
Beaufort County Community College

Cecile Earle
Heald College

Valerie Evans
Cuesta College

Bartlett J. Finney
Park University

Pat Fountain
Coastal Carolina Community College

Marlene Friederich
New Mexico State University, Carlsbad

Christine Foster
Grand Rapids Community College

JoAnn Foth
Milwaukee Area Technical College

Gail Garton
Ozarks Technical Community College

Nanette Clinch Gilson
San Jose State University

Robert Goldberg
Prince George's Community College

Margaret E. Gorman
Cayuga Community College

Judith Graham
Holyoke Community College

Lauren Gregory
South Plains College

Bruce E. Guttman
Katharine Gibbs School, Melville, New York

Susan E. Hall
University of West Georgia

April Halliday
Georgia Piedmont Technical College

Tracey M. Harrison
Mississippi College

Debra Hawhee
University of Illinois

L. P. Helstrom
Rochester Community College

Jack Hensen
Morehead State University

Rovena L. Hillsman
California State University, Sacramento

Karen A. Holtkamp
Xavier University

Michael Hricik
Westmoreland County Community College

Jodi Hoyt
Southeast Technical Institute

Sandie Idziak
University of Texas, Arlington

Karin Jacobson
University of Montana

Bonnie Jeffers
Mt. San Antonio College

Edna Jellesed
Lane Community College

Jane Johansen
University of Southern Indiana

Pamela R. Johnson
California State University, Chico

Edwina Jordan
Illinois Central College

Sheryl E. C. Joshua
University of North Carolina, Greensboro

Diana K. Kanoy
Central Florida Community College

Ron Kapper
College of DuPage

Jan Kehm
Spartanburg Community College

Karen Kendrick
Nashville State Community College

Lydia Keuser
San Jose City College

Linda Kissler
Westmoreland County Community College

Deborah Kitchin
City College of San Francisco

Frances Kranz
Oakland University

Keith Kroll
Kalamazoo Valley Community College

Rose Marie Kuceyeski
Owens Community College

Richard B. Larsen
Francis Marion University

Mary E. Leslie
Grossmont College

Ruth E. Levy
Westchester Community College

Gary R. Lewis
Southwest Florida College

Maryann Egan Longhi
Dutchess Community College

Nedra Lowe
Marshall University

Elaine Lux
Nyack College

Elizabeth MacDonald
Arizona State University

Margarita Maestas-Flores
Evergreen Valley College

Jane Mangrum
Miami-Dade Community College

Maria Manninen
Delta College

Tim March
Kaskaskia College

Paula Marchese
State University of New York, Brockport

Tish Matuszek
Troy University Montgomery

Kenneth R. Mayer
Cleveland State University

Victoria McCrady
University of Texas at Dallas

Karen McFarland
Salt Lake Community College

Pat McGee
Southeast Technical Institute

Bonnie Miller
Los Medanos College

Mary C. Miller
Ashland University

Willie Minor
Phoenix College

Nancy Moody
Sinclair Community College

Suman Mudunuri
Long Beach City College

Nancy Mulder
Grand Rapids Junior College

Paul W. Murphey
Southwest Wisconsin Technical College

Nan Nelson
University of Arkansas Phillips Community College

Lisa Nieman
Indiana Wesleyan University

Jackie Ohlson
University of Alaska, Anchorage

Richard D. Parker
Western Kentucky University

Martha Payne
Grayson County College

Catherine Peck
Chippewa Valley Technical College

Carol Pemberton
Normandale Community College

Carl Perrin
Casco Bay College

Jan Peterson
Anoka-Hennepin Technical College

Susan Peterson
Scottsdale Community College

Kay D. Powell
Abraham Baldwin College

Jeanette Purdy
Mercer County College

Carolyn A. Quantrille
Spokane Falls Community College

Susan Randles
Vatterott College

Diana Reep
University of Akron

Ruth D. Richardson
University of North Alabama

Carlita Robertson
Northern Oklahoma College

Vilera Rood
Concordia College

Rich Rudolph
Drexel University

Rachel Rutledge
Carteret Community College

Joanne Salas
Olympic College

Rose Ann Scala
Data Institute School of Business

Joseph Schaffner
SUNY College of Technology, Alfred

James Calvert Scott
Utah State University

Laurie Shapero
Miami-Dade Community College

Lance Shaw
Blake Business School

Cinda Skelton
Central Texas College

Estelle Slootmaker
Aquinas College

Margaret Smallwood
The University of Texas at Dallas

Clara Smith
North Seattle Community College

Nicholas Spina
Central Connecticut State University

Marilyn St. Clair
Weatherford College

Judy Sunayama
Los Medanos College

Dana H. Swensen
Utah State University

James A. Swindling
Eastfield College

David A. Tajerstein
SYRIT College

Marilyn Theissman
Rochester Community College

Zorica Wacker
Bellevue College

Lois A. Wagner
Southwest Wisconsin Technical College

Linda Weavil
Elan College

William Wells
Lima Technical College

Gerard Weykamp
Grand Rapids Community College

Beverly Wickersham
Central Texas College

Leopold Wilkins
Anson Community College

Anna Williams
College of Central Florida, Ocala

Charlotte Williams
Jones County Junior College

Donald Williams
Feather River College

Janice Willis
College of San Mateo

Almeda Wilmarth
State University of New York, Delhi

Barbara Young
Skyline College

About the Authors

Dr. Mary Ellen Guffey

A dedicated professional, Mary Ellen Guffey has taught business communication and business English topics for over thirty-five years. She received a bachelor's degree, *summa cum laude*, from Bowling Green State University; a master's degree from the University of Illinois, and a doctorate in business and economic education from the University of California, Los Angeles (UCLA). She has taught at the University of Illinois, Santa Monica College, and Los Angeles Pierce College.

Now recognized as the world's leading business communication textbook author, Dr. Guffey corresponds with instructors around the globe who are using her books. She is the founding author of the award-winning *Business Communication: Process and Product*, the leading business communication textbook in this country. She also wrote *Business English*, which serves more students than any other book in its field; *Essentials of College English*; and *Essentials of Business Communication*, the leading text/workbook in its market. Dr. Guffey is active professionally, serving on the review boards of the *Business and Professional Communication Quarterly* and the *Journal of Business Communication*, publications of the Association for Business Communication. She participates in national meetings, sponsors business communication awards, and is committed to promoting excellence in business communication pedagogy and the development of student writing skills.

Dr. Dana Loewy

Dana Loewy taught business communication at California State University, Fullerton for nineteen years. Previously, she also worked as a composition instructor at various Los Angeles area community colleges, thus reaching a solid quarter century of combined experience teaching writing. Dr. Loewy has also lectured abroad, for example, at Fachhochschule Nürtingen, Germany. Having earned a PhD from the University of Southern California in English with a focus on translation, she is a well-published freelance translator, interpreter, and textbook author. Dr. Loewy has collaborated with Dr. Guffey on recent editions of *Business Communication: Process & Product* as well as on *Essentials of Business Communication*.

Fluent in several languages, among them German and Czech, her two native languages, Dr. Loewy has authored critical articles in many areas of interest—literary criticism, translation, business communication, and business ethics. Active in the Association for Business Communication, Dr. Loewy is now focusing on her consulting practice. Most recently she has advised a German bank and a California-based nonprofit organization on communication strategy and effective writing techniques. Dana is also a business etiquette consultant certified by The Protocol School of Washington.

Business Communication in the Digital Age

1

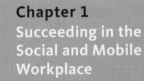

Chapter 1
Succeeding in the Social and Mobile Workplace

Succeeding in the Social and Mobile Workplace

Robert Churchill/GettyImages

Learning Outcomes

After studying this chapter, you should be able to do the following:

1 Describe how strong communication skills will improve your career outlook, strengthen your credibility, and help you succeed in today's competitive digital age marketplace.

2 Confront barriers to effective listening, and start building your listening skills.

3 Explain the features of nonverbal communication, and recognize the importance of improving your nonverbal communication skills.

4 Name five common dimensions of culture, and understand how culture influences communication and the use of social media and communication technology.

5 Discuss strategies that help communicators overcome negative cultural attitudes and prevent miscommunication in today's diverse, mobile, social-media-driven workplace.

1-1 Mastering the Tools for Success in the Twenty-First-Century Workplace

What kind of workplace will you enter when you graduate, and which skills will you need to be successful in it? Expect a fast-paced, competitive, and highly connected digital environment. Communication technology provides unmatched mobility and connects individuals anytime and anywhere in the world. Today's communicators interact using multiple mobile electronic devices and access information stored in remote locations, in the cloud. This mobility and instant access explain why increasing numbers of workers must be available practically around the clock and must respond quickly. Your communication skills will always be on display and will determine your credibility.

This first chapter presents an overview of communication in business today. It addresses the contemporary workplace, listening skills, nonverbal communication, the cultural dimensions of communication, and intercultural job skills. The remainder of the book is devoted to developing specific writing and speaking skills.

1-1a Strong Communication Skills: Your Key to Success

Effective writing skills can be a stepping-stone to great job opportunities; poorly developed writing skills, on the other hand, will derail a career. When competition is fierce, superior communication skills will give you an edge over other job applicants. In survey after survey, recruiters place communication high on their wish lists.[1] In one recent study, employers ranked writing and oral communication among the five top attributes in job seekers, after teamwork and problem-solving skills.[2] Your ability to communicate is a powerful "career sifter."[3] Strong communication skills will make you marketable even in a challenging economic climate.

Perhaps you are already working or will soon apply for your first job. How do your skills measure up? The good news is that you can learn effective communication. This textbook and this course can immediately improve your communication skills. Because the skills you are learning will make a huge difference in your ability to find a job and to be promoted, this will be one of the most important courses you will ever take.

1-1b The Digital Revolution: Why Communication Skills Matter More Than Ever

Since information technology, mobile devices, and social media have transformed the workplace, people in today's workforce communicate more, not less. Thanks to technology, messages travel instantly to distant locations, reaching potentially huge audiences. Work team members can collaborate across vast distances. Moreover, social media are playing an increasingly prominent role in business. In such a hyperconnected world, writing matters more than ever. Digital media require "much more than the traditional literacy of yesterday," and workers' skills are always on display.[5]

As a result, employers seek employees with a broader range of skills and higher levels of knowledge in their field than in the past; hiring standards are increasing.[6] Educators are discussing "essential fluencies"—twenty-first-century skills that include analytical thinking, teamwork, and multimedia-savvy communication.[7] Pew Research found that 90 percent of the Americans polled consider communication the No. 1 skill for a successful life.[8] Billionaire entrepreneur Richard Branson concurs, calling communication "the most important skill any leader can possess."[9] Furthermore, jobs relying heavily on people skills such as communication are less likely to be killed by automation and will offer the most opportunities in the future.[10]

Skills Gap. Unfortunately, a great number of workers can't deliver. More than half of the respondents in an employer survey criticized applicants for their lack of communication, interpersonal, and writing skills. Staffing company Adecco reported that 44 percent of its respondents cited a similar skills gap.[11] Recruiters agree that regardless of the workplace media used, "the ability to communicate an idea, with force and clarity" and with a unique voice is sorely needed.[12] In a PayScale study, 44 percent of bosses felt new graduates lacked writing skills as well as critical-thinking and problem-solving skills (60 percent).[13]

Communication and Employability. Not surprisingly, many job listings require excellent oral and written communication skills. An analysis of 2.3 million LinkedIn profiles revealed that oral and written communication skills were by a large margin the top skill set sought, followed by organization, teamwork, and punctuality.[14] In

LEARNING OUTCOME 1

Describe how strong communication skills will improve your career outlook, strengthen your credibility, and help you succeed in today's competitive digital age marketplace.

OFFICE INSIDER

"Communicating clearly and effectively has NEVER been more important than it is today. Whether it's fair or not, life-changing critical judgments about you are being made based solely on your writing ability."[4]

Victor Urbach, *management consultant*

Note: Small superscript numbers in the text announce information sources. Full citations are near the end of the book. This edition uses a modified American Psychological Association (APA) reference format.

addition, as you will learn in later chapters, recruiters will closely examine your online persona to learn about your communication skills and professionalism. Naturally, they will not hire candidates who write poorly or post inappropriate content.[15] Your reputation and personal credibility are vital assets you must guard.

Techies Write Too. Even in technical fields such as accounting and information technology, you will need strong communication skills. A researcher suggests that "The days of being able to plug away in isolation on a quantitative problem and be paid well for it are increasingly over."[16] In an economy relying on innovation, generating ideas isn't enough; they must be communicated clearly, often in writing.[17] A recruiter in the high-tech industry explains, "Communication is KEY. You can have all the financial tools, but if you can't communicate your point clearly, none of it will matter."[18] A poll of nearly 600 employers showed that they are looking for "communicators with a capital C," people who offer superb speaking, writing, listening, presentation, persuasion, and negotiation skills.[19]

Writing Is in Your Future. Regardless of career choice, you will probably be sending many digital messages, such as the e-mail shown in Figure 1.1. Because electronic mail and other digital media have become important channels of communication

Figure 1.1 Businesslike, Professional E-Mail Message

Uses precise subject line to convey key information quickly

Starts with casual greeting to express friendliness

To: Customer Service Improvement Team
From: Samuel D. Hidalgo <sam.hidalgo@tekmagik–services.com>
Subject: Social Media Strategy Meeting: Wednesday, February 7

Hi, Team,

As recommended at our last meeting, I have scheduled an e-marketing and social media specialist to speak to us about improving our social media responses. Social media consultant Alexis Johnston, founder of Apexx Marketing Solutions, has agreed to discuss ways to turn our social media presence into a competitive advantage. Mark your calendars for the following:

Announces most important idea first with minimal background information

Sets off meeting information for easy recognition and retrieval

Social Media Strategy Meeting
Wednesday, February 7, 11 a.m. to 3 p.m.
Conference Room

In previous meetings our team acknowledged that customers are increasingly turning to our website, blogs, and Facebook pages to locate information, seek support, and connect with us. However, we are experiencing problems in responding quickly and effectively. Ms. Johnston promises to address these concerns. She will also tell us whether we need to establish a presence in additional social media networks. Ms. Johnston will help us decide whether we should hire an in-house social media manager or pay for an external service. To make this meeting most productive, she asks that each team member submit at least three questions or problem areas for discussion.

Provides details about meeting with transition to action requests

Action Requests:

Bullets action requests and places them near message end where readers expect to find them

- Please send three discussion questions to Alan (alan.wong@tekmagik-services .com) by February 2 at 5 p.m. so that he can relay them to Ms. Johnston.

Closes by telling where to find additional information; also expresses appreciation

Because this document shows an internal e-mail, a full signature block is not necessary. Coworkers tend to be connected on the same e-mail system and can easily find one another. E-mails to external audiences require a signature block with full contact information.

- Because we will be ordering box lunches for this meeting, please make your selection on the intranet before February 2.

If you have any questions, drop by my office or send a note. Thanks for your continued efforts to improve our customer service!

Sam

Samuel D. Hidalgo
Director, Customer Service

in today's workplace, all digital business messages must be clear, concise, and professional. Notice that the message in Figure 1.1 is more businesslike and more professional than the quick text or e-mail you might send socially. Learning to write professional digital messages will be an important part of this course.

1-1c What Employers Want: Professionalism

Your future employer will expect you to show professionalism and possess what are often referred to as soft skills in addition to your technical knowledge. Soft skills are essential career attributes that include the ability to communicate clearly, get along with coworkers, solve problems, and take initiative.[20] A PayScale study found that employers considered writing proficiency an indispensable *hard* skill.[21] In a *Wall Street Journal* survey of nearly 900 executives, 92 percent said that soft skills are equally important or more important than technical skills. As a tech sector recruiter put it, "Communications, teamwork, and interpersonal skills are critical—everything we do involves working with other people."[22]

Not every job seeker is aware of the employer's expectations. Some new-hires have no idea that excessive absenteeism or tardiness is grounds for termination. Others are surprised to learn that they are expected to devote their full attention to their duties when on the job. One frustrated Washington, D.C., restaurateur advertised for workers with "common sense." She said "I can teach somebody how to cook soup. But it's hard to teach someone normal manners, or what you consider work ethic."[23]

Projecting and maintaining a professional image can make a real difference in helping you obtain the job of your dreams. Once you get that job, you are more likely to be taken seriously and promoted if you look and sound professional. Don't send the wrong message and risk losing your credibility with unwitting and unprofessional behavior. Figure 1.2 reviews areas you will want to check to be sure you are projecting professionalism. You will learn more about soft skills and professionalism in Chapter 11. The Communication Workshop at the end of this chapter will help you explore your future career and the need for soft skills.

1-1d How Your Education May Determine Your Income

As college tuition rises steeply and student debt mounts, you may wonder whether going to college is worthwhile. Yet the effort and money you invest in earning your college degree will most likely pay off. College graduates earn more, suffer less unemployment, and can choose from a wider variety of career options than workers without a college education. Moreover, college graduates have access to the highest-paying and fastest-growing careers, many of which require a degree.[25] As Figure 1.3 shows, graduates with bachelor's degrees earn nearly three times as much as high school dropouts and are almost four times less likely to be unemployed.[26]

Writing is one aspect of education that is particularly well rewarded. One corporate president explained that many people climbing the corporate ladder are good. When he faced a hard choice between candidates, he used writing ability as the deciding factor. He said that sometimes writing is the only skill that separates a candidate from the competition. A survey of employers confirms that soft skills such as communication ability can tip the scales in favor of one job applicant over another.[27] Your ticket to winning in a competitive job market and launching a successful career is good communication skills.

1-1e Confronting the Challenges of the Information Age Workplace

The workplace is changing profoundly and rapidly. As a businessperson and as a business communicator, you will be affected by many trends, including communication technologies such as social media, expectations of around-the-clock availability, and team projects. Other trends include flattened management hierarchies, global

OFFICE INSIDER

"In a survey conducted by PwC, CEOs cited 'curiosity' and 'open-mindedness' as traits that are becoming increasingly critical. Today's star employees need the full package: hard or technical skills backed up with soft skills and emotional intelligence. It isn't enough to say you're good with people, a resume catch-phrase that's become empty jargon."[24]

Dennis Yang, *chief executive officer of Udemy*

Figure 1.2 Projecting Professionalism When You Communicate

Unprofessional		Professional
Uptalk, a singsong speech pattern, making sentences sound like questions; *like* used as a filler; *go* for *said*; slang; poor grammar and profanity.	Speech habits	Recognizing that your credibility can be seriously damaged by sounding uneducated, crude, or adolescent.
Sloppy messages with incomplete sentences, misspelled words, exclamation points, IM slang, and mindless chatter. E-mail addresses such as *partyanimal@gmail.com, snugglykitty@icloud.com,* or *hotmama@outlook.com.*	E-mail	Messages with subjects, verbs, and punctuation, free from IM abbreviations; messages that are concise and spelled correctly even when brief. E-mail addresses that include a name or a positive, businesslike expression.
Suggestive Twitter handles and user names that point to an immature, unhealthy lifestyle. Posts that reveal political, religious, and other personal leanings.	Internet, social media	Real name Twitter handles and user names that don't sound cute or like chatroom nicknames. Posts in good taste, fit for public consumption.
An outgoing message with strident background music, weird sounds, or a joke message.	Voice mail	An outgoing message that states your name or phone number and provides instructions for leaving a message.
Soap operas, thunderous music, or a TV football game playing noisily in the background when you answer the phone.	Telephone presence	A quiet background when you answer the telephone, especially if you are expecting a prospective employer's call.
Using electronics during business meetings for unrelated purposes or during conversations with fellow employees; raising your voice (cell yell); forcing others to overhear your calls.	Cell phones, tablets	Turning off phone and message notification, both audible and vibrate, during meetings; using your smart devices only for meeting-related purposes.
Sending and receiving text messages during meetings, allowing texting to interrupt face-to-face conversations, or texting when driving.	Texting	Sending appropriate business text messages only when necessary (perhaps when a cell phone call would disturb others).

competition, and a renewed emphasis on ethics. The following overview reveals how communication skills are closely tied to your success in a constantly evolving networked workplace.

- **Social media and changing communication technologies.** New communication technology is dramatically affecting the way workers interact. In our always-connected world, businesses exchange information by e-mail, instant messaging, text messaging, voice mail, powerful laptop computers, netbooks, and smartphones as well as other mobile devices. Satellite communications, wireless networking, teleconferencing, and videoconferencing help workers conduct meetings with associates around the world. Social media sites such as Facebook, Twitter, Instagram, and YouTube as well as blogs, wikis, forums, and peer-to-peer tools help businesspeople collect information, serve customers,

Figure 1.3 The Education Bonus: Higher Income, Lower Unemployment

Education	Median Weekly Earnings	Unemployment Rate
High school dropout	$ 493	8.0%
High school diploma	678	5.4%
Some college, no degree	738	5.0%
Associate's degree	798	3.8%
Bachelor's degree or higher (average)	1,458	2.1%

Source: U.S. Department of Labor, U.S. Bureau of Labor Statistics. (2016, February 5). Employment Projections: Earnings and unemployment rates by educational attainment. Current population survey.

and sell products and services. Figure 1.4 illustrates many technologies you will encounter in today's workplace.

- **Anytime, anywhere availability and nonterritorial offices.** High-speed and wireless Internet access has freed millions of workers from nine-to-five jobs in brick-and-mortar offices. Flexible working arrangements allow them to work at home or on the road. Meet the work shifter, a telecommuter or teleworker who largely remains outside the territorial office. The anytime, anywhere office the work shifter needs requires only a smart mobile device and a wireless connection.[28] If the self-employed are factored in, teleworkers now represent almost 30 percent of the U.S. working adult population.[29] To save on office real estate, some industries provide "nonterritorial" workspaces, or "hot desks." The first to arrive gets the best desk and the corner window.[30] At the same time, 24/7 availability has blurred the line between work and leisure, so that some workers are always on duty.

- **Self-directed work groups and virtual teams. Teamwork has become a reality in business.** Many companies have created cross-functional teams to empower employees and boost their involvement in decision making. You can expect to collaborate with a team in gathering information, finding and sharing solutions, implementing decisions, and managing conflict. You may even become part of a virtual team whose members are in remote locations. Increasingly, organizations are also forming ad hoc teams to solve particular problems. Such project-based teams disband once they have accomplished their objectives.[31] Moreover, parts of our future economy may rely on "free agents" who will be hired on a project basis in what has been dubbed the *gig economy*, a far cry from today's full-time and relatively steady jobs.

- **Flattened management hierarchies.** To better compete and to reduce expenses, businesses have for years been trimming layers of management. This means that as a frontline employee, you will have fewer managers. You will be making decisions and communicating them to customers, to fellow employees, and to executives.

- **Heightened global competition.** Because many American companies continue to move beyond domestic markets, you may be interacting with people from many cultures. To be a successful business communicator, you will need to learn about other cultures. You will also need to develop intercultural skills including sensitivity, flexibility, patience, and tolerance.

- **Renewed emphasis on ethics.** Ethics is once again a hot topic in business. The Great Recession of 2007–2009 was caused largely, some say, by greed and ethical lapses. With the passage of the Sarbanes-Oxley Act, the U.S. government

Figure 1.4 Communication and Collaborative Technologies

alphaspirit/Shutterstock.com

Communication Technologies
Communication Technologies at Work

Cloud Computing, Web 2.0, and Beyond

Increasingly, applications and data are stored in remote locations online, in the cloud. This ability to store and access data on remote servers is called *cloud computing*. Cloud computing means that businesses and individuals no longer need to maintain costly hardware and software in-house; instead, they can centralize data on their own remote servers or pay for digital storage space and software applications offered by providers online. Photo- and video-sharing sites such as Instagram, Flickr, and YouTube keep users' media in the cloud. Similarly, Dropbox, a popular file-synchronization service, and online backup provider Carbonite allow customers to edit and sync files online independent of the device used to access them. Websites and Web applications have shifted from one-way, read-only communication to multidirectional, social, read-write communication. This profound change, dubbed Web 2.0, has allowed workers to participate, collaborate, and network in unprecedented ways. More changes on the horizon include the Internet of things, the storing and making sense of big data, artificial intelligence, and self-driving cars. Continuous automation will make many current jobs obsolete.

Telephony: VoIP

Paul Bradbury/Getty Images

Savvy businesses are switching from traditional phone service to voice over Internet protocol (VoIP). This technology allows callers to communicate using a broadband Internet connection, thus eliminating long-distance and local telephone charges. Higher-end VoIP systems now support unified voice mail, e-mail, click-to-call capabilities, and softphones (Web applications or mobile apps, such as Google Voice, for calling and messaging). Free or low-cost Internet telephony sites, such as the popular Skype and FaceTime, are also increasingly used by businesses, although their sound and image quality is often uneven.

Open Offices

The widespread use of laptop computers, tablets, and other smart devices, wireless technology, and VoIP have led to more fluid, flexible, and open workspaces. Smaller computers and flat-screen monitors enable designers to save space with boomerang-shaped workstations and cockpit-style work surfaces rather than space-hogging corner work areas. Smaller breakout areas for impromptu meetings are taking over some cubicle space, and digital databases are replacing file cabinets. Mobile technology allows workers to be fully connected and productive on the go.

Exactostock / SuperStock

Becoming familiar with modern communication technology can help you succeed on the job. Today's digital workplace is shaped by mobile devices, mobile apps, social media networks, superfast broadband and wireless access, and other technologies that allow workers to share information, work from remote locations, and be more productive in or away from the office. With today's tools you can exchange ideas, solve problems, develop products, forecast performance, and complete team projects any time of the day or night anywhere in the world.

iStock.com/ichaka

Speech Recognition

Computers equipped with speech-recognition software enable users to dictate up to 160 words a minute with accurate transcription. Speech recognition is particularly helpful to disabled workers and to professionals with heavy dictation loads, such as physicians and attorneys. Users can create documents, enter data, compose and send e-mails, browse the Web, and control their notebooks, laptops, and desktops—all by voice. Smart devices can also execute tasks with voice command apps—for example, to dial a call, find a route, or transcribe voice mail.

Denys Prykhodov/Shutterstock.com

Wearable Devices

The most recent trend in mobile computing is wearable devices. Fitbit, Google Glass, Apple Watch, and similar accessories do more than track fitness activities. They are powerful mobile devices in their own right that can sync with other smart electronics.

Smart Mobile Devices and Digital Convergence

Lightweight, ever-smaller devices provide phone, e-mail, Web browsing, and calendar options anywhere there is a cellular or Wi-Fi network. Tablets and smartphones such as Android devices and the iPhone and iPad allow workers to tap into corporate databases and intranets from remote locations. Users can check customers' files, complete orders, collect payment, and send out receipts without returning to the office. The need for separate electronic gadgets is waning as digital smart devices are becoming multifunctional and highly capable. With streaming video on the Web, connectivity between TVs and computers, and networked mobile devices, technology is converging, consolidating into increasingly powerful devices. Many smart devices today are fully capable of replacing digital point-and-shoot still photography and video cameras. Mobile smart devices are also competing with TVs and computers for primacy.

Videoconferencing

Source: Polycom, Inc.

Videoconferencing allows participants to meet in special conference rooms equipped with cameras and television screens. Individuals or groups see each other and interact in real time, although they may be far apart. Faster computers, rapid Internet connections, and better cameras now enable 2 to 200 participants to sit at their own computers or mobile devices and share applications, spreadsheets, presentations, and photos. The technology extends from the popular Internet applications Skype and FaceTime to sophisticated videoconferencing software that delivers HD-quality audio, video, and content sharing.

Hero Images/Getty Images

Web Conferencing

With services such as GoToMeeting, WebEx, and Microsoft Live Meeting, all you need is a computer or a smart device and an Internet connection to hold a meeting (*webinar*) with customers or colleagues in real time. Although the functions are constantly evolving, Web conferencing currently incorporates screen sharing, chats, slide presentations, text messaging, and application sharing.

Mobile Apps

Mobile apps are the software that enables smartphones to run and accomplish amazing feats. Despite their natural size limitations, mobile apps rival the capabilities of full-fledged software applications on laptops, on desktops, and in the cloud.

Electronic Presentations and Data Visualization

Business presentations in PowerPoint, Prezi, or Keynote can be projected from a laptop or tablet, or posted online. Sophisticated presentations may include animation, sound effects, digital photos, video clips, or hyperlinks to Internet sites. In some industries, PowerPoint and other electronic slides (decks) are replacing or supplementing traditional hard-copy reports. Data visualization tools such as SAS can help businesses make sense of increasing amounts of complex data.

Social Media

Broadly speaking, the term *social media* describes technology that enables participants to connect and share in social networks online. For example, tech-savvy companies and individuals use Twitter to issue up-to-date news, link to their blogs and websites, and announce events and promotions. Microblogging services, such as Twitter and Tumblr, also allow businesses to track what is being said about them and their products. Similarly, businesses use social networks such as Facebook, Instagram, and others to

interact with customers and build their brands. Companies may also prospect for talent using social media networks. Efforts to launch corporate social networks have seen mixed results. So far workers have been slow in embracing SharePoint, Jive, Yammer, Telligent, and similar enterprise-grade collaboration platforms, social networks, and community forums.

Collaboration With Blogs, Podcasts, and Wikis

Businesses use *blogs* to keep customers and employees informed and to receive feedback. Company news can be posted, updated, and categorized for easy cross-referencing. An audio or video file streamed online or downloaded to a digital music player is called a *podcast*. A *wiki* is an Internet or intranet site that allows multiple users to collaboratively create and edit digital files as well as media. Information can get lost in e-mails, but wikis provide an easy way to communicate and keep track of what has been said. Wikis for business include Confluence, eXo Platform, Socialtext, and Jive.

Westend61/Getty Images

now requires greater accountability. As a result, businesses are eager to regain public trust by building ethical corporate cultures. Many have written ethical mission statements, installed hotlines, and appointed compliance officers to ensure strict adherence to their high standards and the law.

These trends mean that your communication skills will constantly be on display, and that missteps won't be easily erased or forgotten. Writers of clear and concise messages contribute to efficient operations and can expect to be rewarded.

OFFICE INSIDER

"Did you know?

- It is estimated that more than 50 percent of our work time is spent listening.

- Immediately following a 10-minute presentation, average people retain about half of what they hear and only one quarter after 48 hours.

- Sixty percent of all management problems are related to listening.

- We misinterpret, misunderstand, or change 70 to 90 percent of what we hear."[33]

Valarie Washington, *CEO, Think 6 Results*

1-2 Developing Listening Skills

TV and radio host Larry King said, "I remind myself every morning: Nothing I say this day will teach me anything. So if I'm going to learn, I must do it by listening."[32] In an age that thrives on information and communication technology, listening is an important skill. However, by all accounts most of us are not very good listeners. Do you ever pretend to be listening when you are not? Do you know how to look attentive in class when your mind wanders far away? How about tuning out people when their ideas are boring or complex? Do you find it hard to focus on ideas when a speaker's clothing or mannerisms are unusual?

You probably answered *yes* to one or more of these questions because many of us have poor listening habits. In fact, some researchers suggest that we listen at only 25 to 50 percent efficiency. Such poor listening habits are costly in business and affect professional relationships. Messages must be rewritten, shipments reshipped, appointments rescheduled, contracts renegotiated, and directions restated. Listening skills are important for career success, organization effectiveness, and worker satisfaction. Numerous studies and experts report that good listeners make good managers and are sought after by recruiters.[34]

To develop better listening skills, we must first recognize barriers that prevent effective listening. Then we need to focus on techniques for improving listening skills.

1-2a Overcoming Barriers to Effective Listening

As you have seen, bad habits and distractions can interfere with effective listening. Have any of the following barriers and distractions prevented you from hearing what has been said?

- **Physical barriers.** You cannot listen if you cannot hear what is being said. Physical impediments include hearing disabilities, poor acoustics, and noisy surroundings. It is also difficult to listen if you are ill, tired, or uncomfortable.

- **Psychological barriers.** Everyone brings to the communication process a unique set of cultural, ethical, and personal values. Each of us has an idea of what is right and what is important. If other ideas run counter to our preconceived thoughts, we tend to tune out speakers and thus fail to receive their messages.

- **Language problems.** Unfamiliar words can destroy the communication process because they lack meaning for the receiver. In addition, emotion-laden, or charged, words can adversely affect listening. If the mention of words such as *bankruptcy* or *real estate meltdown* has an intense emotional impact, a listener may be unable to focus on the words that follow.

- **Nonverbal distractions.** Many of us find it hard to listen if a speaker is different from what we view as normal. Unusual clothing or speech mannerisms, body twitches, or a radical hairstyle can cause enough distraction to prevent us from hearing what the speaker has to say.

- **Thought speed.** Because we can process thoughts at least three times faster than speakers can say them, we can become bored and allow our minds to wander.

- **Faking attention.** Most of us have learned to look as if we are listening even when we are not. Such behavior was perhaps necessary as part of our socialization. Faked attention, however, seriously threatens effective listening because it encourages the mind to engage in flights of unchecked fancy. Those who fake attention often find it hard to concentrate even when they want to.

- **Grandstanding.** Would you rather talk or listen? Naturally, most of us would rather talk. Because our own experiences and thoughts are most important to us, we often want to grab the limelight in conversations. We may fail to listen carefully when we are just waiting politely for the next pause so that we can have our turn to speak.

1-2b Building Solid Listening Skills

You can reverse the harmful effects of poor habits by making a conscious effort to become an active listener. This means becoming involved. You can't sit back and hear whatever a lazy mind happens to receive. The following keys will help you become an active and effective listener:

- **Stop talking.** The first step to becoming a good listener is to stop talking. Let others explain their views. Learn to concentrate on what the speaker is saying, not on what your next comment will be.

- **Control your surroundings.** Whenever possible, remove competing sounds. Close windows or doors, turn off TVs and smartphones, and move away from loud people, noisy appliances, or engines. Choose a quiet time and place for listening.

- **Establish a receptive mind-set.** Expect to learn something by listening. Strive for a positive and receptive frame of mind. If the message is complex, think of it as mental gymnastics. It is hard work but good exercise to stretch and expand the limits of your mind.

- **Keep an open mind.** We all sift through and filter information based on our own biases and values. For improved listening, discipline yourself to listen objectively. Be fair to the speaker. Hear what is really being said, not what you want to hear.

- **Listen for main points.** Heighten your concentration and satisfaction by looking for the speaker's central themes. Congratulate yourself when you find them!

- **Capitalize on lag time.** Make use of the quickness of your mind by reviewing the speaker's points. Anticipate what is coming next. Evaluate evidence the speaker has presented. Don't allow yourself to daydream. Try to guess what the speaker's next point will be.

- **Listen between the lines.** Focus both on what is spoken and what is unspoken. Listen for feelings as well as for facts.

- **Judge ideas, not appearances.** Concentrate on the content of the message, not on its delivery. Avoid being distracted by the speaker's looks, voice, or mannerisms.

- **Hold your fire.** Force yourself to listen to the speaker's entire argument or message before responding. Such restraint may enable you to understand the speaker's reasons and logic before you jump to false conclusions.

- **Take selective notes.** In some situations thoughtful notetaking may be necessary to record important facts that must be recalled later. Select only the most important points so that the notetaking process does not interfere with your concentration on the speaker's total message.

- **Provide feedback.** Let the speaker know that you are listening. Nod your head and maintain eye contact. Ask relevant questions at appropriate times. Getting involved improves the communication process for both the speaker and the listener.

LEARNING
OUTCOME 3

Explain the features of non-verbal communication, and recognize the importance of improving your nonverbal communication skills.

1-3 Learning Nonverbal Communication Skills

Psychologist and philosopher Paul Watzlawick claimed that we cannot not communicate.[36] In other words, it's impossible to not communicate. This means that every behavior is sending a message even if we don't use words. The eyes, face, and body convey meaning without a single syllable being spoken.

What Is Nonverbal Communication? Nonverbal communication includes all unwritten and unspoken messages, whether intended or not. These silent signals have a strong effect on receivers. However, understanding them is not simple. Does a downward glance indicate modesty? Fatigue? Does a constant stare reflect coldness? Dullness? Aggression? Do crossed arms mean defensiveness, withdrawal, or just that the person is shivering?

What If Words and Nonverbal Cues Clash? Messages are even harder to decipher when the verbal and nonverbal cues do not agree. What will you think if Scott says he is not angry, but he slams the door when he leaves? What if Alicia assures the hostess that the meal is excellent, but she eats very little? The nonverbal messages in these situations speak louder than the words. In fact, researchers believe that the bulk of any message we receive is nonverbal.

Successful communicators recognize the power of nonverbal messages. Cues broadcast by body language might be helpful in understanding the feelings and attitudes of senders. Be careful, however, before attaching specific meanings to gestures or actions because behavior and its interpretations strongly depend on context and on one's cultural background, as you will see.

1-3a Your Body Sends Silent Messages

Think about how effective nonverbal behavior could benefit your career. Workplace-relevant nonverbal cues include eye contact, facial expression, body movements, time, space, territory, and appearance. These nonverbal cues affect how a message is interpreted, or decoded, by the receiver.

Eye Contact. The eyes have been called the windows to the soul. Even if they don't reveal the soul, the eyes are often the best predictor of a speaker's true feelings. Most of us cannot look another person straight in the eyes and lie. As a result, in North American culture, we tend to believe people who look directly at us. Sustained eye contact suggests trust and admiration; brief eye contact signals fear or stress. Good eye contact enables the message sender to see whether a receiver is paying attention, showing respect, responding favorably, or feeling distress. From the receiver's viewpoint, good eye contact, in North American culture, reveals the speaker's sincerity, confidence, and truthfulness.

Facial Expression. The expression on a person's face can be almost as revealing of emotion as the eyes. Experts estimate that the human face can display over 250,000 expressions.[37] To hide their feelings, some people can control these expressions and maintain so-called poker faces. In North America, however, most of us display our emotions openly. Raising or lowering the eyebrows, squinting the eyes, swallowing nervously, clenching the jaw, smiling broadly—these voluntary and involuntary facial expressions can add to or entirely replace verbal messages.

Posture and Gestures. An individual's posture can convey anything from high status and self-confidence to shyness and submissiveness. Leaning toward a speaker suggests attentiveness and interest; pulling away or shrinking back denotes fear, distrust, anxiety, or disgust. Similarly, gestures can communicate entire thoughts via simple movements. However, the meanings of some of these movements differ in other cultures. Unless you know local customs, they can get you into trouble. In the

United States and Canada, for example, forming the thumb and forefinger in a circle means everything is OK. But in parts of South America, the OK sign is obscene.

In the workplace you can make a good impression by controlling your posture and gestures. When speaking, make sure your upper body is aligned with the person to whom you're talking. Erect posture sends a message of confidence, competence, diligence, and strength. Women are advised to avoid tilting their heads to the side when making an important point to avoid seeming unsure and thus diminishing the impact of the message.[38]

1-3b Time, Space, and Territory Send Silent Messages

In addition to nonverbal messages transmitted by your body, three external elements convey information in the communication process: time, space, and territory.

Time. How we structure and use time tells observers about our personalities and attitudes. For example, when Warren Buffett, industrialist, investor, and philanthropist, gives a visitor a prolonged interview, he signals his respect for, interest in, and approval of the visitor or the topic to be discussed. On the other hand, when David Ing twice arrives late for a meeting, it could mean that the meeting has low priority to David, that he is a self-centered person, or that he has little self-discipline. These are assumptions that typical Americans might make.

Space. How we order the space around us tells something about ourselves and our objectives. Whether the space is a bedroom, a dorm room, or an office, people reveal themselves in the design and grouping of their furniture. Generally, the more formal the arrangement, the more formal and closed the communication style. An executive who seats visitors in a row of chairs across from his desk sends a message of aloofness and a desire for separation. A team leader who arranges chairs informally in a circle rather than in straight rows conveys her desire for a more open exchange of ideas.

Territory. Each of us has a certain area that we feel is our own territory, whether it is a specific spot or just the space around us. Your father may have a favorite chair in which he is most comfortable, a cook might not tolerate intruders in the kitchen, and veteran employees may feel that certain work areas and tools belong to them. We all maintain zones of privacy in which we feel comfortable. Figure 1.5 categorizes the four zones of social interaction among Americans, as formulated by anthropologist Edward T. Hall.[39] Notice that North Americans are a bit standoffish; only intimate friends and family may stand closer than about 1.5 feet. If someone

Figure 1.5 Four Space Zones for Social Interaction

| Intimate Zone (1 to 1½ feet) | Personal Zone (1½ to 4 feet) | Social Zone (4 to 12 feet) | Public Zone (12 or more feet) |

iStock.com/lewkmiller   iStock.com/Dean Mitchell   iStock.com/monkeybusinessimages   © Kablonk Royalty-Free/Inmagine

violates that territory, North Americans feel uncomfortable and may step back to reestablish their space. In the workplace be aware of the territorial needs of others and don't invade their space.

1-3c Appearance Sends Silent Messages

Much like the personal appearance of an individual, the physical appearance of a business document transmits immediate and important nonverbal messages. Ideally, these messages should be pleasing to the eye.

Eye Appeal of Business Documents. The way an e-mail, letter, memo, or report looks can have either a positive or a negative effect on the receiver. Sloppy e-mails send a nonverbal message that you are in a terrific hurry or that you do not care about the receiver. Envelopes—through their postage, quality, and printing—can suggest that the messages they carry are routine, important, or junk mail. Letters and reports can look neat, professional, well organized, and attractive—or just the opposite. In succeeding chapters you will learn how to create business documents that send positive nonverbal messages through their appearance, format, organization, readability, and correctness.

Personal Appearance. The way you look—your clothing, grooming, and posture—transmits an instant nonverbal message about you. Based on what they see, viewers make quick judgments about your status, credibility, personality, and potential. If you want to be considered professional, think about how you present yourself. One management consultant prefers bright-colored dresses, stiletto heels, and bling. But to be perceived as professional, she adopts a more conservative look to match the occasion and the customer: "The success I dress for is that of my *client*."[41] As a businessperson, you will want to think about what your appearance says about you. Although the rules of business attire have loosened up, some workers show poor judgment. You will learn more about professional attire and behavior in later chapters.

WORKPLACE IN FOCUS

The tattoo craze in some U.S. populations continues unabated. Americans spend $1.65 billion on tattoos annually. The Food and Drug Administration estimates that 45 million (14 percent) of Americans have at least one tattoo. The percentages almost triple among U.S. adults aged eighteen through twenty-five and twenty-six through forty (36 and 40 percent). Young people do not fear harming their job prospects, and some studies suggest that attitudes among business professionals are changing slowly.[42] Think twice, however, before displaying "tats" and piercings at work. Conspicuous body art may make you feel distinctive and daring, but what could be the risks for your career?

1-3d Mastering Nonverbal Skills

Nonverbal communication can outweigh words in the way it influences how others perceive you. You can harness the power of silent messages by reviewing the following tips for improving nonverbal communication skills:

- **Establish and maintain eye contact.** Remember that in North America appropriate eye contact signals interest, attentiveness, strength, and credibility.

- **Use posture to show interest.** Encourage interaction by leaning forward, sitting or standing erect, and looking alert.

- **Reduce or eliminate physical barriers.** Move out from behind a desk or lectern; arrange meeting chairs in a circle.

- **Improve your decoding skills.** Watch facial expressions and body language to understand the complete verbal and nonverbal messages being communicated.

- **Probe for more information.** When you perceive nonverbal cues that contradict verbal meanings, politely seek additional cues (*I'm not sure I understand, Please tell me more about . . .,* or *Do you mean that . . .?*).

- **Interpret nonverbal meanings in context.** Make nonverbal assessments only when you understand a situation or a culture.

- **Associate with people from different cultures.** Learn about other cultures to widen your knowledge and tolerance of intercultural nonverbal messages.

- **Appreciate the power of appearance.** Keep in mind that the appearance of your business documents, your business space, and yourself sends immediate positive or negative messages to others.

- **Observe yourself on video.** Ensure that your verbal and nonverbal messages are in sync by recording and evaluating yourself making a presentation.

- **Enlist friends and family.** Ask friends and family members to monitor your conscious and unconscious body movements and gestures to help you become a more effective communicator.

1-4 Recognizing How Culture Influences Communication

LEARNING OUTCOME 4

Name five common dimensions of culture, and understand how culture influences communication and the use of social media and communication technology.

Comprehending the verbal and nonverbal meanings of a message is difficult even when communicators share the same culture. When they come from different cultures, special sensitivity and skills are necessary. Global business, new communication technologies, the Internet, and social media span the world, reducing distances. However, cultural differences still exist and can cause significant misunderstandings.

What Is Culture? For our purposes, *culture* may be defined as the complex system of values, traits, morals, and customs shared by a society. Culture is a powerful operating force that molds the way we think, behave, and communicate. The objective of this section is to broaden your view of culture and open your mind to flexible attitudes so that you can avoid frustration when cultural understanding is necessary. Despite globalization, growing diversity, and social networking, we need to make adjustments and adopt new attitudes.

To help you better understand your culture and how it contrasts with other cultures, we describe five key dimensions of culture: context, individualism, time orientation, power distance, and communication style. The section closes with a look at the interaction between culture and social media.

1-4a High and Low Context

Context is probably the most important cultural dimension and also the most difficult to define. In a model developed by cultural anthropologist Edward T. Hall, context refers to the stimuli, environment, or ambience surrounding an event. Hall arranged cultures on a continuum, shown in Figure 1.6, from low to high in relation to context. This figure also summarizes key comparisons for today's business communicators.

Communicators in low-context cultures (such as those in North America, Scandinavia, and Germany) depend little on the context of a situation and shared experience to convey their meaning. They assume that messages must be explicit, and listeners rely exclusively on the written or spoken word. Low-context cultures tend to be logical, analytical, and action oriented. Business communicators stress clearly articulated messages that they consider to be objective, professional, and efficient. Words are taken literally.

Communicators in high-context cultures (such as those in China, Japan, and Middle Eastern countries) assume that the listener does not need much background information.[43] Communicators in high-context cultures are more likely to be intuitive and contemplative. They may not take words literally. Instead, the meaning of a message may be implied from the social or physical setting, the relationship of the communicators, or nonverbal cues. For example, a Japanese communicator might

Figure 1.6 Comparing Low- and High-Context Cultures

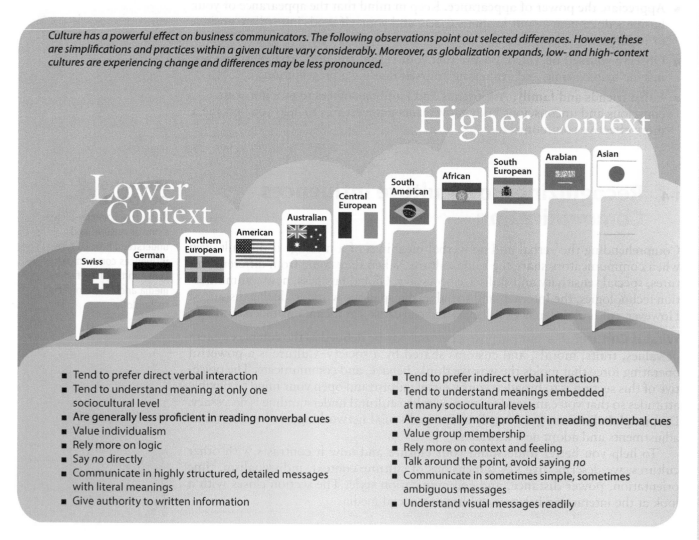

Culture has a powerful effect on business communicators. The following observations point out selected differences. However, these are simplifications and practices within a given culture vary considerably. Moreover, as globalization expands, low- and high-context cultures are experiencing change and differences may be less pronounced.

Higher Context

Lower Context

Asian · Arabian · South European · African · South American · Central European · Australian · American · Northern European · German · Swiss

- Tend to prefer direct verbal interaction
- Tend to understand meaning at only one sociocultural level
- Are generally less proficient in reading nonverbal cues
- Value individualism
- Rely more on logic
- Say *no* directly
- Communicate in highly structured, detailed messages with literal meanings
- Give authority to written information

- Tend to prefer indirect verbal interaction
- Tend to understand meanings embedded at many sociocultural levels
- Are generally more proficient in reading nonverbal cues
- Value group membership
- Rely more on context and feeling
- Talk around the point, avoid saying *no*
- Communicate in sometimes simple, sometimes ambiguous messages
- Understand visual messages readily

say *yes* when he really means *no*. From the context of the situation, his Japanese conversation partner would conclude whether *yes* really meant *yes* or whether it meant *no*. The context, tone, time taken to answer, facial expression, and body cues would convey the meaning of *yes*.[44] In high-context cultures, communication cues are primarily transmitted by posture, voice inflection, gestures, and facial expression.

1-4b Individualism and Collectivism

An attitude of independence and freedom from control characterizes individualism. Members of low-context cultures, particularly North Americans, tend to value individualism. They believe that initiative and self-assertion result in personal achievement. They believe in individual action and personal responsibility, and they desire much freedom in their personal lives.

Members of high-context cultures are more collectivist. They emphasize membership in organizations, groups, and teams; they encourage acceptance of group values, duties, and decisions. They typically resist independence because it fosters competition and confrontation instead of consensus. In group-oriented cultures, such as those in many Asian societies, self-assertion and individual decision making are discouraged. "The nail that sticks up gets pounded down" is a common Japanese saying.[45] Business decisions are often made by all who have competence in the matter under discussion. Similarly, in China managers also focus on the group rather than on the individual, preferring a consultative management style over an autocratic style.[46]

Cultures are complex, of course, and cannot be characterized as totally individualistic or group oriented. To complicate things, group differences may be lessening over time. For example, European-Americans were considered as quite individualistic, whereas African-Americans were deemed less so, and Latinos were believed to be closer to the group-centered dimension. Newer research suggests cultural convergence, a trend toward greater similarity.[47] Figure 1.7 shows selected countries ranked according to their expression of collectivism and individualism as well as power distance.

Figure 1.7 Countries' Ranking in Collectivism, Individualism, and Power Distance

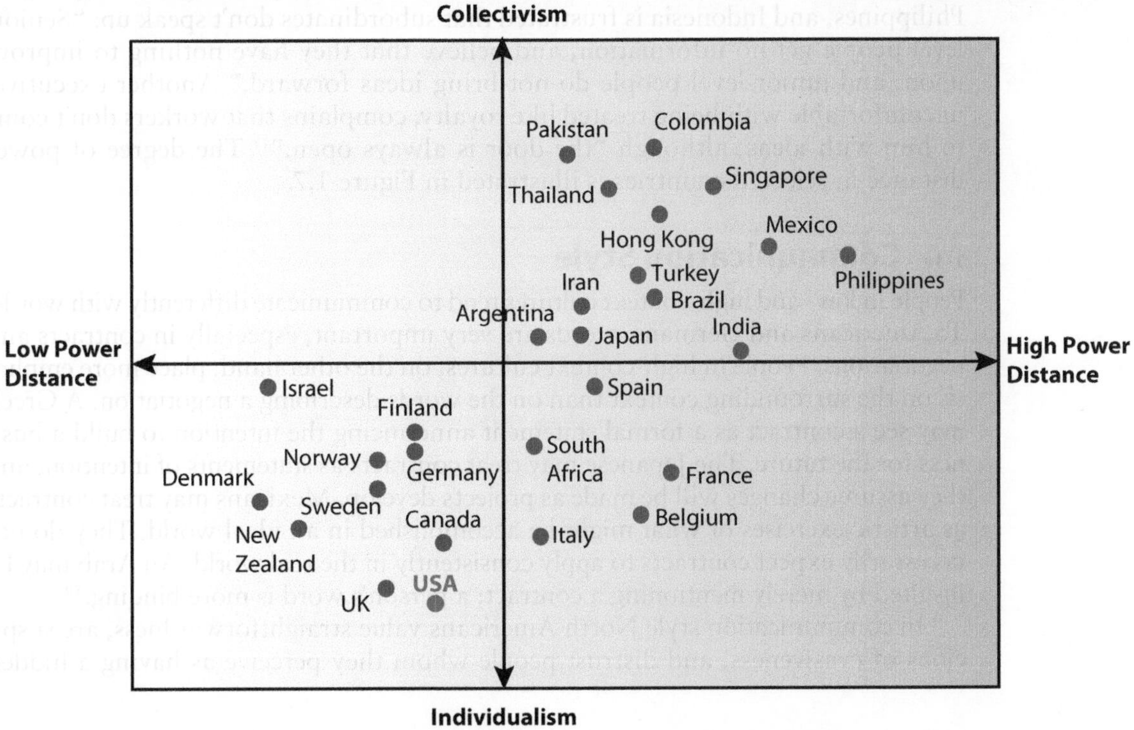

1-4c Time Orientation

North Americans consider time a precious commodity. They correlate time with productivity, efficiency, and money. Keeping people waiting for business appointments is considered a waste of time and also rude.

In other cultures time may be perceived as an unlimited resource to be enjoyed. A North American businessperson, for example, was kept waiting two hours past a scheduled appointment time in South America. She wasn't offended, though, because she was familiar with South Americans' more relaxed concept of time.

The perception of time and how it is used are culturally learned. In some cultures, time is perceived analytically. People account for every minute of the day. In other cultures, time is holistic and viewed in larger chunks. People in Western cultures tend to be more analytical, scheduling appointments at 15- to 30-minute intervals. Those in Eastern cultures tend to be more holistic, planning fewer but longer meetings. People in one culture may look at time as formal and task oriented. In another culture, time is seen as an opportunity to develop interpersonal relationships.

1-4d Power Distance

One important element of culture is power distance, which was first introduced by influential social psychologist Geert Hofstede. The Power Distance Index measures how people in different societies cope with inequality—in other words, how they relate to more powerful or less powerful individuals. In high-power-distance countries, subordinates expect formal hierarchies and embrace relatively authoritarian, paternalistic power relationships. In low-power-distance cultures, however, subordinates may consider themselves as equals of their supervisors. They confidently voice opinions and participate in decision making. Relationships between high-powered people and those with little power tend to be more democratic, egalitarian, and informal.

As you probably guessed, in Western cultures people are more relaxed about social status and the appearance of power.[48] Deference is not generally paid to individuals merely because of their wealth, position, seniority, or age. In many Asian cultures, however, these characteristics are important. Intercultural clashes can erupt in global corporations. A Western executive coach operating in Malaysia, the Philippines, and Indonesia is frustrated that subordinates don't speak up: "Senior-level people get no information, and believe that they have nothing to improve upon, and junior-level people do not bring ideas forward." Another executive, uncomfortable with being treated like royalty, complains that workers don't come to him with ideas, although "the door is always open."[49] The degree of power distance in selected countries is illustrated in Figure 1.7.

1-4e Communication Style

People in low- and high-context cultures tend to communicate differently with words. To Americans and Germans, words are very important, especially in contracts and negotiations. People in high-context cultures, on the other hand, place more emphasis on the surrounding context than on the words describing a negotiation. A Greek may see a contract as a formal statement announcing the intention to build a business for the future. The Japanese may treat contracts as statements of intention, and they assume changes will be made as projects develop. Mexicans may treat contracts as artistic exercises of what might be accomplished in an ideal world. They do not necessarily expect contracts to apply consistently in the real world. An Arab may be insulted by merely mentioning a contract; a person's word is more binding.[50]

In communication style North Americans value straightforwardness, are suspicious of evasiveness, and distrust people whom they perceive as having a hidden agenda or playing their cards too close to the chest.[51] North Americans also tend to be uncomfortable with silence and impatient with delays. Some Asian businesspeople have learned that the longer they drag out negotiations, the more concessions impatient North Americans are likely to make.

1-4f How Technology and Social Media Affect Intercultural Communication

Much has been made of the connectedness that social media and communication technology provide today. With minimal resources, communicators can reach out to larger and more varied audiences than ever before. Social media offer the potential for intercultural engagement. They may overcome cultural differences or reinforce them, depending on their users.

iStock.com/Lesia_G

Social Networking: Blurring Boundaries? What we make of the potential for intercultural connectedness online is as much up to us as it would be at a dinner party where we don't know any of the other guests. "Digital media is an amplifier. It tends to make extroverts more extroverted and introverts more introverted," says Clay Shirky, social media expert at New York University.[52] Some authors believe that social media networks blur cultural gaps, reduce hierarchies, and empower people to change their circumstances.[53] At the same time, the online environment may deepen feelings of isolation; it can make interpersonal contact more difficult because all contact is mediated electronically.[54]

In real life, as online, we instinctively tend to gravitate toward people who seem similar to us, explains Gaurav Mishra, a social media strategist from India: "[H]uman beings have a strong tendency to prefer the familiar, so we pay attention to people with a shared context and treat the rich Twitter public stream as background noise."[55] Twitter and other social media can boost intercultural communication; however, we must be willing to reach out across the boundaries that separate us.

Whether social media networks will allow business communicators to engage across cultures and bridge intercultural differences will depend on the users' attitudes and openness.

Social Networking: Global and Local? Despite the equalizing influence of globalization, regional and cultural differences persist, as those who design media for markets in other countries know. Asian users may prefer muted pastel colors and anime-style graphics that North Americans would find unusual. Conversely, Korean and Japanese employees may balk at being compelled to post photos of themselves on company intranet pages. They opt for avatars or pictures of pets instead, possibly as an expression of personal modesty or expectations of privacy, whereas North Americans believe photos promote cohesion and make them seem accessible.[56]

Marketers and PR agencies understand that they must be aware of cultural differences in the use of digital media in each global market. "Successful campaigns rely on local knowledge," a global media report concludes.[57] If the needs of each market aren't considered, customers may be unhappy and brand perceptions suffer.[58] It remains to be seen whether social networking will slowly erase many of the cultural differences present today or whether distinct national, even local, networks will emerge and survive.[59]

LEARNING
OUTCOME 5

Discuss strategies that help communicators overcome negative cultural attitudes and prevent miscommunication in today's diverse, mobile, social-media-driven workplace.

1-5 Becoming Interculturally Proficient

Being aware of your own culture and how it contrasts with others is a first step in learning intercultural skills. Another important step involves recognizing barriers to intercultural accommodation and striving to overcome them. The digital age economy needs workers who can thrive on diverse teams and interact effectively with customers and clients at home and abroad. This section addresses how to overcome barriers to productive intercultural communication, develop strong intercultural skills, and capitalize on workplace diversity.

1-5a Curbing Ethnocentrism and Stereotyping

The process of understanding and interacting successfully with people from other cultures is often hampered by two barriers: ethnocentrism and stereotyping. These barriers, however, can be overcome by developing tolerance, a powerful and effective aid to communication.

OFFICE INSIDER

"[E]mployers are looking for people who have experienced the world and can bring a global perspective helping us to recognize our common engineering challenges and find solutions together. One way I have become a global citizen is through 'voluntourism.' The term describes trips encompassing both volunteer work and tourism."[60]

Rebecca Delaney,
mechanical engineering team leader, Skidmore, Owings & Merrill

Ethnocentrism. The belief in the superiority of one's own culture is known as *ethnocentrism*. This natural attitude is found in all cultures. Ethnocentrism causes us to judge others by our own values. If you were raised in North America, values such as punctuality and directness probably seem right to you, and you may wonder why the rest of the world doesn't function in the same sensible fashion. A North American businessperson in an Arab or Asian country might be upset at time spent over coffee or other social rituals before any *real* business is transacted. In these cultures, however, personal relationships must be established and nurtured before credible negotiations may proceed.

Stereotypes. Our perceptions of other cultures sometimes cause us to form stereotypes about groups of people. A *stereotype* is an oversimplified perception of a behavioral pattern or characteristic applied uncritically to groups. For example, the Swiss are hardworking, efficient, and neat; Germans are formal, reserved, and blunt; Americans are loud, friendly, and impatient; Canadians are polite, trusting, and tolerant; Asians are gracious, humble, and inscrutable. These attitudes may or may not accurately describe cultural norms. When applied to individual business communicators, however, such stereotypes may create misconceptions and misunderstandings. Look beneath surface stereotypes and labels to discover individual personal qualities.

Tolerance. As global markets expand and as our society becomes increasingly multiethnic, tolerance is critical. *Tolerance* here means learning about beliefs and practices different from our own and appreciating them. It means being open-minded and receptive to new experiences. One of the best ways to develop tolerance is to practice *empathy*, which is defined as trying to see the world through another's eyes. It means being less judgmental and more eager to seek common ground.

One way of promoting greater understanding is to work toward a common goal. An environmental studies center in Israel brings together Jews, Muslims, and Christians to tackle water scarcity in the Middle East, home to 10 of the 15 most water-starved countries in the world. The diverse student body is Jewish Israeli, Arab, and non–Middle Eastern. Aside from caring for the environment, the students attend peace-building forums to discuss race, religion, culture, and politics. The center builds one of the region's scarcest resources—trust.[61]

Getting along well with others is always a good policy, but doubly so in the workplace. Some job descriptions now include statements such as *Must be able to interact with ethnically diverse personnel.*

The suggestions in the following section can help you prevent miscommunication in oral and written transactions across cultures.

1-5b Successful Oral Communication With Intercultural Audiences

When you have a conversation with someone from another culture, you can reduce misunderstandings by following these tips:

- **Use simple English.** Speak in short sentences (under 20 words) with familiar, short words. Eliminate puns, sport and military references, slang, and jargon (special business terms). Be especially alert to idiomatic expressions that can't be translated, such as *face the music* and *hit a home run.*

- **Speak slowly and enunciate clearly.** Avoid fast speech, but don't raise your voice. Overpunctuate with pauses and full stops. Always write numbers for all to see.

- **Encourage accurate feedback.** Ask probing questions, and encourage the listener to paraphrase what you say. Don't assume that a *yes*, a nod, or a smile indicates comprehension or agreement.

- **Check frequently for comprehension.** Avoid waiting until you finish a long explanation to request feedback. Instead, make one point at a time, pausing to check for comprehension. Don't proceed to B until A has been grasped.

- **Observe eye messages.** Be alert to a glazed expression or wandering eyes. These tell you the listener is lost.

- **Accept blame.** If a misunderstanding results, graciously accept the responsibility for not making your meaning clear.

- **Listen without interrupting.** Curb your desire to finish sentences or to fill out ideas for the speaker. Keep in mind that North Americans abroad are often accused of listening too little and talking too much.

- **Smile when appropriate.** The smile is often considered the single most understood and most useful form of communication. In some cultures, however, excessive smiling may seem insincere.

- **Follow up in writing.** After conversations or oral negotiations, confirm the results and agreements with written messages—if necessary, in the local language.

1-5c Successful Written Communication With Intercultural Audiences

When you write to someone from a different culture, you can improve your chances of being understood by following these suggestions:

- **Consider local styles and conventions.** Learn how documents are formatted and how letters are addressed and developed in the intended reader's country. Decide whether to use your organization's preferred format or adjust to local styles.

- **Observe titles and rank.** Use last names, titles, and other signals of rank and status. Send messages to higher-status people; avoid sending copies to lower-rank people.

- **Hire a translator.** Engage a professional translator if (a) your document is important, (b) your document will be distributed to many readers, or (c) you must be persuasive.

- **Use short sentences and short paragraphs.** Sentences with fewer than 20 words and paragraphs with fewer than 8 lines are most readable.

- **Avoid ambiguous wording.** Include relative pronouns (*that, which, who*) for clarity in introducing clauses. Stay away from contractions (especially ones such as *Here's the problem*). Avoid idioms (*once in a blue moon*), slang

(*my presentation really bombed*), acronyms (*ASAP* for "as soon as possible"), abbreviations (*DBA* for "doing business as"), jargon (*input, bottom line*), and sports references (*ballpark figure, slam dunk*). Use action-specific verbs (*buy a printer* rather than *get a printer*).

■ **Cite numbers carefully.** In international trade learn and use the metric system. In citing numbers, use figures (*12*) instead of spelling them out (*twelve*). Always convert dollar figures into local currency. Spell out the month when writing dates. In North America, for example, *March 5, 2019*, might be written as *3/5/19*, whereas in Europe the same date might appear as *5.3.19*.

1-5d Globalization and Workplace Diversity

While North American companies are expanding global operations and adapting to a variety of emerging markets, the domestic workforce is also becoming more diverse. This diversity has many dimensions—race, ethnicity, age, religion, gender, national origin, physical ability, sexual orientation, and others.

No longer, say the experts, will the workplace be predominantly male or Anglo oriented. By 2020 many groups now considered minorities (African-Americans, Hispanics, Asians, Native Americans) are projected to become 36 percent of the U.S. population. Between 2040 and 2050, these groups will reach the majority–minority crossover, the point at which they will represent the majority of the U.S. population.[62] Women will comprise nearly 50 percent of the workforce. Moreover, latest U.S. Census data suggest that the share of the population over sixty-five will jump from 13 percent now to almost 20 percent in 2030.

What do all these changes mean for you? Simply put, your job may require you to interact with colleagues and customers from around the world. You will need to cooperate with individuals and teams. What's more, your coworkers may differ from you in race, ethnicity, gender, age, and other ways.

1-5e Benefits of a Diverse Workforce

As society and the workforce become more diverse, successful communication among the various identity groups brings distinct advantages. Consumers want to deal with companies that respect their values and reflect themselves.

A diverse staff is better able to respond to the increasingly diverse customer base in local and world markets. The CEO of a PR firm embraces a diverse staff and customers: "Our team consists of more than 40 people who collectively speak 20 different languages." Boykiv urges fellow executives to "Tap into the diversity of your workplace to gain a deep understanding of your workforce and your potential customer base."[64]

Many employees work in teams. Leadership and ethics professor Katherine Phillips believes that "Diversity enhances creativity. It encourages the search for novel information and perspectives, leading to better decision making and problem solving."[65] Diverse teams also tend to be good for the bottom line; they are 45 percent more likely to increase market share and 70 percent more likely to capture a new market.[66]

In addition, organizations that set aside time and resources to cultivate and capitalize on diversity will suffer fewer discrimination lawsuits, fewer union clashes, and less government regulatory action. Developing a diverse staff that can work together cooperatively is one of the biggest challenges facing business organizations today.

1-5f Tips for Communicating With Diverse Audiences on the Job

Harmony and acceptance do not happen automatically when people who are dissimilar work together. This means that organizations must commit to diversity. Harnessed effectively, diversity can enhance productivity and propel a company to success. Mismanaged, it can become a drain on a company's time and resources.

How companies deal with diversity will make all the difference in how they compete in a hyperconnected global environment. The following suggestions can help you find ways to improve communication and interaction:

- **Seek training.** If your organization is experiencing diversity problems, awareness-raising sessions may be helpful. Spend time reading and learning about workforce diversity and how it can benefit organizations. Look upon diversity as an opportunity, not a threat. Intercultural communication, team building, and conflict resolution are skills that can be learned in diversity training programs.

- **Understand the value of differences.** Diversity makes an organization innovative and creative. Sameness fosters an absence of critical thinking called *groupthink*. Michael Roth, president of Wesleyan University, believes that "homogeneity kills creativity" and threatens democracy and learning: "We know that diversity is a powerful hedge against the 'rationalized conformity' of groupthink."[67] Diversity can be a powerful antidote.

- **Learn about your cultural self.** Begin to think of yourself as a product of your culture, and understand that your culture is just one among many. Take any opportunity to travel or study abroad, if possible. You will learn much, not only about other cultures but also about your own. Try to stand outside and look at yourself. Do you see any reflex reactions and automatic thought patterns that are a result of your upbringing? These may be invisible to you until challenged by difference. Be sure to keep what works and yet be ready to adapt as environments change. Flexibility is an important survival skill.

- **Make fewer assumptions.** Be careful of seemingly insignificant, innocent workplace assumptions. For example, don't assume that everyone wants to observe the holidays with a Christmas party and a decorated tree. Celebrating only Christian holidays in December and January excludes those who honor Hanukkah, Kwanzaa, and the Lunar New Year. Moreover, in workplace discussions don't assume anything about others' sexual orientation or attitude toward marriage. For invitations, avoid phrases such as *managers and their wives*. *Spouses* or *partners* is more inclusive. Valuing diversity means making fewer assumptions that everyone is like you or wants to be like you.

- **Build on similarities.** Look for areas in which you and others not like you can agree or at least share opinions. Be prepared to consider issues from many perspectives, all of which may be valid. Accept that there is room for various points of view to coexist peacefully. Although you can always find differences, it is much harder to find similarities. Look for common ground in shared experiences, mutual goals, and similar values.[68] Concentrate on your objective even when you may disagree on how to reach it.

Summary of Learning Outcomes

1 **Describe how strong communication skills will improve your career outlook, strengthen your credibility, and help you succeed in today's competitive digital age workplace.**

- Employers hire and promote job candidates who have excellent communication skills; writing skills make or break careers.
- Because workers interact more than ever using communication technology, even technical fields require communication skills.

- New-hires and other employees must project a professional image and possess soft skills.
- Job challenges in the information age include changing communication technologies, mobile 24/7 offices, flatter management, an emphasis on teams, and global competition.

2 Confront barriers to effective listening, and start building your listening skills.

- Most of us are poor listeners; we can learn active listening by removing physical and psychological barriers, overlooking language problems, and eliminating distractions.
- A fast processing speed allows us to let our minds wander; we fake attention and prefer to talk than to listen.
- Poor listening can be overcome as long as we stop talking, focus fully on others, control distractions, keep an open mind, and listen for the speaker's main ideas.
- Capitalizing on lag time, listening between the lines, judging ideas instead of appearances, taking good notes, and providing feedback are other methods for building listening skills.

3 Explain the features of nonverbal communication, and recognize the importance of improving your nonverbal communication skills.

- Be aware of nonverbal cues such as eye contact, facial expression, and posture that send silent, highly believable messages.
- Understand that how you use time, space, and territory is interpreted by the receiver, who also "reads" the eye appeal of your business documents and your personal appearance.
- Build solid nonverbal skills by keeping eye contact, maintaining good posture, reducing physical barriers, improving your decoding skills, and probing for more information.
- Interpret nonverbal meanings in context, learn about other cultures, and understand the impact of appearance—of documents, your office space, and yourself.

4 Name five common dimensions of culture, and understand how culture influences communication and the use of social media and communication technology.

- Culture is a complex system of values, traits, and customs shared by a society; culture molds the way we think, behave, and communicate both offline and online.
- Culture can be described using key dimensions such as context, individualism, time orientation, power distance, and communication style.
- Today's communicators need to be aware of low- and high-context cultures, individualistic versus collectivist societies, differing attitudes toward time, clashing perceptions of power, and varying degrees of reliance on the written word.
- Whether social media and technology can bridge cultural divides and erase differences will depend on the users as much as it would among strangers who meet at a dinner party.

5 Discuss strategies that help communicators overcome negative cultural attitudes and prevent miscommunication in today's diverse, mobile, social-media-driven workplace.

- Beware of ethnocentrism and stereotyping; instead, embrace tolerance and keep an open mind.
- When communicating orally, use simple English, speak slowly, check for comprehension, observe eye messages, accept blame, don't interrupt, smile, and follow up in writing.
- When writing, consider local styles, hire a translator, use short sentences, avoid ambiguous wording, and cite numbers carefully.
- As the domestic workforce becomes more diverse, appreciate diversity as a critical business strategy.
- To communicate well with diverse audiences, seek training, understand the value of diversity, learn about your own culture, make fewer assumptions, and look for similarities.

Chapter Review

1. In what ways are communication skills a path to success or to likely elimination from competition? (L.O. 1)

2. Why are writing skills more important in today's workplace than ever before? (L.O. 1)

3. List six trends in the information age workplace that pose a challenge for business communicators. (L.O. 1)

4. List bad habits and distractions that can act as barriers to effective listening. (L.O. 2)

5. List 11 techniques for improving your listening skills. Be prepared to discuss each. (L.O. 2)

6. How do we send messages to others without speaking? (L.O. 3)

7. What did communication theorist Paul Watzlawick mean when he said that we cannot not communicate? Are the nonverbal signals we are sending easy to read? (L.O. 3)

8. What is culture, and what are five key dimensions that can be used to describe it? (L.O. 4)

9. Name four strategies for communicating with diverse audiences on the job. (L.O. 5)

10. List seven or more suggestions for enhancing comprehension when you are talking with nonnative speakers of English. Be prepared to discuss each. (L.O. 5)

Critical Thinking

11. What could be the career fallout for someone who is unwilling or unable to train to become a better communicator? Can workers today be successful if their writing is and remains poor? (L.O. 1)

12. Why do executives and managers spend more time listening than do workers? (L.O. 2)

13. What arguments could you give for or against the idea that body language is a science with principles that can be interpreted accurately by specialists? (L.O. 3)

14. Imagine that businesspeople from a high-context culture (e.g., Japan or China) meet their counterparts from a low-context culture (the United States) for the first time to negotiate and sign a manufacturing contract. What could go wrong? How about conflicting perceptions of time? (L.O. 4)

15. It is quite natural to favor one's own country over a foreign one. To what extent can ethnocentrism be considered a normal reaction, and when could it become destructive and unproductive? Provide examples to support your answer. (L.O. 5)

Activities and Cases

1.1 Introduce Yourself (L.O. 1)

> Communication Technology > E-Mail > Social Media

Your instructor wants to know more about you, your motivation for taking this course, your career goals, and your writing skills.

YOUR TASK. Send an e-mail or write a memo of introduction to your instructor. See Chapter 5 for formats and tips on preparing e-mails. In your message include the following:

a. Your reasons for taking this class
b. Your career goals (both temporary and long term)
c. A brief description of your employment, if any, and your favorite activities
d. An evaluation and discussion of your current communication skills, including your strengths and weaknesses

Alternatively, your instructor may ask you develop a profile within a learning-management system (e.g., Blackboard or Moodle) to introduce yourself to your classmates. If your class is small, your instructor may challenge you to compose your introduction in 140 or fewer characters (see Chapter 5 for tips on writing Twitter and other microblogging messages).

1.2 Small-Group Presentation: Introduce Team Members (L.O. 1, 2)

> Team

Many business organizations today use teams to accomplish their goals. To help you develop speaking, listening, and teamwork skills, your instructor may assign team projects. One of the first jobs in any team is selecting members and becoming acquainted.

YOUR TASK. Your instructor will divide your class into small groups or teams. At your instructor's direction, either (a) interview another group member and introduce that person to the group or (b) introduce yourself to the group. Think of this as an informal interview for a team assignment or a job. You will want to make notes from which to speak. Your introduction should include information such as the following:

a. Where did you grow up?
b. What work and extracurricular activities have you engaged in?
c. What are your interests and talents? What are you good at doing?
d. What have you achieved?
e. How familiar are you with various computer technologies?
f. What are your professional and personal goals? Where do you expect to be five years from now?
g. Name one thing about you that others might not guess when they first meet you.

To develop listening skills, practice the listening techniques discussed in this chapter and take notes when other students are presenting. In addition to mentioning details about each speaker, be prepared to discuss three important facts about each speaker.

1.3 Social Media Inventory (L.O. 1, 3, 4)

> **Communication Technology** ▸ **E-Mail** ▸ **Social Media** ▸ **Team** ▸ **Web**

The millennials (those born after 1985) do not remember a time without computer technology and cell phones in wide use. People born in the 1990s have only known a society that depends on the Internet and mobile technology. Social media are second nature to most of these young people, who seem to be inseparably attached to their smart devices.

You may live, learn, work, play, network, and shop in the digital world. Even if you are not crazy about the latest gadgets and gizmos, your daily life depends on technology because your cell phone, iPod, TV, DVD player, and other electronics wouldn't exist without it and are increasingly networked.

YOUR TASK. Take stock of your Internet, social media, and other technology use. First establish useful criteria—for example, categories such as consumer electronics, social networking sites, preferred modes of communication with friends and family, and so forth. Within each category, list the technology you use most frequently. For instance, for social media networks and messaging, indicate your use of Facebook, YouTube, Instagram, Messenger, WhatsApp, Twitter, Snapchat, Google+, LinkedIn, and more. How do you use each? Estimate how often you access these sites per day, and indicate the tools you use (e.g., smartphone, tablet, laptop). How much do you text every day? Your instructor may ask you to create at least three categories such as the ones in the preceding list and record your responses in writing. Then compare your three lists within a group of five classmates or in assigned teams. Share your results individually or in teams, either verbally or in writing. Your instructor may ask you to summarize your observations about how plugged in you and your classmates are in a post on a discussion board or in an e-mail.

1.4 Soft Skills: Personal Strengths Inventory (L.O. 1)

When hiring future workers, employers look for hard skills, which are those we learn such as mastery of software applications or accountancy procedures. However, as we have seen in this chapter, businesses are desperate for job candidates equipped with soft skills; some recruiters value soft skills even more than hard skills. Recall that soft skills are interpersonal characteristics, strengths, or other psychological assets a person possesses. Studies have divided soft skills into four categories:

- Thinking and problem solving
- Oral and written communication
- Personal qualities and work ethic
- Interpersonal and teamwork

YOUR TASK. Using the preceding categories to guide you, identify your own soft skills, paying attention to those attributes you think a potential employer would value. Prepare lists of at least four items in each of the four categories. For example, as evidence of problem solving, you might list a specific workplace or student problem you recognized and solved. You will want to weave these words and phrases into cover letters and résumés, which are covered in Chapter 13.

1.5 Rating Your Listening Skills (L.O. 2)

> **Web** ▸

You can learn whether your listening skills are excellent or deficient by completing a brief quiz.

YOUR TASK. Take *Dr. Guffey's Listening Quiz* at **www.cengagebrain.com**. What two listening behaviors do you think you need to work on the most?

1.6 Listening: An In-Person or Virtual Social Media Interview (L.O. 2)

| Communication Technology | E-Mail | Social Media | Team |

How much and to whom do businesspeople listen?

YOUR TASK. Interview a businessperson about his or her workplace listening. Connect with a worker in your circle of friends, family, and acquaintances; in your campus network; at a prior or current job; or via LinkedIn or Facebook. Come up with questions to ask about listening, such as the following: (a) How much active listening do you practice daily? (b) To whom do you listen on the job? (c) How do you know that others are listening or not listening to you? (d) Can you share anecdotes of poor listening that led to negative outcomes? (e) Do you have tips for better listening?

1.7 Listening and Nonverbal Cues: Skills Required in Various Careers (L.O. 2, 3)

| Team |

Do the listening skills and behaviors of individuals differ depending on their careers?

YOUR TASK. Your instructor will divide you into teams and give each team a role to discuss, such as business executive, teacher, physician, police officer, attorney, accountant, administrative assistant, mentor, or team leader. Create a list of verbal and nonverbal cues that a member of this profession would display to indicate that he or she is listening.

1.8 Nonverbal Communication: How Do You Come Across? (L.O. 3)

| Team |

What does your body language say about you? Do you know?

YOUR TASK. Your instructor may pair you up or ask you to form small groups. To find out how others perceive you, ask a classmate or two to critique your use of eye contact, facial expression, and body movements. For two minutes talk about your background, your major, or some other topic that will allow peers to observe your nonverbal cues. Ask your partner or group members to jot down any observations. Another way to analyze your nonverbal style is to record yourself making a presentation. Then study your performance. This way you can make sure your nonverbal cues send the same message as your words. When your instructor asks, share your general impressions—for example, about the duration of eye contact, body posture, voice quality, and other observations.

1.9 Nonverbal Communication: Reading Body Language (L.O. 3)

Can body language be accurately interpreted?

YOUR TASK. What attitudes do the following body movements suggest to you? Do these movements always mean the same thing? What part does context play in your interpretations?

a. Whistling, wringing hands
b. Bowed posture, twiddling thumbs
c. Steepled hands, sprawling sitting position
d. Rubbing hand through hair
e. Open hands, unbuttoned coat
f. Wringing hands, tugging ears

1.10 Nonverbal Communication: How Best to Signal *I Messed Up* (L.O. 3)

| Team |

To promote tranquility on the highways and reduce road rage, motorists submitted the following suggestions. They were sent to a newspaper columnist who asked for a universal nonverbal signal admitting that a driver had goofed.[69]

YOUR TASK. In small groups consider the pros and cons of each of the following gestures intended as an apology when a driver makes a mistake. Why would some fail?

a. Lower your head slightly and bonk yourself on the forehead with the side of your closed fist. The message is clear: *I'm stupid. I shouldn't have done that.*
b. Make a temple with your hands, as if you were praying.
c. Move the index finger of your right hand back and forth across your neck—as if you were cutting your throat.

d. Flash the well-known peace sign. Hold up the index and middle fingers of one hand, making a V, as in victory.
e. Place the flat of your hands against your cheeks, as children do when they have made a mistake.
f. Clasp your hand over your mouth, raise your brows, and shrug your shoulders.
g. Use your knuckles to knock on the side of your head. Translation: *Oops! Engage brain*.
h. Place your right hand high on your chest and pat a few times, like a basketball player who drops a pass or a football player who makes a bad throw. This says, *I'll take the blame*.
i. Place your right fist over the middle of your chest and move it in a circular motion. This is universal sign language for *I'm sorry*.
j. Open your window and tap the top of your car roof with your hand.
k. Smile and raise both arms, palms outward, which is a universal gesture for surrender or forgiveness.
l. Use the military salute, which is simple and shows respect.
m. Flash your biggest smile, point at yourself with your right thumb, and move your head from left to right, as if to say, *I can't believe I did that*.

1.11 Nonverbal Communication: Signals Sent by Casual Attire (L.O. 3)

Communication Technology ▷ **E-Mail** ▷ **Social Media** ▷ **Team** ▷ **Web**

Although many employers allow casual attire, not all employers and customers are happy with the results. To learn more about the implementation, acceptance, and effects of casual-dress programs, select one of the following activities, all of which involve some form of interviewing.

YOUR TASK.

a. In teams, gather information from human resources directors to determine which companies allow casual or dress-down days, how often, and under what conditions. The information may be collected by personal interviews, e-mail, telephone, or instant messaging.
b. In teams, conduct inquiring-reporter interviews. Ask individuals in the community how they react to casual dress in the workplace. Develop a set of standard interview questions.
c. In teams, visit local businesses on both casual days and traditional business-dress days. Compare and contrast the effects of business-dress standards on such factors as the projected image of the company, the nature of the interactions with customers and with fellow employees, the morale of employees, and the productivity of employees. What generalizations can you draw from your findings?

1.12 Nonverbal Communication: Gestures From Around the World (L.O. 3, 4)

Intercultural ▷ **Web**

Gestures play an important role when people communicate. Because culture shapes the meaning of gestures, miscommunication and misunderstanding can easily result in international situations.

YOUR TASK. Use the Web to research the meanings of selected gestures. Make a list of ten gestures (other than those discussed in the text) that have different meanings in different countries. Consider the fingertip kiss, nose thumb, eyelid pull, nose tap, head shake, and other gestures. How are the meanings different in other countries?

1.13 Intercultural Communication: Watching Those Pesky Idioms (L.O. 4)

Intercultural ▷

Many languages have idiomatic expressions that do not always make sense to outsiders.

YOUR TASK. Explain in simple English what the following idiomatic expressions mean. Assume that you are explaining them to nonnative speakers of English.

a. thinking out of the box
b. bottleneck
c. connect the dots
d. hell on wheels
e. drop the ball
f. get your act together
g. stay the course
h. in the limelight
i. low on the totem pole

1.14 Intercultural Communication: Probing Cultural Stereotypes (L.O. 4, 5)

> Intercultural   Team   Web

Generalizations are necessary as we acquire and categorize new knowledge. As long as we remain open to new experiences, we won't be stymied by rigid, stereotypical perceptions of other cultures. Almost all of us are subject to stereotyping by others at some point in our lives, whether we are immigrants, minorities, women, members of certain professions, or Americans abroad. Generally speaking, negative stereotypes sting. However, even positive stereotypes can offend or embarrass because they fail to acknowledge the differences among individuals.

YOUR TASK. Think about a nation or culture about which you have only a hazy idea. Jot down a few key traits that come to mind. For example, you may not know much about the Netherlands and the Dutch people. You may think of gouda cheese, wooden clogs, Heineken beer, tulips, and windmills. Anything else? Then consider a culture with which you are very familiar, whether it is yours or that of a country you visited or studied. For each culture, in one column, write down a few stereotypical perceptions that are positive. Then, in another column, record negative stereotypes you associate with that culture. Share your notes with your team or the whole class, as your instructor may direct. How do you respond to others' descriptions of your culture? Which stereotypes irk you and why? For a quick fact check and overview at the end of this exercise, google the *CIA World Factbook* or *BBC News Country Profiles*.

1.15 Intercultural Communication: Negotiating Diversity in Job Interviews (L.O. 4, 5)

> Intercultural

Today's workforce benefits from diversity, and most businesses have embraced explicit nondiscrimination policies. The U.S. federal government and many state governments have passed legislation that makes it illegal to discriminate based on race, color, creed, ethnicity, national origin, disability, sex, age, and other factors such as sexual orientation and gender identity. Homestay network Airbnb responded to allegations of discrimination with a lengthy nondiscrimination policy. Brian Chesky, CEO and cofounder of Airbnb, insists that inclusion is the platform's foremost goal: "At the heart of our mission is the idea that people are fundamentally good and every community is a place where you can belong. I sincerely believe that [discrimination] is the greatest challenge we face as a company. It cuts to the core of who we are and the values that we stand for."[70]

YOUR TASK. Consider how intercultural differences could affect the communication, for instance, between an interviewer and a job candidate. If negatively, how could the differences and barriers be overcome? Role-play or discuss a potential job interview conversation between the following individuals. After a while summarize your findings, either orally or in writing:

a. A female top executive is interviewing a prospective future assistant, who is male.
b. A candidate with a strong but not disruptive foreign accent is being interviewed by a native-born human resources manager.
c. A manager dressed in a conventional business suit is interviewing a person wearing a turban.
d. A person over fifty is being interviewed by a hiring manager in his early thirties.
e. A recruiter who can walk is interviewing a job seeker who uses a wheelchair.

Grammar/Mechanics Checkup 1

These checkups are designed to improve your grammar and mechanics skills, which include punctuation, spelling, capitalization, and number use. The checkups systematically review all sections of the Grammar/Mechanics Handbook. You will find a set of alternate Bonus Grammar/Mechanics Checkups with immediate feedback on-line. These Bonus G/M Checkups use different content but parallel the items that appear in the textbook. Use the Bonus G/M Checkups to reinforce your learning.

NOUNS

Review Sections 1.02–1.06 in the Grammar/Mechanics Handbook. Then select the correct form to complete each of the following statements. Record the appropriate G/M section and letter to illustrate the principle involved. When you finish, compare your responses with those provided at the bottom of this page. If your answers differ, study carefully the principles shown in parentheses.

_____   **EXAMPLE**   The tennis match turned out to be a battle of the (a) *sex's*, (b) *sexes*.

_____   1. Neither the cities nor the (a) *countys*, (b) *counties* took responsibility for their deteriorating infrastructures.

_____   2. All the (a) *CEOs* (b) *CEO's* at the meeting checked their cell phones constantly.

_____   3. The two high-priced (a) *attornies*, (b) *attorneys* could not agree on the best defense.

_____   4. Were you asked to work on (a) *Sundays*, (b) *Sunday's*?

_____   5. Many (a) *turkies*, (b) *turkeys* had to be destroyed after the virus outbreak.

_____   6. We noticed that the Sanborns and the (a) *Lopez's*, (b) *Lopezes* brought their entire families.

_____   7. Congress established the Small Business Administration in the (a) *1950's*, (b) *1950s*.

_____   8. President Lincoln had four (a) *brothers-in-law*, (b) *brother-in-laws* serving in the Confederate Army.

_____   9. Four of the wooden (a) *benchs*, (b) *benches* must be repaired.

_____   10. Congress conducted several (a) *inquirys*, (b) *inquiries* regarding new taxes.

_____   11. The instructor was surprised to have three (a) *Anthonies*, (b) *Anthonys* in one class.

_____   12. All the mountains and (a) *valleys* (b) *vallies* were visible on Google Earth.

_____   13. The IRS required copies of all documents showing the company's assets and (a) *liabilitys*, (b) *liabilities*.

_____   14. My tablet monitor makes it difficult to distinguish between (a) *i's and l's*, (b) *i s and l s*.

_____   15. The four sisters-in-law joined many other (a) *woman*, (b) *women* fighting for human rights.

1. b (1.05e) 2. a (1.05g) 3. b (1.05d) 4. a (1.05a) 5. b (1.05d) 6. b (1.05b) 7. b (1.05g) 8. a (1.05f) 9. b (1.05b) 10. b (1.05b) 11. b (1.05a) 12. a (1.05d) 13. b (1.05e) 14. a (1.05h) 15. b (1.05c)

Every chapter provides an editing exercise to fine-tune your grammar and mechanics skills. These are the skills that employers frequently find lacking in employees. In this e-mail look for errors in proofreading, grammar, spelling, punctuation, capitalization, word use, and number form. Study the guidelines in the Grammar/Mechanics Handbook in Appendix D, including the lists of Confusing Words and Frequently Misspelled Words.

YOUR TASK. Edit the following (a) by inserting corrections in your textbook or on a photocopy using the proofreading marks in Appendix C or (b) by downloading the message from **www.cengagebrain.com** and correcting at your computer. **Hint:** You should make about 30 edits. Your instructor may ask you to use **Track Changes** as you edit. See the Communication Workshop in Chapter 4 for more information about using **Track Changes**.

To:	Emily Tehrani <etehrani@pioneer.com>
From:	Benjamin Young <byoung@pioneer.com>
Subject:	Guidance as Your Work From Home

Hi, Emily,

I'm happy to learn that you were just granted a leave to work from home, here are some tips on how to be productive while staying in touch with the office.

- **Establish a defined workspace.** Creating a dedicated workspace sends a clear message to others in your house hold that you are doing work.

- **Respond to e-mail.** Check your incoming mail at least 3 times a day. Answer all message promply, and send copys of relevant messages to the appropriate office staff.

- **Transmit all work orders to Rachel.** She will analyze each weeks activitys and update all sales assignments and inventorys.

- **Prepare an end of week report.** Send a summery of your weeks work to me indicating the major accounts you managed.

If you not a big e-mail user get acquainted with it right away and don't be afraid to use it. Please shoot e-mails to any staff member. When you need clarification on a project, or if you just want to keep us updated.

We will continue to hold once a week staff meetings on Friday's at 9 a.m. in the morning. Do you think you can join us for 1 or 2 of these meeting? The next one is on Friday June 9th.

You're sure to enjoy working at home Emily. Following these basic guideline should help you complete your work efficintly and provide the office with adequate communication.

Best wishes,

Ben

Director, Personnel
Pioneer Solutions
byoung@pioneer.com
808-448-3490

Exploring Career Prospects in Your Field With LinkedIn

Where are the jobs? The good news is that, although competitive, the job market is promising and hiring is up. How can you find open positions? As many as 80 percent of candidates snag a job through old-fashioned networking with people they know.[71] However, LinkedIn takes searching and networking online, where the employers are. In a recent poll, nearly 95 percent of recruiting and staffing professionals stated that they used LinkedIn as a recruiting tool.[72]

LinkedIn is the place to find and be found, especially for new grads. It lists well over a million and a half student jobs and internships in addition to millions of full-time jobs.[73] Other social media platforms, such as Facebook, Twitter, Google+, and Glassdoor, as well as popular job boards, are additional job-search tools you can literally manage in the palm of your hand. LinkedIn is an excellent place for any job seeker to learn what is available, what qualifications are necessary, and what salaries are being offered. If you haven't done so already, you will need to develop an effective, professional LinkedIn profile sooner or later.

CAREER APPLICATION. Assume that you are about to finish your degree or certification program and you are now looking for a job. At the direction of your instructor, conduct a survey of online job advertisements in your field. What's available? How much is the salary? What are the requirements?

YOUR TASK

- **Visit LinkedIn.** If you haven't signed up for an account yet, look for the Browse LinkedIn heading on the home page, and click the Jobs link below it. If you have a profile already, go to your home page and click Jobs in the black band on top of the page.

- **Study the opening page.** The interface is clean and uncluttered. If you have previously joined LinkedIn, your search results will be relevant to your profile.

- **Select keyword, category, city, and state.** Decide whether you want to search by a job title (such as *nurse, accountant, project manager*) or a category (such as *Accounting/Finance, Administrative/Clerical, Advertising/Marketing*). Enter your keyword job title or select a category—or do both. Enter a city, state, or region. Click Search.

- **Study the job listings.** Click the links to read more about the job openings.

- **Explore popular job boards.** Try Indeed, the No. 1 job site, offering millions of job listings aggregated from thousands of websites. Indeed accounts for more hires than all the other job boards combined. Other big boards are CareerBuilder, Monster, and CollegeGrad. These sites allow you to search by location and type of job. Become familiar with the sites' search tools, and look for jobs in your field.

- **Select the best ads.** In your career and geographical area, select the three best ads and print them. If you cannot print, take notes on what you find.

- **Analyze the skills required.** How often do the ads you printed mention *communication, teamwork, computer skills,* or *professionalism*? What tasks do the ads mention? What is the salary range identified in these ads for the positions they feature? Tip: Glassdoor offers an insider's look at many companies and positions. Because posts are anonymous, you will find confidential salary data. Your instructor may ask you to submit your findings and/or report to the class.

Communication Workshops (such as the one on this page) provide insight into special business communication topics and skills not discussed in the chapters. Topics include ethics, technology, career skills, and collaboration. Each workshop includes a career application to extend your learning and help you develop skills relevant to the workshop topic.

The Writing Process in the Information Age

Planning Business Messages

iStock.com/GlobalStock

Learning Outcomes

After studying this chapter, you should be able to do the following:

1 Understand the five steps in the communication process.

2 Define the goals of business writing, summarize the 3-x-3 writing process, and explain how it guides a writer.

3 Analyze the purpose of a message, anticipate its audience, and select the best communication channel.

4 Employ expert writing techniques such as incorporating audience benefits, developing the "you" view, and using conversational but professional language.

5 Improve the tone and clarity of a message by using positive and courteous expression, bias-free language, plain words, and precise terms.

2-1 Examining the Communication Process

In the information age, the workplace has become increasingly interconnected. People are exchanging information with a staggering number of messages, most of them in digital form. As a business communicator, you will have an enormous array of communication channels from which to choose, including the latest social media platforms. However, even as we have accepted instant messaging, texting, Twitter, and other interactive media, the nature of communication remains unchanged. No matter how we create or send our messages, the basic communication process consists of the same elements. It starts with an idea that must be transmitted.

In its simplest form, *communication* may be defined as "the transmission of information and meaning from a sender to a receiver." The crucial element in this definition is *meaning*. The process is successful only when the receiver understands an idea as the sender intended it. How does an idea travel from one person to another? It involves a sensitive process, as shown in Figure 2.1. This process can easily be sidetracked resulting in miscommunication. The process of communication, however, is successful when both the sender and the receiver understand the process and how to make it work. In our discussion we are most concerned with professional communication in the workplace so that you can be successful as a business communicator in your career.

Figure 2.1 The Communication Process

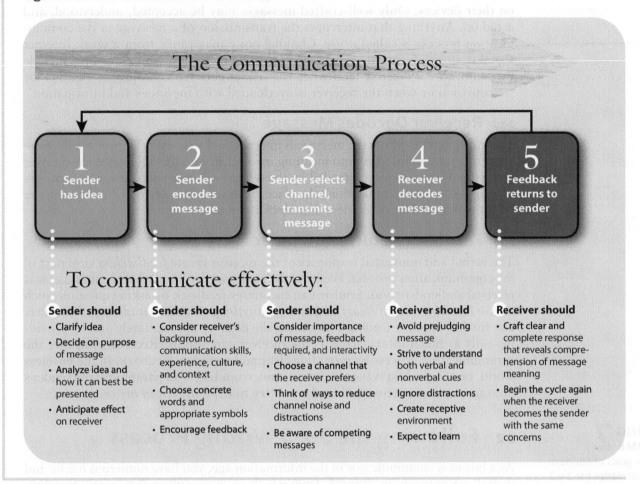

The Communication Process

| 1 Sender has idea | 2 Sender encodes message | 3 Sender selects channel, transmits message | 4 Receiver decodes message | 5 Feedback returns to sender |

To communicate effectively:

Sender should
- Clarify idea
- Decide on purpose of message
- Analyze idea and how it can best be presented
- Anticipate effect on receiver

Sender should
- Consider receiver's background, communication skills, experience, culture, and context
- Choose concrete words and appropriate symbols
- Encourage feedback

Sender should
- Consider importance of message, feedback required, and interactivity
- Choose a channel that the receiver prefers
- Think of ways to reduce channel noise and distractions
- Be aware of competing messages

Receiver should
- Avoid prejudging message
- Strive to understand both verbal and nonverbal cues
- Ignore distractions
- Create receptive environment
- Expect to learn

Receiver should
- Craft clear and complete response that reveals comprehension of message meaning
- Begin the cycle again when the receiver becomes the sender with the same concerns

2-1a Sender Has Idea

The communication process begins when the sender has an idea. The form of the idea may be influenced by complex factors surrounding the sender. These factors include mood, frame of reference, background, culture, and physical makeup, as well as the context of the situation and many other factors. Senders shape their ideas based on their own experiences and assumptions.

2-1b Sender Encodes Idea

The next step in the communication process involves *encoding*. This means converting the idea into words or gestures that will convey meaning. A major problem in communicating any message verbally is that words have different meanings for different people. Recognizing how easy it is to be misunderstood, skilled communicators choose familiar, concrete words. In choosing proper words and symbols, senders must be alert to the receiver's communication skills, attitudes, background, experiences, and culture. Including a smiley face in an e-mail announcement to stockholders may turn them off.

2-1c Sender Selects Channel and Transmits Message

The medium over which the message travels is the *channel*. Messages may be delivered by letter, memorandum, report, announcement, picture, spoken word, fax, Web page, or some other channel. Today's messages are increasingly carried over

LEARNING OUTCOME 1
Understand the five steps in the communication process.

digital networks with much opportunity for distraction and breakdown. Receivers may be overloaded with incoming messages or unable to receive messages clearly on their devices. Only well-crafted messages may be accepted, understood, and acted on. Anything that interrupts the transmission of a message in the communication process is called *noise*. Channel noise may range from a weak Internet signal to sloppy formatting and typos in e-mail messages. Noise may even include the annoyance a receiver feels when the sender chooses an improper channel for transmission or when the receiver is overloaded with messages and information.

2-1d Receiver Decodes Message

The individual for whom the message is intended is the receiver. Translating the message from its symbol form into meaning involves *decoding*. Only when the receiver understands the meaning intended by the sender—that is, successfully decodes the message—does communication take place. Such success is often difficult to achieve because of a number of barriers that block the process.

2-1e Feedback Returns to Sender

The verbal and nonverbal responses of the receiver create *feedback*, a vital part of the communication process. Feedback helps the sender know that the message was received and understood. Senders can encourage feedback by asking questions such as *Am I making myself clear?* and *Is there anything you don't understand?* Senders can further improve feedback by timing the delivery appropriately and by providing only as much information as the receiver can handle. Receivers improve the communication process by providing clear and complete feedback. In the business world, one of the best ways to advance understanding is to paraphrase the sender's message with comments such as *Let me try to explain that in my own words.*

LEARNING OUTCOME 2

Define the goals of business writing, summarize the 3-x-3 writing process, and explain how it guides a writer.

2-2 Following the 3-x-3 Writing Process

As a business communicator in the information age, you have numerous media and digital communication channels from which to choose when you create, transmit, and respond to messages. Nearly all communication, however, revolves around writing. Whether you are preparing a message that will be delivered digitally, orally, or in print, that message requires thinking and writing.

Many of your messages will be digital. A **digital message** may be defined as "a message that is generated, stored, processed, and transmitted electronically by computers using strings of positive and nonpositive binary code (0s and 1s)." That definition encompasses many messages, including e-mail, Facebook posts, tweets, and videos. For our purposes, we focus primarily on messages exchanged on the job. Because writing is central to all business communication, this chapter presents a systematic plan for preparing business messages in the digital era.

2-2a Recognizing Unique Writing Goals for Business Messages

One thing you should immediately recognize about business writing is that it differs from other writing you have done. In preparing high school or college compositions and term papers, you probably focused on discussing your feelings or displaying your knowledge. Your instructors wanted to see your thought processes, and they wanted assurance that you had internalized the subject matter. You may have had to meet a minimum word count. Business writing is definitely not like that! It also differs from personal texts you may exchange with your friends and family. Those messages enabled you to stay connected and express your feelings. In the workplace, however, your writing should have the following characteristics:

- **Purposeful.** You will be writing to solve problems and convey information. You will have a definite strategy to fulfill in each message.

- **Economical.** You will try to present ideas clearly but concisely. Length is not rewarded.
- **Audience oriented.** You will concentrate on looking at a problem from the perspective of the audience instead of seeing it from your own.

These distinctions actually ease your task. You won't be searching your imagination for creative topic ideas. You won't be stretching your ideas to make them appear longer. Writing consultants and businesspeople complain that many college graduates entering the workplace have a conscious—or perhaps unconscious—perception that quantity enhances quality. Wrong! Get over the notion that longer is better. Whether you are presenting your ideas in print, online, or in person, conciseness and clarity are what count in business.

The ability to prepare purposeful, concise, and audience-centered messages does not come naturally. Very few people, especially beginners, can sit down and draft an effective e-mail message, letter, or report without training. However, following a systematic process, studying model messages, and practicing the craft can make nearly anyone a successful business writer or speaker.

2-2b Introducing the 3-x-3 Writing Process

Regardless of what you are writing, the process will be easier if you follow a systematic plan. The 3-x-3 writing process breaks the entire task into three phases: *prewriting*, *drafting*, and *revising*, as shown in Figure 2.2.

To illustrate the writing process, let's say that you own a popular McDonald's franchise. At rush times, you face a problem. Customers complain about the chaotic multiple waiting lines to approach the service counter. You once saw two customers nearly get into a fistfight over cutting into a line. What's more, customers often are so intent on looking for ways to improve their positions in line that they fail to examine the menu. Then they are undecided when their turn arrives. You want to convince other franchise owners that a single-line (serpentine) system would work better. You could telephone the other owners. However, you want to present a serious argument with good points that they will remember and be willing to act on when they gather for their next district meeting. You decide to send a persuasive e-mail that you hope will win their support.

Prewriting. The first phase of the writing process prepares you to write. It involves *analyzing* the audience and your purpose for writing. The audience for your message will be other franchise owners, some highly educated and others not. Your purpose in writing is to convince them that a change in policy would improve customer service. You think that a single-line system, such as that used in banks, would reduce chaos and make customers happier because they would not have to worry about where they are in line.

Prewriting also involves *anticipating* how your audience will react to your message. You are sure that some of the other owners will agree with you, but others might fear that customers seeing a long single line might go elsewhere. In *adapting* your message to the audience, you try to think of the right words and the right tone that will win approval.

Drafting. The second phase involves researching, organizing, and then drafting the message. In *researching* information for this message, you would probably investigate other kinds of businesses that use single lines for customers. You might check your competitors. What are Wendy's and Burger King doing? You might do some calling to see whether other franchise owners are concerned about chaotic lines. Before writing to the entire group, you might brainstorm with a few owners to see what ideas they have for solving the problem.

Once you have collected enough information, you would focus on *organizing* your message. Should you start out by offering your solution? Or should you work up to it slowly, describing the problem, presenting your evidence, and then ending

OFFICE INSIDER

Writing for the *Harvard Business Review*, David Silverman blasts "an educational system that rewards length over clarity." Students learn to overwrite, he says, in hopes that at least some of their sentences "hit the mark." Once on the job, they continue to act as if they were paid by the word, a perception that must be unlearned.[1]

David Silverman, *entrepreneur and business teacher*

Figure 2.2 The 3-x-3 Writing Process

1 Prewriting

Analyze
- What is your purpose?
- What do you want the receiver to do or believe?
- What channel should you choose: face-to-face conversation, group meeting, e-mail, memo, letter, report, blog, wiki, tweet?
- What are the benefits or barriers of each channel?

Anticipate
- What is the audience profile?
- What does the receiver already know?
- Will the receiver's response be neutral, positive, or negative? How will the response affect your organizational strategy?

Adapt
- What techniques can you use to adapt your message to its audience?
- How can you promote feedback?
- What can you do to ensure positive, conversational, and courteous language?

2 Drafting

Research
- Gather data to provide facts.
- Review previous correspondence.
- Search company files for background information.
- Talk with the boss and colleagues.
- Search the Internet.
- What do you need to know to write this message?

Organize
- Organize direct messages with the big idea first, followed by an explanation in the body and an action request in the closing.
- For persuasive or negative messages, use an indirect problem-solving strategy.

Draft
- Prepare a first draft, usually writing quickly.
- Focus on short, clear sentences using the active voice.
- Build paragraph coherence by repeating key ideas, using pronouns, and incorporating appropriate transitional expressions.

3 Revising

Edit
- Edit your message to be sure it is clear, concise, conversational, and readable.
- Revise to eliminate wordy fillers, long lead-ins, redundancies, and trite business phrases.
- Consider using headings and numbered and bulleted lists for quick reading.

Proofread
- Take the time to read the message carefully.
- Look for errors in spelling, grammar, punctuation, names, and numbers.
- Check to be sure the format is consistent.

Evaluate
- Will this message achieve its purpose?
- Does the tone sound pleasant and friendly rather than curt?
- Have you thought enough about the audience to be sure this message is appealing?
- Did you encourage feedback?

with the solution? The final step in the second phase of the writing process is actually *drafting* the letter. At this point many writers write quickly, knowing that they will polish their ideas when they revise.

Revising. The third phase of the process involves editing, proofreading, and evaluating your message. After writing the first draft, you will spend considerable time *editing* the message for clarity, conciseness, tone, and readability. Could parts of it be rearranged to make your point more effectively? This is the time when you look for ways to improve the organization and tone of your message. Next, you will spend time *proofreading* carefully to ensure correct spelling, grammar, punctuation, and format. The final phase involves *evaluating* your message to decide whether it accomplishes your goal.

2-2c Pacing the Writing Process

The time you spend on each phase of the writing process varies depending on the complexity of the problem, the purpose, the audience, and your schedule. On average, you should expect to spend about 25 percent of your time prewriting, 25 percent drafting, and 50 percent revising, as shown in Figure 2.3.

These are rough guides, yet you can see that good writers spend most of their time on the final phase of revising and proofreading. Much depends, of course, on your project, its importance, and your familiarity with it. What is critical to

Figure 2.3 Scheduling the Writing Process

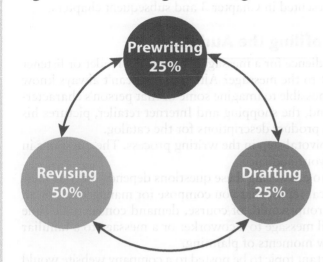

Prewriting 25%

Revising 50%

Drafting 25%

> Although the writing process looks like a linear set of steps, it actually is recursive, enabling writers to revise their work continually as they progress. However, careful planning can avoid wasted time and frustration caused by rethinking and reorganizing during drafting.

remember, though, is that revising is a major component of the writing process even if the message is short.

It may appear that you perform one step and progress to the next, always following the same order. Most business writing, however, is not that rigid. Although writers perform the tasks described, the steps may be rearranged, abbreviated, or repeated. Some writers revise every sentence and paragraph as they go. Many find that new ideas occur after they have begun to write, causing them to back up, alter the organization, and rethink the plan. Beginning business writers often follow the writing process closely. With experience, though, they will become like other good writers and presenters who alter, compress, and rearrange the steps as needed.

2-3 Analyzing the Purpose and Anticipating the Audience

LEARNING OUTCOME 3

Analyze the purpose of a message, anticipate its audience, and select the best communication channel.

Surprisingly, many people begin writing and discover only as they approach the end of a message what they are trying to accomplish. If you analyze your purpose before you begin, you can avoid having to backtrack and start over. The remainder of this chapter covers the first phase of the writing process: analyzing the purpose for writing, anticipating how the audience will react, and adapting the message to the audience.

2-3a Defining Your Purpose

The best way to begin a workplace message is by asking yourself two important questions: (a) Why am I sending this message? and (b) What do I hope to achieve? Your responses will determine how you organize and present your information.

Your message may have both primary and secondary purposes. For college work your primary purpose may be merely to complete the assignment; secondary purposes might be to make yourself look good and to earn an excellent grade. The primary purposes for sending business messages are typically to inform and to persuade. A secondary purpose is to promote goodwill. You and your organization want to look good in the eyes of your audience.

Many business messages do nothing more than *inform*. They explain procedures, announce meetings, answer questions, and transmit findings. Such messages are usually developed directly, as discussed in Chapter 3. Some business messages, however, are meant to *persuade*. These messages attempt to sell products, convince managers, motivate employees, and win over customers. Persuasive messages are often developed indirectly, as presented in Chapter 3 and subsequent chapters.

2-3b Anticipating and Profiling the Audience

A good writer anticipates the audience for a message: What is the reader or listener like? How will that person react to the message? Although one can't always know exactly who the receiver is, it is possible to imagine some of that person's characteristics. A copywriter at Lands' End, the shopping and Internet retailer, pictures his sister-in-law whenever he writes product descriptions for the catalog.

Profiling your audience is a pivotal step in the writing process. The questions in Figure 2.4 will help you profile your audience.

How much time you devote to answering these questions depends on your message and its context. An analytical report that you compose for management or an oral presentation before a big group would, of course, demand considerable time profiling the audience. An e-mail message to a coworker or a message to a familiar supplier might require only a few moments of planning.

Preparing a blog on an important topic to be posted to a company website would require you to think about the local, national, and international audiences that might read that message. Similarly, posting brief personal messages at microblogging sites such as Facebook, Twitter, and Tumblr should make you think about who will read the messages. How much of your day and life do you want to share? Will customers and business partners be reading your posts?

No matter how short your message is, though, spend some time thinking about the people in your audience so that you can tailor your words to them. Remember that your receivers will be thinking, "What's in it for me?" (WIIFM). One of the most important writing tips you can take away from this book is remembering that every message you write should begin with the notion that your audience is thinking WIIFM.

2-3c Tailoring Your Message to the Audience Profile

Profiling your audience helps you make decisions about shaping the message. You will discover what language is appropriate, whether you are free to use specialized technical terms, whether you should explain the background, and so on. Profiling

---

Figure 2.4 Asking the Right Questions to Profile Your Audience

Primary Audience	Secondary Audience

• Who is my primary reader or listener?	• Who might see or hear this message in addition to the primary audience?
• What are my personal and professional relationships with this person?	• How do these people differ from the primary audience?
• How much does this person know about the subject?	• Do I need to include more background information?
• What do I know about this person's education, beliefs, culture, and attitudes?	• How must I reshape my message to make it understandable and acceptable to others to whom it might be forwarded?
• Should I expect a neutral, positive, or negative response to my message?	

the audience helps you decide whether your tone should be formal or informal. Profiling helps you consider whether the receiver is likely to respond positively or negatively to your message, or be neutral about it.

Another consideration in profiling your audience is the possibility of a secondary audience. For example, let's say you start to write an e-mail message to your supervisor, Emily, describing a problem you are having. Halfway through the message, you realize that Emily will probably forward this message to her boss, the vice president. Emily will probably not want to summarize what you said; instead, she may take the easy route and merely forward your e-mail. When you realize that the vice president may see this message, you decide to back up and use a more formal tone. You remove your inquiry about Emily's family, you reduce your complaints, and you tone down your language about why things went wrong. Instead, you provide more background information, and you are more specific in identifying items the vice president might not recognize. Analyzing the task and anticipating the audience help you adapt your message so it will be effective for both primary and secondary receivers.

2-3d Choosing the Best Channel

After identifying the purpose of your message, you will want to choose the most appropriate communication channel. In this digital era, the number of channels continues to expand, as shown in Figure 2.5. Your decision to send an e-mail message, schedule a videoconference, post a note on the company intranet, or use some other channel depends on some of the following factors:

- Importance of the message
- Amount and speed of feedback and interactivity required
- Necessity of a permanent record
- Cost of the channel
- Degree of formality desired
- Confidentiality and sensitivity of the message
- Receiver's preference and level of technical expertise

In addition to these practical issues, you will also consider how rich the channel is. The *richness* of a channel involves the extent to which a channel or medium recreates or represents all the information available in the original message. A richer medium, such as a face-to-face conversation, permits more interactivity and feedback. A leaner medium, such as a letter or an e-mail, presents a flat, one-dimensional message. Richer media enable the sender to provide more verbal and visual cues as well as to tailor the message to the audience.

Figure 2.5 Comparing Rich and Lean Communication Channels

LEARNING OUTCOME 4

Employ expert writing techniques such as incorporating audience benefits, developing the "you" view, and using conversational but professional language.

Choosing the wrong medium can result in a message that is less effective or even misunderstood. If, for example, marketing manager Craig must motivate the sales force to increase sales in the fourth quarter, he is unlikely to achieve his goal if he merely posts an announcement on the office bulletin board, writes a memo, or sends an e-mail. Craig could be more persuasive with a richer channel, such as individual face-to-face conversations or a group meeting to stimulate sales. For sales reps on the road, a richer medium would be a videoconference. In choosing channels, keep in mind two tips: (a) Use the richest media available, and (b) employ richer media for more persuasive or personal communications.

2-4 Adapting to the Audience With Expert Writing Techniques

After analyzing the purpose and anticipating the audience, writers begin to think about how to adapt a message to the task and the audience. Adaptation is the process of creating a message that suits the audience. Skilled communicators employ a number of expert writing techniques such as featuring audience benefits, cultivating a "you" view, and sounding conversational but professional.

2-4a Focusing on Audience Benefits

Focusing on the audience sounds like a modern idea, but actually one of America's early statesmen and authors recognized this fundamental writing principle over 200 years ago. In describing effective writing, Ben Franklin observed, "To be good, it ought to have a tendency to benefit the reader."[3] These wise words have become a fundamental guideline for today's business communicators. Expanding on Franklin's counsel, a contemporary communication consultant gives this solid advice to his business clients: "Always stress the benefit to the audience of whatever it is you are trying to get them to do. If you can show them how you are going to save them frustration or help them meet their goals, you have the makings of a powerful message."[4] Remember, WIIFM!

Adapting your message to the receiver's needs means putting yourself in that person's shoes. This ability to share someone else's feelings is called *empathy*. Empathic senders think about how a receiver will decode a message. They try to give something to the receiver, solve the receiver's problems, save the receiver's money, or just understand the feelings and position of that person. Which version of each of the following ideas is more appealing to the audience?

SENDER FOCUS	AUDIENCE FOCUS
All workers are herewith instructed to complete the enclosed survey so that we can allocate our limited training funds appropriately.	By filling out the enclosed survey, you can be one of the first to sign up for our limited training funds.
Our one-year warranty becomes effective only when we receive an owner's registration.	Your one-year warranty begins working for you as soon as you return your owner's registration.

2-4b Cultivating the "You" View

In concentrating on audience benefits, skilled communicators naturally develop the "you" view. They emphasize second-person pronouns (*you, your*) instead of first-person pronouns (*I/we, us, our*). Whether your goal is to inform, persuade, or promote goodwill, the catchiest words you can use are *you* and *your*. Compare the following examples.

"I/WE" VIEW	"YOU" VIEW
We are requiring all employees to respond to the attached questionnaire about health benefits.	Because your ideas count, please complete the attached questionnaire about health benefits.
I need your account number before I can do anything to address your problem.	Please give me your account number so that I can locate your records and help you solve this problem.

Although you want to focus on the reader or listener, don't overuse or misuse the second-person pronoun *you*. Readers and listeners appreciate genuine interest; on the other hand, they resent obvious attempts at manipulation. The authors of some sales messages, for example, are guilty of overkill when they include *you* dozens of times in a direct-mail promotion. What's more, the word can sometimes create the wrong impression. Consider this statement: *You cannot return merchandise until you receive written approval.* The word *you* appears twice, but the reader may feel singled out for criticism. In the following version, the message is less personal and more positive: *Customers may return merchandise with written approval.*

Another difficulty in emphasizing the "you" view and de-emphasizing *we/I* is that it may result in overuse of the passive voice. For example, to avoid writing *We will give you* (active voice), you might write *You will be given* (passive voice). The active voice in writing is generally preferred because it identifies who is doing the acting. You will learn more about active and passive voice in Chapter 3.

In recognizing the value of the "you" view, however, you don't have to sterilize your writing and totally avoid any first-person pronouns or words that show your feelings. You can convey sincerity, warmth, and enthusiasm by the words you choose. Don't be afraid of phrases such as *I'm happy* or *We're delighted*, if you truly are. When speaking face-to-face, you can show sincerity and warmth with nonverbal cues such as a smile and a pleasant voice tone. In letters, e-mail messages, memos, and other digital messages, however, only expressive words and phrases can show your feelings. These phrases suggest hidden messages that say *You are important, I hear you,* and *I'm honestly trying to please you.*

2-4c Sounding Conversational but Professional

Most business messages replace conversation. That's why an informal, conversational tone is usually more effective than a formal, pretentious tone. Just how informal you can be depends greatly on the workplace. At Google, casual seems to be preferred. In a short message to users describing changes in its privacy policies, Google staff members recently wrote, "we believe this stuff matters."[5] In more traditional organizations, that message probably would have been more formal. The dilemma for you, then, is knowing how casual to be in your writing. We suggest that you strive to be conversational but professional, especially until you learn what your organization prefers.

E-mail, instant messaging, chat, and other short messaging channels such as Twitter enable you and your coworkers to have spontaneous conversations. Don't, however, let your messages become sloppy, unprofessional, or even dangerous. You will learn more about the dangers of e-mail and other digital channels later. At this point, though, we focus on language tone.

WORKPLACE IN FOCUS

Do emojis have a place in communications at work? In a study conducted by the staffing firm Office Team, 19 percent of the manager and employee respondents said they used emojis all the time, whereas 22 percent used them only in casual exchanges, and 26 percent used them sparingly because they didn't seem professional. "Emojis and emoticons are showing up just about everywhere, but that doesn't mean they're always appropriate for the workplace," said Brandi Britton, district president for Office Team.[6] If you were asked to advise recent grads about how to use emojis in workplace messages, what restrictions would you suggest?

To project a professional image, you want to sound educated and mature. Overuse of expressions such as *totally awesome, you know,* and *like,* as well as reliance on unnecessary abbreviations (*BTW* for "by the way"), make a businessperson sound like a teenager. Emojis are fun to pop into personal messages, but think twice before using them at work. See the Workplace in Focus to learn how managers and employees view emojis. Professional messages do not include texting-style abbreviations, slang, sentence fragments, and chitchat. We urge you to strive for a warm, conversational tone that avoids low-level diction. As shown in Figure 2.6, levels of diction range from unprofessional to formal.

Your goal is to convey a warm, friendly tone that sounds professional. Although some writers are too casual, others are overly formal. To impress readers and listeners, they use big words, long sentences, legal terminology, and third-person constructions. Stay away from expressions such as *the undersigned, the writer,* and *the affected party.* You will sound friendlier with familiar pronouns such as *I, we,* and *you.* Compare the following examples:

OVERLY FORMAL	CONVERSATIONAL
Pursuant to yours of the 18th, the undersigned has received your proposal, which will be scrutinized carefully and returned immediately.	I will review your proposal carefully and return my feedback immediately.
Pertaining to your order, we must verify the sizes that your organization requires prior to consignment of your order to our shipper.	We will send your order as soon as we confirm the sizes you need.

UNPROFESSIONAL	PROFESSIONAL
Hey, boss, Gr8 news! Firewall now installed!! BTW, check with me b4 big reveal.	Mr. Watkins, our new firewall software is now installed. Please check with me before announcing it.
Look, dude, this report is totally bogus. And the figures don't look kosher. Show me some real stats. Got sources?	Because the figures in this report seem inaccurate, please submit the source statistics.

Figure 2.6 Levels of Diction

Unprofessional (Low-level diction)	Conversational (Middle-level diction)	Formal (High-level diction)
badmouth	criticize	denigrate
guts	nerve	courage
pecking order	line of command	dominance hierarchy
ticked off	upset	provoked
rat on	inform	betray
rip off	steal	expropriate

2-5 Improving the Tone and Clarity of a Message

As you continue to improve your writing skills, you can use additional expert techniques that improve the tone, clarity, and effectiveness of a message. These skillful techniques include using a positive and courteous tone, bias-free language, plain words, and precise terms. Take a look at Figure 2.7 to see how you can improve an e-mail message by applying numerous professional writing techniques.

2-5a Being Positive Rather Than Negative

One of the best ways to improve the tone of a message is to use positive rather than negative language. Positive language generally conveys more information than negative language does. Moreover, positive messages are uplifting and pleasant to read. Positive wording tells what *is* and what *can be done* rather than what *isn't* and what *can't be done.* For example, *Your order cannot be shipped by January 10* is not nearly as informative as *Your order will be shipped January 15.* An office supply store adjacent to an ice cream parlor in Portland, Maine, posted a sign on its door that reads: *Please enjoy your ice cream before you enjoy our store.* That sounds much more positive and inviting than *No food allowed!*[8]

Using positive language also involves avoiding negative words that create ill will. Some words appear to blame or accuse your audience. For example, opening a letter to a customer with *You claim that* suggests that you don't believe the customer. Other loaded words that can get you in trouble are *complaint, criticism, defective, failed, mistake, problem,* and *neglected.* Also avoid phrases such as *you seem to be unaware of* or *you did not provide* or *you misunderstood* or *you don't understand.* Notice in the following examples how you can revise the negative tone to create a more positive impression.

LEARNING OUTCOME 5
Improve the tone and clarity of a message by using positive and courteous expression, bias-free language, plain words, and precise terms.

NEGATIVE	POSITIVE
Our request for a fitness center will never be approved without senior management support.	Our request for a fitness center could be approved if we obtain senior management support.
You failed to include your credit card number, so we can't mail your order.	We look forward to completing your order as soon as we receive your credit card number.
Your letter of February 2 claims that you returned a defective headset.	Your February 2 letter describes a headset you returned.
Employees cannot park in Lot B until June 1.	Employees may park in Lot B starting June 1.

Figure 2.7 Improving Tone and Clarity of an E-mail

DRAFT

Options... | HTML

To: TechTron Team Members
From: Rayford Williams <ray.williams@techtron.com>
Subject: Company Must Cut Back Employee Driving Trips to Office

Emphasizes sender's rather than receiver's viewpoint →

Our company faces harsh governmental penalties if we fail to comply with the Air Quality Management District's program to reduce the number of automobile trips made by employees.

The aforementioned program stipulates that we offer incentives to entice employees to discontinue driving their vehicles as a means of transportation to and from this place of employment.

← Uses unfamiliar words (*aforementioned, stipulates, entice*)

Presents ideas negatively (*penalty, must not drive, will not be limited, will not be forced*) and assumes driver will be male →

First, we are prepared to offer a full day off without penalty. However, the employee must not drive to work and must maintain a 75 percent vanpool participation rate for six months. Second, we offer a vanpool subsidy of $100 a month, and the vanpool driver will not be limited in the personal use he makes of the vehicle on his own time. Third, employees in the vanpool will not be forced to park in outlying lots.

Pertaining to our need to have you leave your cars at home, all employees are herewith instructed to communicate with Saul Salazar, who will be facilitating the above-referenced program.

← Doesn't use plain language (*pertaining to, herewith, facilitating, above-referenced*)

REVISION

Options... | HTML

To: TechTron Team Members
From: Rayford Williams <ray.williams@techtron.com>
Subject: Company Must Cut Back Employee Driving Trips to Office

Hi, Team,

Opens with "you" view and audience benefits →

Want to earn a full day off with pay, reduce the stress of your commute, and pay a lot less for gas? You can enjoy these and other perks if you make fewer driving trips to the office.

As part of the Air Quality Management District's Trip Reduction Plan, you can enjoy the following benefits by reducing the number of trips you make to work:

Phrases options in bulleted list with "you" view highlighting benefits (*day off, less driving stress, lower gas bill*) →

- **Full Day Off.** If you maintain a 75 percent participation rate in our ride-share program for a six-month period, you will receive one day off with pay.

- **Vanpool Subsidy.** By joining a vanpool, you will receive assistance in obtaining a van along with a monthly $100 subsidy. Even better, if you become a vanpool driver, you will also have unlimited personal use of the vehicle off company time.

- **Preferential Parking.** By coming to work in vanpools, you can park close to the building in reserved spaces.

Repeats audience benefits with conversational tone and familiar words →

Why not help the environment, reduce your gas bill, and enjoy other perks by joining this program? For more information and to sign up, please contact Saul Salazar at saul.salazar@techtron.com before February 1.

Ray

Rayford Williams
Senior Coordinator, Human Resources
ray.williams@techtron.com
(213) 692-9981

2-5b Expressing Courtesy

Maintaining a courteous tone involves not just guarding against rudeness but also avoiding words that sound demanding or preachy. Expressions such as *you should, you must,* and *you have to* cause people to instinctively react with *Oh, yeah?* One remedy is to turn these demands into rhetorical questions that begin with *Will you please. . . .* Giving reasons for a request also softens the tone.

Even when you feel justified in displaying anger, remember that losing your temper or being sarcastic will seldom accomplish your goals as a business communicator: to inform, to persuade, and to create goodwill. When you are irritated, frustrated, or infuriated, keep cool and try to defuse the situation. In dealing with customers in telephone conversations, use polite phrases such as these: *I would be happy to assist you with that, Thank you for being so patient,* and *It was a pleasure speaking with you.*

LESS COURTEOUS	MORE COURTEOUS AND HELPFUL
Can't you people get anything right? This is the second time I've written!	Please credit my account for $340. My latest statement shows that the error noted in my letter of May 15 has not yet been corrected.
Jeremy, you must complete all performance reviews by Friday.	Jeremy, will you please complete all performance reviews by Friday.
Am I the only one who can read the operating manual?	Let's review the operating manual together so that you can get your documents to print correctly next time.

2-5c Applying Bias-Free Language

In adapting a message to its audience, be sure your language is sensitive and bias free. Few writers set out to be offensive. Sometimes, though, we all say things that we never thought could be hurtful. The real problem is that we don't think about words and phrases that stereotype groups of people, such as *the boys in the mail room* or *the girls in the front office*. Be cautious about expressions that might be biased in terms of gender, race, ethnicity, age, and disability.

Generally, you can avoid gender-biased language by choosing alternate language for words involving *man* or *woman*, by using plural nouns and pronouns, or by changing to a gender-free word (*person* or *representative*). Avoid the *his or her* option whenever possible. It's wordy and conspicuous. With a little effort, you can usually find a construction that is graceful, grammatical, and unself-conscious.

Specify age only if it is relevant, and avoid expressions that are demeaning or subjective (such as *spry old codger*). To avoid disability bias, do not refer to an individual's disability unless it is relevant. When necessary, use terms that do not stigmatize people with disabilities. The following examples give you a quick look at a few problem expressions and possible replacements. The real key to bias-free communication, though, lies in your awareness and commitment. Be on the lookout to be sure that your messages do not exclude, stereotype, or offend people.

GENDER BIASED	BIAS FREE
female doctor, woman attorney, cleaning woman	doctor, attorney, cleaner
waiter/waitress, authoress, stewardess	server, author, flight attendant
mankind, man-hour, man-made	humanity, working hours, artificial
office girls	office workers
the doctor . . . he	doctors . . . they
the teacher . . . she	teachers . . . they

"Many people seem to have adopted the expression 'Not a problem' in place of 'You're welcome.'" The problem with this expression is in its negative parts: *not* and *problem*. When it comes to tone, two negatives do not multiply to create a positive."[9]

Lynn Gaertner-Johnston, *business writing blogger, author, expert*

GENDER BIASED	BIAS FREE
executives and their wives	executives and their spouses
foreman, flagman, workman, craftsman	lead worker, flagger, worker, artisan
businessman, salesman	businessperson, sales representative
Each employee had his picture taken.	Each employee had a picture taken. All employees had their pictures taken. Each employee had his or her picture taken.

RACIALLY OR ETHNICALLY BIASED	BIAS FREE
An Indian accountant was hired.	An accountant was hired.
James Lee, an African American, applied.	James Lee applied.

AGE BIASED	BIAS FREE
The law applied to old people.	The law applied to people over sixty-five.
Sally Kay, 55, was transferred.	Sally Kay was transferred.
a sprightly old gentleman	a man
a little old lady	a woman

DISABILITY BIASED	BIAS FREE
afflicted with arthritis, crippled by arthritis	has arthritis
confined to a wheelchair	uses a wheelchair

2-5d Preferring Plain Language and Familiar Words

In adapting your message to your audience, use plain language and familiar words that you think audience members will recognize. Don't, however, avoid a big word that conveys your idea efficiently and is appropriate for the audience. Your goal is to shun pompous and pretentious language. If you mean *begin*, don't say *commence* or *initiate*. If you mean *pay*, don't write *compensate*. By substituting everyday, familiar words for unfamiliar ones, as shown here, you help your audience comprehend your ideas quickly.

UNFAMILIAR	FAMILIAR
commensurate	equal
interrogate	question
materialize	appear
obfuscate	confuse
remuneration	pay, salary
terminate	end

At the same time, be selective in your use of jargon. *Jargon* describes technical or specialized terms within a field. These terms enable insiders to communicate complex ideas briefly, but to outsiders they mean nothing. Human resources professionals, for example, know precisely what's meant by *cafeteria plan* (a benefits option program), but most of us would be thinking about lunch. Geologists refer to *plate tectonics*, and physicians discuss *metastatic carcinomas*. These terms mean little to most of us. Use specialized language only when the audience will understand it. In addition, don't forget to consider secondary audiences: Will those potential receivers understand any technical terms used?

2-5e Using Precise, Vigorous Words

Strong verbs and concrete nouns give receivers more information and keep them interested. Don't overlook the thesaurus (available in print, online, and on your computer) for expanding your word choices and vocabulary. Whenever possible, use precise, specific words, as shown here:

IMPRECISE, DULL	MORE PRECISE
a change in profits	a 25 percent hike in profits a 10 percent plunge in profits
to say	to promise, confess, understand to allege, assert, assume, judge
to think about	to identify, diagnose, analyze to probe, examine, inspect

Summary of Learning Outcomes

1 Understand the five steps in the communication process.

- A sender has an idea.
- The sender encodes (selects) words or symbols to express the idea in a message.
- The message travels over a channel (such as a letter, memorandum, report, announcement, image, tweet, spoken word, or Web page).
- "Noise" (loud sounds, misspelled words, an inappropriate channel, or other distractions) may interfere with the transmission.
- The receiver decodes (interprets) the message and may respond with feedback.

2 Define the goals of business writing, summarize the 3-x-3 writing process, and explain how it guides a writer.

- Business writing should be purposeful, economical, and audience oriented.
- Phase 1 (prewriting): analyze the message, anticipate the audience, and consider how to adapt the message to the audience.
- Phase 2 (drafting): research the topic, organize the material, and draft the message.
- Phrase 3 (revising): edit, proofread, and evaluate the message.
- The 3-x-3 writing process provides a systematic plan that helps writers pace their efforts in creating efficient and effective messages.

3 Analyze the purpose of a message, anticipate its audience, and select the best communication channel.

- Before composing, decide what you hope to achieve.
- Select the appropriate channel to inform, persuade, or convey goodwill.
- After identifying the purpose, visualize both the primary and the secondary audiences.
- Remember that receivers will usually be thinking, "What's in it for me (WIIFM)?"

- Select the best channel by considering (a) the importance of the message, (b) the amount and speed of feedback required, (c) the necessity of a permanent record, (d) the cost of the channel, (e) the degree of formality desired, (f) the confidentiality and sensitivity of the message, and (g) the receiver's preference and level of technical expertise.

4 Employ expert writing techniques such as incorporating audience benefits, developing the "you" view, and using conversational but professional language.

- Look for ways to shape the message from the receiver's, not the sender's, view.
- Apply the "you" view without attempting to manipulate.
- Use conversational but professional language. Strive to convey a warm, friendly tone.
- Avoid expressions such as *totally awesome, you know,* and *like;* use emojis sparingly.

5 Improve the tone and clarity of a message by using positive and courteous expression, bias-free language, plain words, and precise terms.

- Use positive language that tells what can be done rather than what can't be done (*The project will be successful with your support* rather than *The project won't be successful without your support*).
- Be courteous rather than rude, preachy, or demanding.
- Provide reasons for a request to soften the tone of a message.
- Avoid biased language that excludes, stereotypes, or offends people (*lady lawyer, spry old gentleman, confined to a wheelchair*).
- Strive for plain language (*equal* instead of *commensurate*), familiar terms (*end* instead of *terminate*), and precise words (*analyze* instead of *think about*).

Chapter Review

1. What indicates success in the communication process? (L.O. 1)

2. List the five steps in the communication process. How can noise disrupt the process? (L.O. 1)

3. How can a writer make a message *audience oriented* and develop *audience benefits*? Provide an original example. (L.O. 2)

4. List the three phases of the writing process, and summarize what happens in each phase. Which phase requires the most time? (L.O. 2)

5. What seven factors are important in selecting an appropriate channel to deliver a message? What makes one channel richer than another? (L.O. 3)

6. How does profiling the audience help a business communicator prepare a message? (L.O. 3)

7. List three techniques for developing a warm, friendly, and conversational tone in business messages. (L.O. 4)

8. Why is it acceptable to use instant messaging abbreviations (such as *BTW*) and happy faces (emojis) in messages to friends but not in business messages? (L.O. 4)

9. Why does positive language usually tell more than negative language? Give an original example. (L.O. 5)

10. List five examples of gender-biased words and their improved versions. (L.O. 5)

Critical Thinking

11. The use of digital communication has overtaken face-to-face and voice-to-voice communication in the workplace. How has this shift changed the fundamental process of communication? (L.O. 1)

12. Is it necessary to follow a writing process when preparing a short message? A long message? Why or why not? (L.O. 2)

13. In their e-mails, writers sometimes use abbreviations such as *FYI* ("for your information") and *ASAP* ("as soon as possible"). Others sometimes use *LOL* ("laughing out loud"), *4 u* ("for you"), and *gr8* ("great"). What's the difference between these abbreviations, and how do they contribute to one's professional image? (L.O. 4)

14. A grocery clerk helps a customer with purchases to her car, and the clerk says *No problem* or *Not a problem* when thanked. What's the problem with these expressions? What could be said instead? Why do you think some people are now adopting these expressions instead of the conventional *You're welcome*? (L.O. 5)

15. To focus on the "you" view, should writers scrub all uses of *I* and *we* from their writing? Why or why not? (L.O. 4)

Audience Benefits and the "You" View (L.O. 4)

YOUR TASK. Revise the following sentences to emphasize the perspective of the audience and the "you" view.

16. We are taking the proactive step of issuing all our customers new chip-enabled credit cards to replace expired or lost cards and prevent increasingly costly payouts we have suffered from fraud.

17. We take great pride in announcing our new schedule of low-cost, any-day flights to Hawaii.

18. Our strict safety policy forbids us from renting power equipment to anyone who cannot demonstrate proficiency in its use.

19. We're requesting that all employees complete the attached online survey by April 1 so that we may develop a master schedule for summer vacations more efficiently.

20. Our social media engineers are excited to announce a new free app called Fan Boosters that we believe will get fans to share, like, and subscribe to your content.

21. To save the expense of having team trainers set up your training classes in our limited office space, we suggest offering a customized class for your employees right in your own building.

22. Because we take pride in our national policy of selling name brands at discount prices, we can allow store credit but we cannot give cash refunds on returned merchandise.

Conversational but Professional (L.O. 4)

YOUR TASK. Revise the following to make the tone conversational yet professional.

23. As per your recent request, the undersigned is happy to inform you that we are sending you forthwith the procedure manuals you requested.

24. Kindly be informed that it is necessary for you to designate the model number of the appliance before we can submit your order.

25. BTW, Angela went ballistic when the manager accused her of ripping off office supplies.

26. Pursuant to your e-mail of the 12th, please be advised that your shipment was sent April 15.

27. R head honcho wz like totally raggety kuz I wz sick n stuff n mist the team meet. Geez!

28. The undersigned respectfully reminds affected individuals that employees desirous of changing their health plans must do so before December 30.

Positive and Courteous Expression (L.O. 5)

YOUR TASK. Revise the following statements to make them more positive and courteous.

29. Construction on your building is at a standstill because the contractor is unable to pour footings until the soil is no longer soggy.

30. A passport cannot be issued until an application is completed and a recent photo is included.

31. Your message of April 1 claims that the blade in your food processor malfunctioned. Although you apparently failed to read the operator's manual, we are sending you a replacement blade PLUS another manual. Next time read page 18 carefully so that you will know how to attach this blade.

32. Customers are ineligible for the 25 percent discount if they fail to provide the discount code at the time of purchase.

33. As team leader, you apparently failed to remember that you have already assigned me two gigantic and complex research tasks, and now you have dumped another big job on me—one that I can't possibly begin until after I finish the other two jobs.

34. We regret to announce that we can offer the 50 percent discount only to the the first 25 buyers, so act quickly!

Bias-Free Language (L.O. 5)

YOUR TASK. Revise the following sentences to reduce bias (e.g., gender, racial, ethnic, age, and disability).

35. In 18 or more states, an employee has the right to view his employee record.

36. Media Moguls hired Charissa Love, an African-American, for the position of social media coordinator.

37. A skilled assistant proofreads her boss's documents and catches any errors he makes.

38. Curtis is crippled with arthritis, but his crippling rarely interferes with his work.

39. Recently appointed to the commission are a lady lawyer, a Mexican CPA, and two businessmen.

Plain Language and Familiar Words (L.O. 5)

YOUR TASK. Revise the following sentences to use plain language and familiar words.

40. The writer tried to obfuscate the issue with extraneous and superfluous data.

41. To expedite ratification of the agreement, we beseech you to vote in the affirmative.

42. Although the remuneration seems low, it is commensurate with other pay packages.

43. Bank tellers were interrogated after the robbery, but no strong evidence materialized.

44. Researchers dialogued with individual students on campus, but subsequent group interviews proved fruitless.

Precise, Vigorous Words (L.O. 5)

YOUR TASK. From the choices in parentheses, select the most precise, vigorous words.

45. If you find yourself (*performing, doing, juggling*) many tasks, look for ways to reduce your involvement.

46. Rana's outstanding report contains (*a lot of, many, a warehouse of*) helpful data.

47. If necessary, we will (*review, change, reduce*) overtime hours to (*fix, balance, rework*) the budget.

48. The operations manager demanded a (*substantial, 20 percent, big*) reduction in staff travel expenditures.

49. In the courtroom the attorney (*said, alleged, thought*) that the car was stolen.

50. As you requested, we will (*question, interrogate, probe*) our agent.

Selecting Communication Channels (L.O. 3)

YOUR TASK. Using Figure 2.5, suggest the best communication channels for the following messages. Assume that all channels are available. Be prepared to explain your choice.

51. You want to know what team members are available immediately for a quick teleconference meeting. They are all workaholics and glued to their mobile devices.

52. As a manager during a company reorganization, you must tell nine workers that their employment is being terminated.

53. You need to know whether Thomas in Reprographics can produce a rush job for you in two days.

54. A prospective client in Italy wants price quotes for a number of your products—pronto!

55. As assistant to the vice president, you are to explore the possibility of developing internship programs with several nearby colleges and universities.

56. You must respond to a notice from the Internal Revenue Service insisting that you did not pay the correct amount for last quarter's employer's taxes.

Radical Rewrites

From Chapter 2 forward, you will find Radical Rewrite cases. These are poorly written messages that invite you to apply the writing techniques you have been learning. Rewriting is an excellent way to help you build writing skills. It enables you to focus on revising and not on supplying a context or generating imaginary facts. Your instructor's feedback regarding your strengths and challenges will speed your growth as a business communicator. Note that this exercise emphasizes *revising*, not correcting grammar and mechanics.

2.1 Radical Rewrite: Rescuing an Unprofessional Message Written by the Veep (L.O. 4, 5)

The following message from Veronica Dunaway, the vice president of human relations, seeks to help supervisors and managers write safe and helpful performance reviews.

YOUR TASK. Analyze the vice president's message. List at least five weaknesses. Pay special attention to its tone. Your instructor may ask you to revise the e-mail so that it reflects some of the writing techniques you learned in this chapter. How can you make this e-mail more courteous, positive, concise, precise, and audience oriented? Your instructor may ask you to revise this message as a collaboration project using Google Docs or Word's **Track Changes** and **Comment** features.

To: All Supervisors and Departmental Managers
From: Veronica Dunaway <vdunaway@sapphire.com>
Subject: Dangerous Employee Performance Evaluations

All,

This is something I hate to do, but I must warn you that recently one of our employees filed a lawsuit against the company because of comments a supervisor made during a performance evaluation. This did not have to happen. Look, people, you must do better!

Because none of you are dense, here are suggestions you must observe when making evaluations of employees:

You cannot accurately evaluate an employee's performance unless you have a system to measure that performance. That's why the obvious very first step is developing performance standards and goals for each employee. To be effective, these standards and goals must be shared with the employee. However, don't do it orally. Do it in writing.

The performance of each employee must be monitored throughout the year. Keep a log for each worker. Note memorable incidents or projects in which he was involved. But don't just keep favorable comments. I know that many of you are understandably averse to placing negative comments in an employee's file. However, MAN UP! Even negative comments must be included as part of the evaluation process.

Once a year each employee must be formally evaluated in a written performance appraisal—yes, I do mean written! In a face-to-face meeting, let the employee know what you think they did well and what areas the employee may be able to improve. Be specific, give deadlines, be honest, and be realistic.

Giving evaluations can be difficult. With careful preparation, however, the process can be smooth and safe. Don't allow yourself or the company to get involved in any more legal ramifications.

Veronica Dunaway

Vice President, Human Relations | vdunaway@sapphire.com

List at least five weaknesses.

2.2 Selecting Communication Channels (L.O. 3)

YOUR TASK. Using Figure 2.5, suggest the best communication channels for the following messages. Assume that all channels shown are available. Be prepared to explain your choices.

a. As an event planner, you have been engaged to provide information about how to present a charity fashion show, which would include sponsored, crafted, and borrowed outfits and accessories. What is the best channel for conveying your findings to the group that hired you?

b. You want to persuade your friend and company colleague to switch weekend work schedules with you.

c. As the chief of operations, you want to learn which of your project managers in the field are available immediately for a quick teleconference meeting.

d. You need to know whether Ms. Stein in Legal can complete a rush job for you in two days.

e. Your company must inform hundreds of customers of a data security breach.

f. As warehouse manager, you must explain to all employees the details of an upcoming office move that will involve labeling boxes, moving equipment, and keeping track of important information. Some members do not have e-mail.

g. As marketing manager, you want to demonstrate to sales reps in the field a new app that promises to help them analyze trends, forecast future success, and publish daily progress reports. You would like to determine whether they think it's a wise investment.

Grammar/Mechanics Checkup 2

Pronouns

Review Sections 1.07–1.09 in the Grammar Review section of the Grammar/Mechanics Handbook. Select the correct form to complete each of the following statements. Record your answer and the appropriate G/M section to illustrate the principle involved. When you finish, compare your responses with those at the bottom of the page. If your answers differ, study carefully the principles shown in parentheses.

| a | (1.09d) | **EXAMPLE** | The Employee Benefits Committee will make (a) *its*, (b) *their* recommendation soon. |

1. I was expecting Charisse to call. Was it (a) *she*, (b) *her* who left the message?

2. Every player on the girls' team must wear (a) *her*, (b) *their* uniform to be able to play.

3. Every e-mail sent between the CEO and (a) *he*, (b) *him* was revealed in the court case.

4. (a) *Who*, (b) *Whom* did you say would replace the manager?

5. It looks as if (a) *yours*, (b) *your's* is the only report that cites electronic sources correctly.

6. Kevin asked Sierra and (a) *I*, (b) *me*, (c) *myself* to help him complete his research.

7. My friend and (a) *I*, (b) *me*, (c) *myself* were interviewed for the same job.

8. To park your car headed uphill, turn (a) *it's*, (b) *its* front wheels away from the curb and let it roll back a few inches.

9. Give the budget figures to (a) *whoever*, (b) *whomever* asked for them.

10. Everyone except the interviewer and (a) *I*, (b) *me*, (c) *myself* heard the alarm.

11. No one knows that case better than (a) *he*, (b) *him*, (c) *himself*.

12. A proposed budget was sent to (a) *we*, (b) *us* owners before the vote.

13. One of the female travelers left (a) *their*, (b) *her* cell phone on the seat.

14. Isabella and (a) *I*, (b) *myself*, (c) *me* are in charge of the office charity drive.

15. If neither Justin nor I receive confirmation of our itinerary, (a) *him and me*, (b) *he and I* cannot make the trip.

1. a (1.08b) 2. a (1.09b) 3. b (1.08c) 4. a (1.08i) 5. a (1.08i) 6. b (1.08c) 7. a (1.08a) 8. b (1.08d) 9. a (1.08d) 10. b (1.08i) 11. a (1.08f) 12. b (1.08g) 13. b (1.09c) 14. a (1.08a) 15. b (1.08a)

Editing Challenge 2

Every chapter provides an editing exercise to build your grammar and mechanics skills. The following e-mail is a short report about beverage sweeteners from a researcher to his boss. In this message look for errors in proofreading, grammar, spelling, punctuation, capitalization, word use, and number form. Be especially alert to problems with noun plurals, pronouns, and *then/than* and *there/their*. Study the guidelines in the Grammar/Mechanics Handbook (Appendix D), including the lists of Confusing Words and Frequently Misspelled Words. **Hint:** You should make about 30 edits.

YOUR TASK. Edit the following (a) by inserting corrections in your textbook or on a photocopy using proofreading marks in Appendix C or (b) by downloading the message from **www.cengagebrain.com** and correcting at your computer.

To: Chynna Wilson <cwilson@eaton.com>

From: Giovanni Leopold <gleopold@eaton.com>

Subject: New Sweeteners in PepsiCo and Coca-Cola Beverages

Chynna:

As you requested, herewith is the initial report from Joel and I on the topic of beverage sweeteners. As you may all ready know, PepsiCo and Coca-Cola launched two drinks using sweeteners that are new to the market.

Last week Pepsi announced Pepsi True, it's first mid-calorie soda since the failed launch of Pepsi Next more then two years ago. Sweetened with a blend of sugar and stevia, which is a plant-derived sugar substitute Pepsi True contains only 60 calories. Thats 30 percent fewer calorys then regular cola. As sales of low-calorie diet sodas like Diet Pepsi drop, mid-calorie alternatives blend sugar with other sweetners. According to inside information obtained by Joel and I, Pepsi True was tested on the shelves of grocerys, mass merchants, and convenience stores in 5 citys in Florida.

Last month Coca-Cola rolled out Coca-Cola Life which is also sweetened with sugar and stevia. It was successfully tested in the U.K. and South America. In our own in-house research, all of the office gals really liked Life.

BTW, approval from the Food and drug administration did not materialize automatically for these new sweeteners. FDA approval was an issue because studys conducted in the early 1990s suggested that their were possible adverse health affects from the use of stevia-based products. However the herb has been approved for use in 12 countrys.

Both PepsiCo and Coca-Cola eventually received FDA approval, and there products are all ready on the market. Joel and I cannot submit our full report until after him and I complete our investigation in October.

Gio

Giovanni Leopold, Senior Investigator

Research and Development
gleopold@eaton.com
Office: (213) 466-9010
Cell: (213) 358-8893

Perfecting Your Critical-Thinking, Problem-Solving, and Decision-Making Skills

Gone are the days when management expected workers to check their brains at the door and do only as told. Today, you will be expected to use your brain and think critically. You will be solving problems and making decisions. Much of this book is devoted to helping you solve problems and communicate those decisions to management, fellow workers, clients, the government, and the public. Faced with a problem or an issue, most of us do a lot of worrying before identifying the concerns or making a decision. You can convert all that worrying to directed thinking by following these steps:

1. **Identify and clarify the problem.** Your first task is to recognize that a problem exists. Some problems are big and unmistakable, such as failure of an air-freight delivery service to get packages to customers on time. Other problems may be continuing annoyances, such as regularly running out of toner for an office copy machine. The first step in reaching a solution is pinpointing the problem.

2. **Gather information.** Learn more about the problem or situation. Look for possible causes and solutions. This step may mean checking files, calling suppliers, or brainstorming with fellow workers. For example, the air-freight delivery service would investigate the tracking systems of the commercial airlines carrying its packages to determine what is going wrong.

3. **Evaluate the evidence.** Where did the information come from? Does it represent various points of view? What biases could be expected from each source? How accurate is the information? Is it fact or opinion? For example, it is a fact that packages are missing; it is an opinion that they are merely lost and will turn up eventually.

4. **Consider alternatives and implications.** Draw conclusions from the gathered evidence and pose solutions. Then weigh the advantages and disadvantages of each solution. What are the costs, benefits, and consequences? What are the obstacles, and how can they be handled? Most important, what solution best serves your goals and those of your organization? Here is where your creativity is especially important.

5. **Choose the best alternative and test it.** Select an alternative, and try it out to see if it meets your expectations. If it does, put your decision into action. If it doesn't, rethink your alternatives. The freight company decided to give its unhappy customers free delivery service to make up for the lost packages and downtime. Be sure to continue monitoring and adjusting the solution to ensure its effectiveness over time.

CAREER APPLICATION. Let's return to the McDonald's problem, discussed earlier in the chapter, in which customers and some franchise owners are unhappy with the multiple lines for service. Customers don't seem to know where to stand to be the next served. Tempers flare when aggressive customers cut in line, and other customers spend so much time protecting their places in line that they are not ready to order. As a franchise owner, you want to solve this problem. Any new procedures, however, must be approved by a majority of McDonald's owners in your district. You know that McDonald's management believes that the multiline system accommodates higher volumes of customers more quickly than a single-line system does. In addition, customers are turned off when they see a long line.

YOUR TASK

- Individually or with a team, use the critical-thinking steps outlined here. Begin by clarifying the problem.

- Where could you gather information? Would it be wise to see what your competitors are doing? How do banks handle customer lines? Airlines?

- Evaluate your findings and consider alternatives. What are the pros and cons of each alternative?

- With your team, choose the best alternative. Present your recommendation to your class and give your reasons for choosing it.

Organizing and Drafting Business Messages

Courtney Keating/Getty Images

Learning Outcomes

After studying this chapter, you should be able to do the following:

1 Conduct formal and informal research as you apply Phase 2 of the 3-×-3 writing process.

2 Organize information into strategic relationships.

3 Compose the first draft of a message using a variety of sentence types while avoiding sentence fragments, run-on sentences, and comma splices.

4 Emphasize important ideas, employ the active and passive voice strategically, build parallelism, and prevent dangling and misplaced modifiers.

5 Draft well-organized paragraphs that incorporate (a) topic sentences, (b) support sentences, and (c) transitional expressions to build coherence.

3-1 Drafting Workplace Messages

Who me? Write on the job? No way! With today's advances in technology, you may be like others who believe they will never be required to write on the job. The truth is, however, that business, technical, and professional people in this digital age are exchanging more messages than ever before. The more quickly you can put your ideas down and the more clearly you can explain what needs to be said, the more successful and the happier you will be in your career.

Being able to write clearly is also critical to promotions. That's why we devote three chapters to teaching you a tried-and-true writing process, summarized in Figure 3.1 This process guides you through the steps necessary to write rapidly, but more important, clearly. Instead of struggling with a writing assignment and not knowing where to begin or what to say, you can use this effective process both in school and on the job.

Chapter 2 focused on the prewriting stage of the writing process. You studied the importance of using a conversational tone, positive language, plain and courteous expression, and familiar words. This chapter addresses the second stage of the process, which involves gathering information, organizing it into outlines, and drafting messages.

3-1a Beginning the Writing Process by Researching Background Information

No smart businessperson would begin drafting a message before gathering background information. We call this process research, a rather formal-sounding term. For our purposes, however, *research* simply means "collecting information about a certain topic." This is an important step in the writing process because that information helps the writer shape the message. Discovering significant information after a message is half completed often means having to start over and reorganize. To avoid frustration and inaccurate messages, savvy writers collect information that answers several questions:

- What does the receiver need to know about this topic?
- What is the receiver to do?
- How is the receiver to do it?
- When must the receiver do it?
- What will happen if the receiver doesn't do it?

Whenever your communication task requires more information than you have in your head or at your fingertips, you must conduct research. This research may be informal or formal.

3-1b Informal Research Methods

Many routine tasks—such as drafting e-mails, memos, letters, informational reports, and oral presentations—require information that you can collect informally. Where can you find information before starting a project? The following techniques are useful in informal research:

- **Search the company's files.** If you are responding to an inquiry or drafting a routine message, you often can find background information such as previous correspondence in your own files or those of the company. You might consult the company wiki or other digital and manual files. You might also consult colleagues.
- **Talk with the boss.** Get information from the individual giving the assignment. What does that person know about the topic? What slant should you take? What other sources would that person suggest?

OFFICE INSIDER

"With the fast pace of today's electronic communications, one might think that the value of fundamental writing skills has diminished in the workplace. Actually the need to write clearly and quickly has never been more important than in today's highly competitive, technology-driven global economy."[1]

Joseph M. Tucci, *president and chief executive officer of EMC Corporation*

Figure 3.1 The 3-×-3 Writing Process

1 Prewriting

Analyze: Decide on the message purpose. What do you want the receiver to do or believe?

Anticipate: What does the audience already know? How will it receive this message?

Adapt: Think about techniques to present this message most effectively. Consider how to elicit feedback.

2 Drafting

Research: Gather background data by searching files and the Internet.

Organize: Arrange direct messages with the big idea first. For persuasive or negative messages, use an indirect, problem-solving strategy.

Draft: Prepare the first draft, using active-voice sentences, coherent paragraphs, and appropriate transitional expressions.

3 Revising

Edit: Eliminate wordy fillers, long lead-ins, redundancies, and trite business phrases. Strive for parallelism, clarity, conciseness, and readability.

Proofread: Check carefully for errors in spelling, grammar, punctuation, and format.

Evaluate: Will this message achieve your purpose? Is the tone pleasant? Did you encourage feedback?

- **Interview the target audience.** Consider talking with individuals at whom the message is aimed. They can provide clarifying information that tells you what they want to know and how you should shape your remarks. Suggestions for conducting more formal interviews are presented in Chapter 10.

- **Conduct an informal survey.** Gather unscientific but helpful information through questionnaires, telephone surveys, or online surveys. In preparing a report predicting the success of a proposed company fitness center, for example, circulate a questionnaire asking for employee reactions.

- **Brainstorm for ideas.** Alone or with others, discuss ideas for the writing task at hand, and record at least a dozen ideas without judging them. Small groups are especially fruitful in brainstorming because people spin ideas off one another. Use your laptop for a quick, erasable surface to record ideas.

3-1c Formal Research Methods

Long reports and complex business problems generally require formal research methods. Let's say you are part of the management team for an international retailer such as Forever 21, and you have been asked to help launch a new store in Canada. Or, let's assume you must write a term paper for a college class. Both tasks require more data than you have in your head or at your fingertips. To conduct formal research, consider the following research options:

- **Access digital sources.** Torrents of information are available online. Beyond Google, college and public libraries provide digital retrieval services that permit access to a wide array of books, journals, magazines, newspapers, blogs, and other online literature. With so much data drowning today's researchers, they struggle to decide what is current, relevant, and credible. Help is on the way, however! You'll learn more about researching and using electronic sources effectively in Chapter 10.

- **Search manually.** Valuable background and supplementary information is available through manual searching of resources in public and college libraries. These traditional sources include books as well as newspaper, magazine, and journal articles. Other sources are encyclopedias, reference books, handbooks, dictionaries, directories, and almanacs.

- **Investigate primary sources.** To develop firsthand, primary information for a project, go directly to the source. In helping to launch a new Forever 21 outlet in Canada, you might travel to possible sites and check them out. If you need information about how many shoppers pass by a location or visit a shopping center, you might conduct a traffic count. If you need information about consumers, you could search blogs, Twitter, wikis, and Facebook fan pages. To learn more about specific shoppers, you could use questionnaires, interviews, or focus groups. Formal research often includes scientific sampling methods that enable investigators to make accurate judgments and valid predictions.

- **Conduct scientific experiments.** Another source of primary data is experimentation. Instead of merely asking for the target audience's opinion, scientific researchers present choices with controlled variables. Assume, for example, that the management team at Forever 21 wants to know at what price and under what circumstances consumers would purchase jeans from Forever 21 instead of from Abercrombie & Fitch. Instead of jeans, let's say that management wants to study the time of year and type of weather conditions that motivate consumers to begin purchasing sweaters, jackets, and cold-weather gear. The results of such experimentation would provide valuable data for managerial decision making. Because formal research techniques are particularly necessary for reports, you will study resources and techniques more extensively in Unit 4.

3-2 Organizing Information to Show Relationships

LEARNING OUTCOME 2
Organize information into strategic relationships.

Once you have collected information, you must find some way to organize it. Organizing includes two processes: grouping and strategizing. Well-organized messages group similar items together; ideas follow a sequence that helps the reader understand relationships and accept the writer's views. Unorganized messages proceed free-form, jumping from one thought to another. Such messages fail to emphasize important points. Puzzled readers can't see how the pieces fit together, and they become frustrated and irritated. Many communication experts regard poor organization as the greatest failing of business writers. Two simple techniques can help you organize data: the scratch list and the outline.

Some writers make a quick scratch list of the topics they wish to cover in a message. They then compose the message on a computer directly from the scratch list. Most writers, though, need to organize their ideas—especially if the project is complex—into a hierarchy such as an outline. The beauty of preparing an outline is that it gives you a chance to organize your thinking before you get bogged down in word choice and sentence structure. Figure 3.2 shows an outline format.

Direct Strategy for Receptive Audiences. After preparing a scratch list or an outline, think about how the audience will respond to your ideas. When you expect the reader to be pleased, mildly interested, or, at worst, neutral—use the direct strategy. That is, put your main point—the purpose of your message—in the first or second sentence. Dianna Booher, renowned writing consultant, pointed out that typical readers begin any message by thinking, "So what am I supposed to do with this information?" In business writing you have to say, "Reader, here is my point!"[3] As quickly as possible, tell why you are writing. Compare the direct and indirect strategies in the following e-mail openings. Notice how long it takes to get to the main idea in the indirect opening.

INDIRECT OPENING	DIRECT OPENING
For the past several years, our organization has been thinking about how to locate and attract outstanding job candidates whom we could train and who would remain with us for years. One way to do that, as discussed at recent meetings of the Management Council, is to establish an internship program for college students. After considerable investigation, we have voted to begin a pilot program starting next fall.	The Management Council has voted to begin a college internship pilot program next fall.

Figure 3.2 Format for an Outline

Title: Major Idea or Purpose

I. First major component
   A. First subpoint
      1. Detail, illustrations, evidence
      2. Detail, illustrations, evidence
      3. Detail, illustrations, evidence
   B. Second subpoint
      1.
      2.
II. Second major component
   A. First subpoint
      1.
      2.
   B. Second subpoint
      1.
      2.
      3.

Tips for Making Outlines

- Define the main topic in the title.
- Divide the main topic into major components or classifications (preferably three to five).
- Break the components into subpoints.
- Don't put a single item under a major component; if you have only one subpoint, integrate it with the main item above it or reorganize.
- Strive to make each component exclusive (no overlapping).
- Use details, illustrations, and evidence to support subpoints.

Explanations and details follow the direct opening. What's important is getting to the main idea quickly. This direct method, also called *frontloading*, has at least three advantages:

- **Saves the reader's time.** Many of today's businesspeople can devote only a few moments to each message. Messages that take too long to get to the point may lose their readers along the way.

- **Sets a proper frame of mind.** Learning the purpose up front helps the reader put the subsequent details and explanations in perspective. Without a clear opening, the reader may be thinking, "Why am I being told this?"

- **Reduces frustration.** Readers forced to struggle through excessive verbiage before reaching the main idea can become frustrated and begin to resent the writer. Poorly organized messages create a negative impression of the writer.

Typical business messages that follow the direct strategy include routine requests and responses, orders and acknowledgments, nonsensitive memos, e-mails, informational reports, and informational oral presentations. All these tasks have one element in common: none has a sensitive subject that will upset the reader.

Indirect Strategy for Unreceptive Audiences. When you expect the audience to be uninterested, unwilling, displeased, or perhaps even hostile, the indirect strategy is more appropriate. In this strategy you reveal the main idea only after you have offered an explanation and evidence. This approach works well with three kinds of messages: (a) bad news, (b) ideas that require persuasion, and (c) sensitive news, especially when being transmitted to superiors. The indirect strategy has these benefits:

- **Respects the feelings of the audience.** Bad news is always painful, but the trauma can be lessened by preparing the receiver for it.

- **Facilitates a fair hearing.** Messages that may upset the reader are more likely to be read when the main idea is delayed. Beginning immediately with a piece of bad news or a persuasive request, for example, may cause the receiver to stop reading or listening.

- **Minimizes a negative reaction.** A reader's overall reaction to a negative message is generally improved if the news is delivered gently.

Typical business messages that could be developed indirectly include e-mails, memos, and letters that refuse requests, deny claims, and disapprove credit. Persuasive requests, sales letters, sensitive messages, and some reports and oral presentations may also benefit from the indirect strategy. You will learn more about using the indirect strategy in Chapters 7 and 8.

In summary, business messages may be organized directly (with the main idea first) or indirectly. How you expect the audience to respond determines which strategy to use, as illustrated in Figure 3.3. Although these two strategies cover many communication problems, they should be considered neither universal nor inviolate. Every business transaction is distinct. Some messages are mixed: part good news, part bad; part goodwill, part persuasion. In upcoming chapters you will practice applying the direct and indirect strategies in typical situations. Then, you will have the skills and confidence to evaluate communication problems and vary these strategies depending on your goals.

3-3 Drafting With Powerful Sentences

After researching your topic and organizing the data, you are ready to begin drafting. Many writers sputter and can't get started, especially if they haven't completed the preparatory work. Organizing your ideas and working from an outline are very helpful in overcoming writer's block. Composition is also easier if you have a quiet environment in which to concentrate. Businesspeople with messages to compose set aside a given time and allow no calls, visitors, or other interruptions. This is a good technique for students as well.

As you begin writing, think about what style fits you best. Some experts suggest *freewriting*. This technique involves getting your thoughts down quickly and refining them in later versions. As you take up each idea, imagine that you are talking to the reader. If you can't think of the right word, insert a substitute or type *find perfect word later*. Freewriting works well for some writers, but others prefer to move more slowly and think through their ideas more deliberately. Whether you are a speedy or a deliberate writer, keep in mind that you are writing the first draft. You will have time later to revise and polish your sentences.

LEARNING OUTCOME 3
Compose the first draft of a message using a variety of sentence types while avoiding sentence fragments, run-on sentences, and comma splices.

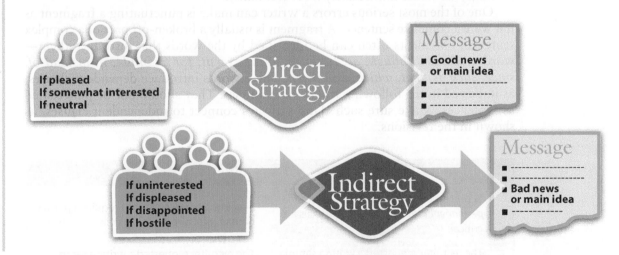

Figure 3.3 Audience Response Determines Direct or Indirect Strategy

3-3a Varying Four Sentence Patterns

Messages that repeat the same sentence pattern soon become boring. To avoid monotony and to add spark to your writing, use a variety of sentence types. You have four sentence types from which to choose: simple, compound, complex, and compound-complex. In the following examples, a single underscore identifies the subject and a double underscore identifies the verb.

Simple Sentence

Contains one complete thought (an independent clause) with a subject and predicate verb:
The entrepreneur saw an opportunity.

Compound Sentence

Contains two complete but related thoughts. May be joined by (a) a conjunction such as *and*, *but*, or *or*; (b) a semicolon; or (c) a conjunctive adverb such as *however*, *consequently*, and *therefore*:
The entrepreneur saw an opportunity, and she responded immediately.
The entrepreneur saw an opportunity; she responded immediately.
The entrepreneur saw an opportunity; consequently, she responded immediately.

Complex Sentence

Contains an independent clause (a complete thought) and a dependent clause (a thought that cannot stand by itself). Dependent clauses are often introduced by words such as *although*, *since*, *because*, *when*, and *if*. When dependent clauses precede independent clauses, they always are followed by a comma:
When the entrepreneur saw the opportunity, she responded immediately.

Compound-Complex Sentence

Contains at least two independent clauses and one dependent clause:
When the entrepreneur saw the opportunity, she responded immediately; however, she needed capital.

3-3b Avoiding Three Common Sentence Faults

As you craft your sentences, beware of three common traps: fragments, run-on (fused) sentences, and comma splices. If any of these faults appears in a business message, the writer immediately loses credibility.

One of the most serious errors a writer can make is punctuating a **fragment** as if it were a complete sentence. A fragment is usually a broken-off part of a complex sentence. Fragments often can be identified by the words that introduce them— words such as *although, as, because, even, except, for example, if, instead of, since, such as, that, which,* and *when*. These words introduce dependent clauses, as italicized in the following fragment examples. They should not be punctuated as sentences. Make sure such clauses always connect to independent clauses, as shown in the revisions.

FRAGMENT	REVISION
Because most transactions require a permanent record. Good writing skills are critical.	Because most transactions require a permanent record, good writing skills are critical.
The recruiter requested a writing sample. *Even though the candidate seemed to communicate well.*	The recruiter requested a writing sample even though the candidate seemed to communicate well.

A second serious writing fault is the **run-on (fused) sentence**. A sentence with two independent clauses must be joined by a coordinating conjunction *(and, or, nor, but)* or by a semicolon (;), or separated into two sentences. Without a conjunction or a semicolon, a run-on sentence results.

RUN-ON SENTENCE	REVISION
Many job seekers prepare traditional résumés some also use digital portfolio websites.	Many job seekers prepare traditional résumés. Some also use digital portfolio websites.
One candidate sent an e-mail résumé another sent a link to her online portfolio.	One candidate sent an e-mail résumé; another sent a link to her online portfolio.

A third sentence fault is a **comma splice**. It results when a writer joins (splices together) two independent clauses with a comma. Independent clauses may be joined with a coordinating conjunction *(and, or, nor, but)* or a conjunctive adverb *(however, consequently, therefore,* and others). Notice that clauses joined by coordinating conjunctions require only a comma. Clauses joined by a conjunctive adverb require a semicolon and a comma. To rectify a comma splice, try one of the possible revisions shown here:

COMMA SPLICE	REVISIONS
Mack preferred his desktop computer, Nadia preferred her tablet.	Mack preferred his desktop computer, but Nadia preferred her tablet.
	Mack preferred his desktop; however, Nadia preferred her tablet.
	Mack preferred his desktop computer. Nadia preferred her tablet.

3-3c Favoring Short Sentences

Because your goal is to communicate clearly, you should strive for sentences that average 20 words. Some sentences will be shorter; some will be longer. The American Press Institute reports that reader comprehension drops off markedly as sentences become longer.[6] Therefore, in crafting your sentences, think about the relationship between sentence length and comprehension.

Sentence Length	Comprehension Rate
8 words	100%
15 words	90%
19 words	80%
28 words	50%

Instead of stringing together clauses with *and, but,* and *however,* break some of those complex sentences into separate segments. Business readers want to grasp ideas immediately. They can do that best when thoughts are separated into short sentences. On the other hand, too many monotonous short sentences will sound choppy and may bore or even annoy the reader. Strive for a balance between longer sentences and shorter ones. Your grammar-checker and spell-checker can show you readability statistics that flag long sentences and give you an average sentence length.

OFFICE INSIDER

On the topic of comma splices, one well-known writing coach says, "Why do intelligent people make the error? I think people worry that they will come across too informally or too plainly if they use [two] short sentences. They believe using 4-to-6-word sentences, especially two of them in a row, can't be professional. But two short, crisp, clear sentences in a row are professional and punchy."[5]

Lynn Gaertner Johnson, *business writing trainer, coach, blogger*

WORKPLACE IN FOCUS

When SeaWorld announced it was ending its controversial policy of breeding captive killer whales, the message needed to be clear and precise. Skillful writers emphasize major ideas by placing them front and center, and the blog post announcing the major policy turnaround at the marine theme park did just that: *We're making historic announcements at SeaWorld, including ending orca breeding, introducing new, inspiring and natural orca encounters, and launching new partnerships to protect oceans and marine animals.* The sentence structure highlights the main news immediately and uses the stylistic writing technique of parallelism to create balance and symmetry. What other strategies can you employ to improve your writing techniques?[7]

LEARNING OUTCOME 4

Emphasize important ideas, employ the active and passive voice strategically, build parallelism, and prevent dangling and misplaced modifiers.

3-4 Mastering Four Skillful Writing Techniques

Business writers can significantly improve their messages by understanding how to use the following techniques strategically: (a) emphasis, (b) active and passive voice, and (c) parallelism. Writers must also beware of dangling and misplaced modifiers.

3-4a Creating Emphasis

When talking with someone, you can emphasize main ideas by speaking more loudly, raising your eyebrows, or shaking your head. When exchanging messages in print or digitally, however, you must use other techniques. In casual messages to friends, you might express emphasis with a single exclamation point. You've probably seen the exuberant posts of bloggers and their followers who include not one but cascades of exclamation points!!!! Doing so in business messages, however, would destroy your credibility and make you look "super unprofessional."[8] Instead of relying on punctuation, skilled business writers achieve emphasis in two ways: visually and stylistically.

Achieving Emphasis Visually. To emphasize an idea in print, a writer may use any of the following visual devices:

Underlining	<u>Underlining</u> draws the eye to a word.
Italics and boldface	Using *italics* or **boldface** conveys special meaning.
Font changes	Selecting a large, small, or different font draws interest.
All caps	Printing words in ALL CAPS is like shouting them.
Dashes	Dashes—used sparingly—can be effective.
Tabulation	Listing items vertically makes them stand out: 1. First item 2. Second item 3. Third item

Other means of achieving visual emphasis include the arrangement of space, color, lines, boxes, columns, titles, headings, and subheadings. Today's software and color printers provide a wonderful array of capabilities for setting off ideas. More tips on achieving emphasis are coming in Chapter 4, in which you will learn about document design.

Achieving Emphasis Through Style. Although visual devices are occasionally appropriate, more often a writer achieves emphasis stylistically. That is, the writer chooses words carefully and constructs sentences skillfully to emphasize main ideas and de-emphasize minor or negative ideas. Here are four suggestions for emphasizing ideas stylistically:

- **Use vivid, not general, words.** Vivid words are emphatic because the reader can picture ideas clearly.

GENERAL	VIVID
The way we seek jobs has changed.	Technology has dramatically changed how job hunters search for positions.
Someone will contact you as soon as possible.	Ms. Hawkins will telephone you before 5 p.m. tomorrow, June 3.

- **Label the main idea.** If an idea is significant, tell the reader.

UNLABELED	LABELED
Consider using Google to look for a job, but also focus on networking.	Consider using Google to look for a job, but, *most important*, focus on networking.
We shop here because of the customer service and low prices.	We like the customer service, but the *primary reason* for shopping here is the low prices.

- **Place the important idea first or last.** Ideas have less competition from surrounding words when they appear first or last in a sentence.

MAIN IDEA LOST	MAIN IDEA EMPHASIZED
Profit-sharing plans are more effective in increasing *productivity* when they are linked to individual performance rather than to group performance.	*Productivity* is more likely to be increased when profit-sharing plans are linked to individual performance rather than to group performance.

- **Give the important idea the spotlight.** Place the main idea in a simple sentence or in an independent clause.

MAIN IDEA LOST	MAIN IDEA CLEAR
Although you are the first trainee we have hired for this program, we had many candidates and expect to expand the program in the future. (The main idea is lost in a dependent clause.)	You are the first trainee we have hired for this program. (Simple sentence)

De-emphasizing When Necessary. To de-emphasize an idea, such as bad news, try one of the following stylistic devices:

- Use general words to de-emphasize harsh words or bad news.

EMPHASIZES HARSH STATEMENT	DE-EMPHASIZES HARSH STATEMENT
Our records indicate that you were recently fired.	Our records indicate that your employment status has recently changed.

- **Subordinate the bad news.** Place the bad news in a dependent clause connected to an independent clause that contains something positive.

EMPHASIZES BAD NEWS	DE-EMPHASIZES BAD NEWS
We cannot issue you credit at this time, but we have a special plan that will allow you to fill your immediate needs on a cash basis.	Although credit cannot be issued at this time, you can fill your immediate needs on a cash basis with our special plan.

3-4b Using the Active and Passive Voice Strategically

In active-voice sentences, the subject (also called the actor) performs the action. In passive-voice sentences, the subject receives the action. Active-voice sentences are more direct because they reveal the performer immediately. They are easier to understand and usually shorter than passive-voice sentences. Most business writing should be in the active voice. However, passive voice is useful to (a) emphasize an action rather than a person, (b) de-emphasize negative news, and (c) conceal the doer of an action.

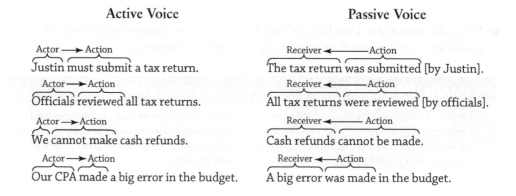

Active Voice

Actor → Action
Justin must submit a tax return.

Actor → Action
Officials reviewed all tax returns.

Actor → Action
We cannot make cash refunds.

Actor → Action
Our CPA made a big error in the budget.

Passive Voice

Receiver ← Action
The tax return was submitted [by Justin].

Receiver ← Action
All tax returns were reviewed [by officials].

Receiver ← Action
Cash refunds cannot be made.

Receiver ← Action
A big error was made in the budget.

3-4c Creating Parallelism

Parallelism is a skillful writing technique that produces balanced writing. Sentences written so that their parts are balanced, or parallel, are easy to read and understand. To achieve parallel construction, use similar structures to express similar ideas. For example, the words *computing, coding, recording,* and *storing* are parallel because the words all end in -*ing*. To express the list as *computing, coding, recording,* and *storage* is disturbing because the last item is not what the reader expects. Try to match nouns with nouns, verbs with verbs, and clauses with clauses. Avoid mixing active-voice verbs with passive-voice verbs. Your goal is to keep the wording balanced in expressing similar ideas.

Chapter 3: Organizing and Drafting Business Messages

LACKS PARALLELISM	ILLUSTRATES PARALLELISM
A wedding planner must arrange for the venue, the flowers, and a person to take videos.	A wedding planner must arrange for the venue, the flowers, and a videographer. (Matches nouns.)
Our primary goals are to increase productivity, reduce costs, and the improvement of product quality.	Our primary goals are to increase productivity, reduce costs, and improve product quality. (Matches verbs.)
We are scheduled to meet in Tampa on January 5, we are meeting in Atlanta on the 15th of March, and in Chicago on June 3.	We are scheduled to meet in Tampa on January 5, in Atlanta on March 15, and in Chicago on June 3. (Matches phrases.)
Marcus audits all accounts lettered A through L; accounts lettered M through Z are audited by Katherine.	Marcus audits all accounts lettered A through L; Katherine audits accounts lettered M through Z. (Matches active voice in clauses.)
Our Super Bowl ads have three objectives: 1. We want to increase product use. 2. Introduce complementary products. 3. Our corporate image will be enhanced.	Our Super Bowl ads have three objectives: 1. Increase product use 2. Introduce complementary products 3. Enhance our corporate image (Matches verbs in listed items.)

OFFICE INSIDER

Good writers don't let their modifiers dangle in public. "Always suspect an -*ing* word of dangling if it's near the front of a sentence; consider it guilty until proved innocent."[9]

Patricia T. O'Conner, *author,* Woe Is I: The Grammarphobe's Guide to Better English in Plain English

3-4d Dodging Dangling and Misplaced Modifiers

For clarity, modifiers must be close to the words they describe or limit. A modifier dangles when the word or phrase it describes is missing from its sentence—for example, *After working overtime, the report was finally finished.* This sentence says that the report was working overtime. Revised, the sentence contains a logical subject: *After working overtime, we finally finished the report.*

A modifier is misplaced when the word or phrase it describes is not close enough to be clear—for example, *Firefighters rescued a dog from a burning car that had a broken leg.* Obviously, the car did not have a broken leg. The solution is to position the modifier closer to the word(s) it describes or limits: *Firefighters rescued a dog with a broken leg from a burning car.*

Introductory verbal phrases are particularly dangerous; be sure to follow them immediately with the words they logically describe or modify. Try this trick for detecting and remedying many dangling modifiers. Ask the question *Who?* or *What?* after any introductory phrase. The words immediately following should tell the reader who or what is performing the action. Try the *Who?* test on the first three danglers here:

DANGLING OR MISPLACED MODIFIER	CLEAR MODIFICATION
Skilled at 3-D printing, the Disney character was easily copied by Jeff.	Skilled at 3-D printing, Jeff easily copied the Disney character.
Working together as a team, the project was finally completed.	Working together as a team, we finally completed the project.
To meet the deadline, the 3D files must be sent by May 1.	To meet the deadline, you must send your 3D files by May 1.
The recruiter interviewed candidates who had excellent computer skills in the morning.	In the morning the recruiter interviewed candidates with excellent computer skills.
As a newbie in our office, we invite you to our Friday after-hours get-together.	As a newbie in our office, you are invited to our Friday after-hours get-together.

3-5 Drafting Well-Organized, Effective Paragraphs

Good business writers develop well-organized paragraphs by focusing on a single main idea. The sentences in their paragraphs cohere, or stick together, through the use of transitional expressions.

3-5a Crafting Topic Sentences

A paragraph is unified when it develops a single main idea. That idea is usually expressed in a topic sentence, which may appear at the beginning, in the middle, or at the end of the paragraph. Business writers generally place the topic sentence first in the paragraph. It tells readers what to expect and helps them understand the paragraph's central thought immediately.

3-5b Developing Support Sentences

Support sentences illustrate, explain, or strengthen the topic sentence. One of the hardest things for beginning writers to remember is that all support sentences in the paragraph must relate to the topic sentence. Any other topics should be treated separately. Support sentences provide specific details, explanations, and evidence. The following example starts with a topic sentence about flexible work scheduling and is followed by three support sentences that explain how flexible scheduling could work. Transitional expressions are italicized.

> **Topic sentence:** Flexible work scheduling could immediately increase productivity and enhance employee satisfaction in our organization.
>
> **Support sentences:** Managers would maintain their regular hours. For many other employees, *however*, flexible scheduling provides extra time to enable them to manage family responsibilities. Feeling less stress, employees are able to focus their attention better at work; *therefore*, they become more relaxed and more productive.

3-5c Building Paragraph Coherence

Paragraphs are coherent when ideas cohere—that is, when the ideas stick together and one idea leads logically to the next. When the author skips from Step 1 to Step 3 and forgets Step 2, the reader is lost. Several techniques will help you keep the reader in step with your ideas.

Sustaining the Key Idea. Repeating a key expression or using a similar one throughout a paragraph helps sustain a key idea. In the following example, notice that the repetition of *guest* and *VIP* connects ideas.

> *Our philosophy holds that every customer is really a* guest. *All new employees are trained to treat* guests *in our theme parks as* VIPs. *We take great pride in respecting our* guests. *As* VIPs*, they are never told what they can or cannot do.*

Dovetailing Sentences. Sentences are dovetailed when an idea at the end of one connects with an idea at the beginning of the next. Dovetailing sentences is especially helpful with dense, difficult topics. It is also helpful with ordinary paragraphs, such as the following:

New hosts and hostesses learn about the theme park and its facilities. *These* facilities *include telephones, food services, bathrooms, and attractions, as well as the location of* offices. *Knowledge of* offices *and the internal workings of the company is required of all staffers.*

Including Pronouns. Familiar pronouns, such as *we, they, he, she,* and *it,* help build continuity, as do demonstrative pronouns, such as *this, that, these,* and *those.* These words confirm that something under discussion is still being discussed. However, be careful with such pronouns. They often need a noun with them to make their meaning clear. In the following example, notice how confusing the pronoun *this* would be if the word *training* were omitted.

All new park employees receive a two-week orientation. They learn that every staffer has a vital role in preparing for the show. This training *includes how to maintain enthusiasm.*

Employing Transitional Expressions. Transitional expressions are another excellent device for showing connections and achieving paragraph coherence. These words, some of which are shown in Figure 3.4, act as verbal road signs to readers and listeners. Transitional expressions enable the receiver to anticipate what's coming, reduce uncertainty, and speed comprehension. They signal that a train of thought is moving forward, being developed, possibly detouring, or ending. As Figure 3.4 shows, transitions can amplify or strengthen a thought, show time or order, clarify ideas, show cause and effect, contradict thoughts, and contrast ideas. Remember that coherence in communication rarely happens spontaneously; it requires effort and skill.

3-5d Controlling Paragraph Length

Although no rule regulates the length of paragraphs, business writers recognize the value of short paragraphs. Paragraphs with eight or fewer printed lines look inviting and readable. Long, solid chunks of print appear formidable. If a topic can't be covered in eight or fewer printed lines (not sentences), consider breaking it into smaller segments.

Figure 3.4 Transitional Expressions to Build Coherence

To Amplify or Strengthen	To Show Time or Order	To Clarify	To Show Cause and Effect	To Contradict	To Contrast
additionally	after	for example	accordingly	actually	as opposed to
accordingly	before	for instance	as a result	but	at the same time
again	earlier	I mean	consequently	however	by contrast
also	finally	in other words	for this reason	in fact	conversely
beside	first	put another way	hence	instead	on the contrary
indeed	meanwhile	that is	so	rather	on the other hand
likewise	next	this means	therefore	still	previously
moreover	now	thus	thus	yet	similarly

Summary of Learning Outcomes

1 Conduct formal and informal research as you apply Phase 2 of the 3-×-3 writing process.

- Apply the second phase of the writing process (prewriting), which includes researching, organizing, and drafting.
- Begin the writing process by researching background information.
- Collect information by answering questions about what the receiver needs to know and what the receiver is to do.
- Conduct informal research for routine tasks by searching the company's digital and other files, talking with the boss, interviewing the target audience, conducting informal surveys, and brainstorming for ideas.
- Conduct formal research for long reports and complex problems by searching digitally or manually, investigating primary sources, and conducting scientific experiments.

2 Organize information into strategic relationships.

- For simple messages, make a quick scratch list of topics; for more complex messages, create an outline.
- To prepare an outline, divide the main topic into three to five major components.
- Break the components into subpoints consisting of details, illustrations, and evidence.
- Organize the information using the direct strategy (with the main idea first) when audiences will be pleased, mildly interested, or neutral.
- Organize information using the indirect strategy (with explanations preceding the main idea) for audiences that will be unwilling, displeased, or hostile.

3 Compose the first draft of a message using a variety of sentence types while avoiding sentence fragments, run-on sentences, and comma splices.

- Decide whether to compose quickly (*freewriting*) or to write more deliberately—but remember that you are writing a first draft.
- Employ a variety of sentence types including simple (one independent clause), complex (one independent and one dependent clause), compound (two independent clauses), and compound-complex (two independent clauses and one dependent clause).
- Avoid fragments (broken-off parts of sentences), run-on sentences (two clauses fused improperly), and comma splices (two clauses joined improperly with a comma).
- Remember that sentences are most effective when they are short (20 or fewer words).

4 Emphasize important ideas, employ the active and passive voice strategically, build parallelism, and prevent dangling and misplaced modifiers.

- Avoid the excessive use of exclamation points as they look unprofessional and destroy credibility.
- Emphasize an idea visually by using underlining, italics, boldface, font changes, all caps, dashes, tabulation, and other devices.
- Emphasize an idea stylistically by using vivid words, labeling it, making it the sentence subject, placing it first or last in the sentence, or removing competing ideas.
- For most business writing, use the active voice by making the subject the doer of the action (*Facebook hired the intern*).
- Use the passive voice (*The intern was fired*) to de-emphasize negative news, to emphasize an action rather than the doer, or to conceal the doer of an action.

- Employ parallelism for balanced construction (*jogging, hiking, and biking* rather than *jogging, hiking, and to bike*).
- Avoid dangling modifiers (*sitting at my computer, the words would not come*) and misplaced modifiers (*I have the report you wrote in my office*).

5 Draft well-organized paragraphs that incorporate (a) topic sentences, (b) support sentences, and (c) transitional expressions to build coherence.

- Build well-organized, unified paragraphs by focusing on a single idea.
- Always include a topic sentence that states the main idea of the paragraph.
- Develop support sentences to illustrate, explain, or strengthen the topic sentence.
- Build coherence by repeating a key idea, using pronouns to refer to previous nouns, and showing connections with transitional expressions (*however, therefore, consequently*).
- Control paragraph length by striving for eight or fewer lines.

Chapter Review

1. What are the three main activities involved in the second phase of the writing process? (L.O. 1)

2. Distinguish between formal and informal methods of researching data for a business message. (L.O. 1)

3. How do you make an outline? (L.O. 2)

4. What is frontloading and what are its advantages? (L.O. 2)

5. Distinguish between the direct and the indirect strategies. When is each appropriate? (L.O. 2)

6. How is a compound sentence different from a complex sentence? Give an example of each. (L.O. 3)

7. Distinguish between achieving emphasis visually and achieving it stylistically. (L.O. 4)

8. Ideally, sentences should be how long? (L.O. 5)

9. What is the difference between a topic sentence and support sentences? (L.O. 5)

10. What rule regulates the length of paragraphs? (L.O. 5)

Critical Thinking

11. A recent PayScale survey revealed a significant gap in perception between managers and new grads. "Overall, the majority of workers (87 percent) feel well prepared (immediately or within 3 months) for their job upon graduation from college. In contrast, only about half of managers (50 percent) feel that employees who recently graduated from college are well prepared for the workforce."[10] The skill most lacking, said the managers, was writing proficiency. What could explain this gap in perception between managers and new grads? (L.O. 1–5)

12. How can bad writing waste a businessperson's time? A researcher asked that question of workers who read business material an average of 25 hours per week (about half of which was e-mail).[11] What writing flaws do you think they named? Should new employees be trained in writing effectively on the job? (L.O. 1–5)

13. Ashley, a twenty-one-year-old college graduate with a 3.5 GPA, was hired for her first job. She was a fast learner on all the software, but her supervisor had to help her with punctuation. On the ninth day of her job, she resigned, saying: "I just don't think this job is a good fit. Commas, semicolons, spelling, typos—those kinds of things just aren't all that important to me. They just don't matter."[12] For what kind of job is Ashley qualified? (L.O. 1–5)

14. Why is audience analysis so important in the selection of the direct or indirect organization strategy for a business message? (L.O. 2)

15. Now that you have studied the active and passive voice, what do you think when someone in government or business says, "Mistakes were made"? Is it unethical to use the passive voice to avoid specifics? (L.O. 4)

Writing Improvement Exercises

Sentence Types (L.O. 3)

YOUR TASK. For each of the numbered sentences, select the letter that identifies its type:

a. Simple sentence
b. Compound sentence
c. Complex sentence
d. Compound-complex sentence

16. Americans pride themselves on their informality. _____

17. When Americans travel abroad on business, their informality may be viewed negatively. _____

18. Informality in Asia often equals disrespect; it is not seen as a virtue. _____

19. The order of first and last names in Asia may be reversed, and this causes confusion to Americans and Europeans. _____

20. When you are addressing someone, ask which name a person would prefer to use; however, be sure you can pronounce it correctly. _____

Sentence Faults (L.O. 3)

YOUR TASK. In the following, identify the sentence fault (fragment, run-on sentence, comma splice). Then revise to remedy the fault.

21. Although they began as a side business for Disney. Destination weddings now represent a major income source.

22. About 2,000 weddings are held yearly. Which is twice the number just ten years ago.

23. Weddings may take place in less than one hour, however the cost may be as much as $5,000.

24. Limousines line up outside Disney's wedding pavilion, ceremonies are scheduled in two-hour intervals.

25. Many couples prefer a traditional wedding others request a fantasy experience.

Emphasis (L.O. 4)

YOUR TASK. For each of the following sentences, circle (a) or (b). Be prepared to justify your choice.

26. Which is more emphatic?

   a. They offer a lot of products.
   b. CyberGuys offers digital, travel, and office accessories.

27. Which is more emphatic?

   a. Increased advertising would improve sales.
   b. Adding $50,000 in advertising would double our sales.

28. Which is more emphatic?

   a. We must consider several factors.
   b. We must consider cost, staff, and safety.

29. Which sentence places more emphasis on product loyalty?

   a. Product loyalty is the primary motivation for advertising.
   b. The primary motivation for advertising is loyalty to the product, although other purposes are also served.

30. Which sentence places more emphasis on the seminar?

   a. An executive training seminar that starts June 1 will include four candidates.
   b. Four candidates will be able to participate in an executive training seminar that we feel will provide a valuable learning experience.

31. Which sentence places more emphasis on the date?

   a. The deadline is April 1 for summer vacation reservations.
   b. April 1 is the deadline for summer vacation reservations.

32. Which is *less* emphatic?

   a. One division's profits decreased last quarter.
   b. Profits in consumer electronics dropped 15 percent last quarter.

33. Which sentence *de-emphasizes* the credit refusal?

   a. We cannot grant you credit at this time, but we welcome your cash business and encouage you to reapply in the future.
   b. Although credit cannot be granted at this time, we welcome your cash business and encourage you to reapply in the future.

34. Which sentence gives more emphasis to leadership?

   a. She has many admirable qualities, but most important is her leadership skill.
   b. She has many admirable qualities, including leadership skill, good judgment, and patience.

35. Which is more emphatic?

   a. We notified three departments: (1) Marketing, (2) Accounting, and (3) Distribution.
   b. We notified three departments:
      1. Marketing
      2. Accounting
      3. Distribution

Active-Voice Verbs (L.O. 4)

YOUR TASK. Business writing is more forceful when it uses active-voice verbs. Revise the following sentences so that verbs are in the active voice. Put the emphasis on the doer of the action. Add subjects if necessary.

EXAMPLE Antivirus software was installed on her computer.

REVISION Rachel installed antivirus software on her computer.

36. A company credit card was used by the manager to purchase office supplies.

37. To protect students, laws were passed in many states that prohibited the use of social security numbers as identification.

38. Checks are processed more quickly by banks because of new regulations.

39. Millions of packages are scanned by FedEx every night as packages stream through its Memphis hub.

Passive-Voice Verbs (L.O. 4)

YOUR TASK. When indirectness or tact is required, use passive-voice verbs. Revise the following sentences so that they are in the passive voice.

EXAMPLE Travis did not submit the proposal before the deadline.

REVISION The proposal was not submitted before the deadline.

40. The folks in Accounting seem to have made a serious error in this report.

41. We cannot ship your order for smart surge protectors until May 5.

42. The government first issued a warning regarding the use of this pesticide more than 15 months ago.

43. Your insurance policy does not automatically cover damage to rental cars.

44. We cannot provide patient care unless patients show proof of insurance.

Parallelism (L.O. 4)

YOUR TASK. Revise the following sentences so that their parts are balanced.

45. (**Hint:** Match verbs.) To improve your listening skills, stop talking, your surroundings should be controlled, be listening for main points, and an open mind must be kept.

46. (**Hint:** Match active voice of verbs.) Alma Cervantes, director of the San Mateo branch, will now supervise all Western Division operations; the Mountain Division will be supervised by our Utah branch director, Diane Macdonald.

47. (**Hint:** Match verb phrases.) Our newly hired employee has started using the computer and to learn her coworkers' names.

48. (**Hint:** Match adjectives.) Training seminars must be stimulating and a challenge.

49. Paperless meetings enable directors to filter vast amounts of data, to search digitally, and cross-references can be linked.

50. We need more trained staff members, office space is limited, and the budget for overtime is much too small.

51. The application for a grant asks for this information: funds required for employee salaries, how much we expect to spend on equipment, and what is the length of the project.

52. Sending an e-mail establishes a more permanent record than to make a telephone call.

Dangling and Misplaced Modifiers (L.O. 4)

YOUR TASK. Revise the following sentences to avoid dangling and misplaced modifiers.

53. When collecting information for new equipment, the Web proved to be my best resource.

54. To win the lottery, a ticket must be purchased.

55. The exciting Mandalay Bay is just one of the fabulous hotels you see strolling along the Las Vegas strip.

56. Angered by slow computer service, complaints were called in by hundreds of unhappy users.

Organizing Paragraph Sentences (L.O. 5)

YOUR TASK. Study the following list of sentences from an interoffice memo to hospital staff.

1. *The old incident report form caused numerous problems and confusion.*

2. *One problem was that employees often omitted important information.*

3. *The Hospital Safety Committee has revised the form used for incident reports.*

4. *Another problem was that inappropriate information was often included that might expose the hospital to liability.*

5. *The Hospital Safety Committee has scheduled a lunchtime speaker to discuss prevention of medication mistakes.*

6. *Factual details about the time and place of the incident are important, but speculation on causes is inappropriate.*

7. *The new form will be available on April 1.*

57. Which sentence should be the topic sentence? _____

58. Which sentence(s) should be developed in a separate paragraph? _____

59. Which sentences should become support sentences? _____

Building Coherent Paragraphs (L.O. 5)

YOUR TASK. Organize the following sentences into coherent paragraphs.

60. Improve the organization, coherence, and correctness of the following paragraph.

We feel that the "extreme" strategy has not been developed fully in the fast-food market. Pizza Hut is considering launching a new product called The Extreme. We plan to price this new pizza at $19.99. It will be the largest pizza on the market. It will have double the cheese. It will also have double the toppings. The plan is to target millennials because pizza is their favorite food. This same target audience that would respond to an extreme product also reacts to low prices. Millennials are the fastest-growing segment in the fast-food market, and they have responded well to other marketing plans using the extreme strategy.

61. Use the following facts to construct a coherent paragraph with a topic sentence and appropriate transitional expressions in the supporting sentences.

- *The federal government will penalize medical practices that don't adopt electronic medical records (EMRs).*
- *Valley Medical Center is considering beginning converting soon.*
- *Converting paper-based records to EMRs will be complex.*
- *Converting will be technically challenging. It will probably be time-consuming and labor-intensive.*
- *Converting should bring better patient care and maybe even lower costs in the long run.*
- *The federal government provides funds to reimburse the cost of adopting the technology.*

62. Use the following facts to construct a coherent paragraph with a topic sentence and appropriate transitional expressions in the supporting sentences.

- *Nearly all teams experience conflict. They should recognize and expect it.*
- *The most effective teams strive to eliminate destructive conflict and develop constructive conflict.*
- *Destructive conflict arises when team members take criticism personally.*
- *Destructive conflict poisons teamwork.*
- *Conflict can become constructive.*

Chapter 3: Organizing and Drafting Business Messages

- *Teams that encourage members to express their opinions may seem to be experiencing conflict when the opinions differ.*
- *Better decisions often result when teams listen to and discuss many views.*

Radical Rewrites

Note: Radical Rewrites are provided at **www.cengagebrain.com** for you to download and revise. Your instructor may show a suggested solution.

Radical Rewrites provide messages that need to be rewritten. Rewriting is an excellent way to help you build writing skills. It enables you to focus on revising and not on supplying a context or generating imaginary facts. Your instructor's feedback regarding your strengths and challenges will speed your growth as a skilled business communicator.

3.1 Radical Rewrite: Improving a Message About Checking References (L.O. 4, 5)

YOUR TASK. Analyze the following e-mail to be sent by the vice president of human resources to all managers. List at least five weaknesses. In addition to grammar faults, pay special attention to dangling modifiers, parallelism, and passive voice. Your instructor may ask you to revise this e-mail so that it reflects writing techniques you learned in this and previous chapters.

To: All Managers
From: Mark Sanchez <marksanchez@zycamindustries>
Subject: Improving Reference-Checking Procedures

With our recent increase in hiring, many of you are reviewing candidates' applications and their references are being checked. Our CEO has asked me to provide all managers with guidance on how to check references to obtain the best information.

Generally, the two ways to check references are by calling or to make an inquiry by writing. Calling is preferred because its easier, can be done more quickly, and calling can reveal more. The main advantage of calling is that people will often provide more valuable information over the phone then they would in writing. However writing does provide stronger documentation. Which can be used to prove that you did your homework. References from former employers are likely to be more valuable than personal references, and can help avoid negligent hiring claims. Educational references should also checked when necessary When calling to check references, several important steps should be followed to obtain the best information:

- Call once to schedule the reference check, then call back when you said you would.
- Plenty of time for the call should be allotted.
- Ask only about job-related information, do not ask inappropriate questions.
- Good notes should be taken, especially in relation to the candidate's former employment.
- At the end, you should summarize and thank the reference for the information.

By following these guidelines, meaningful information can be obtained that will help you make the best hiring decisions.

Mark

Vice President, Human Resources | mark.sanchez@zycamindustries | Office: 455-390-5539 | Cell: 455-290-9760

List at least five weaknesses.

Grammar/Mechanics Checkup 3

Verbs

Review Sections 1.10 –1.15 in the Grammar Review section of the Grammar/Mechanics Handbook. Then study each of the following statements. Underline any verbs that are used incorrectly. In the space provided, write the correct form (or C if correct) and the number of the G/M principle illustrated. When you finish, compare your responses with those provided at the bottom of this page. If your responses differ, study carefully the principles in parentheses.

<u> has </u>   (1.10c)   **EXAMPLE**   Every one of the top-ranking executives <u>have</u> been insured.

—————————   1. Are you convinced that Google's database of customers' messages and private information are secure?

—————————   2. Google's data team have been carefully studying how to shield users from unwarranted government intrusion.

—————————   3. Bank of America, along with most other large national banks, offer a variety of savings plans.

—————————   4. In the next building is the administrative staff and our marketing people.

—————————   5. The city council have unanimously approved the parking fee hike.

—————————   6. If you was in my position, you might agree with my decision.

—————————   7. Everyone except the temporary workers employed during the past year has become eligible for health benefits.

—————————   8. All employees should have went to the emergency procedures demonstration.

—————————   9. The reports have laid on his desk for 11 days and are now overdue.

—————————   10. Either of the flight times are fine with me.

—————————   11. Some of the jury members believes that the prosecution's evidence is not relevant.

    In the space provided, write the letter of the sentence that illustrates consistency in subject, voice, tense, and mood.

—————————   12. a. By carefully following the instructions, much time can be saved.
    b. By carefully following the instructions, you can save much time.

—————————   13. a. All employees must fill out application forms; only then will you be insured.
    b. All employees must fill out application forms; only then will they be insured.

—————————   14. a. First, advertise the position; then, evaluate applications.
    b. First, advertise the position; then, applications must be evaluated.

—————————   15. a. Our manager was a computer whiz who was always ready to help.
    b. Our manager was a computer whiz who is always ready to help.

1. is (1.10c) **2.** has (1.10i) **3.** offers (1.10d) **4.** are (1.10e) **5.** has (1.10e) **6.** were (1.10i) **7.** C (1.12) **8.** gone (1.10h) **9.** lain (1.15) **10.** is (1.10h) **11.** believe (1.10b) **12.** b (1.10b) **13.** b (1.15c—matches subjects) **14.** a (1.15c—matches active voice) **15.** a (1.14b—matches verb tense)

Every chapter provides an editing exercise to build your grammar and mechanics skills. The following letter requires edits in proof-reading, grammar, spelling, punctuation, capitalization, and writing techniques covered in this chapter. Study the guidelines in the Grammar/Mechanics Handbook (Appendix D), including the lists of Confusing Words and Frequently Misspelled Words.

YOUR TASK. Edit the following (a) by inserting corrections in your textbook or on a photocopy using the proofreading marks in Appendix C or (b) by downloading the message from **www.cengagebrain.com** and correcting at your computer.

BODY FITNESS

TRAINING | MASSAGE | WELLNESS

3392 ECONLOCKHATCHEE TRAIL, ORLANDO FL 32822 (407) 551-8791

June 4, 2019

Mr. Allen C. Fineburg
3250 Ponciana Way
Palm Beach Gardens, FL 33410

Dear Mr. Fineberg:

You probably choose Body Fitness because it has became one of the top-rated gyms in the Palm Beach area. Making your work out enjoyable has always been our principal goal. To continue to provide you with the best equipment and programs, your feedback is needed by my partner and myself.

We have build an outstanding program with quality equipment, excellent training programs, and our support staff is very helpful. We feel, however, that we could have a more positive affect and give more individual attention if we could extend our peak usage time. You have probable noticed that attendance at the gym raises from 4 p.m. to 8 p.m. We wish it was possible to accommodate all our customers on their favorite equipment during those hours. Although we can't stretch an hour. We would like to make better use of the time between 8 p.m. and 11 p.m. With more members' coming later, we would have less crush from 4 to 8 p.m. Our exercise machines and strength-training equipment is lying idle later in the evening.

To encourage you to stay later, security cameras for our parking area are being considered by us. Cameras for some inside facilitys may also be added. We have gave this matter a great deal of thought. Although Body Fitness have never had an incident that endangered a member. We have went to considerable trouble to learn about security cameras. Because we think that you will feel more comfortable with them in action.

Please tell us what you think, fill out the enclosed questionnaire, and drop it in the ballot box during your next visit at the desk. We are asking for your feed back about scheduling your workouts, selecting your equipment, and if you would consider coming later in the evening. If you have any other suggestions for reducing the crush at peak times. Please tell us on the enclosed form.

Cordially,

Nicolas Barajas

Nicolas Barajas, Manager

Enclosure

Eight Guidelines for Safe Social Networking

More and more people are becoming accustomed to communicating and sharing information, both business and personal, on Facebook, LinkedIn, Twitter, Instagram, Tumblr, and countless other social media sites. As the popularity of these social networks grows, so do the risks. Savvy business communicators can protect themselves by employing smart practices, such as the following:

- **Beware of privacy settings**. Many sites increasingly give users more control over their settings. Don't assume you must use the default settings. Read the site's privacy policy and use its settings to control who sees your basic information, personal information, photos, friends, and postings. However, sites can change settings anytime without notice. Don't rely solely on privacy settings. Always use discretion in what you post.

- **Check it before you click it**. A sophisticated scam known as *spear phishing* is ensnaring unsuspecting users. Even if a strange message looks as if it's from a friend, remember that hackers may have broken into that person's account. Use an alternate method to reach your friend to confirm the message.

- **Remember that Big Data is watching you**. Whether you are making business contacts or visiting fun sites, you are leaving a digital trail practically forever when you browse the Internet—even in incognito mode! Be mindful of the trail you are leaving when you search and roam.

- **Beware of oversharing**. If your employer visits your Facebook page and notices a flurry of activity while you should be working, you might land in the hot seat. If you report that you're sick and then your Facebook location shows you posting from the local movie theater, this could reveal that you're playing hooky. Additionally, never give details of upcoming holidays nor post holiday snaps while you're away. Criminals scour social networks to find empty houses to burgle.

- **Think twice before "friending."** Don't reject friend request from some coworkers while accepting them from others. Snubbed workers may harbor ill feelings. Don't friend your boss unless he or she friends you first. Send friend requests only once. On the flip side, don't accept every friend or follower request you receive. Connect only with people you know in real life. Criminals create fake online accounts to befriend others and harvest personal information.

- **Be careful of third-party apps**. Polls, quizzes, and games often look innocuous, but signing up for them may be giving scammers permission to access your profile. And if you decide to pay for admission or added perks, you may be providing your credit card and private information to cyber criminals.

- **Limit your LinkedIn info**. Think carefully before posting your full résumé at LinkedIn. Yes, you do want to include enough information to help in a job search, but don't make it easy for identity thieves to use that information, for instance, to fill out a loan application.

- **Don't link accounts**. Many websites and apps allow you to log in with Facebook, rather than creating a separate account. Doing so enables the social network to share all the information it holds about you, including the date and place of your birth and other personal information. Is the temporary convenience worth the risk?

CAREER APPLICATION. Office workers and businesspeople are steeped in technology. Best practices and netiquette rules are a key concern in IT and HR departments. We've presented eight salient tips here for the safe use of social media.

YOUR TASK. In teams discuss the tips presented here. From your own experience, add more suggestions that can make social media users safer. What risky behavior have you experienced or learned about? What violations of netiquette have you seen? Prepare a list of additional helpful tips. Present them using the format shown here, with each statement a command. Submit your list to your instructor and discuss it in class. Consider making a PowerPoint class presentation with original information.

Revising Business Messages

Minerva Studio/iStock/Getty Images

4-1 Stopping to Revise: Applying Phase 3 of the Writing Process

In this fast-paced digital age of e-mailing, texting, and tweeting, the idea of stopping to revise a message would seem to thwart productivity. What? Stop to proofread? Crazy idea! No time! However, sending quick but sloppy business messages not only fails to enhance productivity but also may do just the opposite. Those rushed messages can be confusing and frustrating. They often set into motion a maddening series of back-and-forth queries and responses seeking clarification. To avoid messages that waste time, create confusion, and reduce your credibility, take time to slow down and revise—even short messages.

The final phase of the 3-x-3 writing process focuses on editing, proofreading, and evaluating. Editing means improving the content and sentence structure of your message. Proofreading involves correcting its grammar, spelling, punctuation, format, and mechanics. Evaluating is the process of analyzing whether your message achieves its purpose.

Rarely is the first or even second version of a message satisfactory. Only amateurs expect writing perfection on the first try. The revision stage is your chance to make sure your message says what you mean and makes you look good. Renowned mystery writer Stephen King wisely observed, "To write is human; to edit is divine."

Many professional writers compose the first draft quickly without worrying about language, precision, or correctness. Then they revise and polish extensively.

Learning Outcomes

After studying this chapter, you should be able to do the following:

1 Make business messages more concise by rejecting flabby expressions, long lead-ins, *there is/are* and *it is/was* fillers, redundancies, and empty words, as well as condensing for short social media posts.

2 Enhance clarity in business messages by keeping ideas simple, dumping trite business phrases, cutting clichés, shunning slang and buzzwords, rescuing buried verbs, restraining exuberance, and choosing precise words.

3 Improve readability by applying effective document design including the strategic use of white space, margins, typefaces, fonts, numbered and bulleted lists, and headings.

4 Identify proofreading problem areas, and apply smart techniques to catch mistakes in both routine and complex documents.

5 Evaluate a message to judge its effectiveness.

Other writers, however, prefer to revise as they go—particularly for shorter business documents.

Whether you revise immediately or after a break, you will want to examine your message critically. You should be especially concerned with ways to improve its conciseness, clarity, and readability.

4-1a Cutting the Clutter by Revising for Conciseness

In business, time is indeed money. Translated into writing, this means that concise messages save reading time and, thus, money. In addition, messages that are written directly and efficiently are easier to read and comprehend. In the revision process, look for ways to cut the clutter. Examine every sentence you write. Could the thought be conveyed in fewer words? Your writing will be more concise if you slash flabby expressions, purge unnecessary introductory words, drop fillers, reject redundancies, and eliminate empty words.

Slashing Flabby Expressions. As you revise, strive to slash flabby expressions. This takes conscious effort. Notice the flabbiness in this sentence: *Due to the fact that sales are booming, profits are strong.* It could be said more concisely: *Because sales are booming, profits are strong.* Many flabby expressions can be shortened to one concise word as shown in the following two columns.

Figure 4.1 on the next page illustrates many techniques for writing concisely and also shows how you can revise digital documents with strikethrough formatting and color. If you are revising print documents, use proofreading marks.

FLABBY	CONCISE
as a general rule	generally
at a later date	later
at this point in time	now, presently
despite the fact that	although
due to the fact that, inasmuch as, in view of the fact that	because
feel free to	please
for the period of, for the purpose of	for
in addition to the above	also
in all probability	probably
in the event that	if
in the near future	soon
in very few cases	seldom, rarely
set forth in	in
similar to	like
with regard to	about

Figure 4.1 Revising Digital and Print Documents

Revising Digital Documents Using Strikethrough and Color

~~This is a short note to let you know that, as~~ As you requested, I ~~made an investigation of~~ investigated several of our competitors' websites. Attached ~~hereto~~ is a summary of my findings. ~~of my investigation.~~ I was ~~really~~ most interested in ~~making a comparison of the employment of strategies for~~ comparing marketing ~~strategies~~ as well as ~~the use of~~ navigational graphics ~~used~~ to guide visitors through the sites. ~~In view of the fact that~~ Because we will be revising our own website ~~in the near future~~ soon, I was ~~extremely~~ intrigued by the organization, ~~kind of~~ marketing tactics, and navigation at each ~~and every~~ site I visited.

When revising digital documents, you can use simple word processing tools such as strikethrough and color. In this example, strikethroughs in red identify passages to be deleted. The strikethrough function is located on the Font tab. We used blue to show inserted words, but you may choose any color you prefer.

Revising Printed Documents Using Proofreading Symbols

When revising printed documents, use standard symbols to manually show your revisions.

This is a short note to let you know that, as you requested, I made an investigation of several of our competitors' websites. Attached hereto is a summary of my findings. of my investigation. I was really most interested in making a comparison of the employment of strategies for marketing as well as the use of navigational graphics used to guide visitors through the sites. In view of the fact that Because we will be revising our own website soon in the near future, I was extremely intrigued by the organization, kind of marketing tactics, and navigation at each and every site I visited.

Popular Proofreading Symbols

Delete	℘
Capitalize	≡
Insert	∧
Insert comma	⋏
Insert period	⊙
Start paragraph	¶

Purging Long Lead-Ins. Another way to create concise sentences is to delete unnecessary introductory words. Consider this sentence: *We are using this e-mail to announce that we are considering a flex work schedule.* A more concise and more direct sentence deletes the long lead-in: *We are considering a flex work schedule.* The meat of the sentence often follows the word *that* or *because*, as shown in the following:

WORDY	CONCISE
Please note that this early e-mail is being sent to let everyone know that you may sign up for vacation slots starting on February 1.	You may sign up for vacation slots starting February 1.
This is to inform all customers that lower airfares may be available at our website.	Lower airfares may be available at our website.
I am writing this letter because Professor Kathleen Bent suggested that your organization was hiring trainees.	Professor Kathleen Bent suggested that your organization was hiring trainees.

Dropping Unnecessary *There is/are* and *It is/was* Fillers. In many sentences the expressions *there is/are* and *it is/was* function as unnecessary fillers. In addition to taking up space, these fillers delay getting to the point of the sentence. Eliminate them by recasting the sentence. Many—but not all—sentences can be revised so that fillers are unnecessary.

WORDY	CONCISE
There are more women than men enrolled in college today.	More women than men are enrolled in college today.
It was a Facebook post that revealed the news.	A Facebook post revealed the news.

Rejecting Redundancies. Expressions that repeat meaning or include unnecessary words are redundant. Saying *unexpected surprise* is like saying *surprise surprise* because *unexpected* carries the same meaning as *surprise*. Excessive adjectives, adverbs, and phrases often create redundancies and wordiness. Redundancies do not add emphasis, as some people think. Instead, they identify a writer as inexperienced. As you revise, look for redundant expressions such as the following:

REDUNDANT	CONCISE
absolutely essential	essential
adequate enough	adequate
basic fundamentals	fundamentals *or* basics
collaborate together	collaborate
exactly identical	identical
each and every	each *or* every
necessary prerequisite	prerequisite
new beginning	beginning
refer back	refer
repeat again	repeat
true facts	facts

Eliminating Empty Words. Familiar phrases roll off the tongue easily, but many contain expendable parts. Be alert to these empty words and phrases: *case, degree, the fact that, factor, instance, nature,* and *quality.* Notice how much better the following sentences sound when we remove all the empty words:

~~In the case of~~ Zara, ~~it~~ was able to deliver styles to stores faster than rivals.

Because of ~~the degree of~~ support from upper management, the plan worked.

Are you aware ~~of the fact~~ that millennials may soon make up three quarters of the global workforce?

Except for ~~the instance of~~ Toyota, Japanese imports sagged.

She chose a career in a field that was analytical ~~in nature~~. [OR: She chose a career in an analytical field.]

Student writing in that class is excellent ~~in quality~~.

Also avoid saying the obvious. In the following examples, notice how many unnecessary words we can omit through revision:

> ~~When it arrived,~~ I cashed your check immediately. (Announcing the check's arrival is unnecessary. That fact is assumed in its cashing.)

> As consumers learn more about ingredients ~~and as they become more knowledgeable~~, they are demanding fresher foods. (Avoid repeating information.)

Look carefully at clauses beginning with *that*, *which*, and *who*. They can often be shortened without loss of clarity. Search for phrases such as *it appears that*. These phrases may be reduced to a single adjective or adverb such as *apparently*.

> Changing the name of a _∧*successful* company ~~that is successful~~ is always risky.

> All employees ~~who are among those~~ completing the course will be reimbursed.

> Our _∧*final* proposal, ~~which was~~ slightly altered ~~in its final form~~, was approved.

> We plan to schedule _∧*weekly* meetings ~~on a weekly basis~~.

4-1b Drafting Concise Posts for Social Media Networks

Microblogging is a term you probably haven't heard very often, but chances are you have posted a short message today. As its name suggests, *microblogging* consists of short messages exchanged on social media networks such as Twitter, Facebook, and Tumblr. Businesses are eagerly joining social media networks to see what's being said about them and their products. When they find complaints, they can respond immediately and often solve customer problems. Companies are also using short messaging to make announcements, promote goodwill, and sell their products.

Short messaging may be public or private. Twitter and similar social networks are public channels with messages broadcast to the world. Twitter continues to restrict tweets to 140 characters, but it has changed what counts toward that limit thus slightly expanding expression. Still, brevity is the hallmark of Twitter.

Examples of Company Twitter Messages. Regardless of the short messaging platform, conciseness is critical on Twitter. Your messages must be short—without straying too far from conventional spelling, grammar, and punctuation. Sound difficult? It is, but it can be done, as shown in the following 140-character examples of workplace tweets:

Replying to Customer
@walmart

@PhilMiller We appreciate your sharing your feedback with us. We're very sorry for the inconvenience and understand your frustration. Ani

Sending Helpful Information
@continentalgas

@CleverMom Some boilers can be confusing. Please check our boiler manual to help you figure it out. Try http://po.st/BoilerManual Sarah

Promoting Service Concisely
@ABCbirdandpest

We manage conflict with birds, wildlife, and urban pests proactively and responsibly to ensure our customers' business continuity. bit.ly/feedback2017

Sharing Information
@danaloewy

A new study presents millennials' workplace readiness in a more favorable light. http://fb.me/3suV9QOqL

LEARNING OUTCOME 2

Enhance clarity in business messages by keeping ideas simple, dumping trite business phrases, cutting clichés, avoiding slang and buzzwords, rescuing buried verbs, restraining exuberance, and choosing precise words.

Tips for Writing Concise, Effective Tweets. Your posts will be most effective if you follow these tips:

- Include only main ideas focused on useful information.
- Choose descriptive but short words.
- Personalize your message if possible.
- Be prepared to draft several versions striving for conciseness, clarity, and, yes, even correctness.

It's like playing a game: can you get your message across in only 140 characters? You'll learn more about current communication technology in Chapter 5.

4-2 Enhancing Message Clarity

"Clarity is the most important characteristic of good business writing," claims Grammar Girl podcaster Mignon Fogarty—and we agree![5] A clear message is one that is immediately understood. Fuzzy, long-winded, and careless writing prevents comprehension. Communicators increasingly want to be addressed in a clear and genuine way so that they understand. They comprehend better when information is presented clearly and concisely, as a Dartmouth study about drug facts illustrates in Figure 4.2. Three techniques can improve the clarity of your writing: applying the KISS formula (Keep It Short and Simple), dumping trite business phrases, and avoiding clichés and slang.

4-2a Keep It Short and Simple

To achieve clarity, resist the urge to show off or be fancy. Remember that your goal is not to impress a reader. As a business writer, your goal is to *express*, not *impress*. One way to achieve clear writing is to apply the familiar KISS formula. Use active-voice sentences that avoid indirect, pompous language.

WORDY AND UNCLEAR	IMPROVED
Employees have not been made sufficiently aware of the potentially adverse consequences regarding the use of these perilous chemicals.	Warn your employees about these dangerous chemicals.
In regard to the matter of obtaining optimal results, it is essential that employees be given the implements that are necessary for jobs to be completed satisfactorily.	To get the best results, give employees the tools they need to do the job.

4-2b Dumping Trite Business Phrases

To sound "businesslike," some business writers repeat the same stale expressions that others have used over the years. Your writing will sound fresher and more vigorous if you eliminate these trite phrases or find more original ways to convey the idea.

Figure 4.2 Shorter Advertisement Is Clearer and Easier to Understand

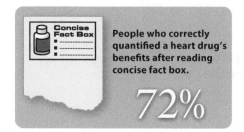

People who correctly quantified a heart drug's benefits after reading concise fact box.

72%

People who correctly quantified a heart drug's benefits after reading the company's long ad.

9%

Consumers understand drug effects better when the information is presented concisely and clearly. A Dartmouth University study revealed that concise fact boxes were superior to the tiny-type, full-page DTC (direct-to-consumer) advertisements that drug manufacturers usually publish.

TRITE PHRASE	IMPROVED
during the period of	during
enclosed please find	enclosed is
every effort will be made	we'll try
in accordance with your wishes	as you wish
in receipt of	have received
please do not hesitate to	please
pursuant to your request	at your request
respond forthwith	respond immediately
thank you in advance	thank you
with the exception of	except
with reference to	about

4-2c Scrapping Clichés

Clichés are expressions that have become exhausted by overuse. Many cannot be explained, especially to those who are new to our culture. Clichés lack not only freshness but also clarity. Instead of repeating clichés such as the following, try to find another way to say what you mean.

at the end of the day	last but not least
better than new	make a bundle
beyond a shadow of a doubt	pass with flying colors
easier said than done	quick as a flash
exception to the rule	shoot from the hip
fill the bill	step up to the plate
first and foremost	think outside the box
good to go	true to form

WORKPLACE IN FOCUS

Buzzwords abound in the business world. Some current expressions are *blue sky thinking* (brainstorming free from practical reality); *at the end of the day* (essentially, finally); *circle back* (rehash an issue), and *core competency* (distinguishable capability). Bloggers find business jargon a favorite target, compiling lists of expressions that they claim are overused, annoying, and meaningless. Others, however, argue that "buzzwords create a common language in the workplace and help foster collaboration and a sense of belonging."[7]

Collect a list of business buzzwords to discuss with your classmates. Can you agree on meanings? Would you use them in business messages? What if your boss and colleagues use expressions that others condemn as buzzwords? Should you use them to fit in?

Don Bayley/E+ /Getty Images

4-2d Shunning Slang and Buzzwords

Slang is composed of informal words with arbitrary and extravagantly changed meanings. These words quickly go out of fashion because they are no longer appealing when everyone begins to understand them. If you want to sound professional, avoid expressions such as *snarky, lousy, blowing the budget, bombed,* and *getting burned.*

Buzzwords are technical expressions that have become fashionable and often are meant to impress rather than express. Business buzzwords include empty terms such as *optimize, incentivize, innovative, leveraging, right-size,* and *paradigm shift.* Countless businesses today use vague rhetoric in the form of phrases such as *cost effective, positioned to perform, solutions-oriented,* and *value-added services with end-to-end fulfillment.*

4-2e Rescuing Buried Verbs

Buried verbs are those that are needlessly converted to wordy noun expressions. Verbs such as *acquire, establish,* and *develop* are made into nouns such as *acquisition, establishment,* and *development.* Such nouns often end in *-tion, -ment,* and *-ance.* Sometimes called *zombie nouns* because they cannibalize and suck the life out of active verbs,[8] these nouns increase sentence length, slow the reader, and muddy the thought. Notice how you can make your writing cleaner and more forceful by avoiding buried verbs and zombie nouns.

BURIED VERBS	UNBURIED VERBS
conduct a discussion of	discuss
create a reduction in	reduce
engage in the preparation of	prepare
give consideration to	consider
make an assumption of	assume
make a discovery of	discover
perform an analysis of	analyze
reach a conclusion that	conclude
take action on	act

4-2f Restraining Exuberance

Occasionally, we show our exuberance with words such as *very, definitely, quite, incredibly, completely, extremely, really, actually,* and *totally.* These intensifiers can emphasize and strengthen your meaning. Overuse, however, makes your writing sound unbusinesslike. Restrain your enthusiasm and guard against excessive use.

EXCESSIVE EXUBERANCE	BUSINESSLIKE
The manufacturer was *extremely* upset to learn that its smartphones were *definitely* being counterfeited.	The manufacturer was upset to learn that its smartphones were being counterfeited.
We *totally* agree that we *actually* did not give his proposal a *very* fair trial.	We agree that we did not give his proposal a fair trial.

4-2g Choosing Clear, Precise Words

As you revise, make sure your words are precise so that the audience knows exactly what you mean. Clear writing creates meaningful images in the mind of the reader. Such writing is sparked by specific verbs, concrete nouns, and vivid adjectives. Foggy messages are marked by sloppy references that may require additional inquiries to clarify their meaning.

LESS PRECISE	MORE PRECISE
She requested that everyone help out.	Our manager begged each team member to volunteer.
They will consider the problem soon.	Our steering committee will consider the recruitment problem on May 15.
We received many responses.	The Sales Division received 28 job applications.
Someone called about the meeting.	Russell Vitello called about the June 12 sales meeting.

4-3 Using Document Design to Improve Readability

LEARNING OUTCOME 3

Improve readability by applying effective document design including the strategic use of white space, margins, typefaces, fonts, numbered and bulleted lists, and headings.

Want to make your readers think you are well organized and intelligent? You can accomplish this by cleverly using document design. You will also enhance the readability of your messages. In the revision process, you have a chance to adjust formatting and make other changes so that readers grasp your main points quickly. Significant design techniques to improve readability include the strategic use of white space, margins, typefaces, fonts, numbered and bulleted lists, and headings for visual impact.

4-3a Employing White Space

Empty space on a page is called *white space*. A page crammed full of text or graphics appears busy, cluttered, and unreadable. You can increase the amount of white space by employing headings, bulleted or numbered lists, and effective margins. Remember that short sentences (20 or fewer words) and short paragraphs (eight or fewer printed lines) improve readability and comprehension. As you revise, think about shortening long sentences. Consider breaking up long paragraphs into shorter chunks.

4-3b Understanding Margins and Text Alignment

Margins determine the white space on the left, right, top, and bottom of a block of type. They define the reading area and provide important visual relief. Business letters and memos usually have side margins of 1 to 1.5 inches.

Your word processing program probably offers four forms of margin alignment: (a) lines align only at the left, (b) lines align only at the right, (c) lines align at both left and right (*justified*), and (d) lines are centered. Nearly all text in Western cultures is aligned at the left and reads from left to right. The right margin may be either *justified* or *ragged right*. The text in books, magazines, and other long works is often justified on the left and right for a formal appearance.

Justified text, however, may require more attention to word spacing and hyphenation to avoid awkward empty spaces or "rivers" of spaces running through a document. When right margins are *ragged*—that is, without alignment or justification—they provide more white space and improve readability. Therefore, you are best served by using left-justified text and ragged-right margins without justification. Centered text is appropriate for headings and short invitations but not for complete messages.

Figure 4.3 Typefaces With Different Personalities for Different Purposes

All-Purpose Sans Serif	Traditional Serif	Happy, Creative Script/Funny	Assertive, Bold Modern Display	Plain Monospaced
Arial	Century	*Brush Script*	**Britannic Bold**	Courier
Calibri	Garamond	Comic Sans	**Broadway**	Letter Gothic
Helvetica	Georgia	*Gigi*	**Elephant**	Monaco
Tahoma	Goudy	Jokerman	**Impact**	Prestige Elite
Univers	Palatino	Lucinda	Bauhaus 93	
Verdana	Times New Roman	Kristen	**SHOWCARD**	

4-3c Choosing Appropriate Typefaces

Business writers today may choose from a number of typefaces on their word processors. A typeface defines the shape of text characters. A wide range of typefaces, as shown in Figure 4.3, is available for various purposes. Some are decorative and useful for special purposes. For most business messages, however, you should choose from *serif* or *sans serif* categories.

Serif typefaces have small features at the ends of strokes. The most common serif typeface is Times New Roman. Other popular serif typefaces are Century, Georgia, and Palatino. Serif typefaces suggest tradition, maturity, and formality. They are frequently used for body text in business messages and longer documents. Because books, newspapers, and magazines favor serif typefaces, readers are familiar with them.

Sans serif typefaces include Arial, Calibri, Gothic, Tahoma, Helvetica, and Univers. These clean characters are widely used for headings, signs, and material that does not require continuous reading. Web designers often prefer sans serif typefaces for simple, pure pages. For longer documents, however, sans serif typefaces may seem colder and less appealing than familiar serif typefaces.

For less formal messages or special decorative effects, you might choose one of the "happy" fonts such as Comic Sans or a bold typeface such as Impact. You can simulate handwriting with a script typeface. Despite the wonderful possibilities available on your word processor, don't get carried away with fancy typefaces. All-purpose sans serif and traditional serif typefaces are most appropriate for your business messages. Generally, use no more than two typefaces within one document.

4-3d Capitalizing on Type Fonts and Sizes

Font refers to a specific style within a typeface family. Here are examples of font styles in the Verdana font family:

CAPITALIZATION	underline
SMALL CAPS	Outline
boldface	Shadow
italics	

Font styles are a mechanical means of adding emphasis to your words. ALL CAPS, Small Caps, and **bold** are useful for headings, subheadings, and single words or short phrases in the text. ALL CAPS, HOWEVER, SHOULD **NEVER** BE USED FOR LONG STRETCHES OF TEXT BECAUSE ALL THE LETTERS ARE THE SAME HEIGHT. This makes it difficult for readers to differentiate words. In addition, excessive use of all caps feels like shouting and irritates readers.

Boldface, *italics*, and <u>underlining</u> are effective for calling attention to important points and terms. Be cautious, however, when using fancy or an excessive number of font styles. Don't use them if they will confuse, annoy, or delay readers.

As you revise, think about type size. Readers are generally most comfortable with 10- to 12-point type for body text. Smaller type enables you to fit more words into a space. Tiny type, however, makes text look dense and unappealing. Slightly larger type makes material more readable. Overly large type (14 points or more) looks amateurish and out of place for body text in business messages. Larger type, however, is appropriate for headings.

OFFICE INSIDER

4-3e Using Numbered and Bulleted Lists for Quick Comprehension

One of the best ways to ensure rapid comprehension is through the use of numbered or bulleted lists. Lists provide high "skim value." This means that readers can browse quickly and grasp main ideas. By breaking up complex information into smaller chunks, lists improve readability, understanding, and retention. They also force the writer to organize ideas and write efficiently.

When revising, look for ideas that could be converted to lists, and follow these techniques to make your lists look professional:

- **Numbered lists:** Use for items that represent a sequence or reflect a numbering system.
- **Bulleted lists:** Use to highlight items that don't necessarily show a chronology.
- **Capitalization:** Capitalize the initial word of each line.
- **Punctuation:** Add end punctuation only if the listed items are complete sentences.
- **Parallelism:** Make all the lines consistent; for example, start each with a verb.

In the following examples, notice that the list on the left presents a sequence of steps with numbers. The bulleted list does not show a sequence of ideas; therefore, bullets are appropriate. Also notice the parallelism in each example. In the numbered list, each item begins with a verb. In the bulleted list, each item follows an adjective/noun sequence. Business readers appreciate lists because they focus attention. Be careful, however, not to use so many that your messages look like grocery lists.

NUMBERED LIST	BULLETED LIST
Create your own website in three easy steps:	Our hosting service features the following:
1. Secure a domain name.	▪ Award-winning designs
2. Choose a Web hosting service.	▪ No-fee hosting
3. Select a design.	▪ Mobile readiness

4-3f Improving Business Messages With Headings

Headings are an effective tool for highlighting information and improving readability. Many business writers think that headings should be reserved for reports; however, headings are also an excellent device for organizing and highlighting information in e-mails and other business messages. Why are they so effective? They encourage the writer to group similar material together. Headings help the reader separate major ideas from details. They enable a busy reader to skim familiar or less important information. They also provide a quick preview or review. Notice how *category headings*, such as those in the following example, immediately help the reader recognize and comprehend the information.

Category Headings

- **Attracting applicants.** We advertise for qualified applicants, and we also encourage current employees to recommend good people.
- **Interviewing applicants.** Our specialized interviews include simulated customer encounters as well as scrutiny by supervisors.
- **Checking references.** We investigate every applicant thoroughly. We contact former employers and all listed references.

In Figure 4.4 on the next page, the writer converts a dense, unappealing e-mail message into an easier-to-read version by applying professional document design. Notice that the all-caps font in the first paragraph makes its meaning difficult to decipher. In the revised version, the writer changed the all-caps font to uppercase and lowercase. One of the best document design techniques in this message is the use of headings and bullets to help the reader see chunks of information in similar groups. All of these improvements are made in the revision process. You can make any message more readable by applying the document design techniques presented here.

LEARNING OUTCOME 4

Identify proofreading problem areas, and apply smart techniques to catch mistakes in both routine and complex documents.

4-4 Catching Errors With Careful Proofreading

Alas, none of us are perfect, and even the best writers sometimes make mistakes. The problem, however, is not making the mistakes; the real problem is not finding and correcting them. Documents with errors affect your credibility and the success of your organization, as illustrated in Figure 4.5.

Once the message is in its final form, it's time to proofread. Don't proofread earlier because you may waste time checking items that eventually will be changed or omitted. Important messages—such as those you send to management or to customers or turn in to instructors for grades—deserve careful revision and proofreading. When you finish a first draft, plan for a cooling-off period. Put the document aside and return to it after a break, preferably after 24 hours or longer. Proofreading is especially difficult because most of us read what we thought we wrote. That's why it's important to look for specific problem areas.

4-4a What to Watch for in Proofreading

Careful proofreaders check for the following problems:

- **Spelling.** Now is the time to consult the dictionary. Is *recommend* spelled with one or two *c*'s? Do you mean *affect* or *effect*? Use your computer spell-checker, but don't rely on it totally.
- **Grammar.** Locate sentence subjects; do their verbs agree with them? Do pronouns agree with their antecedents? Review the principles in the Grammar/ Mechanics Handbook if necessary. Use your computer's grammar-checker, but be suspicious. It's not always correct.
- **Punctuation.** Make sure that introductory clauses are followed by commas. In compound sentences put commas before coordinating conjunctions (*and, or, but, nor*). Double-check your use of semicolons and colons.
- **Names and numbers.** Compare all names and numbers with their sources because inaccuracies are not always visible. Especially verify the spelling of the names of individuals receiving the message. Most of us immediately dislike someone who misspells our name.

Figure 4.4 Improving Readability Through Strategic Document Design and Revision

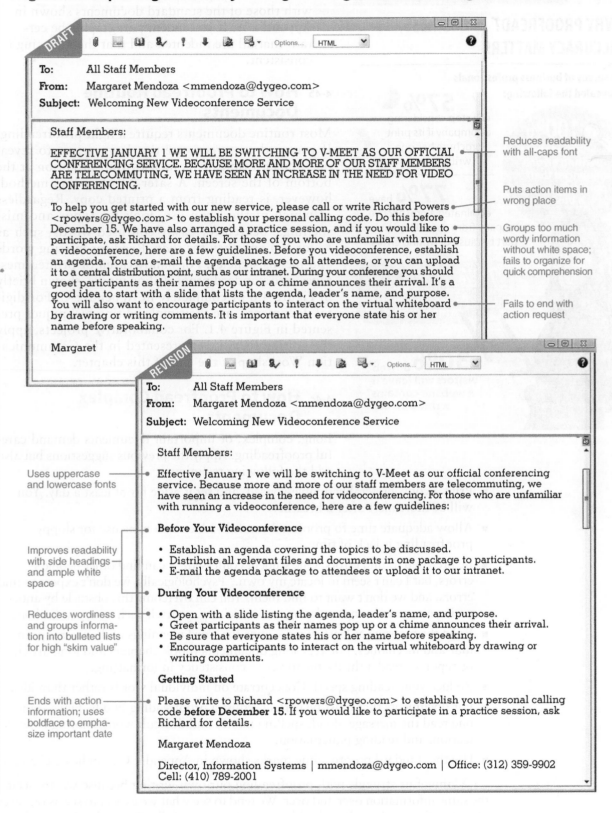

DRAFT

To: All Staff Members
From: Margaret Mendoza <mmendoza@dygeo.com>
Subject: Welcoming New Videoconference Service

Staff Members:

EFFECTIVE JANUARY 1 WE WILL BE SWITCHING TO V-MEET AS OUR OFFICIAL CONFERENCING SERVICE. BECAUSE MORE AND MORE OF OUR STAFF MEMBERS ARE TELECOMMUTING, WE HAVE SEEN AN INCREASE IN THE NEED FOR VIDEO CONFERENCING.

To help you get started with our new service, please call or write Richard Powers <rpowers@dygeo.com> to establish your personal calling code. Do this before December 15. We have also arranged a practice session, and if you would like to participate, ask Richard for details. For those of you who are unfamiliar with running a videoconference, here are a few guidelines. Before you videoconference, establish an agenda. You can e-mail the agenda package to all attendees, or you can upload it to a central distribution point, such as our intranet. During your conference you should greet participants as their names pop up or a chime announces their arrival. It's a good idea to start with a slide that lists the agenda, leader's name, and purpose. You will also want to encourage participants to interact on the virtual whiteboard by drawing or writing comments. It is important that everyone state his or her name before speaking.

Margaret

- Reduces readability with all-caps font
- Puts action items in wrong place
- Groups too much wordy information without white space; fails to organize for quick comprehension
- Fails to end with action request

REVISION

To: All Staff Members
From: Margaret Mendoza <mmendoza@dygeo.com>
Subject: Welcoming New Videoconference Service

Staff Members:

Effective January 1 we will be switching to V-Meet as our official conferencing service. Because more and more of our staff members are telecommuting, we have seen an increase in the need for videoconferencing. For those who are unfamiliar with running a videoconference, here are a few guidelines:

Before Your Videoconference

- Establish an agenda covering the topics to be discussed.
- Distribute all relevant files and documents in one package to participants.
- E-mail the agenda package to attendees or upload it to our intranet.

During Your Videoconference

- Open with a slide listing the agenda, leader's name, and purpose.
- Greet participants as their names pop up or a chime announces their arrival.
- Be sure that everyone states his or her name before speaking.
- Encourage participants to interact on the virtual whiteboard by drawing or writing comments.

Getting Started

Please write to Richard <rpowers@dygeo.com> to establish your personal calling code **before December 15**. If you would like to participate in a practice session, ask Richard for details.

Margaret Mendoza

Director, Information Systems | mmendoza@dygeo.com | Office: (312) 359-9902
Cell: (410) 789-2001

- Uses uppercase and lowercase fonts
- Improves readability with side headings and ample white space
- Reduces wordiness and groups information into bulleted lists for high "skim value"
- Ends with action information; uses boldface to emphasize important date

Figure 4.5 Why Proofread?

WHY PROOFREAD? IN BUSINESS, ACCURACY MATTERS

A survey of business professionals revealed the following:

100% said that writing errors influenced their opinions about a business.

57% will stop considering a company if its print brochure has one writing error.

77% have eliminated a prospective company from consideration in part because of writing errors.

75% thought misspelled words were inexcusable.

30% of Web visitors will leave if a website contains writing errors.

Goodluz/Shutterstock.com

■ **Format.** Be sure that your document looks balanced on the page. Compare its parts and format with those of the standard documents shown in Appendix A. If you indent paragraphs, be certain that all are indented and that their spacing is consistent.

4-4b How to Proofread Routine Documents

Most routine documents require a light proofreading. If you read on screen, use the down arrow to reveal one line at a time. This focuses your attention at the bottom of the screen. A safer proofreading method, however, is reading from a printed copy. Regardless of which method you use, look for typos and misspellings. Search for easily confused words, such as *to* for *too* and *then* for *than*. Read for missing words and inconsistencies. For handwritten or printed messages, use standard proofreading marks, shown briefly in Figure 4.6 or completely in Appendix C. For digital documents, use the simple editing techniques presented in Figure 4.1. For collaborative projects, apply the editing techniques presented in the Communication Workshop at the end of this chapter.

4-4c How to Proofread Complex Documents

Long, complex, or important documents demand careful proofreading. Apply the previous suggestions but also add the following techniques:

■ Print a copy, preferably double-spaced, and set it aside for at least a day. You will be more alert after a breather.

■ Allow adequate time to proofread carefully. A common excuse for sloppy proofreading is lack of time.

■ Be prepared to find errors. One student confessed, "I can find other people's errors, but I can't seem to locate my own." Psychologically, we don't expect to find errors, and we don't want to find them. You can overcome this obstacle by anticipating errors and congratulating, not criticizing, yourself each time you find one.

■ Read the message at least twice—once for word meanings and once for grammar and mechanics. For very long documents (book chapters and long articles or reports), read a third time to verify consistency in formatting.

■ Reduce your reading speed. Concentrate on individual words rather than ideas.

■ For documents that must be perfect, enlist a proofreading buddy. Have someone read the message aloud, spelling names and difficult words, noting capitalization, and reading punctuation.

■ Use the standard proofreading marks shown in Appendix C to indicate changes.

Many of us struggle with proofreading our own writing because we are seeing the same information over and over. We tend to see what we expect to see as our eyes race over the words without looking at each one carefully. We tend to know what is coming next and glide over it. To change the appearance of what you are reading, you might print it on a different colored paper or change the font. If you are proofing on screen, enlarge the page view or change the background color of the screen.

Figure 4.6 Most Common Proofreading Marks

Mark	Meaning	Mark	Meaning
✒	Delete	∧	Insert
≡	Capitalize	#∧	Insert space
/lc	Lowercase (don't capitalize)	∧	Insert punctuation
∩	Transpose	⊙	Insert period
⌒	Close up	¶	Start paragraph

Marked Copy

~~This is to inform you that~~ beginning september 1, the doors
(lc)leading to the West side of the building will have alarms.
Because ~~of the fact that~~ these ~~exits~~ doors also function as fire exits.
they can not ~~actually~~ be locked, consequently, we are instaling
alrarms. Please ~~utilize~~ use the east side exists to avoid setting off
the ear splitting alarms.

4-5 Evaluating the Effectiveness of Your Message

LEARNING OUTCOME 5
Evaluate a message to judge its effectiveness.

As you apply finishing touches, take a moment to evaluate your writing. Remember that everything you write, whether for yourself or someone else, takes the place of a personal appearance. If you were meeting in person, you would be certain to dress appropriately and professionally. The same standard applies to your writing. Evaluate what you have written to be sure that it attracts the reader's attention. Is it polished and clear enough to convince the reader that you are worth listening to? How successful will this message be? Does it say what you want it to? Will it achieve its purpose? How will you know whether it succeeds?

The best way to judge the success of your communication is through feedback. For this reason you should encourage the receiver to respond to your message. This feedback will tell you how to modify future efforts to improve your communication technique.

Your instructor will also be evaluating some of your writing. Although any criticism is painful, try not to be defensive. Look on these comments as valuable advice tailored to your specific writing weaknesses—and strengths. Many businesses today spend thousands of dollars bringing in communication consultants to improve employee writing skills. You are getting the same training in this course. Take advantage of this chance—one of the few you may have—to improve your skills. The best way to improve your skills, of course, is through instruction, practice, and evaluation.

In this class you have all three elements: instruction in the writing process, practice materials, and someone to guide you and evaluate your efforts. Those three elements are the reasons this book and this course may be the most valuable in your entire curriculum. Because it's almost impossible to improve your communication skills alone, take advantage of this opportunity.

Summary of Learning Outcomes

1 Make business messages more concise by rejecting flabby expressions, long lead-ins, *there is/are* and *it is/was* fillers, redundancies, and empty words, as well as condensing for short media posts.

- Eliminate flabby expressions (*at this point in time, for the purpose of, in the event that, this is to inform you*).
- Exclude opening fillers (*there is, there are*), redundancies (*combined together*), and empty words (*in the case of, the fact that*).
- In microblogging messages, include only main ideas, choose descriptive but short words, personalize your message if possible, and be prepared to write several versions striving for conciseness, clarity, and correctness.

2 Enhance clarity in business messages by keeping ideas simple, dumping trite business phrases, cutting clichés, shunning slang and buzzwords, rescuing buried verbs, restraining exuberance, and choosing precise words.

- To be sure your messages are clear, apply the KISS formula: Keep It Short and Simple.
- Avoid foggy, indirect, and pompous language.
- Do not include trite business phrases (*pursuant to your request, enclosed please find, in receipt of*), clichés (*fill the bill, good to go*), slang (*snarky, lousy, bombed*), and buzzwords (*optimize, paradigm shift, incentivize*).
- Avoid burying verbs (*to analyze* rather than *to perform an analysis, to conclude* rather than *to reach a conclusion*). Don't overuse intensifiers that show exuberance (*totally, actually, very, definitely*) but sound unbusinesslike.
- Choose precise words (*the report was well organized* rather than *the report was great*).

3 Improve readability by applying effective document design including the strategic use of white space, margins, typefaces, fonts, numbered and bulleted lists, and headings.

- Enhance readability and comprehension by using ample white space, appropriate side margins, and ragged-right (not justified) margins.
- Use serif typefaces (fonts with small features at the ends of strokes, such as Times New Roman, Century, and Palatino) for body text; use sans serif typefaces (clean fonts without small features, such as Arial, Helvetica, and Tahoma) for headings and signs.
- Choose appropriate font styles and sizes for business messages.
- Provide high "skim value" with numbered and bulleted lists.
- Include headings to add visual impact and aid readability in business messages as well as in reports.

4 Identify proofreading problem areas, and apply smart techniques to catch mistakes in both routine and complex documents.

- In proofreading be especially alert to spelling, grammar, punctuation, names, numbers, and document format.
- Proofread routine documents immediately after completion by reading line by line on the computer screen or, better yet, from a printed draft.
- Proofread more complex documents after a breather.
- Allow adequate time, reduce your reading speed, and read the document at least three times—for word meanings, for grammar and mechanics, and for formatting.

5 Evaluate a message to judge its effectiveness.

- Encourage feedback from the receiver so that you can determine whether your communication achieved its goal.
- Welcome any advice from your instructor on how to improve your writing skills.

Chapter Review

1. How is proofreading different from revising? (L.O. 1)

2. Why should business writers strive for conciseness? (L.O. 1)

3. What's wrong with expressions such as *due to the fact that* and *in view of the fact that*? (L.O. 1)

4. What's wrong with expressions such as *necessary prerequisite* and *big in size*? (L.O. 1)

5. Why should writers avoid the opening *I am sending this e-mail because . . .*? (L.O. 1)

6. Why should writers avoid opening a sentence or clause with *there is* or *there are*? (L.O. 1)

7. What are buried verbs and zombie nouns? Give an original example. Why should writers avoid buried verbs? (L.O. 2)

8. What design techniques can you use to improve the readability of e-mails, memos, letters, and reports? (L.O. 3)

9. In proofreading, why is it difficult to find your own errors? How can you overcome this barrier? (L.O. 4)

10. What are the differences between editing manually and editing digitally? What tools are used for each? (L.O. 4)

Critical Thinking

11. A blogger recently asserted that "the pervasive use of email for business has made the work of writing well even more difficult because it invites—relentlessly—hitting Send before you have thought through, organized, reviewed, and even rewritten your message."[10] Do you agree that the process of writing has become more difficult with e-mail? (L.O. 1–5)

12. You have just submitted a beautifully researched report. But your supervisor focused on the two or three little errors that you missed and gave none of the praise you expected. Was this fair of your supervisor? (L.O. 4, 5)

13. It's easy to use clichés because they just roll off the tongue. What's wrong with tried-and-true expressions such as *it is what it is* and *at the end of the day*? (L.O. 2)

14. Because business writing should have high "skim value," why not write everything in bulleted lists? (L.O. 3)

15. Conciseness is valued in business. However, can messages be too short? (L.O. 1)

Writing Improvement Exercises

Flabby Expressions (L.O. 1)

YOUR TASK. Revise the following sentences to eliminate flabby phrases.

16. We cannot complete the construction at this point in time due to the fact that building costs have jumped at a considerable rate.

17. In the normal course of events, we would seek additional funding; however, in view of the fact that rates have increased, we cannot.

18. In very few cases has it been advisable for us to borrow money for a period of 90 or fewer days.

19. Inasmuch as our sales are increasing in a gradual manner, we might seek a loan in the amount of $50,000.

20. Despite the fact that we have had no response to our bid, we are still available in the event that you wish to proceed with your building project.

Long Lead-Ins (L.O. 1)

YOUR TASK. Revise the following sentences to eliminate long lead-ins.

21. This is an announcement to tell you that parking permits are available in the office.

22. We are sending this memo to notify everyone that anyone who wants to apply for telecommuting may submit an application immediately.

23. I am writing this letter to inform you that your new account executive is Edward Ho.

24. This is to warn you that cyber criminals use sophisticated tools to decipher passwords rapidly.

There is/are and *It is/was* Fillers (L.O. 1)

YOUR TASK. Revise the following sentences to avoid unnecessary *there is/are* and *it is/was* fillers.

25. There is a password-checker that can evaluate your password's strength automatically.

26. It is careless or uninformed individuals who are the most vulnerable to computer hackers.

27. There are computers in Internet cafes, at conferences, and in airport lounges that should be considered unsafe for any personal use.

28. A computer specialist told us that there are keystroke-logging devices that gather information typed on a computer, including passwords.

Redundancies (L.O. 1)

YOUR TASK. Revise the following sentences to avoid redundancies.

29. Because his laptop was small in size, he could carry it everywhere.

30. A basic fundamental of computer safety is to avoid storing your password on a file in your computer because criminals will look there first.

31. The manager repeated again his warning that we must use strong passwords.

32. Although the two files seem exactly identical, we should proofread each and every page.

Trite Business Phrases (L.O. 2)

YOUR TASK. Revise the following sentences to eliminate trite business phrases.

33. Pursuant to your request, I will submit your repair request immediately.

34. Enclosed please find the list of customers that will be used in our promotion.

35. As per your request, we are sending the contract under separate cover.

36. Every effort will be made to proceed in accordance with your wishes.

Jargon, Slang, Clichés, Wordiness (L.O. 2)

YOUR TASK. Revise the following sentences to avoid confusing jargon, slang, clichés, and wordiness.

37. Our manager insists that we must think outside the box in promoting our new kitchen tool.

38. Although we got burned in the last contract, you can be sure we will stand our ground this time.

39. Beyond the shadow of a doubt, our lousy competitor will make another snarky claim that is below the belt.

40. If you refer back to our five-year plan, you will see that there are provisions for preventing blowing the budget.

Buried Verbs (L.O. 2)

YOUR TASK. Revise the following sentences to unbury the verbs.

41. After investigating, the fire department reached the conclusion that the blaze was set intentionally.

42. Our committee promised to give consideration to your proposal at its next meeting.

43. When used properly, zero-based budgeting can bring about a reduction in overall costs.

44. Did our department make an application for increased budget support?

45. The budget committee has not taken action on any projects yet.

46. Homeowners must make a determination of the total value of their furnishings.

Precise, Direct Words (L.O. 2)

YOUR TASK. Revise the following sentences to improve clarity and precision. Use your imagination to add appropriate words.

EXAMPLE They said it was a long way off.

REVISION Management officials announced that the merger would not take place for two years.

47. Someone told us that it would be available for rent soon.

48. Please contact us in the immediate future.

49. An employee from that organization notified us about the change in date for the event.

50. She said that the movie she saw was not very good.

Condensing for Concise Posts: Tweets With Replies (L.O. 1)

YOUR TASK. Read the following Twitter messages and write a 140-character tweet reply to each. Be selective in what you include. Your instructor may show you the actual responses that the company wrote.

51. **@DustinB to @Walmart: Having a terrible time with savings catcher losing my money! Will someone help?** Prepare a response that explains that Walmart can't really fix this problem. But we can refer the customer to our Savings Catcher team at 866-224-1663. Or the customer could e-mail SavCatch@wal-mart.com for assistance.

52. **@NicoleD to @Whole Foods Market: Did you guys discontinue the heavenly super stars gummies ?!?!?!** Prepare a response explaining that you had to check with WFM's private label team to see whether this was a WFM item or a private brand. Unfortunately, you learned that this private brand of gummy candy has been discontinued at Whole Foods Market. However, you will pass along the suggestion in an effort to get this customer's favorite gummies back in the store!

53. **@Courtney88 to @Southwest Air: Absolutely floored by @SouthwestAir. No wonder your bags fly free, there's a chance they'll lose it & can't give you a clue where it is.** Prepare a response that explains that Southwest takes all baggage issues absolutely seriously. Request that the customer send a direct message (DM) with the customer's flight confirmation number. This action will help with the baggage search.

54. **@Tucson79 to @VW: Sunroof on wife's Bug is noisy to the point that may not get VW for next car. Mentioned this at service, still whistles constantly.** Prepare a response based on the following. We can't immediately know the problem, but we do very much want to learn how we may be able to help. We will need you to DM us with the following information: your VIN number and your e-mail address. These pieces of information will enable us to reach out to you.

55. **@RachelD to @CapitalOne. Shout out to @CapitalOne for immediately catching fraudulent activity on my account and resolving it in a 7-minute phone call!** Prepare a response that acknowledges receipt of the tweet but also conveys the goal of CapitalOne to make the lives of customers easier so they can catch up on things like shopping, TV, and movies. Include a winking happy face ;-).

Lists and Headings (L.O. 3)

YOUR TASK. Revise the following sentences and paragraphs using lists and category headings, if appropriate. Improve parallel construction and readability while reducing wordiness.

56. Revise the following paragraph by incorporating a bulleted list.

This information is to let you know that a high-powered MBA program costs hundreds of dollars an hour. However, our program covers the same information. That information includes entrepreneurship tips as well as how to start a business. You will also learn information about writing a business plan and understanding taxes. In addition, our MBA program covers how to go about writing a marketing feasibility study. Another important topic that our program covers is employment benefits plans.

57. Revise the following with a concise introductory paragraph plus a bulleted list of tips.

Unadvertised, or hidden, jobs may make up as much as 80 percent of unfilled openings, according to Fred Coon, a licensed employment agent. To uncover hidden jobs, Coon suggests that those entering the workforce think about joining industry groups. Associations, chambers of commerce, and Toastmasters are excellent places where job applicants can make valuable contacts before they are needed. Coon also suggests talking to insiders. Insights from those already in the industry can help new workers learn how to best chart their career paths. Another way to find hidden jobs is to search company websites. Many companies post openings only on their corporate websites.

58. Revise the following dense, wordy paragraph to create an introductory sentence plus a bulleted list.

We all know that ATMs are quick and convenient for accessing your money, especially if you are having a cash emergency. But not everyone uses an ATM safely. To do so, there are a few procedures that you can follow to feel safe. First, don't use an ATM unless it is located in a well-lit area that is also busy. This is especially important after nightfall. Next, a careful person will look around to see if there are any suspicious people loitering about. It's always wise to use a challenging PIN, which should have more than four letters or numbers. When you approach the ATM machine, check it out. Do you see any false fronts or anything doubtful? Finally, you must always protect your PIN. One way to do that is by placing your hand over the keypad to act as a shield.

59. From the following wordy paragraph, create a concise introductory statement plus a bulleted list with category headings.

This is to inform you that our on-site GuruGeek computer technicians can provide you with fast, affordable solutions to residential and also to small business clients. Our most popular offerings include antivirus security. This service involves having our GuruGeek protect your computer against viruses, worms, and spyware as well as help you avoid e-mail attacks, identity theft, and malicious hacker programs. Our wireless networking service enables you to share Internet access through a single wireless router so that many computer users use one network at the same time. They are all using the same network. Another popular service is data backup and recovery. Our technicians focus on helping small businesses and home users protect their data without making an investment of a lot of time and energy.

Note: Radical Rewrites are provided at **www.cengagebrain.com** for you to download and revise. Your instructor may show a suggested solution.

4.1 Radical Rewrite: Information E-Mail—Negative Announcement (L.O. 1–5)

The following wordy, inefficient, and disorganized message invites department managers to three interviewing sessions to select student interns. However, to be effective, this message desperately needs a radical rewrite.

YOUR TASK. Study the message and list at least five weaknesses. Then revise to avoid excessive wordiness and repetition. Also think about how to develop an upbeat tone and improve readability. Can you condense this sloppy 14-sentence message into 6 efficient sentences plus a list—and still convey all the necessary information?

To:	Management Staff
From:	Nathan Weintraub <nweintraub@bien.com>
Subject:	Interns

Staff:

As you may be aware, we have for the past year been considering changing our approach to interns. Your management council recently made a decision to offer compensation to the interns in our internship program because we learned that in two fields (computer science and information systems) interns are usually paid, which is the norm. However, we will be unable to offer any more than three internships.

In collaboration with our nearby college, we have narrowed the field to six excellent candidates. These six candidates will be interviewed. This is to inform you that you are required to attend three interviewing sessions for these student candidates. Your presence is needed at these sessions to help us avoid making poor selections.

You should mark your calendars for the following three times. We are scheduling the first set of interviews for April 5 to meet in the conference room. Please examine all the candidates' résumés, which are attached, and send me your ranking lists.

The second interviewing session is scheduled for April 8 in Office 22 (the conference room was already scheduled). On April 11 we can finish up in the conference room. All of the meetings will start at 2 p.m. In view of the fact that your projects need fresh ideas and talented new team members, I should not have to urge you to attend and be well prepared.

Nathan Weintraub

Director, Human Resources

List at least five weaknesses.

Adjectives and Adverbs

Review Sections 1.16 and 1.17 of the Grammar/Mechanics Handbook. Then select the correct form to complete each of the following statements. Record the appropriate G/M section and letter to illustrate the principle involved. When you finish, compare your responses with those provided at the bottom of the page. If your answers differ, study carefully the principles shown in parentheses.

_____b_____ (1.17e)   **EXAMPLE**   Surprisingly, most of the (a) *twenty year old*, (b) *twenty-year-old* equipment is still working.

_____ 1.   The newly opened restaurant offered many (a) *tried and true*, (b) *tried-and-true* menu items.

_____ 2.   Although purchased twenty years ago, the equipment still looked (a) *brightly*, (b) *bright*.

_____ 3.   The committee sought a (a) *cost-effective*, (b) *cost effective* solution to the continuing problem.

_____ 4.   How is the Shazam app able to process a song so (a) *quick*, (b) *quickly*?

_____ 5.   Of the two plans, which is (a) *more*, (b) *most* comprehensive?

_____ 6.   Employees may submit only (a) *work-related*, (b) *work related* expenses to be reimbursed.

_____ 7.   Amy and Marusia said that they're planning to open (a) *there*, (b) *their* own business next year.

_____ 8.   Haven't you ever made a (a) *spur of the moment*, (b) *spur-of-the-moment* decision?

_____ 9.   Not all decisions that are made on the (a) *spur of the moment*, (b) *spur-of-the-moment* turn out badly.

_____ 10.   The committee offered a (a) *well-thought-out*, (b) *well thought out* plan to revamp online registration.

_____ 11.   You must complete a (a) *change of address*, (b) *change-of-address* form when you move.

_____ 12.   Employment figures may get (a) *worse*, (b) *worst* before they get better.

_____ 13.   I could be more efficient if my printer were (a) *more nearer*, (b) *nearer* my computer.

_____ 14.   Naturally, our team members felt (a) *bad*, (b) *badly* when our project was canceled.

_____ 15.   The truck's engine is certainly running (a) *smooth*, (b) *smoothly* after its tune-up.

1. b (1.17e) 2. b (1.17c) 3. a (1.17c) 4. b (1.17e) 5. a (1.17d) 6. a (1.16) 7. b (1.17e) 8. b (1.17g) 9. a (1.17e) 10. a (1.17e) 11. b (1.17e) 12. a (1.16) 13. b (1.17b) 14. a (1.16) 15. b (1.17d)

Editing Challenge 4

The following message from a district manager to her boss submits recommendations for launching an employee suggestion plan. However, her enthusiastic message suffers from excessive exuberance, wordiness, lack of parallelism in its list, poor proofreading, a dangling modifier, and other writing faults that require correction.

YOUR TASK. Edit the following (a) by inserting corrections in your textbook or on a photocopy using the proofreading marks in Appendix C or (b) by downloading the message from **www.cengagebrain.com** and correcting at your computer. Your instructor may show you a possible solution.

To: Ryan Karacia <ryan@peterson.com>
From: Amanda Wilmot <amanda@peterson.com>
Subject: Launching an Incredibly Successful Employee Suggestion Program!

Ryan:

Due to the fact that you recently asked me to provide ideas for encouraging employees to make suggestions, I am absolutely delighted to submit the following. You noted that a high level of employee engagement is linked to increased profitability, productivity, and employees are retained longer. I agree totally and completely! After conducting research and interviews, the following ideas came to me on how to make a start for such a program:

- **Obtain senior management buy-in.** To make any suggestion program successful, we must first gain the support of the CEO and all upper management. They must get behind the program and help communicate why it is important to employees as well as to the business.

- **A promotion plan must be developed.** Next we must give the program a name and create initial buzz with a fun launch. Perhaps including a party.

- **Agree on incentive.** A basic fundamental of any suggestion program is the right mix of incentives to encourage employees to share there ideas. Some employees respond to cash prizes, others like perks such as a month of free parking near the front door. One company found that a hand written thank you message from a manger or a mention on the intranet provided sufficient reward for ideas that were good.

- **Educate employees.** The program will never be successful if we are not able to train employees about what types of ideas are sought. A pilot program would be a good idea.

- **A suggestion review team must be set up.** All key departments need to be represented with members to review those ideas and evaluate them as well.

I have many more incredible ideas for launching a suggestion program because I feel that such a program could be very, very successful for our organization. May I make an appointment to discuss these ideas with you farther? I suggest that we actually give serious consideration to taking initial steps to launching a suggestion program.

Best,

Amanda Wilmot
District Manager

Using Google Docs to Collaborate, Revise, and Edit

Collaborative writing and editing projects are challenging. Fortunately, several cloud-based productivity applications are available that enable teams to draft and edit documents in real time. Students will probably be most familiar with the free service **Google Docs**. This Google platform allows users to import or create, share, revise, and comment on an evolving document—from any device. More useful than file-hosting sites such as **Dropbox**, Google Docs lets writers not only privately share Web-based documents, but also edit them. Moreover, team members can message via e-mail from within the program.

At present, Google Docs works seamlessly with MS Word documents that can be imported. Also, files created in Google Docs can be downloaded as Word documents. Edits are recorded in different colors—one for each reviewer. Content to be deleted appears as strikethrough text; new edits match the editor's assigned color, as you can see in Figure 4.7. The collaborators can subsequently accept or reject proposed changes. Clicking on a marginal comment or the corresponding crossed-out text activates horizontal brackets in the editor's color to call attention to the phrase or word under review. In the **Suggesting** mode, team members can point out problematic passages or errors, ask or answer **Suggesting** questions, and share ideas without changing or adding text. The original writer may accept or reject these changes. The multicolored comments

are identified by the individual writers' names and date/time stamps.

One of the notable features is **See revision history**, which enables users not only to view a log of earlier versions of the document, but also to return to and work with those earlier versions. Google Docs automatically saves all changes. Collaborators can choose free storage space on Google Drive.

CAREER APPLICATION. On the job, you will likely be working with others on projects that require written documents. During employment interviews, employers may ask whether you have participated in team projects using collaboration tools. To be able to answer that question favorably, take advantage of this opportunity to work collaboratively on a document using the revising and commenting features provided in the **Editing** and **Suggesting** modes in Google Docs.

YOUR TASK. In pairs, practice collaborative editing. Use Google Docs to revise the Radical Rewrite or Editing Challenge document in this chapter. One team member imports the document into Google Docs, makes the first edits in **Editing** or **Suggesting** mode, and notifies the other team member with the convenient **Share** (or **Email collaborators**) feature that the file is ready for further editing. The team then submits the final document to the instructor—with or without edits showing, depending on the instructor's preference.

Figure 4.7 **Google Docs Aids Collaboration**

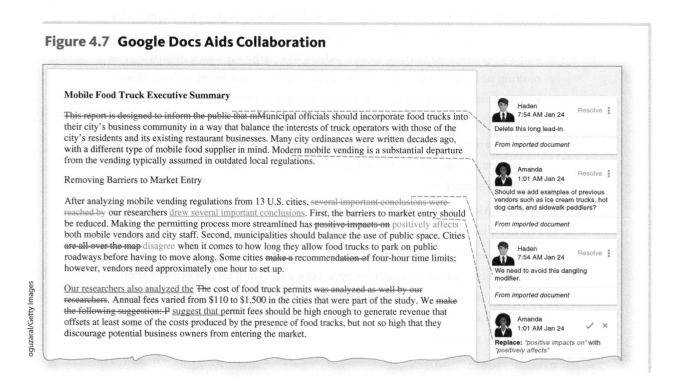

Workplace Communication 3

Pla2na/Shutterstock.com

Rawpixel.com/Shutterstock.com

Short Workplace Messages and Digital Media

racom/Shutterstock.com

Learning Outcomes

After studying this chapter, you should be able to do the following:

1 Understand e-mail, memos, and the professional standards for their usage, structure, and format in the digital era workplace.

2 Explain workplace instant messaging and texting as well as their liabilities and best practices.

3 Identify professional applications of podcasts and wikis.

4 Describe how businesses use blogs to connect with internal and external audiences, and list best practices for professional blogging.

5 Define the advantages and risks of business uses of social media networks.

5-1 Writing Digital Age E-Mail Messages and Memos

We are social and mobile. Communication is rapidly changing in this digital era. The Web has evolved from mere storage of passively consumed information to a dynamic, hyperconnected environment. Users are empowered, active participants who create and edit content, review products, and share information as well as media. To engage, they are increasingly using mobile electronic devices. Messages are shorter and more frequent, and response time is much speedier. Social media

114

platforms such as Facebook, YouTube, Instagram, and Twitter have transformed communication from one-on-one conversations to one-to-many transmissions. Social media and networking apps have also revolutionized the way we keep in touch with friends and family.

In many businesses, desktop computers are becoming obsolete. They are being replaced with ever-smaller laptops, netbooks, smartphones, and tablets. These and other powerful mobile devices access data and applications stored in the *cloud*, in remote networks, not individual computers. Virtual private networks (VPNs) offer secure access to organizations' information from any location in the world. For better or for worse, businesspeople are increasingly connected 24/7.

As a likely digital native, you are probably Internet savvy, but you may need to know how businesses use communication technologies to transmit information. This chapter explores short forms of workplace communication, beginning with e-mail, which many workers love to hate, and memos, which are disappearing but still necessary in many organizations. Focusing on newer media, you will learn about workplace messaging and texting, podcasts, wikis, corporate blogs, and social networking for business. Understanding these workplace technologies and mastering best practices can save you time, reduce blunders, and help you excel as a professional.

5-1a E-Mail: Love It or Hate It—But It's Here to Stay

E-mail in the workplace is unlikely to go away. Despite the growing importance of social media for business, most workplace messages are still sent by e-mail, the most effective digital tool for Internet-using workers.[1] Not only that: the volume of workplace e-mail is expected to grow.[2] Tech expert Alexis Madrigal is one of many staunch defenders of e-mail. "You can't kill email!" he claims. "It's the cockroach of the Internet, and I mean that as a compliment. This resilience is a good thing."[3]

Neither social media, texting, and video chatting, nor phishing, hacking, and spam have diminished the importance of e-mail in the workplace. Not even popular applications such as the collaboration tool Slack are likely to replace e-mail anytime soon.[4] Even Stewart Butterfield, cofounder of the "e-mail killer" Slack, admits he spends up to five hours a day on e-mail and boldly predicts that e-mail will last for millennia.[5]

E-mail has replaced paper memos for many messages inside organizations and some letters to external audiences. A majority of businesspeople (as high as 70 percent) now first open their e-mail on mobile devices.[6] Trailing only text messaging, e-mail is a more widely used smartphone feature than social networking, watching videos, or using navigation.[7] Because you can expect to use e-mail extensively to communicate at work, it's smart to learn how to do it expertly. You may have to adjust the writing practices you currently use for texting and Facebook, but turning out professional e-mails is an easily attainable goal.

5-1b Why Workers Complain About E-Mail

Although e-mail is recognized as the mainstay of business communication, it's not always done well. In a study of 547 business professionals, 81 percent considered ineffective writing a huge time waster. Workplace documents and e-mails, the managers said, were long-winded, disorganized, fuzzy, and jargon-filled.[9] Businesspeople are tired of "untangling a snarl of email threads" and resent "that most people don't take the time to reflect on what they have written or to proofread it before hitting SEND."[10] A *Wall Street Journal* article reported that many business schools were ramping up their writing programs or hiring writing coaches because of complaints about their graduates' skills.[11]

E-Mail Overload. In addition to the complaints about confusing and poorly written e-mails, many people are overwhelmed with too many messages. Currently, the

LEARNING OUTCOME 1

Understand e-mail, memos, and the professional standards for their usage, structure, and format in the digital era workplace.

OFFICE INSIDER

Predictions of e-mail's demise are premature despite fast-growing communication tools such as Slack and Asana: "People use email because it's the best, most reliable way to get anybody on the planet and none of these other tools let you do that; none of them."[8]

Ted Schadler, *VP, senior technology analyst with Forrester Research*

average worker receives 121 e-mails per day or more than 44,000 e-mails per year[12] and checks e-mail 77 times per day; some people peek at their inboxes as often as 373 times daily.[13] Each day approximately 215 billion e-mails are sent across the globe.[14] Some of those messages are unnecessary, such as those that merely confirm receipt of a message or ones that express thanks. The use of *Reply all* adds to the inbox, irritating those who have to plow through dozens of messages that barely relate to them. Others blame e-mail for eliminating the distinction between work life and home life. They feel an urgency to be available 24/7 and respond immediately.

E-Mail—Everlasting Evidence. Still other e-mail senders fail to recognize how dangerous e-mail can be. After deletion, e-mail files still leave trails on servers within and outside organizations. Messages are also backed up on other servers, making them traceable and recoverable by forensic experts. Long-forgotten messages may turn up in court cases as damaging and costly evidence—for example, against German auto executives following Volkswagen's cover-up of its emissions cheating scandal.[16] After the explosion of BP's Deepwater Horizon oil platform, incriminating e-mails prompted the company to agree to a settlement currently at $28 billion.[17]

Organizations can legally monitor their staff's personal e-mail accounts if the workers access them on the company's computer network. Moreover, if employees set up their company's e-mail on their smartphones, they have given their employer the right to remotely delete all personal data on that mobile device.[18] Even writers with nothing to hide should be concerned about what may come back to haunt them. Etiquette expert Daniel Post Senning suggests following the "headline rule": envision what you are writing in an e-mail as a news headline.[19] Also, be sure that you know your organization's e-mail policy before sending personal messages. Estimates suggest that almost 30 percent of bosses have fired an employee for Internet or e-mail-related misuse.[20]

Despite its dark side, e-mail has many advantages and remains a prime communication channel. Therefore, it's to your advantage to learn when and how to use it efficiently and safely.

5-1c Knowing When E-Mail Is Appropriate

E-mail is appropriate for short, informal messages that request information and respond to inquiries. It is especially effective for messages to multiple receivers and messages that must be archived (saved). An e-mail is also appropriate as a cover document when sending longer attachments.

E-mail, however, is not a substitute for face-to-face conversations or telephone calls. These channels are much more successful if your goal is to convey enthusiasm or warmth, explain a complex situation, present a persuasive argument, or smooth over disagreements. One expert gives this wise advice: "Sometimes a conversation is more productive than a chain of emails. If you're frustrated with people's inability to understand what you're getting at, just walk over or pick up the phone."[21] Messages that "require a human moment"—that is, those that are emotional, require negotiation, and relate to personnel—should be delivered in person.[22]

Managers and employees echo this advice. They are adamant about using face-to-face contact, rather than e-mail, for critical work situations such as human resources annual reviews, discipline, and promotions.[23]

5-1d Composing Professional E-Mails

Professional e-mails are quite different from messages you may send to friends. Instead of casual words tossed off in haste, professional e-mails are well-considered messages that usually carry nonsensitive information unlikely to upset readers. Therefore, these messages should be organized directly with the main idea first. The following writing plan will help you create information e-mails quickly.

Information E-Mails

SUBJECT LINE:	Summarize the main idea in condensed form.
OPENING:	Reveal the main idea immediately but in expanded form.
BODY:	Explain and justify the main idea using headings, bulleted lists, and other high-skim techniques when appropriate.
CLOSING:	Include (a) action information, dates, or deadlines; (b) a summary of the message; or (c) a closing thought.

Draft a Compelling but Concise Subject Line. The most important part of an e-mail is its subject line. Avoid meaningless statements such as *Help, Attention,* or *Meeting.* Summarize the purpose of the message clearly and make the receiver want to open the message. Try to include a verb (*Need You to Prepare a Sales Presentation*). Remember that in some instances the subject line can be the entire message (*Meeting Changed from May 3 to May 10*). Also be sure to adjust the subject line if the topic changes after a thread of replies emerges. Subject lines should appear as a combination of uppercase and lowercase letters—never in all lowercase letters or all caps.

Include a Greeting. To help receivers see the beginning of a message and to help them recognize whether they are the primary or secondary receiver, include a greeting. The greeting sets the tone for the message and reflects your audience analysis. For friends and colleagues, try friendly greetings (*Hi, Sandy; Thanks, Sandy; Good morning, Sandy;* or *Greetings, Sandy*). For more formal messages and those to outsiders, include an honorific and last name (*Dear Ms. Richards*).

Organize the Body for Readability and Tone. After drafting an e-mail, ask yourself how you could make your message more readable. Did you start directly? Did you group similar topics together? Could some information be presented with bulleted or numbered lists? Could you add headings—especially if the message contains more than a few paragraphs? Do you see any phrases or sentences that could be condensed? Get rid of wordiness, but don't sacrifice clarity. If a longer sentence is necessary for comprehension, then keep it. To convey the best tone, read the message aloud. If it sounds curt, it probably is.

Close Effectively. At the end of your message, include an action statement with due dates and requests. Although complimentary closes are unnecessary, you might include a friendly closing such as *Many thanks* or *Warm regards.* Do include your name because messages without names become confusing when forwarded or when they are part of a long string of responses.

For most messages to new contacts, and in all external e-mails, include full contact information in a signature block, which your e-mail application can insert

OFFICE INSIDER

"The difficulty of expressive writing isn't new . . . but what's relatively recent is the overwhelming amount of electronic exchanges we have with people whose personalities we only know digitally. Without the benefit of vocal inflections or physical gestures, it can be tough to tell e-sarcastic from e-serious, or e-cold from e-formal, or e-busy from e-angry."[24]

Eric Jaffe, *editor and author*

POOR SUBJECT LINES	IMPROVED SUBJECT LINES
Presentation	Need You to Prepare a Sales Presentation
Division Meeting	Pacific Division Meeting Rescheduled for May 18
Important!	Please Respond to Employee Satisfaction Survey
Parking Permits	New Employee Parking Permits Available From HR

automatically. Figure 5.1 illustrates a typical information e-mail that follows the writing plan and displays proper formatting. It also illustrates how a draft can be revised to improve readability.

Figure 5.1 Creating an Informational E-Mail Message

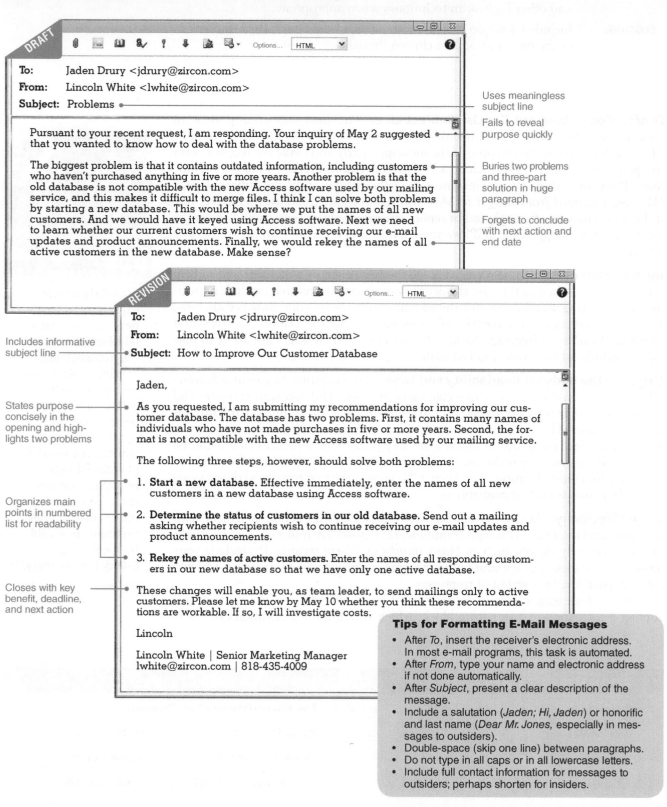

DRAFT

To: Jaden Drury <jdrury@zircon.com>
From: Lincoln White <lwhite@zircon.com>
Subject: Problems

Pursuant to your recent request, I am responding. Your inquiry of May 2 suggested that you wanted to know how to deal with the database problems.

The biggest problem is that it contains outdated information, including customers who haven't purchased anything in five or more years. Another problem is that the old database is not compatible with the new Access software used by our mailing service, and this makes it difficult to merge files. I think I can solve both problems by starting a new database. This would be where we put the names of all new customers. And we would have it keyed using Access software. Next we need to learn whether our current customers wish to continue receiving our e-mail updates and product announcements. Finally, we would rekey the names of all active customers in the new database. Make sense?

Uses meaningless subject line

Fails to reveal purpose quickly

Buries two problems and three-part solution in huge paragraph

Forgets to conclude with next action and end date

REVISION

To: Jaden Drury <jdrury@zircon.com>
From: Lincoln White <lwhite@zircon.com>
Subject: How to Improve Our Customer Database

Jaden,

As you requested, I am submitting my recommendations for improving our customer database. The database has two problems. First, it contains many names of individuals who have not made purchases in five or more years. Second, the format is not compatible with the new Access software used by our mailing service.

The following three steps, however, should solve both problems:

1. **Start a new database.** Effective immediately, enter the names of all new customers in a new database using Access software.

2. **Determine the status of customers in our old database.** Send out a mailing asking whether recipients wish to continue receiving our e-mail updates and product announcements.

3. **Rekey the names of active customers.** Enter the names of all responding customers in our new database so that we have only one active database.

These changes will enable you, as team leader, to send mailings only to active customers. Please let me know by May 10 whether you think these recommendations are workable. If so, I will investigate costs.

Lincoln

Lincoln White | Senior Marketing Manager
lwhite@zircon.com | 818-435-4009

Includes informative subject line

States purpose concisely in the opening and highlights two problems

Organizes main points in numbered list for readability

Closes with key benefit, deadline, and next action

Tips for Formatting E-Mail Messages

- After *To*, insert the receiver's electronic address. In most e-mail programs, this task is automated.
- After *From*, type your name and electronic address if not done automatically.
- After *Subject*, present a clear description of the message.
- Include a salutation (*Jaden; Hi, Jaden*) or honorific and last name (*Dear Mr. Jones,* especially in messages to outsiders).
- Double-space (skip one line) between paragraphs.
- Do not type in all caps or in all lowercase letters.
- Include full contact information for messages to outsiders; perhaps shorten for insiders.

Chapter 5: Short Workplace Messages and Digital Media

5-1e Controlling Your Inbox

Business communicators love to complain about e-mail, and some young people even deny its existence. In the business world, however, e-mail writing IS business writing.[25] Instead of letting your inbox consume your time and crimp your productivity, you can control it by observing a few time-management strategies.

The most important strategy is checking your e-mail at set times, such as first thing in the morning and again after lunch or at 4 p.m. To avoid being distracted, be sure to turn off your audio and visual alerts. No fair peeking! If mornings are your best working times, check your e-mail later in the day. Let your boss and colleagues know about your schedule for responding, or ask to use instant or text messages in urgent situations. Another excellent time-saver is the two-minute rule. If you can read and respond to a message within two minutes, then take care of it immediately. For messages that require more time, flag and add them to your to-do list or schedule them on your calendar. To be polite, send a quick note telling the sender when you plan to respond.

5-1f Replying Efficiently With Down-Editing

When answering e-mail, a useful skill to develop is *down-editing*. This involves inserting your responses to parts of the incoming message. After a courteous opening, your reply message will include only the parts of the incoming message to which you are responding. Delete the sender's message headers, signature, and all unnecessary parts. Your responses can be identified with your initials, if more than one person will be seeing the response. Another efficient trick is to use a different color for your down-edits. It takes a little practice to develop this skill, but the down-edited reply reduces confusion and saves writing and reading time. Figure 5.2 shows a number of additional best practices for managing your e-mail.

5-1g Writing Interoffice Memos

In addition to e-mail, you should be familiar with another workplace document type, the interoffice memorandum. Although e-mail has largely replaced memos, you may still be called on to use the memo format in specific instances. Memos are necessary for important internal messages that (a) are too long for e-mail, (b) require a permanent record, (c) demand formality, or (d) inform employees who may not

---

Figure 5.2 Best Practices for Better E-Mail

Getting Started
- Don't write in another channel—such as IM, social media, or a phone call—might work better.
- Send only content you would want to be published.
- Write compelling subject lines, possibly with names and dates: *Jake: Can You Present at January 10 Staff Meeting?*

Replying
- Scan all e-mails, especially those from the same person. Answer within 24 hours or say when you will.
- Change the subject line if the topic changes. Check the threaded messages below yours.
- Practice down-editing; include only the parts from the incoming e-mail to which you are responding.
- Start with the main idea.
- Use headings and lists.

Observing Etiquette
- Obtain approval before forwarding.
- Soften the tone by including a friendly opening and closing.
- Resist humor and sarcasm. Absent facial expression and tone of voice, humor can be misunderstood.
- Avoid writing in all caps, which is like SHOUTING.

Closing Effectively
- End with due dates, next steps to be taken, or a friendly remark.
- Add your full contact information including social media addresses.
- Edit your text for readability. Proofread for typos or unwanted auto-corrections.
- Double-check before hitting Send.

have work e-mail. Within organizations, memos deliver changes in procedures, official instructions, and reports.

The memo format is particularly necessary for complex, lengthy internal messages. Prepared as memos, long messages are then delivered as attachments to e-mail cover messages. Memos allow for attractive formatting and printing. They seem to function better as permanent records than e-mail messages because the latter may be difficult to locate and may contain a trail of confusing replies. E-mails also may change the origination date whenever the file is accessed, thus making it impossible to know the original date of the message.

When preparing e-mail attachments, be sure that they carry sufficient identifying information. Because the attachment may become separated from the cover e-mail message, it must be fully identified. Preparing the e-mail attachment as a memo provides a handy format that identifies the date, sender, receiver, and subject.

Comparing Memos and E-Mails. Memos have much in common with e-mails. Both usually carry nonsensitive information that may be organized directly with the main idea first. Both have guide words calling for a subject line, a dateline, and the identification of the sender and receiver. To enhance readability, both should be organized with headings, bulleted lists, and enumerated items whenever possible.

Similarities. E-mails and memos both generally close with (a) action information, dates, or deadlines; (b) a summary of the message; or (c) a closing thought. An effective memo or e-mail closing might be *Please submit your written report to me by June 15 so that we can review your data before our July planning session*. In more detailed messages, a summary of main points may be an appropriate closing. If no action request is made and a closing summary is unnecessary, you might end with a simple concluding thought (*I'm glad to answer your questions* or *This sounds like a useful project*).

Differences. You need not close messages to coworkers with goodwill statements such as those found in letters to customers or clients. However, some closing thought is often necessary to avoid sounding abrupt. Closings can show gratitude or encourage feedback with remarks such as *I sincerely appreciate your help* or *What are your ideas on this proposal?* Other closings look forward to what's next, such as *How would you like to proceed?* Avoid closing with overused expressions such as *Please let me know if I may be of further assistance*. This ending sounds mechanical and insincere.

In Figure 5.3, notice how memos are formatted and how they can be created to improve readability with lists, tables, and white space.

LEARNING OUTCOME 2

Explain workplace instant messaging and texting as well as their liabilities and best practices.

5-2 Workplace Messaging and Texting

Instant messaging (IM) and text messaging have become powerful communication tools beyond teens and twentysomethings. IM enables two or more individuals to use the Internet or an intranet (an internal corporate communication platform) to chat in real time by exchanging brief text-based messages. Companies large and small now provide live online chats with customer service representatives, in addition to the usual contact options, such as telephone and e-mail. Popular free messaging apps—for example, Facebook Messenger, WhatsApp, WeChat, Skype, and Snapchat—provide consumers and small businesses with features such as IM, voice and video calls, and photo sharing.

Text messaging, or texting, is another popular means for exchanging brief messages in real time. Usually exchanged via smartphone, texting requires a short message service (SMS) supplied by a cell phone service provider or Wi-Fi access. Both instant and text messages are mostly sent from mobile devices as 68 percent of Americans now own smartphones and depend on them for access not only to voice calls and texting, but also to location-based services, streaming TV or radio, and shopping.[26]

Fueled by online security and legal compliance concerns, business enterprises are combining multiple communication functions behind corporate firewalls. For example, Adobe Systems has developed Unicom. The Unified Communications Tool is an all-in-one internal communication platform connecting coworkers anywhere by chat, Twitter-like microblogging, and employee directory access, as well as by e-mail and phone. Figure 5.4 shows a screenshot of such an integrated internal communication system.

5-2a Impact of Instant Messaging and Texting

Text messaging and IM are convenient alternatives to the telephone and are replacing e-mail for short internal communication. French IT giant Atos reduced e-mail use by 70 percent after shifting its in-house communication over several years to a Facebook-style interface and instant messaging.[27] More than 3.2 billion IM accounts worldwide[28] attest to IM's popularity. Sixty-seven percent of business professionals use IM in the United States.[29]

Figure 5.3 Formatting an Interoffice Memo

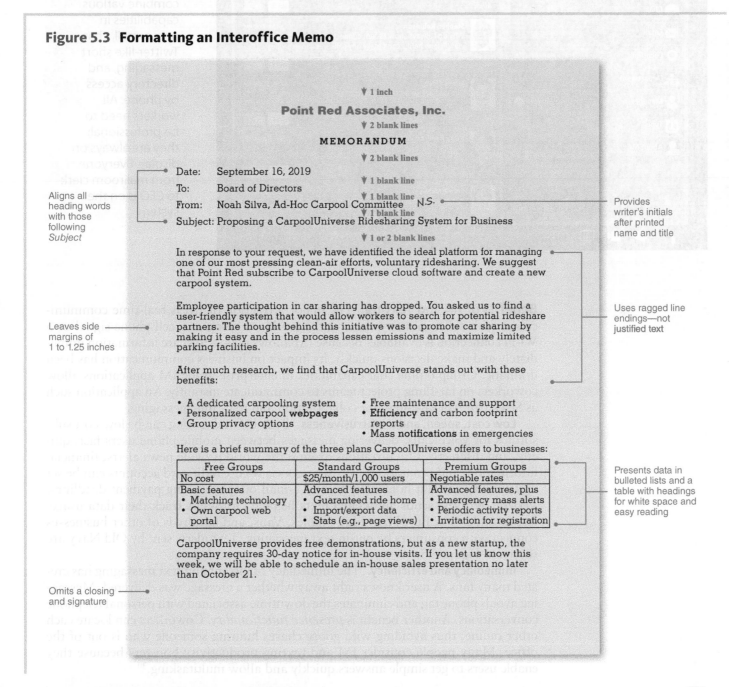

Aligns all heading words with those following *Subject*

Leaves side margins of 1 to 1.25 inches

Omits a closing and signature

▼ 1 inch

Point Red Associates, Inc.

▼ 2 blank lines

MEMORANDUM

▼ 2 blank lines

Date: September 16, 2019
▼ 1 blank line
To: Board of Directors
▼ 1 blank line
From: Noah Silva, Ad-Hoc Carpool Committee *N.S.*
▼ 1 blank line
Subject: Proposing a CarpoolUniverse Ridesharing System for Business

▼ 1 or 2 blank lines

In response to your request, we have identified the ideal platform for managing one of our most pressing clean-air efforts, voluntary ridesharing. We suggest that Point Red subscribe to CarpoolUniverse cloud software and create a new carpool system.

Employee participation in car sharing has dropped. You asked us to find a user-friendly system that would allow workers to search for potential rideshare partners. The thought behind this initiative was to promote car sharing by making it easy and in the process lessen emissions and maximize limited parking facilities.

After much research, we find that CarpoolUniverse stands out with these benefits:

- A dedicated carpooling system
- Personalized carpool **webpages**
- Group privacy options
- Free maintenance and support
- **Efficiency** and carbon footprint reports
- Mass **notifications** in emergencies

Here is a brief summary of the three plans CarpoolUniverse offers to businesses:

Free Groups	Standard Groups	Premium Groups
No cost	$25/month/1,000 users	Negotiable rates
Basic features • Matching technology • Own carpool web portal	Advanced features • Guaranteed ride home • Import/export data • Stats (e.g., page views)	Advanced features, plus • Emergency mass alerts • Periodic activity reports • Invitation for registration

CarpoolUniverse provides free demonstrations, but as a new startup, the company requires 30-day notice for in-house visits. If you let us know this week, we will be able to schedule an in-house sales presentation no later than October 21.

Provides writer's initials after printed name and title

Uses ragged line endings—not justified text

Presents data in bulleted lists and a table with headings for white space and easy reading

Figure 5.4 All-in-One Messaging on an Internal Enterprise Network

To create a platform for secure and legally compliant internal communication, large companies have introduced powerful networks behind corporate firewalls that combine various capabilities in one: e-mail, chat, Twitter-like short messaging, and directory access by phone. All workers need to be professional; they are always on display. Everyone from mailroom clerk to CEO is on the system.

Benefits of IM and Texting. The major attraction of IM is real-time communication with colleagues anywhere in the world—so long as a cell phone signal or a Wi-Fi connection is available. Because IM allows people to share information immediately and make decisions quickly, its impact on business communication has been dramatic. Group online chat capabilities in enterprise-grade IM applications allow coworkers on far-flung project teams to communicate instantly. An application such as Slack can replace e-mail for collaboration and real-time messaging.

Low cost, speed, and unobtrusiveness. Both IM and texting can be low-cost substitutes for voice calls, delivering messages between mobile phone users fast, quietly, and discreetly. Organizations around the world provide news alerts, financial information, and promotions to customers via text. Credit card accounts can be set up to notify account holders by text or e-mail of approaching payment deadlines. Verizon Wireless sends automated texts helping customers track their data usage. Aeropostale, Best Buy, Pizza Hut, Staples, Vans, and hundreds of other businesses connect with consumers by opt-in text messaging. Text alerts sent by Old Navy are shown in Figure 5.5.

Immediacy and efficiency. The immediacy of instant and text messaging has created many fans. A user knows right away whether a message was delivered. Messaging avoids phone tag and eliminates the downtime associated with personal telephone conversations. Another benefit is *presence functionality*. Coworkers can locate each other online, thus avoiding wild goose chases hunting someone who is out of the office. Many people consider IM and texting productivity boosters because they enable users to get simple answers quickly and allow multitasking.[30]

Risks of IM and Texting. Despite their popularity among workers, some organizations forbid employees to use IM and text messaging for a number of reasons. Employers consider instant messaging yet another distraction in addition to the telephone, e-mail, and the Internet. Some organizations also fear that employees using free consumer-grade IM systems will reveal privileged information and company records. The financial sector is particularly vulnerable to charges of impropriety such as insider trading; firms ranging from JPMorgan Chase, Barclays, and Citigroup to RBS have banned IM for external use.[32] Large corporations are protecting themselves by taking instant messaging behind the firewall where they can log and archive traffic.

Liability burden. A worker's improper use of mobile devices while on company business can expose the organization to staggering legal liability. A jury awarded $18 million to a victim struck by a transportation company's big rig whose driver had been checking text messages. Another case resulted in a $21 million verdict to a woman injured by a trucker who had used a cell phone while driving a company truck. A construction firm had to pay $4.75 million to a man injured by a driver using a company-provided cell phone.[33] Overall as many as 34 percent of Americans admit to having texted while driving. In one year alone, 1.3 million crashes, or 23 percent of all collisions, involved cell phones.[34] Unfortunately, 77 percent of young adults are confident that they can safely text and drive.[35]

Security and legal requirements. Companies also worry about phishing (fraudulent schemes), viruses, malware (malicious software programs), and spim (IM spam). Like e-mail, instant and text messages as well as all other electronic records are subject to discovery (disclosure); that is, they can become evidence in lawsuits. Wall Street regulatory agencies NASD, SEC, and NYSE require that IM exchanged between brokers and clients be retained for three to six years, much like e-mail and

OFFICE INSIDER

"[B]ear in mind that messaging sessions can be stored, then copied and pasted elsewhere. . . . The term 'confidential' is somewhat rubbery these days, so . . . stop and think before you hit that enter key."[31]

Michael Bloch, *Taming the Beast, e-commerce development and Web marketing consultant*

Figure 5.5 Old Navy Uses SMS Marketing

Source: Tatango

Old Navy Deal Alerts: Reply Y to agree to 1 automated msg/wk with deals to this number. Not required for purchase. Msg&data rates apply www.oldnavy.com/text

Old Navy Deal Alerts: Thanks, your $5 off $35 offer will be sent to you tomorrow! 1 msg/week. Reply STOP to quit Reply HELP for help. Msg&data rates may apply.

Jacek Lasa/Alamy Stock Photo; Source: Tatango

Old Navy encourages consumers to sign up for its mobile alert program. Once customers opt in by texting their nearest store's number to the dedicated short code 653-689 (old-navy), they receive text messages announcing sneak peeks at new merchandise, rebates, and exclusive offers.

printed documents.[36] Businesses worry that tracking and storing messaging logs to comply with legal requirements may be overwhelming. In addition, IM and texting have been implicated in inappropriate uses such as bullying and the notorious sexting. Currently, banks are terrified that employees will fall prey to spear phishing (clicking links that give hackers access to sensitive information).[37]

5-2b Best Practices for Instant Messaging and Texting

Instant messaging and texting can save time and simplify communication with coworkers and customers. However, before using IM or text messaging on the job, be sure you have permission. Do not download and use software without checking with your supervisor. If your organization does allow IM or texting, you can use it efficiently and professionally by following these guidelines:

- Follow company policies: netiquette rules, code of conduct, ethics guidelines, as well as harassment and discrimination policies.[38]
- Don't disclose sensitive financial, company, customer, employee, or executive data, and don't say anything that could damage your reputation or that of your organization.
- Steer clear of harassment and discriminatory content against classes protected by law (race, color, religion, sex, sexual orientation, national origin, age, and disability).
- Don't forward or link to inappropriate photos, videos, and art.
- Don't text or IM while driving a car; pull over if you must read or send a message.
- Separate business contacts from family and friends; limit personal messaging.
- Avoid unnecessary chitchat and know when to say goodbye.
- Keep your presence status up-to-date, and make yourself unavailable when you need to meet a deadline.
- Use good grammar and correct spelling; shun jargon, slang, and abbreviations, which can be confusing and appear unprofessional.

5-2c Text Messaging and Business Etiquette

Texting is quick and unobtrusive, and for simple routine messages it is often the best alternative to a phone call or e-mail. Given the popularity of text messaging, etiquette experts are taking note.[40] Figure 5.6 summarizes the suggestions they offer for the considerate and professional use of texting.

LEARNING OUTCOME 3

Identify professional applications of podcasts and wikis.

5-3 Making Podcasts and Wikis Work for Business

Empowered by interactivity, individuals wield enormous influence because they can potentially reach huge audiences. Far from being passive consumers, today's Internet users have the power to create Web content; interact with businesses and each other; review products, self-publish, or blog; contribute to wikis; and tag and share images and other files. Businesses often rightly fear the wrath of disgruntled employees and customers, or they curry favor with influential plugged-in opinion leaders, the so-called influencers. Like social media networks, podcasts and wikis are part of the user-centered virtual environment. All these communication technologies are social and mobile, too.

The democratization of the Internet has meant that in the online world, even extreme views reach audiences of thousands or even millions. The dangers are obvious. Fact checking often falls by the wayside, buzz may become more important than truth, and a few keystrokes can destroy a reputation. The latest concern is how

Figure 5.6 Texting Etiquette

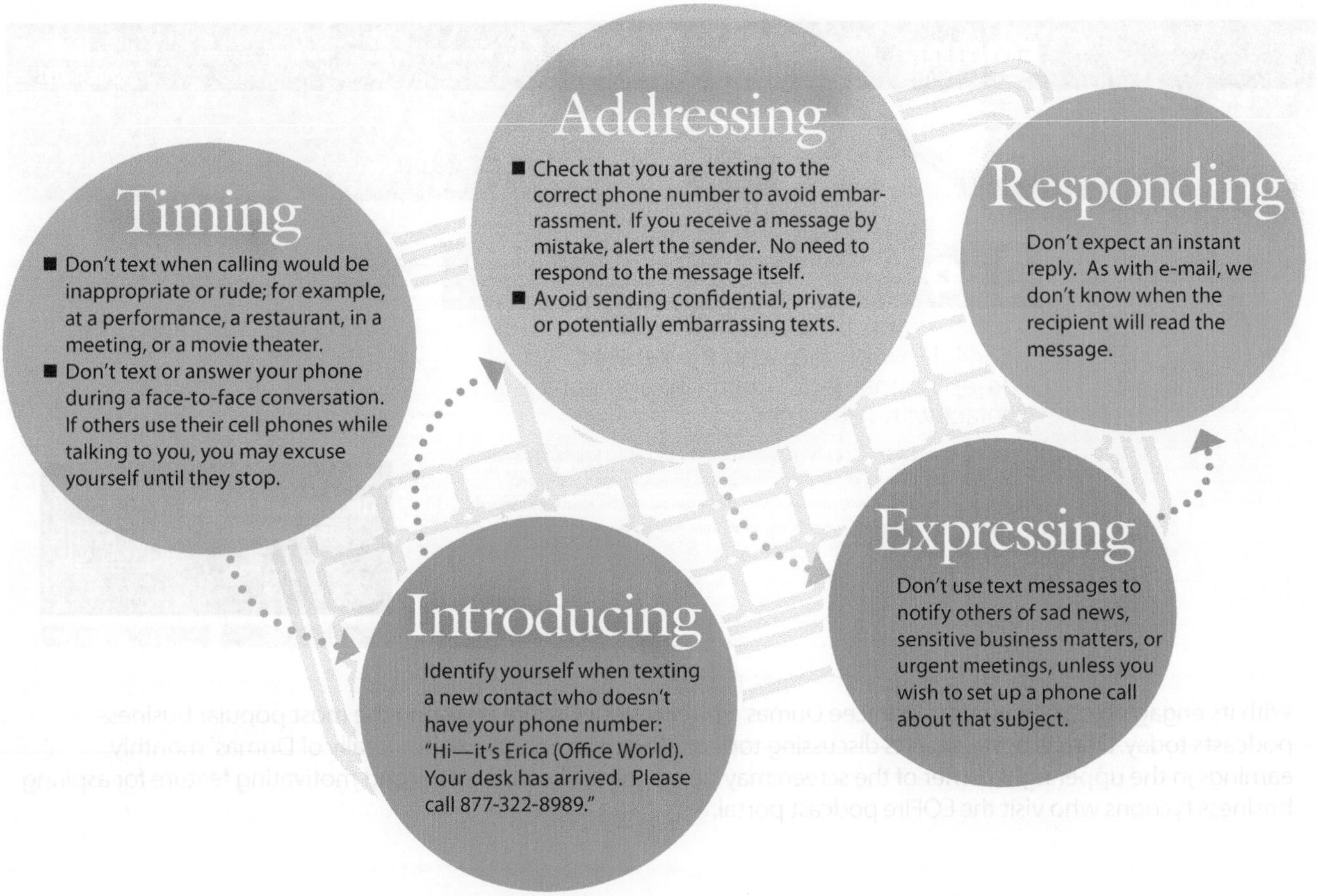

Timing

- Don't text when calling would be inappropriate or rude; for example, at a performance, a restaurant, in a meeting, or a movie theater.
- Don't text or answer your phone during a face-to-face conversation. If others use their cell phones while talking to you, you may excuse yourself until they stop.

Addressing

- Check that you are texting to the correct phone number to avoid embarrassment. If you receive a message by mistake, alert the sender. No need to respond to the message itself.
- Avoid sending confidential, private, or potentially embarrassing texts.

Responding

Don't expect an instant reply. As with e-mail, we don't know when the recipient will read the message.

Introducing

Identify yourself when texting a new contact who doesn't have your phone number: "Hi—it's Erica (Office World). Your desk has arrived. Please call 877-322-8989."

Expressing

Don't use text messages to notify others of sad news, sensitive business matters, or urgent meetings, unless you wish to set up a phone call about that subject.

Internet users can identify *fake news* and evaluate the trustworthiness of a source. This section addresses prudent business uses of podcasts and wikis because you are likely to encounter these and other electronic communication tools on the job.

5-3a Business Podcasts or Webcasts

Perhaps because podcasts are more elaborate to produce and require quality hardware, their use is lagging behind that of other digital media. However, they have their place among contemporary business communication strategies. Although the terms *podcast* and *podcasting* have caught on, they are somewhat misleading. The words *broadcasting* and *iPod* were combined to create the word *podcast*; however, audio and video files can be played on any number of devices, not just Apple's. *Webcasting* for audio content and *vcasting* for video content would be more accurate. Podcasts can extend from short clips of a few minutes to 30-minute or longer digital files. Most are recorded, but some are live. They can be streamed online or downloaded as media files.

How Organizations Use Podcasts. Podcasting has found its place among user groups online. Major news organizations and media outlets podcast radio shows (e.g., National Public Radio, *Harvard Business Review*) and video content such as news and entertainment, from ABC to Fox. Perhaps you are familiar with TED talks, intriguing podcasts on any imaginable topic in technology, entertainment, and design (TED). Entrepreneur On Fire (EOFire), shown in Figure 5.7, provides popular podcasts on many business topics of particular interest to entrepreneurs.

Figure 5.7 Entrepreneur On Fire (EOFire) Podcasts

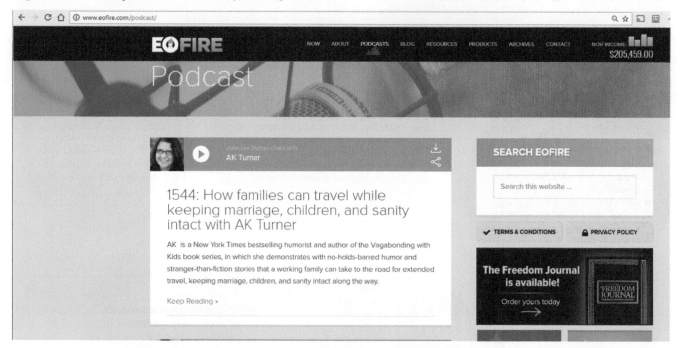

With its engaging daily episodes, John Lee Dumas' Entrepreneur On Fire is among the most popular business podcasts today. Dumas hosts experts discussing topics relevant to entrepreneurs. A tally of Dumas' monthly earnings in the upper right corner of the screen may be a potentially noteworthy and motivating feature for aspiring business tycoons who visit the EOFire podcast portal.

Podcasts are also common in education. You can access instructors' lectures, interviews, and other media files. Apple's iTunes U is perhaps the best-known example of free educational podcasts from prestigious universities. Podcasts encoded as MP3 files can be downloaded to a computer, a smartphone, a tablet, or an MP3 player to be enjoyed on the go, often offline. Businesses are slowly catching on.

Delivering and Accessing Podcasts. Businesses have embraced podcasting for sending audio and video messages that do not require a live presence yet offer a friendly human face. Because they can broadcast repetitive information that does not require interaction, podcasts can replace costlier live teleconferences. IBM is training its sales force with podcasts that are available anytime and providing video podcasts for software engineers and others. Real estate agents such as the Corcoran Group in New York create podcasts to enable buyers to take virtual walking tours of available homes. Human resources policies can also be presented in the form of podcasts for unlimited viewing on demand.

Podcasts are featured on media websites and company portals or shared on blogs and social networking sites, often with links to YouTube and Vimeo. A Pew survey found that podcasting is growing in audience and programming. However, only 21 percent of Americans age twelve and older listened to a podcast in the past month, and half of the respondents didn't know the term *podcasting*.[41]

Experts advise business podcasters first to provide quality content with an authentic voice to build value, and to consider money making second.[42] To browse and learn from popular favorites, search the iTunes Store or free smartphone apps to discover your favorite podcasts, some business related (e.g., Freakonomics Radio, Planet Money, and TED talks).

5-3b Collaborating With Wikis

Wikis are another important feature of our social and mobile virtual environment. A wiki is a cloud-based tool that employs easy-to-use collaborative software to allow multiple users collectively to create, access, and modify documents. Think Wikipedia, the well-known online encyclopedia. You will find wikis in numerous subject categories on the Internet. Wiki editors may be given varying access privileges and control over the cloud-based material. Not surprisingly, some organizations with a top-down culture fear the openness of wikis, and adoption rates have slowed despite the need of larger businesses for rigorous *knowledge management*.[43]

Advantages of Wikis. Two major advantages of wikis come to mind. First, wikis capitalize on *crowdsourcing*, which can be defined as the practice of tapping into the combined knowledge of a large community to solve problems and complete assignments. Second, working on the same content jointly eliminates the infamous problem of version confusion. Most wikis store all changes and intermediate versions of files, so that users can return to previous versions if necessary.

Benefits of corporate wikis include enhancing the reputation of expert contributors, making work flow more easily, and improving an organization's processes.[44] IBM, for example, uses numerous wikis to share documentation for its IBM Collaboration Solutions software and WebSphere products and to interact with the community of adopters.

How Businesses Use Wikis. Enterprises using wikis usually store their internal data on an intranet, a private network. An enterprise-level wiki serves as an easy-to-navigate, efficient central repository of company information, complete with hyperlinks and keywords pointing to related subjects and media. The four main uses of wikis in business, shown in Figure 5.8,[45] range from providing a shared internal knowledge base to storing templates for business documents.

Consider starting a free wiki for your next classroom project requiring teamwork. Browse the Internet for *wiki hosting service* or *wiki farm*. Explore Wikispaces and Wikia—popular free wikis. MindTouch, Yammer, Microsoft Office 365, Atlassian Confluence, and MediaWiki are just some of many enterprise collaboration platforms.[46]

Figure 5.8 Four Main Uses for Business Wikis

The global wiki

For companies with a global reach, a wiki is an ideal tool for information sharing between headquarters and satellite offices. Far-flung team members can easily edit their work and provide input to the home office and each other.

The wiki knowledge base

Teams or departments use wikis to collect and disseminate information to large audiences creating a database for knowledge management. For example, human resources managers may update employee policies, make announcements, and convey information about benefits.

Wikis for meetings

Wikis can facilitate feedback from employees before and after meetings and serve as repositories of meeting minutes. In fact, wikis may replace some meetings, yet still keep a project on track.

Wikis for project management

Wikis offer a highly interactive environment for project information with easy access and user input. All participants have the same information, templates, and documentation readily available.

5-4 Blogging for Business

LEARNING OUTCOME 4

The biggest advantage of business blogs is that they potentially reach a far-flung, vast audience. A blog is a website or social media platform with informal posts and articles on any imaginable topic usually written by one person, although most corporate blogs feature multiple contributors. Typically, readers leave comments. Businesses use blogs to keep customers, employees, and the public at large informed and to interact with them.

Describe how businesses use blogs to connect with internal and external audiences, and list best practices for professional blogging.

Marketing firms and their clients are looking closely at blogs because blogs can invite spontaneous consumer feedback faster and more cheaply than such staples of consumer research as focus groups and surveys. Employees and executives at companies as varied as such as Exxon Mobil, Target, General Motors, Patagonia, and Whole Foods Market maintain blogs. They use blogs to communicate internally with employees and externally with the public. Most recently, 181 (36 percent) of Fortune 500 companies are blogging, and blog use is up again after a downward trend. Researchers note "excitement among . . . corporate giants" around Instagram with its 300 million active users.[47]

In this section you will learn how businesses use blogs. You will also find guidance on professional blogging practices.

5-4a How Companies Blog

Like other social networking tools, corporate blogs create virtual communities, build brands, and develop relationships. In other words, blogs are part of a social media strategy to create *engagement*, resulting in customers' goodwill and brand loyalty. Companies use blogs for public relations, customer relations, crisis communication, market research, viral marketing, internal communication, online community building, and recruiting.

Public Relations, Customer Relations, and Crisis Communication. One of the prominent uses of blogs is to provide up-to-date company information to the media and the public. Blogs can be written by rank-and-file employees or by top managers. Consider these examples: Executive chairman Bill Marriott is an avid blogger. His *Marriott on the Move* blog about leadership, his family history, volunteer work, and more, feels personal and honest. Just one of several General Electric blogs, *Edison's Desk*, operated by GE Global Research, addresses industry insiders and the interested public. In its *Blogger Network*, Best Buy, the electronics retailer, gives a voice to average Joes and Janes who review all kinds of gizmos as brand ambassadors. The Best Buy blog acts as a forum actively soliciting customer input by using *crowdsourcing*—that is, asking the public for ideas.

An organization's blog is a natural forum for late-breaking news, especially when a crisis hits. Jim Murphy, president of General Mills' cereal division, swiftly apologized in an effective blog post just minutes after also publishing a contrite press release about a Cheerios recall.[49] The U.S. Consumer Product Safety Commission maintains official blogs addressing product safety, recalls, and agency activities. Although a blog cannot replace other communication channels in a PR crisis or an emergency, it should be part of the overall effort to soothe the public's emotional reaction with a human voice of reason.

Blog adoption varies across industries. Predictably, semiconductor and electronics makers (56 percent), entertainment firms (50 percent), and general merchandisers (40 percent) are most likely to use blogs, followed by telecommunications firms (36 percent) and commercial banks (22 percent).[50] Social media networks Instagram and LinkedIn have added a blogging feature, a move that may rival stand-alone blogs.

Market Research and Viral Marketing. Because most blogs invite feedback, they can be invaluable sources of opinion and bright ideas from customers as well as industry experts. Starbucks is a Fortune 500 company that understands blogging and crowdsourcing in particular. *My Starbucks Idea* blog, depicted in Figure 5.9, is a public forum for sharing product ideas. Members vote and comment on the suggestions and eliminate poor ideas.

In addition to inviting and monitoring visitor comments on their corporate blogs, large companies employ social media teams. These experts scrutinize the blogosphere for buzz and positive and negative postings about their organizations and products. The term *viral marketing* refers to the rapid spread of messages online, much like infectious diseases that pass from person to person. Marketers realize

Figure 5.9 Starbucks Blog Is Betting on Crowdsourcing

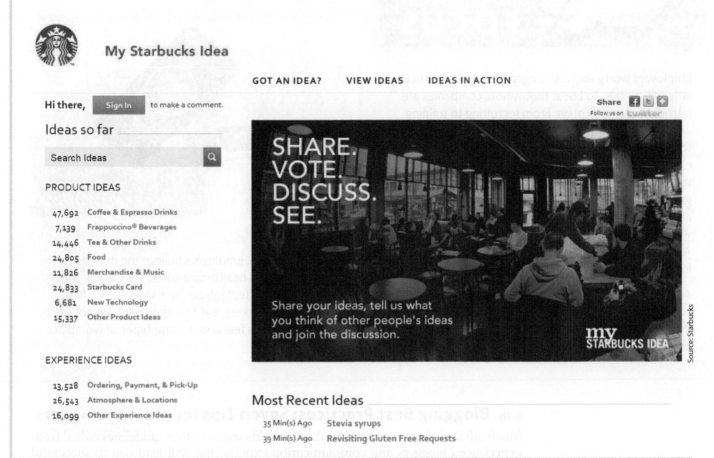

Source: Starbucks

the potential of getting the word out about their products and services in the blogosphere, where their messages are often picked up by well-connected bloggers, the so-called influencers, who boast large audiences. Viral messages must be authentic and elicit an emotional response, but for that very reason they are difficult to orchestrate. Online opinion leaders resent being co-opted by companies using overt hard-sell tactics.

Online Communities. Like Twitter, which is now drawing a loyal core following to businesses and brands, company blogs can attract a devoted community of participants. Such followers want to keep informed about company events, product updates, and other news. In turn, those enthusiasts can contribute new ideas. Few companies enjoy the brand awareness and customer loyalty of Coca-Cola. With its colorful blog *Coca-Cola Conversations*, the soft drink maker shares its rich past ("Coke Bottle 100") and thus deepens Coke fans' loyalty. Coca-Cola's marketing is subtle; the blog is designed to provide a "unique experience" to fans.

Internal Communication and Recruiting. Blogs can be used to keep virtual teams on track and share updates on the road. Members in remote locations can stay in touch by smartphone and other devices, exchanging text, images, sound, and video clips. In many companies, blogs have replaced hard-copy publications in offering late-breaking news or tidbits of interest to employees. Blogs can create a sense of community and stimulate employee participation. Furthermore, blogs mirror the company culture and present a priceless opportunity for job candidates to size up a potential employer and the people working there.

WORKPLACE IN FOCUS

Employers worry about disengaged workers, particularly millennials. To boost motivation, companies are introducing *gamification*. From recruiting to training and development, organizations are adopting gaming to introduce fun, play, and competition. PwC Hungary challenges applicants with Multipoly, a game that tests their workplace readiness. Walmart has used gamification to deliver safety training to 5,000 associates. As they connected emotionally with the game, workers were more likely to follow safety protocols. As in the Boy Scouts, participants' performance is logged as they earn badges and compete.

A related type of workplace surveillance and data collection is *wearable technology*—think heart rate monitors. Wearables measure worker productivity and lifestyle by recording brain activity, movement,

posture, and more. Employers believe the devices can help them save on health-care costs. They argue that lifestyle choices affect job performance. Critics fear poor morale if workers fear that their data are not private.[51] How do you feel about these types of workplace monitoring?

5-4b Blogging Best Practices: Seven Tips for Master Bloggers

Much advice is freely accessible online, but this section offers guidelines culled from experienced bloggers and communication experts that will lead you to successful blog writing. As with any public writing, your posts will be scrutinized; therefore, you want to make the best impression.

Craft a Catchy but Concise Title. The headline is what draws online readers to even click to go your post. Some will be intriguing questions or promises. Online writers often use numbers to structure their posts. Here are some examples: *Six Apps You Don't Want to Miss; 5 Tips to Keep Spear Phishers Out of Your Inbox; Create Powerful Imagery in Your Writing; How Financially Sexy Is Your Household?; The False Choice of Mediocrity.*

Ace the Opening Paragraph. The lead must deliver on the promise of the headline. Identify a need and propose to solve the problem. Ask a relevant question. Say something startling. Tell an anecdote or use an analogy to connect with the reader. The author of How Many Lives Does a Brand Have? opened with this:

> *It's said that cats have nine lives, but how many lives does a brand have? The answer, it seems, is definitely more than one. Recently, in Shanghai, a friend took me to one of the city's most sophisticated luxury malls . . . .[52]*

Provide Details in the Body. Consider the *So what?* and *What's in it for me?* questions. Use vivid examples, quotations and testimonials, or statistics. Structure the body with numbers, bullets, and subheadings. Use expressive action verbs (*buy* for *get; own* for *have; travel* or *jet* for *go*). Use conversational language to sound warm and authentic. Use contractions (*can't* for *cannot; doesn't* for *does not; isn't* for *is not*).

Consider Visuals. Add visual interest with relevant images and diagrams. Keep paragraphs short and use plenty of white space around them. Aim to make the look simple and easy to scan.

Include Calls to Action. Call on readers in the title to do something, or provide a take-away and gentle nudge at the end. Chris Brogan, writing in his blog *Become a Dream Feeder*, had this to say: "So, how will you make your blog into a dream feeder? Or do you do that already? What dreams do your readers have?"[53] Ask open-ended questions or tell the reader what to do: *So, be sure to ask about 360-degree security tactics that aim to stop inbound attacks, but also to block outbound data theft attempts.*

Edit and Proofread. Follow the revision tips in Chapter 4 of this book. Cut any unneeded words, sentences, and irrelevant ideas. Fix awkward, wordy, and repetitious sentences. Edit and proofread as if your life depended on it. Your reputation might. The best blogs are error free.

Respond to Posts Respectfully. Build a positive image online by posting compelling comments on other bloggers' posts. Politely and promptly reply to comments on your site. This reply to Guy Kawasaki's infographic makes a positive observation about the post and adds a valuable thought albeit with a glaring spelling error and missing commas:

> *Great graphic portrayal of the human connection. Three other areas might include 1) use people's first name (something pretty basic but often forgotten) 2) listen before you talk (a great one for bosses when meeting with employees) and 3) don't be afraid to pay complements [sic] when they are warranted.*[55]

If you disagree with a post, do so respectfully. Don't ramble. Remember, your comments may remain online practically forever and could come back to haunt you long after posting. Your blog posts can benefit from the journalistic pattern shown in Figure 5.10 by emphasizing the big news up front, supported by specifics and background information.

5-5 Social Networking for Business

Popular social networking sites such as Facebook and Twitter are used by businesses for similar reasons and in much the same way as podcasts, blogs, and wikis. Social networking sites enable businesses to connect with customers and employees, share company news, and exchange ideas. Social online communities for professional audiences (e.g., LinkedIn), discussed in Chapter 13, help recruiters find talent and encounter potential employees before hiring them. Today, about 84 percent of organizations use social media to recruit suitable candidates.[56]

5-5a Tapping Into Social Media

Clearly, business social networking is a big deal. Globally, a whopping 97 percent of organizations use social media to market themselves.[57] At the same time, workers report that social media play a very small role (4 percent) in their day-to-day job tasks. They list e-mail (61 percent) and the Internet (54 percent) as their most important work tools.[58]

Figure 5.10 Writing a Captivating Blog

Applying the Five Journalistic *Ws* to Blogs

Big Idea First
Who? What? When? Why? How?

Key Facts
Explanations
Evidence
Examples

Background
Details

- Fact check.
- Earn your readers' trust.
- Credit your sources.
- Apply the inverted pyramid.
- Edit, edit, edit.
- Proof, proof, proof.

However, business interest in social networking is not surprising if we consider that the average millennial's smartphone is in use more than three hours a day. Moreover, 71 percent of this desirable Gen Y demographic use social media daily. Older age groups are catching up, though, while also earning higher incomes. Social media users sixty-five and over now comprise 34 percent of that demographic.[59]

Predictably, businesses are trying to adapt and tap the vast potential of social networking. With 79 percent of American adults as users, Facebook is by far the most popular social network, followed by Instagram (32 percent), Pinterest (31 percent), LinkedIn (29 percent), and Twitter (24 percent).[60] A noteworthy 97 percent of Fortune 500 companies are now on LinkedIn, 86 percent have corporate Twitter accounts, and 84 have established a Facebook presence. Instagram use among the Fortune 500 has shot up fivefold in three years reflecting millennials' preferences.[61]

5-5b How Businesses Use Social Media

The key to all the social media is that they thrive in a mobile, interactive, and hyperconnected environment. However, the social Web has also spawned internal networking sites behind corporate firewalls. Tech giant IBM has created Connections, a business social network, to help organizations share knowledge, improve decision making, and foster innovation. Investing heavily in cloud computing to the tune of $16 billion, IBM wants greater employee engagement and productivity.[62]

However, the adoption of enterprise social networks has been slow. It is highest in companies in which the top executives are heavily connected.[63] The advantage of enterprise social media networks is that they are searchable, enabling workers to tag, follow, view activity feeds, and more. Users can access and send information more efficiently than by e-mail alone.[64]

Adopting the Facebook Model. Some companies have found that the Facebook model can be adapted to internal networks, many of which run on the Chatter or Yammer enterprise social networking platforms. For one thing, staff members already intuitively understand how a corporate social network operates because they are familiar with Facebook. Red Robin's Yammer-based corporate social network, dubbed Yummer, gave a voice to employees who normally don't have a say. It led to a better burger recipe and became a mine for creative ideas.[65]

Connecting Far-Flung Workers. Because social networks are about connections, they also enable companies to connect dispersed employees. Rosemary Turner, the president of UPS in northern California, manages a far-flung team of 17,000 workers who drive delivery trucks, work the loading docks, and make sales calls. She uses Twitter to update her team about road conditions but also to highlight employee accomplishments, posing with them in photos that she shares online. UPS employees are comfortable with Twitter; its open dialogue mirrors the transparent company culture and fosters trust.[66]

Crowdsourcing Customers. Social networks and blogs also help companies invite customer input at the product design stage. On its IdeaStorm site, Dell has solicited almost 26,000 new product ideas and suggested improvements, including glossy 4K monitors and improved power cords. Lay's brand is getting a lot of traction for its annual "Do Us a Flavor" contest. One lucky participant wins a cool million dollars for pitching a new potato chip flavor and being chosen by the most Lay's fans.[67] As Figure 5.11 shows, large companies have established successful social media presences.

5-5c Potential Risks of Social Networking for Businesses

Public social networks hold great promise for businesses while also presenting some risk. Most managers want plugged-in employees with strong tech skills. They like to imagine their workers as brand evangelists. They fantasize about their products becoming overnight sensations thanks to viral marketing. However, they also fret about incurring productivity losses, compromising trade secrets, attracting the wrath of huge Internet audiences, and facing embarrassment over inappropriate and damaging employee posts.[68] Moreover, network administrators worry about legal compliance, privacy laws, and the protection of data from malware and cybercrime introduced by employees' sharing.[69]

Businesses take different approaches to the dark side of social networking. Some, such as Zappos, take a hands-off approach and encourage employee online activity. Others, such as IBM, have drafted detailed policies to cover all forms of self-expression online. According to one survey, 80 percent of businesses have social media policies; 36 percent block access to social networking sites, and in most countries, they are well within their legal rights in doing so.[70]

Several top German corporations, including Volkswagen and Porsche, have banned social media outright, fearing a loss of productivity and industrial espionage.[71] However, some experts believe that organizations should embrace positive word-of-mouth testimonials from employees about their jobs, not quash them with rigid policies.[72]

OFFICE INSIDER

"As employees engage in sales and networking across social networks, new pathways into the business open up and cyber criminals know how to exploit them. . . . Many users do not understand how cyber criminals leverage social tools and technologies to gain access to businesses and their data."[73]

Anna Frazzetto, *chief digital technology officer and SVP at Harvey Nash, IT recruiting*

5-5d Using Social Media and Keeping Your Job

Experts agree that, as with any public online activity, users of social networking sites would do well to exercise caution. Privacy is a myth, and sensitive information should not be shared lightly, least of all risqué photographs. Furthermore, refusing friend requests or unfriending coworkers could jeopardize professional relationships.

The advice to think twice before posting online applies to most communication channels used on the job. Among the many risks in cyberspace are inappropriate photographs and tagging. Social media users should always ask permission before

Figure 5.11 The Brands That Rule on Facebook

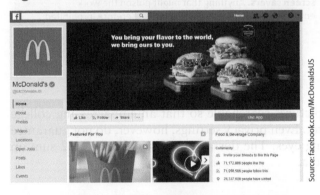

Source: facebook.com/McDonaldsUS

Source: facebook.com/CocaColaUnitedStates

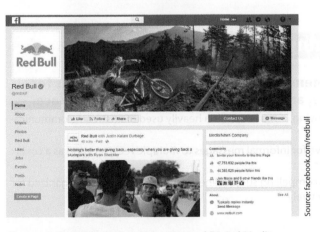

Source: facebook.com/redbull

Facebook has reached 2 billion active monthly users. The nearest social media competitor, YouTube, boasts 1.5 billion users. For comparison, Instagram has 700 million users and LinkedIn 500 million; Twitter claims more than 328 million monthly active users. Facebook allows registered users to create individual home pages as well as group pages based on their interests. The top three brands with the most fans after Facebook itself are Coca-Cola (105.3 million), McDonald's (72.7 million), and Red Bull (48 million).

Figure 5.12 Using Digital Media Like a Pro: Dos and Don'ts

DON'TS — Avoid questionable content, personal documents, and file sharing

Don't spread rumors, gossip, and negative defamatory comments. Because all digital information is subject to discovery in court, avoid unprofessional content and conduct, including complaints about your employer, customers, and employees.

Don't download and share cartoons, video clips, photos, and art. Businesses are liable for any recorded digital content regardless of the medium used.

Don't open unfamiliar attachments. Attachments with executable files or video files may carry viruses, spyware, or other malware (malicious programs).

Don't download free software and utilities to company machines. Employees can unwittingly introduce viruses, phishing schemes, and other cyber bugs.

Don't store your music and photos on a company machine (or server) and don't watch streaming videos. Capturing precious company bandwidth for personal use is a sure way to be shown the door.

Don't share files, and avoid file-sharing services. Clarify whether you may use Google Docs and other services that offer optional file sharing. Stay away from distributors or pirated files such as LimeWare.

DOs — Know workplace policies and use media only for work-related purposes

Learn your company's rules. Some companies require workers to sign that they have read and understand Internet and digital media use policies. Being informed is your best protection.

Avoid sending personal e-mail, instant messages, or texts from work. Even if your company allows personal use during lunch or after hours, keep it to a minimum. Better yet, wait to use your own electronic devices away from work.

Separate work and personal data. Keep information that could embarrass you or expose you to legal liability on your personal storage devices, on hard drives, or in the cloud, never on your office computer.

Be careful when blogging, tweeting, or posting on social networking sites. Unhappy about not receiving a tip, a Beverly Hills waiter lost his job for tweeting disparaging remarks about an actress. Forgetting that his boss was his Facebook friend, a British employee was fired after posting, "OMG, I HATE MY JOB!" and calling his supervisor names.

Keep sensitive information private. Use privacy settings, but don't trust the "private" areas on Facebook, Twitter, Flickr, and other social networks.

Avoid pornography, sexually explicit jokes, or inappropriate screen savers. Anything that might poison the work environment is a harassment risk and, therefore, prohibited.

---

tagging someone. Tags make pictures searchable so that an embarrassing college incident may resurface years later. Even privacy settings, however, do not guarantee complete protection from prying eyes. The dos and don'ts in Figure 5.12 sum up best practices for all digital media.

Summary of Learning Outcomes

1 Understand e-mail, memos, and the professional standards for their usage, structure, and format in the digital era workplace.

- Although sometimes annoying, e-mail remains a heavily used mainstream communication channel.
- E-mail is especially effective for informal messages to multiple receivers and as a cover document for attachments.
- Business e-mails feature a compelling subject line, include a greeting, are organized for readability, and close effectively.

- Memos are still used for internal messages that are too long for e-mail, require a lasting record, demand formality, or inform workers who don't have e-mail.
- Like e-mails, memos carry nonsensitive information and include a subject line, a date-line, and the names of senders and receivers.

2 Explain workplace instant messaging and texting as well as their liabilities and best practices.

- Individuals use the Internet or corporate intranets to exchange brief text-based messages, which requires a cellular connection, Wi-Fi, or a VoIP service.
- The benefits of messaging are low cost, speed, unobtrusiveness, immediacy, and efficiency.
- The risks of messaging include legal liability, security breaches, and compliance issues.
- Best practices for messaging include minding policies, protecting sensitive data, pulling over to message, separating personal and work contacts, and using correct language.

3 Identify professional applications of podcasts and wikis.

- Whether as short clips or longer digital files, audio as well as video podcasts offer a friendly human face and can replace costlier live teleconferences.
- A wiki is an Internet- or intranet-based collaborative software tool that allows multiple users to create, access, and modify documents.
- Wikis can help teams solve problems and complete assignments while preventing version confusion.

4 Describe how businesses use blogs to connect with internal and external audiences, and list best practices for professional blogging.

- External or internal corporate blogs help create virtual communities, build brands, and develop relationships.
- Companies use blogs for public relations, customer relations, crisis communication, market research, viral marketing, online community building, internal communication, and recruiting.
- Best practices include crafting a catchy title and intriguing opening, providing details in the body, using visuals, calling for action, editing carefully, and commenting respectfully.

5 Define the advantages and risks of business uses of social media networks.

- Social networking sites enable businesses to connect with customers and employees, share news, exchange ideas, and boost their brand images.
- In addition to Facebook, Twitter, and other very public social media, many businesses also run private social networks behind corporate firewalls.
- The risks of social media use in business include productivity losses, leaked trade secrets, angry Internet audiences, security breaches, and damaging employee posts.
- Savvy users should keep privacy settings up-to-date, avoid risqué images, handle friend requests tactfully, and beware of tagging.

Chapter Review

1. Briefly describe what it means to be social and mobile in the workplace today. (L.O. 1)

2. Why is workplace e-mail unlikely to go away? (L.O. 1)

3. Why do many workers complain about e-mail? (L.O. 1)

4. What are the risks of instant messaging and texting? (L.O. 2)

5. List five best practices for using IM and texting that you consider most important. (L.O. 2)

6. How do organizations use and deliver podcasts? (L.O. 3)

7. Explain what a wiki is and list its advantages. (L.O. 3)

8. How do companies use blogs? (L.O. 4)

9. What seven tips would you give to a beginning blogger? (L.O. 4)

10. Name potential risks of social networks for businesses. (L.O. 5)

Critical Thinking

11. The eminent sociologist Zygmunt Bauman had this to say about social media: "Most people use social media not to unite, not to open their horizons wider, but on the contrary, to cut themselves a comfort zone where the only sounds they hear are the echoes of their own voice, where the only things they see are the reflections of their own face. Social media are very useful, they provide pleasure, but they are a trap."[75] Do you agree? Why or why not? How do you use social media networks? (L.O. 5)

12. On Martin Luther King Jr. Day, four Oklahoma State University students tweeted a group selfie; two of the students were wearing blackface, causing outrage on campus. In another incident, several students were expelled from a Texas university for posting a Snapchat video of a peer in blackface, wearing baggy clothes, sporting exaggerated lips, and making offensive racial jokes.[76] Comment on these incidents in the light of the students' eventual job search. What advice would you give your peers about posting on social media? (L.O. 5)

13. Are common abbreviations such as *lol* and *imho* and all-lowercase writing acceptable in texting or instant messaging for business? (L.O. 2)

14. Traditional mainstream media act as so-called gatekeepers that vet the news and decide what kind of content gets published. However, social media networks have changed the game. Now anyone with an Internet connection can publish anything, even fake news, and reach vast audiences in mere seconds. What are the benefits and dangers of this unprecedented access and speed of distribution? (L.O. 5)

15. Some marketers employ machines to inflate the number of likes and fans online.[77] So-called bot networks (*botnets*) operate large numbers of fake accounts on Facebook, Instagram, and Twitter. A rental agency based in Washington, D.C., went from two fans to almost 15,000 within a few days. How do you feel about companies and their brands pretending they have actual traffic on their sites and buying likes? (L.O. 5)

Writing Improvement Exercises

Message Openers and Subject Lines (L.O. 1)

YOUR TASK. Compare the following sets of message openers. Circle the letter of the opener that illustrates a direct opening. Write an appropriate subject line for each opening paragraph.

16. An e-mail requesting sign-up for a leadership seminar on mediation:

   a. Organization leaders are responsible for creating a work environment that enables people to thrive. If turf wars, disagreements, and differences of opinion escalate into interpersonal conflict, you must intervene immediately. In conflict-ridden situations, your mediation skill and interventions are critical. If you sign up for one of our upcoming HR Workplace Conflict Resolution seminars, you will be able to polish these crucial managerial skills.

   b. Please sign up for one of the upcoming HR Workplace Conflict Resolution seminars for executives to keep your mediation skills sharp. Organization leaders are responsible for creating a work environment that enables people to thrive. If turf wars, disagreements, and differences of opinion escalate into interpersonal conflict, you must intervene immediately. In conflict-ridden situations, your mediation skill and interventions are critical.

   Subject line:

17. An e-mail announcing a low-cost day-care program:

   a. Employees interested in enrolling their children in our new low-cost day-care program are invited to attend an HR orientation on January 18.

   b. For several years we have studied the possibility of offering a day-care option for those employees who are parents. Until recently, our management team was unable to agree on the exact parameters of this benefit, but now some of you will be able to take advantage of this option.

   Subject line:

18. A memo announcing flexible policies to help employees create a healthy work-life balance:

   a. Effective February 1, all our employees will be able to benefit from new opportunities for achieving a healthy work-life balance. ReSource Partners, Inc., will begin to offer flexible work schedules, paid time off, and company-sponsored family events and activities. The pursuit of work-life balance reduces the stress employees experience. When they spend the majority of their days on work-related activities and feel as if they are neglecting the other important aspects of their lives, stress and unhappiness result.

   b. Work-life balance is a concept that supports the efforts of employees to split their time and energy between work and the other important aspects of their lives. Work-life balance is a daily effort to make time for family, friends, community participation, spirituality, personal growth, self-care, and other personal activities, in addition to the demands of the workplace. ReSource Partners, Inc.'s management team has thought long and hard about providing a healthy work-life balance for employees.

   Subject line:

19. A memo announcing a new policy:

   a. It has come to our attention that some staff members write blogs, sometimes publicly addressing sensitive company information. Although we respect the desire of employees to express themselves and would like to continue allowing the practice, we have decided to adopt a new policy providing binding rules to ensure the company's and the bloggers' safety.

   b. The following new policy for blog authors will help staff members create posts that maintain the integrity of the company's sensitive information and keep writers safe.

   Subject line:

Bulleted and Numbered Lists (L.O. 1)

E-mails and memos frequently contain numbered lists (for items in a sequence) or bulleted lists. Study how the following wordy paragraph was revised into a more readable format with a list:

BEFORE REVISION:

Our office could implement better environmental practices such as improving energy efficiency and reducing our carbon footprint. Here are three simple things we can do to make our daily work practices greener. For one thing, we can power down. At night we should turn off monitors, not just log off our computers. In addition, we could "Light Right." This means installing energy-efficient lighting throughout the office. A final suggestion has to do with recycling. We could be recycling instantly if we placed small recycling bins at all workstations and common use areas.

AFTER REVISION:

Our office could use energy more efficiently and reduce our carbon footprint in three simple ways:

- **Power down:** Turn off monitors rather than just logging off our computers.
- **Light right:** Install energy-efficient lighting throughout the office.
- **Recycle instantly:** Place small recycling bins at all workstations and common use areas to encourage recycling.

YOUR TASK. Revise the following wordy, unorganized paragraphs. Include an introductory statement followed by a bulleted or numbered list. Look for ways to eliminate unnecessary wording.

20. Because all casual clothing is not suitable for the office, these guidelines will help you determine what is appropriate to wear to work. Slacks that are similar to Dockers and other makers of cotton or synthetic material pants, wool pants, flannel pants, and attractive dress synthetic pants are acceptable. Casual dresses and skirts hemmed at the knee and lower or slits at or below the knee are acceptable. Dress and skirt length should be at a length at which you can sit comfortably in public. Casual shirts and blouses, dress shirts and blouses, sweaters, tops, golf-type shirts, tunics, and turtlenecks are acceptable attire for work. Most suit jackets or sport jackets are also acceptable attire for the office. Conservative athletic or walking shoes, loafers, clogs, sneakers, boots, flats, dress heels, and leather deck-type shoes are acceptable for work.

21. Our attorney made a recommendation that we consider several things to avoid litigation in regard to sexual harassment. The first thing he suggested was that we take steps regarding the establishment of an unequivocal written policy prohibiting sexual harassment within our organization. The second thing we should do is make sure training sessions are held for supervisors regarding a proper work environment. Finally, some kind of official procedure for employees to lodge complaints is necessary. This procedure should include investigation of complaints.

Radical Rewrites

Note: Radical Rewrites are provided at **www.cengagebrain.com** for you to download and revise. Your instructor may show a suggested solution.

5.1 Radical Rewrite: Information E-mail—Hastily Written Message Needs Drastic Revision (L.O. 1)

Bien, Inc., is considering launching an internship program, and Nathan Weintraub, manager of Human Resources, seeks information from members of the management team.

YOUR TASK. Study the first draft of his hastily written message and list at least five weaknesses. Then revise it to create a concise, clear message. Consider patterning your revision on Figure 5.1 in this chapter.

> **To:** Danika Benoit <dbenoit@bien.com>
> **From:** Nathan Weintraub <nweintraub@bien.com>
> **Subject:** Interns?
>
> Hi, Danika,
>
> You may remember that some time ago our management team here at Bien talked about an internship program. The topic has come up again at this time, and I'm taking this opportunity to ask you to please answer some questions about whether this is a good idea or not. As our organization continues to expand, interns might make sense. But there are many points that we need to discuss, and I've put together a few questions that I think we should cover at the next management meeting. Please mark your calendar to meet on March 14 at 9 a.m. in the morning.
>
> First, we really need to discuss whether an internship program is advantageous to us here at Bien. In addition, what are the disadvantages? Next, what are some of the ramifications legally of hosting an internship program here in our state? Another question that enters my mind is whether we should pay interns. Do they receive college credit instead? I wonder if that serves as satisfactory compensation. Finally, we need to discuss where this program would be launched within Bien. What departments would pilot such a program?
>
> I hope you will give careful thought to these questions and come prepared to discuss.
>
> Nathan Weintraub
>
> Manager, Human Resources | nweintraub@bien.com | Cell: 566.201.9033

List at least five weaknesses.

5.2 Radical Rewrite: Information E-Mail—Tips for Conferencing (L.O. 1)

Gabriel Lugo, a blogger and Web conferencing expert, responds to a request from Samantha Staiger, who wants advice for an article she is writing. Gabriel's advice is good, but his message is poorly organized, contains grammar and other errors, and is hard to read.

YOUR TASK. Analyze the following message and list at least five weaknesses. Then revise it if your instructor advises.

To: Samantha Staiger <sstaiger@realtopublications.com>
From: Gabriel Lugo <gabe@gabesworldblog.com>
Subject: Your Request

Dear Samantha Staiger:

Hey, thanks for asking me to make a contribution to the article you are preparing and working up for *Networking Voices*. Appreciate this opportunity! Although you asked me to keep it brief, I could give you an extensive, comprehensive list of dos and don'ts for Web conferencing. If you want this, let me know.

As an alternative to in-person meetings, Web conferencing is increasingly popular. Here's five tips for your article. First and foremost, plan ahead. All participants should be notified of things like the date, time, and duration. It's your job to send log-ins, passwords, and printed documents by e-mail. My next advise is about identifying yourself. Don't assume that attendees will automatically recognize your voice. The first few times you speak, its good to state your name.

Another tip has to do with muting (turning off) your phone. Believe me, there's nothing worse than barking dogs, side conversations. And worst of all is the sound of toilets flushing during a conference. Ick!

You should play with your microphone and speakers until you sound good. And of course, don't shuffle papers. Don't eat. Don't move things while your speaking.

My final tip involves using a lobby slide to open. This is a slide that tells the meeting details. Such as the start time, audio information, and the agenda. This lobby slide should go up about 10 to 15 minutes before the meeting begins.

Hope this helps!

Gabe

Gabriel Lugo | Gabe's World Blog | gabe@gabesworldblog.com |

List at least five weaknesses.

Activities and Cases

5.3 Instant Messaging: Live Chat Training at TransGlobal Airlines (L.O. 2)

> Communication Technology   > E-Mail   > Team   > Web

Live chat operators who help customers by exchanging instant messages with them in real time play an important role in customer service. The goal of providing such direct communication online is to inform and troubleshoot, but also to build a lasting relationship with customers. Ideally, by being cordial, professional, and helpful, live chat operators can contribute significantly to turning customers into fans of the company or brand. Representatives must sound authentic and human. TransGlobal Airlines is training its representatives with hypothetical customer service scenarios. Following are two logs of chats by trainees who were asked to respond to a customer, Alex, in an online chat.

YOUR TASK. Carefully review the logs of the conversations between Alex and Representative 1 as well as Representative 2. Individually or as a team, critique Rep 1 and Rep 2 in class or in an e-mail to your instructor summarizing your observations. Support your views with examples. For instance, you could comment on the representatives' courtesy, helpfulness, tone, or writing skills. Then, if your instructor asks you to rewrite this chat, try your hand at being Representative 3 and apply some of the lessons you have learned in this chapter and Chapter 4. **Tip:** Create a table to approximate the dialogue in an online chat. Note that sometimes the same person may write two or more comments in a row instead of waiting for a reply to the first one.

Representative 1

Rep: Hey, Alex, what's shakin' in Atlanta? What do you need?

Alex: Hi.

Rep: Perf to have you here. Hiw can I hlep?

Alex: Your award-travel system sucks!! I'm so tired of wasting time on your website!

Rep: Whoa! Chill!?. Why diss our system. What trasnpired

Alex: What happened is that I keep getting an error message just before I click Purchase. I tried many times.

Alex: What point are award miles when they can't be redeemed??

Rep: Where... what Just a sec I'm on another chat. Whats wrong?

Alex: I am planning a business trip to London with some of my 500k frequent flyer miles. Whenever I choose the itinierary, fill in payment information for the taxes etc, I hit Purchase and an Error !!! pops up. I can't finish the booking. So annoying! Who has the time??

Rep: How v nice to be able to go to London Wow, 500k miles? I can see your search in our systm. Lemme try it for you. Leave technology to a milenial! [Pause]

Rep: Nope! it doesn't work Sorry. System is new and has glitches.

Alex: Why on earth do you roll out something that's full of bugs, why waste my time??

Rep: Yasss, good question tbh. Listen I can try to get on this and will let you go now. When I make the booking I will give you a buzz first. then shoot you an email. Our tech boss has a blog for complaints. You should give him an earful there!! He says he wants to hear from our ticked off customers. Will send you the link too. Oh and I will save you money, no live booking fees.

Alex: Okay. That's a relief. Thanks. I'll be awaiting your call and e-mail.

Rep: Anything else I can do??

Alex: No, gotta run! Bye

Rep: Cheers!

Representative 2

Rep: Good day, dear sir! We are honored to serve esteemed customers like you.

Alex: Hi.

Rep: How can we be of assistance?

Alex: Your award-travel system sucks!! I'm so tired of wasting time on your website!

Rep: We are so very sorry to hear that your customer experience is less than stellar, sir!

Alex: What happened is that I keep getting an error message just before I click Purchase. I tried many times.

Alex: What point are award miles when they can't be redeemed??

Rep: Would you be so kind and describe the precise nature of your issue?

Alex: I am planning a business trip to London with some of my 500k frequent flyer miles. Whenever I choose the itinierary, fill in payment information for the taxes etc, I hit Purchase and an Error !!! pops up. I can't finish the booking. So annoying! Who has the time??

Rep: When you visited our website, we saw your credentials and search parameters. I shall attempt to complete the booking in your stead. [Pause]

Rep: I'm truly inconsolable, sir. It appears that I am unable to complete the transaction using our new system. I might need to escalate the problem to my supervisor.

Alex: Why on earth do you roll out something that's full of bugs, why waste my time??

Rep: Please stay calm, sir. We are trying our best to serve you. As one of America's most respected airlines, we take customer service very seriously. Allow me to keep trying to complete the transaction gratis, without live booking fees. I shall telephone you and communicate via e-mail once the booking is completed. You will also receive a link that will allow you to share your expe-rience with our CTO.

Alex: Okay. That's a relief. Thanks. I'll be awaiting your call and e-mail.

Rep: May we do even more to provide excellent service, sir?

Alex: No, gotta run! Bye

Rep: Have an enjoyable day, sir. Goodbye!

5.4 Information/Procedure Message: Parking Guidelines With a Smile (L.O. 1)

> E-Mail

As Adelle Justice, director of Human Resources, you must remind both day-shift and swing-shift employees of the company's parking guidelines. Day-shift employees must park in Lots A and B in their assigned spaces. If they have not registered their cars and received their white stickers, the cars will be ticketed.

Day-shift employees are forbidden to park at the curb. Swing-shift employees may park at the curb before 3:30 p.m. Moreover, after 3:30 p.m., swing-shift employees may park in any empty space—except those marked Tandem, Handicapped, Vanpool, Car Pool, or Management. Day-shift employees may loan their spaces to other employees if they know they will not be using them.

One serious problem is lack of registration (as evidenced by white stickers). Registration is done by Employee Relations. Any car without a sticker will be ticketed. To encourage registration, Employee Relations will be in the cafeteria May 12 and 13 from 11:30 a.m. to 1:30 p.m. and from 3 p.m. to 5 p.m. to take applications and issue white parking stickers.

YOUR TASK. Write an information/procedure e-mail or memo to employees that reviews the parking guidelines and encourages them to get their cars registered. Use listing techniques, and strive for a tone that fosters a sense of cooperation rather than resentment.

5.5 Information Message: Great News! Floating Holidays at Westend Chemical (L.O. 1)

> **E-Mail**

A floating holiday is a perk that employers provide as a nod to religious diversity, employee satisfaction, and work-life balance.[78] In the United States, employers are not required to offer paid holidays, paid vacation, or even paid sick leave. However, most full-time employees expect such compensation for time not worked as part of their benefits package. Hourly and contract employees don't usually receive paid holidays.

In addition to at least seven to nine common paid holidays—for example, Independence Day, Labor Day, and Thanksgiving Day—some employers offer one or two floating holidays per year that employees take as needed. For instance, workers can take a paid day off to participate in elections, celebrate a birthday, attend a family reunion, take a parent-teacher day, or commemorate religious holidays. Without floating holidays, employees would need to take personal days or paid vacation days to spend with family or devote to worship.

Westend Chemical in Queensport, Tennessee, has decided to provide two annual floating days that can be taken anytime, without blackout periods; managers must work with employees so that the workers can take these days off as they need them. The floating holidays do not accrue (i.e., they must be taken in each calendar year); however, unused days are paid out at year's end or when a worker leaves the company. A floating holiday is a relatively inexpensive morale booster.

YOUR TASK. As a human resources trainee, draft an e-mail or memo to all employees informing them about this welcome benefit that's effective immediately. Rely on the information in the scenario, but do not copy. Consider using some of the techniques introduced in Chapter 4.

5.6 Information Message: Establishing Wiki Rules (L.O. 3)

> **Communication Technology** ▸ **E-Mail** ▸ **Social Media** ▸ **Web**

Wikipedia, the most famous wiki platform, tends to pop up at the top of most Internet searches. However, the Internet is teeming with wiki sites or wikifarms hosting countless wiki communities with millions of pages. Popular platforms are Wikia, Wikispaces, PBworks, and Google Sites. All offer free accounts inviting users to browse or start their own wikis on any imaginable topic of interest. One notable online community is Wikibiz on Wikia, which is currently seeking competent business users to edit over 200 articles. It's not hard to understand how businesses benefit from wikis for providing documentation, establishing a knowledge base, collaborating on and editing articles, and communicating in forums and chats. But what makes a valuable contributor?

Whether they contribute to a wiki on the Internet or at work, participants should try to abide by the conventions of polite society, yet even commonsense rules are often broken. Valued users show respect and avoid ambiguous language. They don't attack or harshly criticize other contributors. They aren't trolls (annoying individuals who post irrelevant or controversial comments that anger fellow users and disrupt a discussion). Because expression online allows for little subtlety, wiki editors know that words can be misinterpreted. Members of online communities form deep bonds and dislike contributors they consider vicious or mean.

Wiki users must verify their facts and pay attention to correct grammar and spelling. Every comment a member contributes is published on the Internet and available to any reader. If the wiki is on the intranet behind a firewall, an ill-conceived comment is for the whole company to see. Sloppiness causes embarrassment or worse. Wikipedia, a wiki that is trying to marry credibility with its desire for openness, tightened the rules for editors after incursions of Internet vandals who posted inaccurate information. Errors introduced by cyber attacks and innocent errors alike are often perpetuated by readers who blindly trust wiki content.

Any new user needs to read and follow the guidelines for contributors and give credit where credit is due. Every contribution must fit into the group effort in style, content, and format. Newbies should ask for help if necessary. Big egos and effective collaboration don't go hand in hand. Contributors are part of a team, not individual authors who can expect recognition or maintain control over their writing. Sources must be cited to avoid plagiarism. Users of copyrighted material must follow fair use guidelines or ask for explicit permission.

YOUR TASK. Your boss, Evan Bell, sent you the preceding information about wikis, their terms of use, and community guidelines. Because you are a new trainee, the manager wants you to try your hand at drafting his memo to all staff to prepare everyone for the launch of the new wiki. He asks you to extract relevant behavior guidelines from the text and summarize them in several actionable rules for the soon-to-be-deployed corporate wiki. Employees are also expected to attend a mandatory wiki training. The sign-up deadline for this training is May 24. To sign up and obtain answers to technical questions, employees need to get in touch with Joanna Bridge in the IT department. Her e-mail address is *jbridge@futrtech.com*. In your memo or e-mail to future company wiki users, present the content in a visually appealing format. Try to emulate the information documents shown in Figures 5.1 and 5.3. Paraphrase; don't just cut and paste from the text!

5.7 Information Message: Rescheduling Interviews (L.O. 1)

E-Mail

Your boss, Pete Rollins, has scheduled three appointments to interview applicants for the position of project manager. All of these appointments are for Thursday, August 22. However, he now must travel to Miami that week. He asks you to reschedule these appointments for one week later. He also wants a brief background summary for each candidate.

Although frustrated, you call each interviewee and are lucky to arrange these times. Diego Abrego, who has been a project manager for nine years with Summit Enterprises, agrees to come at 10:30 a.m. Edna Kerber, who is a systems analyst and a consultant to many companies, will come at 11:30 a.m. Maya Oliva, who has an MA degree and six years of experience as a senior project coordinator at High Point Industries, will come at 9:30 a.m. You are wondering whether Mr. Rollins forgot to include Kimberly Yang, operations personnel officer, in these interviews. Ms. Yang usually is part of the selection process.

YOUR TASK. Write an e-mail or memo to Mr. Rollins including all the information he needs. Make your message easy to scan and visually appealing.

5.8 Instant Messaging: Practicing Your Professional IM Skills (L.O. 2)

Communication Technology ▸ **Social Media** ▸ **Web** ▸ **Team**

In this role-playing group activity, you will showcase your professional instant messaging skills. Guided by your instructor, you will simulate one of several typical business scenarios—for example, responding to a product inquiry, training a new-hire, troubleshooting with a customer, or making an appointment. For each scenario, two or more students chat professionally with only a minimal script to practice on-the-spot, yet courteous professional interactions by IM. Your instructor will determine which client software or app you will need and provide brief instructions to prepare you for your role.

If you don't have instant messaging software on your computer or smart device yet, download the application first—for example, AIM, Google Hangouts, Skype, or IM aggregators such as Trillian or Pidgin that allow you to chat with people using IM clients or apps. All IM software enables users to share photos and large media files. You can make voice calls and use webcam video as well. These advanced features turn IM software into a simple conferencing tool and video phone. You can connect with users around the world as long as they have the same software. Unlike calling landlines or cell phones, peer-to-peer voice calls are free. Most IM clients also offer mobile apps for your smartphone, so that you can IM or call other users while you are away from a computer. WhatsApp, Facebook Messenger, QQ, WeChat, and Skype are just a few of the most popular apps. You may want to use a computer because downloading and saving chat sessions is easier on a computer than on a smartphone.

YOUR TASK. Open the IM or chat program your instructor chooses. Follow your instructor's directions closely as you role-play the business situation you were assigned with your partner or team. The scenario will involve two or more people who will communicate by instant messaging in real time.

5.9 Analyzing a Podcast (L.O. 3)

Communication Technology ▸ **E-Mail** ▸ **Social Media** ▸ **Web**

Browsing the podcasts at iTunes, you stumble across the Quick and Dirty Tips series, specifically Money Girl, who dispenses financial advice. You sign up for the free podcasts that cover a variety of business topics. You can also visit the website Quick and Dirty Tips or interact with Laura D. Adams on her Money Girl Facebook page. Alternatively, examine the advice conveyed via podcast, the Web, Facebook, and Twitter by clever Grammar Girl Mignon Fogarty.

YOUR TASK. Pick a Money Girl podcast that interests you. Listen to it or obtain a transcript on the website and study it for its structure. Is it direct or indirect? Informative or persuasive? How is it presented? What style does the speaker use? How useful is the information? At your instructor's request, write an e-mail about the podcast you analyzed. Alternatively, if your instructor allows, you could also send a very concise summary of the podcast by text message from your cell phone or by tweet to your instructor. Try limiting yourself to 140 characters to practice conciseness, although Twitter now allows longer messages.

5.10 Recording a Simple Audio Podcast (L.O. 3)

Communication Technology ▸ **Social Media** ▸ **Web**

Do you want to try your hand at producing a podcast? As you have seen, some businesses create short audio or video podcasts on focused, poignant subjects. The following process describes how to create a simple podcast:

Select software. In addition to free offline software (e.g., Audacity or GarageBand for Mac), Adobe Audition provides sophisticated features for a monthly subscription. However, check with your college to see whether it contracts with Adobe to make Creative Cloud available free or at a low cost to students and instructors.

Obtain hardware. For good sound quality, you may need a sophisticated microphone and other equipment. The recording room must be properly shielded against noise, echo, and other interference. Many universities and some libraries provide recording booths.

Organize the message. Make sure your broadcast has a beginning, middle, and end. Build in some redundancy. Previews, summaries, and transitions are important to help your audience follow the message.

Choose an extemporaneous or scripted delivery. Extemporaneous delivery means that you prepare, but you use only brief notes. It usually sounds more spontaneous and natural than reading from a script, but it can also lead to redundancy, repetition, and flubbed lines.

Prepare and practice. Practice before recording. Editing audio or video is difficult and time-consuming. Try to get your recording right, so that you won't have to edit much.

Publish your message. Once you post the MP3 podcast to your course website or blog, you can introduce it and request feedback from your audience.

YOUR TASK. Create a short podcast about a business-related subject you care about. Producing a simple podcast does not require sophisticated equipment. With free or inexpensive recording, editing, and publishing software such as Audacity or GarageBand, you can inform customers, mix your own music, or host interviews. Any digital recorder can be used to create a quality no-frills podcast if the material is scripted and well rehearsed.

5.11 Blogging: Learning From Master Bloggers (L.O. 4)

Communication Technology ▶ E-Mail ▶ Social Media ▶ Web

Visit the blogs of Seth Godin, Chris Brogan, Guy Kawasaki, Bill Marriott, and other acclaimed bloggers. See what tricks of the trade you can adopt and make work for you.

YOUR TASK. You may be asked to write a blog entry detailing your analysis of the professional blogs you have examined. Apply the best practices for professional business blogs outlined in this chapter. Remember to offer a catchy title that will attract browsers or, in this case, your peers in class and your instructor. Share helpful advice in easy-to-read numbered items and, if applicable, provide links to other relevant articles. To motivate readers to respond, ask questions at the end of your blog entry.

5.12 Composing a Personal Blog Entry (L.O. 4)

Communication Technology ▶ Social Media ▶ Web

Review the guidelines for professional blogging in this chapter. Find a recent social media-related study or survey, and target an audience of business professionals who may wish to know more about social networking. Search for studies conducted by respected organizations and businesses such as Pew Research Center, Robert Half International, Burson-Marsteller, ePolicy Institute, and U.S. government agencies, as applicable. As you plan and outline your post, follow the advice provided in this chapter. Although the goal is usually to offer advice, you could also weigh in with your opinion regarding a controversy. For example, do you agree with companies that forbid employees to use company computers for social networking? Do you agree that millennials are losing social skills because of excessive online connectivity?

YOUR TASK. Compose a one-page blog entry in MS Word and submit it in hard copy. Alternatively, post it to the discussion board on the class course-management platform, or e-mail it to your instructor, as appropriate. Because you will be using outside sources, be careful to paraphrase correctly. Visit Chapter 10 to review how to put ideas into your own words with integrity.

5.13 Reviewing Corporate Blogs (L.O. 4)

Communication Technology ▶ E-Mail ▶ Social Media ▶ Web

Here is your opportunity to view and evaluate a corporate blog. As we have seen, about 36 percent of Fortune 500 companies, or 181, are blogging, and researchers note a slight increase in corporations with active public blogs. The companies and their CEOs who do blog can impart valuable lessons.

YOUR TASK. Within your favorite browser, search for *CEO bloggers, index of corporate blogs, index of CEO blogs*, and similar keywords. You will likely end up at CEO Bloggers, on CEO.com, at CEOBlogger on CEOExpress, and at other sites that may list the top 10 or so most popular corporate blogs penned by a CEO. Select a corporate or CEO blog you find interesting, browse the posts, and read some of the content. Furthermore, note how many of the points the blog makes match the guidelines in this book. If your instructor directs, write a brief information memo or e-mail summarizing your observations about the business blog, its style, the subjects covered, and so forth.

5.14 Monitoring Twitter Feeds and Facebook Posts (L.O. 5)

> Communication Technology > Social Media > Web

Many large companies monitor Twitter and Facebook posts. They have discovered social media as a tool for averting public relations disasters. Domino's Pizza is an often-cited case. The company deftly responded with a coordinated social media campaign to counter the fallout from a damaging prank. Two employees had posted a disgusting YouTube video showing them engaging in several health code violations.[79] Despite initial damage, the company was able to regain its customers' trust.

IHOP, JetBlue, Nordstrom, Coca-Cola, and others are quick to apologize to irate customers and to correct problems that blow up on Twitter or in other social media. But businesses can also score points by putting Internet trolls in their place. When a snarky Twitter user unfairly accused Wendy's of freezing its beef despite the company's established practices, the fast-food chain casually shot back. Wendy's Twitter team earned praise from *Adweek* for its quick wit and for standing up to the provocateur, who later ditched his or her Twitter account amid embarrassment.[80] Experts predict that by 2020, 90 percent of companies will rely on social media for customer service.[81] Tech company Hewlett-Packard (HP) is ready. It provides customer support on social media in 95 countries and in seven languages. "Our research shows that 72 percent of customers expect a response within an hour," says Kriti Kapoor, global head of social media customer care. She believes that 70 percent of customers who receive a fast response are likely to advocate the HP brand.[82]

YOUR TASK. You are one of three social media interns working for Kriti Kapoor at HP. Your job is to comb through tweets and Facebook posts to find those that are both positive about and critical of your company and to inform your boss about any that could end up hurting HP's image. Deciding which post could cause trouble is difficult, given that even with tracking software, you may need to scan hundreds of posts every day. You know that if many users retweet, or redistribute the news, the problem may get out of hand. Create a Twitter account and search for posts about HP or any other company your instructor may assign. Make a list of three positive and three negative tweets. Recommend or draft responses to them. If you identify a trend, make a note of it and report it either in class or in writing as directed by your instructor.

5.15 Social Media: Quitting Cold Turkey? (L.O. 5)

> Communication Technology > Social Media > Web

Could you give up your electronic toys for 24 hours without withdrawal symptoms? How about quitting social media cold turkey for a week? Thirty days? Would you be able to survive unplugged from all media? Headlines decrying social media addiction litter the Internet. Self-declared social media junkies detail the lessons they learned after renouncing their gadgets for a "detox," "sabbatical," "purge," or "dramatic spree." Those who go offline describe feelings of emptiness, boredom, loneliness, depression, and anxiety. Some are baffled by their digital friends reacting to their abstinence with coercion, cajoling—even scorn![83]

In one study a class of 200 students at the University of Maryland, College Park, went media free for 24 hours and then blogged about the experience.[84] Some did sound like addicts going cold turkey: *In withdrawal. Frantically craving. Very anxious. Extremely antsy. Miserable. Jittery. Crazy.* One student lamented: *I clearly am addicted and the dependency is sickening.* In the absence of technology that anchors them to friends and family, students felt bored and isolated. One wrote: *I felt quite alone and secluded from my life. Although I go to a school with thousands of students, the fact that I was not able to communicate with anyone via technology was almost unbearable.*

The study reveals a paradigm shift in human interaction. Some users are viscerally wedded to electronic toys, so much so that technology has become an indispensable part of their lives. Electronically abstinent students stated that they spent more time on course work, took better notes, and were more focused. As a result, they said they learned more and became more productive. They also reported that they spent more time with loved ones and friends face-to-face. Life slowed down and the day seemed much longer to some.

YOUR TASK. Discuss in class, in a chat, or in an online post the following questions: Have you ever unplugged? What was that experience like? Could you give up your smartphone, iPod, TV, car radio, online magazines and newspapers, and computer (no texting, no Facebook, or IM) for a day or longer? What would you do instead? Is there any harm in not being able to unplug?

Prepositions and Conjunctions

Review Sections 1.18 and 1.19 in the Grammar Review section of the Grammar/Mechanics Handbook. Then select the correct form to complete each of the following statements. Record the appropriate G/M section and letter to illustrate the principle involved. When you finish, compare your responses with those provided at the bottom of the page. If your answers differ, study carefully the principles shown in parentheses.

___b_____ (1.18a)   **EXAMPLE**   a. When do you expect to graduate college?
b. When do you expect to graduate from college?

_____ 1. a. The new manager is more creative than the last.
b. The new manager is more creative then the last.

_____ 2. a. Don't you hate when your cell rings with marketing messages?
b. Don't you hate it when your cell rings with marketing messages?

_____ 3. a. If the company called you, than it must be looking at your résumé.
b. If the company called you, then it must be looking at your résumé.

_____ 4. a. Ethnocentrism is when you believe your culture is best.
b. Ethnocentrism involves the belief that your culture is best.

_____ 5. a. Business messages should be clear, correct, and written with conciseness.
b. Business messages should be clear, correct, and concise.

_____ 6. a. What type of computer monitor do you prefer?
b. What type computer monitor do you prefer?

_____ 7. a. Do you know where the meeting is at?
b. Do you know where the meeting is?

_____ 8. a. Did you send an application to the headquarters in Los Angeles or to the branch in San Diego?
b. Did you apply to the Los Angeles headquarters or the San Diego branch?

_____ 9. a. Shelby said she graduated high school last year.
b. Shelby said she graduated from high school last year.

_____ 10. a. She had a great interest, as well as a profound respect for, historical homes.
b. She had a great interest in, as well as a profound respect for, historical homes.

_____ 11. a. Volunteers should wear long pants, bring gloves, and sunscreen should be applied.
b. Volunteers should wear long pants, bring gloves, and apply sunscreen.

_____ 12. a. His PowerPoint presentation was short, as we hoped it would be.
b. His PowerPoint presentation was short, like we hoped it would be.

_____ 13. a. An ethics code is where a set of rules spells out appropriate behavior standards.
b. An ethics code is a set of rules spelling out appropriate behavior standards.

_____ 14. a. Please keep the paper near the printer.
b. Please keep the paper near to the printer.

_____ 15. a. A behavioral interview question is when the recruiter says, "Tell me about a time . . . ."
b. A behavioral interview question is one in which the recruiter says, "Tell me about a time . . . ."

1. a (1.19d) **2.** b (1.19c) **3.** b (1.19d) **4.** b (1.19d) **5.** b (1.19c) **6.** a (1.19a) **7.** b (1.18a) **8.** b (1.18c) **9.** b (1.18a) **10.** b (1.18e) **11.** b (1.19a)
12. a (1.19b) **13.** b (1.19c) **14.** a (1.18b) **15.** b (1.19c)

Editing Challenge 5

Every chapter provides an editing exercise to fine-tune your grammar and mechanics skills.

The following e-mail requires edits that address grammar, punctuation, conciseness, lead-ins, parallelism, listing techniques, and other writing issues. Study the guidelines in the Grammar/Mechanics Handbook (Appendix D), including the lists of Confusing Words and Frequently Misspelled Words.

YOUR TASK. Edit the following (a) by inserting corrections in your textbook or on a photocopy using the proofreading marks in Appendix C or (b) by downloading the message from **www.cengagebrain.com** and correcting at your computer.

To: Department Heads, Managers, and Supervisors
From: Garth Hawkins <garth.hawkins@xcelsolutions>
Subject: Submitting Appraisals of Performance by June 1

This is just a reminder to all of your to say that performance appraisals for all you employees must be submitted by June first. These appraisal are especially important and essential this year because of job changes, new technologys, and because of office reorganization.

To complete your performance appraisal in the most effective manner, you should follow the procedures described in our Employee Manual. Let me briefly make a review of those procedures;

- Be sure each and every employee has a performance plan with three or 4 main objective.
- For each objective make an assessment of the employee on a scale of 5 (consistently exceeds requirements) to 0 (does not meet requirements.
- You should identify three strengths that he brings to the job.
- Name three skills that he can improve. These should pertain to skills such as Time Management rather then to behaviors such as habitual lateness.
- You should meet with the employee to discuss the appraisal.
- Then be sure to obtain the employees signature on the form.

We look upon appraisals as a tool for helping each worker assess his performance. And enhance his output. Please submit and send each employees performance appraisal to my office by June first. If you would like to discuss this farther, please do not hesitate to call me.

Garth Hawkins, Director
Human Resources
garth.hawkins@xcelsolutions
Office: 805-433-5890
Cell: 439-220-3990

Should Employers Curb Social Media, E-Mail, and Other Internet Use?

Most employees today have Internet access and carry smartphones and tablets to work. Should they be able to use their own devices or work computers for social media posting, online shopping, private messages, and personal work, as well as to listen to music and play games?

But It's Harmless

Office workers have discovered that it is far easier to shop online than to race to malls and wait in line. To justify her online shopping at work, one employee, a recent graduate, said, "Instead of standing at the water cooler gossiping, I shop online." She went on to say, "I'm not sapping company resources by doing this."[85]

A recent Pew Internet survey revealed that more than a third of workers say they use social media on the job to "take a mental break from work," while 27 percent like to connect with friends and family; 42 percent deny that social media use is distracting, while 56 percent agree that it is distracting, with 30 percent agreeing strongly.

Some experts don't believe in monitoring employee social media use, especially if it happens off the clock: "The only time employers have a legal *duty* to monitor employee communications is when the employer has reason to believe that the employee is engaged in illegal conduct."[86] One HR professional believes that monitoring is essentially futile because "A slacking employee will not become a star performer just because you limit his or her social media access; he or she will just find another way to slack off."[87]

Companies Cracking Down

Most employers, however, see it differently. One survey reported that 28 percent of employers have fired workers for Internet use that wasn't work related such as online shopping and Facebook visits.[88] Research firm Gartner found that digital surveillance at work is increasing; 60 percent of organizations are planning to join social media networks expressly to monitor their employees.[89] UPS discovered an employee running a personal business from his office computer. Lockheed Martin fired an employee who disabled its entire company network for six hours because of an e-mail heralding a holiday event that the worker sent to 60,000 employees. Companies worry about not only lost productivity, but also litigation, security breaches, and other electronic disasters from accidental or intentional misuse of computer systems.

What's Reasonable?

Some companies (e.g., Volkswagen and Porsche) impose a zero tolerance policy, prohibiting any personal use of company equipment. Ameritech Corporation tells employees that computers and other company equipment are to be used only for business purposes. Companies such as Boeing, however, have issued guidelines allowing some personal use of e-mail and the Internet. The company strictly prohibits chain letters, obscenity, and political and religious solicitation.

CAREER APPLICATION. As an administrative assistant at Live IT, Inc., in Seattle, Washington, you have just received an e-mail from your boss asking for your opinion. Many employees have been accessing social media sites, shopping online, and using instant messaging. One person received four personal packages from UPS in one morning. Although reluctant to do so, management is considering installing monitoring software that not only tracks Internet use but also blocks social media, messaging, porn, hate, and game sites.

YOUR TASK

- In teams or as a class, discuss the problem of workplace abuse of social media, e-mail, instant messaging, online shopping, and other Internet browsing. Should full personal use be allowed?

- Are computers with Internet access similar to other equipment such as telephones?

- Should employees be allowed to access the Internet for personal use as long as they limit it to their own mobile devices?

- Should management be allowed to monitor all Internet use?

- Should employees be warned if Internet activities including e-mail are to be monitored?

- What reasons can you give to support an Internet crackdown by management?

- What reasons can you give to oppose a crackdown?

Decide whether you support or oppose the crackdown. Explain your views in an e-mail or a memo to your boss, Don Kawamoto, at *dkawamoto@live-it.net*

Positive and Neutral Messages

EHStock/Getty Images

Learning Outcomes

After studying this chapter, you should be able to do the following:

1 Name the channels through which typical positive and neutral messages travel in the digital era—e-mails, memos, and business letters—and explain how business letters should be formatted.

2 Compose direct messages that make requests, respond to inquiries online and offline, and deliver step-by-step instructions.

3 Prepare messages that make direct claims and voice complaints, including online posts.

4 Write adjustment messages that salvage customers' trust and promote further business.

5 Craft special messages that foster goodwill and convey kindness.

6-1 Routine Messages: E-Mails, Memos, and Letters

In the workplace most messages are positive or neutral and, therefore, direct. Positive messages are straightforward; they help workers conduct everyday business. Such routine messages include simple requests for information or action, replies to customers, and explanations to coworkers. Other types of routine messages are instructions, direct claims, and complaints.

E-mails, memos, and letters are the channels most frequently used. In addition, businesses today must listen and respond to social media. At the same time, in some industries, memos continue to be an important channel of communication within organizations, whereas letters are a vital paper-based external channel.

Chapter 5 discussed e-mails as well as memos and focused on their format and safe, professional use. This chapter will familiarize you with the direct writing plans for positive messages whether electronic or paper based. First, though, you will learn when writing a business letter is appropriate and how to format such a letter.

6-1a Understanding Business Letters

Despite the advent of e-mail, social networking, and other digital communication technologies, in certain situations letters are still the preferred channel of communication for delivering messages *outside* an organization. Such letters go to suppliers, government agencies, other businesses, and, most important, customers.

You may think that everybody is online, but at an Internet penetration rate in North America of 89 percent,[1] a portion of the U.S. population is still unplugged. In some regions of the world, Internet access may be spotty. Just as they are eager to connect with a majority of consumers online, businesses continue to give letters to customers a high priority. After all, letters, too, encourage product feedback, project a favorable image of the organization, promote future business, and signal greater formality.

Whether you send a business letter will depend on the situation and the preference of your organization. Business letters are necessary when the situation (a) demands a permanent record; (b) requires confidentiality; (c) calls for formality and sensitivity; and (d) favors a persuasive, well-considered presentation.

Providing a Permanent Record. Many business transactions require a permanent record. For example, when a company enters into an agreement with another company, business letters introduce the agreement and record decisions and points of understanding. Business letters deliver contracts, explain terms, exchange ideas, negotiate agreements, answer vendor questions, and maintain customer relations.

Safeguarding Confidentiality. Business letters are confidential. They are less likely than electronic media to be intercepted, misdirected, forwarded, retrieved, or otherwise inspected by unintended recipients. Today's business communicators know how risky it is to entrust confidential and sensitive information to digital channels.

Conveying Formality and Sensitivity. Business letters presented on company stationery communicate formality and importance not possible with e-mail. They look important, as illustrated in Figure 6.1. Letters carry a nonverbal message that the writer considered the message to be significant and values the recipient.

Delivering Persuasive, Well-Considered Messages. Business letters represent deliberate, thoughtful communication. Letters can persuade people to change their actions, adopt new beliefs, make donations, contribute their time, and try new products. Direct-mail letters remain a powerful tool to promote services and products, boost online and retail traffic, and enhance customer relations. You will learn more about writing persuasive and sales messages in Chapter 8.

6-1b Formatting Business Letters

A letter's appearance and format reflect the writer's carefulness and experience. A short letter bunched at the top of a sheet of paper, for example, looks as though it were prepared in a hurry or by an amateur.

For your letters to make a good impression, you need to select an appropriate format. The block style shown in Figure 6.1 is a popular format. In this style the parts of a letter—dateline, inside address, optional subject line, body, and so on—are set

LEARNING OUTCOME 1

Name the channels through which typical positive and neutral messages travel in the digital era—e-mails, memos, and business letters—and explain how business letters should be formatted.

OFFICE INSIDER

"The old-fashioned personal business letter—written on pristine, high-quality paper, sealed in an envelope, and delivered by post or by hand—remains the single most impressive written ambassador for your company. A letter has a dignity that cannot be equaled by electronic mail or faxed correspondence."[2]

The Emily Post Institute, "Effective Business Letters"

Figure 6.1 Formatting a Direct Response Letter—Block Style

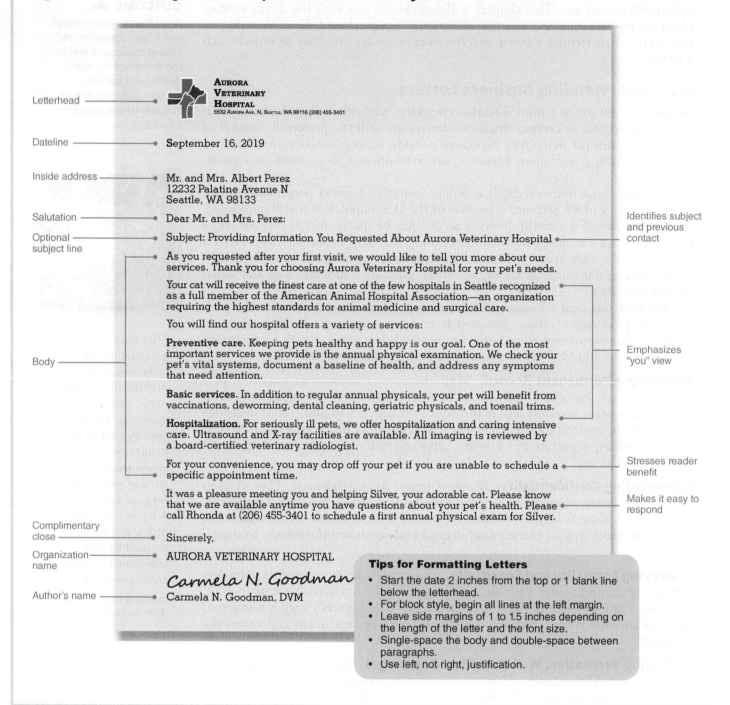

Letterhead

**AURORA
VETERINARY
HOSPITAL**
5532 Aurora Ave. N, Seattle, WA 98116 (206) 455-3401

Dateline

September 16, 2019

Inside address

Mr. and Mrs. Albert Perez
12232 Palatine Avenue N
Seattle, WA 98133

Salutation

Dear Mr. and Mrs. Perez:

Optional subject line

Subject: Providing Information You Requested About Aurora Veterinary Hospital

Identifies subject and previous contact

As you requested after your first visit, we would like to tell you more about our services. Thank you for choosing Aurora Veterinary Hospital for your pet's needs.

Your cat will receive the finest care at one of the few hospitals in Seattle recognized as a full member of the American Animal Hospital Association—an organization requiring the highest standards for animal medicine and surgical care.

You will find our hospital offers a variety of services:

Body

Preventive care. Keeping pets healthy and happy is our goal. One of the most important services we provide is the annual physical examination. We check your pet's vital systems, document a baseline of health, and address any symptoms that need attention.

Emphasizes "you" view

Basic services. In addition to regular annual physicals, your pet will benefit from vaccinations, deworming, dental cleaning, geriatric physicals, and toenail trims.

Hospitalization. For seriously ill pets, we offer hospitalization and caring intensive care. Ultrasound and X-ray facilities are available. All imaging is reviewed by a board-certified veterinary radiologist.

For your convenience, you may drop off your pet if you are unable to schedule a specific appointment time.

Stresses reader benefit

It was a pleasure meeting you and helping Silver, your adorable cat. Please know that we are available anytime you have questions about your pet's health. Please call Rhonda at (206) 455-3401 to schedule a first annual physical exam for Silver.

Makes it easy to respond

Complimentary close

Sincerely,

Organization name

AURORA VETERINARY HOSPITAL

Carmela N. Goodman

Author's name

Carmela N. Goodman, DVM

Tips for Formatting Letters

- Start the date 2 inches from the top or 1 blank line below the letterhead.
- For block style, begin all lines at the left margin.
- Leave side margins of 1 to 1.5 inches depending on the length of the letter and the font size.
- Single-space the body and double-space between paragraphs.
- Use left, not right, justification.

flush left on the page. The letter is arranged on the page so that it is framed by white space. Most letters have margins of 1 to 1.5 inches.

In preparing business letters, use ragged-right margins; that is, don't allow your computer to justify the right margin and make all lines end evenly. Unjustified margins improve readability, say experts, by providing visual stops and by making it easier to tell where the next line begins. Although book publishers use justified right margins, as you see on this page, your letters should be ragged right. Study Figure 6.1 for more tips on making your letters look professional. If you have questions about letter formats, see Appendix A.

6-2 Typical Request, Response, and Instruction Messages

LEARNING OUTCOME 2

Compose direct messages that make requests, respond to inquiries online and offline, and deliver step-by-step instructions.

In the workplace positive or neutral messages take the form of e-mails, memos, and letters. Brief positive or neutral messages are also delivered by instant messaging, texting, and social media. When you need information from a team member in another office, you might send an e-mail or use IM. If you must explain a new procedure for ordering supplies and rank-and-file workers do not have company e-mail, you would write a memo. When you welcome a new customer or respond to a customer letter asking about your products, you would prepare a letter.

Requests and replies may be transmitted in e-mails, memos, letters, or social media posts. You might, for example, receive an inquiry via Twitter or Facebook about an upcoming product launch. These kinds of routine messages follow a similar pattern, as shown in the following writing plan.

Direct Request Messages

OPENING: Ask the most important question, express a polite command, or state the main idea.

BODY: Explain the request logically and courteously. Ask other questions if necessary.

CLOSING: Request a specific action with an end date, if appropriate, and express appreciation.

6-2a Creating Request Messages

When you write messages that request information or action and you think your request will be received positively, *frontload* your message, which means start with the main idea. Readers tend to look at the opening and closing first. As a writer, then, you should capitalize on this tendency by putting the most significant statement first. The first sentence of a direct request is usually a question or a polite command.

Big Idea First. An e-mail inquiring about hotel accommodations, shown in Figure 6.2, begins immediately with the most important idea: Can the hotel provide meeting rooms and accommodations for 150 people? If several questions must be asked, you have two choices. You can ask the most important question first, as shown in Figure 6.2. An alternate opening begins with a summary statement, such as *Please answer the following questions about providing meeting rooms and accommodations for 150 people from April 18 through April 24*. If written as a letter, this direct request would most commonly be attached to an e-mail or faxed.

Providing Details. The body of a message that requests information or action provides necessary details. Remember that the quality of the information obtained from a request depends on the clarity of the inquiry. If you analyze your needs, organize your ideas, and frame your request logically, you are likely to receive a meaningful answer that doesn't require a follow-up message. Whenever possible, focus on benefits to the reader (*To ensure that you receive the exact sweater you want, send us your color choice*). To improve readability, itemize the appropriate information in bulleted or numbered lists. Notice that the questions in Figure 6.2 are bulleted, and they are parallel. That is, they use the same balanced construction.

Closing With Appreciation and an Action Request. In the closing tell the reader courteously what is to be done. If timing is important, set an end date to take action

Figure 6.2 Customer Direct Request E-Mail

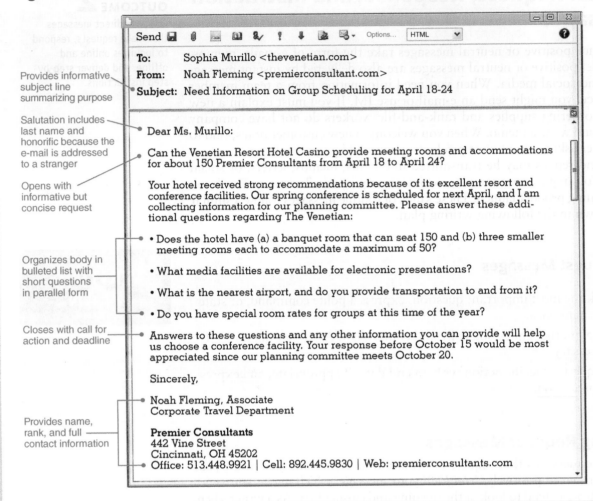

Provides informative subject line summarizing purpose

Salutation includes last name and honorific because the e-mail is addressed to a stranger

Opens with informative but concise request

Organizes body in bulleted list with short questions in parallel form

Closes with call for action and deadline

Provides name, rank, and full contact information

Send · Options... · HTML

To: Sophia Murillo <thevenetian.com>
From: Noah Fleming <premierconsultant.com>
Subject: Need Information on Group Scheduling for April 18-24

Dear Ms. Murillo:

Can the Venetian Resort Hotel Casino provide meeting rooms and accommodations for about 150 Premier Consultants from April 18 to April 24?

Your hotel received strong recommendations because of its excellent resort and conference facilities. Our spring conference is scheduled for next April, and I am collecting information for our planning committee. Please answer these additional questions regarding The Venetian:

• Does the hotel have (a) a banquet room that can seat 150 and (b) three smaller meeting rooms each to accommodate a maximum of 50?

• What media facilities are available for electronic presentations?

• What is the nearest airport, and do you provide transportation to and from it?

• Do you have special room rates for groups at this time of the year?

Answers to these questions and any other information you can provide will help us choose a conference facility. Your response before October 15 would be most appreciated since our planning committee meets October 20.

Sincerely,

Noah Fleming, Associate
Corporate Travel Department

Premier Consultants
442 Vine Street
Cincinnati, OH 45202
Office: 513.448.9921 | Cell: 892.445.9830 | Web: premierconsultants.com

---

and explain why. You can save the reader time by spelling out the action to be taken. Avoid overused endings such as *Thank you for your cooperation* (trite), *Thank you in advance for . . .* (trite and presumptuous), and *If you have any questions, do not hesitate to call me* (suggests that you didn't make yourself clear).

Showing appreciation is always appropriate, but try to do so in a fresh and efficient manner. For example, you could hook your thanks to the end date (*Thanks for returning the questionnaire before May 5, when we will begin tabulation*). You might connect your appreciation to a reader benefit (*We are grateful for the information you will provide because it will help us serve you better*). You could briefly describe how the information will help you (*I appreciate this information that will enable me to . . .*). When possible, make it easy for the reader to comply with your request (*Reply to this e-mail and provide your answers in the body of the message*).

6-2b Responding to Requests

Often, your messages will respond directly and favorably to requests for information or action. A customer wants information about a product. A supplier asks to arrange a meeting. An employee inquires about a procedure, or a manager requests your input on a marketing campaign. In complying with such requests, apply the same direct pattern you used in making requests, as shown in the following writing plan.

Response Messages

SUBJECT LINE: Summarize the main information from your reply. (A subject line is optional in letters.)

OPENING: Start directly by responding to the request with a summary statement.

BODY: Provide additional information and details in a readable format.

CLOSING: Add a concluding remark, summary, or offer of further assistance.

A customer reply letter that starts with an effective (optional) subject line, as shown in Figure 6.1, helps the reader recognize the topic immediately. The subject line refers in abbreviated form to previous correspondence and/or summarizes a message (*Subject: Providing Information You Requested About Aurora Veterinary Hospital*).

In the first sentence of a direct reply, deliver the information the reader wants. Avoid wordy, drawn-out openings (*I am responding to your e-mail of December 1, in which you request information about . . .*). More forceful and more efficient is an opener that answers the inquiry directly (*Here is the information you wanted about . . .*). When agreeing to a request for action, announce the good news promptly (*Yes, I will be happy to speak to your business communication class about . . .*).

OFFICE INSIDER

When answering several questions or providing considerable data, arrange the information logically and make it readable by using graphic devices such as lists, tables, headings, boldface, or italics. When customers or prospective customers inquire about products or services, your response should do more than merely supply helpful answers. Try to promote your organization and products, as Figure 6.1 does. Be sure to present the promotional material with attention to the "you" view and reader benefits (*Your cat will receive the finest care at one of the few hospitals in Seattle recognized as a full member of the American Animal Hospital Association*).

In concluding a response message, refer to enclosures if they are provided (*The attached list summarizes our recommendations. We wish you all the best in redesigning your social media presence.*). If further action is requested or required, help the reader with specifics as Figure 6.1 shows (*Please call Rhonda at (206) 455–3401 to schedule a first annual physical exam for Silver*). To prevent abruptness, include a pleasant closing remark that shows your willingness to help. Tailor your remarks to fit the message and the reader. Avoid signing off with clichés (*If I may be of further assistance, don't hesitate to . . .*). In an e-mail provide your full contact information to enable the reader to follow up, as the writer in Figure 6.2 does.

"When project requirements, business cases, IT strategies, supplier contracts and other documents are not clearly written, they are likely to be misinterpreted. The result is often additional work, with cost overruns, systems that don't meet user needs, legal disputes and other problems. Even a simple email requesting a 2:00 call can be misinterpreted if the time zone is not specified and callers are in different parts of the world."[3]

Bart Perkins, *managing partner at Leverage Partners, Inc.*

6-2c Reacting to Customer Comments Online

We live in an age when vocal individuals can start a firestorm of criticism online or become powerful brand ambassadors who champion certain products. Therefore, businesses must listen to social media comments about themselves and, if necessary, respond. You may wonder how companies know when to respond, and how. This invaluable knowledge is an evolving field and, some would say, a minefield that can cause disastrous missteps and missed opportunities.

However, social media marketing experts are developing guidelines to provide organizations with tools for strategic decision making in various situations. Businesses can't control the conversation without disabling fans' comments on their Facebook walls or blogs, but they can respond in a way that benefits customers, prevents the problem from snowballing, and shines a positive light on the organizations.

Embracing Customer Comments. Customer reviews online are opportunities for savvy businesses to improve their products or services and may serve as a free and efficient *crowdsourced* quality-control system. Retailers such as Walmart, Amazon, and L.L. Bean use powerful software to sift through billions of social media posts and product reviews. The data offer real-time feedback that may help clear up supply chain bottlenecks, expose product flaws, and improve operating instructions.[4] Companies had better listen: over 95 percent of consumers state they are influenced by what other people say about businesses on social media; 90 percent of purchase decisions are driven by recommendations of friends and family.[5]

However, businesses are far from perfect in delivering social customer service. The average response time for online complaints is 7 hours and 12 minutes. Most customers, however, expect a reply on Twitter within 60 minutes although 58 percent never receive an answer at all.[6] Nordstrom, Macy's, and Hollister top Facebook, Twitter, and Instagram in responsiveness. Nordstrom responds the fastest, in a blistering 17 seconds.[7]

Adopting Best Practices for Replying to Online Posts. Social media experts say that not every comment on the Web merits a response. They recommend responding to posts only when you can add value—for example, by correcting false information or providing customer service. Additional guidelines for professional responses to customer comments are summarized in Figure 6.3.

6-2d Composing Instruction Messages

Instruction messages describe how to complete a task. You may be asked to write instructions about how to access cloud-based information, order supplies, file a grievance, or hire new employees. Instructions must use plain English and be especially clear. Instructions are different from policies and official procedures, which establish rules of conduct to be followed within an organization. We are most concerned with creating messages that clearly explain how to complete a task. Like requests and responses, instruction messages follow a straightforward, direct approach.

Figure 6.3 Responding to Customers Online

As businesses increasingly interact with their customers and the public online, they are developing rules of engagement and best practices.

Be positive.
- Respond in a friendly, upbeat, yet professional tone.
- Correct mistakes politely.
- Do not argue, insult, or blame others.

Be honest.
- Own up to problems and mistakes.
- Tell customers when and how you will improve the situation.

Be timely.
- Respond to e-mail in less than 24 hours, as fast as possible on social media.

Be transparent.
- State your name and position with the business.
- Personalize and humanize your communication.

Be helpful.
- Point users to valuable information on your website or other approved websites.
- Follow up with users when new information is available.

Creating Step-by-Step Instructions. Before writing instructions for a process, be sure you understand the process completely. Practice doing it yourself. The following writing plan will get you started:

Instruction Messages

SUBJECT LINE: Summarize the content of the message.

OPENING: Expand the subject line by stating the main idea concisely in a full sentence.

BODY: List the steps in the order in which they are to be carried out. Arrange the items vertically with numbers. Begin each step with an action verb using the imperative (command) mood.

CLOSING: Request a specific action, summarize the message, or present a closing thought. If appropriate, include a deadline and a reason.

The most effective way to list directions is to use command language, which is called the *imperative mood*. Think recipes, owner manuals, and assembly instructions. The imperative mood differs from the *indicative mood* in that it requests an action, whereas the indicative mood describes a statement; both are shown here:

INDICATIVE MOOD	IMPERATIVE (COMMAND) MOOD
The contract should be sent immediately.	Send the contract immediately.
The first step involves downloading the app.	Download the app first.
A survey of employees is necessary to learn what options they prefer.	Survey employees to learn the options they prefer.

If you are asked to prepare a list of instructions that is not part of a message, include a title, such as How to *Access Cloud-Based Information*. Include an opening paragraph explaining why the instructions are needed.

Revising Message Delivering Instructions. Figure 6.4 shows the first draft of an interoffice memo written by Brian Belmont. His memo was meant to announce a new method for employees to follow in requesting equipment repairs. However, the tone was negative, the explanation of the problem rambled, and the new method was unclear. Finally, Brian's first memo was wordy and filled with clichés (*do not hesitate to call*). By explaining clearly and changing his tone, Brian was able to improve his memo.

Provide clear explanations. Brian realized that his original explanation of the new procedure was confusing. To clarify the instructions, he itemized and numbered the steps. Each step begins with an action verb in the imperative (command) mood (*Log in, Indicate, Select, Identify,* and *Print*). It is sometimes difficult to force all the steps in a list into this kind of command language. Brian struggled, but he finally found verbs that worked.

Why should you go to so much trouble to make lists and achieve parallelism? Because readers can comprehend what you have said much more quickly. Parallel language also makes you look professional and efficient.

Figure 6.4 Memo Delivering Instructions

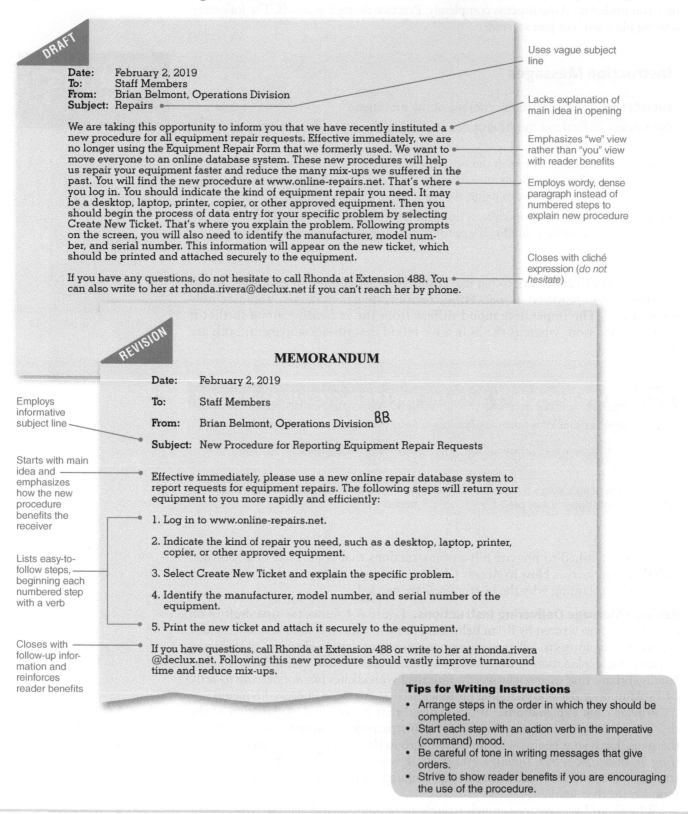

DRAFT

Date: February 2, 2019
To: Staff Members
From: Brian Belmont, Operations Division
Subject: Repairs

We are taking this opportunity to inform you that we have recently instituted a new procedure for all equipment repair requests. Effective immediately, we are no longer using the Equipment Repair Form that we formerly used. We want to move everyone to an online database system. These new procedures will help us repair your equipment faster and reduce the many mix-ups we suffered in the past. You will find the new procedure at www.online-repairs.net. That's where you log in. You should indicate the kind of equipment repair you need. It may be a desktop, laptop, printer, copier, or other approved equipment. Then you should begin the process of data entry for your specific problem by selecting Create New Ticket. That's where you explain the problem. Following prompts on the screen, you will also need to identify the manufacturer, model number, and serial number. This information will appear on the new ticket, which should be printed and attached securely to the equipment.

If you have any questions, do not hesitate to call Rhonda at Extension 488. You can also write to her at rhonda.rivera@declux.net if you can't reach her by phone.

Uses vague subject line

Lacks explanation of main idea in opening

Emphasizes "we" view rather than "you" view with reader benefits

Employs wordy, dense paragraph instead of numbered steps to explain new procedure

Closes with cliché expression (do not hesitate)

REVISION

MEMORANDUM

Date: February 2, 2019

To: Staff Members

From: Brian Belmont, Operations Division B.B.

Subject: New Procedure for Reporting Equipment Repair Requests

Effective immediately, please use a new online repair database system to report requests for equipment repairs. The following steps will return your equipment to you more rapidly and efficiently:

1. Log in to www.online-repairs.net.

2. Indicate the kind of repair you need, such as a desktop, laptop, printer, copier, or other approved equipment.

3. Select Create New Ticket and explain the specific problem.

4. Identify the manufacturer, model number, and serial number of the equipment.

5. Print the new ticket and attach it securely to the equipment.

If you have questions, call Rhonda at Extension 488 or write to her at rhonda.rivera@declux.net. Following this new procedure should vastly improve turnaround time and reduce mix-ups.

Employs informative subject line

Starts with main idea and emphasizes how the new procedure benefits the receiver

Lists easy-to-follow steps, beginning each numbered step with a verb

Closes with follow-up information and reinforces reader benefits

Tips for Writing Instructions
- Arrange steps in the order in which they should be completed.
- Start each step with an action verb in the imperative (command) mood.
- Be careful of tone in writing messages that give orders.
- Strive to show reader benefits if you are encouraging the use of the procedure.

Watch your tone. In the revision Brian improved the tone considerably. The frontloaded idea is introduced with a *please*, which softens an order. The subject line specifies the purpose of the memo. Instead of dwelling on past procedures and failures (*we are no longer using* and *many mix-ups in the past*), Brian revised his message to explain constructively how reporting should be handled.

When writing messages that deliver instructions, be careful of tone. Today's managers and team leaders seek employee participation and cooperation. These goals can't be achieved, though, if the writer sounds like a dictator. Avoid making accusations and fixing blame. Rather, explain changes, give reasons, and suggest benefits to the reader. Assume that employees want to contribute to the success of the organization and to their own achievement. Notice in the Figure 6.4 revision that Brian tells readers that they will save time and reduce mix-ups if they follow the new method.

6-3 Direct Claims and Complaints

In business, things can and do go wrong—promised shipments are late, warrantied goods fail, and service is disappointing. When consumers must lodge a complaint or when they need to identify or correct a wrong, the message is called a claim. Because straightforward *claims* are those to which you expect the receiver to agree readily, use a direct approach, as shown in the following writing plan.

Direct Claims

WRITING PLAN

OPENING: Describe clearly the desired action.

BODY: Explain the claim, tell why it is justified, and provide details describing the desired action.

CLOSING: End pleasantly with a goodwill statement, and include an end date and action request, if appropriate.

Increasingly, consumers resort to telephone calls, they e-mail their claims, or—as we have seen—they vent their peeves in online posts. Large companies can afford to employ social media specialists who monitor and respond to comments. However, small and midsized businesses often have few options other than Google Alerts and their own limited forays into social networking.

This is why in an age of digital communication, claims written as letters of complaint still play an important role even as they are being replaced by telephone calls, e-mails, and social media posts. Depending on the circumstances, letters more convincingly establish a record of what happened. Some business communicators opt for letters they can either attach to e-mail messages or fax. Regardless of the channel, straightforward claims use a direct approach. Claims that require a persuasive response are presented in Chapter 8.

6-3a Stating a Clear Claim in the Opening

When you, as a consumer, have a legitimate claim, you can expect a positive response from a company. Smart businesses want to hear from their customers. They know that retaining a customer is far less costly than recruiting a new customer.

Open your claim with a compliment, a point of agreement, a statement of the problem, a brief review of action you have taken to resolve the problem, or a clear statement of the action you want. You might expect a replacement, a refund, a new order, credit to your account, correction of a billing error, free repairs, or cancellation of an order. When the remedy is obvious, state it immediately (*Please correct an erroneous double charge of $59 to my credit card for Laplink migration software. I accidentally clicked the Submit button twice*).

When the remedy is less obvious, you might ask for a change in policy or procedure or simply for an explanation (*Because three of our employees with confirmed reservations were refused rooms September 16 in your hotel, please clarify your policy regarding reservations and late arrivals*).

6-3b Explaining and Supporting a Claim

In the body of a claim message, explain the problem and justify your request. Provide the necessary details so that the problem can be corrected without further correspondence. Avoid becoming angry or trying to fix blame. Bear in mind that the person reading your message is seldom responsible for the problem. Instead, state the facts logically, objectively, and unemotionally; let the reader decide on the causes.

If you choose to send a letter by postal mail, include copies of all pertinent documents such as invoices, sales slips, catalog descriptions, and repair records. Of course, those receipts and other documents can also be scanned and attached to an e-mail. If using paper mail, send copies and *not* your originals, which could be lost.

When service is involved, cite the names of individuals you spoke to and the dates of calls. Assume that a company honestly wants to satisfy its customers—because most do. When an alternative remedy exists, spell it out (*If you are unable to offer store credit, please apply the second amount of $59 to your Turbo Speed software and a Laplink USB cable that I would like to buy too*).

6-3c Concluding With an Action Request

End a claim message with a courteous statement that promotes goodwill and summarizes your action request. If appropriate, include an end date (*I hope you understand that mistakes in ordering online sometimes occur. Because I have enjoyed your prompt service in the past, I hope that you will be able to issue a refund or store credit by May 3*).

Finally, in making claims, act promptly. Delaying claims makes them appear less important. Delayed claims are also more difficult to verify. By taking the time to put your claim in writing, you indicate your seriousness. A written claim starts a record of the problem, should later action be necessary. Save a copy of your message, whether paper or electronic.

6-3d Completing the Message and Revising

When Jade Huggins received a statement showing a charge for a three-year service warranty that she did not purchase, she was furious. She called the store but failed to get satisfaction. She decided against voicing her complaint online because she wished for a quick resolution and doubted that the small business would notice her social media post. She chose to write an e-mail to the customer service address featured prominently on the MegaMedia website.

You can see the first draft of Jade's direct claim e-mail in Figure 6.5. This draft gave her a chance to vent her anger, but it accomplished little else. The tone was belligerent, and the writer assumed that the company intentionally mischarged her. Furthermore, Jade failed to tell the reader how to remedy the problem. The revision, also shown in Figure 6.5, tempered the tone, described the problem objectively, and provided facts and figures. Most important, it specified exactly what Jade wanted to be done.

6-3e Posting Complaints and Reviews Online

Social media experts advise that consumers exhaust all other options for complaints with the company before venting online.[10] Just as you probably wouldn't complain to the Better Business Bureau without giving a business at least one chance to respond, you shouldn't express dissatisfaction just to let off steam online. Although it may feel good temporarily to rant, most businesses want to please their customers and welcome an opportunity to right a wrong.

Figure 6.5 Direct E-Mail Claim

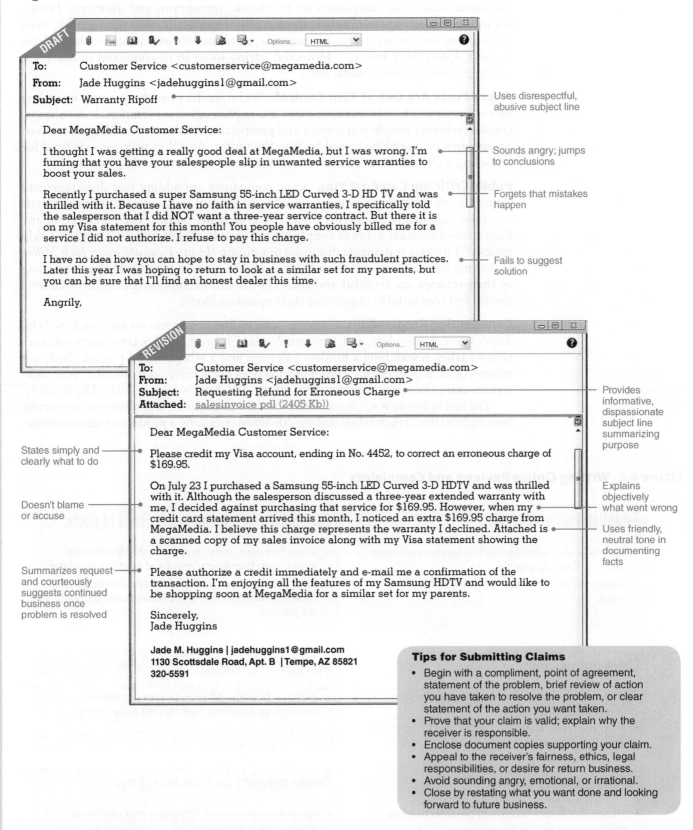

DRAFT

To: Customer Service <customerservice@megamedia.com>
From: Jade Huggins <jadehuggins1@gmail.com>
Subject: Warranty Ripoff *Uses disrespectful, abusive subject line*

Dear MegaMedia Customer Service:

I thought I was getting a really good deal at MegaMedia, but I was wrong. I'm fuming that you have your salespeople slip in unwanted service warranties to boost your sales. *Sounds angry; jumps to conclusions*

Recently I purchased a super Samsung 55-inch LED Curved 3-D HD TV and was thrilled with it. Because I have no faith in service warranties, I specifically told the salesperson that I did NOT want a three-year service contract. But there it is on my Visa statement for this month! You people have obviously billed me for a service I did not authorize. I refuse to pay this charge. *Forgets that mistakes happen*

I have no idea how you can hope to stay in business with such fraudulent practices. Later this year I was hoping to return to look at a similar set for my parents, but you can be sure that I'll find an honest dealer this time. *Fails to suggest solution*

Angrily,

REVISION

To: Customer Service <customerservice@megamedia.com>
From: Jade Huggins <jadehuggins1@gmail.com>
Subject: Requesting Refund for Erroneous Charge *Provides informative, dispassionate subject line summarizing purpose*
Attached: salesinvoice pdl (2405 Kb))

Dear MegaMedia Customer Service:

States simply and clearly what to do — Please credit my Visa account, ending in No. 4452, to correct an erroneous charge of $169.95.

Doesn't blame or accuse — On July 23 I purchased a Samsung 55-inch LED Curved 3-D HDTV and was thrilled with it. Although the salesperson discussed a three-year extended warranty with me, I decided against purchasing that service for $169.95. However, when my credit card statement arrived this month, I noticed an extra $169.95 charge from MegaMedia. I believe this charge represents the warranty I declined. Attached is a scanned copy of my sales invoice along with my Visa statement showing the charge. *Explains objectively what went wrong* *Uses friendly, neutral tone in documenting facts*

Summarizes request and courteously suggests continued business once problem is resolved — Please authorize a credit immediately and e-mail me a confirmation of the transaction. I'm enjoying all the features of my Samsung HDTV and would like to be shopping soon at MegaMedia for a similar set for my parents.

Sincerely,
Jade Huggins

Jade M. Huggins | jadehuggins1@gmail.com
1130 Scottsdale Road, Apt. B | Tempe, AZ 85821
320-5591

Tips for Submitting Claims

- Begin with a compliment, point of agreement, statement of the problem, brief review of action you have taken to resolve the problem, or clear statement of the action you want taken.
- Prove that your claim is valid; explain why the receiver is responsible.
- Enclose document copies supporting your claim.
- Appeal to the receiver's fairness, ethics, legal responsibilities, or desire for return business.
- Avoid sounding angry, emotional, or irrational.
- Close by restating what you want done and looking forward to future business.

Increasingly, businesses are beefing up their customer service with social media specialists who field complaints on Facebook, Instagram, and Twitter.[11] Travelers in particular expect nearly instant replies from airlines to their gripes, even minor ones, on Twitter. Delta, for example, employs 40 staff members who address roughly 3,000 daily tweets.[12] However, letting loose in ill-conceived online comments exposes you to multiple risks.

Angry Posts Are Out of Your Control. Social media posts have a way of ending up in the wrong hands, making vicious complainers seem irrational. As always, consider whether people you respect and prospective employers would approve. Even anonymous posts can be traced back to the writer. An Ohio waitress was fired for schooling a customer—a Facebook acquaintance—on how to tip properly.[13]

Public Criticism Can Cost You. Some companies are adding non-disparagement clauses in fine print to consumer contracts. As a result, businesses and professionals can take individuals to court for negative comments online. The Dallas company Prestigious Pets sued a Texas couple for thousands of dollars over a negative Yelp review.[14] Libelous statements disguised as opinion (*In my view attorney Jack Miller is stealing $4,000 from his clients*) can get consumers in trouble. However, as long as their reviews are truthful and their claims can be supported, online reviewers should feel comfortable expressing their opinions freely.

Commenting Responsibly. Shoppers read online comments on sites such as Yelp, TripAdvisor, Angie's List, and Amazon. A solid 74 percent of U.S. consumers read user reviews when researching a product category, and a whopping 88 percent check out reviews of local businesses.[15] Even if posting does not achieve your objective, your well-written complaint or review may help others. You have a responsibility. Use it wisely.

The tips in Figure 6.6, gleaned from *Consumer Reports*, will allow you to exercise your right to free speech while staying safe when critiquing a product or service online.

Figure 6.6 Writing Online Reviews and Complaints

Establish your credibility.

- Zero in on your objective and make your comment as concise as possible.
- Focus only on the facts and be able to support them.

Consider the reach and permanence of posts.

- Know that your review may be posted indefinitely, even if you change your mind and modify a post later.
- Be open; even anonymous comments can be tracked down. Privacy policies do not protect writers from subpoenas.

Check posting rules.

- Understand what's allowed by reading the terms and conditions on the site.
- Keep your complaint clean, polite, and to the point.

Accept offers to help.

- Reply if a business offers to help or discuss the problem; update your original post as necessary.

Provide balanced reviews.

- To be fair, offset criticism with positives to show that you are a legitimate consumer.
- Suggest improvements even in glowing reviews; all-out gushing is suspicious and not helpful.

Refuse payment for favorable critiques.

- Never accept payment to change your opinion or your account of the facts.
- Comply with requests for a review if you are a satisfied customer.

6-4 Adjustment Messages

LEARNING OUTCOME 4

Write adjustment messages that salvage customers' trust and promote further business.

Even the best-run and best-loved businesses occasionally receive claims or complaints from consumers. When a company receives a claim and decides to respond favorably, the message is called an *adjustment*. Most businesses make adjustments promptly: they replace merchandise, refund money, extend discounts, send coupons, and repair goods. In fact, social media have shortened the response time drastically to mere hours, sometimes minutes, not days.

Businesses make favorable adjustments to legitimate claims for two reasons. First, contract and tort law protects consumers for recovery of damages. If, for example, you find an insect in a package of frozen peas, the food processor of that package is bound by contractual law to replace it. If you suffer injury, the processor may be liable for damages. Second, most organizations genuinely want to satisfy their customers and retain their business.

In responding to customer claims, you must first decide whether to grant the claim. Unless the claim is obviously fraudulent or excessive, you will probably grant it. When you say *yes*, your adjustment message will be good news to the reader. Deliver that good news by using the direct strategy. When your response is *no*, the indirect pattern might be more appropriate. Chapter 7 discusses the indirect pattern for conveying negative news. You have three goals in adjustment messages:

- Rectifying the wrong, if one exists
- Regaining the confidence of the customer
- Promoting further business

A positive adjustment message follows the direct strategy described in the following writing plan.

Adjustment Messages

WRITING PLAN

SUBJECT LINE: Identify the previous correspondence and refer to the main topic.

OPENING: Grant the request or announce the adjustment immediately.

BODY: Provide details about how you are complying with the request. Try to regain the customer's confidence. Apologize, if appropriate, but don't admit negligence.

CLOSING: End positively with a forward-looking thought; express confidence about future business relations. Include a sales promotion, if appropriate. Avoid referring to unpleasantness.

6-4a Revealing Good News Up Front

Instead of beginning with a review of what went wrong, present the good news in an adjustment message immediately. When Leslie Bartolome-Williams responded to the claim of customer Daramis Services about a missing shipment, her first draft, shown at the top of Figure 6.7, was angry. No wonder. Daramis Services apparently had provided the wrong shipping address, and the goods were returned. Once Leslie and her company decided to send a second shipment and comply with the customer's claim, however, she had to give up the anger. Her goal was to regain the goodwill and the business of the customer. The improved version of her letter announces that a new shipment will arrive shortly.

If you decide to comply with a customer's claim, let the receiver know immediately. Don't begin your message with a negative statement (*We are very sorry that you are having trouble with your dishwasher*). This approach reminds the reader of

Figure 6.7 Customer Adjustment Letter

DRAFT

Dear Sir:

Your complaint letter dated May 17 has reached my desk. I assure you that we take all inquiries about missing shipments seriously. However, you failed to supply the correct address.

After receiving your complaint, our investigators looked into your problem shipment and determined that it was sent immediately after we received the order. According to the shipper's records, it was delivered to the warehouse address given on your stationery: 5261 Motor Avenue SW, Lakewood, WA 98433. Unfortunately, no one at that address would accept delivery, so the shipment was returned to us. I see from your current stationery that your company has a new address. With the proper address, we probably could have delivered this shipment.

Although we feel that it is entirely appropriate to charge you shipping and restocking fees, as is our standard practice on returned goods, in this instance we will waive those fees. We hope this second shipment finally catches up with you at your current address.

Sincerely,

Fails to reveal good news immediately and blames customer

Creates ugly tone with negative words and sarcasm

Sounds grudging and reluctant in granting claim

REVISION

 Allied Control Technology
4166 SE Stanley Avenue
Portland, OR 97206

Phone: (503) 777-3183
Fax: (503) 777-5167
Web: www.act-or.com

May 22, 2019

Mr. Elias Vysocky
Daramis Services
2749 Ninth Street SW
Lakewood, WA 98499

Dear Mr. Vysocky:

Subject: Your May 17 Letter About Your Purchase Order

Your second shipment of the Blu-ray players, video game consoles, and other electronics that you ordered April 18 is on its way and should arrive on May 29.

The first shipment of this order was delivered May 3 to 5261 Motor Avenue SW, Lakewood, WA 98433. When no one at that address would accept the shipment, it was returned to us. Now that I have your letter, I see that the order should have been sent to 2749 Ninth Street SW, Lakewood, WA 98499. When an order is undeliverable, we usually try to verify the shipping address by telephoning the customer. Somehow the return of this shipment was not caught by our normally painstaking shipping clerks. You can be sure that I will investigate shipping and return procedures with our clerks immediately to see if we can improve existing methods.

Your respect is important to us, Mr. Vysocky. Although our rock-bottom discount prices have enabled us to build a volume business, we don't want to be so large that we lose touch with valued customers like you. Over the years our customers' respect has made us successful, and we hope that the prompt delivery of this shipment will retain yours.

Sincerely,

Leslie Bartolome-Williams

Leslie Bartolome-Williams
Distribution Manager

c Steve Richman
   Shipping Department

Uses customer's name in salutation

Announces good news immediately

Regains confidence of customer by explaining what happened and by suggesting plans for improvement

Closes confidently with genuine appeal for customer's respect

the problem and may rekindle the heated emotions or unhappy feelings experienced when the claim was written. Instead, focus on the good news. The following openings for various messages illustrate how to *frontload* the good news:

> *You're right! We agree that the warranty on your KitchenPro Model SH68T55 dishwasher should be extended for six months.*

> *You will be receiving shortly a new iPhone to replace the one that shattered when dropped recently.*

> *Please take your portable Admiral microwave oven to Ajax Appliance Service, 530 Calafia Street, Glendale, where it will be repaired at no cost to you.*

In announcing that you will make an adjustment, do so without a grudging tone—even if you wonder whether the claim is legitimate. Once you decide to comply with the customer's request, do so happily. Avoid halfhearted or reluctant responses (*Although the Admiral microwave works well when used properly, we have decided to allow you to take yours to Ajax Appliance Service for repair at our expense*).

6-4b Explaining Compliance in the Message Body

In responding to claims, most organizations want to do more than just make the customer happy. They want to stand behind their products and services; they want to do what is right.

In the body of the message, explain how you are complying with the claim. In all but the most routine claims, also seek to regain the customer's trust. You might reasonably expect that a customer who has experienced difficulty with a product, with delivery, with billing, or with service has lost faith in your organization. Rebuilding that faith is important for future business.

How to rebuild lost confidence depends on the situation and the claim. If procedures need to be revised, explain what changes will be made. If a product has defective parts, tell how the product is being improved. If service is faulty, describe genuine efforts to improve it. Notice in Figure 6.7 that the writer promises to investigate shipping procedures to prevent future mishaps.

Sometimes the problem is not with the product but with the way consumers use it. In other instances customers misunderstand warranties or inadvertently cause delivery and billing mix-ups. Remember that rational and sincere explanations will do much to regain the confidence of unhappy customers. In your explanation avoid emphasizing negative words such as *trouble, regret, misunderstanding, fault, defective, error, inconvenience,* and *unfortunately.* Keep your message positive and upbeat.

6-4c Deciding Whether to Apologize

Whether to apologize is debatable. Attorneys generally discourage apologies fearing that they admit responsibility and can trigger lawsuits. However, both judges and juries tend to look on apologies favorably. Thirty-six U.S. states have passed *apology laws* that allow an expression of regret without fear that those statements would be used as a basis for liability in court.[17] Some public relations and business writing experts caution that apologies are counterproductive and merely remind the customer of unpleasantness. Some have even argued that public apologies stoke a firestorm on the Internet, whereas riding out the crisis may allow hate to fizzle.[18] If, however, apologizing seems natural, do so.

People like to hear apologies. It raises their self-esteem, shows the humility of the writer, and acts as a form of "psychological compensation."[19] Don't, however, fall back on the familiar phrase *I'm sorry for any inconvenience we may have caused.* It sounds mechanical and insincere. Instead, try something like this: *We understand the frustration our delay has caused you* or *We're sorry you didn't receive better service.* If you feel that an apology is appropriate, say you're sorry early and briefly.

You will learn more about delivering effective apologies in Chapter 7, when we discuss negative messages.

The primary focus of an adjustment message is on how you are complying with the request, how the problem occurred, and how you are working to prevent its recurrence.

6-4d Using Sensitive Language

The language of adjustment messages must be particularly sensitive, because customers are already upset. Here are some don'ts:

- Don't use negative words or phrases such as *trouble, regret, misunderstanding, fault, error, inconvenience*, and *you claim*.
- Don't blame customers—even when they may be at fault.
- Don't blame individuals or departments within your organization; it's unprofessional.
- Don't make unrealistic promises; you can't guarantee that the situation will never recur.

To regain the confidence of your reader, consider including resale information. Describe a product's features and any special applications that might appeal to the reader. Promote a new product if it seems appropriate.

6-4e Showing Confidence in the Closing

End positively by expressing confidence that the problem has been resolved and that continued business relations will result. You might mention the product in a favorable light, suggest a new product, express your appreciation for the customer's business, or anticipate future business. It's often appropriate to refer to the desire to be of service and to satisfy customers. Notice how the following closings illustrate a positive, confident tone.

> *Thanks for writing. Your satisfaction is important to us. We hope that this refund check convinces you that service to our customers is our No. 1 priority. Our goals are to earn your confidence and continue to justify that confidence with quality products and excellent service.*

> *You were most helpful in informing us of this situation and permitting us to correct it. We appreciate your thoughtfulness in writing to us.*

> *Your Dell Netbook will come in handy whether you are connecting with friends, surfing the Internet, listening to music, watching movies, or playing games. What's more, you can add a Total Defense Premium Security package and a deluxe carrying bag for a little more. Take a look at the enclosed booklet detailing the big savings for essential technology on a budget. We value your business and look forward to your future orders.*

Although the direct pattern works for many requests and replies, it obviously won't work for every situation. With more practice and experience, you will be able to alter the pattern and adapt your skills to other communication problems.

LEARNING OUTCOME 5

Craft special messages that foster goodwill and convey kindness.

6-5 Goodwill Messages

Many communicators are intimidated when they must write goodwill messages expressing thanks, recognition, and sympathy. Finding the right words to express feelings is often more difficult than writing ordinary business documents. That is why writers tend to procrastinate when it comes to goodwill messages. Sending a ready-made card or picking up the telephone is easier than writing a message.

Remember, though, that the personal sentiments of the sender are more expressive and more meaningful to readers than are printed cards or oral messages. Taking the time to write gives more importance to our well-wishing. Personal notes also provide a record that can be reread, savored, and treasured.

In expressing thanks, recognition, or sympathy, you should always do so promptly. These messages are easier to write while the situation is fresh in your mind. They also mean more to the recipient. A prompt thank-you note carries the hidden message that you care and that you consider the event to be important. Instead of learning writing plans for each goodwill message—whether thanks, congratulations, praise, or sympathy—we recommend that you concentrate on the five Ss. Goodwill messages should have the following characteristics:

- **Selfless.** Focus the message solely on the receiver, not the sender. Don't talk about yourself; avoid such comments as *I remember when I. . . .*
- **Specific.** Personalize the message by mentioning specific incidents or characteristics of the receiver. Telling a colleague *Great speech* is much less effective than *Great story about McDonald's marketing in Moscow.* Take care to verify names and other facts.
- **Sincere.** Let your words show genuine feelings. Rehearse in your mind how you would express the message to the receiver orally. Then transform that conversational language to your written message. Avoid pretentious, formal, or flowery language (*It gives me great pleasure to extend felicitations on the occasion of your firm's twentieth anniversary*).
- **Spontaneous.** Keep the message fresh and enthusiastic. Avoid canned phrases (*Congratulations on your promotion, Good luck in the future*). Strive for directness and naturalness, not creative brilliance.
- **Short.** Although goodwill messages can be as long as needed, try to accomplish your purpose in only a few sentences. Remembering an individual is most important. Such caring does not require documentation or wordiness. Individuals and business organizations often use special note cards or stationery for brief messages.

6-5a Saying Thank You

When someone has done you a favor or when an action merits praise, you need to extend thanks or show appreciation. Letters of appreciation may be written to customers for their orders, to hosts for their hospitality, to individuals for kindnesses performed, to employees for a job well done, and especially to customers who complain. After all, whether in social media posts, by e-mail, or on paper, complaints are actually providing you with free consulting reports from the field. Complainers who feel that their complaints were heard often become the greatest promoters of an organization.[21]

Because the receiver will be pleased to hear from you, you can open directly with the purpose of your message. The letter in Figure 6.8 thanks a speaker who addressed a group of marketing professionals. Although such thank-you notes can be short, this one is a little longer because the writer wants to lend importance to the receiver's efforts. Notice that every sentence relates to the receiver and offers enthusiastic praise. By using the receiver's name along with contractions and positive words, the writer makes the letter sound warm and conversational.

Written notes that show appreciation and express thanks are significant to their receivers. Although messages that express thanks may be as long as the letter shown in Figure 6.8, you generally write a short note on special notepaper or heavy card stock. The following messages provide models for expressing thanks for a gift, for a favor, for hospitality, and for employee contributions.

Expressing Thanks for a Gift. When expressing thanks, tell what the gift means to you. Use sincere, simple statements.

Figure 6.8 Thank-You Letter for a Favor

Global Marketing Association
10995 LeConte Avenue, Suite 203
Los Angeles, CA 90024
WWW.GLOBALMARKETINGASSOCIATION.COM

October 28, 2019

Ms. Rebecca Lennox
Vice President, Marketing
Toys "R" Us, Inc.
One Geoffrey Way
Wayne, NJ 07470-2030

Dear Ms. Lennox:

The Los Angeles chapter of the Global Marketing Association extends its ●————— *Opens directly with the purpose of message and thanks*
sincere thanks to you for a most entertaining and enlightening presentation on October 25.

Personalizes the message with specific references to the presentation ●—————
Your description of the expansion of Toys "R" Us into China mesmerized our members, particularly when you spoke about the demands of the Chinese culture. We were surprised to learn that some toy companies—notably Mattel— have struggled in China because parents seem to prefer burying their children in school books, and *play* is a four-letter word. As a result, your company has had to emphasize educational toys to win over the fiercest of strict tiger moms. You told us that affluent Chinese consumers prefer toy microscopes, building blocks, and other educational toys rather than Barbie dolls.

In addition to your good advice about entering the Chinese market, we enjoyed ●————— *Spotlights the reader's talents*
your sense of humor and jokes—as you must have recognized from the uproarious laughter. What a great routine you do on faulty translations!

Concludes with compliments and gratitude ●—————
We're grateful, Ms. Lennox, for the stimulating and instructive evening you provided for our marketing professionals.

Cordially,

Adam L. Russo

Adam L. Russo
Program Chair, GMA

ALR: mef

Thanks, Sheila, to you and the other members of the department for honoring me with the elegant Lalique crystal vase at the party celebrating my twentieth anniversary with the company. The height and shape of the vase are perfect to hold roses and other bouquets from my garden. Each time I fill it, I will remember your thoughtfulness in choosing this lovely gift for me.

Sending Thanks for a Favor. In showing appreciation for a favor, explain the importance of the gesture to you.

I sincerely appreciate your filling in for me last week when I was too ill to attend the planning committee meeting for the long-term cost-cutting initiative. Without your participation, much of my preparatory work would have been lost. Knowing that competent and generous individuals like you are part of our team, Gary, is a great comfort. Moreover, counting you as a friend is my very good fortune. I'm grateful to you.

Extending Thanks for Hospitality. When you have been a guest, send a note that compliments the fine food, charming surroundings, warm hospitality, excellent host, and good company.

> *Dan and I want you to know how much we enjoyed the dinner party for our department that you hosted Saturday evening. Your charming home and warm hospitality, along with the lovely dinner and sinfully delicious chocolate dessert, combined to create a truly memorable evening. Most of all, though, we appreciate your kindness in cultivating togetherness in our department. Thanks, Jennifer, for being such a special person.*

Recognizing Employees for Their Contributions. A letter that recognizes specific employee contributions makes the person feel appreciated even if it is not accompanied by a bonus check.

> *Mike, I am truly impressed by how competently you led your team through the complex SpaceOne project. Thanks to your leadership, team members stayed on target and met their objectives. Your adept meeting facilitation, use of an agenda, and quick turnaround of meeting minutes kept the project on track. However, most of all I appreciate the long hours you put in to hammer out the final report.*

6-5b Replying to Goodwill Messages

Should you respond when you receive a congratulatory note or a written pat on the back? By all means! These messages are attempts to connect personally; they are efforts to reach out, to form professional and/or personal bonds. Failing to respond to notes of congratulations and most other goodwill messages is like failing to say *You're welcome* when someone says *Thank you*. Responding to such messages is simply the right thing to do. Do not, though, minimize your achievements with comments that suggest you don't deserve the praise or that the sender is exaggerating your good qualities.

Answering a Congratulatory Note. In responding to congratulations, keep it short and simple.

> *Thanks for your kind words regarding my award, and thanks, too, for forwarding me the link to the article online. I truly appreciate your warm wishes.*

Responding to Praise. When acknowledging a pat-on-the-back note, use simple words in conveying your appreciation.

> *Your note about my work made me feel good. I'm grateful for your thoughtfulness.*

6-5c Expressing Sympathy and Writing Condolences

Most of us can bear misfortune and grief more easily when we know that others care. Sympathy notes, though, are probably more difficult to write than any other kind of message. Commercial sympathy cards make the task easier—but they are far less meaningful than personal notes. Grieving friends want to know what you think—not what Hallmark's card writers think.

Conveying Sympathy. To help you get started, you can always glance through cards expressing sympathy. They will supply ideas about the kinds of thoughts you might wish to convey in your own words. In writing a sympathy note, (a) refer to the death or misfortune sensitively, using words that show you understand what a crushing blow it is; (b) in the case of a death, praise the deceased in a personal way; (c) offer assistance without going into excessive detail; and (d) end on a reassuring, forward-looking note. Sympathy messages may be typed, although handwriting seems more personal. In either case, use quality paper stock or personal stationery.

Sending Condolences. Mention the loss tactfully, recognize good qualities of the deceased, assure the receiver of your concern, offer assistance, and conclude on a reassuring note.

We are deeply saddened, Vanessa, to learn of the death of your husband. Will's kind nature and friendly spirit endeared him to all who knew him. He will be missed. Although words seem empty in expressing our grief, we want you to know that your friends at QuadCom extend their profound sympathy to you. If we may help you or lighten your load in any way, you have but to call.

We know that the treasured memories of your many happy years together, along with the support of your family and many friends, will provide strength and comfort in the months ahead.

Like other goodwill messages, personal expressions of sympathy should be acknowledged by the recipient. If the grieving person is not able to respond, a family member or a friend can take on the task of expressing thanks.

6-5d Using E-Mail for Goodwill Messages

In expressing thanks or responding to goodwill messages, handwritten notes are most impressive and personal. However, if you frequently communicate with the receiver by e-mail and if you are sure your note will not get lost, then sending an e-mail goodwill message is acceptable, according to the Emily Post Institute and other experts.[22]

To express sympathy immediately after learning of a death or accident, you might precede a phone call or a written condolence message with an e-mail. E-mail is a fast and nonintrusive way to show your feelings. However, advises the Emily Post Institute, immediately follow with a handwritten note. Remember that e-mail messages are quickly gone and forgotten. Handwritten or printed messages remain and can be savored. Your thoughtfulness is more lasting if you take the time to prepare a handwritten or printed message on notepaper or personal stationery.

Summary of Learning Outcomes

1 **Name the channels through which typical positive and neutral messages travel in the digital era—e-mails, memos, and business letters—and explain how business letters should be formatted.**

- Most workplace messages are positive or neutral; therefore, adopt the direct strategy. Positive messages are routine; they help workers conduct everyday business.
- Write a letter when the situation (a) demands a permanent record, (b) requires confidentiality, (c) calls for formality, and (d) favors a well-considered presentation.
- Format your letters carefully. Select the block style, leave enough white space, and set margins of 1 to 1.5 inches. Don't justify the right margin.

2 **Compose direct messages that make requests, respond to inquiries online and offline, and deliver step-by-step instructions.**

- In requests, frontload key information because readers look at the opening and closing first. Provide details in the body, and close with appreciation and a call for action.
- When complying with requests, be direct. Sum up the main idea in the subject line; open directly; provide details in the body; and end with a brief conclusion, a summary, or an offer of help.
- Expect to listen to social media comments about your business; if necessary, respond to benefit customers, prevent escalation, and present your organization in a positive light.

- Be direct and divide instructions into steps in the correct order, arrange items vertically with numbers, and begin each step with an action verb in the imperative mood.

3 Prepare messages that make direct claims and voice complaints, including online posts.

- Open a claim by describing the desired action; explain and justify your claim. Conclude pleasantly with a goodwill statement, a date, and an action request, if appropriate.

- In making claims, act promptly. Delaying claims makes them appear less important and makes them difficult to verify.

- When posting complaints online, keep in mind that you can't prevent angry reactions to your posts, and that public criticism could cost you; use the power inherent in commenting publicly responsibly.

4 Write adjustment messages that salvage customers' trust and promote further business.

- Favorable responses to claims are called adjustments. In adjustment messages announce the good news up front, explain how you are complying with the request in the message body, and end positively.

- Understand that the three goals in adjustment messages are rectifying wrongs, regaining the confidence of the customer, and promoting further business.

- When appropriate, apologize early and briefly. Don't use negative language, don't blame customers or coworkers, and don't make unrealistic promises.

- Show confidence in the closing; end positively by expressing confidence that the problem has been resolved and that continued business relations will result.

5 Craft special messages that foster goodwill and convey kindness.

- Write goodwill messages to express thanks, recognition, and sympathy; dispatch goodwill notes promptly to show that the reader is important to you.

- Make your goodwill messages selfless, specific, sincere, spontaneous, and short.

- Answer congratulatory notes and respond to praise in simple words that convey your appreciation.

- When expressing condolences, mention the loss tactfully, recognize good qualities of the deceased, assure the receiver of your concern, offer assistance, and end on a reassuring note.

- Sending an e-mail goodwill message is acceptable; however, follow up with a handwritten note.

Chapter Review

1. Describe the types of positive and neutral messages and why they follow the direct approach. (L.O. 1)

2. When are letters still the best choice ahead of e-mail, social networking, and other electronic communication technologies? (L.O. 1)

3. What should you include in the closing of a request message? (L.O. 2)

4. Why do savvy businesses embrace customer comments online? (L.O. 2)

5. How should businesspeople respond to online posts? (L.O. 2)

6. How should instructions be written? Give an example. (L.O. 2)

7. What is a claim? When should it be straightforward? (L.O. 3)

8. What are a writer's three goals in composing an adjustment message? (L.O. 4)

9. What are five characteristics of goodwill messages? (L.O. 5)

10. What are four groups of people to whom business communicators might write letters of appreciation? (L.O. 5)

Critical Thinking

11. As you have seen in this chapter, some businesses seek to protect themselves from negative online reviews by slipping non-disparagement clauses into their terms of service. Then, in some cases, they sue the authors of negative posts. Lawmakers have taken note, and a new law might void such statements in small print.[23] Is trying to silence online reviewers fair, or are businesses within their rights to protect from illegitimate, damaging complaints? (L.O. 2, 3)

12. Why is it smart to remain cool when making a claim, and how should one go about it? (L.O. 3)

13. Why is it important to regain the trust of a customer in an adjustment message? How can it be done? (L.O. 4)

14. Why should you respond when you receive a congratulatory note or some other written pat on the back and how? (L.O. 5)

15. Is it fair for creditors to continue reporting late payments after the payments have been made? What do you think about experts' suggestion that people with credit blemishes write a sincere "goodwill" letter to creditors asking for compassion and requesting that the records of their late payments be erased? (L.O. 5)

Improving Subject Lines and Opening Sentences (L.O. 2)

YOUR TASK. Revise the following wordy openings for messages so that they are more direct and concise. Write an appropriate subject line and opening sentence for each one.

16. Hello! My name is Garrick Williams, and I just saw the terrific website for your organization, Green Living Spaces, which I understand is one of the world's leading health and wellness companies. I have a number of questions about selling your products and earning commissions. At your website I learned about the possibility of gaining affiliate status, which I am definitely interested in, but I still have many questions not answered at your site.

    Subject line:

    Opening sentence:

17. This is to inform you that your letter of April 4 has been circulated to me, as I am in charge of such requests. After your inquiry, I looked into the matter of supplying your firm with suffocation warning bags. Yes, we do carry these bags in various sizes. They alert customers to potential child hazards. Due to the fact that these bags are required by many government agencies, we keep them constantly in stock. They are compliant with FDA and USDA regulations. On each bag is a message that is printed in English, Spanish, and French. You will find that items slip easily into these poly bags that are open-ended. According to my records, they are available for immediate shipment.

    Subject line:

    Opening sentence:

18. I have received your message of January 5 asking whether or not our company has an employee recognition program. You inquired about whether we had such a program and whether we found it effective. I can answer in the affirmative to both queries! We do indeed have a recognition program because we have learned that small surprises and tokens of appreciation spread throughout the year help employees feel valued all year long. You asked if we would be willing to give you advice on starting such a program. We feel so strongly about our program that we would be happy to share our system, which is effective in rewarding behavior that we want to see repeated. Our program provides rewards that are simple, immediate, and powerfully reinforcing.

    Subject line:

    Opening sentence:

19. Please allow me to introduce myself. I am Marquis Jones, and I am assistant to the director of Employee Relations at United Anesthesia Associates. We place nurse anesthetists in hospitals. Each year we try to recognize outstanding staff members during Customer Service Week. I understand you provide an Idea Guide and that you sell special recognition gifts. I have a number of questions about them.

    Subject line:

    Opening sentence:

20. Your complaint message about our Mesa/Boogie BQ6 Russian matched pair guitar amplifier tubes that were broken in transit to you has been directed to me for response. Thank you for telling us immediately about this mishap with your Order No. 6090. We also thank you for your thoughtfulness in noting the damage carefully on the express receipt. That information is very helpful. We are sending a replacement shipment of your entire order by prepaid express and expect that it will arrive by February 20 to replace your stock of guitar amp tubes.

    Subject line:

    Opening sentence:

Writing Instructions (L.O. 2)

YOUR TASK. Revise each of the following wordy, dense paragraphs into a set of concise instructions. Include a short introductory sentence.

21. A number of employees have asked about how to make two-sided copies on our copy machine. Here's what to do. The copy for side 1 of the original goes face down on the document glass. Then the document cover should be closed. Next you should select the quantity that you require. To copy side 1, you should then press Start. Now you remove the first original and place the second original face down on the document glass. The document cover should be closed. Now you remove side 1 copy from the output tray. It should be inserted face down into the paper bypass tray. Then select the alternate paper tray and press Start.

22. Many young people today complain that they find it difficult to obtain and keep good credit. Here are five suggestions that will help you obtain credit and maintain a good credit score. One thing I like to suggest first is getting a gas store card. These cards are easier to get than regular credit cards. What's great about them is that you can establish a credit history by making small payments in full and on time. To maintain good credit, you should always pay your bills on time. Delinquencies are terrible. They create the biggest negative effect on a credit score. If you already have credit cards, your balance should be paid down. If you can't afford to do that, you might take a loan from a family member or friend. If you have unused credit card accounts, don't close them. I know it sounds as if you should, but actually, canceling a card can lower your score. Don't do it! Finally, never max out your credit cards. A good rule of thumb to follow is to keep your balance below 30 percent of your credit limit.

6.1 Radical Rewrite: Information Request Letter? Workstation Security (L.O. 2)

The following letter requests information, but its disorderly and illogical presentation makes the reader work too hard to comprehend what is being requested. Based on what you have learned in this chapter, what needs to be done to rewrite this poor request?

YOUR TASK. Analyze the letter and list its weaknesses. Then list the steps in the writing plan for a direct request. If your instructor directs, revise the letter following that plan.

Current date

Mr. Kyle Gregory, Sales Manager
Micro Supplies and Software
830 North Meridian Street
Indianapolis, IN 46205

Dear Sir:

Our insurance rates will be increased in the near future due to the fact that we don't have security devices on our computer equipment. Local suppliers were considered, but at this point in time none had exactly what we wanted. That's why I am writing to see whether or not you can provide information and recommendations regarding equipment to prevent the possible theft of office computers and printers. In view of the fact that our insurance carrier has set a deadline of April 1, we need fast action.

Our office now has 18 computer workstations along with twelve printers. We need a device that can be used to secure separate computer components to desks or counters. Would you please recommend a device that can secure a workstation consisting of a computer, monitor, and keyboard. We wonder if professionals are needed to install your security devices and to remove them. We are a small company, and we don't have a staff of maintenance people.

One problem is whether the devices can be easily removed when we need to move equipment around. We are, of course, very interested in the price of each device. What about quantity discounts, if you offer them.

Until such time as we hear from you, thank you in advance for your attention to this matter.

Sincerely,

List at least five weaknesses.

Outline a Writing Plan for a Direct Request

- **Opening**:
- **Body**:
- **Closing**:

6.2 Radical Rewrite: Instruction E-Mail—Tips for Avoiding Hackers (L.O. 2)

The following wordy and poorly expressed e-mail from a CEO discusses a growing problem for organizations: how to avoid the loss of valuable company data to hackers.

YOUR TASK. Study the e-mail, list its weaknesses, and then rewrite it in the form of an instruction message. Is it better to use bullets or numbers for an internal list?

To:	Staff Members
From:	G. B. Goldman <gbgoldman@firstfederalsavings.com>
Subject:	Hackers!

Staff Members:

This is to inform you that, like other banks, we are afraid of hackers. We fear that employees will expose valuable information to hackers without realizing what they are doing. Because of our fear, we have consulted cybersecurity experts, and they gave us much good advice with new procedures to be followed. Here are the procedures suggested by experts:

1. We don't want you to leave out-of-office messages. These voice mail or e-mails might explain when you will be away. Such messages are a red flag to hackers telling them that your computer is vacant and not being monitored.

2. Because smartphones can be lost or stolen, don't snap photos of company documents. Phones may be lost or stolen, and our data might be compromised.

3. Although small memory devices (thumb drives) are handy and easy to use, you may be inclined to store company files or information on these drives. Don't do it. They can easily be lost, thus exposing our company information.

4. Using work e-mail addresses for social media is another problem area. When you post details about your job, hackers can figure out an organization's best target.

5. Phishing links are the worst problem. Any request for password information or any requests to click links should be viewed with suspicion. Never click them. Even messages that seem to be from high-level officials or the human resources department within our own company can be sophisticated, realistic fakes. Examples include a request to click a link to receive a package or to download a form from within the company.

We want to let you all know that within the next two months, we plan to begin implementing a program that will educate and train employees with regard to what to avoid. The program will include fake phishing messages. The program will be explained and you will learn more from your managers in training workshops that are scheduled to begin September 1.

G. B. Goldman, CEO First Federal Savings and Loan | gbgoldman@firstfederalsaving.com | 678–405–3302

List at least five weaknesses.

6.3 Radical Rewrite: Adjustment Letter—Sagging Canvas Needs Restretching (L.O. 4)

When a company received an expensive office painting with sags in the canvas, it complained. The seller, Central Park Gallery, responded with the following adjustment letter. How can it be improved?

YOUR TASK. Analyze the letter. List its weaknesses. If your instructor directs, revise the letter.

Current date

Ms. Sharon Nickels
2459 Drew Street
Clearwater, FL 33765

Dear Ms. Nickels:

Your letter has been referred to me for reply. You claim that the painting recently sent by Central Park Gallery arrived with sags in the canvas and that you are unwilling to hang it in your company's executive offices.

I have examined your complaint carefully, and, frankly, I find it difficult to believe because we are so careful about shipping, but if what you say is true, I suspect that the shipper may be the source of your problem. We give explicit instructions to our shippers that large paintings must be shipped standing up, not lying down. We also wrap every painting in two layers of convoluted foam and one layer of Perf-Pack foam, which we think should be sufficient to withstand any bumps and scrapes that negligent shipping may cause. We will certainly look into this.

Although it is against our policy, we will in this instance allow you to take this painting to a local framing shop for restretching. We are proud that we can offer fine works of original art at incredibly low prices, and you can be sure that we do not send out sagging canvases.

Sincerely,

List at least five weaknesses.

6.4 Responding to Online Posts (L.O. 2, 3)

> Social Media > Web

YOUR TASK. Decide whether to respond to the following online posts.[24] If you believe you should respond, compose a concise Facebook reply following the guidelines in this chapter. Your instructor may also direct that you rewrite some of the posts themselves, if necessary.

a. Dani posted this to the Box and Barrel Facebook site: *So sad!! Ran to my store to pick up Pumpkin Yippee Pie mix and it's all sold out. :(And all sold out online also! Bummer. I knew I should've bought more! LOL)....*

b. Carrie posted this comment on the Zappos Facebook site: *I ordered a few things on the 20th and opted for next day shipping...but UPS says expected delivery date is the 30th! -:-(*

c. Steve wrote the following to upscale men's clothing purveyor Brooks Brothers: *I first began shopping at Brooks Brothers about six years ago. I had read a book on menswear called "Style" by Russell Smith. He made mention to brass collar stays. I could not find them in Canada. I wandered into a Brooks Brothers store in Michigan and asked, "You don't sell brass collar stays do you?" The salesman said, "Of course." I bought collar stays, shirts and pajamas that day. A devoted customer I became. You can imagine how happy I am that Brooks Brothers has come to Canada. Bienvenue! Welcome!*

d. Allison posted this message on Geico's Facebook page: *I just wanted to thank Geico for all your support on a claim I filed. The service was excellent at one of your body repair shops and also, your customer service is top notch: calls, emails, and not to mention the site which gives you all details possible like pictures, status of the claim, easy contact us section, upload of files. GREAT WEBSITE and SERVICE. Geico has me in GOOD HANDS, not Allstate :-)*

e. Mikaela posted this request for information on the Facebook page of her favorite resort hotel, Monte Carlo Resort & Casino in Las Vegas: *Will the pool still be opened this weekend?*

6.5 Direct Request: Seeking a Social Media Specialist (L.O. 2)

> E-Mail > Social Media > Web

As the director of corporate communication for HomeCenter, a large home supply store, you are charged with looking into the possible hiring of a social media specialist. You know that other companies have both profited from and been hurt by fast-moving viral news. Social media experts, companies hope, can monitor cyberspace and be ready to respond to both negative and positive messages. They can help build a company's brand and promote its online reputation. They can also develop company guidelines for employee use and encourage staffers to spread the good word about the organization.

To learn more about social media jobs, you decide to go to Doug Goodwin, who was recommended as a social media consultant by your CEO John Brauburger. You understand that Mr. Goodwin has agreed to provide information and will be paid by HomeCenter. The CEO wants you to explore the possibilities. You decide that this is not a matter that can be handled quickly by a phone call. You want to get answers in writing.

Many issues concern you. For one thing, you are worried about the hiring process. You are not sure about a reasonable salary for a social media expert. You don't know where to place that person within your organizational structure. Would the media expert operate out of corporate communications, marketing, customer service, or exactly where? Another thing that disturbs you is how to judge a candidate. What background would you require? How will you identify the best candidate? And what about salary? Should HomeCenter pay a full-time salary for doing what most people consider to be fun?[25]

YOUR TASK. Compose an e-mail inquiry to *doug.goodwin@mediaresources.com.* Explain your situation and list specific questions. Mr. Goodwin is not an employment source; he is a consultant who charges for his information and advice. Make your questions clear and concise. You realize that Mr. Goodwin would probably like to talk on the phone or visit you, but make clear that you want a written response, so that you can have a record of this information to share when you report to the CEO.

6.6 Direct Request: Puppies, Philanthropy, and PR (L.O. 2)

As an assistant in the Community Involvement Program of your corporation, you have been given an unusual task. Your boss wants to expand the company's philanthropic and community relations mission and especially employee volunteerism. She heard about Southwestern Guide Dogs, a program in which volunteers raise puppies for 14 to 18 months for guide dog training. She thinks this would be an excellent outreach program for the company's employees. They could give back to the community in their role as puppy raisers. To pursue the idea, she asks you to request information about the program and ask whether a company could sponsor a program encouraging employees to act as volunteers. She hasn't thought it through very carefully and relies on you to raise logical questions, especially about who covers the cost of raising puppies.

YOUR TASK. Write a direct request letter to Clea Zayas, Southwestern Guide Dogs, 500 Caja Del Rio Road, Santa Fe, NM 87507. Include an end date and a reason.

6.7 Direct Request: Planning a Winter Retreat in Vail, Colorado (L.O. 2)

> E-Mail   >   Web

Your employer, Pointer Media Group of Columbus, Ohio, has had an excellent year, and the CEO, Jeremy Pointer, would like to reward the troops for their hard work with a rustic yet plush winter retreat. The CEO wants his company to host a four-day combination conference/retreat/vacation for his 55 marketing and media professionals with their spouses or significant others at some spectacular winter resort.

One of the choices is Vail, Colorado, a famous ski resort town with steep slopes and dramatic mountain views. As you investigate the options in Vail, you are captivated by the Four Seasons Resort and Residences Vail, a five-star property with an outdoor pool, indoor and outdoor hot tubs, ski-in/ski-out access, a ski concierge, two acclaimed gourmet restaurants, and an amply equipped gym and fitness center. Other amenities include an on-site spa with massage and treatment rooms, a sauna, and facial and body treatments. Bathrooms feature separate bathtubs and showers, double sinks, and bathrobes. For business travelers, the hotel offers complimentary wired high-speed Internet access, complimentary wireless Internet access, and multiline phones as well as the use of two desktop computers.

The website of the Four Seasons Resort and Residences Vail is not very explicit on the subject of business and event facilities, so you decide to jot down a few key questions. You estimate that your company will require about 50 rooms. You will also need two conference rooms (to accommodate 25 participants or more) for one and a half days. You want to know about room rates, conference facilities, A/V equipment in the conference rooms, Internet access, and entertainment options for families. You have two periods that would be possible: December 16–20 or January 13–17. You realize that both are peak times, but you wonder whether you can get a discounted group rate. You are interested in entertainment in Vail, and in tours to the nearby national parks. Eagle County Airport is 36 miles away, and you would like to know whether the hotel operates a shuttle. Also, one evening the CEO will want to host a banquet for about 85 people. Mr. Pointer wants a report from you by September 13.

YOUR TASK. Write a well-organized direct request letter or e-mail to Kiersten Dunn, Sales Manager, Four Seasons Resort and Residences Vail, One Vail Road, Vail, Co 81657.

6.8 Direct Response: Chesapeake Sail & Canvas Receives a Poor Customer Rating on Yelp (L.O. 2)

> E-Mail   >   Social Media   >   Web

Yelp, the social network for consumer reviews and local searches, logs approximately 89 million monthly unique visitors and has listed 121 million reviews at this time.[26] Many users rely on what they hope to be real reviews by real people, as the company claims. They wish to make more informed buying decisions based on Yelp reviews. Barry Gregg, owner of Chesapeake Sail & Canvas in Annapolis, Maryland, watches his Yelp reviews. Currently, he has six reviews, all five stars. Imagine his surprise when he recently received only one star from Angela K.:

> *Chesapeake Sail & Canvas does good work, but it seems to have become a casualty of its own success. The company is unresponsive when you call and e-mail. I will take my business elsewhere because after 3 weeks, I still haven't heard about that estimate for my marine canvas. I had left a voice mail message and sent an e-mail. No response. I called again and was received as if my request were outlandish when I expressed the hope of getting a quote that same week. Since then, silence. Not cool. And I am a repeat customer. . . . People, fortunately there are other businesses out there!*

The writer says she is a returning customer. Barry sighs because he is really shorthanded. His administrative assistant has been sick a lot lately, and inquiries have gone unanswered; communication has been poor. Business is booming, and he does not have enough qualified installers; as a result, weeks elapse before his small crew gets around to completing a job. Barry searches his files and finds Angela's job completed four years ago. Harbor had made custom cockpit cushions, a dodger, a sail cover, and smaller canvas items for Angela's 30-foot Catalina sailboat, a $5,000 job.

YOUR TASK. Consider Barry's options. Should he respond to the one negative review? What could be the consequences of ignoring it? If you believe that Barry should respond, discuss first how. He has the disgruntled customer's e-mail, phone number, and street address. He could post a reply on Yelp to provide a commentary to the bad review. If your instructor directs, plan a strategy for Barry and respond to the customer in the way you believe is best for Barry and his business.

6.9 Direct Response: Interviewing at Marmont & Associates (L.O. 2)

> E-Mail

Carl Mekeel, founder and CEO of Marmont & Associates, is a busy architect. As he expands his business, he is looking for ecologically conscious designers who can develop sustainable architecture that minimizes the negative environmental impact of buildings. His company has an open position for an environmental architect/designer. Three candidates were scheduled to be interviewed on March 14. However, Mr. Mekeel now finds he must be in Dallas during that week to consult with the builders of a 112-unit planned golf course community. He asks you, his office manager, to call the candidates, reschedule for March 28 or March 29, and prepare a memo with the new times as well as a brief summary of the candidates' backgrounds.

Fortunately, you were able to reschedule all three candidates. Scott Hogarth will come on March 29 at 11 a.m. Mr. Hogarth specializes in passive solar energy and has two years of experience with SolarPlus, Inc. He has a bachelor's degree from the University of Southern California. Christine Lindt has a master's degree from Boise State University and worked for five years as an architect planner for Boise Builders, with expertise in sustainable building materials. She will come on March 28 at 2 p.m. Without a degree but with ten years of building experience, Jerry Rodriguez is scheduled for March 28 at 10 a.m. He is the owner of Green Building Consulting and has experience with energy efficiency, sustainable materials, domes, and earth-friendly design. You are wondering whether Mr. Mekeel forgot to include Phil Barker, his partner, who usually helps make personnel selections.

YOUR TASK. Prepare a memo (or e-mail if your instructor directs) to Mr. Mekeel with all the information he needs in the most readable format. Consider using a three-column table format for the candidate information.

6.10 Instruction Message: E-Mail Inviting Down-Editing Needs Revision (L.O. 2)

> **E-Mail**

The following message, which originated in an international technology company, was intended to inform new team members about their upcoming move to a different office location. But its stream-of-consciousness thinking and jumbled connections leave the receiver confused as to what is expected and how to respond.

YOUR TASK. Study the message. Then revise it with (a) a clear introduction that states the purpose of the message, (b) a body with properly announced lists, and (c) a conclusion that includes a call to action and a deadline. Improve the organization by chunking similar material together. What questions must be answered? What tasks should be performed? Should this message use more of a "you" view? In addition, make it easy for receivers to respond. Receivers will be down-editing—that is, returning the message with their responses (in another color) interspersed among the listed items.

Hello everyone,

We'll be moving new team members into a new location next week so there are things we need you to do to be ready for the move. For one thing, let me know which Friday you want your personal items moved. The possibilities are November 8 and 15. Also, if you have an ergonomic desk or chair you want moved, let me know. By the way, we'll be sending boxes, labels, tape and a move map four or five days before the move date you choose, so let me know if this timeframe allows you enough time to pack your belongings. And if you are bringing office equipment from your current team to the new team, let me know. Remember that company policy allows you to take a workstation/laptop from your current team to the new workstation. So check with your admin and let me know what office equipment you will be bringing. Incidentally, your new workstation will have a monitor and peripherals.

You'll need to do some things before the movers arrive. Make sure you put foam pads around your valuable, fragile items and then box them up. This includes things such as IT plaques, glass, or anniversary glass sculptures. If the glass things break, replacing them is expensive and the cost center is responsible for replacement. You may want to move them yourself and not have the movers do it.

Another thing—make sure you pack up the contents of all gray filing cabinets because movers do not move those. Also, write on the move map the number and delivery location of whiteboards, corkboards, and rolling cabinets. Most important, make sure you add a name label to all your belongings, such as desk phones, docking stations, peripherals, monitors, tables, ergonomic desks, ergonomic chairs, etc. If you see old move labels on recycled boxes, remove them or cross them out.

Get back to me ASAP. And by the way, the movers will arrive between 4 p.m. and midnight on the move date.

Thank you

6.11 Instruction Message: How to Copy Pictures and Text From PDF Documents (L.O. 2)

As a summer intern in the Marketing Department at Jovanovic Laboratory Supply, Inc., in Bozeman, Montana, you have been working on the company's annual catalog. You notice that staffers could save a lot of valuable time by copying images and text from the old edition and inserting them into the new document. Your boss, Marketing Director Jenny Zhang, has received numerous inquiries from staffers asking how to copy text and images from previous editions. You know that this can be done, and you show a fellow worker how to do it using a PDF feature called Take a Snapshot. Marketing Director Zhang decides that you are quite a tech-savvy student. Because she has so much confidence in you, she asks you to draft a memo detailing the steps for copying images and text passages from portable document format (PDF) files.

You start by viewing the **Edit** pull-down menu in an open PDF document. Depending on the Acrobat version, a feature called **Take a Snapshot** can be seen. It is preceded by a tiny camera icon and a check mark when the tool is activated. To copy content, you need to select the part of the PDF document that you want to capture. The cursor will change its shape once the feature is activated. Check what shape it acquires. With the left mouse button, click the location where you want to copy a passage or image. At the same time, you need to drag the mouse over the page in the direction you want. A selected area appears that you can expand and reduce, but you can't let go of the left mouse button. Once you release the left mouse button, a copy of the selected area will be made. You can then paste the selected area into a blank Microsoft Office document, whether Word, Excel, or PowerPoint. You can also take a picture of an entire page.

YOUR TASK. Prepare a memo addressed to Marketing Department staff members for the signature of Jenny Zhang. Practice the steps described here in abbreviated form, and arrange all necessary instructions in a logical sequence. You may need to add steps not noted here. Remember, too, that your audience may not be as computer literate as you are, so ensure that the steps are clear and easy to follow.

6.12 Direct Claim: A Not-So-Smart TV (L.O. 3)
> E-Mail

After you receive an unexpected bonus, you decide to indulge and buy a new 4K Ultra HD TV. You conduct research to compare prices and decide on an Insignia 50-inch LED HD TV Model NS-50DR710. You find a great deal at Digital Depot for $399.99 plus tax. Although the closest store is a 30-minute drive, the price is so good you decide it's worth the trip. You sell your old TV on Craig's List to make room for the Insignia and spend several hours installing the new set. It works perfectly, but the next day when you turn it on, nothing happens. You check everything, but no matter what you do, you can't get a picture. You're irritated! You are without a TV and have wasted hours hooking up the Insignia. Assuming it's just a faulty set, you pack up the TV and drive back to Digital Depot. You have no trouble returning the item and come home with a second Insignia TV.

Again you install the TV, and again you enjoy your new purchase. But a few days later, you have no picture for a second time. Now you are fuming! Not looking forward to your third trip to Digital Depot, you repack the Insignia television and return it. The customer service representative tries to offer you another Insignia model, but you decline. You point out all the trouble you have been through and say you would prefer a more reliable TV from a different manufacturer that is the same size and in the same price range as the Insignia. Digital Depot carries a Samsung (Model UN50KU6300) that fits your criteria, but at $749.99, it is more than you had budgeted. You feel that after all the problems you have endured, Digital Depot should sell you the Samsung at the same price as the Insignia. However, when you call to discuss the matter, you learn that the local sales manager isn't authorized to make this decision. You are told to submit a written request to the regional office.

YOUR TASK. Write a direct claim e-mail to Christopher Sanchez, Regional Manager at Digital Depot, in New Orleans, Louisiana, asking him to sell you the TV for less than the advertised price.

6.13 Direct Claim: Door Fell Short! (L.O. 3)
> E-Mail

The owner of New Century Interiors, Sue Ewerth, recently worked on the custom Chicago home of an NBA basketball player. He requested an oversized 12-foot mahogany entry door. Sue ordered by telephone the solid mahogany door ("Cape Cod") from American Wood Products on May 17. When it arrived on June 28, her carpenter gave her the bad news. Magnificent as it was, the huge door was cut too small. Instead of measuring a total of 12 feet 2 inches, the door measured 11 feet 10 inches. In Sue's carpenter's words, "No way can I stretch that door to fit this opening!" Sue had waited four weeks for this hand-crafted custom door, and her client wanted it installed immediately. Sue's carpenter said, "I can rebuild this opening for you, but I'm going to have to charge you for my time." His extra charge came to $940.50.

Sue feels that the people at American Wood Products should reimburse her for this amount since it was their error. In fact, Sue actually saved them a bundle of money by not returning the door. She has decided to write to American Wood Products and enclose a copy of her carpenter's bill. She wonders whether she should also include a copy of the invoice, even though it does not show the exact door measurements. New Century Interiors is a good customer of American Wood Products, having used its quality doors and windows on many other jobs. Sue is confident that the company will grant this claim.

YOUR TASK. Draft a claim letter for Sue Ewerth's signature. Address it to Bryan Mumm, Operations Manager, American Wood Products, 4230 North Superior Street, Lincoln, NE 68521. Ms. Ewerth may ask you to fax the letter. Or, if your instructor directs, write an e-mail instead and mention the scanned documents you are sending.

6.14 Direct Claim: Asking Customer Service to Fix Snafu (L.O. 3)
> E-Mail

Have you ever bought a product that didn't work as promised? Have you been disappointed in service at a bank, restaurant, department store, discounter, or from an online merchant? Remember that smart companies want to know what their customers think, especially if a product could be improved.

YOUR TASK. Select a product or service that has disappointed you. Write a claim letter requesting a refund, replacement, explanation, or whatever seems reasonable. Generally, such letters are addressed to customer service departments. For claims about food products, be sure to include bar code identification from the package, if possible. Your instructor may ask you to mail this letter or attach a digital copy to a cover e-mail addressed to the company. Search for the customer service e-mail address online. When you receive a response, share it with your class.

6.15 Adjustment: Responding to TV Claim (L.O. 4)

E-Mail

Christopher Sanchez is Regional Manager at Digital Depot in New Orleans, Louisiana. He received an e-mail from Thomas Heffernan, a frustrated customer who is demanding a steep price match for all his trouble with two new 4K Ultra HD televisions that both malfunctioned (see **Activity 6.12**). He had bought an Insignia 50-inch 4K Ultra HD TV Model NS-50DR710 at Digital Depot for $399.99 plus tax. After installing it, he found, much to his chagrin, that the TV set failed the very next day. Wanting a new TV as soon as possible, he drove 30 minutes to the same Digital Depot store to exchange the faulty model for another Insignia NS-50DR710.

A few days later, this TV also conked out. Again Thomas had to return the TV set, but this time he insisted on exchanging it for a different brand, a comparable Samsung 4K Ultra HD TV (Model UN50KU6300). However, the Samsung TV cost $749.99, nearly twice as much as the Insignia. The e-mail landed in Mr. Sanchez's inbox because the lower-level sales managers were not authorized to grant an adjustment of such magnitude.

Mr. Sanchez empathizes with the customer, but the price difference is substantial. He decides to grant the adjustment as long as Mr. Heffernan forgoes the latest 4K Ultra HD model with a 2160p resolution and instead accepts a conventional Samsung 1080p HD TV that costs $449.99. Alternatively, Mr. Sanchez can offer the customer for $499.99 a substantially reduced soon-to-be-discontinued Samsung 4K Ultra HD TV, a floor model. Of course, Mr. Heffernan could also try his luck with another Insignia 4K Ultra HD TV that would require no additional payment.

YOUR TASK. Because he wants to respond promptly to the frustrated customer, Mr. Sanchez asks you to write an adjustment e-mail to Thomas Heffernan (theffernan@gmail.com) and explain his options. Copy the store manager, Herbert Greene, who has called Mr. Sanchez about Mr. Heffernan's request.

6.16 Adjustment: Responding to Door Claim (L.O. 4)

E-Mail

As Bryan Mumm, operations manager, American Wood Products, you have a problem. Your firm manufactures quality precut and custom-built doors and frames. You have received a letter from Sue Ewerth (described in **Activity 6.13**), an interior designer. Her letter explained that the custom mahogany door ("Cape Cod") she received was cut to the wrong dimensions. She ordered an oversized door measuring 12 feet 2 inches. The door that arrived was 11 feet 10 inches.

Ms. Ewerth kept the door because her client, an NBA basketball player, insisted that the front of the house be closed up. Therefore, she had her carpenter resize the door opening. He charged $940.50 for this corrective work. She claims that you should reimburse her for this amount, since your company was responsible for the error. You check her May 17 order and find that the order was filled correctly. In a telephone order, Ms. Ewerth requested the Cape Cod double-entry door measuring 11 feet 10 inches, and that is what you sent. Now she says that the doors should have been 12 feet 2 inches.

Your policy forbids refunds or returns on custom orders. Yet, you remember that around May 15 you had two new people working the phones taking orders. It is possible that they did not hear or record the measurements correctly. You don't know whether to grant this claim or refuse it. But you do know that you must look into the training of telephone order takers and be sure that they verify all custom order measurements. It might also be a good idea to confirm all phone orders by e-mail, IM, or text message.

Ms. Ewerth is a successful interior designer who has provided American Wood Products with a number of orders. You value her business but aren't sure how to respond. You would like to remind her that American Wood Products has earned a reputation as a premier manufacturer of wood doors and frames. Your doors feature prime woods, meticulous craftsmanship, and award-winning designs. What's more, the engineering is ingenious. You also have a wide range of classic designs.

YOUR TASK. Decide how to treat this claim and then respond to Sue Ewerth, New Century Interiors, 4808 W Victoria Street, Chicago, IL 60646. You might mention that you have a new line of greenhouse windows that are available in three sizes. Include a brochure describing these windows. Alternatively, at your instructor's discretion, you could write an e-mail and refer Ms. Ewerth to your website (www.americanwood-products.com), which features the new line of windows.

6.17 Goodwill Message: U.S. President's Statement on Fidel Castro's Death (L.O. 5)

E-Mail > **Social Media**

Diplomacy is often a delicate dance between harsh political realities and basic human decorum. When Cuban strongman Fidel Castro died at age ninety, heads of state all over the world responded with the obligatory sympathy messages. President Barack Obama followed accepted practice despite the rocky relations between the U.S. and Cuba and the ongoing embargo. Here is Obama's statement:

> *At this time of Fidel Castro's passing, we extend a hand of friendship to the Cuban people. We know that this moment fills Cubans—in Cuba and in the United States—with powerful emotions, recalling the countless ways in which Fidel Castro altered the course of individual lives, families, and of the Cuban nation. History will record and judge the enormous impact of this singular figure on the people and world around him.*

> *For nearly six decades, the relationship between the United States and Cuba was marked by discord and profound political disagreements. During my presidency, we have worked hard to put the past behind us, pursuing a future in which the relationship between our two countries is defined not by our differences but by the many things that we share as neighbors and friends—bonds of family, culture, commerce, and common humanity. This engagement includes the contributions of Cuban Americans, who have done so much for our country and who care deeply about their loved ones in Cuba.*

> *Today, we offer condolences to Fidel Castro's family, and our thoughts and prayers are with the Cuban people. In the days ahead, they will recall the past and also look to the future. As they do, the Cuban people must know that they have a friend and partner in the United States of America.*

YOUR TASK. Regardless of your political views, examine the features in this goodwill message. In a concise social media post or an e-mail, evaluate whether it conforms to the guidelines discussed in this chapter.

6.18 Goodwill Message: Extending Sympathy to a Spouse (L.O. 5)

YOUR TASK. Imagine that the spouse of a coworker recently died in an automobile accident. Write the coworker a letter of sympathy.

6.19 Goodwill Message: Thank You for a Glowing Letter of Recommendation (L.O. 5)

E-Mail

One of your instructors has complied with your urgent request for a letter of recommendation and has given you an enthusiastic endorsement. Regardless of the outcome of your application, you owe thanks to all your supporters. Respond promptly after receiving this favor. Also, you can assume that your instructor is interested in your progress. Let him or her know whether your application was successful.

YOUR TASK. Write an e-mail or, better yet, a letter thanking your instructor. Remember to make your thanks specific so that your words are meaningful. Once you know the outcome of your application, use the opportunity to build more goodwill by writing to your recommender again.

6.20 Goodwill Message: Responding to Good Wishes by Saying Thank You (L.O. 5)

YOUR TASK. Write a short note thanking a friend who sent you good wishes when you recently completed your degree.

Commas 1

Review the Grammar Review section of the Grammar/Mechanics Handbook Sections 2.01–2.04. Then select the correctly punctuated sentences and record their letters in the space provided. Record also the appropriate G/M guidelines to illustrate the principles involved. When you finish, compare your responses with those provided at the bottom of the page. If your answers differ, study carefully the appropriate guideline.

___a___   (2.01)

EXAMPLE
a. The association considered holding its conference in Atlanta, St. Louis, or Chicago.
b. The association considered holding its conference in Atlanta, St. Louis or Chicago.

_____ 1. a. Reasonable people adapt themselves to the world; unreasonable people however attempt to adapt the world to themselves.
b. Reasonable people adapt themselves to the world; unreasonable people, however, attempt to adapt the world to themselves.

_____ 2. a. We are certain Mr. Ferratta, that your UPS delivery will arrive before 11 a.m.
b. We are certain, Mr. Ferratta, that your UPS delivery will arrive before 11 a.m.

_____ 3. a. Our software helps your employees be more creative collaborative and productive.
b. Our software helps your employees be more creative, collaborative, and productive.

_____ 4. a. Amazon closed distribution centers in McDonough, Georgia, and Grand Forks, North Dakota, to save money.
b. Amazon closed distribution centers in McDonough, Georgia and Grand Forks, North Dakota to save money.

_____ 5. a. By the way, the best things in life aren't things.
b. By the way the best things in life aren't things.

_____ 6. a. The last council meeting was held on March 23, 2018 in Boise.
b. The last council meeting was held on March 23, 2018, in Boise.

_____ 7. a. Mr. Avila, Mrs. Kim and Ms. Longo were all promoted.
b. Mr. Avila, Mrs. Kim, and Ms. Longo were all promoted.

_____ 8. a. The shipment addressed to Lone Star Industries, 6920 Fondren Road, Houston, TX 77074, arrived two weeks late.
b. The shipment addressed to Lone Star Industries, 6920 Fondren Road, Houston, TX, 77074, arrived two weeks late.

_____ 9. a. The manager feels, nevertheless, that the support of all employees is critical.
b. The manager feels nevertheless, that the support of all employees is critical.

_____ 10. a. Successful teams encourage open communication, resolve conflict fairly and promote interaction among members.
b. Successful teams encourage open communication, resolve conflict fairly, and promote interaction among members.

1. b (2.03) **2.** b (2.02) **3.** b (2.01) **4.** a (2.04c) **5.** a (2.04c) **6.** b (2.03) **7.** b (2.01) **8.** a (2.04b) **9.** a (2.04b) **10.** b (2.01)

Every chapter provides an editing exercise to fine-tune your grammar and mechanics skills. The following e-mail requires edits that address proofreading, grammar, spelling, punctuation (especially commas), capitalization, word use, and other writing issues. Study the guidelines in the Grammar/Mechanics Handbook (Appendix D), including the lists of Confusing Words and Frequently Misspelled Words.

YOUR TASK. Edit the following (a) by inserting corrections in your textbook or on a photocopy using the proofreading marks in Appendix C or (b) by downloading the message from **www.cengagebrain.com** and correcting at your computer.

To: Amy Weaver <aweaver@iriscompanies.com>

From: Marco Nava <marco.nava@abitechnologies.com>

Subject: Your September 20 Inquiry About WorkZone Software

Dear Mr. Weaver:

Yes we do offer personel record-keeping software specially designed for small businesses like your's. Here's answers to your three questions about this software,

1. Our WorkZone software provide standard employee forms so that you are always in compliance with current goverment regulations.
2. You recieve an interviewers guide for structured employee interviews and you also receive a scripted format for checking references by telephone.
3. Yes, you can up date your employees records easy without the need for additional software, hardware or training. As a matter of fact everything you need is immediately available.

Our WorkZone software was professionally designed to provide you with expert forms for interviewing, verifying references, recording attendance, evaluating performance and tracking the status of your employees. We even provide you with step by step instructions, and suggested procedures. You can treat your employees as if you had a Professional human resources specialist right on your staff.

Because important changes in laws and regulations are constantly being made every business needs to have details in one place. One major step toward compliance is having these details clearly accessible.

To try out WorkZone in your office for 30 days risk-free just make an appointment by clicking **here**. We look forward Ms. Weaver to demonstrating WorkZone to you personal in the comfort of your office.

Best wishes,

Marco Nava
marco.nava@abitechnologies
Product Development
455-309-2091
www.abitechnologies.com

Choosing Tools for Doing the Right Thing

In composing messages or engaging in other activities on the job, business communicators can't help being torn between conflicting loyalties. Do we tell the truth and risk our jobs? Do we show loyalty to friends even if it means bending the rules? Should we be tactful or totally honest? Is it our duty to make a profit or be socially responsible?

Acting ethically means doing the right thing *given the circumstances*. Each set of circumstances requires analyzing issues, evaluating choices, and acting responsibly. Resolving ethical issues is never easy, but the task can be made less difficult if you know how to identify key issues. The following questions may be helpful.

- **Is the action legal?** No matter who asks you to do it or how important you feel the result will be, avoid anything that is prohibited by law. Bribing a buyer to secure a large order is illegal, even if you suspect that others in your field do it and you know that without the kickback you will lose the sale.

- **Would you do it if you were on the opposite side?** Looking at both sides of an issue helps you gain perspective. By weighing both sides of an issue, you can arrive at a more equitable solution.

- **Can you rule out a better alternative?** Would the alternative be more ethical? Under the circumstances, is the alternative feasible?

- **Would a trusted advisor agree?** Suppose you feel ethically bound to report accurate information to a client—even though your boss has ordered you not to do so. Talking about your dilemma with a coworker or with a colleague in your field might give you helpful insights and lead to possible alternatives.

- **Would your family, friends, employer, or coworkers approve?** If the thought of revealing your action publicly produces cold sweats, your choice is probably not a wise one. Losing the faith of your friends or the confidence of your customers is not worth whatever short-term gains you might realize.

CAREER APPLICATION. One of the biggest accounting firms uses an ethical awareness survey that includes some of the following situations. You may face similar situations with ethical issues on the job or in employment testing.

YOUR TASK. In teams or individually, decide whether each of the following ethical issues is (a) very important, (b) moderately important, or (c) unimportant. Then decide whether you (a) strongly approve of, (b) are undecided about, or (c) strongly disapprove of the action taken.[27] Apply the ethical tools presented here to determine whether the course of action is ethical. What alternatives might you suggest?

- **Recruiting.** You are a recruiter for your company. Although you know company morale is low, the turnover rate is high, and the work environment in many departments is deplorable, you tell job candidates that it is a great place to work.

- **Training program.** Your company is offering an exciting training program in Hawaii. Although you haven't told anyone, you plan to get another job shortly. You decide to participate in the program anyway because you have never been to Hawaii. One of the program requirements is that participants must have "long-term career potential" with the firm.

- **Thievery.** As a supervisor, you suspect that one of your employees is stealing. You check with a company attorney and find that a lie detector test cannot be legally used. Then you decide to scrutinize the employee's records. Finally, you find an inconsistency in the employee's records. You decide to fire the employee, although this inconsistency would not normally have been discovered.

- **Downsizing.** As part of the management team of a company that makes potato chips, you face the rising prices of potatoes. Rather than increase the cost of your chips, you decide to decrease slightly the size of the bag. Consumers are less likely to notice a smaller bag than a higher price.

Negative Messages

wavebreakmedia/Shutterstock.com

Learning Outcomes

After studying this chapter, you should be able to do the following:

1 Understand the strategies of business communicators in conveying negative news.

2 Compare the techniques and ethics of the direct and indirect strategies in communicating unfavorable news.

3 Explain the components of effective negative messages, including opening with a buffer, apologizing, showing empathy, presenting the reasons, cushioning the bad news, and closing pleasantly.

4 Apply effective techniques for refusing typical requests or claims, as well as for presenting bad news to customers in print or online.

5 Describe and apply effective techniques for delivering bad news within organizations.

7-1 Communicating Negative News Effectively

Even well-managed businesses can run into trouble. Goods are not delivered, products fail to perform as expected, service is poor, billing gets fouled up, or customers are misunderstood. You may have to write messages declining proposals, explaining service outages, describing data breaches, announcing price increases, refusing requests for donations, turning down invitations, or responding to unhappy customers. You might have to apologize for mistakes in orders or pricing, the rudeness of employees, overlooked appointments, faulty accounting, defective products, or jumbled instructions. As a company representative, you may have to respond to complaints posted for the world to see on Twitter, Facebook, or complaint websites.

The truth is that everyone occasionally must deliver negative news in business. Because bad news disappoints, irritates, and sometimes angers the receiver, such messages must be written carefully. The bad feelings associated with disappointing news can generally be reduced if the receiver (a) knows the reasons for the rejection, (b) feels that the news was revealed sensitively, and (c) believes that the matter was treated seriously and fairly.

In this chapter you will learn when to use the direct strategy and when to use the indirect strategy to deliver bad news. You will study the goals of business communicators in working with unfavorable news and learn techniques for achieving those goals.

7-1a Identifying Your Goals in Communicating Negative News

LEARNING OUTCOME 1

Understand the strategies of business communicators in conveying negative news.

Delivering bad news is not the happiest communication task you may have, but it can be gratifying if you do it effectively. As a business communicator working with bad news, you will have many goals. Here's how to achieve them:

- **Explain clearly and completely.** Your goal is to make your readers understand and, in the best case, accept the bad news. Recipients should not have to call or write to clarify your message.

- **Project a professional image.** Even when irate customers sound threatening and overstate their claims, you should strive to stay calm, use polite language, and respond with clear explanations of why a negative message was necessary.

- **Convey empathy and sensitivity.** Use language that respects the receiver but also attempts to reduce bad feelings. When appropriate, accept blame and apologize without creating legal liability for your organization or yourself.

- **Be fair.** When you can show that the decision was fair, impartial, and rational, receivers are far more likely to accept the negative news.

- **Maintain friendly relations.** A final goal is to demonstrate your desire to continue pleasant relations with the receivers and to regain their confidence.

These goals are ambitious, and, frankly, you may not achieve them all. However, many communicators have found the strategies and techniques you are about to learn helpful in conveying disappointing news sensitively and safely. With experience, you will be able to vary these strategies and adapt them to your organization's specific communication tasks.

7-2 Analyzing Negative News Strategies

LEARNING OUTCOME 2

Compare the techniques and ethics of the direct and indirect strategies in communicating unfavorable news.

Bad news in business can be difficult to categorize. To successfully convey bad news, writers must carefully consider the audience, purpose, and context. Experienced business communicators understand that their approaches to negative news must be flexible.[1] As a business writer in training, you have at your disposal two basic strategies for delivering negative news: direct and indirect, as compared in Figure 7.1.

Which approach is best suited for your particular message? One of the first steps you will take before delivering negative news is analyzing how your receiver will react to this news. In earlier chapters we discussed applying the direct strategy to positive and neutral messages. In this chapter we expand on that advice and offer additional considerations to help you decide which strategy to use.

7-2a When to Use the Direct Strategy

The direct strategy saves time and is preferred by some who consider it to be more professional and even more ethical than the indirect strategy. The direct strategy may be more effective in situations such as the following:

- **When the bad news is not damaging.** If the bad news is insignificant (such as a small increase in cost) and doesn't personally affect the receiver, then the direct strategy makes sense.

- **When the receiver may overlook the bad news.** Changes in service, new policy requirements, and legal announcements—these critical messages may require boldness to ensure attention.

- **When the organization or receiver prefers directness.** Some companies and individuals expect all internal messages and announcements—even bad news—to be straightforward and presented without frills.

Figure 7.1 Comparing the Direct and Indirect Strategies for Negative Messages

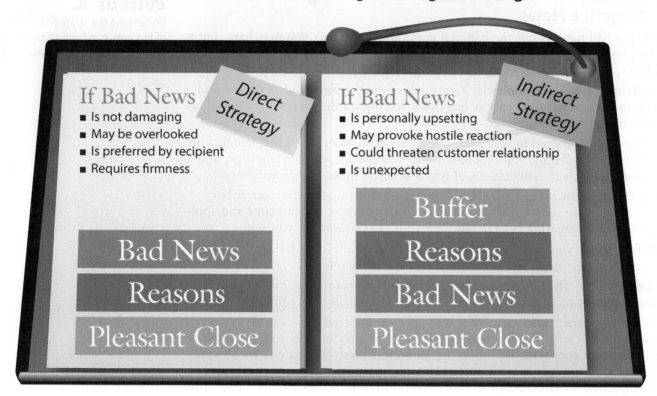

- **When firmness is necessary.** Messages that must demonstrate determination and strength should not use delaying techniques. For example, the last in a series of collection letters that seek payment on an overdue account may require a direct opener.

Security breach messages provide a good example of how to employ the direct strategy in delivering bad news. Notice in Figure 7.2 that the writer, Garrett Blake, is fairly direct in announcing that consumer identity information was lost at Well Point Federal Credit Union.

Although he does not blurt out "your information has been compromised," the writer does announce a potential identity theft problem in the first sentence. He then explains that a hacker attack has compromised roughly a quarter of customer accounts. In the second paragraph, he recommends that credit union customer Geoff Ferguson take specific corrective action to protect his identity and offers helpful contact information. The tone is respectful and serious. The credit union's letter is modeled on an FTC template that was praised for achieving a balance between a direct and indirect opening.[2]

7-2b When to Use the Indirect Strategy

The indirect strategy does not reveal the bad news immediately. This strategy, at least theoretically, enables you to keep the reader's attention until you have been able to explain the reasons for the bad news. Some writing experts suggest that the indirect strategy "ill suits today's skeptical, impatient, even cynical audience."[3] Others have argued the relative merits of both approaches and their effects on the receiver.[4] To be sure, in social media, bluntness seems to dominate public debate. Directness is equated with honesty; hedging, with deceit.

Regardless, many communicators prefer to use the indirect strategy to soften negative news. Whereas good news can be revealed quickly, bad news may be easier to accept when broken gradually. Here are typical instances in which the indirect strategy works well:

- **When the bad news is personally upsetting.** If the negative news involves the receiver personally, such as a layoff notice, the indirect strategy makes sense. Telling an employee that he or she no longer has a job is probably best done in person and by starting indirectly and giving reasons first. When a company has made a mistake that inconveniences or disadvantages a customer, the indirect strategy also makes sense.

Figure 7.2 Announcing Bad News Directly: Security Breach Letter

Well Point™
FEDERAL CREDIT UNION

1530 S GOVERNORS AVENUE, DOVER, DE 19905
www.wellpointfcu.com   302-448-2101

September 5, 2019

Mr. Geoff Ferguson
206 South Salisbury Avenue
Salisbury, MD 21801

Dear Mr. Ferguson:

Uses modified direct strategy because urgent action is needed to prevent identity theft

We are contacting you about a potential problem involving identity theft. On August 30, names, encrypted social security numbers, birth dates, and e-mail addresses of fewer than 25 percent of accounts were compromised in an apparent hacker attack on our website. Outside data security experts are working tirelessly to identify the causes of the breach as well as prevent future intrusions into our system. Immediately upon detecting the attack, we notified the local police authorities as well as the FBI. We also alerted the three major credit-reporting agencies.

We recommend that you place a fraud alert on your credit file. A fraud alert tells creditors to contact you before they open any new accounts or change your existing accounts. Please call any one of the three major credit bureaus. As soon as one credit bureau confirms your fraud alert, the others are notified to place fraud alerts. All three credit reports will be sent to you, free of charge.

Suggests recommended steps and provides helpful information about credit-reporting agencies

Equifax	Experian	TransUnion
800-685-1111	888-397-3742	800-680-7289

Gives reasons for the recommended action, provides contact information, and offers additional pointers

Even if you do not find any suspicious activity on your initial credit reports, the Federal Trade Commission (FTC) recommends that you check your credit reports periodically. Victim information sometimes is held for use or shared among a group of thieves at different times. Checking your credit reports periodically can help you spot problems and address them quickly.

If you find suspicious activity on your credit reports or have reason to believe your information is being misused, call 518-584-5500 and file a police report. Get a copy of the report; many creditors want the information it contains to absolve you of the fraudulent debts. You also should file a complaint with the FTC at www.ftc.gov/idtheft or at 1-877-ID-THEFT (877-438-4338).

Ends by providing more helpful information, company phone number, and offer of one year of free credit monitoring

Please visit our website at www.wellpointfcu.com/databreach for updates on the investigation, or call our privacy hotline at 800-358-4422. Affected customers will receive free credit-monitoring services for one year.

Sincerely,

Garrett Blake

Garrett Blake
Customer Service

- **When the bad news will provoke a hostile reaction.** When your message will irritate or infuriate the recipient, the indirect method may be best. It begins with a buffer and reasons, thus encouraging the reader to finish reading or hearing the message. A blunt announcement may make the receiver stop reading.

- **When the bad news threatens the customer relationship.** If the negative message may damage a customer relationship, the indirect strategy may help salvage the customer bond. Beginning slowly and presenting reasons that explain what happened can be more helpful than directly announcing bad news or failing to adequately explain the reasons.

- **When the bad news is unexpected.** Readers who are totally surprised by bad news tend to have a more negative reaction than those who expected it. If a company suddenly closes an office or a plant and employees had no inkling of the closure, that bad news would be better received if it were revealed cautiously with reasons first.

Whether to use the direct or indirect strategy depends largely on the situation, the reaction you expect from the audience, and your goals. The indirect approach does not guarantee that recipients will be pleased, because, after all, bad news is just that—bad. However, many communicators prefer to use it because they believe that revealing bad news slowly and indirectly shows sensitivity to the receiver. By preparing the receiver, you tend to soften the impact. Moreover, although social media users may favor the direct approach, the majority of negative messages are still conveyed indirectly. To apply the indirect strategy effectively, you may use four parts, as shown in Figure 7.3.

7-2c Keeping the Indirect Strategy Ethical

You may worry that the indirect organizational strategy is unethical or manipulative because the writer deliberately delays the main idea. Now, consider the alternative. Breaking bad news bluntly can cause pain and hard feelings. By delaying bad news, you soften the blow somewhat, as well as ensure that your reasoning will be read while the receiver is still receptive. One psychologist recognized the significance of the indirect strategy when she stated, "If the *why* of my *no* is clear and understandable, it's less likely that the other person will take it as being a *no* to them."[6] In using the indirect strategy, your motive is not to deceive the reader or hide the news. Rather, it is to be a compassionate, yet effective communicator.

The key to ethical communication lies in the motives of the sender. Unethical communicators *intend to deceive*. Although the indirect strategy provides a setting in which to announce bad news, it should not be used to avoid or misrepresent the truth. For example, the Internet is rife with bogus offers such as skin care products promising to deliver the fountain of youth. Some offer miraculous

Figure 7.3 Four-Part Indirect Strategy for Bad News

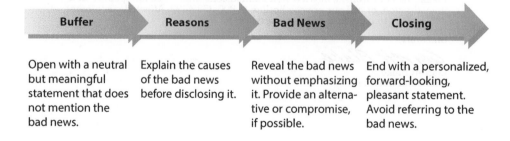

Buffer	Reasons	Bad News	Closing
Open with a neutral but meaningful statement that does not mention the bad news.	Explain the causes of the bad news before disclosing it.	Reveal the bad news without emphasizing it. Provide an alternative or compromise, if possible.	End with a personalized, forward-looking, pleasant statement. Avoid referring to the bad news.

Chapter 7: Negative Messages

weight loss with the help of green coffee bean extract or raspberry ketone supplements, to name just two of the current scams. Unscrupulous marketers advertise on trusted websites of national news organizations and falsely claim endorsements by Oprah Winfrey and Dr. Oz, says Truth in Advertising, a nonprofit dedicated to stamping out deceptive advertising.[7] As you will see in Chapter 8, misleading, deceptive, and unethical claims are never acceptable. In fact, many are simply illegal.

7-3 Composing Effective Negative Messages

LEARNING OUTCOME 3

Explain the components of effective negative messages, including opening with a buffer, apologizing, showing empathy, presenting the reasons, cushioning the bad news, and closing pleasantly.

Even though it may be impossible to make the receiver happy when delivering negative news, you can reduce resentment by structuring your message sensitively. Most negative messages contain some or all of these parts: buffer, reasons, bad news, and closing. Figure 7.4 presents these four components of the indirect strategy in greater detail. This section also discusses apologies and how to convey empathy in delivering bad news.

7-3a Opening Indirect Messages With a Buffer

A buffer is a device to reduce shock or pain. To buffer the pain of bad news, begin with a neutral but meaningful statement that makes the reader continue reading. The buffer should be relevant and concise and provide a natural transition to the explanation that follows. The situation, of course, will help determine what you should put in the buffer. Avoid trite buffers such as *Thank you for your e-mail*.

Not all business communication authors agree that buffers increase the effectiveness of negative messages. However, many cultures appreciate softening bad news. Following are some possibilities for opening indirect bad-news messages.

Best News. Start with the part of the message that represents the best news. For example, a message to customers who purchased mobile device insurance announced a progressive rate increase that was tied to the replacement value of each smart device. Only customers with very expensive handsets will experience price increases. You might start by reminding customers about the value of insuring a mobile device: *As a reminder, your Premium Electronics Protection provides the benefit of a replacement device when your smartphone is accidentally damaged,*

Figure 7.4 Delivering Bad News Sensitively

Buffer	Reasons	Bad News	Closing
• Best news • Compliment • Appreciation • Agreement • Facts • Understanding • Apology	• Cautious explanation • Reader or other benefits • Company policy explanation • Positive words • Evidence that matter was considered fairly and seriously	• Embedded placement • Passive voice • Implied refusal • Compromise • Alternative	• Forward look • Information about alternative • Good wishes • Freebies • Resale • Sales promotion

including liquid damage, loss, theft, and malfunction. Although devices are becoming increasingly expensive, no changes will be made to your deductible amount or coverage.

Compliment. Praise the receiver's accomplishments, organization, or efforts, but do so with honesty and sincerity. For instance, in a message declining an invitation to speak, you could write: *Phi Beta Delta has my sincere admiration for its fundraising projects on behalf of hungry children. I am honored that you asked me to speak Friday, October 11.*

Appreciation. Convey thanks for doing business, for sending something, for showing confidence in your organization, for expressing feelings, or simply for providing feedback. Suppose you had to draft a letter that refuses employment. You could say: *I appreciated learning about the hospitality management program at Cornell and about your qualifications in our interview last Friday.* Avoid thanking the reader, however, for something you are about to refuse.

Agreement. Make a relevant statement with which both you and the receiver can agree. A letter that rejects a loan application might read: *We both realize how much plummeting crude oil prices on the world market have devastated domestic oil production.*

Facts. Provide objective information that introduces the bad news. For example, in a memo announcing cutbacks in the hours of the employee cafeteria, you might say: *During the past five years, the percentage of employees eating breakfast in our cafeteria has dropped from 32 percent to 12 percent.*

Understanding. Show that you care about the reader. Notice how in this e-mail to customers announcing a product defect, the writer expresses concern: *We know that you expect superior performance from all the products you purchase from OfficeMall. That's why we are writing personally about the P65X printer cartridges you recently ordered.*

7-3b Apologizing

You learned about making apologies in adjustment messages in Chapter 6. We expand that discussion here because apologies are often part of negative-news messages. An *apology* is defined as an "admission of blameworthiness and regret for an undesirable event."[9] Apologies to customers are especially important if you or your company erred. They cost nothing, and they go a long way in soothing hard feelings.

Why apologize? Because sincere apologies work and may even affect the bottom line. A study suggested that CEOs who appeared genuinely sad, not merely contrite, in videos saw their companies' stock prices rise after an apology. Conversely, leaders who smiled while apologizing were perceived as insincere, and their companies' stock prices dropped.[10] The following pointers can help you apologize effectively in business messages:

- **Apologize promptly and sincerely.** Credibility suffers when a public figure delays an apology and responds only after causing an outrage. Also, people dislike apologies that sound hollow (*We regret that you were inconvenienced* or *We are sorry that you are disturbed*). Focusing on your regret does not convey sincerity; explaining what you will do to prevent recurrence of the problem does.

- **Accept responsibility.** One CEO was criticized for the following weak apology after angrily and publicly firing an employee: "It was an emotional response at the start of a difficult discussion dealing with many people's careers and livelihoods. . . . [I] apologized for the way the matter was handled at the meeting."

schatzy/Shutterstock.com

"The purpose of an apology is not to restore trust, but to confirm to others that we deserve it," says best-selling author and speaker Joseph Grenny.

Source: Grenny, J. (2016, October 21). What a real apology requires. *Harvard Business Review*. Retrieved from https://hbr.org/2016/10/what-a-real-apology-requires

Communication experts faulted this apology because it did not acknowledge responsibility or show remorse.[11]

- **Use good judgment.** Before admitting blame, it might be wise to consult a superior or the company legal counsel to avoid litigation.

Consider these poor and improved apologies:

Poor apology: We apologize if anyone was affected.

Improved apology: I apologize for the frustration our delay caused you. As soon as I received your message, I began looking into the cause of the delay and realized that our delivery tracking system must be improved.

Poor apology: We regret that you are unhappy with the price of frozen yogurt purchased at one of our self-serve scoop shops.

Improved apology: We are genuinely sorry that you were disappointed in the price of frozen yogurt recently purchased at one of our self-serve scoop shops. Your opinion is important to us, and we appreciate your giving us the opportunity to look into the problem you describe.

7-3c Showing Empathy

One of the hardest things to do in apologies is to convey sympathy and empathy. As discussed in Chapter 2, *empathy* is the ability to understand and enter into the feelings of another. Recently, a simple typo crippled Amazon's Simple Storage Service (S3) platform and caused a service disruption in Northern Virginia sending ripple effects across the Internet. The online retailer was quick to explain how the outage occurred and acknowledged the inconvenience customers suffered: "[W]e want to apologize for the impact this event caused for our customers. While we are proud of our long track record of availability with Amazon S3, we know how critical this service is to our customers, their applications and end users, and their businesses. We will do everything we can to learn from this event and use it to improve our availability even further."[12]

You can express empathy in many ways, as illustrated in the following:

- In writing to an unhappy customer: *We did not intentionally delay the shipment, and we sincerely regret the disappointment and frustration you must have suffered.*

- In laying off employees: *It is with great regret that we must take this step. Rest assured that I will be more than happy to write letters of recommendation for anyone who asks.*

- In responding to a complaint: *I am deeply saddened that our service failure disrupted your sale, and we will do everything in our power to respond to any future outages promptly.*

- In showing genuine feelings: *You have every right to be disappointed. I am truly sorry that. . . .*

OFFICE INSIDER

"Empathy is not a soft nurturing value but a hard commercial tool that every business needs as part of their DNA. Our aim is to make every interaction our customers have with us an individual one."[13]

René Schuster, *chief operating officer, VimpelCom, formerly CEO of Telefónica Germany*

7-3d Presenting the Reasons

Providing an explanation reduces feelings of ill will and improves the chances that readers will accept the bad news. Without sound reasons for denying a request, refusing a claim, or revealing other bad news, a message will fail, no matter how cleverly it is organized or written. For example, if you must deny a customer's request, as part of your planning before writing, you analyze the request and decide to refuse it for specific reasons. Where do you place your reasons? In the indirect strategy, the reasons appear before the bad news. In the direct strategy, the reasons appear immediately after the bad news.

Explaining Clearly. If the reasons are not confidential and if they will not create legal liability, you can be specific: *Growers supplied us with a limited number of patio roses, and our demand this year was twice that of last year.* In responding to a billing error, explain what happened: *After you informed us of an error on your January bill, we investigated the matter and admit the mistake was ours. Until our new automated system is fully online, we are still subject to human error. Rest assured that you will see a credit on your next bill.* In refusing a speaking engagement, tell why the date is impossible: *On January 15 we have a board of directors meeting that I must attend.* Don't, however, make unrealistic or dangerous statements in an effort to be the good guy: *Although we can't contribute now, we expect increased revenues next year and promise a generous gift then.*

Citing Reader or Other Benefits, if Plausible. Readers are more open to bad news if in some way, even indirectly, it may help them. In refusing a client's request for a 3 percent discount, Fred Warmbier, owner of Ohio-based Finishing Technology, Inc., argued as follows: "We are working to keep our prices from going up, even though the costs of our materials, utilities, labor—and health insurance—are increasing. Our prices are competitive and fair, and in most cases we really can't afford to lower them"—without passing the burden on to customers. Warmbier says that clients who go after lower prices often return because his competitors engage in "unsustainable" practices "such as compromising on quality or cutting corners on health coverage."[14]

Readers also accept bad news more readily if they recognize that someone or something else benefits, such as other workers or the environment: *Although we would like to consider your application, we prefer to fill managerial positions from within.* Avoid trying to show reader benefits, though, if they appear insincere: *To improve our service to you, we are increasing our brokerage fees.*

Explaining Company Policy. Readers resent blanket policy statements prohibiting something: *Company policy prevents us from hiring outside job candidates* or *Contract bids may be accepted from local companies only.* Instead of hiding behind company policy, gently explain why the policy makes sense: *We prefer to promote from within because it rewards the loyalty of our employees. In addition, we have found that people familiar with our organization make the quickest contribution to our team effort.* By offering explanations, you demonstrate that you care about readers and are treating them as important individuals.

Choosing Positive Words. Because the words you use can affect a reader's response, choose carefully. Remember that the objective of the indirect strategy is holding the reader's attention until you have had a chance to explain the reasons justifying the bad news. To keep the reader in a receptive mood, avoid expressions with punitive, demoralizing, or otherwise negative connotations. Stay away from such words as *cannot, claim, denied, error, failure, fault, impossible, mistaken, misunderstand, never, regret, rejected, unable, unwilling, unfortunately,* and *violate.*

Showing Fairness and Serious Intent. In explaining reasons, show the reader that you take the matter seriously, have investigated carefully, and are making an unbiased decision. Receivers are more accepting of disappointing news when they feel that their requests have been heard and that they have been treated fairly. In canceling funding for a program, board members provided this explanation: *As you know, the publication of* Urban Artist *was funded by a renewable annual grant from the National Endowment for the Arts. Recent cutbacks in federally sponsored city arts programs have left us with few funds. Because our grant has been discontinued, we have no alternative but to cease publication of* Urban Artist. *The board has searched long and hard for some other viable funding, but every avenue of recourse has been closed before us. Accordingly, June's issue will be our last.*

7-3e Cushioning the Bad News

Although you can't prevent the disappointment that bad news brings, you can reduce the pain somewhat by breaking the news sensitively. Be especially considerate when the reader will suffer personally from the bad news. A number of thoughtful techniques can cushion the blow.

Positioning the Bad News Strategically. Instead of spotlighting it, sandwich the bad news between other sentences, perhaps among your reasons. Don't let the refusal begin or end a paragraph; the reader's eye will linger on these high-visibility spots. Another technique that reduces shock is putting a painful idea in a subordinate clause: *Although another candidate was hired, we appreciate your interest in our organization and wish you every success in your job search.* Subordinate clauses often begin with words such as *although, as, because, if,* and *since.*

Using the Passive Voice. Passive-voice verbs enable you to depersonalize an action. Whereas the active voice focuses attention on a person (*We don't give cash refunds*), the passive voice highlights the action (*Cash refunds are not given because …*). Use the passive voice for the bad news. In some instances you can combine passive-voice verbs and a subordinate clause: *Although franchise scoop shop owners cannot be required to lower their frozen yogurt prices, we are happy to pass along your comments for their consideration.*

Highlighting the Positive. As you learned earlier, messages are far more effective when you describe what you can do instead of what you can't do. Rather than *We will no longer allow credit card purchases*, try a more positive appeal: *We are now selling gasoline at discount cash prices.*

Implying the Refusal. It is sometimes possible to avoid a direct refusal. Often, your reasons and explanations leave no doubt that a request has been denied. Explicit refusals may be unnecessary and at times cruel. In this refusal to contribute to a charity, for example, the writer never actually says *no*: *Because we will soon be moving into new offices in Glendale, all our funds are earmarked for relocation costs. We hope that next year we will be able to support your worthwhile charity.* The danger of an implied refusal, of course, is that it is so subtle that the reader misses it. Be certain that you make the bad news clear, thus preventing the need for further correspondence.

Suggesting a Compromise or an Alternative. A refusal is not so depressing—for the sender or the receiver—if a suitable compromise, substitute, or alternative is available. In denying permission to a group of students to visit a historical private residence, for instance, this writer softens the bad news by proposing an alternative: *Although private tours of the grounds are not given, we do open the house and its gardens for one charitable event in the fall.* You can further reduce the impact of the bad news by refusing to dwell on it. Present it briefly (or imply it), and move on to your closing.

7-3f Closing Pleasantly

After explaining the bad news sensitively, close the message with a pleasant statement that promotes goodwill. The closing should be personalized and may include a forward look, an alternative, good wishes, freebies, resale information, or a sales promotion. *Resale* refers to mentioning a product or service favorably to reinforce the customer's choice. For example, *you chose our best-selling model.*

Forward Look. Anticipate future relations or business. A letter that refuses a contract proposal might read: *Thanks for your bid. We look forward to working with your talented staff when future projects demand your special expertise.*

An Alternative. If an alternative exists, you might end your letter with follow-through advice. For example, in a letter rejecting a customer's demand for replacement of landscaping plants, you might say: *I will be happy to give you a free inspection and consultation. Please call 301-746-8112 to arrange a date for my visit.* In a message to a prospective home buyer: *Although the lot you saw last week is now sold, we do have two lots with excellent views that are available at a slightly higher price.* In reacting to an Internet misprint: *Please note that our website contained an unfortunate misprint offering $850-per-night Bora Bora bungalows at $85. Although we cannot honor that rate, we are offering a special half-price rate of $425 to those who responded.*

Good Wishes. A letter rejecting a job candidate might read: *We appreciate your interest in our company, and we extend to you our best wishes in your search to find the perfect match between your skills and job requirements.*

Freebies. When customers complain—primarily about food products or small consumer items—companies often send coupons, samples, or gifts to restore confidence and promote future business. In response to a customer's complaint about a frozen dinner, you could write: *Your loyalty and your concern about our frozen entrées are genuinely appreciated. Because we want you to continue enjoying our healthy* *and convenient dinners, we are enclosing a coupon that you can take to your local market to select your next Green Valley entrée.*

Resale or Sales Promotion. When the bad news is not devastating or personal, references to resale information or promotion may be appropriate: *The computer workstations you ordered are unusually popular because of their stain-, heat-, and scratch-resistant finishes. To help you locate hard-to-find accessories for these workstations, we invite you to visit our website where our online catalog provides a huge selection of surge suppressors, multiple outlet strips, security devices, and computer accessories.*

Avoid endings that sound canned, insincere, inappropriate, or self-serving. Don't invite further correspondence (*If you have any questions, do not hesitate...*), and don't refer to the bad news. To review these suggestions for delivering bad news sensitively, take another look at Figure 7.4, Delivering Bad News Sensitively.

7-4 Refusing Typical Requests and Claims

When you must refuse typical requests, first think about how the receiver will react to your refusal and decide whether to use the direct or the indirect strategy. As you advance in your career, you may receive requests for favors or contributions. You may have to say *no* to customer claims or invitations to give presentations. You may also deal with disappointment and anger. If you have any doubt, use the indirect strategy and the following writing plan:

Refusing Typical Requests and Claims

WRITING PLAN

BUFFER: Start with a neutral statement on which both reader and writer can agree, such as a compliment, appreciation, a quick review of the facts, or an apology. Try to include a key idea or word that acts as a transition to the reasons.

REASONS: Present valid reasons for the refusal, avoiding words that create a negative tone.

BAD NEWS: De-emphasize the bad news, use the passive voice, accentuate the positive, or imply a refusal. Suggest a compromise, alternative, or substitute, if possible. The alternative may be part of the bad-news section or part of the closing.

CLOSING: Renew good feelings with a positive statement. Avoid referring to the bad news. Include resale or sales promotion material, if appropriate. Look forward to continued business.

7-4a Rejecting Requests for Favors, Money, Information, and Action

LEARNING OUTCOME 4

Apply effective techniques for refusing typical requests or claims, as well as for presenting bad news to customers in print or online.

Requests for favors, money, information, and action may come from charities, friends, or business partners. Many are from people representing worthy causes, and you may wish you could comply. However, resources are usually limited. In a letter from Delta Management Associates, shown in Figure 7.5, the company must refuse a request for a donation to a charity. Following the indirect strategy, the letter begins with a buffer acknowledging the request. It also praises the good works

Figure 7.5 Refusing a Donation Request

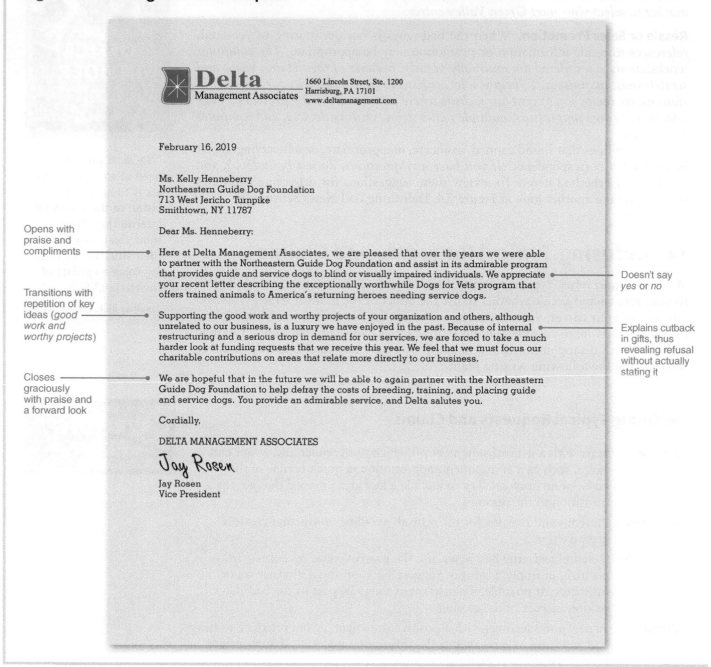

Opens with praise and compliments

Transitions with repetition of key ideas (*good work and worthy projects*)

Closes graciously with praise and a forward look

1660 Lincoln Street, Ste. 1200
Harrisburg, PA 17101
www.deltamanagement.com

February 16, 2019

Ms. Kelly Henneberry
Northeastern Guide Dog Foundation
713 West Jericho Turnpike
Smithtown, NY 11787

Dear Ms. Henneberry:

Here at Delta Management Associates, we are pleased that over the years we were able to partner with the Northeastern Guide Dog Foundation and assist in its admirable program that provides guide and service dogs to blind or visually impaired individuals. We appreciate your recent letter describing the exceptionally worthwhile Dogs for Vets program that offers trained animals to America's returning heroes needing service dogs.

Supporting the good work and worthy projects of your organization and others, although unrelated to our business, is a luxury we have enjoyed in the past. Because of internal restructuring and a serious drop in demand for our services, we are forced to take a much harder look at funding requests that we receive this year. We feel that we must focus our charitable contributions on areas that relate more directly to our business.

We are hopeful that in the future we will be able to again partner with the Northeastern Guide Dog Foundation to help defray the costs of breeding, training, and placing guide and service dogs. You provide an admirable service, and Delta salutes you.

Cordially,

DELTA MANAGEMENT ASSOCIATES

Jay Rosen

Jay Rosen
Vice President

Doesn't say *yes* or *no*

Explains cutback in gifts, thus revealing refusal without actually stating it

of the charity and uses those words as a transition to the second paragraph. In the second paragraph, the writer explains why the company cannot donate. Notice that the writer reveals the refusal without actually stating it (*Because of internal restructuring and a serious drop in demand for our services, we are forced to take a much harder look at funding requests that we receive this year*). This gentle refusal makes it unnecessary to be blunter in stating the denial.

In some donation refusal letters, the reasons may not be fully explained: *Although we can't provide financial support at this time, we all unanimously agree that the Make-A-Wish Foundation contributes a valuable service to sick children.* The emphasis is on the foundation's good deeds rather than on an explanation for the refusal. Businesses that are required to write frequent refusals might prepare a template, changing a few variables as needed.

7-4b Dealing With Disappointed Customers in Print

Businesses must occasionally respond to disappointed customers. Whenever possible, these problems should be dealt with immediately and personally. Most business professionals strive to control the damage and resolve such problems in the following manner[17]:

- Call or e-mail the individual immediately.
- Describe the problem and apologize.
- Explain why the problem occurred, what they are doing to resolve it, and how they will prevent it from happening again.
- Promote goodwill by following up with a print message that documents the phone call.

Written messages are important (a) when personal contact is impossible, (b) to establish a record of the incident, (c) to formally confirm follow-up procedures, and (d) to promote good relations. Dealing with problems immediately is very important in resolving conflict and retaining goodwill.

A bad-news follow-up letter is shown in Figure 7.6. Consultant Kimberly Haydn found herself in the embarrassing position of explaining why she had given out the name of her client to a salesperson. The client, C & C Resources International, had hired her firm, MKM Consulting Associates, to help find an appropriate service for outsourcing its payroll functions. Without realizing it, Kimberly had mentioned to a potential vendor (ABS Payroll Services, Inc.) that her client was considering hiring an outside service to handle its payroll. An overeager salesperson from ABS Payroll Services immediately called on C & C, thus angering the client.

Kimberly Haydn first called her client to explain and apologize. She was careful to control her voice and rate of speaking. She also followed up with the letter shown in Figure 7.6. The letter not only confirms the telephone conversation but also adds the right touch of formality. It sends the nonverbal message that the writer takes the matter seriously and that it is important enough to warrant a hard-copy letter.

Many consumer problems are still handled with letters, either written by consumers as complaints or by companies in response. However, e-mail and social networks are also firmly established as channels for delivering complaints and negative messages.

7-4c Managing Negative News and Reviews Online

Today's impatient, hyperconnected consumers eagerly embrace the idea of delivering their complaints to social networking sites rather than calling customer service departments. Why rely on word of mouth or send an e-mail to a company about poor service or a defective product when you can jump online and shout your grievance to the entire world? Internet sites such as Complaints.com and Ripoff Report, and specialty message boards such as Cruise Critic, encourage consumers to quickly share complaints about stores, products, and services. Twitter, Facebook, Angie's List, TripAdvisor, Yelp, and many more enable consumers to voice their displeasure with negative posts and reviews. Why? Consumers may receive faster responses to tweets than to customer service calls.[19]

How can organizations respond to negative posts and reviews online? Experts suggest the following pointers:

- **Verify the situation.** Investigate to learn what happened. If the complaint is legitimate and your organization fouled up, it's best to fess up. Admit the problem and try to remedy it.
- **Respond quickly and constructively.** Offer to follow up offline; send your contact information. Be polite and helpful.

Figure 7.6 Bad-News Follow-Up Message

MKM Consulting Associates

350 Tijeras Avenue NW
Albuquerque, NM 87102

(505) 842-0971
www.mkmconsulting.com

May 7, 2019

Mr. Roger Martinez
Director, Administrative Operations
C & C Resources International
2740 Harper Drive NE, Ste. 310
Santa Fe, NM 87506

Dear Mr. Martinez:

[Opens with agreement and apology] You have every right to expect complete confidentiality in your transactions with an independent consultant. As I explained in yesterday's telephone call, I am very distressed that you were called by a salesperson from ABS Payroll Services, Inc. This should not have happened, and I apologize to you again for inadvertently mentioning your company's name in a conversation with a potential vendor, ABS Payroll Services, Inc.

[Takes responsibility and promises to prevent recurrence] All clients of MKM Consulting are assured that their dealings with our firm are held in the strictest confidence. Because your company's payroll needs are so individual and because you have so many contract workers, I was forced to explain how your employees differed from those of other companies. Revealing your company name was my error, and I take full responsibility for the lapse. I can assure you that it will not happen again. I have informed ABS Payroll Services that it had no authorization to call you directly and that its actions have forced me to reconsider using its services for my future clients. **[Explains what caused the problem and how it was resolved]**

[Closes with forward look] A number of other payroll services offer outstanding programs. I'm sure we can find the perfect partner to enable you to outsource your payroll responsibilities, thus allowing your company to focus its financial and human resources on its core business. I look forward to our next appointment when you may choose from a number of excellent payroll outsourcing firms.

Sincerely,

Kimberly Haydn

Kimberly Haydn
Partner

Tips for Resolving Problems and Following Up

- Whenever possible, call or see the individual involved.
- Describe the problem and apologize.
- Explain why the problem occurred.
- Take responsibility, if appropriate.
- Explain what you are doing to resolve it.
- Explain what you are doing to prevent recurrence.
- Follow up with a message that documents the personal contact.
- Look forward to positive future relations.

- **Consider freebies.** Suggest a refund or a discount on future services. Dissatisfied customers often write a second, more positive review if they have received a refund.

- **Learn how to improve.** Look upon online comments as opportunities for growth and improvement. See complaining customers as real-time focus groups that can provide valuable insights.

- **Accept the inevitable.** Recognize that nearly every business will experience some negativity, especially on today's readily accessible social media sites. Do what you can to respond constructively, and then move on.

  For advice on answering online comments, see Chapter 6.

7-4d Denying Claims

Customers occasionally want something they are not entitled to or something you can't grant. Because these customers are often unhappy with a product or service, they are emotionally involved. Messages that say *no* to emotionally involved receivers will probably be your most challenging communication task. As publisher Malcolm Forbes observed, "To be agreeable while disagreeing—that's an art."[20]

Fortunately, the reasons-before-refusal plan helps you be empathic and artful in breaking bad news. Obviously, in denial messages you will need to adopt the proper tone. Don't blame customers, even if they are at fault. Avoid *you* statements that sound preachy (*You would have known that cash refunds are impossible if you had read your contract*). Use neutral, objective language to explain why the claim must be refused. Consider offering resale information to rebuild the customer's confidence in your products or organization.

In Figure 7.7 the writer denies the customer's claim for the difference between the price the customer paid for speakers and the price he saw advertised locally (which would have resulted in a whopping cash refund of $500). Although the online retailer does match any advertised lower price, the price-matching policy applies *only* to exact models. This claim must be rejected because the advertisement the customer submitted showed a different, older speaker model.

The e-mail to Chris Dandron opens with a buffer that agrees with a statement in the customer's e-mail. It repeats the key idea of product confidence as a transition to the second paragraph. Next comes an explanation of the price-matching policy. The writer does not assume that the customer is trying to pull a fast one. Nor does he suggest that the customer is a dummy who didn't read the price-matching policy. The safest path is a neutral explanation of the policy along with precise distinctions between the customer's speakers and the older ones. The writer also gets a chance to resell the customer's speakers and demonstrate what a quality product they are. By the end of the third paragraph, it is evident to the reader that his claim is unjustified.

OFFICE INSIDER

"Any declarative sentence starting with 'you' when talking to a customer is best avoided—it comes across as shaking your finger at the customer, and no one wants to feel like we're talking to our mother! Better choices are 'We can' or 'Let's do this together' or 'What I could suggest is.'"[21]

Kristin Robertson, *KR Consulting, Inc.*

7-5 Managing Bad News Within Organizations

A tactful tone and a reasons-first approach help preserve friendly relations with customers. These same techniques are also useful when delivering bad news within organizations. Interpersonal bad news might involve telling the boss that something went wrong or confronting an employee about poor performance. Organizational bad news might involve declining profits, lost contracts, harmful lawsuits, public relations controversies, and policy changes. Whether you use a direct or an indirect strategy in delivering that news depends primarily on the anticipated reaction of the audience. Generally, bad news is better received when reasons are given first. Within organizations, you may find yourself giving bad news in person or in writing.

LEARNING OUTCOME 5

Describe and apply effective techniques for delivering bad news within organizations.

7-5a Delivering Bad News in Person

Whether you are an employee or a supervisor, you may have the unhappy responsibility of delivering bad news. First, decide whether the negative information is newsworthy. For example, trivial, noncriminal mistakes or one-time bad behaviors are best left alone. However, fraudulent travel claims, consistent hostile behavior, or failing projects must be reported.[22] For example, you might have to tell the boss that the team's computer picked up a virus that caused it to lose all its important files. Similarly, as a team leader or supervisor, you might be required to confront an underperforming employee. If you know that the news will upset the receiver,

Figure 7.7 E-Mail Denying a Claim

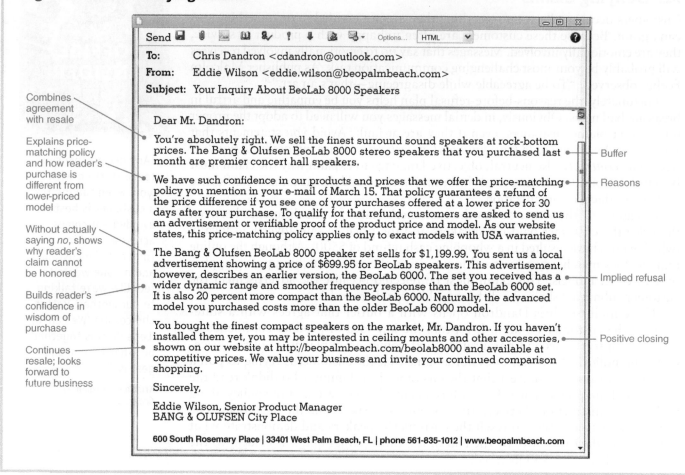

Combines agreement with resale

Explains price-matching policy and how reader's purchase is different from lower-priced model

Without actually saying no, shows why reader's claim cannot be honored

Builds reader's confidence in wisdom of purchase

Continues resale; looks forward to future business

To: Chris Dandron <cdandron@outlook.com>
From: Eddie Wilson <eddie.wilson@beopalmbeach.com>
Subject: Your Inquiry About BeoLab 8000 Speakers

Dear Mr. Dandron:

You're absolutely right. We sell the finest surround sound speakers at rock-bottom prices. The Bang & Olufsen BeoLab 8000 stereo speakers that you purchased last month are premier concert hall speakers. — **Buffer**

We have such confidence in our products and prices that we offer the price-matching policy you mention in your e-mail of March 15. That policy guarantees a refund of the price difference if you see one of your purchases offered at a lower price for 30 days after your purchase. To qualify for that refund, customers are asked to send us an advertisement or verifiable proof of the product price and model. As our website states, this price-matching policy applies only to exact models with USA warranties. — **Reasons**

The Bang & Olufsen BeoLab 8000 speaker set sells for $1,199.99. You sent us a local advertisement showing a price of $699.95 for BeoLab speakers. This advertisement, however, describes an earlier version, the BeoLab 6000. The set you received has a wider dynamic range and smoother frequency response than the BeoLab 6000 set. It is also 20 percent more compact than the BeoLab 6000. Naturally, the advanced model you purchased costs more than the older BeoLab 6000 model. — **Implied refusal**

You bought the finest compact speakers on the market, Mr. Dandron. If you haven't installed them yet, you may be interested in ceiling mounts and other accessories, shown on our website at http://beopalmbeach.com/beolab8000 and available at competitive prices. We value your business and invite your continued comparison shopping. — **Positive closing**

Sincerely,

Eddie Wilson, Senior Product Manager
BANG & OLUFSEN City Place

600 South Rosemary Place | 33401 West Palm Beach, FL | phone 561-835-1012 | www.beopalmbeach.com

---

OFFICE INSIDER

"E-mail and blogging have become such a part of our DNA that people take for granted that it's an OK way to communicate. But actually it's depersonalizing. It chops us off from who we thought we were."[24]

Ruth Luban, *employment counselor and author of* Are You a Corporate Refugee? A Survival Guide for Downsized, Disillusioned, and Displaced Workers

the reasons-first strategy is most effective. When the bad news involves one person or a small group nearby, you should generally deliver that news in person. Here are pointers on how to do so tactfully, professionally, and safely[23]:

- **Gather all the information.** Cool down and have all the facts before marching in on the boss or confronting someone. Remember that every story has two sides.

- **Prepare and rehearse.** Outline what you plan to say so that you are confident, coherent, and dispassionate.

- **Explain: past, present, future.** If you are telling the boss about a problem such as a computer crash, explain what caused the crash, the current situation, and how and when you plan to fix it.

- **Consider taking a partner.** If you fear a "shoot the messenger" reaction, especially from your boss, bring a colleague with you. Each person should have a consistent and credible part in the presentation. If possible, take advantage of your organization's internal resources. To lend credibility to your view, call on auditors, inspectors, or human resources experts.

- **Think about timing.** Don't deliver bad news when someone is already stressed or grumpy. Experts also advise against giving bad news on Friday afternoon when people have the weekend to dwell on it.

- **Be patient with the reaction.** Give the receiver time to vent, think, recover, and act wisely.

7-5b Refusing Workplace Requests

Occasionally, managers must refuse requests from employees. In Figure 7.8 you see the first draft and revision of a message responding to a request from a key specialist, Kevin Peterson. He wants permission to attend a conference. However, his timing is bad; he must be present at budget planning meetings scheduled for the same two weeks. Normally, this matter would be discussed in person. However, Kevin has been traveling among branch offices, and he just hasn't been in the office recently.

The vice president's first inclination was to dash off a quick e-mail, as shown in the Figure 7.8 draft, and tell it like it is. However, the vice president realized that this message was going to hurt and that it had possible danger areas. Moreover, the message misses a chance to give Kevin positive feedback. Notice that Emily's revision carefully employs a buffer, gives a rational explanation, and closes positively with an alternative and gratitude.

Figure 7.8 Refusing an Internal Request

DRAFT

To: Kevin Peterson <kpeterson@polaris-tech.com>
From: Emily Garcia <egarcia@polaris-tech.com>
Subject: Request

Kevin,

Announces the bad news too quickly and painfully —
This is to let you know that attending that conference in October is out of the question. Perhaps you didn't remember that budget planning meetings are scheduled for that month.

Overemphasizes the refusal and apology —
We really need your expertise to help keep the updating of our telecommunications network on schedule. Without you, the entire system—which is shaky at best— might fall apart. I'm really sorry to have to refuse your request to attend the conference. I know this is small thanks for the fine work you have done for us. Please accept our humble apologies.

Gives reasons, but includes a potentially dangerous statement about the "shaky" system

Makes a promise that might be difficult to keep —
In the spring I'm sure your work schedule will be lighter, and we can release you to attend a conference at that time.

REVISION

To: Kevin Peterson <kpeterson@polaris-tech.com>
From: Emily Garcia <egarcia@polaris-tech.com>
Subject: Your Request to Attend October Conference

Kevin,

Buffer: Includes sincere praise —
The entire Management Council and I are pleased with the exceptional leadership you have provided in setting up video transmission to our regional offices. Because of your genuine professional commitment, I can understand your desire to attend the conference of the Telecommunication Specialists of America October 21-25 in Phoenix.

Transition: Uses date to move smoothly from buffer to reasons

Reasons: Explains why refusal is necessary
Bad news: Implies refusal —
The last two weeks in October have been set aside for budget planning. As you and I know, we have only scratched the surface of our teleconferencing projects for the next five years. Because you are the specialist and we rely heavily on your expertise, we need you here for these planning sessions.

Closing: Contains realistic alternative —
If you are able to attend a similar conference in the spring and if our workloads permit, we will try to send you then. You are a valuable team member, Kevin, and we are grateful for the quality leadership you provide to the entire Information Systems team.

Sincerely,

Emily

7-5c Announcing Bad News to Employees and the Public

In an age of social media, damaging information can rarely be contained for long. Executives can almost count on it to be leaked. Corporate officers who fail to communicate effectively and proactively may end up on the defensive and face an uphill battle trying to limit the damage. Many of the techniques used to deliver bad news personally are useful when organizations face a crisis or must deliver bad news to their workers and other stakeholders.

Keeping Communication Open and Honest. Smart organizations involved in a crisis prefer to communicate the news openly to employees and other stakeholders. A crisis might involve serious performance problems, a major relocation, massive layoffs, a management shakeup, or public controversy. Instead of letting rumors distort the truth, managers ought to explain the organization's side of the story honestly and promptly.

Choosing the Best Communication Channel. Morale can be destroyed when employees learn of major events affecting their jobs through the grapevine or from news accounts—rather than from management. When bad news must be delivered to individual employees, management may want to deliver the news personally. With large groups, however, this is generally impossible. Instead, organizations deliver bad news through multiple channels, ranging from hard-copy memos to digital media. Such electronic messages can take the form of intranet posts, e-mails, videos, webcasts, internal as well as external blogs, and voice mail.

WRITING PLAN

Announcing Negative News to Employees

BUFFER: Start with a neutral or positive statement that transitions to the reasons for the bad news. Consider opening with the best news, a compliment, appreciation, agreement, or solid facts. Show understanding.

REASONS: Explain the logic behind the bad news. Provide a rational explanation using positive words and displaying empathy. If possible, mention reader benefits.

BAD NEWS: Position the bad news so that it does not stand out. Be positive, but don't sugarcoat the bad news. Use objective language.

CLOSING: Provide information about an alternative, if one exists. If appropriate, describe what will happen next. Look forward positively.

Draft of Intranet Post. The draft of the intranet blog post shown in Figure 7.9 announces a substantial increase in the cost of employee health care benefits. However, the message suffers from many problems. It announces jolting news bluntly in the first sentence. Worse, it offers little or no explanation for the steep increase in costs. It also sounds insincere (*We did everything possible...*) and arbitrary. In a final miscue, the writer fails to give credit to the company for absorbing previous health cost increases.

Revision of Intranet Post. The revision of this bad-news message shows the indirect strategy and improves the tone considerably. Notice that it opens with a relevant, upbeat buffer regarding health care—but says nothing about increasing costs. For a smooth transition, the second paragraph begins with a key idea from the opening (*comprehensive package*). The reasons section discusses rising costs

Figure 7.9 Announcing Bad News to Employees

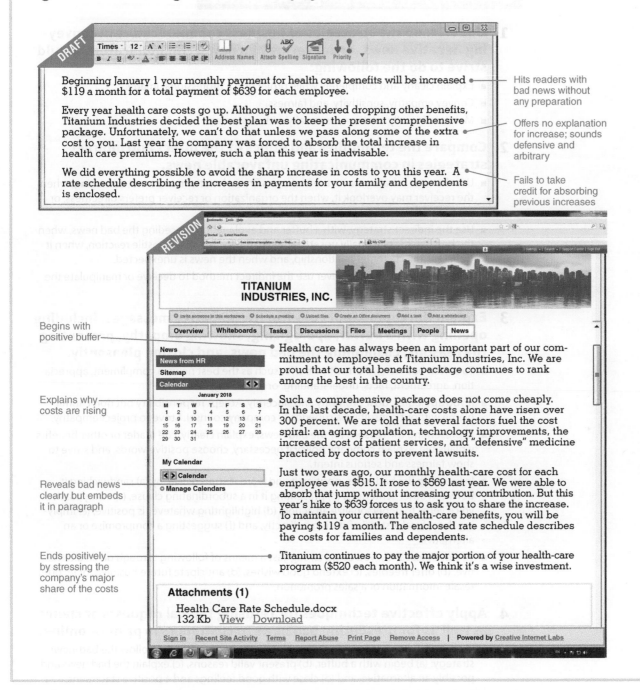

DRAFT

Beginning January 1 your monthly payment for health care benefits will be increased $119 a month for a total payment of $639 for each employee.

Hits readers with bad news without any preparation

Every year health care costs go up. Although we considered dropping other benefits, Titanium Industries decided the best plan was to keep the present comprehensive package. Unfortunately, we can't do that unless we pass along some of the extra cost to you. Last year the company was forced to absorb the total increase in health care premiums. However, such a plan this year is inadvisable.

Offers no explanation for increase; sounds defensive and arbitrary

We did everything possible to avoid the sharp increase in costs to you this year. A rate schedule describing the increases in payments for your family and dependents is enclosed.

Fails to take credit for absorbing previous increases

REVISION

TITANIUM INDUSTRIES, INC.

Overview | Whiteboards | Tasks | Discussions | Files | Meetings | People | News

News
News from HR
Sitemap
Calendar

January 2018

M	T	W	T	F	S	S
1	2	3	4	5	6	7
8	9	10	11	12	13	14
15	16	17	18	19	20	21
22	23	24	25	26	27	28
29	30	31				

My Calendar
Calendar
Manage Calendars

Begins with positive buffer

Health care has always been an important part of our commitment to employees at Titanium Industries, Inc. We are proud that our total benefits package continues to rank among the best in the country.

Explains why costs are rising

Such a comprehensive package does not come cheaply. In the last decade, health-care costs alone have risen over 300 percent. We are told that several factors fuel the cost spiral: an aging population, technology improvements, the increased cost of patient services, and "defensive" medicine practiced by doctors to prevent lawsuits.

Reveals bad news clearly but embeds it in paragraph

Just two years ago, our monthly health-care cost for each employee was $515. It rose to $569 last year. We were able to absorb that jump without increasing your contribution. But this year's hike to $639 forces us to ask you to share the increase. To maintain your current health-care benefits, you will be paying $119 a month. The enclosed rate schedule describes the costs for families and dependents.

Ends positively by stressing the company's major share of the costs

Titanium continues to pay the major portion of your health-care program ($520 each month). We think it's a wise investment.

Attachments (1)

Health Care Rate Schedule.docx
132 Kb View Download

Sign in Recent Site Activity Terms Report Abuse Print Page Remove Access | Powered by Creative Internet Labs

with explanations and figures. The bad news (*you will be paying $119 a month*) is clearly presented but embedded within the paragraph. Throughout, the writer strives to show the fairness of the company's position. The ending, which does not refer to the bad news, emphasizes how much the company is paying and what a wise investment it is.

The entire message demonstrates a kinder, gentler approach than that shown in the first draft. Of prime importance in breaking bad news to employees is providing clear, convincing reasons that explain the decision. Parallel to this internal blog post, the message was also sent by e-mail. In smaller companies in which some workers do not have company e-mail, a hard-copy memo would be posted prominently on bulletin boards and in the lunchroom.

Summary of Learning Outcomes

1 **Understand the strategies of business communicators in conveying negative news. In delivering bad news, communicators should strive to do the following:**
- Explain clearly and completely while projecting a professional image.
- Convey empathy, sensitivity, and fairness.
- Maintain friendly relations, especially with customers.

2 **Compare the techniques and ethics of the direct and indirect strategies in communicating unfavorable news.**
- Use the direct strategy, with the bad news first, when the news is not damaging, when the receiver may overlook it, when the organization or receiver prefers directness, or when firmness is necessary.
- Use the indirect strategy, with a buffer and explanation preceding the bad news, when the bad news is personally upsetting, when it may provoke a hostile reaction, when it threatens the customer relationship, and when the news is unexpected.
- To avoid being unethical, never use the indirect method to deceive or manipulate the truth.

3 **Explain the components of effective negative messages, including opening with a buffer, apologizing, showing empathy, presenting the reasons, cushioning the bad news, and closing pleasantly.**
- To soften bad news, start with a buffer such as the best news, a compliment, appreciation, agreement, facts, understanding, or an apology.
- If you apologize, do it promptly and sincerely. Accept responsibility but don't admit blame without consulting a superior or company counsel. Strive to project empathy.
- In presenting the reasons for the bad news, explain clearly, cite reader or other benefits if plausible, explain company policy if necessary, choose positive words, and strive to show fairness and serious intent.
- In breaking the bad news, position it and word it strategically by (a) sandwiching it between other sentences, (b) presenting it in a subordinating clause, (c) using passive-voice verbs to depersonalize an action, (d) highlighting whatever is positive, (e) implying the refusal instead of stating it directly, and (f) suggesting a compromise or an alternative.
- To close pleasantly, you could (a) suggest a means of following through on an alternative, (b) offer freebies, (c) extend good wishes, (d) anticipate future business, or (e) offer resale information or a sales promotion.

4 **Apply effective techniques for refusing typical requests or claims, as well as for presenting bad news to customers in print or online.**
- In rejecting requests for favors, money, information, and action, follow the bad-news strategy: (a) begin with a buffer, (b) present valid reasons, (c) explain the bad news and possibly an alternative, and (d) close with good feelings and a positive statement.
- To deal with disappointed customers in print, (a) call or e-mail the individual immediately; (b) describe the problem and apologize; (c) explain why the problem occurred, what you are doing to resolve it, and how you will prevent it from happening again; and (d) promote goodwill with a follow-up message.
- To handle negative posts and reviews online, (a) verify the situation, (b) respond quickly and constructively, (c) consider giving freebies such as refunds or discounts, (d) learn to improve by considering people who made negative comments as real-time focus groups, and (e) be prepared to accept the inevitable and move on.
- To deny claims, (a) use the reasons-before-refusal plan, (b) don't blame customers (even if they are at fault), (c) use neutral objective language to explain why the claim must be refused, and (d) consider offering resale information to rebuild the customer's confidence in your products or organization.

5 Describe and apply effective techniques for delivering bad news within organizations.

- To deliver workplace bad news in person, (a) gather all the information; (b) prepare and rehearse; (c) explain the past, present, and future; (d) consider taking a partner; (e) choose the best time to deliver the news; and (f) be patient with the reaction.
- In announcing bad news to employees and to the public, strive to keep the communication open and honest, choose the best communication channel, and consider applying the indirect strategy.
- Be positive, but don't sugarcoat the bad news; use objective language.

Chapter Review

1. How can the bad feelings associated with disappointing news be reduced? (L.O. 1)

2. What are your goals in communicating negative news, and how can you achieve them? (L.O. 1)

3. What is the primary difference between the direct and the indirect strategies? (L.O. 2)

4. When would you be more inclined to use the direct strategy in delivering bad news? (L.O. 2)

5. What is a buffer? Name five or more techniques to buffer the opening of a bad-news message. (L.O. 3)

6. Why should you apologize to customers if you or your company erred? What is the best way to do it? (L.O. 3)

7. Describe the writing plan for refusing typical requests and claims. (L.O. 4)

8. How can negative online comments be turned into positive growth for an organization? (L.O. 4)

9. How can a subordinate tactfully, professionally, and safely deliver upsetting news personally to a superior? (L.O. 5)

10. What are some channels that large organizations may use to deliver bad news to employees? (L.O. 5)

Critical Thinking

11. Why might it be shortsighted to bluntly refuse lending money or issue credit cards to people without a credit history—such as young students—or to consumers with less-than-stellar credit? (L.O. 1–4)

12. Robert Bies, professor of management at Georgetown University, believes that an important ethical guideline in dealing with bad news is never to shock the recipient: "Bad news should never come as a surprise. Failure to warn senior leadership of impending bad news, such as poor sales or a loss of a major client, is a cardinal sin. So is failure to warn subordinates about mistakes in their performance and provide an opportunity for them to make corrections and improve."[25] Discuss the motivation of people who keep quiet and struggle with dispensing bad news. (L.O. 1–3)

13. Should organizations fear websites where consumers post negative messages about products and services? What actions can companies take in response to this potential threat? (L.O. 4)

14. Consider times when you have been aware that others were using the indirect strategy in writing or speaking to you. How did you react? (L.O. 2)

15. What might be some advantages and disadvantages to being let go remotely, if any? Why might it be a good idea to rein in one's frustration and anger? (L.O. 5)

Writing Improvement Exercises

Passive-Voice Verbs (L.O. 3)

Passive-voice verbs may be preferable in breaking bad news because they enable you to emphasize actions rather than personalities. Compare these two refusals:

EXAMPLE   **Active voice:** We cannot send any employees to the Las Vegas conference this year.

Passive voice: No employees can be sent to the Las Vegas conference this year.

Revise the following refusals so that they use passive-voice instead of active-voice verbs.

16. We will no longer be accepting credit cards for purchases under $5.

17. Our hospital policy forbids us to examine patients until we have verified their insurance coverage.

18. We cannot offer health and dental benefits until employees have been on the job for 12 months.

19. The manager and I have made arrangements for the investors to have lunch after the tour.

20. Because management now requires more stringent security, we are postponing indefinitely requests for company tours.

Subordinate Clauses (L.O. 3)

You can further soften the effect of bad news by placing it in an introductory subordinate clause that begins with *although, since,* or *because.* The emphasis in a sentence is on the independent clause. Instead of saying *We cannot serve you on a credit basis,* try *Although we cannot serve you on a credit basis, we invite you to take advantage of our cash discounts and sale prices.* Revise the following so that the bad news is de-emphasized in a dependent clause that precedes an independent clause.

21. We are sorry to report that we are unable to ship your complete order at this time. However, we are able to send two corner workstations now; you should receive them within five days.

22. Unfortunately, we no longer print a complete catalog. However, we now offer all of our catalog choices at our website, which is always current.

23. We appreciate your interest in our organization, but we are unable to extend an employment offer to you at this time.

24. The state does not allow smoking within 5 feet of a state building. However, we have set aside three lawful outdoor smoking areas.

Implying Bad News (L.O. 3)

Bad news can be de-emphasized by implying a refusal instead of stating it directly. Compare these refusals:

EXAMPLE **Direct refusal:** We cannot send you a price list, nor can we sell our lawn mowers directly to customers. We sell only through dealers, and your dealer is HomeCo.

Implied refusal: Our lawn mowers are sold only through dealers, and your dealer is HomeCo.

Revise the following refusals so that the bad news is implied. If possible, use passive-voice verbs and subordinate clauses to further de-emphasize the bad news.

25. We cannot ship our fresh fruit baskets c.o.d. Your order was not accompanied by payment, so we are not shipping it. We have it ready, though, and will rush it to its destination as soon as you call us with your credit card number.

26. Unfortunately, we find it impossible to contribute to the fund-raising campaign this year. At present all the funds of my organization are needed to lease new equipment and offices for our latest branch in Atlanta. We hope to be able to support this endeavor in the future.

27. Your team cannot schedule a retreat for the week of May 15. Too many staffers will be working on the Osgood Project, which will not be completed until June 1.

Note: Radical Rewrites are provided at **www.cengagebrain.com** for you to download and revise. Your instructor may show a suggested solution.

7.1 Radical Rewrite: Request Refusal—Nuptials Nixed at Napa Inn (L.O. 1–4)

The following poorly written letter turns down the request of a bride-to-be seeking to reserve the popular Napa Valley Inn as a venue for her wedding. How can this letter be made less disappointing?

YOUR TASK. Analyze the message. List its weaknesses, and then outline an appropriate writing plan. If your instructor directs, revise the message.

February 5, 2019

Ms. Sonya Capretta
2459 Sierra Avenue
Fresno, CA 93710

Dear Ms. Capretta:

We regret to inform you that the wedding date you request in your letter of February 2 at the Napa Valley Inn is unavailable. Unfortunately, we are fully booked for all of the Saturdays in June, as you probably already suspected.

June is our busiest month, and smart brides make their reservations many months—even years—in advance. That's because the Napa Valley Inn is the ideal romantic getaway for weddings. With unparalleled cuisine and service, along with panoramic Napa Valley and vineyard views, our inn offers a unique, intimate ambiance in a breathtaking location for your special event.

We apologize if we have caused you any inconvenience. However, if you could change your wedding date to the middle of the week, we would try to accommodate your party. We do have a few midweek spots open in June, but even those dates are rapidly filling up. With 45 Mediterranean-style rooms and suites, each with its own sunny private terrace, the Napa Valley Inn is the perfect location for you and your partner to begin your married lives. Afternoon ceremonies typically begin at 11 a.m., while golden sunsets at the Napa Valley Inn offer a romantic prelude of the evening to come. Evening ceremonies usually begin at 6 p.m. I'm available if you want to arrange something.

Sincerely,

1. List at least five weaknesses.

2. Outline a writing plan for a request refusal:

7.2 Radical Rewrite: Bad News to Employees—Software Is Strictly Business (L.O. 1–3, 5)

Anna He Wong must refuse the request of some staff engineers. They want access keys for home use of the latest version of Adobe Creative Cloud, a licensed cloud-based suite of apps and services that includes Photoshop, Illustrator, and InDesign. Although priced for small businesses, starting at $29.99 per month per user, the cost for licenses adds up. The company cannot finance Creative Cloud licenses for home use.

YOUR TASK. Analyze Anna's message. It suffers from many writing faults that you have studied. List its weaknesses. If your instructor directs, revise the message.

To: Staff computer users
From: Anna He Wong <ahwong@csb.com>
Subject: Adobe Creative Cloud Access Codes Are Expensive!

Unfortunately, I cannot buy extra licenses for the latest Adobe Creative Cloud apps and services for home use. Or for any other use. Some staffers have asked for this privilege. Which is cost prohibitive.

This cloud-based suite of applications has many outstanding features, and I would be happy to demonstrate some of it to anyone who drops by the Document Production Department. Purchasing access to this software for private use would be too expensive. Like many cloud-based software titles, Adobe Creative Cloud is subscription based, per month, per user. We cannot use access keys for more than one computer each. The access keys are unique. Definitely not for home use! If you stop and think about it, it makes a lot of sense. Software companies need to provide unique access codes because otherwise they wouldn't be in business long. Eventually, they would not earn enough money to stay in business. Or to develop new software.

This e-mail is to inform you that we cannot provide extra licenses for Adobe Creative Cloud access due to the fact that we agreed to limit use to work-related projects only. Thank you for your cooperation.

Anna He Wong, Manager

Document Production

List at least five weaknesses.

Activities and Cases

7.3 Request Refusal: Rising Phoenix Team Sinks Application (L.O. 1–4)

> E-Mail   > Web

Adobe Systems Incorporated is known for its community involvement and corporate social responsibility efforts. This is why, like most large companies, the software giant receives many requests for sponsorships of charity events and community projects. True to its innovative spirit, the software company has streamlined the application process by providing an online sponsorship request form on its website.

You work in Corporate Affairs/Community Relations at Adobe and periodically help decide which nonprofits obtain support. Just yesterday you received an e-mail from Rising Phoenix of Portland, Oregon, a dragon boat racing team of breast cancer survivors. The ancient Chinese sport has spread around the globe with competitions held not only in Asia but also in many Western countries. Dragon boat racing has gained popularity in North America among breast cancer patients who bond with fellow survivors, engage in healthy competition, and exercise regularly on the water. Synchronicity and technique are more important than brute strength, which is the main reason even recreational paddlers enjoy this fast-growing water sport.

The survivor team would like Adobe to sponsor a dragon boat festival in Portland in less than a month, an event potentially drawing at least 20 survivor teams that would compete against each other. Your company is already funding several cancer charities and has a policy of sponsoring many causes. Naturally, no corporate giving program has infinite funds, nor can it green-light every request. Adobe steers clear of religious, political, and "pornographic" events. The team judging the sponsorship entries wants to ensure that each proposal reaches audiences affiliated with Adobe. Most important, applicants must submit their requests at least six weeks before the event.

YOUR TASK. As a junior staff member in Corporate Affairs/Community Relations, write an e-mail to Rising Phoenix captain Jenny Johnson (jjohnson@risingphoenix.org) refusing her initial request and explaining the Adobe sponsorship philosophy and submission rules.

7.4 Request Refusal: Turning Down an Award-Winning Charity (L.O. 1–4)

As a vice president of a financial services company, you serve many clients and they sometimes ask your company to contribute to their favorite charities. You recently received a letter from Elliana Larios asking for a substantial contribution to Interval House Crisis Shelters & Centers for Victims of Domestic Violence. On visits to your office, she has told you about the model charity's programs to provide comprehensive domestic violence services in over 70 languages to individuals and families in Los Angeles County and Orange County. Elliana herself is active as one of many Interval House volunteers who help ensure the safety of people who are battered, abused, or at risk; create public awareness about the epidemic of violence; and mobilize the community to prevent and end violence.

You are impressed by this highly decorated charity, recognized with over 500 awards, including four Presidential Awards and four Governor's Awards. You sincerely want to support Interval House and its good work. However, your company has suffered setbacks, and you can't be as generous as you have been in the past. Ms. Larios wrote a special letter to you asking you to become a Key contributor, with a pledge of $2,000.

YOUR TASK. Write a refusal letter that maintains good relations with your client. Address it to Ms. Elliana Larios, 1450 Opechee Way, Glendale, CA 91208.

7.5 Request Refusal: I'm Flattered, But I Can't Speak to Your Club (L.O. 1–4)

As an assistant to Pamela Eyring, you must help her refuse an invitation to speak at Wysocki College in Boston. The business associations on campus pooled their resources and decided to invite Ms. Eyring to give a talk on campus about the importance of soft skills. A sought-after TV commentator and media personality, Ms. Eyring owns The Protocol School of Washington, a training center for etiquette consultants and protocol officers. For over two decades, she was chief of protocol at a prominent military base. Since acquiring The Protocol School of Washington, she has established herself as a frequent contributor to Reuters, *The Wall Street Journal*, *The New York Times*, *Forbes*, *Entrepreneur*, and other important publications. An authority on business etiquette, she is often featured on radio and TV programs such as the *Today Show*, CNN, and ABC Radio Network. A member of several business and professional associations, Ms. Eyring receives many invitations to speak as an authority on business etiquette and as an award-winning entrepreneur and leader.

Ms. Eyring likes to speak to young students, mostly pro bono or for a nominal fee, but during the spring semester she is too busy with starting her new location in Dubai, United Arab Emirates, with organizing a meeting of the Women Presidents Organization, and with writing a book on dining like a diplomat. Ms. Eyring might be able to deliver her presentation some other time, or she could send Robert Hickey, her deputy director and senior trainer.

YOUR TASK. In Ms. Eyring's name, refuse the invitation but suggest an alternative. Send your letter to Chelsea Landry, Associated Students, Wysocki College, 246 Bay State Road, Boston, MA 02215.

7.6 Request Refusal: Can't Evict Noisy Tenant (L.O. 1–4)
> Web

As the owner of Edgewood Towne Center, you must respond to the request of Charles Costerisan, one of the tenants in your three-story office building. Mr. Costerisan, a CPA, demands that you immediately evict a neighboring tenant who plays loud music throughout the day, interfering with Mr. Costerisan's conversations with clients and with his concentration. The noisy tenant, Timothy Brenner, seems to operate an entertainment booking agency and spends long hours in his office. You know you can't evict Mr. Brenner because, as a legal commercial tenant, he is entitled to conduct his business. However, you might consider adding soundproofing, an expense that you would prefer to share with Mr. Brenner and Mr. Costerisan. You might also discuss limiting the time of day that Mr. Brenner could make noise.

YOUR TASK. Before responding to Mr. Costerisan, you decide to find out more about commercial tenancy. Use the Web to search the keywords *commercial eviction*. Then develop a course of action. In a letter to Mr. Costerisan, deny his request but retain his goodwill. Tell him how you plan to resolve the problem. Write to Charles Costerisan, CPA, Suite 200, Edgewood Towne Center, 300 Frandor Avenue, Lansing, MI 48912. Your instructor may also ask you to write an appropriate message to Mr. Timothy Brenner, Suite 220.

7.7 Claim Denial: Pricey Prescription Eyewear Left on Plane (L.O. 1–4)

Pacific Southern Airlines (PSA) had an unhappy customer. Cynthia Mercier-Walters flew from Philadelphia, Pennsylvania, to Phoenix, Arizona. The flight stopped briefly at Hartsfield-Jackson Atlanta International Airport, where she got off the plane for half an hour. When she returned to her seat, her $400 prescription reading glasses were gone. She asked the flight attendant where the glasses were, and the attendant said they probably were thrown away since the cleaning crew had come in with big bags and tossed everything in them. Ms. Mercier-Walters tried to locate the glasses through the airline's lost-and-found service, but she failed.

Then she wrote a strong letter to the airline demanding reimbursement for the loss. She felt that it was obvious that she was returning to her seat. The airline, however, knows that an overwhelming number of passengers arriving at hubs switch planes for their connecting flights. The airline does not know who is returning. What's more, flight attendants usually announce that the plane is continuing to another city and that passengers who are returning should take their belongings. Cabin cleaning crews speed through planes removing newspapers, magazines, leftover foods, and trash. Airlines feel no responsibility for personal items left in cabins.[26]

YOUR TASK. As a staff member of the Customer Relations Department of Pacific Southern Airlines, deny the customer's claim but retain her goodwill using techniques learned in this chapter. The airline never refunds cash, but it might consider travel vouchers for the value of the glasses.

Remember that apologies cost nothing. Write a claim denial to Ms. Cynthia Mercier-Walters, 8400 S 51st Avenue, Glendale, AZ 85301.

7.8 Claim Denial: Whining on the Web (L.O. 1-4)

> E-Mail > Social Media > Web

The growth of social networking has also spawned many websites dedicated to customer reviews and complaints—for example, Angie's List, which profiles local service companies, contractors, and professionals. More specifically, companies such as Cruise Critic focus solely on vacation travel by ship. Visit Complaints.com, Ripoff Report, or another complaint site. Study ten or more complaints about products or companies (e.g., iPhone, Starbucks, Delta Air Lines).

YOUR TASK. Select one complaint and, as a company employee, respond to it employing some of the techniques presented in this chapter. Submit a copy of the complaint along with your response to your instructor. Your instructor may request that you write an e-mail or a letter.

7.9 Claim Denial: Sorry—Smokers Must Cough Up Cash (L.O. 1-4)

Recently the Century Park Hotel embarked on a two-year plan to provide enhanced value and improved product quality to its guests. It always strives to exceed guest expectations. As part of this effort, Century Park Hotel has been refurbishing many rooms with updated finishes. The new carpet, paint, upholstery, and draperies, however, absorb the heavy odor of cigarette smoke. To protect the hotel's investment, Century Park enforces a strict nonsmoking policy for its nonsmoking rooms.

Century Park makes sure that guests know about its policy regarding smoking in nonsmoking rooms. It posts a notice in each non-smoking room, and it gives guests a handout from the manager detailing its policy and the consequences for smoking in nonsmoking rooms. The handout clearly says, "Should a guest opt to disregard our nonsmoking policy, we will process a fee of $150 to the guest's account." For those guests who prefer to smoke, a smoking accommodation can be provided.

On May 10 Wilson M. Weber was a guest in the hotel. He stayed in a room clearly marked "Nonsmoking." After he left, the room cleaners reported that the room smelled of smoke. According to hotel policy, a charge of $150 was processed to Mr. Weber's credit card. Mr. Weber has written to demand that the $150 charge be removed. He doesn't deny that he smoked in the room. He just believes that he should not have to pay.

YOUR TASK. As hotel manager, deny Mr. Weber's claim. You would certainly like to see Mr. Weber return as a Century Park Hotel guest, but you cannot budge on your smoking policy. Address your response to Mr. Wilson M. Weber, 634 Wetmore Avenue, Everett, WA 98201.

7.10 Customer Bad News: Pick a Price Hike (L.O. 1-4)

Select a product or service that you now use (e.g., Internet or cable service, water or electricity, propane or natural gas, cell or landline phone, car insurance). Assume that the provider must raise its rates and that you are the employee who must notify customers. Should you use a letter, e-mail, company website, or blog? Decide whether you should use the direct or indirect strategy. Gather as much information as you can about the product or service. What, if anything, justifies the increase? What benefits can be cited?

YOUR TASK. Prepare a rate increase announcement. Submit it along with a memo explaining your rationale for the strategy you chose.

7.11 Customer Bad News: Blunder in Scheduling Fairytale Thorncrown Chapel Wedding (L.O. 1-4)

As the wedding planner at Eureka Springs Weddings in Arkansas, you just discovered a terrible mistake. Two weddings have been scheduled for the same Saturday in June. How could this have happened? You keep meticulous records, but six months ago, you were away for two weeks. Another employee filled in for you. She apparently didn't understand the scheduling system and lined up two weddings for the renowned Thorncrown Chapel on June 16. The month of June, of course, is the busiest month of the year. Weddings in the beautiful glass cathedral in the woods are usually booked for two years in advance, and it can handle only one wedding a day.

It's now January, and Candy Schonwald, one of the brides-to-be called to check on her arrangements. That's when you discovered the mistake. However, you didn't reveal the blunder to Candy on the telephone. From experience, you know how emotional brides can be when their plans go awry. Now you must decide what to do. Your manager has given you complete authority in scheduling weddings, and you know he would back nearly any decision you make to rectify the mistake. Unfortunately, the historic 1886 Crescent Hotel & Spa and 1905 Basin Park Hotel wedding venues are booked for June Saturdays. However, you do have some midweek openings for the Thorncrown Chapel in early June. If one of the brides could change to midweek, you might offer one free night in a sumptuous bridal suite at the storied Crescent Hotel & Spa to smooth ruffled feathers.

With its 6,000 square feet of glass and 425 windows, Thorncrown Chapel offers a dreamlike setting for unforgettable wedding celebrations that feel outdoors while providing the comfort of indoor air conditioning. Brides, grooms, and their guests can enjoy the historic Castle in the Sky, a palatial hotel perched atop West Mountain in the Ozarks, a Victorian hotel surrounded by hundreds of Victorian cottages, ample green space, and hidden trails.

YOUR TASK Decide what course of action to take. The two brides-to-be are Candy Schonwald, 614 Pirkle Ferry Road, Cumming, GA 30040, and Debbie Hungeling, 4590 Clairmont Road, Atlanta, GA 30346. In a memo to your instructor, explain your response strategy. If you plan a phone call, outline what you plan to say. If your instructor requests, write a letter and copy your instructor.

7.12 Customer Bad News: Selecting Sturdy Stepper for Snap Fitness Gym (L.O. 1–4)

> **E-Mail**

You are delighted to receive a large order from Lawrence Holder at Snap Fitness Gym. This order includes two Lifecycle Trainers (at $1,295 each), four Pro Abdominal Boards (at $295 each), three Tunturi Muscle Trainers (at $749 each), and three Dual-Action StairClimbers (at $1,545 each).

You could ship immediately except for one problem. The Dual-Action StairClimber is intended for home use, not for gym or club use. Customers like it because they say it is more like scaling a mountain than climbing a flight of stairs. With each step, users exercise their arms to pull or push themselves up. Its special cylinders absorb shock so that no harmful running impact results. However, this model is not what you would recommend for gym use. You feel Mr. Holder should order your premier stair climber, the LifeStep (at $2,395 each). This unit has sturdier construction and is meant for heavy use. Its sophisticated electronics provide a selection of customer-pleasing programs that challenge muscles progressively with a choice of workouts. It also quickly multiplies workout gains with computer-controlled interval training. Electronic monitors inform users of step height, calories burned, elapsed time, upcoming levels, and adherence to fitness goals. For gym use the LifeStep is clearly better than the Dual-Action StairClimber. The bad news is that the LifeStep is considerably more expensive. You get no response when you try to call Mr. Holder to discuss the problem. Should you ship what you can, or hold the entire order until you learn whether he wants the Dual-Action StairClimber or the LifeStep? Or perhaps you should substitute the LifeStep and send only two of them.

YOUR TASK. Decide what to do and write a letter to be faxed or send an e-mail to Lawrence Holder, Snap Fitness Gym, 1212 Bahama Drive, Richmond, KY 40475.

7.13 Employee Bad News: No More Help With Sky-High Tuition (L.O. 1–5)

> **E-Mail**

Lea Tyra, a hardworking bank teller, has sent an e-mail request asking that the company create a program to reimburse the tuition and book expenses for employees taking college courses. Although some companies have such a program, Unified Federal Bank has not felt that it could indulge in such an expensive employee perk. Moreover, the CEO is not convinced that companies see any direct benefit from such programs. Employees improve their educational credentials and skills, but what is to keep them from moving that education and those skill sets to other employers? Unified Federal has over 200 employees. If even a fraction of them started classes, the company could see a huge bill for the cost of tuition and books.

Because the bank is facing stiff competition and its profits are sinking, the expense of such a program makes it out of the question. In addition, it would involve administration—applications, monitoring, and record keeping. It is just too much of a hassle. When employees were hard to hire and retain, companies had to offer employment perks. With a fluctuating job market, however, such inducements are unnecessary.

YOUR TASK. As director of Human Resources, send an individual e-mail response to Lea Tyra. The answer is a definite *no*, but you want to soften the blow and retain the loyalty of this conscientious employee.

7.14 Employee Bad News: Saying Goodbye to Gourmet Meals and Perks (L.O. 1–5)

> **Communication Technology**

When high-tech start-up Minx first hit the technology scene, it created a big splash. Its music-streaming and voice control technology promised to revolutionize the field. It attracted $500,000 in seed money, suggesting that it could hire the best talent and create amazing new products. But Minx quickly fell off the fast track. It spent nearly $400,000 on a Bluetooth product that sold only 28 units. In addition, a botched security update resulted in the company's having to conduct a nationwide recall of one of its smart products. However, other products have been successful, and the company is not facing bankruptcy.

Initially, Minx offered amazing perks to attract the best and brightest talent. It provided an in-house chef with free gourmet meals, unlimited snacks, on-site acupuncture, and free yoga classes. Its offices were pet-friendly, and new employees received a $10,000 cash signing bonus. To counter the long hours that the tech world notoriously demands of its workers, Minx offered relaxation areas with table tennis and foosball tables. Unfortunately, cash flow problems after a recent acquisition have made it necessary for Minx to pull back on its employee perks. Although no staff members are being released, the in-house chef has to go, along with on-site acupuncture, yoga classes, and the $10,000 signing bonus. However, it's still a good place to work, and camaraderie is high.

YOUR TASK. As a communications trainee in the CEO's office, you have been asked to draft an intranet post or a memo to employees announcing the bad news. Explain the cutbacks that affect current employees. Employ the bad-news techniques taught in this chapter. What could soften this bad news?

7.15 Employee Bad News: No Social Media at Work (L.O. 1–5)

> **E-Mail**

Your manager at MarketingMind, a successful midsized public relations agency, is concerned that the youngest employees may be oversharing on Facebook, Instagram, Twitter, and other popular social media platforms. Two supervisors have complained that they spotted inappropriate photos on Facebook posted by a small group of millennials on the company payroll. This group of twenty-somethings is close-knit. Its members maintain friendships outside the office and in cyberspace. They are smart and plugged in, but they seem to have trouble recognizing boundaries of age and authority. They party every weekend, which is code for a lot of drinking, marijuana use, and even salacious escapades—all of which the young workers generously document with smartphone cameras on the spot and occasionally in real time. Sometimes they share snarky comments about their workplace, such as "Rough day at work" or "Talked to the most idiotic client ever!" On top of that, the young people think nothing of friending their colleagues and supervisors. Their friends rank in the hundreds; some in the group have exceeded 1,000 friends on Facebook and Instagram.

MarketingMind has embraced cutting-edge technology because the management believes that information sharing and collaboration tools can lead to networking opportunities and, if used correctly, to increased productivity. The company maintains a permissive stance toward Internet use, but concern is growing that the young people are headed for trouble. The abuses continue despite the company's comprehensive Internet and social media use policy, which was widely disseminated. Probably the biggest risk MarketingMind fears is the leaking of confidential information on social networking sites. The managers also complain that the millennials spend too much time on social media during office hours. Your boss is becoming impatient. After several meetings, the management decides to disallow social media use during work hours and to caution all employees against dangerous breaches of company policy and social media netiquette.

YOUR TASK. Draft an e-mail for the signature of your boss, Emma P. Sharpe, Director, Human Resources. Your message should remind all employees about the existing social networking policy and tactfully yet clearly announce the end of social media use at the office. The prohibition is effective immediately. Your message should also warn about the pitfalls of oversharing online.

Commas 2

Review the Grammar/Mechanics Handbook Sections 2.05–2.09. Then select the correctly punctuated sentence and record its letter in the space provided. Record also the appropriate G/M guideline to illustrate the principle involved. When you finish, compare your responses with those provided at the bottom of the page. If your answers differ, study carefully the appropriate guideline.

_____a_____ (2.06a)   EXAMPLE   a. When U.S. organizations engage in overseas business, they must train their staffs accordingly.
b. When U.S. organizations engage in overseas business they must train their staffs accordingly.

_____ 1. a. If you are based in Chicago, and working with a sales office in Australia you will be dealing with a 17-hour time difference.
b. If you are based in Chicago and working with a sales office in Australia, you will be dealing with a 17-hour time difference.

_____ 2. a. One international support person works with time zones around the world, and she keeps several clocks set to different zones.
b. One international support person works with time zones around the world and she keeps several clocks set to different zones.

_____ 3. a. Dealing with the unfamiliar is less challenging if you are patient, and if you are able to avoid becoming irritated at misunderstandings.
b. Dealing with the unfamiliar is less challenging if you are patient and if you are able to avoid becoming irritated at misunderstandings.

_____ 4. a. Lourdes Luna, who was recently transferred to the parent company in France, quickly became fluent in French.
b. Lourdes Luna who was recently transferred to the parent company in France, quickly became fluent in French.

_____ 5. a. The imaginative promising software company opened its offices April 22 in Paris.
b. The imaginative, promising software company opened its offices April 22 in Paris.

_____ 6. a. Any sales associate who earns at least 1,000 recognition points this year, will be honored with a bonus vacation trip to Tahiti.
b. Any sales associate who earns at least 1,000 recognition points this year will be honored with a bonus vacation trip to Tahiti.

_____ 7. a. Sonia Soto, the marketing manager for Avon International, frequently engages in video-conferences that span time zones.
b. Sonia Soto, the marketing manager for Avon International frequently engages in video-conferences that span time zones.

_____ 8. a. In a period of less than six weeks Ms. Soto made several trips to the West Coast and to Asia.
b. In a period of less than six weeks, Ms. Soto made several trips to the West Coast and to Asia.

_____ 9. a. When you are working with foreign clients for whom English is a second language you may have to speak slowly and repeat yourself.
b. When you are working with foreign clients for whom English is a second language, you may have to speak slowly and repeat yourself.

_____ 10. a. To be most successful, you must read between the lines and learn to pick up on different cultural vibes.
b. To be most successful, you must read between the lines, and learn to pick up on different cultural vibes.

1. b (2.06a) 2. a (2.05) 3. b (2.05) 4. a (2.06c) 5. b (2.08) 6. b (2.06c) 7. a (2.09) 8. b (2.07) 9. b (2.07) 10. a (2.07)

Every chapter provides an editing exercise to fine-tune your grammar and mechanics skills. The following letter requires edits that address grammar, concise wording, sentence structure, punctuation (especially commas), and other writing issues. Study the guidelines in the Grammar/Mechanics Handbook (Appendix D), including the lists of Confusing Words and Frequently Misspelled Words.

YOUR TASK. Edit the following (a) by inserting corrections in your textbook or on a photocopy using proofreading marks in Appendix C or (b) by downloading the message from **www.cengagebrain.com** and correcting at your computer.

PIONEER WATER DISTRICT

November 15, 2019

Ms. Ann Neethirajan
4783 Haven Avenue
Alta Loma, CA 91737

Dear Mr. Neethirajan:

This is to let you know that our top priority at the Pioneer Water District is to provide safe and reliable water to over 93,000 people here in Pioneer Valley. Providing accurate regular water bills to our customers homes and businesses' every month is an integral part of our service. Since the launch of a new billing system we have experienced problems in delivering bills in a manner that is timely. We apologize for the inconvenience and frustration this may have caused you. However we want you to know that we are doing everything we can to resolve this billing issue as quick as possible.

About two years ago we began researching new billing systems in response to our customers requests for more flexible convenient payment methods. Such as online billing and the ability to make credit card payments. Customers also expressed interest in improved access to water use information and online tools. After an extensive vendor search and vetting process we engaged Excel Water Management to implement a new billing system to meet our customers needs.

Unfortunately since making the transition we have experienced unexpected and unacceptable implementation challenges. We are extremely disapointed and frustrated with the impact that the new billing plan has had on our customers. Without question some of our customers has not received the reliably scheduled billing service that they expect, and that we are committed to providing.

Please be assured that we are working in a diligent manner to fix these problems to protect our customers interests, keep our costs low and provide water bills on a timely basis.

We appreciate you ongoing patience and understanding while we work to resolve this billing issue. If you are interested in following our efforts please visit our website for regular progress updates, www.pioneerwater.com.

Sincerely,

Mason R. Lennox, Manager

Saying *No* Across Cultures

As you have learned in this chapter, Americans generally prefer to present negative messages indirectly to minimize disappointment. Other cultures may treat bad news differently, as illustrated in the following:

- British writers tend to be straightforward with bad news, seeing no reason to soften its announcement.

- In Germany business communicators occasionally use buffers but tend to present bad news directly.

- In Latin American countries, the question is not how to organize negative messages but whether to present them at all. It is considered disrespectful and impolite to report bad news to superiors. Therefore, reluctant employees may fail to report accurately any negative situations to their bosses.

- In Thailand the negativism represented by a refusal is completely alien; the word *no* does not exist. In many cultures negative news is offered with such subtlety or in such a positive light that it may be overlooked or misunderstood by literal-minded Americans.

- In many Asian and some Latin cultures, one must look beyond an individual's actual words to understand what is really being communicated. One must consider the communication style, the culture, and especially the context. Consider the following phrases and their possible meanings:

Phrase	Possible Meaning
I agree.	I agree with 15 percent of what you say.
We might be able to . . .	Not a chance!
We will consider . . .	*We* will consider, but the real decision maker will not.
That is a little too much.	That is outrageous!
Yes.	Yes, I'm listening. *OR:* Yes, you have a good point. *OR:* Yes, I understand, but I don't necessarily agree.

CAREER APPLICATION. Interview fellow students or work colleagues who are from other cultures. Collect information by asking the following questions:

- How is negative news handled in your culture?

- How would typical business communicators refuse a request for a business favor (such as a contribution to a charity)?

- How would typical business communicators refuse a customer's claim?

- How would an individual be turned down for a job?

YOUR TASK. Report the findings of your interviews in class discussion or in a memo report. In addition, collect samples of foreign business letters. You might search the Internet for sample business letters in other languages with the help of foreign students. Alternatively, you might ask your campus admissions office or local export/import companies whether they would be willing to share business letters written in English from other countries. Compare letter styles, formats, tone, and writing strategies. How do these elements differ from those in typical North American business letters?

Persuasive Messages

goodluz/Shutterstock.com

8-1 Understanding Persuasion in a Social and Mobile Age

Contemporary businesses have embraced leaner corporate hierarchies, simultaneously relying on teams, eliminating division walls, and blurring the lines of authority. As teams and managers are abandoning the traditional command structure, excellent persuasive skills are becoming ever more important at work. Effective businesspeople must try to *influence* others.[1] However, getting others to do what we want isn't easy. Persuasion is needed when we are making more than routine demands and facing skeptical audiences.

Experts say that an American adult on average endures as many as 5,000 advertisement and brand exposures a day.[2] As citizens and consumers, we need to be alert to persuasive practices and how they influence behavior. Being informed is our best defense. For better or for worse, social media networks have put power into the hands of many. Persuasion guru B. J. Fogg points out that social media enable individuals or groups to reach virtually limitless audiences and practice "mass interpersonal persuasion."[3] In an age of so-called alternative facts and alleged fake news, responsible citizens must be skeptical consumers of information.

You have already studied techniques for writing routine request messages that require minimal persuasion. This chapter focuses on messages that require deliberate and skilled persuasion in the workplace. It also addresses selling, both offline and online.

Learning Outcomes

After studying this chapter, you should be able to do the following:

1 Explain digital age persuasion and identify time-proven persuasive techniques.

2 Craft persuasive messages that request actions.

3 Write compelling claims and deliver successful complaints.

4 Understand interpersonal persuasion at work, and compose persuasive messages within organizations.

5 Create effective and ethical direct-mail and e-mail sales messages.

8-1a How Has Persuasion Changed in the Digital Age?

The preoccupation with persuasion is not new. From the days of Aristotle in ancient Greece and Machiavelli in Renaissance Italy, philosophers, politicians, and business-people have longed to understand the art of influencing others. However, persuasion in the twenty-first century is different from persuasion in previous historic periods in distinct ways.[4] The most striking developments, summarized in this section, are less than three decades old.

The Volume and Reach of Persuasive Messages Have Exploded. Although full awareness and engagement are difficult to measure, experts estimate that the average American adult is exposed to 362 ads alone each day, not to mention many other daily persuasive appeals.[5] TV, radio, the Internet, and mobile devices blast myriad messages to the far corners of the earth. Past Pew Research studies show that the United States is generally seen favorably by people around the globe despite a complex political climate,[6] due, perhaps, to America's pervasive popular culture.

Persuasive Messages Spread at Warp Speed. Popular TV shows such as *The Big Bang Theory*, the action drama *NCIS*, and the *Crime Scene Investigation* franchise are global phenomena.[7] Popular music and social media engage fans worldwide. Furthermore, election year campaign buzz also traveled at dizzying speed and was followed around the world.

Organizations of All Stripes Are in the Persuasion Business. Companies, ad agencies, PR firms, social activists, lobbyists, marketers, and more spew persuasive messages. Although outspent by corporations that can sink millions into image campaigns, activists of various political leanings use social networks to galvanize their followers.

Persuasive Techniques Are More Subtle and Misleading. Instead of a blunt, pushy hard-sell approach, persuaders play on emotions by using flattery, empathy, nonverbal cues, and likability appeals. They are selling images and lifestyles, not products.[9] In this age of spin, the news media are increasingly infiltrated by

WORKPLACE IN FOCUS

Professional persuaders try to generate "a distinct kind of automatic, mindless compliance" in people, a "willingness to say yes without thinking first," believes psychologist Robert B. Cialdini. The best-selling author of *Influence* cautions: "The ever-accelerating pace and informational crush of modern life will make . . . unthinking compliance more and more prevalent in the future. It will be increasingly important for the society, therefore, to understand the how and why of automatic influence." What does this mean for you as a consumer and participant in social media?[10]

Dimitri Vervitsiotis/Photographer's Choice/Getty Images

Figure 8.1 Effective Persuasion Techniques

Establish credibility
- Show that you are truthful, experienced, and knowledgeable.
- Use others' expert opinions and research to support your position.

Make a reasonable, specific request
- Make your request realistic, doable, and attainable.
- Be clear about your objective. Vague requests are less effective.

Tie facts to benefits
- Line up plausible support such as statistics, reasons, and analogies.
- Convert the supporting facts into specific audience benefits.

Recognize the power of loss
- Show what others stand to lose if they don't agree.
- Know that people dread losing something they already possess.

Expect and overcome resistance
- Anticipate opposition from conflicting beliefs, values, and attitudes.
- Be prepared to counter with well-reasoned arguments and facts.

Share solutions and compromise
- Be flexible and aim for a solution that is acceptable to all parties.
- Listen to people and incorporate their input to create buy-in.

partisan interests and spread messages masquerading as news. Political bloggers opine, frequently dispensing with the careful fact checking expected of mainstream media.

Persuasion Is More Complex and Impersonal. American consumers are more diverse and don't necessarily think alike. To reach them, marketers carefully study target groups and customize their appeals. Technology has increased the potential for distortion. People can "mash up" content, give it meanings the source never intended, and blast it into the world in seconds.

You probably recognize how important it is not only to become a skilled persuader, but also to identify devious messages and manipulation attempts directed at you. The delivery channels may have changed, but the principles of effective, time-tried persuasion outlined in Figure 8.1 still apply today.

When you want your ideas to prevail, start thinking about how to present them. Listeners and readers will be more inclined to accept what you are offering if you focus on important strategies, outlined in Figure 8.1 and further discussed throughout this chapter.

8-2 Planning and Writing Persuasive Requests

LEARNING OUTCOME 2
Craft persuasive messages that request actions.

Direct request and claim messages, such as those you wrote in Chapter 6, are straightforward and, therefore, can be direct. Persuasive requests, on the other hand, are generally more effective when they are indirect. Reasons and explanations should precede the main idea. To overcome possible resistance, the writer lays a logical foundation before delivering the request. A writing plan for persuasive requests requires deliberate development.

Persuasive Requests

OPENING: Capture the reader's attention and interest. Describe a problem, make an unexpected statement, suggest reader benefits, offer praise or compliments, or ask a stimulating question.

BODY: Build interest. Explain logically and concisely the purpose of the request. Prove its merit. Use facts, statistics, expert opinion, examples, and specific details. Focus on the reader's direct and indirect benefits. Reduce resistance. Elicit a desire to comply. Anticipate objections, offer counterarguments, establish credibility, demonstrate competence, and show the value of your proposal.

CLOSING: Motivate action. Ask for a particular action. Make the action easy to take. Show courtesy, respect, and gratitude.

In this chapter you will learn to apply the preceding writing plan to (a) messages that request actions, (b) claims and adjustment requests that may meet with opposition, (c) messages intended to persuade subordinates and supervisors, and (d) direct-mail and e-mail sales messages.

8-2a Crafting an Effective Persuasive Message

Convincing someone to change a belief or to perform an action when that person is reluctant requires planning and skill—and sometimes a little luck. A written request may require more preparation than a face-to-face request, but it can be more effective. For example, you may ask a well-known businessperson to make a presentation to your club. You may ask a company to encourage its employees to participate in a charity drive. Such messages require skill in persuasion.

Figure 8.2 shows a persuasive request from Danuta Hajek. Her research firm seeks to persuade other companies to complete a questionnaire revealing salary data. In most organizations, salary information is strictly confidential. What can Danuta do to convince strangers to part with such private information?

Analyzing the First Draft. The hurriedly written first version of the request in Figure 8.2 suffers from many faults. It fails to pique the interest of the reader in the opening. It also provides an easy excuse for Mr. Janssen to refuse (*filling out surveys can be tedious*). In the body, Mr. Janssen doesn't receive any incentive to accept the request. The writing is self-serving and offers few specifics. In addition, the draft does not anticipate objections and fails to suggest counterarguments. Last, the closing does not motivate action by providing a deadline or a final benefit.

Revising the First Draft. In the revised version shown in Figure 8.2, to gain attention, Danuta poses two short questions that spotlight the need for salary information. To build interest and establish trust, she states that Herron & Hogan Research has been collecting business data for a quarter century and has received awards. She ties her reasonable request to audience benefits.

LEARNING OUTCOME 3
Write compelling claims and deliver successful complaints.

8-3 Writing Effective Persuasive Claims and Complaints

As their name suggests, complaints deliver bad news. Some complaint messages just vent anger. However, if the goal is to change something (and why bother to write except to motivate change?), then persuasion is necessary. Persuasive claim

Figure 8.2 Persuasive Request

 DRAFT

Dear Mr. Janssen:

We need your help in collecting salary data for today's workers. Herron & Hogan Research has been collecting business data for 25 years, and we have received awards for accuracy. We know that filling out surveys can be tedious, but the results are very useful.
— *Fails to pique interest; provides easy excuse*

Companies trust the survey data we compile. We have been in this business long enough to know how important comparative salary data are to most organizations. Filling out our questionnaire will not take very long. If you wish, we could send you some of the results showing not only salaries, but also perks and other benefits.
— *Does not promote direct and indirect benefits*

Please fill out the enclosed questionnaire and call us if you have any questions. Thank you for your cooperation.
— *Does not anticipate objections; fails to motivate action*

 REVISION

HERRON & HOGAN RESEARCH
435 N Tampa Street, Tampa, FL 33602, www.hhresearch.com
PH 813.878.2300
FAX 813.878.4359

May 18, 2019

Mr. Gregory S. Janssen
Mellon Wealth Management
444 First Street South, Suite 450
St. Petersburg, FL 33701

Dear Mr. Janssen:

Poses two short questions related to the reader —
Would you like access to more reliable salary data than Glassdoor has to offer? Has your company ever lost a valued employee to another organization that offered 20 percent more in salary for the same position?
— *Gains attention*

Presents reader benefit tied to request explanation; establishes credibility —
To remain competitive in hiring and to retain qualified workers, companies rely on survey data showing current salaries. Herron & Hogan Research has been collecting business data for a quarter century and has been honored by the American Management Association for its accurate data. We need your help in collecting salary data for today's workers. Information from the enclosed questionnaire will supply companies like yours with such data.
— *Builds interest*

Anticipates and counters resistance to confidentiality and time/effort objections —
Your information, of course, will be treated confidentially. The questionnaire takes but a few moments to complete, and it can provide substantial dividends for professional organizations just like yours that need comparative salary data.
— *Elicits desire and reduces resistance*

Offers free salary data as a direct benefit —
To show our gratitude for your participation, we will send you free comprehensive salary surveys for your industry and your metropolitan area. Not only will you find basic salaries, but you will also learn about bonus and incentive plans, special pay differentials, expense reimbursements, and perquisites such as a company car and credit card.
— *Appeals to professionalism, an indirect benefit*

Provides deadline and a final benefit to prompt action —
Comparative salary data are impossible to provide without the support of professionals like you. Please complete the questionnaire and return it in the prepaid envelope before June 1, our spring deadline. Participating in this survey means that you will no longer be in the dark about how much your employees earn compared with others in your industry.
— *Motivates action*

Sincerely yours,

HERRON & HOGAN RESEARCH

Danuta Hajek

Danuta Hajek
Director, Survey Research

Enclosures

and complaint messages may involve damaged products, mistaken billing, inaccurate shipments, warranty problems, limited return policies, insurance snafus, faulty merchandise, and so on.

An effective claim message makes a reasonable and valid request, presents a logical case with clear facts, and has a moderate tone. Anger and emotion are not effective persuaders.

8-3a Developing a Logical Claim Message

Strive for logical development in a claim message. You might open with sincere praise, an objective statement of the problem, a point of agreement, or a quick review of what you have done to resolve the problem. Then you can explain precisely what happened or why your claim is legitimate. Don't provide a blow-by-blow chronology of details; just hit the highlights. Be sure to enclose copies of relevant invoices, shipping orders, warranties, and payments. Close with a clear statement of what you want done: a refund, replacement, credit to your account, or other action. Be sure to think through the possibilities and make your request reasonable.

8-3b Using a Moderate Tone

The tone of your message is important. Don't suggest that the receiver intentionally deceived you or intentionally created the problem. Rather, appeal to the receiver's sense of responsibility and pride in the company's good name. Calmly express your disappointment in view of your high expectations of the product and of the company. Communicating your feelings without rancor is often the strongest appeal.

Denise Blanchard's e-mail, shown in Figure 8.3, follows the persuasive strategy as she seeks credit for two VoIP (voice over Internet protocol) office systems. Actually, she was quite upset because her company was counting on these new Internet systems to reduce its phone bills. Instead, the handsets produced so much static that incoming and outgoing calls were all but impossible to hear. The full setup also proved to be too complex for the small business.

What's more, Denise was frustrated that the Return Merchandise Authorization form she filled out at the company's website seemed to sink into a dark hole in cyberspace. She had reason to be angry! However, Denise resolved to use a moderate tone in writing her complaint e-mail because she knew that a calm, unemotional tone would be more effective. She opted for a positive opening, a well-documented claim, and a request for specific action in the closing.

8-4 Crafting Persuasive Messages in Digital Age Organizations

The lines of authority are blurry in today's information age workplaces, and the roles of executives are changing. Technology has empowered rank-and-file employees who can turn to their companies' intranets and don't need their managers to be information providers—formerly a crucial managerial role. Starbucks CEO Howard Schultz calls his employees *partners*, suggesting equality, at least in attitude.[12] Amazon-owned Internet shoe seller Zappos is even experimenting with replacing traditional teams and managers with fully empowered employee *circles*.[13]

This huge shift in authority is affecting both the strategies for creating, and the tone of, workplace persuasive messages. You may still want to be indirect if you hope to persuade your boss to do something he or she will be reluctant to do; however, your boss, in turn, will be less likely to rely on the power of

Figure 8.3 Persuasive Claim (Complaint) E-Mail

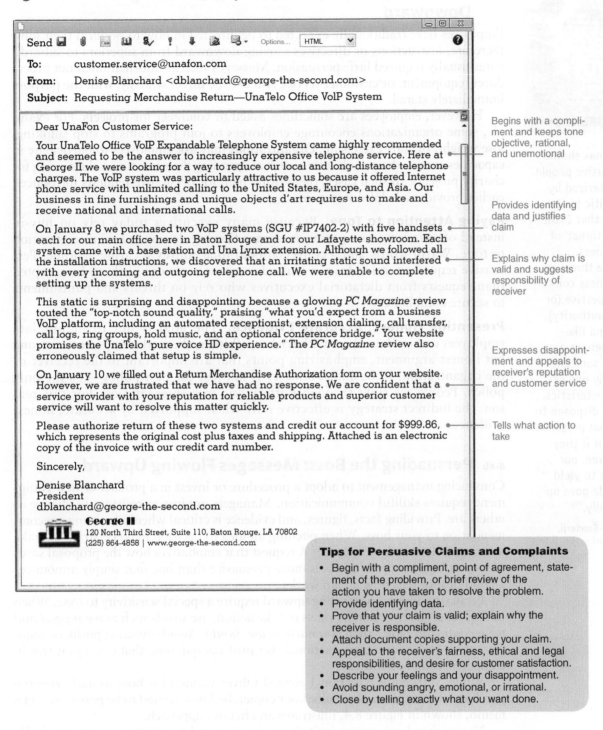

Send ⊟ 📎 🖼 📇 🔍 ! ⬇ 📋 📭 ▾   Options...   HTML ▾   ❓

To: customer.service@unafon.com
From: Denise Blanchard <dblanchard@george-the-second.com>
Subject: Requesting Merchandise Return—UnaTelo Office VoIP System

Dear UnaFon Customer Service:

Your UnaTelo Office VoIP Expandable Telephone System came highly recommended and seemed to be the answer to increasingly expensive telephone service. Here at George II we were looking for a way to reduce our local and long-distance telephone charges. The VoIP system was particularly attractive to us because it offered Internet phone service with unlimited calling to the United States, Europe, and Asia. Our business in fine furnishings and unique objects d'art requires us to make and receive national and international calls.

On January 8 we purchased two VoIP systems (SGU #IP7402-2) with five handsets each for our main office here in Baton Rouge and for our Lafayette showroom. Each system came with a base station and Una Lynxx extension. Although we followed all the installation instructions, we discovered that an irritating static sound interfered with every incoming and outgoing telephone call. We were unable to complete setting up the systems.

This static is surprising and disappointing because a glowing *PC Magazine* review touted the "top-notch sound quality," praising "what you'd expect from a business VoIP platform, including an automated receptionist, extension dialing, call transfer, call logs, ring groups, hold music, and an optional conference bridge." Your website promises the UnaTelo "pure voice HD experience." The *PC Magazine* review also erroneously claimed that setup is simple.

On January 10 we filled out a Return Merchandise Authorization form on your website. However, we are frustrated that we have had no response. We are confident that a service provider with your reputation for reliable products and superior customer service will want to resolve this matter quickly.

Please authorize return of these two systems and credit our account for $999.86, which represents the original cost plus taxes and shipping. Attached is an electronic copy of the invoice with our credit card number.

Sincerely,

Denise Blanchard
President
dblanchard@george-the-second.com

George II
120 North Third Street, Suite 110, Baton Rouge, LA 70802
(225) 864-4858 | www.george-the-second.com

Annotations:
- Begins with a compliment and keeps tone objective, rational, and unemotional
- Provides identifying data and justifies claim
- Explains why claim is valid and suggests responsibility of receiver
- Expresses disappointment and appeals to receiver's reputation and customer service
- Tells what action to take

Tips for Persuasive Claims and Complaints
- Begin with a compliment, point of agreement, statement of the problem, or brief review of the action you have taken to resolve the problem.
- Provide identifying data.
- Prove that your claim is valid; explain why the receiver is responsible.
- Attach document copies supporting your claim.
- Appeal to the receiver's fairness, ethical and legal responsibilities, and desire for customer satisfaction.
- Describe your feelings and your disappointment.
- Avoid sounding angry, emotional, or irrational.
- Close by telling exactly what you want done.

position and just issue commands. Rather, today's executives increasingly opt for participatory management and bank on persuasion to achieve buy-in from subordinates.[15]

This section focuses on messages flowing downward and upward within organizations. Horizontal messages exchanged among coworkers resemble the persuasive requests discussed earlier in requesting actions.

LEARNING OUTCOME 4

Understand interpersonal persuasion at work, and compose persuasive messages within organizations.

8-4a Persuading Employees: Messages Flowing Downward

Employees have traditionally expected to be directed in how to perform their jobs; therefore, instructions or directives moving downward from superiors to subordinates usually required little persuasion. Messages such as information about procedures, equipment, or customer service still use the direct strategy, with the purpose immediately stated.

However, employees are sometimes asked to volunteer for projects. For example, some organizations encourage employees to join programs to stop smoking, lose weight, or start exercising. Organizations may ask employees to participate in capacities outside their work roles—such as spending their free time volunteering for charity projects. In such cases, the writing plan for persuasive requests introduced earlier provides a helpful structure.

Paying Attention to Tone. Because many executives today rely on buy-in instead of exercising raw power, messages flowing downward require attention to tone. Warm words and a conversational tone convey a caring attitude. Persuasive requests coming from a trusted superior are more likely to be accepted than requests from dictatorial executives who rely on threats and punishments to secure compliance.

Presenting Honest, Accurate Evidence. The goal is not to manipulate employees or to seduce them with trickery. Rather, the goal is to present a strong but honest argument, emphasizing points that are important to the receiver or the organization. In business, honesty is not just the best policy—it's the only policy. People see right through puffery and misrepresentation. For this reason, the indirect strategy is effective only when supported by accurate, honest evidence.

8-4b Persuading the Boss: Messages Flowing Upward

Convincing management to adopt a procedure or invest in a product or new equipment requires skillful communication. Managers are just as resistant to change as others are. Providing facts, figures, and evidence is critical when submitting a recommendation to your boss. When pitching an idea to decision makers, strive to make a strong dollars-and-cents case.[17] A request that emphasizes how the proposal saves money or benefits the business is more persuasive than one that simply announces a good deal or tells how a plan works.

Persuasive messages traveling upward require a special sensitivity to tone. When asking supervisors to change views or take action, use words such as *we suggest* and *we recommend* rather than *you must* or *we should*. Avoid sounding pushy or argumentative. Strive for a conversational, yet professional, tone that conveys warmth, competence, and confidence.

When Marketing Assistant Leonard Oliver wanted his boss to authorize the purchase of a multifunction color laser copier, he knew he had to be persuasive. His memo, shown in Figure 8.4, illustrates an effective approach.

Notice that Leo's memo isn't short. A successful persuasive message typically takes more space than a direct message because proving a case requires evidence. In the end, Leo chose to send his memo as an e-mail attachment accompanied by a polite, short e-mail message because he wanted to keep the document format in MS Word intact. He also felt that the message was too long to paste into his e-mail program. The subject line announces the purpose of the message without disclosing the actual request.

The strength of the persuasive document in Figure 8.4 is in the clear presentation of comparison figures showing how much money the company can save by purchasing a remanufactured copier.

Figure 8.4 Persuasive Message Flowing Upward

To: Arron Raphael <arron.raphael@adama-machining.com>
From: Leonard Oliver <leonard.oliver@adama-machining.com>
Subject: Saving Time and Money on Copying and Printing
Attached: Refurbished color copiers.docx (10 KB)

Arron,

Attached is a brief document that details our potential savings from purchasing a refurbished color laser copier. After doing some research, I discovered that these sophisticated machines aren't as expensive as one might think.

Please look at my calculations and let me know what you suggest that we do to improve our in-house production of print matter and reduce both time and cost for external copying.

Leo

Leonard Oliver
Marketing Assistant • Adama Machining, Inc.
800 South Santa Fe Blvd. • City of Industry, CA 91715
213.680.3000 office / 213.680.3229 fax
leonard.oliver@adama-machining.com

Serves as cover e-mail to introduce attached memo in MS Word

Opens with catchy subject line

Does not reveal recommendation but leaves request for action to the attached memo

Provides an electronic signature with contact information

↓ 1 inch
MEMORANDUM
↓ 2 blank lines

Date: April 9, 2019 ↓ 1 blank line

To: Arron Raphael, Vice President ↓ 1 blank line

From: Leonard Oliver, Marketing ↓ 1 blank line

Subject: Saving Time and Money on Copying
↓ 1 or 2 blank lines

Describes topic without revealing request

We are losing money on our current copy services and wasting the time of employees as well. Because our aging Canon copier is in use constantly and can't handle our growing printing volume, we find it increasingly necessary to send major jobs out to Copy Quick. Moreover, whenever we need color copies, we can't handle the work ourselves. Just take a look at how much we spend each month for outside copy service:

Summarizes problem

Copy Costs: Outside Service
10,000 B&W copies/month made at Copy Quick	$ 700.00
1,000 color copies/month, $0.25 per copy (avg.)	250.00
Salary costs for assistants to make 32 trips	480.00
Total	$1,430.00

Uses headings and columns for easy comprehension

To save time and money, I have been considering alternatives. Large-capacity color laser copiers with multiple features (copy, e-mail, fax, LAN fax, print, scan) are expensive. However, reconditioned copiers with all the features we need are available at attractive prices. From Copy City we can get a fully remanufactured Xerox copier that is guaranteed and provides further savings because solid-color ink sticks cost a fraction of laser toner cartridges. We could copy and print in color for roughly the same cost as black and white. After we make an initial payment of $300, our monthly costs would look like this:

Proves credibility of request with facts and figures

Copy Costs: Remanufactured Copier
Paper supplies for 11,000 copies	$160.00
Ink sticks and copy supplies	100.00
Labor of assistants to make copies	150.00
Monthly financing charge for copier (purchase price of $3,105 – $300 amortized at 10% with 36 payments)	93.74
Total	$503.74

As you can see, a remanufactured Xerox 8860MFP copier saves us more than $900 per month. For a limited time Copy City is offering a free 15-day trial offer, a free copier stand (a $250 value), free starter supplies, and free delivery and installation. We have office space available, and my staff is eager to add a second machine.

Provides more benefits

Highlights most important benefit

Counters possible resistance

Please call me at Ext. 630 if you have questions. This copier is such a good opportunity that I have prepared a purchase requisition authorizing the agreement with Copy City. With your approval before May 4, we could have our machine by May 14 and start saving time and more than $900 every month. Fast action will also help us take advantage of Copy City's free start-up incentives.

Makes it easy to grant approval

Repeats main benefit with motivation to act quickly

LEARNING
OUTCOME **5**
Create effective and ethical
direct-mail and e-mail sales
messages.

8-5 Creating Effective Sales Messages in Print and Online

The best sales messages, whether delivered by postal mail or by e-mail, have much in common. They use persuasion to promote products and services. Marketing professionals analyze and perfect every aspect of a sales message to encourage consumers to read and act on the message. This section presents techniques developed by experts for drafting effective sales messages, in print and online.

Sales letters and other physical mailpieces, such as postcards, flyers, self-mailers, product samples, and brochures, are called direct mail. Usually part of multichannel marketing campaigns, direct-mail promotions—sales letters in particular—are a powerful means to make sales, generate leads, boost retail traffic, solicit donations, and direct consumers to websites.

Direct mail is an ideal channel for personalized, tangible, three-dimensional messages that are less invasive than telephone solicitations and less reviled than unsolicited e-mail. Neuroscience-based studies show that tangible mail appears to have a greater emotional impact than digital mail. MRI scans, eye tracking, and other indicators of emotional engagement suggest that physical materials "have a deeper and longer-lasting effect than digital ads on instilling desire for products and services."[18] Figure 8.5 juxtaposes the most relevant features of traditional direct-mail and online sales messages.

8-5a Betting on Highly Targeted, Relevant Direct Mail

Although not as flashy as social media campaigns, direct mail still works as long as it is personalized and relevant.[19] Experts know that most recipients do look at their direct mail and respond to it; in fact, 79 percent of consumers act on direct

Figure 8.5 Persuasive Sales Techniques in the Digital Age

Characteristics of Traditional Versus Online Sales Messages

Traditional Direct Mail (Sales Letter)	E-Commerce (E-Mail, Social Media Messages)
Creating static content (hard copy)	Creating dynamic digital content
Anticipating a single response (inquiry, sale)	Creating engagement instead of selling overtly
Resorting to "spray-and-pray" approach	Building one-to-one relationships and communities around brands
Single communication channel	Multiple communication channels
Limited response	Potentially unlimited responses
Monologue	Dialogue, potential for mass diffusion
Private response	Public, shared response
Asynchronous (delayed) response	Instant, real-time response possible
Passive	Interactive, participatory
Promoter-generated content	User-generated content
The needs of target groups must be anticipated and met in advance.	Consumers expect that brands understand their unique needs and deliver.
Direct mail is preferred for information about insurance, financial services, and health care; excellent channel for offline customers.	Savvy brands respond nimbly to customer participation; today's sophisticated consumers dislike "hard sell."

GREEN BELGIUM MAILING
WITHOUT WATER, KNOWLEDGE CAN'T FLOW.

To mark World Water Day, this mailing was sent out to companies and the press.
The letter inside can only be read when held under water - proving that water really is the source of all knowledge.

Source: Green Belgium Mailing

To commemorate World Water Day, this expensive, selectively targeted mailpiece, Green Belgium Mailing, drives home a memorable and nearly irresistible message about the importance of clean water. The message can be read only if submerged in water. In an example of ingenious branding, the ad agency behind this creative campaign, Duval Guillaume of Antwerp, Belgium, subscribes to this scrappy motto: "We are a small global agency with big brave clients."

mail immediately, whereas only 45 percent deal with e-mail right away.[21] Now more money goes to digital and interactive marketing ($77 billion) than to traditional direct-mail marketing ($46 billion),[22] and digital marketing is forecast to reach $120 billion by 2021.[23] The ever-increasing spending on digital and mobile advertising reflects the channels where the eyeballs are. Nevertheless, savvy marketers keep direct mail, "the golden child of the print media family,"[24] in their marketing mix.

Professionals who specialize in traditional direct-mail services have made it a science. They analyze a market, develop an effective mailing list, study the product, prepare a sophisticated campaign aimed at a well-defined target audience, and motivate the reader to act. You have probably received many direct-mail pieces, often called junk mail. Promotional mailings such as sales letters, postcards, catalogs, and brochures now comprise almost 60 percent of all postal mail sent.[25] Chances are they will keep coming because even tech-centered millennials respond positively to it,[26] and the mail will be a lot more relevant to you and your spending habits.

8-5b Considering the Value of Sales Letters

Because sales letters are usually written by specialists, you may never write one on the job. Why learn how to write a sales letter? Learning the techniques of sales writing will help you be more successful in any communication that requires persuasion and promotion. What's more, you will recognize sales strategies directed at you, which will make you a more perceptive consumer of ideas, products, and services.

Your primary goal in writing a sales message is to get someone to devote a few moments of attention to it. You may be promoting a product, a service, an idea, or yourself. In each case the most effective messages follow the AIDA strategy illustrated in Figure 8.6: (a) gain attention, (b) build interest, (c) elicit desire and reduce resistance, and (d) motivate action.

Figure 8.6 The AIDA Strategy for Sales Messages

	STRATEGY	CONTENT	SECTION
A	Attention	Captures attention, creates awareness, makes a sales proposition, prompts audience to read on	Opening
I	Interest	Describes central selling points, focuses not on features of product/service but on benefits relevant to the reader's needs	Body
D	Desire	Reduces resistance, reassures the reader, elicits the desire for ownership, motivates action	Body
A	Action	Offers an incentive or gift, limits the offer, sets a deadline, makes it easy for the reader to respond, closes the sale	Closing

WRITING PLAN

Sales Messages: AIDA

OPENING: Gain *attention*. Offer something valuable; promise a benefit to the reader; ask a question; or provide a quotation, fact, product feature, testimonial, startling statement, or personalized action setting.

BODY: Build *interest*. Describe central selling points and make rational and emotional appeals. Elicit *desire* in the reader and reduce resistance. Use testimonials, money-back guarantees, free samples, or performance tests.

CLOSING: Motivate *action*. Offer a gift, promise an incentive, limit the offer, set a deadline, or guarantee satisfaction.

Gaining Attention in Sales Messages. One of the most critical elements of a sales message is its opening paragraph. This opener should be short (one to five lines), honest, relevant, and stimulating. Marketing pros have found that eye-catching typographical arrangements or provocative messages, such as the following, can hook a reader's attention:

- **Offer:** *Subscribe now and get a free iPad to enjoy your programming on the go!*
- **Promise:** *Now you can raise your sales income by 50 percent or even more with the proven techniques found in. . . .*
- **Question:** *Why wait in the Starbucks line for a pitiful paper cup when for $20 you can have the Chiseled Chrome Coffee Cup, a handsome stylish tumbler of your own to refill every morning?*
- **Quotation or proverb:** *Necessity is the mother of invention.*
- **Fact:** *The Greenland Eskimos ate more fat than anyone in the world. And yet . . . they had virtually no heart disease.*
- **Product feature and its benefit:** *The Atlas sock is made from cotton, polyester, and carbonized coffee. Yup! Coffee helps filter odor, but equally important, the sock uses pressure mapping and thermal imaging to create a ridiculously comfortable sock!*
- **Startling statement:** *Bigger houses cost less.*
- **Personalized action setting:** *It's 4:30 p.m. and you have to make a decision. You need everybody's opinion, no matter where they are. Before you pick up your phone and call them one at a time, pick up this card: WebEx Teleconference Services.*

Other openings calculated to capture attention include a solution to a problem, an anecdote, a personalized statement using the receiver's name, or a relevant current event.

Building Interest With Rational and Emotional Appeals. In this phase of your sales message, you should describe clearly the product or service. In simple language emphasize the central selling points that you identified during your prewriting analysis. Those selling points can be developed using rational or emotional appeals.

Rational appeals are associated with reason and intellect. They translate selling points into references to making or saving money, increasing efficiency, or making the best use of resources. In general, rational appeals are appropriate when a product is expensive, long-lasting, or important to health, security, or financial success.

Emotional appeals relate to status, ego, and sensual feelings. Appealing to the emotions is sometimes effective when a product is inexpensive, short-lived, or nonessential. Many clever sales messages, however, combine emotional and rational strategies for a dual appeal. Consider these examples:

Rational Appeal
You can buy the things you need and want, pay household bills, pay off higher-cost loans and credit cards—as soon as you are approved and your Choice-Credit card account is opened.

Emotional Appeal
Leave the urban bustle behind and escape to sun-soaked Tahiti! To recharge your batteries with an injection of sun and surf, all you need is your bathing suit, a little suntan lotion, and your ChoiceCredit card.

Dual Appeal
New ChoiceCredit cardholders are immediately eligible for a $200 travel certificate and additional discounts at fun-filled resorts. Save up to 40 percent while lying on a beach in picturesque, sun-soaked Bora Bora, the year-round luxury resort.

Leigh J/Shutterstock.com

Public service announcements (PSAs) about distracted driving use different strategies in their messages. Some PSAs cite statistics as a rational appeal; others show horrific accidents as a scare tactic. Recently, a New Zealand advertising agency used humor in its PSA to discourage using a phone while driving. As a cover of Lionel Richie's "Hello" plays, a series of young drivers reach for their phones but are blocked when the front seat passenger grabs the driver's hand. The driver appears shocked as the passenger looks on with adoring eyes. The tag line reads: "Put me first. Drive phone free." Is humor an effective strategy for a PSA aimed at distracted drivers?

A physical description of your product is not enough, however. Zig Ziglar, thought by some to be America's greatest salesperson, pointed out that no matter how well you know your product, no one is persuaded by cold, hard facts alone. In the end, people buy because of product benefits.[27] Your job is to translate those cold facts into warm feelings and reader benefits.

A feature is what your product is or does; a benefit is how the audience can use it. Let's say a sales message promotes a hand cream made with aloe and cocoa butter extracts, along with vitamin A. Those facts become *Nature's hand helpers—including soothing aloe and cocoa extracts, along with firming vitamin A—form invisible gloves that protect your sensitive skin against the hardships of work, harsh detergents, and constant environmental assaults.*

Reducing Resistance and Building Desire. Marketing specialists use a number of techniques to overcome resistance and build desire. When price is an obstacle, consider these suggestions:

- Delay mentioning price until after you have created a desire for the product.
- Show the price in small units, such as the price per issue of a magazine.
- Demonstrate how the reader saves money—for instance, by subscribing for two or three years.
- Compare your prices with those of a competitor.

In addition, you need to anticipate objections and questions the receiver may have. When possible, translate these objections into selling points (*If you are worried about training your staff members on the new software, remember that our offer includes $1,000 worth of on-site one-on-one instruction*). Be sure, of course, that your claims are accurate and do not stretch the truth. Other techniques to overcome resistance and prove the credibility of the product include the following:

- **Testimonials:** *"I never stopped eating, yet I lost 107 pounds."—Tina Rivers, Greenwood, South Carolina*
- **Names of satisfied users** (with permission, of course): *Enclosed is a partial list of private pilots who enthusiastically subscribe to our service.*
- **Money-back guarantee or warranty:** *We offer the longest warranties in the business—all parts and service on-site for five years!*
- **Free trial or sample:** *We are so confident that you will like our new accounting program that we want you to try it absolutely free.*
- **Performance tests, polls, or awards:** *Our TP-3000 was named Best Internet Phone, and Etown.com voted it Smartphone of the Year.*

Motivating Action at the Conclusion of a Sales Message. All the effort put into a sales message goes to waste if the reader fails to act. To make it easy for readers to act, you can provide a reply card, a stamped and preaddressed envelope, a toll-free telephone number, a smartphone-readable matrix barcode, a simple Web address, or a promise of a follow-up call. Because readers often need an extra push, consider including additional motivators, such as the following:

- **Offer a gift:** *You will receive a free iPad mini with the purchase of any new car.*
- **Promise an incentive:** *With every new, paid subscription, we will plant a tree in one of America's Heritage Forests.*
- **Limit the offer:** *Only the first 100 customers receive free travel mugs.*
- **Set a deadline:** *You must act before June 1 to take advantage of these low prices.*
- **Guarantee satisfaction:** *We will return your full payment if you are not entirely satisfied—no questions asked.*

The final paragraph of the sales message carries the punch line. This is where you tell readers what you want them to do and give them reasons for doing it. Most sales messages also include postscripts because they make irresistible reading. Even readers who might skim over or bypass paragraphs are drawn to a P.S. Therefore, use a postscript to reveal your strongest motivator, to add a special inducement for a quick response, or to reemphasize a central selling point.

8-5c Putting Together All the Parts of a Sales Message

Direct mail is highly effective, because it cuts through the clutter of sales appeals. It can be personalized, directed to very specific target audiences, and filled with more complex messages than other advertising media can. Physical sales messages have the highest household response rate (3.7 percent), ahead of e-mail (1 percent) and social media (1 percent).[28] However, direct mail is expensive. That's why crafting and assembling all the parts of a sales message are so critical.

Figure 8.7 shows a sales letter addressed to individuals and families who may need health insurance. To prompt the reader to respond to the mailing, the letter incorporates the effective four-part AIDA strategy. The writer first establishes the need for health coverage. Then she develops a rational central selling point (*a variety of affordable health plans for every budget offered without sales pressure and medical jargon*) and repeats this selling point in all the components of the letter. This sales letter saves its strongest motivator—a free heart-rate monitor for the first 30 callers—for the high-impact P.S. line.

Although you want to be persuasive in sales letters, you must guard against overstepping legal and ethical boundaries. Be sure to check out the Communication Workshop at the end of this chapter to see examples of what is legal and what is not.

8-5d Writing Successful E-Mail Sales Messages

E-mail remains the primary channel for brand communication today. Seventy percent of consumers favor e-mail when interacting with brands—over direct mail, SMS, and other marketing messages.[30] E-mail is the most used digital channel for customer communication (51 percent),[31] and 77 percent of consumers prefer permission-based marketing through e-mail.[32] E-mails cost between $11 and $15 per consumer response versus about $19 per response for traditional direct mail.[33]

Much like traditional direct mail, e-mail marketing can attract new customers, keep existing ones, encourage future sales, cross-sell, and cut costs. However, e-marketers can create and send a promotion in half the time it takes to print and distribute a traditional message. To reach today's consumer, marketers must target their e-mails well if they wish to even get their messages opened.

Meet Chef James Barry. The owner of Wholesome2Go, an organic-food home-delivery service, knows that to achieve success today, he must cultivate relationships, not just push products.[34] A former personal chef for celebrities, James engages his clients by maintaining a website, tweeting updates, and posting on his Facebook, Instagram, and Pinterest pages. Wholesome2Go also has a YouTube channel. Frequently, Chef James sends persuasive e-mails such as the one shown in Figure 8.8 that follows the four-part AIDA strategy.

On a practical level, you want to show how your persuasive message solves a problem, achieves a personal or work objective, or just makes life easier for your audience. Chef James understands that New Year's resolutions to eat healthy food and lose weight might reduce resistance to his offer.

When adapting persuasive requests to your audience, consider these questions that receivers will very likely be asking themselves: *Why should I? What's in it for me? What's in it for you? Who cares?*

8-5e Best Practices for Online Sales Messages

The goal of a persuasive message is to convert the receiver to your ideas and motivate action. To accomplish this feat in the age of social media, persuaders seek to build relationships with their audiences. Even so, a message without a clear purpose is doomed. Too often, inexperienced writers reach the end of the first draft of a message before discovering exactly what they want the receiver to think or do.

The first rule of e-marketing is to communicate only with those who have given permission. By sending messages only to opt-in folks, you greatly increase your open rate—e-mails that will be opened and perhaps read. E-mail users detest spam. However, receivers are surprisingly receptive to offers tailored specifically to them.

OFFICE INSIDER

"The best form of marketing is the kind that does not feel like marketing. I'm going to buy from the brands that sell to me the least."[29]

Giselle Abramovich, *senior editor at the media company Digiday*

Figure 8.7 ProHealth Sales Letter

ProHealth
Insurance you can count on

June 17, 2019

Mr. Owen Van Dijk
329 South Pine Street
Portland, OR 97204

Dear Mr. Van Dijk:

Choose our health plans if you want VALUE!

Confused about health insurance? You're not alone.

Call a licensed expert at **(877) 522-0417.**

Visit us online at **www.prohealth.com.**

Return the completed reply card to us by mail.

(Addresses common fear) Do you think you can't afford quality health insurance? Let us try to change your mind. ProHealth offers attractive health plans that fit a range of budgets, needs, and lifestyles. Whether you're a recent graduate, self-employed, retiring early, or working without health insurance, one of our plans could be right for you. *(Gains attention)*

(Establishes need for health insurance) Health care needs can rise at any time in life, even in healthy and fit individuals. Anyone can succumb to an infectious disease or become sidelined by an accident. Knowing that such an event won't break the bank will give you peace of mind. *(Builds interest)*

(Emphasizes central selling point and reader benefits) **Choose from a variety of plans and benefits at affordable rates, starting at $110.** Our individual and family plans feature important benefits to keep you healthy:

- Preventive care comes at no additional cost, including your annual exam!
- Generic and brand-name prescription drug coverage will save you money every time.
- Chiropractic care, acupuncture, and rehabilitation coverage will help keep you in shape.
- A range of deductible options that work for your budget will put coverage within reach.
- Optional dental, vision, and life insurance coverage will protect you from unexpected expense.

(Elicits desire and reduces resistance)

Visit our website **www.prohealth.com** for lots of ideas on how you can achieve your wellness goals. Learn about discount programs that help you save money and achieve a healthier lifestyle—at no additional charge.

(Repeats central sales pitch in last two paragraphs) **Compare ProHealth plans when you're ready. No obligation. No pressure. Simple!** Call us at **(877) 522-0417**, and we will answer your questions in clear, easy-to-understand language, without medical or bureaucratic jargon. We promise. No sales types will hound you, either. That's a promise too. *(Motivates action)*

Stay well,

Deena Heathman

Deena Heathman
Director of Individual and Family Care

(Spotlights free offer in P.S. to prompt immediate reply) P.S. Call **(877) 522-0417** <u>today</u> for your free quote or to apply for coverage. The first 30 callers will receive a <u>free</u> heart-rate monitor. We're here to help improve the health of the people we serve.

Remember that today's customer is somebody—not just anybody. Marketers must make it easy for the recipient to unsubscribe.

Some differences between traditional sales messages and e-marketing are obvious when you study Figure 8.8. Online sales messages are shorter than direct-mail messages, feature colorful graphics, and occasionally even come with sound or video clips. They offer a richer experience to readers who can click hyperlinks at will to access content that interests them. When such messages are sent out as ads or periodic e-newsletters, they may not have salutations or closings. Rather, they may resemble Web pages.

Here are a few guidelines that will help you create effective e-mail sales messages:

- **Craft a catchy subject line.** Include an audience-specific location (*Lucky Dragon in Vegas Opens Soon!*); ask a meaningful question (*What's Your*

Figure 8.8 How Wholesome2Go Engages the Audience

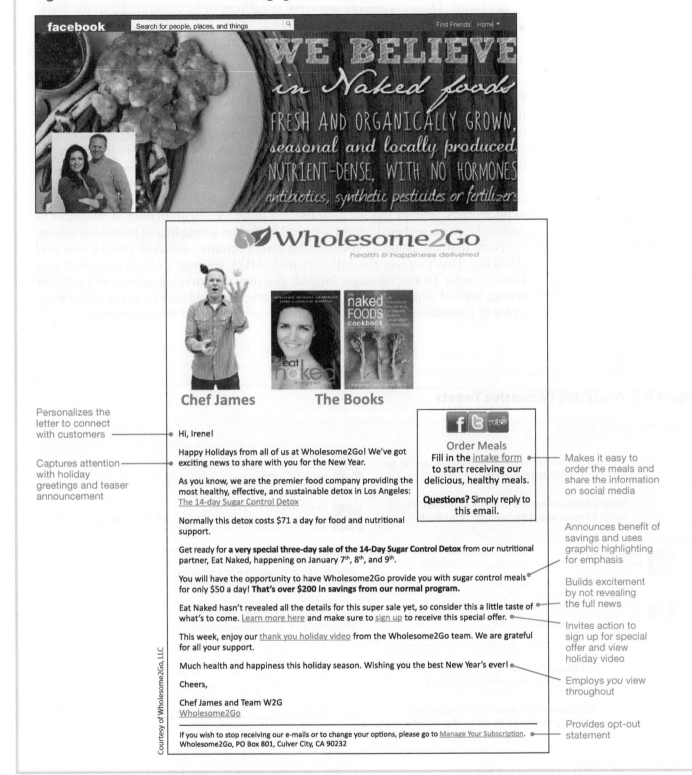

Personalizes the letter to connect with customers

Captures attention with holiday greetings and teaser announcement

Hi, Irene!

Happy Holidays from all of us at Wholesome2Go! We've got exciting news to share with you for the New Year.

As you know, we are the premier food company providing the most healthy, effective, and sustainable detox in Los Angeles: The 14-day Sugar Control Detox

Normally this detox costs $71 a day for food and nutritional support.

Get ready for **a very special three-day sale of the 14-Day Sugar Control Detox** from our nutritional partner, Eat Naked, happening on January 7th, 8th, and 9th.

You will have the opportunity to have Wholesome2Go provide you with sugar control meals for only $50 a day! **That's over $200 in savings from our normal program.**

Eat Naked hasn't revealed all the details for this super sale yet, so consider this a little taste of what's to come. Learn more here and make sure to sign up to receive this special offer.

This week, enjoy our thank you holiday video from the Wholesome2Go team. We are grateful for all your support.

Much health and happiness this holiday season. Wishing you the best New Year's ever!

Cheers,

Chef James and Team W2G
Wholesome2Go

If you wish to stop receiving our e-mails or to change your options, please go to Manage Your Subscription.
Wholesome2Go, PO Box 801, Culver City, CA 90232

Order Meals
Fill in the intake form to start receiving our delicious, healthy meals.

Questions? Simply reply to this email.

Makes it easy to order the meals and share the information on social media

Announces benefit of savings and uses graphic highlighting for emphasis

Builds excitement by not revealing the full news

Invites action to sign up for special offer and view holiday video

Employs *you* **view throughout**

Provides opt-out statement

Courtesy of Wholesome2Go, LLC

Dream Vacation?); and use no more than 50 characters. Promise realistic solutions. Offer discounts or premiums.

- **Keep the main information "above the fold."** E-mails should be top heavy. Primary points should appear early in the message to capture the reader's attention.
- **Make the message short, conversational, and focused.** Because on-screen text is taxing to read, be brief. Focus on one or two central selling points only.

- **Sprinkle testimonials throughout the copy.** Consumers' own words are the best sales copy. These comments can serve as callouts or be integrated into the copy.
- **Provide a means for opting out.** It's polite and a good business tactic to include a statement that tells receivers how to be removed from the sender's mailing database.

8-5f Writing Short Persuasive Messages Online

Increasingly, writers are turning to social networks to promote their businesses, further their causes, and build their online personas. As we have seen, social media are not primarily suited for overt selling; however, tweets and other online posts can be used to influence others and to project a professional, positive online presence.

Typically, organizations and individuals with followers post updates of their events, exploits, thoughts, and experiences. In persuasive tweets and posts, writers try to pitch offers, prompt specific responses, or draw the attention of their audiences to interesting events and media links. Figure 8.9 displays a sampling of persuasive tweets.

Note that the compact format of a tweet requires extreme conciseness and efficiency. Don't expect the full four-part AIDA strategy to be represented in a 140-character Twitter message. Instead, you may see attention-getters and calls for action, both of which must be catchy and intriguing. Regardless, many of the principles of persuasion discussed in this chapter apply even to micromessages.

Figure 8.9 Analyzing Persuasive Tweets

Tweet promoting professional services by offering the reader a general benefit

Sandra Zimmer @sandrazimmer
Coaching for authentic presentations, public speaking & **persuasive messages** to help you shine. tinyurl.com/m5hrrx
Expand ← Reply ⇄ Retweet ★ Favorite

Tweet offering a freebie to promote a book and urging action by restricting the availability of the freebie

Jessica Brody @JessicaBrody
5 autographed copies of UNREMEMBERED (UK edition) are up for grabs on Free Book Friday teens this week! Check it out! ow.ly/k5k6M

Delta @Delta
Be sure to enter our Kick It in NYC contest before the curtain closes. Enter now! oak.ctx.ly/r/1nwv pic.twitter.com/CRHxOwKe
View photo ← Reply ⇄ Retweet ★ Favorite

An airline creating urgency by suggesting that time to enter a contest is running out

James Barry @ChefJamesBarry
The Sugar Control Detox is coming and at an insanely low price! This opportunity is available to everyone, no... fb.me/S2XDfTXB
View media ← Reply ⇄ Retweet ★ Favorite

Teaser tweet by a small business owner announcing an upcoming promotion

A nonprofit organization requesting political action of advocacy for a popular cause

Army of Women @ArmyofWomen
Think #breastcancer should be a Nat. priority? Tell the president HERE:ow.ly/dnMd3
Expand ← Reply ⇄ Retweet ★ Favorite

Prominent philanthropist tweeting to motivate giving by reassuring followers of charities' merit

Bill Gates @BillGates
Make your donations count. @CharityNav provides great information on the impact non-profits are actually having. b-gat.es /ThLBLJ
Expand

Mike Bloomberg @MikeBloomberg
I've joined @Instagram. Follow me here: instagram.com /mikebloomberg
Expand

Tweet by a notable public figure announcing his new social network account and inviting followers along

Guy Kawasaki @GuyKawasaki
Are you a writer? Here are some fantastic resources available free today as a download on the APE website.... fb.me/10bBh8apK
Expand ← Reply ⇄ Retweet ★ Favorite

Tweet by well-known businessperson offering a free resource using an attention-getter

Summary of Learning Outcomes

1 Explain digital age persuasion and identify time-proven persuasive techniques.

- Business communicators need to use persuasion when making more than routine demands and facing a skeptical audience.
- Digital age persuasion is prolific, widespread, far-reaching, and fast-moving.
- Persuasive techniques today are more subtle and misleading than those used in the past, as well as more complex and impersonal.
- Effective persuaders establish credibility; make a specific, reasonable request; tie facts to benefits; recognize the power of loss; anticipate and overcome resistance; share solutions; and compromise.

2 Craft persuasive messages that request actions.

- Convincing a reluctant person requires planning and skill and sometimes a little luck.
- The writing plan for persuasive requests consists of an opening that captures the reader's attention; a body that establishes credibility, builds interest, and proves the merit of the request by using specific details; and a closing that motivates action while showing courtesy.

3 Write compelling claims and deliver successful complaints.

- Complaints and some persuasive claims deliver bad news; some vent anger, yet persuasion is necessary to effect change.
- Persuasive claims and complaints may involve damaged products, billing errors, wrong shipments, warranty problems, limited return policies, or insurance snafus.
- Employing a moderate tone, claim/complaint messages need to be logical and open with praise, a statement of fact or agreement, and a quick review of what was done to resolve the problem.
- In the body, writers highlight what happened and why the claim/complaint is legitimate; they enclose supporting documents such as invoices, shipping orders, warranties, and payments.
- The closing specifies what is to be done (e.g., a refund, replacement, or credit).

4 Understand interpersonal persuasion at work, and compose persuasive messages within organizations.

- Today's executives try to achieve buy-in from subordinates instead of forcing them to do things such as volunteer for projects or join programs that require lifestyle changes.
- Messages flowing downward require attention to tone and rely on honest, accurate evidence.
- Messages to management should provide facts, figures, and evidence and make strong dollars-and-cents cases for proposed ideas using a warm, professional tone.

5 Create effective and ethical direct-mail and e-mail sales messages.

- Whether delivered by postal mail or by e-mail, marketers design sales messages to encourage consumers to read and act on the message.
- Sales letters are still an important part of multichannel marketing campaigns that can make sales, generate leads, boost retail traffic, solicit donations, and direct consumers to websites.
- The AIDA writing plan consists of an opening that gains attention, a body that builds interest and elicits desire, and a closing that motivates action by setting a deadline or presenting an incentive or a limited offer.
- Skilled e-marketers create catchy subject lines, start with the most important points, make the message conversational and focused, use testimonials, and allow readers to opt out.
- Short persuasive posts and tweets concisely pitch offers, prompt responses, and draw attention to events and media links. Principles of persuasion apply even to micromessages.

Chapter Review

1. What developments have made persuasive skills ever more important at work, and when is persuasion generally needed? (L.O. 1)

2. List effective persuasion techniques. (L.O. 1)

3. Describe the writing plan for persuasive requests and its components. (L.O. 2)

4. What do claim/complaint messages typically involve, and how should they be crafted? (L.O. 3)

5. How can you ensure that your claim/complaint message is developed logically? (L.O. 3)

6. Describe situations when managers might want to persuade employees instead of just telling them what to do. (L.O. 4)

7. What is the four-part AIDA writing plan for sales messages, and what does the acronym stand for? (L.O. 5)

8. What distinguishes rational, emotional, and dual appeals in persuasion? (L.O. 5)

9. Name the best practices for e-marketers hoping to write effective e-mail sales messages. (L.O. 5)

10. Describe the purpose and characteristics of persuasive tweets and other online posts. (L.O. 5)

Critical Thinking

11. Many consumers rely on product reviews posted online, presumably by ordinary citizens describing their authentic experiences. Unfortunately, though, Amazon and Yelp, the most prominent of the many Internet review sites, have been called out for fake and paid-for reviews. Amazon has threatened to sue people posting fake public reviews.[35] Why is it important that online reviews or testimonials be trustworthy? (L.O. 1, 5)

12. The word *persuasion* turns some people off. What negative connotations can it have? (L.O. 1, 5)

13. What are some of the underlying motivations that prompt individuals to agree to requests that do not directly benefit themselves or their organizations? (L.O. 3)

14. How are direct-mail and e-mail sales messages similar, and how are they different? (L.O. 5)

15. Los Angeles–based clothing company Barabas used the name and likeness of brutal Mexican drug kingpin Joaquin "El Chapo" Guzmán on its website, flanked by photos of attractive male models wearing the same distinctive cotton shirts of the Fantasy and Crazy Paisley lines. The all-caps announcement read: "EL CHAPO GUZMAN WEARING BARABAS SHIRT!"[36] Barabas' excitement about its infamous customer met with criticism, but the company couldn't keep the $128 shirts on the shelves.[37] At one point Internet traffic crashed the Barabas website. Public outrage ultimately prompted the clothier to remove overt references to El Chapo and his photos. Is it ethical to resort to such extreme means to drive sales? (L.O. 1, 5)

Writing Improvement Exercises

Direct and Indirect Strategies

YOUR TASK. For each of the following situations, check the appropriate writing strategy.

Direct Strategy	Indirect Strategy	
_____	_____	16. A request from a sales representative to confirm an appointment for a product presentation
_____	_____	17. An announcement urging employees to participate in an optional program to feed homeless people at a nearby shelter over Thanksgiving
_____	_____	18. An e-mail message to employees telling them that the company parking lot will be closed for one week while it is being resurfaced
_____	_____	19. A letter to a cleaning service demanding a refund for sealing a dirty tiled floor and damaging a fresh coat of paint

Direct Strategy	Indirect Strategy	
_____	_____	20. A request for information about new features of a cloud-based backup system for office files
_____	_____	21. A letter to a drugstore requesting permission to display posters advertising a college fund-raising car wash
_____	_____	22. A request for a refund by a buyer who purchased the wrong software but failed to uninstall it within the mandatory two-week return period.
_____	_____	23. A message to your accountant asking her to reconsider her fee, which you think is exorbitant, considering that it was a bad year for your business
_____	_____	24. A letter from a property owner to a nearby business asking it to prohibit mobile catering service trucks from gathering outside the business at lunchtime
_____	_____	25. A memo to employees announcing a new procedure for submitting travel expenses.

Radical Rewrites

Note: Radical Rewrites are provided at **www.cengagebrain.com** for you to download and revise. Your instructor may show a suggested solution.

8.1 Radical Rewrite: Customer Lodges Passionate but Ineffectual Complaint (L.O. 1–3)

The following claim letter delivers a passionate but largely ineffectual complaint. Its insulting tone does little to persuade the receiver to meet the writer's demands. Can you administer a radical rewrite that might make the request more successful?

YOUR TASK. Analyze this poorly written claim letter, and list at least five weaknesses. If your instructor directs, revise it.

Current date

Mr. Lance Lazarovich
Duplicating Systems
5409 Fondren Road
Houston, TX 77807

Dear Ripoff Specialists:

Let me lay the facts on the line. Sadly, my company recently purchased four of your Color Laser Jet Pro TFP500 photocopiers, which seemed logical at the time. They promised out-of-the-box networked printing, 2-sided copies, fax, and color scanning. This was perfect for my growing engineering firm. Your sales lady Taylor Noack assured us that the TFP500 could handle our high volume of 3,000 copies a day. This sounded unlikely since the sales brochure suggested that the TFP500 was meant for 500 copies a day. Regardless, we listened to what Ms. Noack told us. Unfortunately, that was a big mistake. Our four TFP500 copiers are down every day, and my employees are screaming at me to do something. Because these machines are still under warranty, they do eventually get repaired. However, we can't deal with so much downtime.

After losing faith in your Ms. Noack, I called the district manager, Christopher Lopez. I suggested that we trade in our four TFP500 copiers (which cost $2,300 each) for two TFP1000 models (at $12,500 each). However, Mr. Lopez said he would have to charge 50 percent depreciation on our TFP500 copiers. That's a colossal rip-off! Any reasonable person would think that 20 percent depreciation is more sensible because we've had the machines only three months. Ms. Noack said she would get back to me, but I haven't heard from her since.

Now I'm forced to write to your headquarters because I have had no luck with either Ms. Noack or Mr. Lopez, and I need to see some action on these machines. If you understood anything about business, you would see what a sweet deal I'm offering. I'm willing to stick with your company and purchase your most expensive model—but I can't take such a steep loss on the TFP500 copiers. These copiers are relatively new; you should be able to sell them with no trouble. And think of all the money you will save by not having your repair technicians making constant trips to service our underpowered TFP500 copiers! Please respond immediately, or I may be forced to engage our attorney.

Sincerely yours,

List at least five weaknesses.

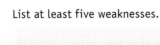

8.2 Radical Rewrite: Poor Persuasive Message Flowing Upward—A Plea for Better Meetings (L.O. 1, 2, 4)

The following e-mail message suffers from many writing faults, including poor tone and ineffective persuasive strategy. It originated with a manager and is addressed to her boss.

YOUR TASK. List at least five writing weaknesses. Then revise the message implementing an effective persuasive strategy. See Chapter 11 for suggestions about improving meetings. Consider volunteering to help develop and carry out the policy being requested.

To:	Kellie King <kking@xfactorsolutions.com>
From:	Jason Williams <jwilliams@xfactorsolutions.com>
Subject:	Dismal, Depressing Meetings

Good morning!

I wonder if you have any idea of how annoying meetings are around here. We seem to have endless meetings that drag on and on forever. I myself attended five meetings within the building but also was forced to participate in three more conference call meetings. And that was just last week! Nearly every one of those meetings was poorly run. Some should never have been called because they merely announced information after a decision had already been made. Some could easily have been handled in an e-mail. Sometimes I think our meetings are really opportunities to socialize under the guise of "work." Our meetings are huge time sucks.

I hope you don't mind if I level with you and tell it like it is. Something needs to be done about the lost productivity and sagging employee morale around here. No one likes to waste valuable time attending poorly run or unnecessary meetings. Apparently, our managers have not been trained in how to conduct meetings, although I realize that all of them are professional and have business training.

What we need is a meeting policy or something like that. We need some guidelines or training about how to conduct meetings. Has anyone thought of that? I can think of many ways to improve meetings. Could we please talk about this?

Jason Williams
Project Manager

List at least five weaknesses.

8.3 Radical Rewrite: Favor Request—Facebook Flub? (L.O. 1, 2, 5)

A student chose Facebook to request a recommendation from his professor. The following message suffers from many writing faults, including poor tone and flawed persuasive strategy.

YOUR TASK. Analyze the Facebook message and list at least five weaknesses. If your instructor directs, revise the message. Decide whether to use Facebook, of which the receiver is a member, or a conventional e-mail to make this request.

To: Tom Janowski
Subject: Letter of Rec
Message: Hey, Prof!!

How's it goin? You still travel to Europe a lot? You and me talked about Poland alot because my family is originally Polish. You remember me, don't ya? I jus wanted to know would you write a letter of recommendation for me? I'm applying for the MBA program. I was always helpin you out with distriuting papers and sat upfront. Never missed a class.

Anyhoo, I was wondering if you'd write me a ltter. In case you wonder, I had you in FAll 2017 for business writting. best class I ever took. Oh, I need it real soon, on Friday this week??

Call me on my cell 215 622-9763 or use FB. Thanx.

Steven

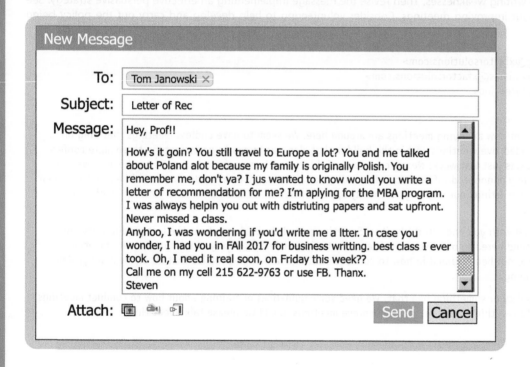

List at least five weaknesses.

8.4 Persuasive Request: Inviting an Alumna to Speak (L.O. 1, 2)

> **E-Mail**

As public relations director for the Business and Accounting Association on your campus, you have been asked to find a keynote speaker for the first meeting of the school year. The owner of a successful local firm, TempHelp4You, is an alumna of your university. You think not only that many students would enjoy learning about how she started her business, but also that some might like to sign up with her temporary help agency. She would need to prepare a 30-minute speech and take questions after the talk. The event will be held from noon until 1:30 p.m. on a date of your choosing in Branford Hall. You can offer her lunch at the event and provide her with a parking permit that she can pick up at the information kiosk at the main entrance to your campus. You need to have her response by a deadline you set.

YOUR TASK. Write a direct-approach e-mail to Marion Minter in which you ask her to speak at your club's meeting. Send it to mminter@temphelp4you.com.

8.5 Persuasive Request: How to Ask for a Letter of Recommendation (L.O. 1, 2)

> **E-Mail**

As a student, you will need letters of recommendation to find a job, to apply for a scholarship or grant, or to enter graduate school. Naturally, you will consider asking one or several of your college instructors. You talk to Paul, a senior you know, to find out how to get a busy professor to write you an effective letter. Paul has the following advice:

- Ask only instructors who have had the opportunity to observe your performance and may still remember you fondly. Two to five years after you attended a course of 20 to 40 students, your teachers may not recall you at all.
- Contact only instructors who can sing your praises. If your grades were poor, the endorsement won't be glowing. Some instructors refuse to write recommendations for mediocre students.

Make it easy for your instructors to agree to your request and to write a solid letter promptly by following these guidelines:

- Make the first request in person; your former instructor will be more likely to remember you.
- Introduce yourself by name and try to point out something memorable you did to help your professor recall your performance.
- Have a hard copy of the job description, scholarship information, grant requirements, or graduate school application ready, or direct the instructor to a website.
- Carry a copy of a recent polished résumé, or promise to e-mail these documents and any other information to help your recommender recall you in a professional setting and understand what you need.
- Confirm any agreement by e-mail promptly, and set a firm yet reasonable deadline by which the letter must be received. Don't expect to get a letter if you ask at the last minute.
- Gently nudge by e-mail to remind the recommender when the deadline is approaching.

YOUR TASK. Write a persuasive request by e-mail asking your instructor (or supervisor or manager) to write you a letter of recommendation for a job application, grant, scholarship, or graduate school application. Provide all relevant information to make it easy for your reader to write a terrific letter. Explain any attachments.

8.6 Persuasive Request: Asking the Boss to Pick up the Tab for Tuition (L.O. 1, 2, 4)

> **Communication Technology** > **Team**

After working a few years, you would like to extend your college education on a part-time basis. You know that your education can benefit your employer, but you can't really afford the fees for tuition and books. You have heard that many companies offer reimbursement for tuition and books when employees complete approved courses with a grade of *C* or higher.

YOUR TASK. In teams discuss the best way to approach an employer whom you wish to persuade to start a tuition and books reimbursement program. How could such a program help the employer? Remember that the most successful requests help receivers see what's in it for them. What objections might your employer raise? How can you counter them? After discussing strategies in teams face-to-face or online, write a team memo or individual memos to your boss (at a company where you now work or one with which you are familiar). Persuade her or him to act on your persuasive request.

8.7 Persuasive Request: Providing Suitable Suits to Interviewees (L.O. 1, 2, 4)

> **E-Mail**

You saw an interesting article describing a Suitable Suits program at Barnard College. Its College of Career Development kept a closet filled with 21 crisp black suits that students could borrow for job interviews. Students made appointments with the office and agreed to dry clean the suits before returning them. At Barnard the program was paid for with a grant from a prominent financial firm. You think that a Suitable Suits program is worth exploring with your dean.

YOUR TASK. Write a persuasive message requesting an appointment with your dean to discuss a Suitable Suits program at your school. You don't have all the answers and you are not sure how such a program would operate, but you think the idea is worth discussing. Can you convince the dean to see you? Should you write an e-mail or a letter?

8.8 Persuasive Claim: Overpriced Hotel Breakfast in Las Vegas (L.O. 3)

As regional manager for a national restaurant chain, you and two other employees attended a sales conference in Las Vegas, Nevada. You stayed at the Aria Resort & Casino because your company recommends that employees use this hotel during annual industry meetings. Generally, your employees have liked their accommodations, and the rates have been within your company's budget.

Now, however, you are unhappy with the charges you see on your company's credit statement from Aria Resort & Casino. When your department's administrative assistant made the reservations, she was assured that you would receive the weekend rates and that a hot breakfast—in the hotel's Italian restaurant, Carbone—would be included in the rate. So you and the other two employees went to the restaurant and ordered a hot meal from the menu.

When you received the credit statement, though, you saw a charge for $153 for three champagne buffet breakfasts at Carbone. You hit the ceiling! For one thing, you didn't have a buffet breakfast and certainly no champagne. The three of you got there so early that no buffet had been set up. You ordered pancakes and sausage, and for this you were billed $40 each. What's worse, your company may charge you personally for exceeding the maximum per diem rates.

In looking back at this event, you remember that other guests on your floor were having a continental breakfast in a lounge on your floor. Perhaps that's where the hotel expected all guests on the weekend rate to eat. However, your administrative assistant had specifically asked about this matter when she made the reservations, and she was told that you could order breakfast from the menu at the hotel's Italian restaurant, Carbone.

YOUR TASK. You want to straighten out this problem, and you can't do it by telephone because you suspect that you will need a written record of this entire mess. Online you have tried in vain to find an e-mail address for guest relations at Aria. Write a persuasive claim to Customer Service, Aria Resort & Casino, 3730 Las Vegas Boulevard, Las Vegas, NV 89158. Should you include a copy of the credit card statement showing the charge?

8.9 Persuasive Claim: Wretched Print Job (L.O. 3)

As president of Unicorn Travel, you brought a very complex print job to the Primera Printers in Rochester, New York. It took almost 15 minutes to explain the particulars of this job to the printer. When you left, you wondered whether all of the instructions would be followed precisely. You even brought in your own special paper, which added to the cost of printing. When you got the job back (a total of 1,500 sheets of paper) and returned to your office, you discovered a host of problems. One of the pages had 300 copies made on cheap 20-pound paper. This means that the printer must have run out of your special paper and substituted something else for one of the runs. The printer also made copies of your original photos and graphics, so that all the final prints were run from second-generation prints, which reduced the quality of the graphics enormously. What's more, many of the sheets were poorly or improperly cut. In short, the job was unacceptable.

Because you were desperate to complete the job, you allowed the print shop to repeat the job using its paper supply. When you inquired about the cost, the counter person Hugh was noncommittal. He said you would have to talk to the owner, who worked in the Rochester shop. The repeat print job turned out fairly well, and you paid the full price of $782. But you are unhappy, and Hugh sensed that Primera Printers would not see Unicorn Travel again as a customer. He encouraged you to write to the owner and ask for an adjustment.

YOUR TASK. Write a claim letter to Mr. Mitch Spiro, Primera Printers, 240 State Street, Rochester, NY 14608. What is a reasonable claim to make? Do you simply want to register your unhappiness, or do you want a refund? Supply any needed information.

8.10 Persuasive Organizational Message Flowing Upward: Four-Day Weekend Now!

(L.O. 4)

> E-Mail > Team > Web

Some companies and municipalities are switching to a four-day workweek to reduce traffic congestion, air pollution, and stressed employees. Compressing the workweek into four 10-hour days sounds pretty good to you. You would much prefer having Friday free to schedule medical appointments and take care of family business, in addition to leisurely three-day weekends.

As a manager at Skin Essentials, a mineral-based skin care products and natural cosmetics company, you are convinced that the company's 200 employees could switch to a four-day workweek with many resulting benefits. For one thing, they would save on gasoline and commute time. You know that many cities and companies have already implemented a four-day workweek with considerable success. You took a quick poll of immediate employees and managers and found that 80 percent thought that a four-day workweek was a good idea. One said, "This would be great! Think of what I could save on babysitting and lunches!"

YOUR TASK. With a group of other students, conduct research on the Web and discuss your findings. What are the advantages of a four-day workweek? What organizations have already tried it? What appeals could be used to persuade management to adopt a four-day workweek?

What arguments could be expected, and how would you counter them? Individually or as a group, prepare a one-page persuasive e-mail or memo addressed to the Skin Essentials Management Council. Decide on a goal. Do you want to suggest a pilot study? Should you meet with management to present your ideas? How about starting a four-day workweek immediately?

8.11 Persuasive Organizational Message Flowing Upward: Consider This Idea (L.O. 4)

> E-Mail

In your own work or organization experience, identify a problem for which you have a solution. Should a procedure be altered to improve performance? Would a new or different piece of equipment or software help you perform your work better? Could some tasks be scheduled more efficiently? Are employees being used most effectively? Could customers be better served by changing something? Do you want to work other hours or perform other tasks? Do you deserve a promotion? Do you have a suggestion to improve profitability?

YOUR TASK. Once you have identified a situation requiring persuasion, write a memo or an e-mail to your boss or organization head. Use actual names and facts. Employ the concepts and techniques in this chapter to help you convince your boss that your idea should prevail. Include concrete examples, anticipate objections, emphasize reader benefits, and end with a specific action to be taken.

8.12 Persuasive Organizational Message Flowing Downward: Avoiding Costly Shipping Charges (L.O. 4)

As office manager of a Sacramento footwear and apparel company, write a memo persuading your shipping employees to reduce express delivery fees. Your FedEx and other shipping bills have been sky high, and you feel that staff members are overusing these services to please their favorite distributors. They don't consider less expensive options, such as sharing shipping costs with the recipient.

If shipping staff members plan ahead and allow enough time, they can use UPS or FedEx ground service, which takes three to five days and is much cheaper. You wonder whether staff members consider whether the recipient would mind waiting a few days longer for the merchandise in exchange for prices remaining low. When is overnight shipment justified? You would like to reduce overnight delivery services voluntarily by 50 percent over the next two months. Unless a sizable reduction occurs, the CEO threatens severe restrictions in the future.

YOUR TASK. Address your memo to all staff members. What other ways could employees reduce shipping costs?

8.13 Persuasive Organizational Message Flowing Downward: Volunteering for Urban Farming (L.O. 4)

> E-Mail > Web

As employee relations manager of Whole Foods Market in Brooklyn, New York, one of your tasks is to promote Gotham Greens. This company has partnered with Whole Foods to establish the nation's first commercial-scale rooftop greenhouse. Demand for locally grown greens in densely populated areas such as New York has prompted Gotham Greens to establish a hydroponic greenhouse on the roof of the Whole Foods Gowanus store to grow organic, non-GMO greens. You must recruit 12 coworkers who will volunteer to help operate the rooftop greenhouse, interact with visitors interested in urban farming, and teach community families about healthy eating. The goal is to help feed the community by starting more rooftop urban gardens and eventually perhaps even turn a modest profit.

Whole Foods Market volunteers will be expected to attend training sessions and then to instruct participating members of the community. In return, employees will receive two hours of release time per week to work on their urban farming project. The program has been very successful thus far, and the interest in community gardens is growing.

YOUR TASK. Learn more about urban farming by searching the Web. Then write a persuasive memo or e-mail with convincing appeals that will bring you 12 volunteers to work with Whole Foods and Gotham Greens on urban farming projects.

8.14 Identifying the AIDA Strategy in Sales Messages (L.O. 5)
> E-Mail

YOUR TASK. Select a one- or two-page sales letter or promotional e-mail received by you or a friend. If you are unable to find a sales message, your instructor may have a collection. Study the sales message and then answer these questions:

a. What techniques capture the reader's attention?
b. Is the opening effective? Explain.
c. What is the central selling point?
d. Does the message use rational, emotional, or a combination of appeals? Explain.
e. What reader benefits are suggested?
f. How does the message build interest in the product or service?
g. How is price handled?
h. How does the message anticipate reader resistance and offer counterarguments?
i. What action is the reader to take? How is the action made easy?
j. What motivators spur the reader to act quickly?

8.15 Sales Message: Subscribing to Organic Greens (L.O. 5)
> E-Mail

Many consumers worry about what's in their food. They fear conventional factory farming, wish to be good stewards of the environment, and desire a sustainable lifestyle. Wholesome organic food can increasingly be found on the shelves of mainstream supermarkets. Even big-box stores such as Costco—not just health food stores such as Mother's Market, Sprouts Farmers Market, and Whole Foods Market—are capitalizing on the farm-to-table trend. Weekly farmers' markets selling local produce and fruit are common across America.

But even busy urbanites who don't like to travel to shop can embrace healthier fare by subscribing to farm-fresh veggies and fruit online for home delivery. Services such as Fair & Fresh Farming in Montana, themselves organic farmers since 1976, partner with other organic farms to offer customizable boxes with several service and delivery options. Because these co-op-type outfits benefit from economies of scale, their prices, although higher than those of conventional markets, are not exorbitant. The delivery services also offer priceless convenience. Subscribers can customize their boxes on the Fair & Fresh Farming website, or they can let the farmers select the content for them.

The advantages of receiving weekly boxes filled with healthy seasonal produce include fresh, delicious taste, wholesome food that's free of herbicides and pesticides, and less time spent in traffic by ordering a custom box online each week or less frequently. In addition, subscribers are supporting small family farms that supply local, in-season fruit and veggies instead of buying greens that are flown halfway around the world. Depending on location, subscribers receive their boxes on Tuesday or Wednesday if they order a box by 10 a.m. on Sunday. For Thursday or Friday delivery, orders must be placed by 10 a.m. on Tuesday. New members receive 20 percent off their first order.

YOUR TASK. Write a sales message—a letter or an e-mail—for the signature of Marketer-in-Chief Martina Sabatini, Fair & Fresh Farming, 513 East Valentine Road, Glendive, MT 59330. Provide an enticing but accurate explanation of the service, and invite your reader to subscribe. Focus on audience benefits.

8.16 Sales Message: Promoting Products and Services (L.O. 5)
> E-Mail

Identify a situation in your current job or a previous one in which a sales message is or was needed. Using suggestions from this chapter, write an appropriate sales message that promotes a product or service. Use actual names, information, and examples. If you have no work experience, imagine a business you would like to start, such as data processing, pet grooming, car detailing, cleaning, tutoring, specialty knitting, balloon decorating, delivery service, child or elder care, gardening, or lawn care.

YOUR TASK. Write a sales letter or an e-mail marketing message selling your product or service to be distributed to your prospective customers. Be sure to tell them how to respond. You don't need to know HTML or have a Constant Contact account to craft a concise and eye-catching online sales message. Try designing it in Microsoft Word and saving it as a Web page (go to the **File** tab and select **Save as**; then in the **Save as type line**, select **Web page**). Consider adding graphics or photos—either your own or samples borrowed from the Internet. As long as you use them for this assignment and don't publish them online, you are not violating copyright laws.

8.17 Analyzing Tweets: Persuasive Micromessages (L.O. 1, 5)

> Communication Technology > E-Mail > Social Media > Web

As you have learned in this chapter, the time-tried AIDA sales technique is alive and well even in 140-character Twitter messages. Of course, we can't expect to find all four parts in a single tweet.

YOUR TASK. Study the following tweets and describe the persuasive techniques they employ. **Hint:** You may find that Twitter users rely on attention-getters, calls for action, emotional appeals, incentives, and testimonials. They may also create urgency to stoke readers' interest. Chat about your findings in class or on your favorite course-management platform. Your instructor may ask you to collect your own examples of persuasive tweets or other social media posts and discuss their frequency as well as effectiveness. After you have collected a sample large enough to allow you to generalize, compose an e-mail or post about your observations.

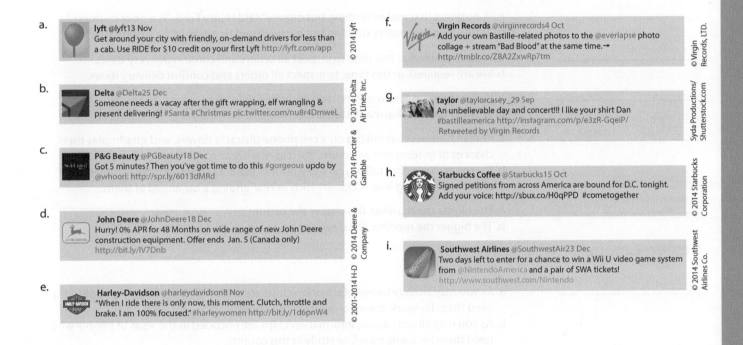

a.
lyft @lyft13 Nov
Get around your city with friendly, on-demand drivers for less than a cab. Use RIDE for $10 credit on your first Lyft http://lyft.com/app
© 2014 Lyft

b.
Delta @Delta25 Dec
Someone needs a vacay after the gift wrapping, elf wrangling & present delivering! #Santa #Christmas pic.twitter.com/nu8r4DmweL
© 2014 Delta Air Lines, Inc.

c.
P&G Beauty @PGBeauty18 Dec
Got 5 minutes? Then you've got time to do this #gorgeous updo by @whoorl: http://spr.ly/6013dMRd
© 2014 Procter & Gamble

d.
John Deere @JohnDeere18 Dec
Hurry! 0% APR for 48 Months on wide range of new John Deere construction equipment. Offer ends Jan. 5 (Canada only) http://bit.ly/IV7Dnb
© 2014 Deere & Company

e.
Harley-Davidson @harleydavidson8 Nov
"When I ride there is only now, this moment. Clutch, throttle and brake. I am 100% focused." #harleywomen http://bit.ly/1d6pnW4
© 2001-2014 H-D

f.
Virgin Records @virginrecords4 Oct
Add your own Bastille-related photos to the @everlapse photo collage + stream "Bad Blood" at the same time.→ http://tmblr.co/Z8A2ZxwRp7tm
© Virgin Records, LTD.

g.
taylor @taylorcasey_29 Sep
An unbelievable day and concert!!! I like your shirt Dan #bastilleamerica http://instagram.com/p/e3zR-GqeiP/ Retweeted by Virgin Records
Syda Productions/ Shutterstock.com

h.
Starbucks Coffee @Starbucks15 Oct
Signed petitions from across America are bound for D.C. tonight. Add your voice: http://sbux.co/H0qPPD #cometogether
© 2014 Starbucks Corporation

i.
Southwest Airlines @SouthwestAir23 Dec
Two days left to enter for a chance to win a Wii U video game system from @NintendoAmerica and a pair of SWA tickets! http://www.southwest.com/Nintendo
© 2014 Southwest Airlines Co.

8.18 Writing Persuasive Tweets and Posts (L.O. 1, 5)

> Social Media > Web

Being able to compose effective and concise micromessages and posts will positively contribute to your professional online persona.

YOUR TASK. Brainstorm to identify a special skill you have, an event you want others to attend, a charitable cause dear to your heart, or a product you like. Applying what you have learned about short persuasive messages online, write your own 140-character persuasive tweet or post. Use Figure 8.9 as a starting point and model.

8.19 Taking Aim at Puffery in Advertising (L.O. 1, 5)

> Communication Technology > Social Media > Web

As discussed in the Communication Workshop at the end of this chapter, puffery in advertising may be tacky, but it is not illegal. Few of us take claims seriously that shout *the best pizza in town, the largest selection of electronics, the ultimate fresh breath, the world's juiciest hamburgers, the biggest pie money can buy,* or *coldest beer.* After all, such exaggerated claims cannot be proven and do not fool anyone.

Serious, quantifiable claims, however, must be backed up with evidence or they could mean litigation: "Our chicken has less fat than a hamburger. It's better for you."[38] This bold claim was investigated, and the fried chicken restaurant had to stop using it in its advertising. Yes, the fried chicken had a little less total fat than a hamburger, but it contained more harmful transfat, sodium, and cholesterol, making it higher in calories—a decidedly unhealthy alternative. As the Federal Trade Commission points out, a restaurant can compare itself to others, but it must tell the truth.

YOUR TASK. Look for examples of puffery, and find ads that would need to prove their claims. How can you tell which is which? Discuss examples in class or in an online forum set up for your class.

Commas 3

Review the Grammar/Mechanics Handbook Sections 2.10–2.15. Then select the correctly punctuated sentence and record its letter in the space provided. Also record the appropriate G/M guideline to illustrate the principle involved. When you finish, compare your responses with those provided at the bottom of the page. If your answers differ, study carefully the appropriate guideline.

_____b____(2.12)_____

EXAMPLE
a. It was the manager, not the president who signed the check.
b. It was the manager, not the president, who signed the check.

_____ 1. a. "A business that makes nothing but money" said Henry Ford, "is a poor business."
b. "A business that makes nothing but money," said Henry Ford, "is a poor business."

_____ 2. a. We are required at this time to inspect all orders and confirm delivery dates.
b. We are required, at this time, to inspect all orders and confirm delivery dates.

_____ 3. a. We interviewed Shawna Patterson on June 2 didn't we?
b. We interviewed Shawna Patterson on June 2, didn't we?

_____ 4. a. Research shows that talking on a cell phone distracts drivers, and quadruples their chances of getting into accidents, such as rear-ending a car ahead of them.
b. Research shows that talking on a cell phone distracts drivers and quadruples their chances of getting into accidents such as rear-ending a car ahead of them.

_____ 5. a. The bigger the monitor, the clearer the picture.
b. The bigger the monitor the clearer the picture.

Review Commas 1, 2, 3

_____ 6. a. As you may already know information chips are encoded in the visas of people who need them for work, travel, or study in this country.
b. As you may already know, information chips are encoded in the visas of people who need them for work, travel, or study in this country.

_____ 7. a. We think, however, that the new passports will be issued only to diplomats, and other government employees beginning in August.
b. We think, however, that the new passports will be issued only to diplomats and other government employees beginning in August.

_____ 8. a. A widely discussed study of productivity that was conducted by authoritative researchers revealed that workers in the United States are more productive than workers in Europe or Japan.
b. A widely discussed study of productivity, that was conducted by authoritative researchers, revealed that workers in the United States are more productive than workers in Europe or Japan.

_____ 9. a. America's productivity secrets which were discussed in the report were not bigger companies, more robots or even brainier managers.
b. America's productivity secrets, which were discussed in the report, were not bigger companies, more robots, or even brainier managers.

_____ 10. a. As a matter of fact, the report said that America's productivity resulted from a capitalistic system of unprotected, hands-off competition.
b. As a matter of fact, the report said that America's productivity resulted from a capitalistic system of unprotected hands-off competition.

1. b (2.14a) **2.** a (2.15) **3.** b (2.15) **4.** b (2.14b) **5.** a (2.15) **6.** b (2.06a, 2.01) **7.** b (2.03) **8.** a (2.15) **9.** b (2.06c, 2.01) **10.** b (2.03, 2.08)

Every chapter provides an editing exercise to fine-tune your grammar and mechanics skills.

The following letter requires edits that address proofreading, grammar, concise wording, punctuation (especially commas), capitalization, word use, and other writing issues. Study the guidelines in the Grammar/Mechanics Handbook (Appendix D), including the lists of Confusing Words and Frequently Misspelled Words.

YOUR TASK. Edit the following (a) by inserting corrections in your textbook or on a photocopy using proofreading marks in Appendix C or (b) by downloading the message from **www.cengagebrain.com** and correcting at your computer.

May 14, 2019

Mr. Jeremy Roper, General Manager
Monterey Plaza Hotel and Spa
440 Cannery Row
Monterey, CA 93940

Dear Mr. Roper:

I'm writing this letter to let you know that the wait staff at the Monterey Plazas popular Schooner Bistro restaurant would like to bring to your attention a serious problem. Even when us servers have gave good service some customer's leave no tip. Many of us have gotten together and decided to bring the problem and a possible solution to your attention per this letter.

Restaurants such as the famous French Laundry which is ranked as the countries finest restaurant, now add a 20 percent tip to the bill. All service charges go to the house and every one is paid a salary from that. Other restaurants are also printing gratuity guidelines on checks. In fact American Express now provides a calculation feature on it's terminals so that restaurants can chose the tip levels they want printed. In Europe a service charge of up to 20 percent is auto calculated, and added to a check.

Us servers are of the opinion that a suggested tip printed on checks would work good here at Schooner Bistro. We know that we give good service but some customers forget to tip. By printing a suggested tip on the check we remind them so that they won't forget. A printed suggested tip also does the math for them which is a advantage for customer's who are not to good with figures. In addition many of our customers are tourists from Europe. Who don't understand our tipping system.

Printing suggested tips on checks not only helps customers but also proves to the staff that you support them in there goal to recieve decent wages for the hard work they do. A few customers might resist, however these customers can always cross out the printed tip if they wish. If you have any doubts about the plan we could try it for a 6-month period, and monitor customers reactions.

We erge you to begin printing a suggested 20 percent tip on each customers bill. Our American express terminals are all ready equipt to do this. Please let us know your feelings about this proposal because its a serious concern to us.

Sincerely,

Joshua Rubin

Joshua Rubin
Server, Schooner Bistro

What's Legal and What's Not in Sales Messages and Online Reviews

In promoting products and writing sales messages, be careful about the words you use and the claims you make. Avoid paid reviews. How far can you go in praising and selling your product?

- **Puffery**. You might see advertisements that make proclamations such as *We make the world's best burger*. Called *puffery*, such promotional claims are not taken literally by reasonable consumers. Such subjective statements are accepted as puffery because they puff up, or exaggerate. Surprisingly, this kind of sales exaggeration is not illegal. However, when sales claims consist of objective statements that cannot be verified (*Our burgers were voted the best in town*), they become deceptive advertising.

- **Deceptive advertising**. If you write that three out of four dentists recommend your toothpaste, you had better have competent and reliable scientific evidence to support the claim. Such a claim goes beyond puffery and requires proof. According to a U.S. government report, as many as 20 percent of dietary supplements in the United States featured labels that made illegal claims to cure or treat diseases such as cancer and AIDS.[39] Similarly, the creator of the popular Lumosity brain-training games, Lumos Labs, settled a lawsuit for $2 million over allegedly unfounded claims that the games could stave off dementia and reduce cognitive impairment from stroke and attention-deficit/hyperactivity disorder.[40] In a litigious society, marketers who exaggerate are often taken to court.

- **Celebrities**. The unauthorized use of a celebrity's name, likeness, or nickname is not permitted in sales messages. Hollywood stars George Clooney and Julia Roberts joined forces to sue two audiovisual companies for misusing their names and images in selling projectors and entertainment systems.[41] The latest twist is social media posts. Award-winning actress Katherine Heigl sued a drugstore chain for $6 million for tweeting a photo of her leaving a store and this text: "Love a quick #DuaneReade run? *Even @KatieHeigl* can't resist shopping #NYC's favorite drugstore."[42] Heigl's photo was also posted on the company's Facebook page. The actress sued for false advertising and violation of her rights of privacy and publicity.

- **Misleading promises**. Multilevel marketing companies such as Herbalife frequently invite scrutiny. Recently, an investment firm released a video that confirmed suspicions. Senior Herbalife distributors acknowledged that their business model results in "eventual deception" and that Herbalife uses "a level of inauthenticity" to lure new recruits into the scheme.[43] Similarly, the shoe company Skechers had to pay $40 million to settle charges that it misled consumers. One advertisement promised that its Resistance Runners would raise "'muscle activation' by up to 85 percent for posture-related muscles," and "71 percent for one of the muscles in the buttocks."[44] A director of the Federal Trade Commission (FTC) said that for millions of consumers "the only thing that got a workout was their wallet."[45]

- **Paid online reviews**. The FTC also mandates full disclosure when a merchant and a promoter have a financial relationship. Legacy Learning Systems paid $250,000 to settle charges that it hired reviewers to recommend its videos on the Web.[46] Amazon and other online retailers have policies against buying positive reviews. Nonetheless, experts estimate that about one third of all Internet consumer reviews are fake.[47] Dishonest bad reviews can be damaging to a company's reputation. FTC commissioners have the legal authority to fine and even shut down a business for fake testimonials or misleading reviews.[48]

CAREER APPLICATION. Bring to class at least three promotional e-mails, sales letters, social media posts, or advertisements that may represent issues described here. What examples of puffery can you identify? Are claims substantiated by reliable evidence? What proof is offered? Do any of your examples include names, images, or nicknames of celebrities? How likely is it that the celebrity authorized this use? Have you ever received unwanted merchandise as part of a sales campaign? What were you expected to do with it?

Business Reports and Proposals— Best Practices

4

Pla2na/Shutterstock.com

GaudiLab/Shutterstock.com

Informal Reports

Stuart Jenner/Getty Images

Learning Outcomes
After studying this chapter, you should be able to do the following:

1 Explain informational and analytical report functions, organizational strategies, and writing styles.

2 Describe typical report formats and understand the significance of effective headings.

3 Identify the problem that the report addresses, define the report purpose, and collect significant secondary and primary information to solve the problem.

4 Prepare short informational reports that describe routine tasks.

5 Prepare short analytical reports that solve business problems.

9-1 Preparing Reports in the Digital Age

Business reports are an integral part of actively managing any company. Because digital age organizations face a world of intense competition and constant technological change, efficient reporting plays a critical role in helping managers sift through huge amounts of data to make decisions. Whether a company decides to launch a new product, expand into new markets, reduce expenses, improve customer service, or increase its social media presence, decisions are usually based on information submitted in reports. Routine reports keep managers informed about work in progress. Focused reports help managers analyze the challenges they face before recommending solutions. In the digital age, the amount of data expands exponentially by the minute; report writers are challenged to make sense of it.

Business reports range widely in length, purpose, and delivery mode. Some are short, informal bulleted lists with status updates. Others are formal 100-page financial forecasts. Routine reports may be generated weekly or monthly, whereas focused reports cover specific problems or situations. Report findings may be presented orally in a meeting or shared electronically on Web platforms. Many reports today are delivered digitally in e-mail messages, PDF (portable document format) files, or slide decks. These files can then be accessed on a company's intranet, posted on the Internet, or saved on cloud servers off-site.

The worldwide sales of Coca-Cola soda are sinking, but no need to panic, says the company. Although global soda consumption fell, the total beverage sales for Coca-Cola expanded by 2 percent last quarter. Analysis of sales data revealed that alternative beverages such as the company's teas, juices, and bottled water grew in popularity. In addition, the company learned that the sale of smaller cans and bottles of soda actually made Coca-Cola more money than the sale of larger ones did. Moreover, the company is acquiring a soy-beverage brand in Latin America as well as investing in a line of organic aloe-water beverages. What types of reports can help Coca-Cola managers organize and interpret data to make strategic decisions that offset sagging soda sales?

This chapter examines the functions, organizational strategies, writing styles, and formats of typical business reports. It also introduces the report-writing process and discusses methods of collecting, documenting, and illustrating data. Some reports provide information only; others analyze and make recommendations. Although reports vary greatly in length, content, form, and formality level, they all have one or more of the following purposes: *to convey information, answer questions*, and *solve problems*.

LEARNING OUTCOME 1

Explain informational and analytical report functions, organizational strategies, and writing styles.

9-1a Basic Report Functions

In terms of what they do, most reports fit into one of two broad categories: informational reports and analytical reports.

Informational Reports. Reports that present data without analysis or recommendations are primarily informational. For such reports, writers collect and organize facts, but they do not analyze the facts for readers. A trip report describing an employee's visit to a trade show, for example, is informational. Weekly bulleted status reports about an ongoing project are also informational. Other reports that present information without analysis include monthly sales reports, status updates, and government compliance reports.

Analytical Reports. Reports that provide data or findings, analyses, and conclusions are analytical. If requested, writers also supply recommendations. Analytical reports may intend to persuade readers to act or change their beliefs. For example, if you were writing a yardstick report that compares several potential manufacturing locations for a new automobile plant, you would compare the locations using the same criteria and then provide a recommendation. Other reports that provide recommendations are feasibility studies (e.g., for expansion opportunities) and justification reports (e.g., for buying equipment or changing procedures).

AP Images/Jon Elswick

9-1b Organizational Strategies

Like other business messages, reports may be organized directly or indirectly. The reader's anticipated reaction and the content of a report determine its organizational strategy, as illustrated in Figure 9.1. In long reports, such as corporate annual reports, some parts may be organized directly whereas other parts are arranged indirectly.

Analytical reports may also be organized directly, especially when readers are supportive of or familiar with the topic. Many busy executives prefer this strategy because it gives them the results of the report immediately. They don't have to spend time wading through the facts, findings, discussion, and analyses to get to the two items they are most interested in—the conclusions and recommendations.

Direct Strategy When you place the purpose for writing close to the beginning of a report, the organizational strategy is direct. Informational reports, such as the one shown in Figure 9.2, are usually arranged directly. They open with an introduction, which is followed by the facts and a summary. In Figure 9.2 the writer sends this report to respond to a request for information about complying with job safety procedures. The report opens with an introduction followed by a bulleted list of compliance data. The report ends with a summary and a forward look.

Indirect Strategy. The organizational strategy is indirect when the conclusions and recommendations, if requested, appear at the end of the report. Such reports usually begin with an introduction or description of the problem, followed by facts and explanations. They end with conclusions and recommendations. This strategy is helpful when readers are unfamiliar with the problem or when they must be persuaded. When readers may be disappointed in or hostile toward the report's findings, an indirect strategy works best. The writer is more likely to retain the reader's interest by first explaining, justifying, and analyzing the facts and then making recommendations. This strategy also seems most rational to readers because it follows the normal thought process: problem, alternatives (facts), solution.

Figure 9.1 Audience Analysis and Report Organization

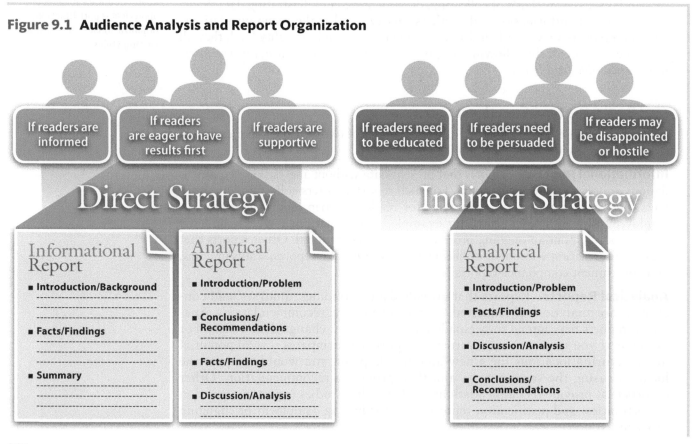

254

Figure 9.2 Informational Safety Compliance Report—Letter Format

ATLAS MANUFACTURING CO.
15910 BRATTON ROAD, AUSTIN, TX 78728

Uses letterhead stationery for informal report addressed to an outsider

August 10, 2019

Mr. Richard Wattenburg
Texas Occupational Safety Department
1033 La Posada Drive
Austin, TX 78752

Dear Mr. Wattenburg:

Includes subject line for quick comprehension

Subject: Job Safety and Standard Operating Procedures at Atlas Manufacturing Co.

Here is the report you requested regarding our job safety and operating procedures. As you suggested, we followed your instructions to outline plant safety responsibilities for all personnel. This report, along with diagrams and manuals, is now available at each workstation. It has also been circulated to all employees and is posted on all department bulletin boards.

As instructed, we hired a firm to translate our safety manuals into the languages spoken on the plant floor. In addition, we are working on a plan to ensure regular updating of the manuals. Specific procedures are as follows:

Organizes information into bulleted segments to concisely present an overview of separate safety concerns

- The binding manager will stand in front of the department near the binding equipment to observe employees operating the equipment and working near the machinery. The manager will direct employees out the employee entrance or through the main office, in case of a fire.
- The fabrication manager will be responsible for the proper shutdown of all equipment before shifts end. Press operators and injection operators will perform shutdown of ovens and extruders.
- The production supervisor will go to the junction at the binding and finishing cells to ensure that (a) work areas are clutter free, (b) proper attire is worn, and (c) safety equipment is working properly.
- In the supplies room, the forklift operator on each shift will inspect the forklift for any visible damage.
- In the assembly area, the shift supervisor will ensure that employees are directed out of the building through the east hallway.

Presents facts without analysis or recommendations

We hope these procedures are satisfactory since we seek the utmost safety for our employees. Should you have any questions or further suggestions, please call me at 512-928-5498 or send an e-mail to sjohnson@atlasmfg.com. With these measures now in place, we trust that we will pass the September inspection with flying colors.

Closes politely with contact information and a look forward

Sincerely,

Sally Johnson

Sally Johnson
Vice President, Operations

Tips for Writing Letter Reports
- Use letter format for short informal reports sent to outsiders.
- Organize the report into an introduction, body, and summary closing.
- Single-space the body.
- Double-space between paragraphs.
- Create side margins of 1 to 1.25 inches.

9-1c Informal and Formal Writing Styles

Like other business messages, reports can range from informal to formal depending on their purpose, audience, and setting. Research reports from consultants to their clients tend to be more formal. Such reports must project objectivity, authority, and impartiality. However, depending on the industry, a report to a boss describing a trip to a conference is normally informal.

An office worker once called a grammar hotline service with this problem: "We've just sent a report to our headquarters, and it was returned with this comment, 'Put it in the third person.' What does this mean?" The hotline experts explained that management apparently wanted a more formal writing style, using third-person constructions (*the company* or *the researcher* instead of *we* and *I*). Figure 9.3, which compares the characteristics of formal and informal report-writing

Figure 9.3 Report-Writing Styles

	INFORMAL WRITING STYLE	FORMAL WRITING STYLE
Appropriate Use	• Short, routine reports • Reports for familiar audiences • Noncontroversial reports • Internal use reports • Internal announcements and invitations	• Lengthy, formal reports and proposals • Research studies • Controversial or complex reports • External use reports • Formal invitations
Overall Effect	• Friendly tone • Relationship building • Casual	• Objectivity and accuracy • Sense of professional distance between writer and reader
Writing Style Characteristics	• Use of first-person pronouns *(I, we, me, my, us, our)* • Use of contractions *(can't, don't)* • Emphasis on active-voice verbs *(I conducted the study)* • Shorter sentences • Familiar words • Conversational language	• Use of third person *(the researcher, the writer)* (depends on the circumstances) • Absence of contractions *(cannot, do not)* • Use of passive-voice verbs *(the study was conducted)* • Professional, respectful language • Absence of humor and figures of speech • Elimination of "editorializing" (author's opinions and perceptions)

styles, can help you decide which style is appropriate for your reports. Note that, increasingly, formal report writers use contractions and active-voice verbs. Today, report writers try to avoid awkward third-person references to themselves as *the researchers* or *the authors* because it sounds stilted and outdated.

LEARNING OUTCOME 2
Describe typical report formats and understand the significance of effective headings.

9-2 Report Formats and Heading Levels

The overall design of a formatted report should be visually appealing and professional looking. Reports in the conventional workplace may be presented in a number of formats. Their design should include a hierarchy of meaningful headings that highlight major points, allowing readers to see the flow of ideas. Many corporations use templates or reporting software to standardize the look of their report in terms of formats and heading levels.

9-2a Typical Report Formats

Reporting in digital age organizations remains a critical but challenging key to business success as the amount of data continually expands. Many types of reports coexist and vary greatly by sector or industry. The format of a report depends on its length, topic, audience, and purpose. After considering these elements, you will probably choose from among the following formats.

Digital Formats and PDF Files. Writers routinely save and distribute reports as portable document format (PDF) files. This file type, invented by Adobe, condenses documents while preserving the formatting and graphics. A report created with Microsoft Word, Excel, or PowerPoint can easily be saved as a PDF file. A PDF report might include links to external websites, a nice advantage over printed reports. Web-based reports may feature engaging multimedia effects, such as interactive charts and video.

Digital Slide Decks. Many business writers deliver their report information in digital slideshows, also called slide decks. These slides can be sent by e-mail, embedded on the Web, or posted on a company intranet. When used in reporting, slide decks may have more text than typical presentation slides. Photographs, tables, charts, and other visuals make slide decks more inviting to read than print pages of dense report text. Not surprisingly, communicators in marketing, technology, media, entertainment, and consulting are fond of using slide deck reports to summarize their statistics and other findings. Figure 9.4 shows several slides from global marketing company ExactTarget analyzing the Internet market in Germany.

Infographics. Infographics, short for information graphics, are visual representations of data or information. They can display complex information quickly and clearly, and they may be easier to understand than written text. Infographics are also affordable and effortlessly shared on social media platforms. In fact, good infographics can go viral when viewers embed and spread the word about them in their blogs and on their social media networks. Infographics, as discussed later in this chapter, can tell compelling stories that help all types of businesses attract and inform consumers.

E-Mail and Memo Formats. Many reports are attached to e-mails, posted online, or, if short, embedded in the body of e-mails. For short informal reports that stay within organizations, the memo format may still be appropriate. Memo reports begin with essential background information, using standard headings: *Date, To, From,* and *Subject.* Memo reports differ from regular memos in length, use of headings, and deliberate organization. Today, memo reports are rarely distributed in hard copy; more likely they are shared electronically as PDF files.

Forms and Templates. Office workers use digital forms that are usually made available on the company intranet or the Internet. Such electronic templates are suitable for repetitive data, such as monthly sales reports, performance appraisals, merchandise inventories, and personnel and financial reports. Employees can customize and fill in the templates and forms. Then they distribute them electronically or print them. Using standardized formats and headings saves a writer time and ensures that all necessary information is included.

Letter Format. The letter format for short informal reports (usually eight or fewer pages) addressed outside an organization can still be found in government agencies, real estate companies, and accounting firms. Prepared on office stationery, a letter report contains a date, inside address, salutation, and complimentary close, as shown earlier in Figure 9.2. Although they may carry information similar to that found in correspondence, letter reports usually are longer and show more careful organization than typical letters. They also may include headings to guide the reader through the content, and they may come with attachments. Like memo reports, letter reports are also likely to be sent to clients as PDF files.

Manuscript Format. For longer, more formal reports, use the manuscript format. These reports are usually printed on plain paper without letterhead. They begin with a title followed by systematically displayed headings and subheadings. You will see examples of proposals and formal reports using the manuscript format in Chapter 10.

9-2b Effective Report Headings

Descriptive headings assist readers in comprehending the organization of a report. Viewers can see major ideas at a glance. Moreover, headings provide resting points for the mind and for the eye, breaking up large chunks of text into manageable and readable segments.

Figure 9.4 Informal Reports Delivered as Slide Decks

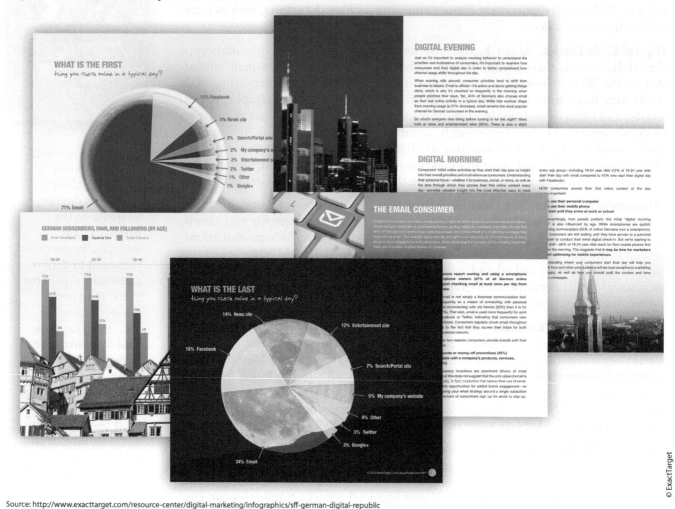

Source: http://www.exacttarget.com/resource-center/digital-marketing/infographics/sff-german-digital-republic

Report writers may use functional or talking headings, examples of which are shown in Figure 9.5. Functional headings are one- or two-word labels that show the sections of a report but provide little insight about the contents. Functional headings are sometimes useful for routine reports.

Talking headings provide more information and spark interest. Writers must make sure, however, that talking headings contribute to the overall organization and flow of ideas. With some planning, headings can combine the best attributes of both functional and talking. The best strategy for creating helpful talking headings is to write a few paragraphs first and then generate a talking heading that covers those paragraphs. To create effective report headings, follow these basic guidelines:

- **Construct a clear hierarchy of heading levels.** A hierarchy refers to the level of importance of the headings in a document. Some reports have one level of heading and others may have three. A heading's placement, size, and font should match those of the other headings in the same level. Writers may use varying font styles and sizes, but the hierarchy must be clear to the reader. Remember, too, that reports are easier to follow when they use no more than three heading levels.

- **Capitalize and emphasize carefully.** A writer might choose to use all capital letters for main titles, such as a report or chapter title. For first- and second-level headings, they follow the traditional rules for headings: capitalize the first letter of main words such as nouns, verbs, adjectives, adverbs, and so on. Do not

Figure 9.5 Distinguishing Among Functional, Talking, and Combination Headings

Functional Headings	Talking Headings	Combination Headings

• Background
• Findings
• Personnel
• Production Costs
	• Lack of Space and Cost
	  Compound Parking Program
	• Survey Shows Support for
	  Parking Fees
		• Introduction: Lack of Parking
		  Reaches Crisis Proportions
		• Parking Recommendations:
		  Shuttle and New Structures

capitalize articles (*a, an, the*), conjunctions (*and, but, or, nor*), and prepositions with three or fewer letters (*in, to, by, for*) unless they are the first or last words in the heading. Headings generally appear in bold font, as shown in Figure 9.6.

- **Create grammatically equal heading levels.** Try to create headings that are grammatically equal, or parallel, within the same level. For example, *Developing Product Teams* and *Presenting Plan to Management* are parallel headings; they both begin with an action word ending in *-ing*. *Development of Product Teams* and *Presenting Plan to Management* are not parallel headings.

- **For short reports use one or two heading levels.** In a short report, first-level headings might be bold and left-aligned; second-level headings might be bold paragraph headings.

- **Include at least one heading per report page, but don't end the page with a stand-alone heading.** Headings increase the readability and add visual appeal to report pages. Try to use at least one heading per page to break up blocks of text and reveal the content's topic. If a heading at the bottom of a page gets separated from the text that follows, move that heading to the top of the following page.

- **Apply punctuation correctly.** A stand-alone bold heading does not require end punctuation. A paragraph heading, on the other hand, is followed by a period, which separates it from the text that follows.

- **Keep headings short but clear.** One-word headings are emphatic but not always clear. For example, the heading *Project* does not adequately describe the expectations of a summer internship project for a Texas oil company. A better heading would be [*Company name*] *Internship Expectations*. Keep your headings brief (no more than eight words), but make them meaningful. Clarity is more important than brevity.

9-3 Identifying the Problem, Defining the Purpose, and Collecting Data

LEARNING OUTCOME 3
Identify the problem that the report addresses, define the report purpose, and collect significant secondary and primary information to solve the problem.

Because business reports are systematic attempts to compile data, answer questions, and solve problems, you'll want to be methodical in achieving those goals. Following are guidelines that will help you identify the report problem and purpose as well as gather relevant data.

9-3a Determine the Problem and Purpose

The first step in writing a report is analyzing or determining the problem the report will address. Preparing a written problem statement helps clarify the task. Suppose a pharmaceutical company wants to investigate the problem of high transportation costs for its sales representatives. Some sales reps visit clients using company-leased

Figure 9.6 Levels of Headings

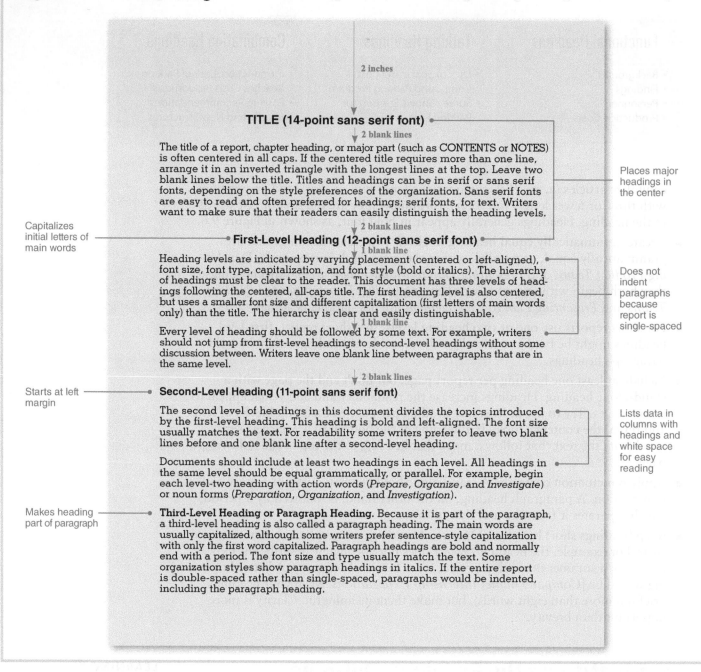

Capitalizes initial letters of main words

Starts at left margin

Makes heading part of paragraph

2 inches

TITLE (14-point sans serif font)

2 blank lines

The title of a report, chapter heading, or major part (such as CONTENTS or NOTES) is often centered in all caps. If the centered title requires more than one line, arrange it in an inverted triangle with the longest lines at the top. Leave two blank lines below the title. Titles and headings can be in serif or sans serif fonts, depending on the style preferences of the organization. Sans serif fonts are easy to read and often preferred for headings; serif fonts, for text. Writers want to make sure that their readers can easily distinguish the heading levels.

2 blank lines

First-Level Heading (12-point sans serif font)

1 blank line

Heading levels are indicated by varying placement (centered or left-aligned), font size, font type, capitalization, and font style (bold or italics). The hierarchy of headings must be clear to the reader. This document has three levels of headings following the centered, all-caps title. The first heading level is also centered, but uses a smaller font size and different capitalization (first letters of main words only) than the title. The hierarchy is clear and easily distinguishable.

1 blank line

Every level of heading should be followed by some text. For example, writers should not jump from first-level headings to second-level headings without some discussion between. Writers leave one blank line between paragraphs that are in the same level.

2 blank lines

Second-Level Heading (11-point sans serif font)

The second level of headings in this document divides the topics introduced by the first-level heading. This heading is bold and left-aligned. The font size usually matches the text. For readability some writers prefer to leave two blank lines before and one blank line after a second-level heading.

Documents should include at least two headings in each level. All headings in the same level should be equal grammatically, or parallel. For example, begin each level-two heading with action words (*Prepare, Organize,* and *Investigate*) or noun forms (*Preparation, Organization,* and *Investigation*).

Third-Level Heading or Paragraph Heading. Because it is part of the paragraph, a third-level heading is also called a paragraph heading. The main words are usually capitalized, although some writers prefer sentence-style capitalization with only the first word capitalized. Paragraph headings are bold and normally end with a period. The font size and type usually match the text. Some organization styles show paragraph headings in italics. If the entire report is double-spaced rather than single-spaced, paragraphs would be indented, including the paragraph heading.

Places major headings in the center

Does not indent paragraphs because report is single-spaced

Lists data in columns with headings and white space for easy reading

cars; others drive their own cars and are reimbursed for expenses. The leasing agreements for 12 cars expire in three months. The company wants to investigate the transportation choices and report the findings before the leases are renewed. The following problem statement helps clarify the reason for the report:

> **Problem statement:** *The leases on all company cars will expire in three months. The company must decide whether to renew them or develop a new policy regarding transportation for sales reps. Expenses and reimbursement paperwork for employee-owned cars is excessive.*

A statement of purpose further defines the report's purpose and scope. To begin, develop questions that help clarify the purpose: Should the company compare the costs of buying and leasing cars? Should the company gather current data on reimbursement costs for those driving personal cars? Will the report writers evaluate the data and recommend a course of action? Should the sales reps' reactions be considered? Then write a statement of purpose that answers the questions.

Statement of purpose: *To recommend a plan that provides sales reps with cars to be used in their calls. The report will compare costs for three plans: outright ownership, leasing, and compensation for employee-owned cars. Data will include the sales reps' reactions to each plan.*

Preparing a written purpose statement is a good idea because it limits the scope and provides a standard that keeps the project on target. In writing useful purpose statements, choose action verbs telling what you intend to do: *analyze, choose, investigate, compare, justify, evaluate, explain, establish, determine,* and so on. Notice that the preceding purpose statement uses the action verbs *recommend* and *compare.*

Some reports require only a simple statement of purpose (e.g., *to investigate expanded teller hours, to select a manager from among four candidates, to describe the position of accounts supervisor*). Many assignments, though, require expanded purpose statements.

9-3b Collect Information From Secondary and Primary Sources

One of the most important steps in writing a report is that of collecting information (research). A good report is based on solid, accurate, verifiable facts. This factual information falls into two broad categories: primary and secondary. Primary data result from firsthand experience and observation. Secondary data come from reading what others have experienced or observed and recorded. Typical sources of both primary and secondary factual information for informal reports are (a) company records, (b) printed material, (c) electronic resources, (d) observation, (e) surveys and questionnaires, and (f) interviews.

Company Records. Many business reports begin with an analysis of company records and files. These records reveal past performance and methods used to solve previous problems. You can collect pertinent facts that will help determine a course of action.

Printed Material. Although some print resources are also available online, libraries should not be overlooked as an excellent source for many types of print resources. Some information in libraries is available only in print. Print sources include books, newspapers, and periodicals, such as magazines and journals.

Digital Resources. An extensive source of current and historical information is available from digital resources. From a computer or mobile device, you can access information provided by government sites, news media, periodicals, nonprofits, and businesses. Business researchers are also using Facebook comments, Twitter feeds, forum messages, and blog posts to gather information. For short informal reports, you will probably gather most of your data from online resources. Chapter 10 provides more detailed suggestions about online research and Web search tools.

Observation. In the absence of secondary sources, a primary source of data for many problems comes from personal observation and experience. For example, if you were writing a report on the need for a comprehensive policy on the use of social media, you might observe employees to see whether they are checking their social networks during the workday or sharing potentially damaging company information on their blogs, on Facebook, and on other social networks. Observation might yield incomplete results, but it is nonetheless a valid form of data collection.

Surveys and Questionnaires. When a report requires current user or customer feedback, you can collect the data efficiently and economically by using surveys and questionnaires. This is another primary source of information. For example, if

Gathering and analyzing survey data for business reports has never been easier. One cloud-based tool has turned the task of conducting surveys into a lot of monkey business—literally. SurveyMonkey provides online templates and easy methodologies so that anyone can create a survey and get results quickly. Yet, it's so powerful that more than 20 million people around the world, including 99 percent of the Fortune 500 companies, have used it to gather survey-related information. One human resources manager said that the "360 degree feedback survey we created is sent to employees, managers, and even customers. The insights it provides are invaluable." What other uses of surveys are commonly found in business?[2]

you were part of a committee investigating the success of an employee carpooling program, you might gather data by distributing a questionnaire to the employees themselves. See Chapter 10 for more information about surveys.

Interviews. Talking with individuals directly concerned with the problem produces excellent firsthand information if published sources are not available. For example, if you would like to find ways to improve the hiring process of your company, you might interview your company's human resources director or several of the department hiring managers for the most accurate and relevant information. Interviews allow you to gather data from experts in their fields.

LEARNING OUTCOME 4

Prepare short informational reports that describe routine tasks.

9-4 Preparing Short Informational Reports

Now that you are familiar with the basics of gathering data, you are ready to organize that information into short informational or analytical reports. Informational reports often describe periodic, recurring activities (such as monthly sales or weekly customer calls) as well as situational, nonrecurring events (such as trips, conferences, and special projects). Short informational reports may include safety compliance reports, such as that illustrated in Figure 9.2, and summaries of longer publications. Most informational reports have one thing in common: a neutral or receptive audience. The readers of informational reports do not need to be persuaded; they simply need to be informed.

You can expect to write many informational reports as an entry-level or middle-management employee. These reports generally deliver nonsensitive data and are therefore written directly. Although the writing style is usually conversational and informal, the report contents must be clear to all readers. All headings, lists, and graphics should help readers grasp major ideas immediately.

The principles of conciseness, clarity, courtesy, and correctness discussed in earlier chapters apply to report writing as well. Your ability to write effective reports can boost your visibility in a company and promote your advancement.

9-4a Trip, Convention, and Conference Reports

Employees sent on business trips to conventions and conferences typically submit reports to document the events they attended and what they learned. Organizations may require documentation to show that their money was well spent in funding the travel. These reports often inform management about business trends, procedures, legal requirements, or other information that would affect their operations and products.

When writing a trip or conference report, you must select the most relevant material and organize it directly and coherently. Generally, it is best not to use chronological sequencing (*in the morning we did X, at lunch we heard Y, and in the afternoon we did Z*). Instead, you should focus on three to five topics in which your reader will be interested. These items become the body of the report. Then simply add an introduction and a closing, and your report is organized. Here is a general outline for trip, conference, and convention reports:

- Begin by identifying the event (name, date, and location) and previewing the topics that were discussed.
- In the body, summarize the main topics that might benefit others in the organization. Use headings and bullets to enhance readability.
- Close by expressing appreciation, mentioning the value of the trip or event, and offering to share the information.
- Itemize your expenses, if requested, on a separate sheet.

Sofia Murillo was encouraged by her boss Colson Carpenter to attend a two-day conference in San Diego focused on tips for increasing sales through social media. Sofia's report, shown in Figure 9.7, emphasizes four strategies that could help her company use social media to improve customer service as well as to increase sales.

9-4b Progress, or Interim, Reports

Continuing projects often require progress, or interim, reports to give status updates on the project. These reports may be external (advising customers regarding the headway of their projects) or internal (informing management of the status of activities). Follow this pattern when writing a progress report:

- Specify the purpose and nature of the project in the opening.
- Provide background information if it gives the reader a better perspective.
- Describe the work completed so far.
- Explain the work currently in progress, including names, activities, methods used, and locations.
- Describe current and anticipated problems. If possible, include possible remedies.
- Discuss future plans and completion dates in the closing.

As a location manager for her company, Victoria Van Wijk frequently writes progress reports, such as the one shown in Figure 9.8. Producers want to know what she

Figure 9.7 Conference Report—Memo Format

Introduces message in clear subject line

Describes important points in the body with category headings for easy skimming

Closes by expressing appreciation and offering to share the information

Provides the name, date, location, and leader of the event; also previews topics

---

MEMORANDUM

Date: May 14, 2019

To: Colson Carpenter, Marketing Manager

From: Sofia Murillo, Marketing Specialist *S. M.*

Subject: Conference Report: Boosting Sales Through Social Media

As you suggested, I am submitting this brief report summarizing important strategies presented at the conference titled "Boosting Sales Through Social Media." Held in San Diego on May 4 and 5, the conference was led by Kari Abrams, director, Media Relations Specialists. She stressed that large businesses set aside huge budgets for social media marketing, but small businesses can achieve the same success by focusing on a few strategies, such as these:

- **Establish genuine personal engagement.** For many consumers today, a company Facebook page or Twitter handle is their first stop. In addition to promoting product deals, use these platforms to establish loyal, long-term customers. Urge your customers to recount their enthusiasm about favorite items before, during, and after a purchase. Offer reward points for sharing, liking, or commenting on the product or for referring a friend.

- **Prioritize customer service.** When customers have a complaint, strive to resolve it immediately. Assign staff members to respond to all queries within 12 hours. If your staff is limited, consider investing in social media monitoring tools, which we would be happy to discuss with you.

- **Recognize the power of a hashtag.** You don't need sophisticated technology to produce results with a tweet. Twitter allows users to feature products that link directly to their Amazon shopping carts so that they can purchase the item later. Your tweets can include a compelling visual, a promo code, and a purchase link.

- **Take advantage of selling on social channels.** Increasingly, online channels provide "buy" buttons enabling users to make purchases directly, seamlessly, and securely from within social networks. In fact, social-driven retail sales are growing at a faster rate than they are on all other online channels.

These are just a few of the many strategies Ms. Abrams presented. I thoroughly enjoyed the conference and thank the company for allowing me to attend. If you would like me to present these and additional strategies for improving customer service and sales through social media, please know that I am eager to do so.

Tips for Formatting Memo Reports

- Use memo stationery or plain paper with "Memorandum" centered 1 or 2 inches from the top.
- Leave side margins of 1 to 1.25 inches.
- Sign your initials on the *From* line.
- Use an informal, conversational style.
- Include side headings and bulleted lists to enhance readability.
- For long memo reports, consider sending as an attachment to an e-mail.

---

is doing, and a phone call does not provide a permanent record. She provides background information to inform the director of location instructions she is following. She then includes information about what she is currently doing and what she plans to do next. Victoria is up front about possible complications and concludes by giving a completion date. She chose to use bold paragraph headings to make the report's sequence easy to follow. She also chose to follow the headings with a colon rather than a period.

9-4c Minutes of Meetings

Minutes summarize the proceedings of meetings. Most businesses post team meeting minutes to intranet sites soon after the meeting ends. The notes are then accessible to everyone who attended or who missed the meeting. Companies often use in-house

Figure 9.8 Progress Report

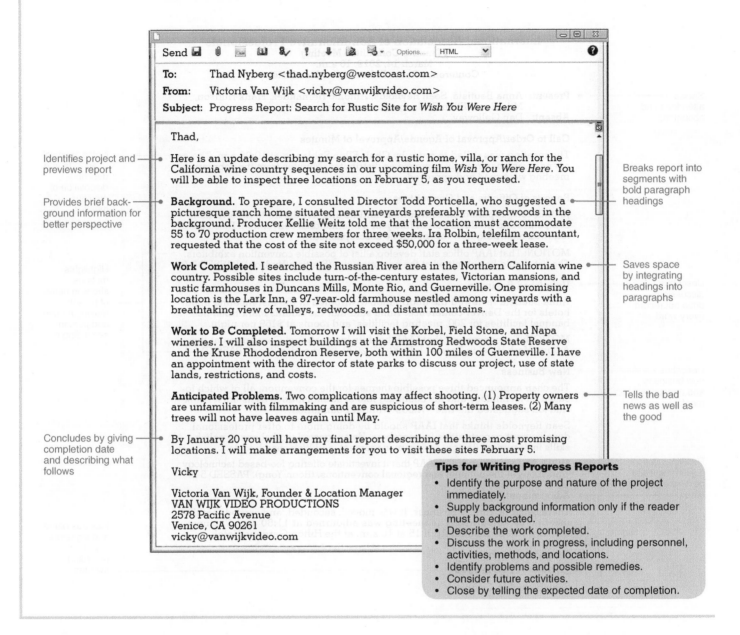

Identifies project and previews report

Provides brief background information for better perspective

Concludes by giving completion date and describing what follows

Breaks report into segments with bold paragraph headings

Saves space by integrating headings into paragraphs

Tells the bad news as well as the good

To: Thad Nyberg <thad.nyberg@westcoast.com>
From: Victoria Van Wijk <vicky@vanwijkvideo.com>
Subject: Progress Report: Search for Rustic Site for *Wish You Were Here*

Thad,

Here is an update describing my search for a rustic home, villa, or ranch for the California wine country sequences in our upcoming film *Wish You Were Here*. You will be able to inspect three locations on February 5, as you requested.

Background. To prepare, I consulted Director Todd Porticella, who suggested a picturesque ranch home situated near vineyards preferably with redwoods in the background. Producer Kellie Weitz told me that the location must accommodate 55 to 70 production crew members for three weeks. Ira Rolbin, telefilm accountant, requested that the cost of the site not exceed $50,000 for a three-week lease.

Work Completed. I searched the Russian River area in the Northern California wine country. Possible sites include turn-of-the-century estates, Victorian mansions, and rustic farmhouses in Duncans Mills, Monte Rio, and Guerneville. One promising location is the Lark Inn, a 97-year-old farmhouse nestled among vineyards with a breathtaking view of valleys, redwoods, and distant mountains.

Work to Be Completed. Tomorrow I will visit the Korbel, Field Stone, and Napa wineries. I will also inspect buildings at the Armstrong Redwoods State Reserve and the Kruse Rhododendron Reserve, both within 100 miles of Guerneville. I have an appointment with the director of state parks to discuss our project, use of state lands, restrictions, and costs.

Anticipated Problems. Two complications may affect shooting. (1) Property owners are unfamiliar with filmmaking and are suspicious of short-term leases. (2) Many trees will not have leaves again until May.

By January 20 you will have my final report describing the three most promising locations. I will make arrangements for you to visit these sites February 5.

Vicky

Victoria Van Wijk, Founder & Location Manager
VAN WIJK VIDEO PRODUCTIONS
2578 Pacific Avenue
Venice, CA 90261
vicky@vanwijkvideo.com

Tips for Writing Progress Reports
- Identify the purpose and nature of the project immediately.
- Supply background information only if the reader must be educated.
- Describe the work completed.
- Discuss the work in progress, including personnel, activities, methods, and locations.
- Identify problems and possible remedies.
- Consider future activities.
- Close by telling the expected date of completion.

templates for recording meeting minutes. Formal, traditional minutes, illustrated in Figure 9.9, are written for more formal meetings and legislative bodies. If you are assigned to take minutes, you will want to follow this general pattern:

- Begin with the name of the group, as well as the date, time, and place of the meeting.
- Identify the names of attendees and absentees.
- State whether the previous minutes were approved or revised.
- Record briefly the discussions of old business, new business, announcements, and committee reports.
- Include the precise wording of motions; record the votes and actions taken.
- Conclude with the name of the person recording the minutes. Formal minutes may require a signature.

Figure 9.9 Formal Meeting Minutes

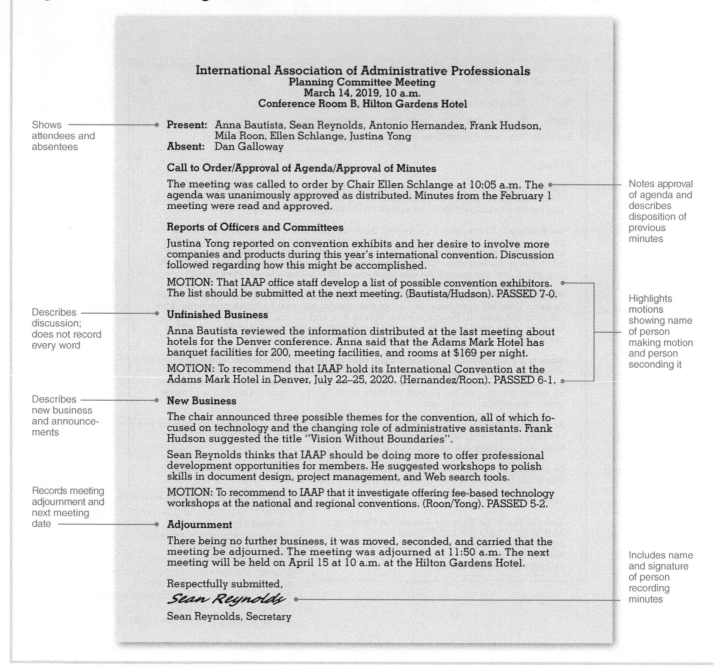

Shows attendees and absentees

Describes discussion; does not record every word

Describes new business and announcements

Records meeting adjournment and next meeting date

International Association of Administrative Professionals
Planning Committee Meeting
March 14, 2019, 10 a.m.
Conference Room B, Hilton Gardens Hotel

Present: Anna Bautista, Sean Reynolds, Antonio Hernandez, Frank Hudson, Mila Roon, Ellen Schlange, Justina Yong
Absent: Dan Galloway

Call to Order/Approval of Agenda/Approval of Minutes

The meeting was called to order by Chair Ellen Schlange at 10:05 a.m. The agenda was unanimously approved as distributed. Minutes from the February 1 meeting were read and approved.

Reports of Officers and Committees

Justina Yong reported on convention exhibits and her desire to involve more companies and products during this year's international convention. Discussion followed regarding how this might be accomplished.

MOTION: That IAAP office staff develop a list of possible convention exhibitors. The list should be submitted at the next meeting. (Bautista/Hudson). PASSED 7-0.

Unfinished Business

Anna Bautista reviewed the information distributed at the last meeting about hotels for the Denver conference. Anna said that the Adams Mark Hotel has banquet facilities for 200, meeting facilities, and rooms at $169 per night.

MOTION: To recommend that IAAP hold its International Convention at the Adams Mark Hotel in Denver, July 22–25, 2020. (Hernandez/Roon). PASSED 6-1.

New Business

The chair announced three possible themes for the convention, all of which focused on technology and the changing role of administrative assistants. Frank Hudson suggested the title "Vision Without Boundaries".

Sean Reynolds thinks that IAAP should be doing more to offer professional development opportunities for members. He suggested workshops to polish skills in document design, project management, and Web search tools.

MOTION: To recommend to IAAP that it investigate offering fee-based technology workshops at the national and regional conventions. (Roon/Yong). PASSED 5-2.

Adjournment

There being no further business, it was moved, seconded, and carried that the meeting be adjourned. The meeting was adjourned at 11:50 a.m. The next meeting will be held on April 15 at 10 a.m. at the Hilton Gardens Hotel.

Respectfully submitted,

Sean Reynolds

Sean Reynolds, Secretary

Notes approval of agenda and describes disposition of previous minutes

Highlights motions showing name of person making motion and person seconding it

Includes name and signature of person recording minutes

9-4d Summaries

A summary compresses the main points from a book, report, article, website, meeting, or convention. A summary saves time by reducing a report or article by 85 to 95 percent. Employees are sometimes asked to write summaries that condense technical reports, periodical articles, or books so that a reader can skim the main ideas quickly. Students may be asked to write summaries of articles or chapters to sharpen their writing skills and confirm their knowledge of reading assignments.

CEO Tucker Trabold asked his administrative assistant Maria Maffei to search for current information on CEO involvement in social networks. Maria found an article that identified the social profiles of every CEO on the Fortune 500 list and their participation in the six most popular networks: Twitter, Facebook, LinkedIn,

Figure 9.10 Article Summary

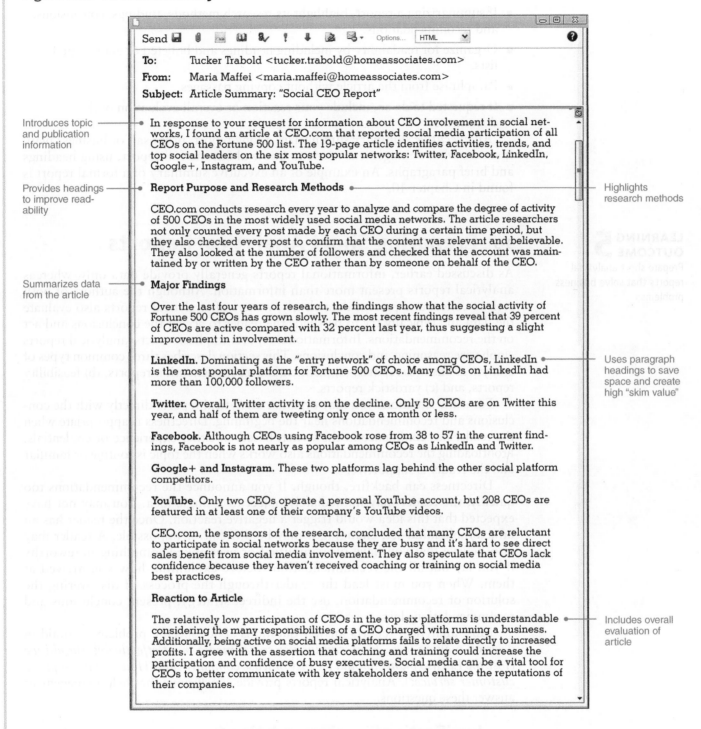

Send [toolbar icons] Options... HTML

To: Tucker Trabold <tucker.trabold@homeassociates.com>
From: Maria Maffei <maria.maffei@homeassociates.com>
Subject: Article Summary: "Social CEO Report"

Introduces topic and publication information →

In response to your request for information about CEO involvement in social networks, I found an article at CEO.com that reported social media participation of all CEOs on the Fortune 500 list. The 19-page article identifies activities, trends, and top social leaders on the six most popular networks: Twitter, Facebook, LinkedIn, Google+, Instagram, and YouTube.

Provides headings to improve readability →

Report Purpose and Research Methods ← *Highlights research methods*

CEO.com conducts research every year to analyze and compare the degree of activity of 500 CEOs in the most widely used social media networks. The article researchers not only counted every post made by each CEO during a certain time period, but they also checked every post to confirm that the content was relevant and believable. They also looked at the number of followers and checked that the account was maintained by or written by the CEO rather than by someone on behalf of the CEO.

Summarizes data from the article →

Major Findings

Over the last four years of research, the findings show that the social activity of Fortune 500 CEOs has grown slowly. The most recent findings reveal that 39 percent of CEOs are active compared with 32 percent last year, thus suggesting a slight improvement in involvement.

LinkedIn. Dominating as the "entry network" of choice among CEOs, LinkedIn ← *Uses paragraph headings to save space and create high "skim value"* is the most popular platform for Fortune 500 CEOs. Many CEOs on LinkedIn had more than 100,000 followers.

Twitter. Overall, Twitter activity is on the decline. Only 50 CEOs are on Twitter this year, and half of them are tweeting only once a month or less.

Facebook. Although CEOs using Facebook rose from 38 to 57 in the current findings, Facebook is not nearly as popular among CEOs as LinkedIn and Twitter.

Google+ and Instagram. These two platforms lag behind the other social platform competitors.

YouTube. Only two CEOs operate a personal YouTube account, but 208 CEOs are featured in at least one of their company's YouTube videos.

CEO.com, the sponsors of the research, concluded that many CEOs are reluctant to participate in social networks because they are busy and it's hard to see direct sales benefit from social media involvement. They also speculate that CEOs lack confidence because they haven't received coaching or training on social media best practices,

Reaction to Article

The relatively low participation of CEOs in the top six platforms is understandable ← *Includes overall evaluation of article* considering the many responsibilities of a CEO charged with running a business. Additionally, being active on social media platforms fails to relate directly to increased profits. I agree with the assertion that coaching and training could increase the participation and confidence of busy executives. Social media can be a vital tool for CEOs to better communicate with key stakeholders and enhance the reputations of their companies.

Google+, Instagram, and YouTube. Shown in Figure 9.10, her report includes headings to highlight the article's main ideas. She concluded with her overall reaction to the article. Summary reports of all types follow these general guidelines:

- State the main idea or purpose as well as the source of the document being summarized.
- Explain why the article was written.

- Include major points but omit illustrations, examples, and references.
- If summarizing a report, highlight its research methods, findings, conclusions, and recommendations.
- Organize for readability by including headings and bulleted or enumerated lists.
- Paraphrase from the article without copying passages.
- If requested to do so, include your reaction or overall evaluation of the document.

An *executive summary* summarizes a long report, proposal, or business plan. It covers what management needs to know about the full report, using headings and brief paragraphs. An example of an executive summary of a formal report is found in Chapter 10.

LEARNING OUTCOME 5

Prepare short analytical reports that solve business problems.

9-5 Preparing Short Analytical Reports

As discussed earlier, informational reports generally provide data only, whereas analytical reports present more than information. Although the authors of both seek to collect and present data clearly, writers of analytical reports also evaluate the data and typically try to persuade the reader to accept the conclusions and act on the recommendations. Informational reports emphasize facts; analytical reports emphasize reasoning and conclusions. This section describes three common types of analytical business reports: (a) justification/recommendation reports, (b) feasibility reports, and (c) yardstick reports.

For some situations you may organize analytical reports directly with the conclusions and recommendations near the beginning. Directness is appropriate when the reader has confidence in the writer, based on either experience or credentials. Frontloading the recommendations also works when the topic is routine or familiar and the reader is supportive.

Directness can backfire, though. If you announce the recommendations too quickly, the reader may immediately object to a single idea. You may not have expected that this idea would trigger a negative reaction. Once the reader has an unfavorable mind-set, changing it may be difficult or impossible. A reader may also believe that you have oversimplified or overlooked something noteworthy if you lay out all the recommendations before explaining how you arrived at them. When you must lead the reader through the process of discovering the solution or recommendation, use the indirect strategy: present conclusions and recommendations last.

Most analytical reports answer questions about specific problems and aid in decision making (e.g., *How can we use social media most effectively? Should we close the El Paso plant? Should we buy or lease company cars? How can we improve customer service?*). Analytical reports provide conclusions that help management answer these questions.

9-5a Justification/Recommendation Reports

Both managers and employees must occasionally write reports that justify or recommend actions, such as buying equipment, changing a procedure, hiring an employee, consolidating departments, or investing funds. These reports may also be called *internal proposals* because their persuasive nature is similar to that of external proposals (presented in Chapter 10). Large organizations sometimes prescribe how these reports should be organized and formatted; they often use forms with conventional headings. When you are free to select an organizational plan yourself, however, let your audience and topic determine your choice of the direct or indirect strategy.

Direct Strategy. For nonsensitive topics and recommendations that will be agreeable to readers, you can organize directly according to the following sequence:

1. Identify the problem or need briefly.
2. Announce the recommendation, solution, or action concisely and with action verbs.
3. Explain more fully the benefits of the recommendation or steps necessary to solve the problem.
4. Include a discussion of pros, cons, and costs.
5. Conclude with a summary specifying the recommendation and necessary action.

Indirect Strategy. When a reader may oppose a recommendation or when circumstances suggest caution, do not rush to reveal your recommendation. Consider using the following sequence for an indirect approach to your recommendations:

1. Refer to the problem in general terms, not to your recommendation, in the subject line.
2. Describe the problem or need your recommendation addresses. Use specific examples, supporting statistics, and authoritative quotes to lend credibility to the seriousness of the problem.
3. Discuss alternative solutions, beginning with the least likely to succeed.
4. Present the most promising alternative (your recommendation) last.
5. Show how the advantages of your recommendation outweigh its disadvantages.
6. Summarize your recommendation. If appropriate, specify the action it requires.
7. Ask for authorization to proceed if necessary.

Noel Navarro, an executive assistant at a large petroleum and mining company in Grand Prairie, Texas, received a challenging research assignment. Her boss, the director of Human Resources and Welfare, asked her to investigate ways to persuade employees to quit smoking. Here is how she described her task: "We banned smoking many years ago inside our buildings and on the premises, but we never tried very hard to get smokers to actually kick their habits. My job was to gather information about the problem and learn how other companies have helped workers stop smoking. The report would go to my boss, but I knew he would pass it along to the management council for approval."

Continuing her explanation, Noel said, "If the report were just for my boss, I would put my recommendation up front, because I'm sure he would support it. However, the management council may need to be persuaded because of the costs involved—and because some of them are smokers. Therefore, I put the alternative I favored last. To gain credibility, I footnoted my sources. I had enough material for a ten-page report, but I kept it to two pages in keeping with our company report policy." Noel chose APA style to document her sources. Although she prepared the report as a memo, she sent it as an attachment to an e-mail message.

9-5b Feasibility Reports

Feasibility reports examine the practicality and advisability of following a course of action. They answer this question: Will this plan or proposal work? Feasibility reports typically are internal reports written to advise on matters such as consolidating departments, offering a wellness program to employees, or hiring an outside firm to handle a company's accounting or social media presence. These reports may also be written by consultants called in to investigate a problem. The focus of these reports is on the decision: rejecting or proceeding with the proposed option. Your role as a report writer is usually not to persuade the reader to accept the decision;

your role is to present information objectively. In writing feasibility reports, consider these suggestions:

- Announce the decision immediately.
- Provide a description of the background and problem necessitating the proposal.
- Discuss the benefits of the proposal.
- Describe the problems that may result.
- Calculate the costs associated with the proposal, if appropriate.
- Show the time frame necessary for implementing the proposal.
- Conclude with an action request if appropriate.

Figure 9.11 Justification/Recommendation Report, APA Style

Date: November 17, 2019

To: Keith Kunin, Vice President, Human Resources

From: Noel Navaro, Executive Assistant ᴎᴎᴧ

Subject: Analysis of Employee Smoking Cessation Programs

At your request, I have examined measures that encourage employees to quit smoking. As company records show, approximately 23 percent of our employees still smoke, despite the antismoking and clean-air policies we adopted in 2015. To collect data for this report, I studied professional and government publications; I also inquired at companies and clinics about stop-smoking programs.

[Margin note left: Avoids revealing recommendation immediately]

[Margin note right: Introduces purpose of report, tells method of data collection, and previews organization]

This report presents data describing the significance of the problem, three alternative solutions, and a recommendation based on my investigation.

[Margin note left: Uses headings that combine function and description]

Significance of Problem: Health Care and Productivity Losses

Employees who smoke are costly to any organization. The following statistics show the effects of smoking for workers and for organizations:

- Absenteeism is 40 to 50 percent greater among smoking employees.
- Accidents are two to three times greater among smokers.
- Bronchitis, lung and heart disease, cancer, and early death are more frequent among smokers (Arhelger, 2019, p. 4).

[Margin note right: Documents data sources for credibility, uses APA style citing author and year in the text]

Although our clean-air policy prohibits smoking in the building, shop, and office, we have done little to encourage employees to stop smoking. Many workers still go outside to smoke at lunch and breaks. Other companies have been far more proactive in their attempts to stop employee smoking. Many companies have found that persuading employees to stop smoking was a decisive factor in reducing their health insurance premiums. Following is a discussion of three common stop-smoking measures tried by other companies, along with a projected cost factor for each (Rindfleisch, 2018, p. 4).

Alternative 1: Literature and Events

The least expensive and easiest stop-smoking measure involves the distribution of literature, such as "The Ten-Step Plan" from Smokefree Enterprises and government pamphlets citing smoking dangers. Some companies have also sponsored events such as the Great American Smoke-Out, a one-day occasion intended to develop group spirit in spurring smokers to quit. "Studies show, however," says one expert, "that literature and company-sponsored events have little permanent effect in helping smokers quit" (Mendel, 2017, p. 108).

Cost: Negligible

Figure 9.11 Continued

Alternative 2: Stop-Smoking Programs Outside the Workplace

Local clinics provide treatment programs in classes at their centers. Here in Houston we have the Smokers' Treatment Center, ACC Motivation Center, and New-Choice Program for Stopping Smoking. These behavior-modification stop-smoking programs are acknowledged to be more effective than literature distribution or incentive programs. However, studies of companies using off-workplace programs show that many employees fail to attend regularly and do not complete the programs.

    Cost: $1,200 per employee, three-month individual program ●————— Highlights costs for
        (Your-Choice Program)   easy comparison
        $900 per employee, three-month group session

Alternative 3: Stop-Smoking Programs at the Workplace

Many clinics offer workplace programs with counselors meeting employees in ●————— Arranges
company conference rooms. These programs have the advantage of keeping a   alternatives so that
firm's employees together so that they develop a group spirit and exert pressure   most effective
on each other to succeed. The most successful programs are on company   is last
premises and also on company time. Employees participating in such programs had a 72 percent greater success record than employees attending the same stop-smoking program at an outside clinic (Honda, 2017, p. 35). A disadvantage of this arrangement, of course, is lost work time—amounting to about two hours a week for three months.

    Cost: $900 per employee, two hours per week of release time for three months

Conclusions and Recommendation ●————— Summarizes
findings and ends
with specific
recommendation

Smokers require discipline, counseling, and professional assistance to kick the nicotine habit, as explained at the American Cancer Society website ("Guide to Quitting Smoking," 2018). Workplace stop-smoking programs on company time are more effective than literature, incentives, and off-workplace programs. If our goal is to reduce health care costs and lead our employees to healthful lives, we should invest in a workplace stop-smoking program with release time for smokers. Although the program temporarily reduces productivity, we can expect to recapture that loss in lower health care premiums and healthier employees.

Reveals
recommendation
only after
discussing all
Therefore, I recommend that we begin a stop-smoking treatment program on ●— alternatives
company premises with two hours per week of release time for participants for three months.

Lists all references
in APA Style ————————————————————— **References**

Magazine ————— Arhelger, Z. (2018, November 5). The end of smoking. *The World of Business*,
                    pp. 3–8.

Website article ————— Guide to quitting smoking. (2018, October 17). Retrieved from the American
                    Cancer Society http://www.cancer.org

Journal article ————— Honda, E. M. (2017). Managing anti-smoking campaigns: The case for company
                    programs." *Management Quarterly*, *32*(2), 29–47. Retrieved from
                    http://search.ebscohost.com/

Book ————— Mendel, I. A. (2017). *The puff stops here.* Chicago: Science Publications, p. 108.

Newspaper article ————— Rindfleisch, T. (2018, December 4). Smoke-free workplaces can help smokers
                    quit, expert says." *Evening Chronicle*, p. 4.

Brenda Tchakerian, human resources director for a large financial services firm in St. Louis, Missouri, wrote the feasibility report shown in Figure 9.12. Because she discovered that the company was losing time and money as a result of personal e-mail and Internet use by employees, she talked with vice president Damian Gorman about employee-monitoring software. Rather than take time away from

Figure 9.12 Feasibility Report

Figure 9.12 Continued

RUIZ FINANCIAL SERVICES LLP
MEMORANDUM

Date: October 3, 2019
To: Damian Gorman, Vice President
From: Brenda Tchakerian, Director, Human Resources *B.T.*
Subject: Feasibility of Implementation of Internet Monitoring Program

Explains reason for report and outlines its organization

As you suggested, we hired a consultant to investigate the feasibility of implementing a plan to monitor employee Internet use. The consultant reports that such a plan is workable and could be fully implemented by February 1. This report discusses the background, benefits, problems, costs, and time frame of the plan.

Reveals decision immediately

Background: Current Misuse of Internet Privileges. Currently we allow employees Internet access for job-related tasks. Many use social media—specifically, Facebook, Twitter, and LinkedIn—to communicate with clients and the public. However, some employees use this access for personal reasons, resulting in lowered productivity, higher costs, and a strain on the network. Therefore, we hired an outside consultant who suggested an Internet-monitoring program.

Describes problem and background

Evaluates positive and negative aspects of proposal objectively

Benefits of Plan: Appropriate Use of Social Media and the Internet. The proposed plan calls for installing Internet-monitoring software such as NetGuard or eMonitor. We would fully disclose to employees that this software will be tracking their online activity. We would also teach employees what social media and Internet use is appropriate. In addition to increased productivity, lowered costs, and improved network performance, this software will also help protect our company against loss of intellectual property, trade secrets, and confidential information.

Employee Acceptance. One of the biggest problems will be convincing employees to accept this new policy without feeling that their privacy is being violated. However, proper training will help employees understand the appropriate use of social media and the Internet.

Costs. Implementing the monitoring plan involves two direct costs. The first is the initial software cost of $500 to $1,100, depending on the package we choose. The second cost involves employee training and trainer fees. However, the expenditures are within the project's budget.

Presents costs and schedule; omits unnecessary summary

Time Frame. Selecting the software package will take about two weeks. Preparing a training program will require another three weeks. Once the program is started, the breaking-in period will take at least three months. By February 1 the Internet-monitoring program will be fully functional resulting in increased productivity, decreased costs, lowered liability, and improved network performance.

Please let me know by October 15 whether you would like additional information about monitoring social media and Internet programs.

Concludes with action request

Brenda's regular duties to have her investigate software programs, the vice president suggested that she hire a consultant to analyze the situation and present a plan. When the consultant's work was completed, the vice president wanted to know whether the consultant's plan was feasible. Although Brenda's feasibility report is only one page long, it provides all the necessary information: background, benefits, employee acceptance, costs, and time frame.

9-5c Yardstick Reports

Yardstick reports examine problems with two or more solutions. To determine the best solution, the writer establishes criteria by which to compare the alternatives. The criteria then act as a yardstick against which all the alternatives are measured, as shown in Figure 9.13. The yardstick approach is effective for companies that must establish specifications for equipment purchases and then compare each manufacturer's product with the established specs. The yardstick approach is also effective when exact specifications cannot be established.

For example, a yardstick report might help a company decide on an inexpensive job perk. Perks are nontraditional benefits that appeal to current and future employees. Popular job perks include free food and beverages, flexible scheduling and telecommuting options, on-site gyms, and fitness classes. A yardstick report may help a company decide what job perks make the most sense. If the company wants to encourage long-term wellness, it might consider offering employees discounted fitness club memberships, on-site yoga classes, or ergonomic workstations. The yardstick report would describe and compare the three alternatives in terms

Figure 9.13 Yardstick Report

Date: March 2, 2019
To: Vinay P. Devaki, Director, Operations
From: Alexis Broussard, Benefits Administrator *AB*
Subject: Choosing Outplacement Plan

Here is the report you requested investigating the possibility of CompuTech's use of outplacement services. It discusses the problem of counseling services for discharged staff and establishes criteria for selecting an outplacement agency. It then evaluates three prospective agencies and presents a recommendation based on that evaluation.

Introduces purpose and gives overview of report organization

Problem: Counseling Discharged Staff

Discusses background briefly because readers already know the problem

In an effort to reduce costs and increase competitiveness, CompuTech will begin a program of staff reduction that will involve releasing up to 20 percent of our workforce over the next 12 to 24 months. Many of these employees have been with us for ten or more years, and they are not being released for performance faults. These employees deserve a severance package that includes counseling and assistance in finding new careers.

Solution and Alternatives: Outplacement Agencies

Uses dual headings, giving function and description

Numerous outplacement agencies offer discharged employees counseling and assistance in locating new careers. This assistance minimizes not only the negative feelings related to job loss but also the very real possibility of litigation. Potentially expensive lawsuits have been lodged against some companies by unhappy employees who felt they were unfairly released.

Announces solution and the alternatives it presents

In seeking an outplacement agency, we should find one that offers advice to the sponsoring company as well as to dischargees. The law now requires certain procedures, especially in releasing employees over forty. CompuTech could unwittingly become liable to lawsuits because our managers are uninformed of these procedures. I have located three potential outplacement agencies appropriate to serve our needs: Gray & Associates, Right Access, and Careers Plus.

Establishing Criteria for Selecting Agency

Tells how criteria were selected

In order to choose among the three agencies, I established criteria based on professional articles, discussions with officials at other companies using outplacement agencies, and interviews with agencies. Here are the four groups of criteria I used in evaluating the three agencies:

1. Counseling services—including job search advice, résumé help, crisis management, corporate counseling, and availability of full-time counselors

2. Administrative and research assistance—including availability of administrative staff, librarian, and personal computers

3. Reputation—based on a telephone survey of former clients and listing with a professional association

4. Costs—for both group programs and executive services

Creates four criteria for use as yardstick in evaluating alternatives

Figure 9.13 Continued

Discussion: Evaluating Agencies by Criteria

Each agency was evaluated using the four criteria just described. Data comparing the first three criteria are summarized in Table 1.

Table 1

A COMPARISON OF SERVICES AND REPUTATIONS
FOR THREE LOCAL OUTPLACEMENT AGENCIES

Places table close to spot where it is first mentioned

	Gray & Associates	Right Access	Careers Plus
Counseling services			
Résumé advice	Yes	Yes	Yes
Crisis management	Yes	No	Yes
Corporate counseling	Yes	No	No
Full-time counselors	Yes	No	Yes
Administrative, research assistance			
Administrative staff	Yes	Yes	Yes
Librarian, research library	Yes	No	Yes
Personal computers	Yes	No	Yes
Listed by National Association of Career Consultants	Yes	No	Yes
Reputation (telephone survey of former clients)	Excellent	Good	Excellent

Summarizes complex data in table for easy reading and reference

Counseling Services

All three agencies offered similar basic counseling services with job-search and résumé advice. They differed, however, in three significant areas.

Right Access does not offer crisis management, a service that puts the discharged employee in contact with a counselor the same day the employee is released. Experts in the field consider this service especially important to help the dischargee begin "bonding" with the counselor immediately. Immediate counseling also helps the dischargee learn how to break the news to family members. Crisis management can be instrumental in reducing lawsuits because dischargees immediately begin to focus on career planning instead of concentrating on their pain and need for revenge. Moreover, Right Access does not employ full-time counselors; it hires part-timers according to demand. Industry authorities advise against using agencies whose staff members are inexperienced and employed on an "as-needed" basis.

Highlights the similarities and differences among the alternatives

In addition, neither Right Access nor Careers Plus offers regular corporate counseling, which I feel is critical in training our managers to conduct terminal interviews. Careers Plus, however, suggested that it could schedule special workshops if desired.

Administrative and Research Assistance

Both Gray & Associates and Careers Plus offer complete administrative services and personal computers. Dischargees have access to staff and equipment to assist them in their job searches. These agencies also provide research libraries, librarians, and databases of company information to help in securing interviews.

Does not repeat obvious data from table

---

of (a) costs, (b) long-term benefits, and (c) expected participation level. After interviewing employees and talking to people whose companies offer similar benefits, report writers would compare the alternatives and recommend the most workable job perk.

The real advantage to yardstick reports is that alternatives can be measured consistently using the same criteria. Writers using a yardstick approach typically do the following:

- Begin by describing the problem or need.
- Explain possible solutions and alternatives.
- Establish criteria for comparing the alternatives; tell how the criteria were selected or developed.
- Discuss and evaluate each alternative in terms of the criteria.
- Draw conclusions and make recommendations.

Figure 9.13 Continued

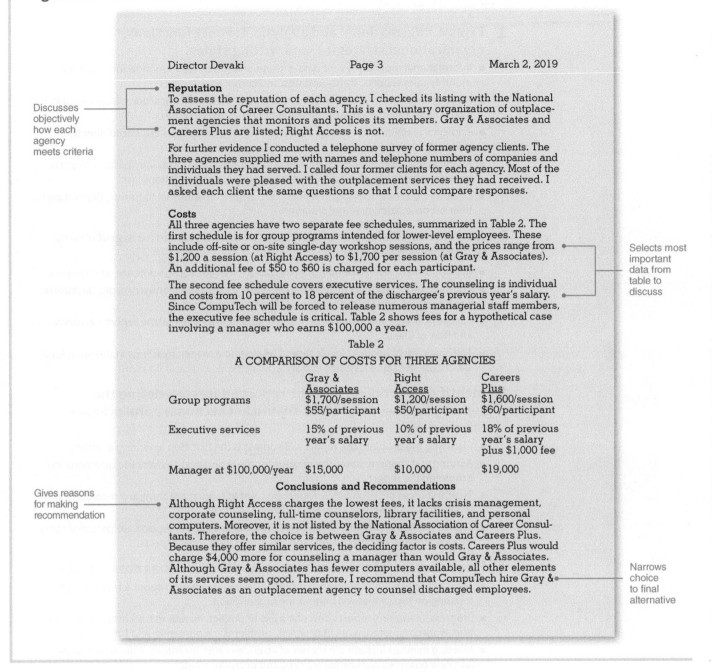

Discusses objectively how each agency meets criteria

Director Devaki   Page 3   March 2, 2019

Reputation

To assess the reputation of each agency, I checked its listing with the National Association of Career Consultants. This is a voluntary organization of outplacement agencies that monitors and polices its members. Gray & Associates and Careers Plus are listed; Right Access is not.

For further evidence I conducted a telephone survey of former agency clients. The three agencies supplied me with names and telephone numbers of companies and individuals they had served. I called four former clients for each agency. Most of the individuals were pleased with the outplacement services they had received. I asked each client the same questions so that I could compare responses.

Costs

All three agencies have two separate fee schedules, summarized in Table 2. The first schedule is for group programs intended for lower-level employees. These include off-site or on-site single-day workshop sessions, and the prices range from $1,200 a session (at Right Access) to $1,700 per session (at Gray & Associates). An additional fee of $50 to $60 is charged for each participant.

Selects most important data from table to discuss

The second fee schedule covers executive services. The counseling is individual and costs from 10 percent to 18 percent of the dischargee's previous year's salary. Since CompuTech will be forced to release numerous managerial staff members, the executive fee schedule is critical. Table 2 shows fees for a hypothetical case involving a manager who earns $100,000 a year.

Table 2

A COMPARISON OF COSTS FOR THREE AGENCIES

	Gray & Associates	Right Access	Careers Plus
Group programs	$1,700/session $55/participant	$1,200/session $50/participant	$1,600/session $60/participant
Executive services	15% of previous year's salary	10% of previous year's salary	18% of previous year's salary plus $1,000 fee
Manager at $100,000/year	$15,000	$10,000	$19,000

Conclusions and Recommendations

Gives reasons for making recommendation

Although Right Access charges the lowest fees, it lacks crisis management, corporate counseling, full-time counselors, library facilities, and personal computers. Moreover, it is not listed by the National Association of Career Consultants. Therefore, the choice is between Gray & Associates and Careers Plus. Because they offer similar services, the deciding factor is costs. Careers Plus would charge $4,000 more for counseling a manager than would Gray & Associates. Although Gray & Associates has fewer computers available, all other elements of its services seem good. Therefore, I recommend that CompuTech hire Gray & Associates as an outplacement agency to counsel discharged employees.

Narrows choice to final alternative

Alexis Broussard, benefits administrator for computer manufacturer CompuTech, was called on to write the report in Figure 9.13 comparing outplacement agencies. These agencies counsel discharged employees and help them find new positions; fees are paid by the former employer. Alexis knew that downsizing and outsourcing would take place in the next two years. Her task was to compare outplacement agencies and recommend one to management.

Alexis gathered information about three outplacement agencies and wanted to organize it systematically using a yardstick report. She chose to evaluate each agency using the following categories: counseling services, administrative and research assistance, reputation, and costs. Alexis showed the results of her research in Tables 1 and 2 in Figure 9.13. She used the criteria as headings and discussed how each agency met, or failed to meet, each criterion. Making a recommendation was easy once Alexis had created the tables and compared the agencies.

Summary of Learning Outcomes

1 **Explain informational and analytical report functions, organizational strategies, and writing styles.**

- Informational reports present data without analysis or recommendations, such as monthly sales reports, status updates, and compliance reports.
- Analytical reports provide data or findings, analyses, and conclusions. Examples include justification, recommendation, feasibility, and yardstick reports.
- Audience reaction and content determine whether a report is organized directly or indirectly.
- Reports organized directly reveal the purpose and conclusions immediately; reports organized indirectly place the conclusions and recommendations last.
- Like other business messages, reports can range from informal to formal, depending on their purpose, audience, and situation.

2 **Describe typical report formats and understand the significance of effective headings.**

- Report formats vary, depending on the report's length, topic, audience, and purpose.
- Common report formats include e-mail, letter, memo, and manuscript; digital reports can be created and shared as slide decks and infographics.
- Report headings add visual appeal and readability; they reveal the report's organization and flow of ideas.
- The hierarchy of heading levels should be clear to a reader; headings in the same level should use the same font size and style, placement, and capitalization.

3 **Identify the problem that the report addresses, define the report purpose, and collect significant secondary and primary information.**

- Clarifying the problem the report will address is the first step in writing a report.
- A purpose statement states the reasons for the report and answers the questions that prompted the report.
- Typical sources of secondary information used in reports are company records, books, journals, magazines, newspapers, and Web resources.
- Typical sources of primary, or firsthand, information used in reports are personal observations, surveys, questionnaires, and interviews with topic experts.

4 **Prepare short informational reports that describe routine tasks.**

- Trip, convention, and conference reports present information about a trip or event, focusing on topics that will benefit the organization.
- Progress, or interim, reports describe a job or project, including background information, work completed, work in progress, problems encountered, and future plans.
- Meeting minutes include the names of attendees and absentees, a discussion of old and new business, committee reports, and decisions made.
- Summaries of longer publications include the name, date, and author of the publication plus an outline of the main ideas along with a description of research methods, findings, conclusions, and recommendations.

5 **Prepare short analytical reports that solve business problems.**

- Analytical reports, such as justification/recommendation, feasibility, and yardstick reports, evaluate information, draw conclusions, and make recommendations.
- Justification/recommendation reports are organized directly when the reader is supportive and indirectly when the reader needs persuasion to accept the recommendations.
- Feasibility reports are written directly and examine the practicality and advisability of following a course of action.
- Yardstick reports examine problems by using a standard set of criteria to compare several alternatives before recommending a solution.

Chapter Review

1. Why are reports indispensable documents in business? (L.O. 1)

2. Describe seven typical formats used for reports. Be prepared to discuss each. (L.O. 2)

3. What is the chief difference between primary and secondary data? (L.O. 3)

4. Name six sources of factual information for informal reports. (L.O. 3)

5. Why is it important to write a purpose statement before beginning to compose a report? (L.O. 3)

6. Explain the purpose of each of the following informational reports. (L.O. 4)

   a. Trip or conference report

   b. Progress report

   c. Minutes of meetings

   d. Summary

7. Explain the purpose of each of the following analytical reports. (L.O. 5)

   a. Justification/recommendation report

   b. Feasibility report

   c. Yardstick report

8. Your supervisor wants to know the main points of a recent review in an influential online magazine discussing the latest Apple product. What report category and format would be appropriate? (L.O. 2, 4)

9. Your team was assigned to write a report explaining how your company, a racing bicycle manufacturer, can comply with the International Cycling Union's regulations before bikes go into production. Your boss wants to know what you have done thus far. What report category and format would be appropriate? (L.O. 2, 4)

10. You represented your company at the Green Building Conference held by the National Association of Home Builders in Salt Lake City, Utah. Your supervisor asked for a written description of the latest trends. What report category and format would be appropriate? (L.O. 2, 4)

Critical Thinking

11. How would you determine whether to use the direct strategy or the indirect strategy for any company report you are writing? (L.O. 1)

12. Why would you want to start your research with secondary data rather than gathering primary data right away? (L.O. 3)

13. How might technology shape business report formats and their delivery in the future? (L.O. 1–5)

14. How can report writers ensure that they present their topics objectively and credibly? (L.O. 1–5)

15. What are the purposes of headings? Describe three heading types discussed in this chapter. (L.O. 2)

Activities and Cases

9.1 Informational Report: Recording Information From Your Work Experience (L.O. 4)

Select a position you now hold or one that you have held in the past. If you have not been employed, choose a campus, professional, or community organization to which you belong. You may also select an internship or a volunteer experience.

YOUR TASK. Write an informational memo report to your instructor describing your current or former employment, an internship or volunteer experience, or your involvement in a professional or community group. Introduce the report by describing the organization's products or services, its history and leadership, and its primary location. In the body of the report, add your title and job responsibilities, including the skills you need or needed to perform the job. Then describe the value and skills you gained from this experience. Your memo report should be single-spaced and 1 1/2 to 2 pages long. Add a meaningful subject line and descriptive headings for each section of the report.

9.2 Informational Report: Choosing a Fabulous Company to Work For (L.O. 4)
> Web

You are intrigued by *Fortune's* annual list of the 100 best companies to work for. Although it's a long shot, you decide that you want to work for one of them. You read the good news that many of them are hiring, so you begin searching for a company that has possibilities for you. After narrowing the list, you hone in on one that seems like the best fit.

YOUR TASK. Select a company from *Fortune's* list of 100 best companies to work for. It may be a dream, but you are curious about working there. Note the reasons *Fortune* added this company to the list, and note the company's ranking out of 100. Then review the company's website and gather information about the company's mission and goals, history, products, services, and current news releases. Find out where the home office is located, who leads the company, and how many employees work there. After researching the company, list your reasons for wanting to work there. In a memo report to your instructor, summarize your research findings. State the purpose, add appropriate section headings, and conclude with your thoughts on why you think this company is a good employment choice.

9.3 Informational Report: Investigating a Career Path (L.O. 4)
> Web

You are interested in exploring your career options to make sure you have the right skill set for your chosen field and that the future in that field looks promising. One of the best places to search is the latest *Occupational Outlook Handbook* compiled by the U.S. Bureau of Labor Statistics. Using your favorite browser, search for *Occupational Outlook Handbook A-Z Index*. Within the index, search for your desired occupation. The *Occupational Outlook Handbook* is a highly respected resource whether you are choosing a career or changing careers.

YOUR TASK. Write an informational memo report to your instructor that describes your desired career. In the report, summarize the information found in the *Handbook* about the nature of the work, working conditions, necessary qualifications, and the outlook for this career. Also summarize relevant information about typical salary ranges for this occupation. Add an appropriate introductory paragraph that describes the purpose of the report, and conclude with a brief paragraph summarizing what you learned from this investigation. For instance, after this investigation, do you still feel this career is a good fit for you? State your reasoning.

9.4 Summary: Briefing the Boss (L.O. 4)

> Web

Like many executives, your boss is too rushed to read long journal or business articles. However, she is eager to keep up with developments in her field. She asks you to submit to her one summary every month on an article of interest to help her stay abreast of research in her field.

YOUR TASK. In your field of study, select a professional journal, such as the *Journal of Management*. With the help of a research database, search for articles in your target journal. Select an interesting article that is at least five pages long, and write a summary in memo format. Include an introduction that might begin with *As you requested, I am submitting this summary of. . . .* Identify the author, article title, journal, and date of publication. Explain the purpose of the article. Summarize three or four of the most important findings. Your boss would also like a concluding statement indicating your reaction to the article. Address your memo to Marilyn Edelman.

9.5 Progress Report: A Work in Progress (L.O. 4)

Think about someone who supports your decision to pursue your education and earn a degree. You want to let that person know how you are doing on your journey to complete your education. You decide to write a report describing your progress.

YOUR TASK. Prepare a progress report in letter format to a relative or friend who is supportive of your educational pursuits. You may organize the report as follows: (a) Describe your progress toward your educational goal; (b) summarize the work you have completed thus far; (c) discuss the work currently in progress, including your successes and challenges; and (d) outline your plans to accomplish your goal.

9.6 Progress Report: Checking In With Your Instructor (L.O. 4)

> E-Mail

If you are working on a lengthy formal or informal report for either this chapter or Chapter 10, you may want to keep your instructor informed of your progress and record any setbacks.

YOUR TASK. Send your instructor an e-mail report detailing the progress you are making on your long report assignment. Discuss (a) the purpose of the report, (b) the work already completed, (c) the work currently in progress, (d) problems encountered, (e) future activities, and (f) your schedule for completing the report.

9.7 Recommendation Report: What Philanthropic Projects Are Trending? (L.O. 5)

> Web

Great news! GeekTech, the start-up company where you work, has become enormously successful. Now the owner wants to support a philanthropic program. He appoints you to research philanthropic opportunities and recommend one. The owner is highly interested in projects that ease poverty and increase education in high-poverty regions. He is also interested in knowing what projects other companies are supporting. Based on this information, what projects can you recommend to the owner?

YOUR TASK. The owner wants you to investigate the philanthropic projects at 20 high-profile companies of your choice. Visit their websites and study programs such as volunteerism, matching funds, and charitable donations. In a recommendation report, discuss five of the best programs and recommend one that could serve as a philanthropic project for your company. Address your memo report to Jason Franco.

9.8 Justification/Recommendation Report: Developing a Social Media Use Policy (L.O. 5)

> Social Media   Team   Web

A social media usage policy is a set of rules developed by organizations to regulate the use of social media by employees. As a manager in a midsized engineering firm, you see the need to draft such a policy. You have received reports that employees are using the Internet and social media sites during work hours to check Facebook and Twitter, look for jobs on LinkedIn, shop on eBay, and even play games online. You have also received reports that some employees have posted inappropriate comments about the company on Facebook. You have reason to worry about inappropriate behavior, declining productivity, security problems, and liability issues. The executive council now wants to establish a social media policy, in addition to the already existing Internet policy, to clarify their policies on social media use and acceptable behavior. You are aware that the executive council needs to know that acceptable use of social media pertains to employees at work and at home. You decide to talk with other managers about the problem and to look at other companies' social media policies. You'll report your findings in a justification/recommendation report.

YOUR TASK. As a team, discuss the need for comprehensive social media use policies in general. Search for information about other firms' social media policies. Read about companies that are currently facing lawsuits over employees' inappropriate messages on social media networks. Find out what areas your policy should cover. Should the policy include guidelines for behavior on Facebook, Twitter, blogs, and wikis? Each member of the team should present and support his or her ideas regarding what should be included in the policy. Individually or as a team, write a convincing justification/recommendation report in memo format to the executive council based on the conclusions you draw from your research and discussion. Because you are recommending action, decide whether your approach should be direct or indirect.

9.9 Feasibility Report: Health and Wellness Perks (L.O. 5)

> Web

Your company is considering adding some health and wellness perks that will interest current and future employees. Perks are benefits that are added above and beyond the normal medical coverage and sick pay. These wellness perks help in recruiting and retaining talented employees. You work for a smaller company that cannot compete with the great perks offered by giant companies such as Google and Amazon. However, small- and medium-sized companies are now adding health and wellness perks at little or no expense. You've been assigned to research and select three health and wellness perks that could be incorporated into your company's culture immediately. The company has a training room on-site for classes and a large lunchroom for lunchtime activities. You might consider the following options: a company-sponsored softball league, lunchtime walking groups, weekend hikes and bike trips, lunchtime classes on health and nutrition, or weekly yoga and cross-training classes. Search online for other possibilities, and be ready to suggest three company perks to your supervisor. Estimate the approximate costs associated with these perks, including administration costs. Then suggest an appropriate time frame for implementation.

YOUR TASK. Select three health and wellness perks that can be offered to employees at little or no cost. Write a memo report investigating the feasibility of adding the three perks. Begin by stating the decision to add them. Then discuss the background leading up to the decision and the benefits of such programs. Estimate the approximate costs associated with each option, including administration costs, if any. Then suggest an appropriate time frame for implementation.

9.10 Minutes: Taking Notes for a Friend (L.O. 4)

Attend an organized meeting at your school, in your community, in city government, or for a professional organization. Take notes and record the proceedings as if you were covering the meeting for a friend who could not attend.

YOUR TASK. Write the meeting minutes including all the data necessary and following the instructions in this chapter. Focus on committee reports, old and new business, motions and votes, decisions made, and action items for future meetings. Include the organization's name and the date, time, and location of the meeting in the heading.

9.11 Meeting Minutes: Team Meeting Notes (L.O. 4)

> Team

When working on a formal report with a team, volunteer to take notes at a team meeting and be prepared to share the meeting minutes with your instructor, if requested. Follow the instructions in this chapter for meeting minutes.

YOUR TASK. Record the proceedings of a team meeting for a group project. Record the date and time of the meeting, the attendees' names, discussion items, decisions made, and the date of the next meeting.

9.12 Yardstick Report: Choosing a Live Chat Solution (L.O. 5)

> Web

As an intern for a midsized online marketing company that sells outdoor and recreational clothing and equipment, you are anxious to comply with a request from the vice president of marketing. He wants to add a live chat feature on the company website to improve customer service with online shoppers. He is aware that online shoppers frequently accept invitations to chat live when they need help or have questions. What's more, they often turn into buyers. He asks you to research the most popular live chat software options, compare the features and monthly costs, and recommend one that the company could implement quickly.

YOUR TASK. Write a memo yardstick report to Vice President of Marketing Jon Stokes that compares the options. Search online for live chat support software, and look at several sources that list the most popular options for small and midsized companies. Choose five of the most frequently mentioned options, and compare them in terms of (a) monthly or yearly costs, (b) main features, and (c) ratings or reviews. Follow the instructions in this chapter for writing yardstick reports. Briefly discuss the background for the report, list the live chat alternatives, and compare them using the established criteria. Your comparison data may work best in a table. Draw conclusions and recommend a live chat solution that you believe will best meet the needs of the company.

9.13 Article or Infographic Summary: Current Social Media Marketing Trends (L.O. 4)

Social Media ▶ Web ▶

With the rise of social media in business, your supervisor wants to stay abreast of the latest social media marketing trends. He asks you to research this topic and list the current trends with a brief explanation of each. You will format this document as an article summary.

YOUR TASK. Search for an article or infographic that addresses current or future social media marketing trends. In a memo report addressed to your boss, Jin Le, summarize the main ideas presented in the article or infographic. Be sure to identify the author, article title, publication name, and date of the article. If your source is an infographic, follow a similar procedure and identify the title, sponsoring website, source, and date, if available. Conclude with your overall opinion of the article or infographic.

9.14 Report Topics for Informal Reports (L.O. 4, 5)

Team ▶ Web ▶

A list of over 100 report topics is available at **www.cengagebrain.com**. The topics are divided into the following categories: accounting, finance, human resources, marketing, information systems, management, and general business/education/campus issues. You can collect information for many of these reports by using electronic databases and the Web. Your instructor may assign them as individual or team writing projects. All require critical thinking in collecting and organizing information into logical reports.

YOUR TASK. As directed by your instructor, select a topic from the report list at **www.cengagebrain.com**.

Grammar/Mechanics Checkup 9

Semicolons and Colons

Review Sections 2.16–2.19 in the Grammar/Mechanics Handbook. Then select the correctly punctuated sentence and record its letter in the space provided. Also record the appropriate G/M guideline to illustrate the principle involved. When you finish, compare your responses with those provided at the bottom of the page. If your answers differ, study carefully the appropriate guideline.

| a (2.16b) | **EXAMPLE** | a. Sales meetings during prosperous times focused on entertainment; meetings today focus on training and motivation. |
| | | b. Sales meetings during prosperous times focused on entertainment, meetings today focus on training and motivation. |

_____ 1. a. Green technologies have gained a strong following, consequently, many industries favor green products and recycling programs.
 b. Green technologies have gained a strong following; consequently, many industries favor green products and recycling programs.

_____ 2. a. Cash resulting from holiday product sales does not arrive until January; therefore, our cash flow becomes critical in November and December.
 b. Cash resulting from holiday product sales does not arrive until January, therefore, our cash flow becomes critical in November and December.

_____ 3. a. We must negotiate short-term financing during the following months: October, November, and December.
 b. We must negotiate short-term financing during the following months; October, November, and December.

_____ 4. a. The largest American corporations offering financial services are: Bank of America and J. P. Morgan Chase.
 b. The largest American corporations offering financial services are Bank of America and J. P. Morgan Chase.

5. _____ a. A supermarket probably requires no short-term credit, a seasonal company such as a ski resort, however, typically would need considerable short-term credit.
   b. A supermarket probably requires no short-term credit; a seasonal company such as a ski resort, however, typically would need considerable short-term credit.

6. _____ a. We offer three basic types of short-term lines of credit: commercial, paper, and single-payer credit.
   b. We offer three basic types of short-term lines of credit; commercial, paper, and single-payer credit.

7. _____ a. Speakers at the conference on credit include the following businesspeople: Melanie Rey, financial consultant, American Investments, Daniel Owens, comptroller, NationsBank, and Kristen Byers, legal counsel, Fidelity Financial.
   b. Speakers at the conference on credit include the following businesspeople: Melanie Rey, financial consultant, American Investments; Daniel Owens, comptroller, NationsBank; and Kristen Byers, legal counsel, Fidelity Financial.

8. _____ a. Many methods are used to calculate finance charges; for example, average daily balance, adjusted balance, two-cycle average daily balance, and previous balance.
   b. Many methods are used to calculate finance charges: for example, average daily balance, adjusted balance, two-cycle average daily balance, and previous balance.

9. _____ a. Apple earns most of its income from the following: Macs, iPads, and iPhones.
   b. Apple earns most of its income from the following; Macs, iPads, and iPhones.

10. _____ a. Texting is more intrusive than e-mail, use it only when response time is important.
    b. Texting is more intrusive than e-mail; use it only when response time is important.

1. b (2.16a) 2. a (2.16a) 3. a (2.17a) 4. b (2.17a, 2.01) 5. b (2.17b) 6. a (2.16d, 2.03) 7. b (2.16c) 8. a (2.16c) 9. a (2.17a, 2.01) 10. b (2.16b)

282   Chapter 9: Informal Reports

Editing Challenge 9

Every chapter provides an editing exercise to fine-tune your grammar and mechanics skills. The following progress report requires edits that address proofreading, grammar, spelling, punctuation, concise wording, parallelism, and other writing issues. Study the guidelines in the Grammar/Mechanics Handbook (Appendix D), including the lists of Confusing Words and Frequently Misspelled Words.

YOUR TASK. Edit the following (a) by inserting corrections in your textbook or on a photocopy using the proofreading marks in Appendix C or (b) by downloading the message from **www.cengagebrain.com** and correcting at your computer. Your instructor may show you a possible solution.

To: Saul Salazar <ssalazar@compassrealty.com>

From: Brooke Burgess <bburgess@alliedcontractors.com>

Subject: Progress Report on Construction of San Diego Branch Office

---

Dear Mr. Salazar:

Construction of Compass Realtys San Diego branch office has entered Phrase 3. Although we are one week behind the contractors original schedule the building should be already for occupancy on April 1.

Past Progress

Phase 1 involved development of the architects plans, this task was completed on July 1. Phase two involved submission of the plans for county building department approval. A copy of the plans were then given to the following two contractors for the purpose of obtaining an estimate, Jack Jones Contractors and Titan Builders. The lower bidder was Jack Jones Contractors, consequently this firm began construction on August 15.

Present Status

Phase three includes initial construction work. We have completed the following work as of November 9

- Demolition of the existing building at 3389 Magnolia Street
- Excavation of foundation footings for the building and for the surrounding wall
- Steel reinforcing rods installed in building pad and wall
- Pouring of the concrete foundation

Jack Jones Contractors indicated that it was one week behind schedule for several reasons. The building inspectors required more steel reinforcement then was showed on the architects blueprings. In addition excavation of the footings required more time then the contractor anticipated because the 18-inch footings were all below grade.

Future Schedule

In spite of the fact that we lost time in Phrase 3 we are substantially on target for the completion of this office building by March 1. Phase 4 includes the following activities, framing, drywalling, and installation of plumbing. If you have questions call me at 213-488-7802.

Brooke Burgess,

Project Manager

Allied Contractors
bburgess@alliedcontractors.com
3690 Market Street
San Diego, CA 91005
213-488-7802

Best Practices for Highly Successful Team Writing Projects

Participating in group presentations and collaborating on written reports will help you develop the kinds of teamwork skills that employers prize. Although sometimes frustrating, team projects can be highly successful and rewarding when members follow best practices such as those presented here.

Preparing to Work Together

Before beginning the project, meet as a team and establish roles and ground rules by doing the following:

- Select a team leader to coordinate and manage the project and a recorder to write and distribute the ground rules and take notes on each meeting's accomplishments.

- Decide whether your team will be governed by consensus (everyone must agree) or by majority rule.

- Compare team members' schedules, gather contact information, and agree on meeting times.

- Decide how to involve those who miss a meeting.

- Discuss the value of sharing diverging opinions. When multiple viewpoints are shared, a better product results. Talk openly about conflict and how it should focus on issues, not on people.

- Discuss how to deal with members who do not meet deadlines or do their part.

Planning the Document

Once you have established ground rules, you are ready to discuss the project and the resulting document.

- Establish the document's specific purpose and identify the main issues involved.

- Discuss the audience(s) for the document and what appeal would help it achieve its purpose.

- Write a detailed outline of the report. What parts will be assigned to each team member? What graphics and visuals are needed?

- Develop a work plan. Set deadlines for submitting the early drafts, for integrating the parts into one document, and for proofreading the final draft.

- Decide what fonts and format you will use in the final document. Will the report need a cover sheet, a table of contents, or a list of citations?

Collecting Information

- As a group, brainstorm ideas for gathering relevant information.

- Establish deadlines for collecting information from primary and secondary sources.

- Discuss ways to ensure the accuracy and currency of the information collected.

Organizing, Writing, and Revising

As the project progresses, your team may wish to modify some of its earlier decisions.

- Review the proposed outline and adjust if necessary.

- Share the first drafts and have all members review them. Make sure all writers are using the same format, heading styles, and font sizes.

- Appoint the strongest writer to integrate all the parts, striving for a consistent voice. The report should read as if it were written by one person.

Editing and Evaluating

- Review the document's overall design, format, and heading levels. Is the report organized so that it is easy to follow?

- Although all members should review and suggest edits to the final document, assign a strong writer to copyedit the report for grammar and punctuation correctness and consistency.

- Evaluate the final document. Discuss whether it fulfills its purpose and meets the needs of the audience.

Using Online Collaboration Tools

Consider using Google Docs or another document management and editing tool. Some writers prefer to create drafts in Microsoft Word and use the **Track Changes** feature to gather comments from multiple readers. Search online or ask educators and project managers what document-sharing platforms they prefer.

CAREER APPLICATION. Select a topic from the suggested activities in this chapter or from Report Topics at **www.cengagebrain**. Assume that you are preparing the report as a team project. If you are working on a long report, your instructor may ask you to prepare individual progress reports as you develop your topic.

YOUR TASK

- Form a team of two to five members, and prepare to work together by following the suggestions in this workshop.

- Plan your report by establishing its purpose, analyzing the audience, writing a detailed outline, developing a work plan, and deciding how you want the final document to look.

- Collect information, organize it, and write the first draft.

- Offer to proofread and comment on the drafts of team members.

Your instructor may assign grades not only for the final report but also for team effectiveness and your individual contribution, as evaluated by fellow team members.

Proposals and Formal Reports

Learning Outcomes

After studying this chapter, you should be able to do the following:

1 Understand the importance, types, and components of informal and formal proposals.

2 Describe the preparation of formal reports, including their components, work plan, organizational strategies, and editing.

3 Collect primary and secondary information being careful to assess its credibility.

4 Identify the purposes and techniques of documentation in business reports as well as how to avoid plagiarism.

5 Convert report data into meaningful visual aids and graphics.

6 Describe the content of typical formal report components.

10-1 Preparing Business Proposals

A *proposal* is a written offer to solve problems, provide services, or sell products. Proposals can mean life or death for a business. Why are they so important? A well-written proposal can generate millions of dollars of income for big companies. Multimillion-dollar aerospace and engineering firms depend on proposals to compete for business. People running smaller businesses—such as electricians, contractors, plumbers, and interior designers—also depend on proposals to sell their services and products.

LEARNING OUTCOME 1

Understand the importance, types, and components of informal and formal proposals.

10-1a Types of Business Proposals

Writers prepare proposals for various reasons, such as asking for funds or promoting products and services to customers. Some proposals are brief; some are lengthy and complex. A proposal recipient could be a manager inside your company or a potential client outside your company. All types of proposals share two significant characteristics: (a) they use easy-to-understand language, and (b) they show the value and benefits of the product or services being recommended. Proposals may be classified as (a) informal or formal, (b) internal or external, and (c) solicited or unsolicited.

Informal or Formal. Informal proposals are short reports, often formatted as memos or letters. Proposal sections can vary, but an informal proposal might include the following parts: (a) an introduction or description of the problem, (b) pertinent background information or a statement of need, (c) the proposal benefits and schedule for completion, (d) the staffing requirements, (e) a budget analysis, and (f) a conclusion that may include an authorization request. Figure 10.2 illustrates an informal letter proposal to a Texas dentist who sought to improve patient satisfaction. The research company submitting the proposal describes the benefits of a patient survey to gather data about the level of patient satisfaction. As you can see, the proposal contains the basic components of an informal proposal.

Formal proposals differ from informal proposals not in style but in size and format. Formal proposals respond to big projects and may range from 5 to 200 or more pages. In addition to the six basic parts of informal proposals, formal proposals may contain some or all of these additional parts: (a) a copy of a request for proposal (RFP), (b) a letter of transmittal, (c) an abstract or executive summary, (d) a title page, (e) a table of contents, (f) a list of figures, and (g) an appendix. Figure 10.1 shows the typical sections included in informal and formal proposals.

Internal or External. Proposal writers may submit internal proposals to management when they see benefits in changing a company policy, purchasing equipment, or adding new products and services. A company decision maker will review the proposal and accept or reject the idea. Internal proposals may resemble justification and

Figure 10.1 Components of Informal and Formal Proposals

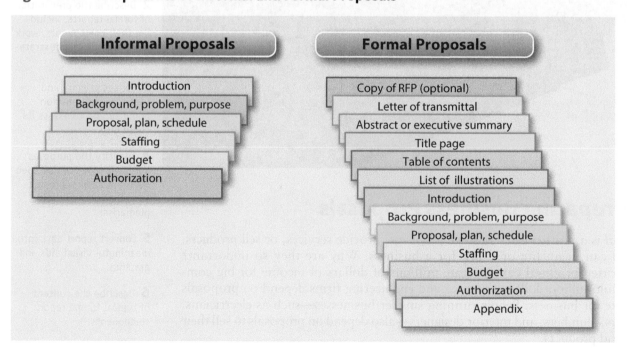

Informal Proposals	Formal Proposals
Introduction	Copy of RFP (optional)
Background, problem, purpose	Letter of transmittal
Proposal, plan, schedule	Abstract or executive summary
Staffing	Title page
Budget	Table of contents
Authorization	List of illustrations
	Introduction
	Background, problem, purpose
	Proposal, plan, schedule
	Staffing
	Budget
	Authorization
	Appendix

recommendation reports, as discussed in Chapter 9. Most proposals, however, are external and addressed to clients and customers outside the company. An external sales proposal to a client would show how the company's goods or services would solve a problem or benefit the client.

Another type of external proposal is a *grant proposal*, written to obtain funding from agencies that support worthwhile causes. The Ronald McDonald House Charities, for example, receives many requests in the form of grant proposals from organizations seeking support for their charitable causes. The accompanying Workplace in Focus describes some of its current support goals.

Solicited (RFP) or Unsolicited. When government organizations or businesses have a specific need, they prepare a *request for proposal (RFP)*, a document that specifies their requirements. Government agencies as well as private businesses use RFPs to solicit competitive bids from vendors. RFPs ensure that bids are comparable and that funds are awarded fairly. The city of Raleigh, North Carolina, prepared an RFP seeking bids for a $490,000 contract to tear down a fire station and replace it with a new, modern facility.[1] Companies responding to solicited proposals are careful to follow the RFP instructions explicitly, which might include following a specific proposal format.

Enterprising companies looking for work or special challenges might submit unsolicited proposals. Both large and small companies are likely to use RFPs to solicit bids on their projects. This enables them to compare prices from various companies on their projects. Not only do they want a good price from their project bidders, but also they want the legal protection offered by proposals, which are considered legal contracts.

When writing proposals, remember that they must be persuasive, not merely mechanical descriptions of what you can do. Like the persuasive sales messages discussed in Chapter 8, effective proposals must (a) get the reader's attention, (b) emphasize how your methods and products will benefit the reader, (c) showcase your expertise and build credibility, and (d) present ideas clearly and logically, making it easy for the reader to understand.

WORKPLACE IN FOCUS

Over the past 25 years, The Ronald McDonald House Charities has awarded more than $100 million in response to grant proposals submitted by nonprofit organizations. Going forward, it plans to focus on the oral health needs of children ages 0 to 6 in the United States and on reducing maternal and child mortality in the first six months of life in Africa, South Asia, and Latin America. It will work with a select group of nonprofit organizations around the world that are already making a positive impact on children. Skilled grant writers are among the most in-demand professionals today. A grant writer is a vital connecting link between a funder and the grant seeker. What skills do you think a grant proposal writer must have?

McDonald's Kinderhilfe

Bastian Kienitz/Shutterstock.com

10-b Components of Informal Proposals

Informal proposals may be presented in manuscript format (usually no more than ten pages) with a cover page, or they may take the form of short (two-to four-page) letters. Sometimes called *letter proposals*, they usually contain six principal components: introduction, background, proposal, staffing, budget, and authorization. Both informal and formal proposals contain these six basic parts. The titles, or headings, of the components of informal proposals may vary, but the goals of the components are standard. Each of the following components of a typical informal proposal serves a purpose and contributes to its overall success.

Introduction. Most proposals begin with a brief explanation of the reasons for the proposal and then highlight the writer's qualifications. To make an introduction more persuasive, strive to provide a hook, such as the following:

- Hint at extraordinary results with details to be revealed shortly.
- Promise low costs or speedy results.
- Mention a remarkable resource (e.g., well-known authority, new computer program, well-trained staff) available exclusively to you.
- Identify a serious problem (worry item) and promise a solution, to be explained later.
- Specify a key issue or benefit that you feel is the heart of the proposal.

Before writing the proposal shown in Figure 10.2, Ronald Bridger analyzed the request of Texas dentist Louisa Canto and decided that she was most interested in improving service to her patients. However, Ron did not hit on this hook until he had written a first draft and had come back to it later. It's not a bad idea to put off writing the proposal introduction until after you have completed other parts. In longer proposals the introduction also describes the scope and limitations of the project, as well as outlining the organization of the material to come.

Background, Problem, and Purpose. The background section identifies the problem and discusses the goals or purposes of the project. In an unsolicited proposal, your goal is to convince the reader that a problem exists. Therefore, you must present the problem in detail, discussing such factors as revenue losses, failure to comply with government regulations, or decreased customer satisfaction.

In a solicited proposal, your aim is to persuade the reader that you understand the reader's issues and that you have a realistic solution. If an RFP is involved, follow its requirements precisely and use the company's language in your description of the problem. For example, if the RFP asks for *the design of a maintenance program for wireless communication equipment*, do not call it a *customer service program for wireless products*. The background section might include segments titled *Statement of Need, Basic Requirements, Most Critical Tasks,* or *Important Secondary Problems.*

Proposal, Plan, and Schedule. In the proposal section itself, you would explain your plan for solving the problem. In some proposals this is tricky because you want to disclose enough of your plan to secure the contract, while being cautious about providing so much information that your services will not be needed. Without specifics, though, your proposal has little chance, so you must decide how much to reveal.

The proposal section often includes an implementation plan. If research is involved, state what methods you will use to gather the data. Remember to be persuasive by showing how your methods and products will benefit the reader. For example, show how the initial investment will pay off later. The proposal might even promise specific *deliverables*—tangible things your project will produce for the customer. A proposal deliverable might be a new website design or an online marketing plan. To add credibility, also specify how the project will be managed and audited. Most writers also include a schedule or timetable of activities showing the proposal's benchmarks for completion.

Staffing. The staffing section of a proposal describes the qualifications of the staff that will complete the work as well as the credentials and expertise of the project leaders. In other words, this section may include the size and qualifications of the support staff. This section is a good place to endorse and promote your staff. The client sees that qualified people will be on board to implement the project. Even résumés may be included in this section. Experts, however, advise proposal writers against including generic résumés that have not been revised to mirror the RFP's requirements. Only well-tailored résumés will inspire the kind of trust in a team's qualifications that is necessary if a proposal is to be accepted.[3]

Budget. A central item in most proposals is the budget, a list of proposed project costs. Some proposal writers title this section *Statement of Costs*. You need to

Figure 10.2 Informal Letter Proposal

Quintile
RESEARCH

May 30, 2019

Louisa Canto, D.D.S.
2002 Medical Plaza Drive #300
The Woodlands, TX 77380

Dear Dr. Canto:

(annotation left: Uses opening paragraph in place of introduction)

Understanding the views of your patients is the key to meeting their needs. Quintile Research is pleased to propose a plan to help you become even more successful by learning what patients expect of your practice, so that you can improve your services.

(annotation right: Grabs attention with hook that focuses on key benefit)

Background and Goals

We know that you have been incorporating a total quality management system in your practice. Although you have every reason to believe that your patients are pleased with your services, you may want to give them an opportunity to discuss what they like and possibly don't like about your office. Specifically, your purposes are to survey your patients to (a) determine the level of their satisfaction, (b) elicit their suggestions for improvement, (c) learn more about how they discovered you, and (d) compare your preferred and standard patients.

(annotation right: Identifies four purposes of survey)

(annotation left: Announces heart of proposal)

Proposed Plan

On the basis of our experience in conducting many local and national customer satisfaction surveys, Quintile proposes the following plan:

(annotation left: Divides total plan into logical segments for easy reading)

Survey. We will develop a short but thorough questionnaire probing the data you desire. Although the survey instrument will include both open-ended and close-ended questions, it will concentrate on the latter. Close-ended questions enable respondents to answer easily; they also facilitate systematic data analysis. The questionnaire will gauge patients' views of courtesy, professionalism, billing accuracy, friendliness, and waiting time. After you approve it, the questionnaire will be sent to a carefully selected sample of 300 patients whom you have separated into groupings of preferred and standard.

(annotation right: Describes procedure for solving problem or achieving goals)

Analysis. Survey data will be analyzed by demographic segments, such as patient type, age, and gender. Using state-of-the-art statistical tools, our team of seasoned experts will study (a) satisfaction levels, (b) the reasons for satisfaction or dissatisfaction, and (c) the responses of your preferred compared to standard patients.

Report. You will receive a final report with the key findings clearly spelled out, Dr. Canto. Our expert staff will draw conclusions based on the results. The report will include tables summarizing all responses, divided into preferred and standard clients.

Figure 10.2 Continued

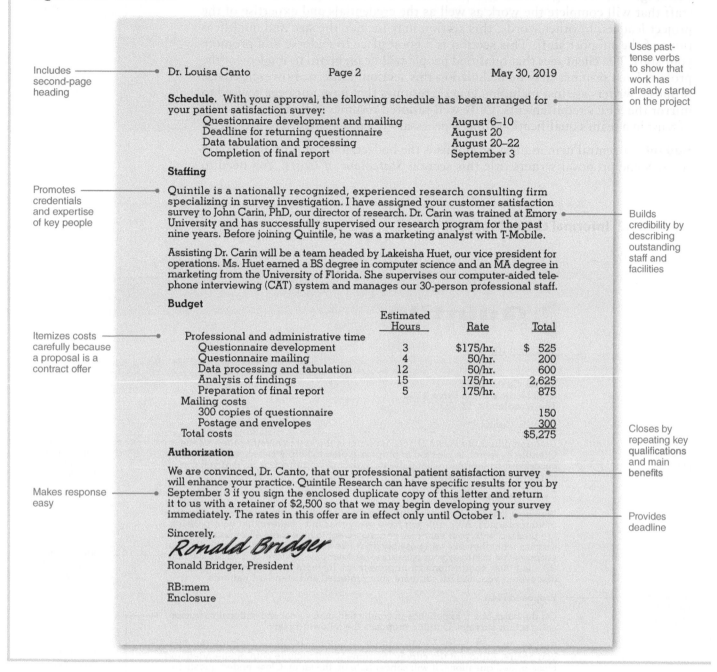

Includes second-page heading

Dr. Louisa Canto   Page 2   May 30, 2019

Uses past-tense verbs to show that work has already started on the project

Schedule. With your approval, the following schedule has been arranged for your patient satisfaction survey:

Questionnaire development and mailing	August 6–10
Deadline for returning questionnaire	August 20
Data tabulation and processing	August 20–22
Completion of final report	September 3

Staffing

Promotes credentials and expertise of key people

Quintile is a nationally recognized, experienced research consulting firm specializing in survey investigation. I have assigned your customer satisfaction survey to John Carin, PhD, our director of research. Dr. Carin was trained at Emory University and has successfully supervised our research program for the past nine years. Before joining Quintile, he was a marketing analyst with T-Mobile.

Builds credibility by describing outstanding staff and facilities

Assisting Dr. Carin will be a team headed by Lakeisha Huet, our vice president for operations. Ms. Huet earned a BS degree in computer science and an MA degree in marketing from the University of Florida. She supervises our computer-aided telephone interviewing (CAT) system and manages our 30-person professional staff.

Budget

Itemizes costs carefully because a proposal is a contract offer

	Estimated Hours	Rate	Total
Professional and administrative time			
Questionnaire development	3	$175/hr.	$ 525
Questionnaire mailing	4	50/hr.	200
Data processing and tabulation	12	50/hr.	600
Analysis of findings	15	175/hr.	2,625
Preparation of final report	5	175/hr.	875
Mailing costs			
300 copies of questionnaire			150
Postage and envelopes			300
Total costs			$5,275

Authorization

Makes response easy

We are convinced, Dr. Canto, that our professional patient satisfaction survey will enhance your practice. Quintile Research can have specific results for you by September 3 if you sign the enclosed duplicate copy of this letter and return it to us with a retainer of $2,500 so that we may begin developing your survey immediately. The rates in this offer are in effect only until October 1.

Closes by repeating key qualifications and main benefits

Provides deadline

Sincerely,

Ronald Bridger

Ronald Bridger, President

RB:mem
Enclosure

prepare this section carefully because it represents a contract; you cannot raise the project costs later—even if your costs increase.

In the proposal shown in Figure 10.2, Ronald Bridger justified the budget for his firm's patient satisfaction survey by itemizing the costs. Whether the costs in a proposal are itemized or treated as a lump sum depends on the reader's needs and the proposal's goals.

Conclusion and Authorization. The closing section should remind the reader of the proposal's key benefits and make it easy for the reader to respond. It might also include a project completion date as well as a deadline beyond which the proposal offer will no longer be in effect. Writers of informal proposals often refer to this as a request for approval or authorization. The conclusion of the proposal in Figure 10.2 mentions a key benefit as well as a deadline for approval.

10-2 Preparing Formal Business Reports

LEARNING OUTCOME 2

Describe the preparation of formal reports, including their components, work plan, organizational strategies, and editing.

A *formal report* may be defined as a document in which a writer analyzes findings, draws conclusions, and makes recommendations intended to solve a problem. Formal business reports are similar to formal proposals in length, organization, and tone. Instead of making an offer, however, formal reports represent the product of thorough investigation and analysis. They present ordered information to decision makers in business, industry, government, and education. Informal and formal business reports have similar components, as shown in Figure 10.3, but, as might be expected, formal reports have more sections.

10-2a Steps to Follow in Writing Formal Business Reports

Writing a formal report is a difficult task. It requires planning, researching, and organizing. Because this is a complex process, writers are most successful when they follow specific steps, as outlined in the following sections.

Determine the Purpose and Scope of the Report. Like proposals and informal reports, formal reports begin with a purpose statement. Preparing a written purpose statement is helpful because it defines the focus of the report and provides a standard that keeps the project on target. Study the following purpose statement and notice the use of action words (*adding, writing,* and *establishing*):

> **Simple purpose statement:** *To recommend adding three positions to our sales team, writing a job description for the sales team leader, and establishing recruitment guidelines for sales team hiring.*

You can determine the scope of the report by defining the problem or problems that will be researched and analyzed. Then examine your limitations by considering these questions: How much time do you have to complete the report? How accessible is the data you need? How thorough should your research be, and what boundaries will help you limit the scope of this report? If interviews or surveys are appropriate, how many people should you contact, and what questions should you ask?

Figure 10.3 Components of Informal and Formal Reports

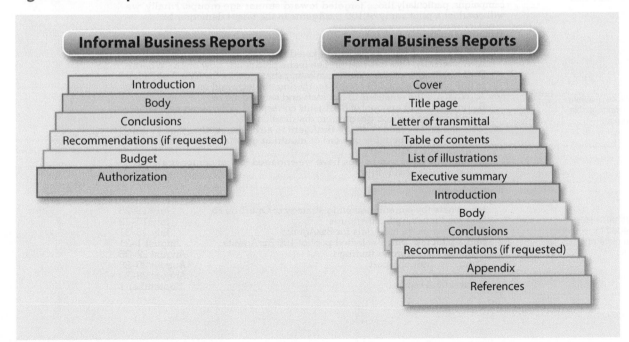

Informal Business Reports
- Introduction
- Body
- Conclusions
- Recommendations (if requested)
- Budget
- Authorization

Formal Business Reports
- Cover
- Title page
- Letter of transmittal
- Table of contents
- List of illustrations
- Executive summary
- Introduction
- Body
- Conclusions
- Recommendations (if requested)
- Appendix
- References

Anticipate the Needs of the Audience. Your goal is to present key findings that are relevant to your audience. Keep in mind that the audience may or may not be familiar with the topic. If you were reporting to a targeted audience of human resources managers, the following facts gathered from an employee survey would be considered relevant: *According to the company survey completed by 425 of our 515 employees, 72 percent of employees are currently happy with their health benefits package.*

Decide on a Work Plan and Appropriate Research Methods. A work plan is a tentative schedule that guides the investigation. This plan includes a clear problem statement, a purpose statement, and a description of the research methods to be used. A good work plan also involves a tentative outline of the report's major sections and a logical work schedule for completion of major tasks, as illustrated in Figure 10.4.

Figure 10.4 Work Plan for a Formal Report

WORK PLAN FOR LEE JEANS ONE TRUE FIT LINE

Statement of Problem. Many women between the ages of 18 and 34 have trouble finding jeans that fit. Lee Jeans hopes to remedy that situation with its One True Fit line. We want to demonstrate to Lee that we can create a word-of-mouth campaign that will help it reach its target audience.

Defines purpose, scope, limits, and significance of report

Statement of Purpose. The purpose of this report is to secure an advertising contract from Lee Jeans. We will examine published accounts about the jeans industry and Lee Jeans in particular. In addition, we will examine published results of Lee's current marketing strategy. We will conduct focus groups of women in our company to generate campaign strategies for our pilot study of 100 BzzAgents. The report will persuade Lee Jeans that word-of-mouth advertising is an effective strategy to reach women in this demographic group and that BzzAgent is the right company to hire. The report is significant because an advertising contract with Lee Jeans would help our company grow significantly in size and stature.

Research Strategy (Sources and Methods of Data Collection)

Describes primary and secondary data

We will gather information about Lee Jeans and the product line by examining published marketing data and conducting focus group surveys of our employees. In addition, we will gather data about the added value of word-of-mouth advertising by examining published accounts and interpreting data from previous marketing campaigns, particularly those targeted toward similar age groups. Finally, we will conduct a pilot study of 100 BzzAgents in the target demographic.

Tentative Outline

Factors problem into manageable chunks

  I. How effectively has Lee Jeans marketed to the target population?
    A. Historically, who has bought Lee Jeans products? How often? Where?
    B. How effective are the current marketing strategies for the One True Fit line?
  II. Is this product a good fit for our marketing strategy and our company?
    A. What are the reactions of our staff and sample survey?
    B. How well does our pool of BzzAgents correspond to the target demographic in terms of age and geographic distribution?
  III. Why should Lee Jeans engage BzzAgent to advertise its One True Fit line?
    A. What are the benefits of word of mouth in general and for this demographic in particular?
    B. What previous campaigns have we engaged in that demonstrate our company's credibility?

Work Schedule

Estimates time needed to complete report tasks

Investigate the current marketing strategy of One True Fit	July 15–25
Test product using focus groups	July 15–22
Create campaign materials for BzzAgents	July 18–31
Run a pilot test with a selected pool of 100 BzzAgents	August 1–21
Evaluate and interpret findings	August 22–25
Compose draft of report	August 26–28
Revise draft	August 28–30
Submit final report	September 1

Conduct Research Using Primary and Secondary Sources. Formal report writers conduct most of their research using *secondary sources*—that is, information that has been previously analyzed and compiled. Books, articles, Web documents, podcasts, correspondence, and annual reports are examples of secondary sources. In contrast, writers may conduct some of their research using primary sources—information and data gathered from firsthand experience. Interviews, observations, surveys, questionnaires, and meetings are examples of primary research. Research methods are discussed later in this chapter in the section "Collecting Information Through Primary and Secondary Research."

Organize, Analyze, and Draw Conclusions. Formal report writers should organize their information logically and base their recommendations on solid facts to impress decision makers. They should analyze the findings and make sure they are relevant to the report's purpose.

When organizing your ideas, place your main topics and subtopics into an outline format as shown in Figure 10.5.

As you sort through your information, decide what information is substantiated and credible. Give readers only the information they need. Then arrange that information using one of the strategies shown in Figure 10.6. For example, if a company wants to design its own online surveys, management may request a report that compares the best survey software solutions. In this case, the compare/contrast strategy helps the report writer organize the data and compare the features and costs of each survey tool.

Figure 10.5 Outline Format

FORMS OF BUSINESS OWNERSHIP

I. Sole proprietorship
  A. Advantages of sole proprietorsship
    1. Minimal capital requirements
    2. Control by owner
  B. Disadvantages of sole proprietorsship
    1. Unlimited liability
    2. Limited management talent

II. Partnership
  A. Advantages of partnership
    1. Access to capital
    2. Management talent
    3. Ease of formation
  B. Disadvantages of partnership
    1. Unlimited liability
    2. Personality conflicts

Figure 10.6 Strategies for Organizing Report Findings

Strategy Type	Data Arrangement	Useful Application
Chronological	Arrange information in a time sequence to show history or development of topic.	Useful in showing time relationships, such as five-year profit figures or a series of events leading to a problem
Geographical	Organize information by geographic regions or locations.	Appropriate for topics that are easily divided into locations, such as East Coast, Northwest, etc.
Topic/Function	Arrange by topics or functions. May use a prescribed, conventional format.	Works well for topics with established categories or for recurring reports
Compare/Contrast	Present problem and show alternative solutions. Use consistent criteria. Show how the solutions are similar and different.	Best used for "before and after" scenarios or when comparing alternatives
Importance	Arrange from least to most important, lowest to highest priority, or lowest to highest value, etc.	Appropriate when persuading the audience to take a specific action or change a belief
Simple/Complex	Proceed from simple to more complex concepts or topics.	Useful for technical or abstract topics
Best Case/Worst Case	Describe the best and the worst possible scenarios.	Useful when dramatic effect is needed to achieve results; helpful when audience is uninterested or uninformed

Conclude the report by summarizing your findings, drawing conclusions, and making recommendations. The way you conclude depends on the purpose of your report and what the reader needs. A well-organized report with conclusions based on solid data will impress management and other decision makers.

Design Graphics to Clarify the Report's Message. Presenting numerical or quantitative data visually helps your reader understand information readily. Trends, comparisons, and cycles are easier to comprehend when they are expressed graphically. These visual elements in reports draw attention, add interest, and often help readers gain information quickly. Visuals include drawings, graphs, maps, charts, photographs, and tables. This topic is covered in more depth in the section "Incorporating Meaningful Visual Aids and Graphics" later in this chapter.

10-2b What to Review When Editing Formal Business Reports

The final step in preparing a formal business report involves editing and proofreading. Because the reader is the one who determines the report's success, review the report as if you were the intended audience. Pay particular attention to the following elements:

- **Format.** Look at the report's format and assess the report's visual appeal.
- **Consistency.** Review the report for consistency in margins, page numbers, indents, line spacing, and font style.
- **Graphics.** Make sure all graphics have meaningful titles, are clear, and are placed in the report near the words that describe them.
- **Heading levels.** Check the heading levels for consistency in font style and placement. Headings and subheadings should be meaningful and help the reader follow the report's logic.
- **Accuracy.** Review the content for accuracy and clarity. Make sure all facts are documented.
- **Mechanics.** Correct all grammar, punctuation, capitalization, and usage errors. These errors will damage your credibility and might cause the reader to mistrust the report's content.

LEARNING OUTCOME 3
Collect primary and secondary information being careful to assess its credibility.

10-3 Collecting Information Through Primary and Secondary Research

Research, or the gathering of information, is one of the most important steps in writing a report. Because a report is only as good as its data, you will want to spend considerable time collecting data before you begin writing.

As you analyze a report's purpose and audience, think about your research strategy and what data you will need to support your argument or explain your topic. Will the audience need a lot of background or contextual information? Will your readers value or trust statistics, case studies, or expert opinions? Will they want to see information from interviews or surveys?

Data sources fall into two broad categories, primary and secondary. Primary data result from gathering original data from firsthand experience, interviews, surveys, experiments, or direct observation. Secondary data result from reading what others have published, experienced, or observed. To illustrate, consider an experiment at Texas A&M Transportation Institute. Investigators conducted primary research when they compared the reaction time of drivers who texted manually with those who used a voice-to-text app. Although texting drivers may believe they're being more careful when they use the hands-free method, the results indicated no safety advantage. Driver response times were significantly delayed no matter which texting method was used.[4] This primary data becomes secondary information when others report the findings.

We discuss secondary data first because that is where nearly every research project should begin. In most cases something has already been written about your topic. Reviewing secondary sources can save time and effort and prevent you from reinventing the wheel. Most secondary material is available either in print or electronically.

Print Resources. Although we are seeing a steady movement away from print data and toward electronic data, print sources are still the most visible part of most libraries. Much information is available only in print.

By the way, if you are an infrequent library user, begin your research by talking with a reference librarian about your project. Librarians won't do your research for you, but they will steer you in the right direction. Many librarians help you understand their computer, cataloging, and retrieval systems by providing advice, brochures, handouts, and workshops.

Books. Although quickly outdated, books provide excellent historical, in-depth data. Like most contemporary sources, books can be located through online listings.

Periodicals. Magazines, pamphlets, and journals are called *periodicals* because of their recurrent, or periodic, publication. Journals are compilations of scholarly articles. Articles in journals and other periodicals are extremely useful because they are concise, limited in scope, and current. Current publications are digitized and available in full text online, often as PDF documents.

Indexes. University libraries today offer online access to *The Readers' Guide to Periodical Literature*, an index now offered by EBSCO, a major provider of online databases. Contemporary business writers rely almost totally on electronic indexes and research databases to locate references, abstracts, and full-text articles from magazines, journals, and newspapers, such as *The New York Times*. When using Web-based online indexes, follow the on-screen instructions or ask for assistance from a librarian. Once you locate usable references, print a copy of your findings, save them to a flash drive or in a cloud-based storage location such as Dropbox, or send them to your e-mail address.

Research Databases. As a writer of business reports today, you will probably begin your secondary research with electronic resources. Online databases have become the staple of secondary research. Most writers turn to them first because they are fast and easy to use. You can conduct detailed searches without ever leaving your office or home.

A *database* is a collection of information stored digitally so that it is accessible by computer or mobile electronic devices and searchable. Databases provide bibliographic information (titles of documents and brief abstracts) and full-text documents. Databases contain a rich array of magazine, newspaper, and journal articles, as well as newsletters, business reports, company profiles, government data, reviews, and directories. The five databases most useful to business writers are ABI/INFORM Complete (ProQuest), Business Source Premier (EBSCO), JSTOR Business, Factiva (Dow Jones), and LexisNexis Academic. Figure 10.7 shows the ABI/INFORM Complete search menu.

Efficient search strategies take time to master. Therefore, get advice from a librarian. Remember that college and public libraries as well as some employers offer free access to several commercial databases, sparing you the high cost of individual subscriptions.

Figure 10.7 ABI/INFORM Complete (ProQuest) Search Result Page

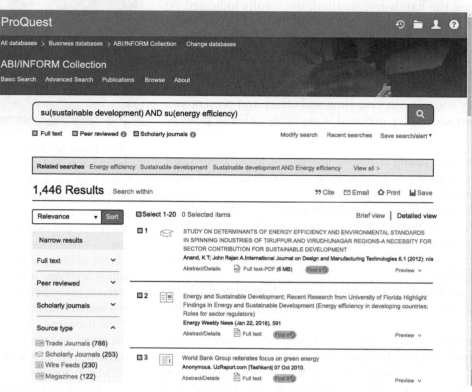

ABI/INFORM (ProQuest) indexes over 4,000 journals and features more than 3,000 full-text documents about business topics. Users can access newspapers, magazines, reports, dissertations, book reviews, scholarly journals, and trade publications. Figure 10.7 shows that the search terms *sustainable development* and *energy efficiency* brought up 1,446 search results. When retrieving too many results, savvy researchers further narrow their search to retrieve a more manageable number.

10-3a The Web

If you are like most adults today, you probably use the Web for entertainment and work every day. You may have a Facebook or Instagram page and may look up directions on Google Maps. In this section we examine the Web as an effective research tool.

Web Search Tools. Finding what you are looking for on the Web is hopeless without powerful, specialized search tools, such as Google, Bing, Yahoo Search, and Ask.

To get the most from Google, try the Advanced search feature. It resembles the query fields in research databases and allows you to narrow your searches more effectively than you can when you rely on a simple search and thus obtain only the most popular results that Google displays first.

Applying Internet Search Strategies and Techniques. To conduct a thorough search for the information you need, build a (re)search strategy by understanding the tools available. Figure 10.8 outlines several effective search techniques.

Wikipedia and Other Encyclopedias. College-level research requires you to use general encyclopedia information only as a starting point for more in-depth research. That means you will not cite Wikipedia, Ask, general encyclopedias, search engines, or similar references in your writing. Their information is too fluid and too general. However, these information-packed sites often provide their own references (bibliographies) that you can employ in your research. Locate the original sources of information rather than condensed reference articles.

10-3b Credibility of Internet Sources

Most Internet users tend to assume that any information turned up by a search engine has somehow been evaluated as part of a valid selection process. Wrong! Unlike library-based research, information at many sites has not undergone the

Figure 10.8 Useful Internet Search Techniques

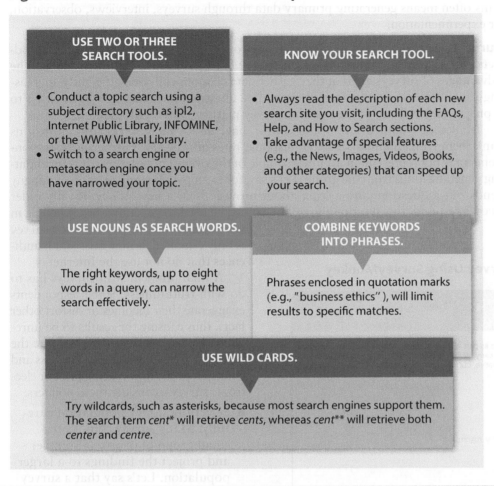

USE TWO OR THREE SEARCH TOOLS.

- Conduct a topic search using a subject directory such as ipl2, Internet Public Library, INFOMINE, or the WWW Virtual Library.
- Switch to a search engine or metasearch engine once you have narrowed your topic.

KNOW YOUR SEARCH TOOL.

- Always read the description of each new search site you visit, including the FAQs, Help, and How to Search sections.
- Take advantage of special features (e.g., the News, Images, Videos, Books, and other categories) that can speed up your search.

USE NOUNS AS SEARCH WORDS.

The right keywords, up to eight words in a query, can narrow the search effectively.

COMBINE KEYWORDS INTO PHRASES.

Phrases enclosed in quotation marks (e.g., "business ethics"), will limit results to specific matches.

USE WILD CARDS.

Try wildcards, such as asterisks, because most search engines support them. The search term *cent** will retrieve *cents*, whereas *cent*** will retrieve both *center* and *centre*.

editing or scrutiny of scholarly publication procedures. The information we read in journals and most reputable magazines is reviewed, authenticated, and evaluated.

Information on the Web is much less reliable than information from traditional sources. Blogs and discussion forum entries illustrate this problem. They change constantly and may disappear fast, so that your source can't be verified. Many don't provide any references, or they reveal sources that are either obscure or suspect. Even worse, today we hear of fake news websites that publish hoaxes, propaganda, and disinformation. Academic researchers prefer lasting, scholarly sources.

To use the Internet meaningfully, you must scrutinize what you find and check who authored and published it. The Communication Workshop at the end of this chapter provides a comprehensive list of questions to ask when checking the currency, authority, content, and accuracy of a website.

10-3c Primary Research Sources

Although you will start nearly every business report assignment by sifting through secondary sources, you will probably need primary data to add credibility and show the bigger picture. Business reports that solve specific current problems typically rely on primary, firsthand data. If, for example, management wants to discover the cause of increased employee turnover in its Seattle office, it might investigate employment trends in Seattle, prepare an employee survey about job satisfaction, and interview management for another perspective. Providing answers to business problems often means generating primary data through surveys, interviews, observation, or experimentation.

Surveys. Surveys collect data from groups of people. Before developing new products, for example, companies often survey consumers to learn their needs. The advantages of surveys are that they gather data economically and efficiently. Increasingly, consumers are asked to fill out online questionnaires and are taken either to a proprietary website or the popular survey platform SurveyMonkey.

Mailed or e-mailed surveys, of course, have disadvantages. Because most of us rank them with junk mail or spam, response rates may be low. Furthermore, respondents may not represent an accurate sample of the overall population, thus invalidating generalizations from the group. Let's say, for example, that an insurance company sends out a questionnaire asking about provisions in a new policy. If only older people respond, the questionnaire data cannot be used to generalize what people in other age groups might think. If a survey is only e-mailed, it may miss small audiences that do not use the Internet.

A final problem with surveys has to do with truthfulness. Some respondents exaggerate their incomes or distort other facts, thus causing the results to be unreliable. Nevertheless, surveys may be the best way to generate data for business and student reports. In preparing print or electronic surveys, consider these pointers:

- **Select the survey population carefully.** Many surveys question a small group of people (a sample) and project the findings to a larger population. Let's say that a survey of your class reveals that the majority prefer cheese pizza. Can you then say that all students on your campus (or in the nation) prefer cheese pizza? To be able to generalize from a survey, you need to make the sample large enough.

- **Explain why the survey is necessary.** In a cover letter or an opening paragraph, describe the need for the survey. Suggest how someone or something other than you will benefit. If appropriate, offer to send recipients a copy of the findings.

- **Consider incentives.** If the survey is long, persuasive techniques may be necessary. Response rates can be increased by offering money (such as a $1 bill), coupons, gift certificates, books, or other gifts.

- **Limit the number of questions.** Resist the temptation to ask for too much. Request only information you will use.

Figure 10.9 Preparing a Survey Using SurveyMonkey

Greendale College Bookstore

STUDENT SURVEY

The Greendale College Bookstore wants to do its part in protecting the environment. Each year we give away 45,000 plastic bags for students to carry off their purchases. We are considering changing from plastic to cloth bags or some other alternative, but we need your views.

1. What is your gender?

O Female
O Male

2. How many units are you currently carrying?

O 15 or more units
O 9 to 14 units
O 8 to fewer units

3. How many times have you visited the bookstore this semester?

O 0 times
O 1 time
O 2 times
O 3 times
O 4 or more times

4. Indicate your concern for the environment.

O Very concerned
O Concerned
O Unconcerned

5. To protect the environment, would you be willing to change to another type of bag when buying books?

O Yes
O No

6. Indicate your feeling about the following alternatives.

For major purchases the bookstore should:

	Agree	Undecided	Disagree
Continue to provide plastic bags.	O	O	O
Provide no bags; encourage students to bring their own bags.	O	O	O
Provide no bags; offer cloth bags at reduced price (about $3).	O	O	O

- **Use questions that produce quantifiable answers.** Check-off, multiple-choice, yes-no, and scale (or rank-order) questions, some of which are illustrated in Figure 10.9, provide quantifiable data that are easily tabulated. When questions elicit variable data, give interviewees a list of possible responses, as shown in item 6.

- **Avoid leading or ambiguous questions.** The wording of a question can dramatically affect responses to it.[6] When respondents were asked, "Are we spending too much, too little, or about the right amount on *assistance to the poor?*" 13 percent responded *Too much.* When the same respondents were asked, "Are we spending too much, too little, or about the right amount on *welfare?*" 44 percent responded *Too much.* Because words have different meanings for different people, you must strive to use objective language and pilot test your questions with typical respondents. Ask neutral questions (*Do CEOs earn too much, too little, or about the right amount?*).

- **Make it easy for respondents to return the survey.** Researchers often provide prepaid self-addressed envelopes or business-reply envelopes. Survey software such as SurveyMonkey helps users develop simple, template-driven questions and allows survey takers to follow a link to take the survey online.

- **Conduct a pilot study.** Try the questionnaire with a small group so that you can remedy any problems. In the survey shown in Figure 10.9, female students generally favored cloth bags and were willing to pay for them. Male students opposed purchasing cloth bags. By adding a gender category, researchers could verify this finding. The pilot study also revealed the need to ensure an appropriate representation of male and female students in the survey.

Interviews. Some of the best report information, particularly on topics about which little has been written, comes from individuals. These individuals are usually experts or veterans in their fields. Consider both in-house and outside experts for business reports. Tapping these sources will call for in-person, telephone, or online interviews. To elicit the most useful data, try these techniques:

- **Locate an expert.** Ask managers and individuals who are considered to be most knowledgeable in their areas. Check membership lists of professional organizations, and consult articles about the topic. Most people enjoy being experts or at least recommending them. You could also *crowdsource* your question in social media; that is, you could pose the query to your network to get input from your contacts.

- **Prepare for the interview.** Learn about the individual you are interviewing, and make sure you can pronounce the interviewee's name. Research the background and terminology of the topic. Let's say you are interviewing a corporate communication expert about producing an in-house newsletter. You ought to be familiar with terms such as *font* and software such as MS Publisher and InDesign. In addition, be prepared by making a list of questions that pinpoint your focus on the topic. Ask the interviewee if you may record the talk. Familiarize yourself with the recording device beforehand.

- **Maintain a professional attitude.** Call before the interview to confirm the arrangements, and then arrive on time. Be prepared to take notes if your recorder fails (and remember to ask permission beforehand if you want to record). Use your body language to convey respect.

- **Ask objective and friendly questions.** Adopt a courteous and respectful attitude. Don't get into a debating match with the interviewee, and don't interrupt. Remember that you are there to listen, not to talk! Use open-ended questions to draw experts out.

- **Watch the time.** Tell interviewees in advance how much time you expect to need for the interview. Don't overstay your appointment. If your subject rambles, gently try to draw him or her back to the topic; otherwise, you may run out of time before asking all your questions.

- **End graciously.** Conclude the interview with a general question, such as *Is there anything you would like to add?* Express your appreciation, and ask permission to telephone later if you need to verify points.

Observation and Experimentation. Some kinds of primary data can be obtained only through firsthand observation and investigation. If you determine that you need observational data, decide what or whom to observe and how often those observations are necessary. For example, if you want to learn more about an organization's telephone customer service, you might observe how long a typical caller waits before a customer service rep answers the call. To observe, arrive early enough to introduce yourself and set up any equipment. If you are recording, secure permissions beforehand. In addition, take notes, not only of the events or actions but also of the settings. Experimentation produces data suggesting causes and effects. Informal experimentation might be as simple as a pretest and posttest in a college course. Did students learn in the course?

Scientists and professional researchers undertake more formal experimentation. They control variables to test their effects. Assume, for example, that Hershey's wants to test the hypothesis (a tentative assumption) that chocolate provides an emotional lift. An experiment testing the hypothesis would separate depressed people into two groups: the chocolate eaters (the experimental group) and the chocolate deprived (the control group). Such experiments are not done haphazardly, however. Valid experiments require sophisticated research designs.

LEARNING OUTCOME 4

Identify the purposes and techniques of documentation in business reports as well as how to avoid plagiarism.

10-4 Documenting Information

In writing business reports, you will often build on the ideas and words of others. In Western culture, whenever you borrow the ideas of others, you must give credit to your information sources. This is called *documentation*.

10-4a The Purposes of Documentation

As a careful writer, you should take pains to document report data properly for the following reasons:

- **To strengthen your argument.** Including good data from reputable sources will convince readers of your credibility and the logic of your reasoning.

- **To protect yourself against charges of plagiarism.** Acknowledging your sources keeps you honest. *Plagiarism*, which is unethical and in some cases illegal, is the act of using others' ideas without proper documentation.

- **To instruct the reader.** Citing references enables readers to pursue a topic further and make use of the information themselves.

- **To save time.** The world of business moves so quickly that words and ideas must often be borrowed—which is very acceptable when you give credit to your sources.

10-4b Intellectual Theft: Plagiarism

Plagiarism of words or ideas is a serious offense and can lead to loss of a job. Famous historians, several high-level journalists, and even college professors[7] have suffered grave consequences for copying from unnamed sources. Your instructor may use a commercial plagiarism detection service such as Turnitin, which cross-references much of the information on the Web, looking for documents with identical phrasing.

The result, an "originality report," shows the instructor whether you have been accurate and honest.

You can avoid charges of plagiarism as well as add clarity to your work by knowing what to document and by developing good research habits. First, however, let's consider the differences between business and academic writing with respect to documentation.

10-4c Academic Documentation and Business Practices

In the academic world, documentation is critical. Especially in the humanities and sciences, students are taught to cite sources by using quotation marks, parenthetical citations, footnotes, and bibliographies. College term papers require full documentation to demonstrate that a student has become familiar with respected sources and can cite them properly in developing an argument. Giving credit to the authors is extremely important. Students who plagiarize risk a failing grade in a class and even expulsion from school.

In business, however, documentation and authorship are sometimes viewed differently. Business communicators on the job may find that much of what is written does not follow the standards they learned in school. In many instances individual authorship is unimportant. For example, employees may write for the signature of their bosses. The writer receives no credit. Similarly, teams turn out documents for which none of the team members receive individual credit. Internal business reports, which often include chunks of information from previous reports, also don't give credit. Even information from outside sources may lack detailed documentation. However, if facts are questioned, business writers must be able to produce their source materials.

Although both internal and external business reports are not as heavily documented as school assignments or term papers, business communication students are well advised to learn proper documentation methods. In the workplace, stealing the ideas of others and passing them off as one's own can be corrosive to the business because it leads to resentment and worse.

10-4d What to Document

When you write reports, especially in college, you are continually dealing with other people's ideas. You are expected to conduct research, synthesize ideas, and build on the work of others. But you are also expected to give proper credit for borrowed material. To avoid plagiarism, you must give credit whenever you use the following[8]:

- Another person's ideas, opinions, examples, or theory
- Any facts, statistics, graphs, and drawings that are not common knowledge
- Quotations of another person's actual spoken or written words
- Paraphrases of another person's spoken or written words
- Visuals, images, and any kind of electronic media

Information that is common knowledge requires no documentation. For example, the statement *The Wall Street Journal is a popular business newspaper* would require no citation. Statements that are not common knowledge, however, must be documented. The following statement would require a citation because most people do not know these facts: *On Forbes' list of America's fastest-growing cities, Cape Coral/Fort Myers, Florida, took the top spot with a growth rate of 3.39 percent last year.*[9] Someone went to the trouble and expense of assembling this original data and now *owns* it. Sources for such proprietary information—in this case, statistics reported by a newspaper or magazine—must be cited. Even if you summarize data in your own words, you must cite the source.

10-4e The Fine Art of Paraphrasing

In writing reports and using the ideas of others, you will probably rely heavily on *paraphrasing*, which means restating an original passage in your own words and in your own style. To do a good job of paraphrasing, follow these steps:

1. Read the original material intently to comprehend its full meaning.
2. Write your own version without looking at the original.
3. Avoid repeating the grammatical structure of the original and merely replacing words with synonyms.
4. Reread the original to be sure you covered the main points but did not borrow specific language.

To better understand the difference between plagiarizing and paraphrasing, study the following passages. Notice that the writer of the plagiarized version uses the same grammatical construction as the source and often merely replaces words with synonyms. Even the acceptable version, however, requires a reference to the source author.

Source

We have seen, in a short amount of time, the disappearance of a large number of household brands that failed to take sufficient and early heed of the software revolution that is upending traditional brick-and-mortar businesses and creating a globally pervasive digital economy.[10]

Plagiarized version

Many trusted household name brands disappeared very swiftly because they did not sufficiently and early pay attention to the software revolution that is toppling traditional physical businesses and creating a global digital economy. (Saylor, 2012)

Acceptable paraphrase

Digital technology has allowed a whole new virtual global economy to blossom and very swiftly wipe out some formerly powerful companies that responded too late or inadequately to the disruptive force that has swept the globe. (Saylor, 2012)

10-4f When and How to Quote

On occasion, you will want to use the exact words of a source, but beware of overusing quotations. Documents that contain pages of spliced-together quotations suggest that writers have few ideas of their own. Wise writers and speakers use direct quotations for three purposes only:

- To provide objective background data and establish the severity of a problem as seen by experts
- To repeat identical phrasing because of its precision, clarity, or aptness
- To duplicate exact wording before criticizing

When you must use a long quotation, try to summarize and introduce it in your own words. Readers want to know the gist of a quotation before they tackle it. For example, to introduce a quotation discussing the shrinking staffs of large companies, you could precede it with your words: *In predicting employment trends, Charles Waller believes the corporation of the future will depend on a small core of full-time employees.* To introduce quotations or paraphrases, use wording such as the following:

According to Waller, . . .
Waller argues that . . .
In his recent study, Waller reported . . .

Use quotation marks to enclose exact quotations, as shown in the following: *"The current image,"* says Charles Waller, *"of a big glass-and-steel corporate headquarters on landscaped grounds directing a worldwide army of tens of thousands of employees may soon be a thing of the past"* (2013, p. 51).

10-4g Citation Formats

You can direct readers to your sources with parenthetical notes inserted into the text and with bibliographies. The most common citation formats are presented by the Modern Language Association (MLA), the American Psychological Association (APA), and the Chicago Manual of Style (CMS). Learn more about using MLA and APA formats in Appendix B.

10-5 Incorporating Meaningful Visual Aids and Graphics

LEARNING OUTCOME 5
Convert report data into meaningful visual aids and graphics.

After collecting and interpreting information, you need to consider how best to present it. If your report contains complex data and numbers, you may want to consider graphics such as tables and charts. These graphics clarify data, create visual interest, and make numerical data meaningful. By simplifying complex ideas and emphasizing key data, well-constructed graphics make key information easier to remember. However, the same data can be shown in many forms; for example, in a chart, table, or graph. That's why you need to know how to match the graphic with your objective and how to incorporate it into your report.

10-5a Matching Graphics and Objectives

To develop the best graphics, you must decide what data you want to highlight and which graphics are most appropriate given your objectives. Tables? Bar charts? Pie charts? Line charts? Surface charts? Flowcharts? Organizational charts? Pictures? Figure 10.10 summarizes appropriate uses for each type of graphic. The following sections discuss each type in more detail.

Figure 10.10 Matching Graphics to Objectives

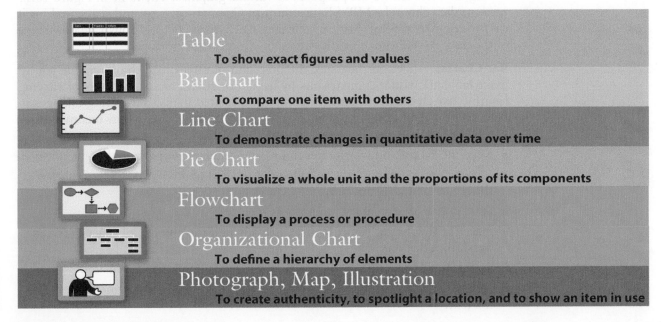

Table
To show exact figures and values

Bar Chart
To compare one item with others

Line Chart
To demonstrate changes in quantitative data over time

Pie Chart
To visualize a whole unit and the proportions of its components

Flowchart
To display a process or procedure

Organizational Chart
To define a hierarchy of elements

Photograph, Map, Illustration
To create authenticity, to spotlight a location, and to show an item in use

Figure 10.11 Table Summarizing Precise Data

	Theme Parks	Motion Pictures	DVDs & Blu-ray Discs	Total
Figure 1 MPM ENTERTAINMENT COMPANY Income by Division (in millions of dollars)				
2014	$15.8	$39.3	$11.2	$66.3
2015	18.1	17.5	15.3	50.9
2016	23.8	21.1	22.7	67.6
2017	32.2	22.0	24.3	78.5
2018 (projected)	35.1	21.0	26.1	82.2

Source: *Industry Profiles* (New York: DataPro, 2017) 225.

Tables. Probably the most frequently used graphic in reports is the table. Because a table presents quantitative or verbal information in systematic columns and rows, it can clarify large quantities of data in small spaces. Although tables do not readily display trends, they enable you to effectively organize raw data collected from surveys or interviews. The following tips will help you produce effective tables, one of which is shown in Figure 10.11.

- Place titles and labels at the top of the table.
- Arrange items in a logical order (alphabetical, chronological, geographical, highest to lowest), depending on what you need to emphasize.
- Provide clear headings for the rows and columns.
- Identify the units in which figures are given (percentages, dollars, units per worker hour) in the table title, in the column or row heading, with the first item in a column, or in a note at the bottom.
- Make long tables easier to read by shading alternate lines or by leaving a blank line after groups of five.
- Place tables as close as possible to the place where they are mentioned in the text.

   Figure 10.10 shows the purposes of various graphics. The table in Figure 10.11 presents data about the MPM Entertainment Company over several years, making it easy to compare several divisions. Figures 10.12 through 10.15 illustrate how some of the data for MPM can be illustrated in various chart formats.

Bar Charts. Although they lack the precision of tables, bar charts enable you to make emphatic visual comparisons by using horizontal or vertical bars of varying lengths. Bar charts are useful for comparing related items, illustrating changes in data over time, and showing segments as a part of the whole. Many techniques for constructing tables also hold true for bar charts. Here are a few more tips:

- Keep the length and width of each bar and segment proportional.
- Include a total figure in the middle or at the end of the bar if the figure helps the reader and does not clutter the chart.
- Start dollar or percentage amounts at zero.
- Place the first bar at some distance (usually half the amount of space between bars) from the *y*-axis.
- Avoid showing too much information, to avoid clutter and confusion.
- Place each bar chart as close as possible to the place where it is mentioned in the text.

Figure 10.12 Horizontal Bar Chart

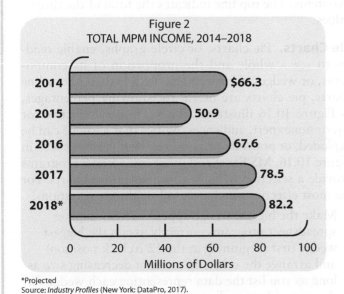

Figure 2
TOTAL MPM INCOME, 2014–2018

2014 $66.3
2015 50.9
2016 67.6
2017 78.5
2018* 82.2

0   20   40   60   80   100
Millions of Dollars

*Projected
Source: *Industry Profiles* (New York: DataPro, 2017).

Figure 10.13 Segmented 100 Percent Bar Chart

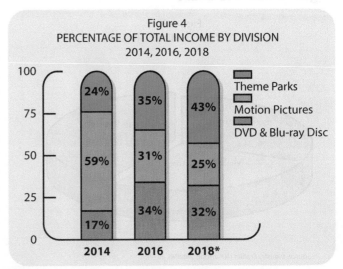

Figure 4
PERCENTAGE OF TOTAL INCOME BY DIVISION
2014, 2016, 2018

Theme Parks
Motion Pictures
DVD & Blu-ray Disc

2014: 24%, 59%, 17%
2016: 35%, 31%, 34%
2018*: 43%, 25%, 32%

*Projected
Source: *Industry Profiles* (New York: DataPro, 2017).

Figure 10.14 Multiple Line Chart

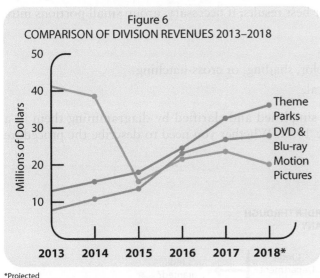

Figure 6
COMPARISON OF DIVISION REVENUES 2013–2018

Theme Parks
DVD & Blu-ray
Motion Pictures

2013 2014 2015 2016 2017 2018*

*Projected
Source: *Industry Profiles* (New York: DataPro, 2017).

Figure 10.15 Segmented Line (Area) Chart

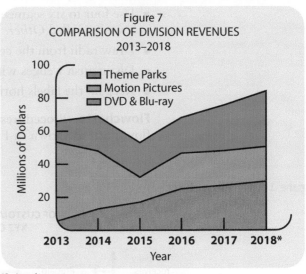

Figure 7
COMPARISION OF DIVISION REVENUES
2013–2018

Theme Parks
Motion Pictures
DVD & Blu-ray

2013 2014 2015 2016 2017 2018*
Year

*Projected
Source: *Industry Profiles* (New York: DataPro, 2017).

Line Charts. The major advantage of line charts is that they show changes over time, thus indicating trends. The vertical axis is typically the dependent variable; and the horizontal axis, the independent one. Multiple line charts compare items, such as two or more data sets, using the same variable (Figure 10.14). Segmented line charts (Figure 10.15), also called surface charts, illustrate how the components of a whole change over time. To prepare a line chart, follow these tips:

■ Begin with a grid divided into squares.

■ Arrange the time component (usually years) horizontally across the bottom; arrange values for the other variable vertically.

■ Draw small dots at the intersections to indicate each value at a given year.

■ Connect the dots and add color if desired.

■ To prepare a segmented (surface) chart, plot the first value (say, DVD and Blu-ray disc income) across the bottom; add the next item (say, motion picture income) to the first figures for every increment; for the third item (say, theme

Figure 10.16 Pie Chart

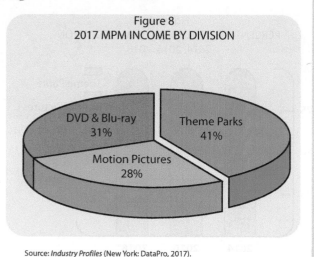

Figure 8
2017 MPM INCOME BY DIVISION

Theme Parks 41%

DVD & Blu-ray 31%

Motion Pictures 28%

Source: *Industry Profiles* (New York: DataPro, 2017).

park income), add its value to the total for the first two items. The top line indicates the total of the three values.

Pie Charts. Pie charts, or circle graphs, enable readers to see a whole and the proportion of its components, or wedges. Although less flexible than bar or line charts, pie charts are useful for showing percentages, as Figure 10.16 illustrates. They are very effective for lay, or nonexpert, audiences. Notice that a wedge can be exploded, or popped out, for special emphasis, as seen in Figure 10.16. MS Excel and other spreadsheet programs provide a selection of three-dimensional pie charts. For the most effective pie charts, follow these suggestions:

- Make the biggest wedge appear first. Computer spreadsheet programs correctly assign the biggest wedge first (beginning at the 12 o'clock position) and arrange the others in order of decreasing size as long as you list the data representing each wedge on the spreadsheet in descending order.
- Include, if possible, the actual percentage or absolute value for each wedge.
- Use four to six segments for best results; if necessary, group small portions into a wedge called *Other*.
- Draw radii from the center.
- Distinguish wedges with color, shading, or cross-hatching.
- Keep all the labels horizontal.

Flowcharts. Procedures are simplified and clarified by diagramming them in a flowchart, as shown in Figure 10.17. Whether you need to describe the procedure

Figure 10.17 Flowchart

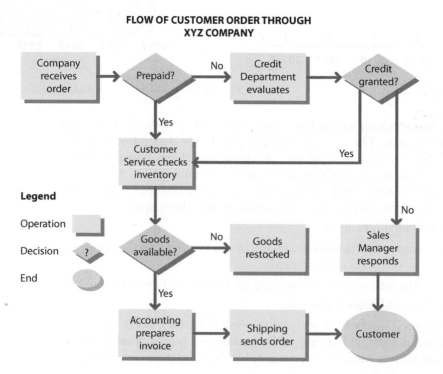

FLOW OF CUSTOMER ORDER THROUGH
XYZ COMPANY

Company receives order → Prepaid? — No → Credit Department evaluates → Credit granted?

Prepaid? — Yes → Customer Service checks inventory

Credit granted? — Yes → Customer Service checks inventory

Credit granted? — No → Sales Manager responds

Customer Service checks inventory → Goods available? — No → Goods restocked

Goods available? — Yes → Accounting prepares invoice → Shipping sends order → Customer

Sales Manager responds → Customer

Legend

Operation

Decision ?

End

for handling a customer's purchase, highlight steps in solving a problem, or display a problem with a process, flowcharts help the reader visualize the process. Traditional flowcharts use the following symbols:

- Ovals to designate the beginning and end of a process
- Diamonds to designate decision points
- Rectangles to represent major activities or steps

Organizational Charts. Many large organizations are so complex that they need charts to show the chain of command, from the boss down to the line managers and employees. Organizational charts provide such information as who reports to whom, how many subordinates work for each manager (the span of control), and what channels of official communication exist. These charts may illustrate a company's structure—for example, by function, customer, or product. They may also be organized by the work being performed in each job or by the hierarchy of decision making.

Photographs, Maps, and Illustrations. Some business reports include photographs, maps, and illustrations to serve specific purposes. Photos, for example, add authenticity and provide a visual record. An environmental engineer may use photos to document hazardous waste sites. Maps enable report writers to depict activities or concentrations geographically, such as dots indicating sales reps in states across the country. Illustrations and diagrams are useful in indicating how an object looks or operates. A drawing showing the parts of a printer with labels describing their functions, for example, is more instructive than a photograph or verbal description.

Infographics An *infographic* is a visual representation of complex information in a format that is easy to understand. Compelling infographics tell a story by combining images and graphic elements, such as charts and diagrams. The best infographic design is informative and entertaining. As shown in Figure 10.18, Michael Anderson created stylized charts in his infographic résumé to display his experience, education, and skills as a graphic designer. Infographics are frequently built around basic types of graphical elements such as bar, line, and pie charts. Although art makes an infographic visually appealing, the most important element of an infographic is accuracy: the data must be accurate and presented fairly. Because infographics tend to be complex and colorful, they are commonly shared in online environments.

10-5b Incorporating Graphics in Reports

Used appropriately, graphics make reports more interesting and easier to understand. In putting graphics into your reports, follow these suggestions for best effects:

- **Evaluate the audience.** Consider the reader, the content, your schedule, and your budget. Because graphics take time to create and can be costly to print in color, think carefully before deciding how many to use. Six charts in an internal report to an executive may seem like overkill; however, in a long technical report to outsiders, six may be too few.
- **Use restraint.** Don't overuse color or decorations. Although color can effectively distinguish bars or segments in charts, too much color can be distracting and confusing. Remember, too, that colors themselves sometimes convey meaning: red suggests deficits or negative values; blue suggests calmness and authority; and yellow may suggest warning.
- **Be accurate and ethical.** Double-check all graphics for accuracy of figures and calculations. Be certain that your visuals aren't misleading—either accidentally or intentionally. Manipulation of a chart scale can make trends look steeper and more dramatic than they really are. Moreover, be sure to cite sources when you use someone else's facts.

Figure 10.18 Infographic Résumé

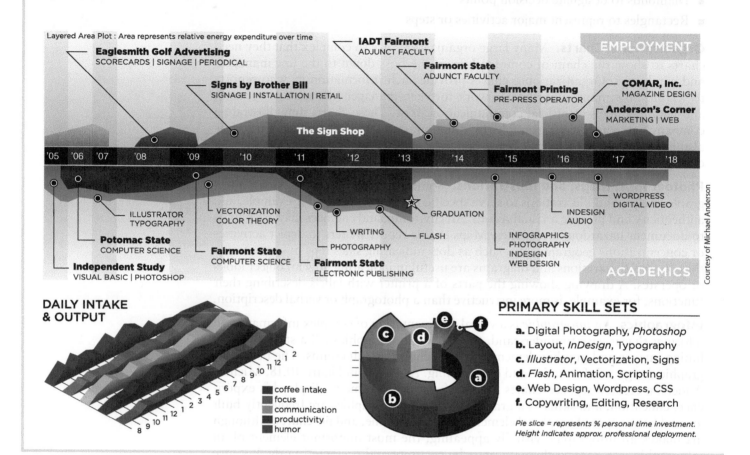

Courtesy of Michael Anderson

- **Introduce a graph meaningfully.** Refer to every graphic in the text, and place the graphic close to the point where it is mentioned. Most important, though, help the reader understand the significance of the graphic. You can do this by telling your audience what to look for or by summarizing the main point of the graphic. Don't assume the reader will automatically reach the same conclusions you reached from a set of data. Instead of saying, *The findings are shown in Figure 3*, tell the reader what to look for: *Two thirds of the responding employees, as shown in Figure 3, favor a flextime schedule.* The best introductions for graphics interpret them for readers.

- **Choose an appropriate caption or title style.** Like reports, graphics may use talking titles or generic, descriptive titles. Talking titles are more persuasive; they tell the reader what to think.

LEARNING OUTCOME 6
Describe the content of typical formal report components.

10-6 Understanding Formal Report Components

In many ways formal business reports are longer versions of the analytical business reports presented in Chapter 9. Because of their length and complexity, formal business reports include more sections than routine informal business reports do.

To compare the components of informal and formal reports, see Figure 10.3. In this section, we focus on formal report components.

10-6a Front Matter Components

The front matter of a formal report refers to the preliminary sections before the body section. Some front matter components are optional, but they typically appear in the following order: (a) report cover (optional), (b) title page, (c) letter or memo of transmittal (optional), (d) table of contents, (e) list of figures or tables (optional), and (f) executive summary. Writers often number these sections with lowercase Roman numerals; the title page, however, is normally not numbered. These components make it easy for the reader to find specific information quickly.

Title Page. The format of title pages may vary, but title pages often include the following elements:

- *Name* of the report, often in uppercase letters (no underscore and no quotation marks)
- *Presented to* (or *Submitted to*) followed by the name, title, and organization of the individual receiving the report
- *Prepared by* (or *Submitted by*) followed by the author's name and title
- Date of submission

Letter or Memo of Transmittal. Generally written on organization stationery, a letter or memorandum of transmittal may introduce a formal report. A transmittal letter or memo uses the direct strategy and is usually less formal than the report itself. The transmittal document typically (a) announces the topic of the report and tells how it was authorized; (b) briefly describes the project; (c) highlights the report's findings, conclusions, and recommendations; and (d) closes with appreciation for the assignment or instruction for follow-up actions. If a report is going to various readers, you would prepare a special transmittal letter or memo for each reader.

Table of Contents. The table of contents shows the main sections in the report and their page numbers. The proper title is *Contents* or *Table of Contents*. The table of contents includes front matter items, the body section's main headings and subheadings, and back matter sections, such as the appendix. Major headings are left-aligned, and leaders (spaced dots) help guide the eye to the page numbers.

List of Figures. For reports with many figures or tables, you may wish to list the figures to help readers locate them easily. This list may appear on the same page as the table of contents, space permitting. For each figure or table, include a title and page number.

Executive Summary. The purpose of an executive summary is to present an overview of the longer report for people who may not have time to read the entire document. Generally, an executive summary is prepared by the author of the report. However, you might be asked to write an executive summary of a published report or article written by someone else. In either case, the writer's goal is to summarize the report's major sections, such as the purpose, background, conclusions, and recommendations. Readers often go straight to the executive summary and look for the recommendations before glancing at the full report.

10-6b Body Components

Body components of formal reports typically include the introduction and body sections. In the introduction, the writer briefly describes the report's contents. In the body, the longest and most substantive section, the writer discusses the problem and findings before presenting analyses, conclusions, and recommendations.

Introduction. Formal reports begin with an introduction to announce the topic and to set the stage for the reader. A good report introduction typically covers the following elements, although not necessarily in this order:

- **Background:** Events leading up to the problem or need
- **Problem or purpose:** An explanation of the problem or need that motivated the report
- **Significance:** An account of the significance or importance of the report topic, which may include quotes from experts, journals, or Web resources
- **Scope:** Boundaries of the report, defining what will be included or excluded
- **Organization:** A road map or structure of the report

Beyond these minimal introductory elements, consider adding any of the following information that may be relevant to your readers:

- **Authorization:** The name of whoever commissioned the report and its intended audience
- **Literature review:** A summary of other publications on this topic
- **Sources and methods:** A description of secondary sources (periodicals, books, databases) and methods of collecting primary data
- **Key terms:** Definitions of important and unfamiliar terms used in the report

Report Body (Findings and Analyses). The body is the principal section in a formal report. It discusses, analyzes, interprets, and evaluates the research findings or solution to the initial problem. This is where you show the evidence that justifies your conclusions. Organize the body into main categories following your original outline.

The body section contains clear headings that explain each major section. Headings may be functional or talking. Functional heads (such as *Results of the Survey*, *Analysis of Findings*, or *Discussion*) help readers identify the general purpose of the section. Such headings are useful for routine reports or for sensitive topics that may upset readers. Talking heads (for example, *Findings Reveal Revenue and Employment Benefits*) are more descriptive and informative.

Conclusions and Recommendations. Writers know that the conclusions and recommendations section is most important to a reader. This section tells what the findings mean, particularly in terms of solving the original problem. Some writers prefer to intermix their conclusions with the analysis of the findings. Other writers place the conclusions before the body so that busy readers can examine them immediately. Still other writers combine the conclusions and recommendations. Most writers, though, present the conclusions after the body because readers expect this sequence. To improve readability, you may present the conclusions in a numbered or bulleted list.

10.6c Back Matter Components

The back matter of most reports includes a reference section and one or more appendixes. The reference section includes a bibliography of sources, and the appendix contains supplemental information or source documents. In organizing the back matter sections, use standard Arabic numerals to number the pages.

Works Cited, References, or Bibliography. If you use the MLA (Modern Language Association) referencing format, list all sources of information alphabetically in a section titled *Works Cited*. If you use the APA (American Psychological Association) format, list your sources in a section called *References*. Your listed sources must correspond to in-text citations in the report whenever you are borrowing words or ideas from published and unpublished resources.

Regardless of the documentation format, you must include the author, title, publication, date of publication, page number, and other significant data for all ideas or quotations used in your report. Whether to include the URLs for electronic

Figure 10.19 Quick View of Selected Pages From the Formal Report

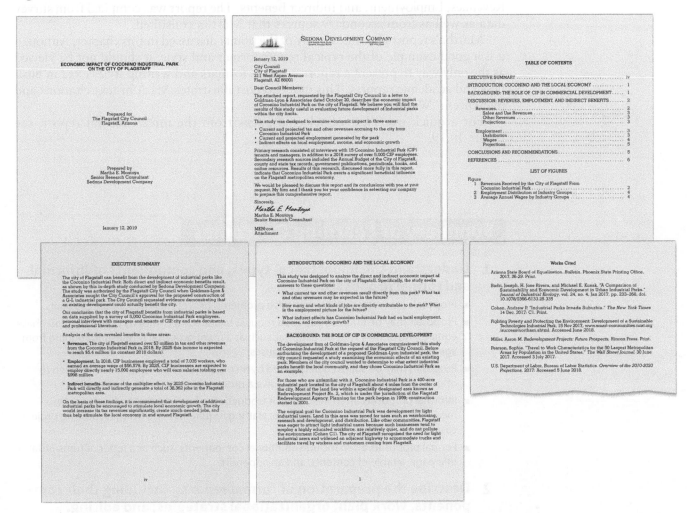

references depends on the guidelines of your documentation format or your company's preference. Appendix B of this textbook contains additional documentation models and information.

Appendixes. Incidental or supplemental materials belong in appendixes at the end of a formal report. These materials are relevant to some readers but not to all. They may also be too bulky to include in the text. Appendixes may include survey forms, copies of other reports, tables of data, large graphics, and related correspondence. If multiple appendixes are necessary, they are listed consecutively, such as *Appendix A, Appendix B,* and *Appendix C.*

10-6d Model Formal Report With MLA Format

A complete formal report illustrating all of the parts is available online. To see a complete formal report illustrating nearly all the parts, visit the Student Companion Website at **cengage.brain.com.**

In this formal report, Martha Montoya, senior research consultant with Sedona Development Company, examined the economic impact of a local industrial park on the city of Flagstaff, Arizona.

The city council hired consultants to evaluate Coconino Industrial Park and to assess whether future commercial development would stimulate further economic growth. Martha Montoya subdivided the economic impact into three parts: Revenues, Employment, and Indirect Benefits. The report was compiled from survey data as well as from secondary sources that Martha consulted.

Martha's report illustrates many of the points discussed in this chapter. Although it is a good example of the typical report format and style, it should not be viewed as the only way to present a report. Various formats and writing styles exist in business and academic reports. This model report illustrates MLA in-text citations and references ("Works Cited").

For a quick overview of selected pages from the model formal report, see Figure 10.19.

Summary of Learning Outcomes

1 Understand the importance, types, and components of informal and formal proposals.

- Proposals are written offers that solve problems, provide services, or sell products.
- Proposals may be internal, such as a request to change a company policy or to purchase equipment; or they may be external, such as a grant proposal requesting funding from agencies that support worthwhile causes.
- Proposals may be solicited (requested by an organization) or unsolicited (written to offer a service, request funding, or solve a problem).
- Informal proposals often include an introduction; a background and purpose statement; a proposal, plan, and schedule; staffing requirements; a budget showing project costs; and a conclusion.
- Formal proposals often include additional components, such as a letter of transmittal, a title page, a table of contents, and an appendix.

2 Describe the preparation of formal reports, including their components, work plan, organizational strategies, and editing.

- A formal report is a document that analyzes findings, draws conclusions, and makes recommendations intended to solve a problem.
- Writers determine the purpose and scope of the report, anticipate the needs of the audience, prepare a work plan, decide on appropriate research methods, conduct research using secondary and primary sources, organize findings, draw conclusions, and design graphics.
- Writers proofread and edit formal reports by reviewing the format, spacing and font consistency, graphics placement, heading levels, data accuracy, and mechanics.

3 Collect primary and secondary information being careful to assess its credibility.

- Nearly every research project should begin with secondary data including print resources.
- Print resources include books, periodicals, and indexes.
- Research databases (such as ProQuest, EBSCO, JStor, and Factiva) enable researchers to access in-depth data without ever leaving their offices or homes.
- The most successful researchers know their search tools and apply smart Internet strategies.
- Good writers assess the credibility of each Web resource by evaluating its currency (last update), author or sponsoring organization, content, purpose, and accuracy.
- Report writers gather data from primary sources by distributing surveys, conducting interviews, and collecting data from firsthand observation.

4 Identify the purposes and techniques of documentation in business reports as well as how to avoid plagiarism.

- Documenting sources means giving credit to information sources.
- Documenting is necessary to strengthen an argument, protect against charges of plagiarism, instruct the reader, and save time.
- In the academic world, documentation is critical. In business, reports are less heavily documented; however, writers still may need to cite their sources.
- Common citation formats include the Modern Language Association (MLA), the American Psychological Association (APA), and the Chicago Manual of Style (CMS).

5 Convert report data into meaningful visual aids and graphics.

- Graphics clarify data, add visual interest, and make complex data easy to understand; they should be placed close to where they are referenced.
- Tables show quantitative information in systematic columns and rows; they require meaningful titles, bold column headings, and logical data arrangement.
- Bar charts and line charts show visual comparisons using horizontal or vertical bars or lines of varying lengths; pie charts show a whole and the proportion of its components.
- Flowcharts diagram processes and procedures, organizational charts show a company's chain of command and structure, and infographics visually illustrate complex information.
- To incorporate graphics into reports, evaluate the audience, use restraint in colors and decorations, be accurate and ethical, introduce a graph meaningfully, and choose an appropriate caption or title style.
- Infographics, popular in online environments, combine images and graphic elements to visually illustrate information in an easy-to-understand format.

6 Describe the content of typical formal report components.

- Front matter components of formal reports often include a title page, letter or memo of transmittal, table of contents, list of figures, and executive summary.
- Body components of formal reports include the introduction, the body, and the conclusions and recommendations.
- The principal section of a formal report is the body; it discusses, analyzes, interprets, and evaluates the research findings before drawing conclusions.
- Back matter components of a formal report include a bibliography, which may be a works-cited or reference page, and any appendixes.

Chapter Review

1. What is an RFP and what purpose does it serve? (L.O. 1)

2. What is a hook in a proposal, and why is it part of the introduction? (L.O. 1)

3. Name five possible parts of a work plan for a formal report. (L.O. 2)

4. Why are formal reports written in business? Give an original example of a business-related report. (L.O. 2)

5. If the Internet is one of the greatest sources of information, why must researchers exercise caution when using its sources? (L.O. 3)

6. What are the differences between primary and secondary sources? Which should a researcher seek first? Give an example of each. (L.O. 3)

7. What is the difference between plagiarizing and paraphrasing? What techniques can a writer employ to paraphrase effectively? (L.O. 4)

8. Briefly compare the advantages and disadvantages of illustrating data with charts (bar and line) versus tables. (L.O. 5)

9. What is the purpose of an executive summary? (L.O. 6)

10. What are the three major parts of a formal report, and what components are found in each? (L.O. 6)

Critical Thinking

11. What category of proposal, solicited or unsolicited, is more likely to succeed, and why? (L.O. 1)

12. What is the difference between conclusions and recommendations in a report? (L.O. 2)

13. Why must researchers document their sources meticulously? (L.O. 4)

14. How can report writers decide what type of graphic to use in a report? (L.O. 5)

15. Is information obtained on the Web as reliable as information obtained from journals, newspapers, and magazines? (L.O. 3)

10.1 Proposal: Pinpoint That Workplace Problem (L.O. 1)

The ability to spot problems before they turn into serious risks is prized by most managers. Drawing on your internship and work experience, can you identify a problem that could be solved with a small to moderate financial investment? Look for issues such as a lack of lunch or break rooms for staff; badly needed health initiatives such as gyms or sport club memberships; low-gas-mileage, high-emission company vehicles; a little effort to achieve sustainability; or a lack of recycling efforts.

YOUR TASK. Discuss with your instructor the workplace problem you have identified. Make sure you choose a relatively weighty problem that can be lessened or eliminated with a minor expenditure. Strive to explain how the benefits merit the cost. Address your unsolicited letter or memo proposal to your current or former boss and copy your instructor.

10.2 Proposal: Lending a Hand With Proposal Writing (L.O. 1, 2)

> E-Mail > Web

Many new companies with services or products to offer would like to land corporate or government contracts. However, they are intimidated by the proposal and RFP processes. Your friend, Christie, who has started her own designer uniform company, has asked you for help. Her goal is to offer her colorful yet functional uniforms to hospitals and clinics. Before writing a proposal, however, she wants to see examples and learn more about the process.

YOUR TASK. Use the Web to find at least two examples of business proposals. Don't waste time on sites that want to sell templates or books. Find actual examples. Try **http://www.bplans.com/samples/sba.cfm**. Then prepare an e-mail or memo to Christie in which you do the following:

a. Identify two sample business proposals.
b. Outline the parts of each proposal.
c. Compare the strengths and weaknesses of each proposal.
d. Draw conclusions. What can Christie learn from these examples?

10.3 Grant Writing: Learning From Nonprofits (L.O. 1, 2)

> Web

Nonprofit organizations frequently seek grant writers, and you would like to gain experience in this area. You've heard that they pull down good salaries, and one day you might even decide to become a professional grant/proposal writer. However, you first need experience. You saw a Web listing from The Actors Theatre Workshop advertising for a grant writer to "seek funding for general operating expenses and program-related funding." A grant writer would "develop proposals, generate boilerplates for future applications, and oversee a writing team." This listing sounds good, but you need a local position.

YOUR TASK. Search the Web for local nonprofits. Alternatively, your instructor may already know of local groups seeking grant writers, such as a United Way member agency, an educational institution, or a faith-based organization. Talk with your instructor about an assignment. Your instructor may ask you to submit a preliminary memo report outlining ten or more guidelines you expect to follow when writing proposals and grants for nonprofit organizations.

10.4 Service Learning: Write Away! (L.O. 1–6)

> E-Mail > Web

Your school may be one that encourages service learning, a form of experiential learning. You could receive credit for a project that bridges academic and nonacademic communities. Because writing skills are in wide demand, you may have an opportunity to simultaneously apply your skills, contribute to the community, and expand your résumé. The National Service-Learning Clearinghouse describes service learning as "a teaching and learning strategy that integrates meaningful community service with instruction and reflection to enrich the learning experience, teach civic responsibility, and strengthen communities."[11] You can access thousands of Clearinghouse resources at **gsn.nylc.org/clearinghouse**. The Web offers many sites devoted to examples of students engaging in service-learning projects.

YOUR TASK. Research possible service-learning projects in this class or another. Your instructor may ask you to submit a memo or e-mail message analyzing your findings. Describe at least four completed service-learning projects that you found in your research. Draw conclusions about what made them successful or beneficial. What kinds of similar projects might be possible for you or students in your class? Your instructor may use this as a research project or turn it into a hands-on project by having you find a service organization in your community that needs trained writers.

10.5 Unsolicited Proposal: Requesting Funding for Your Campus Business Club (L.O. 1)

Professional associations often have student-organized chapters on college campuses. Let's say you are a member of a campus business club, such as the Society for the Advancement of Management (SAM), the American Marketing Association (AMA), the American Management Association (AMA), the Accounting Society (AS), the International Association of Administrative Professionals (IAAP), or the Association of Information Technology Professionals (AITP). Your club or association has managed its finances well, and therefore, it is able to fund monthly activities. However, membership dues are insufficient to cover any extras. You see the need for a special one-time seminar with a panel of experts or a keynote speaker that would benefit many business students. For example, you see value in inviting a panel of recruiters to come and discuss current job requirements and hiring processes. You must now request funding for this event.

YOUR TASK. Write an unsolicited letter or memo proposal to your program chair or business division dean to request one-time funding to cover the costs associated with this event. Identify your need or problem, provide the details of the event, mention the ways this event will benefit the attendees, support your claims with evidence, and provide a budget. Think ahead about costs associated with printing, appreciation gifts for the presenters, food and beverage needs, and other miscellaneous expenses.

10.6 Primary Research: Seeking Customer Feedback Through an Online Survey (L.O. 3)

> Web

Companies use surveys to continually improve their products and services. As a sales manager in a store selling wireless devices and electronics, you are interested in your customers' opinions about your sales associates, product quality, and loyalty to your products. You plan to conduct a survey and use the results in an upcoming training workshop for your sales associates. You have obtained the e-mail addresses of customers who have opted in for product updates and reviews. You plan to design your own survey and want to get ideas by looking at examples of surveys and templates.

YOUR TASK. Search for free customer service survey templates, study the questions, and add the URL of the surveys you reviewed. Then design a customer service survey with a mix of seven or eight typical multiple-choice, scale, or open-ended questions.

10.7 Formal Business Report: Gathering Data for International Expansion (L.O. 3)

> Intercultural   Team   Web

U.S. businesses are expanding into foreign markets with manufacturing plants, sales offices, and branches abroad. Many Americans, however, have little knowledge of or experience with people from other cultures. To prepare for participation in the global marketplace, you are to collect information for a report focused on an Asian, Latin American, European, or African country where English is not regularly spoken. Before selecting the country, though, consult your campus international student program for volunteers who are willing to be interviewed. Your instructor may make advance arrangements with international student volunteers.

YOUR TASK. In teams of three to five, collect information about your target country from electronic databases, the Web, and other sources. Then invite an international student representing your target country to be interviewed by your group. Alternatively, you could interview a faculty member who hails from another country. Prepare and know your interview questions and be courteous; people like to talk about themselves, but no one wants to waste time.

As you conduct primary and secondary research, investigate the topics listed in Figure 10.20. Confirm what you learn in your secondary research by talking with your interviewee. When you complete your research, write a report for the CEO of your company (make up a name and company). Assume that your company plans to expand its operations abroad. Your report should advise the company's executives of the social customs, family life, attitudes, religions, education, and values of the target country. Remember that your company's interests are business oriented; do not dwell on tourist information. Write your report individually or in teams.

10.8 Citations: Citing Secondary Resources Using MLA Format (L.O. 4)

> E-Mail

You will want to stay up-to-date on your career field by reading, saving current articles, and bookmarking valuable resources. Think about a current business topic related to your professional field that you would like to learn more about. This is your chance to learn more about, gather tips and strategies about, and follow current trends in your field of interest.

YOUR TASK. Look for three current (within the last two years) secondary research sources on a topic related to your field of study. In a memo or e-mail to your instructor, write a one-paragraph summary of each article or resource. Then list the citations for your three resources using MLA standards. The citations should follow the format used on a works-cited page with citations in alphabetical order and using the hanging indent style.

Figure 10.20 Intercultural Interview Topics and Questions

Social Customs

- How do people react to strangers? Are they generally friendly? Hostile? Reserved?
- How do people greet each other?
- What are the appropriate manners when you enter a room? Bow? Nod? Shake hands with everyone?
- How are names used for introductions? Is it appropriate to inquire about one's occupation or family?
- What are the attitudes toward touching?
- How does one express appreciation for an invitation to another's home? Bring a gift? Send flowers? Write a thank-you note? Are any gifts taboo?
- Are there any customs related to how or where one sits?
- Are any facial expressions or gestures considered rude?
- How close do people stand when talking?
- What is the attitude toward punctuality in social situations? In business situations?
- What are acceptable eye contact patterns?
- What gestures indicate agreement? Disagreement?

Family Life

- What is the basic unit of social organization? Basic family? Extended family?
- Do women work outside of the home? In what occupations?

Housing, Clothing, and Food

- Are there differences in the kinds of housing used by different social groups? Differences in location? Differences in furnishings?
- What occasions require special clothing?
- Are some types of clothing considered taboo?
- What is appropriate business attire for men? For women?
- How many times a day do people eat?
- What types of places, food, and drink are appropriate for business entertainment? Where is the seat of honor at a table?

Class Structure

- Into what classes is society organized?
- Do racial, religious, or economic factors determine social status?
- Are there any minority groups? What is their social standing?

Political Patterns

- Are there any immediate threats to the political survival of the country?
- How is political power manifested?
- What channels are used for expressing political opinions?
- What information media are important?
- Is it appropriate to talk politics in social situations?

Religion and Folk Beliefs

- To which religious groups do people belong? Is one predominant?
- Do religious beliefs influence daily activities?
- Which places are considered sacred? Which objects? Which events?
- How do religious holidays affect business activities?

Economic Institutions

- What are the country's principal products?
- Are workers organized in unions?
- How are businesses owned? By family units? By large public corporations? By the government?
- What is the standard work schedule?
- Is it appropriate to do business by telephone? By computer?
- How has technology affected business procedures?
- Is participatory management used?
- Are there any customs related to exchanging business cards?
- How is status shown in an organization? Private office? Secretary? Furniture?
- Are businesspeople expected to socialize before conducting business?

Value Systems

- Is competitiveness or cooperation more prized?
- Is thrift or enjoyment of the moment more valued?
- Is politeness more important than honesty?
- What are the attitudes toward education?
- Do women own or manage businesses? If so, how are they treated?
- What are your people's perceptions of Americans? Do Americans offend you? What has been hardest for you to adjust to in the United States? How could Americans make this adjustment easier for you?

10.9 Who Gets Hurt? Examining Infamous Plagiarism Scandals (L.O. 4)

> Team   > Web

Have you ever wondered who gets hurt when students, teachers, journalists, scientists, and other authors are dishonest researchers and writers? Occasionally we read about people who plagiarize their work, try to cheat their way through college, invent news features, copy from others, or fabricate research results.

Former British surgeon Andrew Wakefield published an article in the reputable medical journal *The Lancet* that seemed to provide evidence that a common immunization against measles, mumps, and rubella (MMR) could cause autism. Wakefield had fabricated evidence and was found guilty of professional misconduct. He lost his license to practice as a medical doctor. His fraudulent research, however, caused a precipitous drop in vaccinations in the United Kingdom and Ireland. In the words of one pediatrician, "That paper killed children."[12] Many American parents still refuse to vaccinate their kids and are causing the spread of diseases that had been eradicated in the United States.[13]

A Harvard researcher's purposely nonsensical research paper, consisting of randomly generated text accompanied by two fake authors, was accepted by 17 of 37 medical journals. Journals publishing such bogus research are called predatory publishers. A prominent bioethicist calls such practices "publication pollution."[14]

YOUR TASK. If your instructor directs, individually or as a team, investigate the cases of Andrew Wakefield, Joachim Boldt, Stephen Ambrose, Jayson Blair, Doris Kearns Goodwin, Jonah Lehrer, Kaavya Viswanathan, or other infamous plagiarists. Alternatively, you could focus on the case of 200 professors from 50 universities implicated in a massive publishing scam in South Korea.[15] Consider the authors' transgressions, their excuses, and the consequences of their actions. As a team, gather your individual research results, compare notes, and summarize your insights in a memo report to your instructor. This assignment could also be turned into a formal report if the investigation is expanded to include more detailed discussions and more cases.

10.10 Plagiarism, Paraphrasing, and Citing Sources (L.O. 4)

One of the biggest challenges for student writers is paraphrasing secondary sources correctly to avoid plagiarism.

YOUR TASK. For each of the following, read the original passage. Analyze the paraphrased version. List the weaknesses in relation to what you have learned about plagiarism and the use of references. Then write an improved version.

a. **Original Passage** When the Tesla Model S launched four years ago, the all-electric luxury sedan certainly had its critics. Many of them were executives at German luxury carmakers, quick to dismiss the upstart American carmaker as a quixotic but doomed effort. But as the Model S won plaudits, achieved respectable sales, and captured the public's imagination, that attitude has changed. And that was before Tesla racked up nearly 400,000 reservations for its Model 3 sedan, which is expected to compete with German mainstays like the Audi A4 and BMW 3-Series. Now, Audi, BMW, Mercedes-Benz, and Porsche are downright worried about Tesla. "Tesla has promised a lot but has also delivered most of it," Dieter Zetsche—chairman of Mercedes parent Daimler—said earlier this month.[16]

   Paraphrased Passage Upon the launch of its Model S, Tesla had many detractors; most were executives at German car companies selling luxury cars. They dismissed the new California-based carmaker as a doomed effort. That attitude has changed as the Model S won praise, racked up considerable sales, and impressed the general public. Most recently, Tesla secured 400,000 early reservations for its Model 3, which will compete with German luxury cars such as the Audi A4 and the BMW 3-Series. Now that Tesla has promised a lot but has also delivered most of it, said Daimler chairman Dieter Zetsche, the German carmakers Audi, Mercedes-Benz, Porsche, and BMW are pretty worried about Tesla.

b. **Original Passage** Lurking behind chartjunk is contempt both for the information and for the audience. Chartjunk promoters imagine that numbers and details are boring, dull, and tedious, requiring ornament to enliven. Cosmetic decoration, which frequently distorts the data, will never salvage an underlying lack of content. If the numbers are boring, then you've got the wrong numbers. Credibility vanishes in clouds of chartjunk; who would trust a chart that looks like a video game?[17]

   Paraphrased Passage Chartjunk creators hold the information they are conveying and their audience in contempt because they believe that statistical details are dull, unimaginative, and tedious and need to be spruced up with decorations. Purely ornamental design elements distort the data and cannot cover up a lack of content. If the statistics are boring, then they are the wrong statistics. Chartjunk kills credibility. Readers cannot trust a chart that looks like a video game.

c. **Original Passage** Developing casual online game titles can be much less risky than trying to create a game that runs on a console such as an Xbox. Casual games typically cost less than $200,000 to produce, and production cycles are only six months to a year. There's no shelf space, packaging, or CD production to pay for. Best of all, there's more room for innovation.[18]

   Paraphrased Passage The development of casual online games offers less risk than creating games running on Xbox and other consoles. Usually, casual games are cheaper, costing under $200,000 to create and 6 to 12 months to produce. Developers save on shelf space, packaging, and CD production too. Moreover, they have more freedom to innovate.

10.11 Selecting Graphics (L.O. 5)

YOUR TASK. Identify the best graphics forms to illustrate the following data.

a. Potential new residential development project
b. Annual restaurant industry sales figures
c. Government unemployment data by industry and sector, in percentages
d. Figures showing the distribution of the H3N2 strain of type A flu virus in humans by state
e. Figures showing the process of delivering water to a metropolitan area
f. Figures showing what proportion of every state tax dollar is spent on education, social services, transportation, debt, and other expenses
g. Academic, administrative, and operation divisions of a college, from the president to department chairs and division managers
h. Figures comparing the sales of smartphones, tablets, and laptops over the past five years

10.12 Evaluating Graphics (L.O. 5)

> E-Mail Web

YOUR TASK. Select four graphics from newspapers or magazines in hard copy or online. Look in *The Wall Street Journal, USA Today, Bloomberg Businessweek, U.S. News & World Report, Fortune, Forbes*, or other business news publications. Add the title and the source of each graphic. In an e-mail or memo to your instructor, critique each graphic based on what you have learned in this chapter. Do you think the graphic could have been expressed more effectively in text? How effective are the labels and headings used in this graphic? Did color add clarity? If used, describe the placement and effectiveness of a legend. Is the appropriate graphic form used? What is your overall impression of the effectiveness of the graphic?

10.13 Creating a Bar Chart and Writing a Title (L.O. 5)

> Web

YOUR TASK. Create a bar chart comparing the current number of Internet users (by millions) in the following eight countries: United States, India, Japan, Brazil, Indonesia, China, United Kingdom, and Russia. Find statistics within the last year and name the source of your information. Arrange the bars according to the country with the highest number of users to the lowest. Add a chart title and appropriate labels.

10.14 Formal Report: Comparing Before Buying (L.O. 2–6)

> Team Web

Study a consumer product that you or a business might consider buying. This might be a notebook or laptop, smartphone, digital camera, widescreen TV, espresso machine, car, combination print/scan/fax machine, powerful office printer, or some other product.

YOUR TASK. Use at least four primary and four secondary sources to research your product. Your primary research will be in the form of interviews with individuals (owners, users, salespeople, technicians) in a position to comment on attributes of your product. Secondary research will be in the form of print or electronic sources, such as magazine articles, marketing websites with user reviews, and company websites. Use electronic databases and the Web to find appropriate articles. Your report should analyze and discuss at least three comparable models or versions of the target product. Decide what criteria you will use to compare the models, such as price, features, warranty, and service. Create at least one original graphic to display report data. Include the following components in the report: table of contents, executive summary, introduction (including background, purpose, scope of the report, and research methods), findings (organized by comparison criteria), summary of findings, conclusions, recommendations, and bibliography. Address the report to your instructor. You may work individually, in pairs, or in teams.

10.15 Report Topics for Proposals and Formal Reports (L.O. 1–6)

> Team Web

A list of nearly 100 **Report Topics** is available at the Student Companion Website accessed at **www.cengagebrain.com**. The topics are divided into the following categories: accounting, finance, personnel/human resources, marketing, information systems, management, and general business/education/campus issues. You can collect information for many of these reports by searching the Internet. Your instructor may assign topics as individual or team projects. All involve research and critical thinking in organizing information, drawing conclusions, and making recommendations. The topics are appropriate for proposals and formal business reports.

YOUR TASK. As directed by your instructor, select a topic from the report list at **www.cengagebrain.com**.

Apostrophes

Review Sections 2.20–2.22 in the Grammar/Mechanics Handbook. In the space provided, write the letter of the correctly punctuated sentence. Also record the appropriate G/M guideline for the principle involved. When you finish, compare your responses with those provided at the bottom of the page. If your answers differ, study carefully the appropriate guideline.

_b_   (2.20b)   **EXAMPLE**   In just two (a) _years_, (b) _years'_ time, you could finish your degree.

_____ 1. Did you know that (a) Susan Campbell's, (b) Susan Campbells, (c) Susan Campbells' proposal was accepted?

_____ 2. The company plans to double its earnings in three (a) years, (b) year's, (c) years' time.

_____ 3. Everyone wondered how (a) Louis', (b) Louis's, (c) Louis laptop could have disappeared.

_____ 4. Professor (a) Sanchez's, (b) Sanchezes, (c) Sanchezes' quizzes always came on Fridays.

_____ 5. Several (a) employees', (b) employee's, (c) employees records were accidentally lost.

_____ 6. The last (a) witness's, (b) witnesses, (c) witness' testimony was the most convincing to the jury.

_____ 7. (a) Lisa, (b) Lisas', (c) Lisa's smoking led to health problems.

_____ 8. I always get my (a) moneys, (b) money's, (c) monies worth at my favorite restaurant.

_____ 9. Three local (a) companies, (b) company's, (c) companies' went out of business last month.

_____ 10. In one (a) months, (b) month's time we hope to have our new website up and running.

1. a (2.20a) 2. c (2.20b) 3. b (2.20b) 4. a (2.21) 5. a (2.21) 6. a (2.20b) 7. c (2.22) 8. b (2.20b) 9. a (2.20b) _companies_ is plural, not possessive) 10. b (2.20a)

320   Chapter 10: Proposals and Formal Reports

Every chapter provides an editing exercise to fine-tune your grammar and mechanics skills. The following executive summary requires edits that address spelling, grammar, punctuation, concise wording, and other issues. Study the guidelines in the Grammar/Mechanics Handbook (Appendix D), including the lists of Confusing Words and Frequently Misspelled Words.

YOUR TASK. Edit the following (a) by inserting corrections in your textbook or on a photocopy using proofreading marks in Appendix C or (b) by downloading the message from **www.cengagebrain.com** and correcting at your computer.

HOW PURE IS BOTTLED WATER?

EXECUTIVE SUMMARY

Problem

Because bottled water is widely considered to be a purer choice then tap water, bottled water has become a billion-dollar-a-year business in the United states. Millions of consumer's use bottled water as there primary source of drinking water. Although most bottled water is of good quality some bottled water contains bacterial contaminants. Reassurances from the water industrys executives that bottled water is totally safe may be false.

Summary of Findings

Commissioned by the National Resource's Defense Commission this report analyzes tests of bottled water. The tests revealed that most bottled water is not contaminated, however after testing more then 1,000 bottles, we found that about one fourth were contaminated at levels violating many states limits. Bottled water contaminated with microbes may raise public health issues, and todays consumers are rightfully concerned.

There are government bottled water regulations and programs that have serious deficiencys. Under the FDAs control, the regulation of most bottled water is left to ill-equipped and under staffed state governments. In spite of the fact that voluntary bottled water industry controls are commendable. They are an inadequate substitute for strong goverment rules. FDA officials has stated that bottled water regulation carries a low priority. In addition the marketing of bottled water can be misleading. However the long term solution to drinking water problems are to fix tap water rather than switching to bottled water.

Recommendations

Based on our tests and analysis we submit the following reccomendations:

1. Fix tap water quality so that consumers' will not resort to bottled water.
2. Establish the publics right to know about the contents of bottled water.
3. Require FDA inspections of all bottling facilities and there water sources.
4. Institute a penny per bottle fee to ensure bottled water safety.
5. Bottled water certification should be introduced.

Evaluating the Credibility of Web Documents: Let the Reader Beware

Evaluating a website's credibility requires critical thinking and a good eye. Savvy Web users start the evaluation process by thinking about how they found the site in the first place. They may have accessed the site from the results page of a search engine or by following a link from a reputable site. Perhaps the site was recommended by a friend, which would add credibility. The processes for finding Web information may vary, but the reader alone is responsible for determining the validity, truthfulness, and integrity of that information. Because anyone with a computer and an Internet connection can publish on the Web, the reader must beware and wisely question all Web content.

Unlike the content of journals, magazines, and newspapers found in research-oriented libraries, the content of most websites has not been reviewed by skilled editors. Some Web pages do not show authorship, credentials, or sponsoring organizations. The content cannot be verified. These sites have low credibility.

As a frequent Web user, you must learn to critically examine Web information for credibility. The following checklist of questions about authorship, publisher or sponsor, currency, content quality, and accuracy and organization will help you critically assess the validity of Web information.

Authorship

- Who authored this page or article?
- Are the author's credentials easily found? If not, check the author's credentials online.
- Is the author affiliated with a reputable organization?
- Is the author's contact information, such as an e-mail address, easily found?
- Are the About page and the Contact page easy to spot?

Publisher or Sponsor

- What organization publishes or sponsors this Web page? Is the publisher reputable?
- What domain is used in the URL? The domain name gives clues about who published the document (e.g., .com, .org, .edu, .gov, .net).
- Is the site published or sponsored in another country? Look for a two-letter code in the URL: .uk, .au, .br, .hu, .mx, .ca, .in.

Currency

- When was the Web page published or last updated? Readers expect this information at the bottom of the page.
- Is this a website that requires current, updated information (e.g., science, medicine, current events)?

- Are all links on this Web page current and working? Broken links are red flags.

Content Quality

- What is the purpose of the Web page? For example, does the page entertain, inform, persuade, sell, or express satire?
- Who is the intended audience of the page, based on its content, tone, and style?
- Do you see evidence of bias, and does the author acknowledge the bias?
- Does the site link to other reputable sites? Do those sites in turn link back to the site in question?
- Does the page contain distracting graphics or fill the screen with unwanted ads and pop-ups?

Accuracy and Organization

- Does the information appear to be well researched?
- If the site contains statistics and facts, are sources, dates, and/or citations provided?
- Is the information well organized with main points clearly presented?
- Is the site well designed and easy to navigate? Good design adds credibility.
- Does the page have broken links or graphics that don't load?
- Are the graphics appropriately placed and clearly labeled?
- Does the site have spelling, grammar, or usage errors? Careless errors are red flags.

CAREER APPLICATION. As interns in a news-gathering service, you have been asked to assess the quality of the following websites. Think about whether you would recommend these sites as trustworthy sources of information.

- Beef Nutrition (**http://www.beefnutrition.org**)
- Edmunds (**http://www.edmunds.com**)
- EarthSave (**http://www.earthsave.org**)
- The White House (**http://www.whitehouse.net**)
- The White House (**http://www.whitehouse.gov**)
- The Anaheim White House Restaurant (**http://www.anaheimwhitehouse.com**)
- National Anti-Vivisection Society (**http://www.navs.org**)
- PETA (**http://www.peta.org**)
- WebMD (**http://www.webmd.com**)
- Petrol Direct (**http://www.petroldirect.com**)
- Smithsonian (**http://www.si.edu**)
- Hootsuite (**https://hootsuite.com**)

- Bureau of Sasquatch Affairs (**http://zapatopi.net/bsa**)
- Mint (**https://www.mint.com**)
- DHMO.org (**http://www.dhmo.org**)
- Lonely Planet (**http://www.lonelyplanet.com**)
- Drudge Report (**http://www.drudgereport.com**)
- American Cancer Society (**http://www.cancer.org**)
- The Onion (**http://www.theonion.com**)
- Pacific Northwest Tree Octopus (**http://zapatopi.net/treeoctopus**)

YOUR TASK. If you decide to use teams, divide the preceding list among team members. If you are working individually, select four of the sites. Analyze each site using the checklist of questions in each category. Then summarize your evaluation of each site in a memo or e-mail report addressed to your boss (your instructor). Your report may also become part of a team presentation or a class discussion. Add a comment about whether you would recommend this site for researchers of news articles. Be careful—even a hoax site can seem reputable and trustworthy at first glance. Be careful not to label sites as good or bad. Even biased sites may have large audiences and some merit.

Professionalism, Teamwork, Meetings, and Speaking Skills

Chapter 11
Professionalism at Work: Business Etiquette, Ethics, Teamwork, and Meetings

Chapter 12
Business Presentations

Pla2na/Shutterstock.com

LuckyImages/Shutterstock.com

Professionalism at Work: Business Etiquette, Ethics, Teamwork, and Meetings

Kzenon/Shutterstock.com

Learning Outcomes

After studying this chapter, you should be able to do the following:

1 Build your credibility and gain a competitive advantage by developing professionalism, an ethical mind-set, and business etiquette skills.

2 Use your voice as a communication tool, master face-to-face workplace interaction, foster positive relations on the job, and accept as well as provide constructive criticism gracefully.

3 Practice professional telephone skills and polish your voice mail etiquette.

4 Understand the importance of teamwork in the digital era workplace, and explain how you can contribute positively to team performance.

5 Discuss effective practices and technologies for planning and participating in productive face-to-face meetings and virtual meetings.

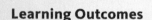

11-1 Developing Professionalism and Business Etiquette Skills at the Office and Online

As you have seen in Chapter 1, soft skills are the hallmark of a professional. Often cited when soft skills are discussed, a businesslike, professional demeanor and good manners are among the top skills recruiters seek in applicants. Employers prefer professional and courteous job candidates over those who lack these skills and traits.

Business etiquette is more about attitude than about formal rules of behavior. This attitude is a desire to show others consideration and respect. It includes a desire to make others feel comfortable. Sometimes called *employability skills* or *key competencies*, these soft skills are desirable in all business sectors and job positions.[1]

Can you learn how to be professional, civil, and courteous? Of course! This section gives you a few pointers. Next, you will be asked to consider the link between professional and ethical behavior on the job. Finally, by protecting your reputation offline and online, you can become the kind of professional that recruiters are looking to hire.

11-1a Understanding Professionalism and the Cost of Incivility

What exactly is professionalism? The term *professionalism* and its synonyms, such as *business etiquette* or *business protocol, soft skills, social intelligence, polish*, and *civility*, all have one element in common. They describe *desirable workplace behavior*. Businesses have an interest in employees who get along and deliver positive results that enhance profits and boost the company's image. In the digital age, professionalism also means maintaining *personal credibility* and a *positive online presence*, a subject we discussed in Chapters 1 and 5 and will revisit in Unit 6, Employment Communication.

As workloads increase and face-to-face meetings decline, bad behavior is becoming alarmingly common in the American workplace.[2] One survey of 20,000 employees showed that 54 percent don't feel respected by their leaders. However, those who do feel respected reported 92 percent more focus, 56 percent better health, and 55 percent more engagement.[3] Rude behavior affects thinking skills and helpfulness; in short, workers' performance suffers.[4] These embattled workers worry about incidents, think about changing jobs, and cut back their efforts on the job. Employers, of course, suffer from the resulting drop in productivity and exodus of talent. Workplace rudeness also turns customers away.[5]

Not surprisingly, businesses are responding to increasing incidents of *desk rage* and *cyberbullying* in American workplaces. Many organizations have established protocol procedures or policies to enforce civility. Following are a few traits and skills that define professional behavior to foster positive workplace relations.

Civility. Management professor Christine Porath, who has studied workplace behavior for two decades, defines rising incivility at work as "any rude, disrespectful or insensitive behavior that people feel runs counter to the norms of their workplace."[6] The need to combat uncivil behavior gave rise to several nonprofit organizations: The Civility Initiative at Johns Hopkins University defines its mission as "assessing and promoting the significance of civility, manners, and politeness in contemporary society."[7] The Institute for Civility in Government was founded in response to a heated, polarized political climate in the United States, and the Civility Institute in Canada conducts research in social psychology and wishes to "encourage a broad discussion of civility and its complex and powerful role in human relations."[8]

Polish. You may hear businesspeople refer to someone as being *polished* or displaying *polish* when dealing with others. In her book with the telling title *Buff and Polish: A Practical Guide to Enhance Your Professional Image and Communication Style*, corporate trainer Kathryn J. Volin explains that polish includes making first impressions, shaking hands, improving one's voice quality, listening, presenting well, and more.

A more recent mentoring book, *Polished*, by Calvin Purnell Jr., addresses, among other things, appearance, character, and focus but also keeping one's digital footprint clean. You will find pointers on developing many of these valuable traits of a polished business professional in this textbook and also in the Communication Workshop at the end of this chapter.

Business and Dining Etiquette. Proper business attire, dining etiquette, and other aspects of your professional presentation can make or break your interview. Even a seemingly harmless act such as sharing a business meal can have a huge impact on your career. In the words of a Fortune 500 executive, "Eating is not an executive skill . . . but it is especially hard to imagine why anyone negotiating a rise to the top would consider it possible to skip mastering the very simple requirements . . . what else did they skip learning?"[10] Business meals are almost always strategic; your dining partner may want to see how you treat the waitstaff and whether you might embarrass yourself during client visits. "Etiquette is thinking about the other people you're with," says etiquette consultant Dennis Cornell. "It's about respecting them."[11] In short, you will be judged on more than your college-bred expertise.

Social Intelligence. Occasionally you may encounter the expression *social intelligence*. In the words of one of its modern proponents, it is "the ability to get along well with others and to get them to cooperate with you."[12] Social intelligence points to a deep understanding of culture and life that helps us negotiate interpersonal

OFFICE INSIDER

"Live the reputation you want to see online. These days, everything you do or say, even in a moment of weakness or in private, ends up online. It's impossible to live one life and project another, so remember your current or future business before posting that provocative picture on Facebook. The Internet sees the good, the bad and the ugly."[9]

Martin Zwilling, *start-up mentor, angel investor*

and social situations. This type of intelligence can be much harder to acquire than simple etiquette. Social intelligence requires us to interact well, be perceptive, show sensitivity toward others, and grasp a situation quickly and accurately.

Soft Skills. Perhaps the most common definition of important interpersonal habits is *soft skills,* as opposed to *hard skills,* a term for the technical knowledge in your field. In a survey of managers, more than 60 percent cited soft skills as the most important factor in evaluating an employee's on-the-job performance, followed by hard skills (32 percent) and social media skills (7 percent). The top three soft skills on the managers' wish list were the ability to prioritize work, a positive attitude, and teamwork skills.[13] A CareerBuilder survey revealed that the top three most desirable soft skills in job candidates were a strong work ethic, dependability, and a positive attitude.[14]

Employers want managers and employees who are comfortable with diverse coworkers, listen actively to customers and colleagues, make eye contact, and display good workplace manners. Your long-term success depends on how well you communicate with your boss, coworkers, and customers and whether you can be an effective and contributing team member.

Simply put, all these attempts to explain proper behavior at work aim at identifying traits that make someone a good employee and a compatible coworker. You will want to achieve a positive image on the job and online to maintain a solid reputation. For the sake of simplicity, in the discussion that follows, the terms *professionalism, business etiquette,* and *soft skills* are used largely as synonyms.

11-1b Relating Professional Behavior to Ethics

A broad definition of professionalism also encompasses another crucial quality in a businessperson: *ethics,* or *integrity.* You may have a negative view of business after learning of corporate scandals swirling around well-established businesses such as Wells Fargo, Volkswagen, GM, or Mylan, maker of the Epipen. However, for every company that captures the limelight for misconduct, hundreds or even thousands of others operate honestly and serve their customers and the public well. The overwhelming majority of businesses wish to recruit ethical and polished graduates.

The difference between ethics and etiquette is minimal in the workplace. Ethics professor Douglas Chismar—and Harvard professor Stephen L. Carter before him—suggests that no sharp distinction between ethics and etiquette exists. How we approach the seemingly trivial events of work life reflects our character and attitudes when we handle larger issues. Our conduct should be consistently ethical and professional. Professor Chismar believes that "we each have a moral obligation to treat each other with respect and sensitivity every day."[16] He calls on all of us to make a difference in the quality of life, morale, and productivity at work.

Figure 11.1 summarizes the many components of professional workplace behavior[17] and identifies six main dimensions that will ease your entry into the world of work.

11-1c Gaining an Etiquette Edge in a Networked World

An awareness of courtesy and etiquette can give you a competitive edge in the job market. Etiquette, civility, and goodwill efforts may seem out of place in today's fast-paced offices. However, when two candidates have equal qualifications, the one who appears to be more polished and professional is more likely to be hired and promoted.

In the networked professional environment of the digital era, you must manage and guard your reputation—at the office and online. How you present yourself in the virtual world, meaning how well you communicate and protect your brand, may very well determine how successful your career will be. Thoughtful blog posts, astute comments on LinkedIn and Facebook, as well as competent e-mails will enhance your credibility and show your professionalism.

From meetings and interviews to company parties and golf outings, nearly all workplace-related activities involve etiquette. Take Your Dog to Work Day, the ever-popular morale booster that keeps workers chained to their pets instead of the desk, has a unique set of guidelines to help maximize fun. For employees at the nearly one in five U.S. businesses that allow dogs at work, etiquette gurus say pets must be well behaved, housebroken, and free of fleas to participate in the four-legged festivity. Before bringing a dog to the office, check with immediate neighbors to see if any are allergic to dogs. Remember, too, that dogs must be not be allowed to wander around

freely. At Amazon, dogs are required to be on-leash except when they're in an office with the door closed or behind a baby gate. Why is it important to follow proper business etiquette?

Figure 11.1 The Six Dimensions of Professional Behavior

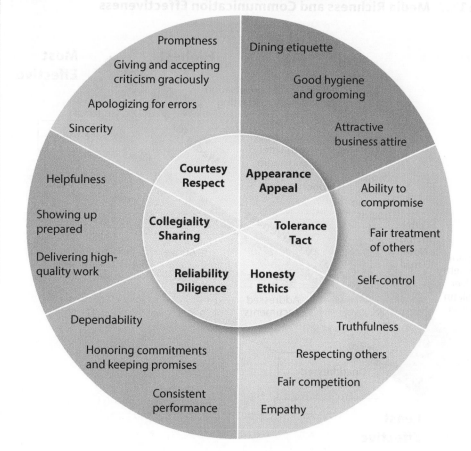

Courtesy Respect
- Promptness
- Giving and accepting criticism graciously
- Apologizing for errors
- Sincerity

Appearance Appeal
- Dining etiquette
- Good hygiene and grooming
- Attractive business attire

Collegiality Sharing
- Helpfulness
- Showing up prepared
- Delivering high-quality work

Tolerance Tact
- Ability to compromise
- Fair treatment of others
- Self-control

Reliability Diligence
- Dependability
- Honoring commitments and keeping promises
- Consistent performance

Honesty Ethics
- Truthfulness
- Respecting others
- Fair competition
- Empathy

OFFICE INSIDER

"Unprofessional conduct around the office will eventually overflow into official duties. Few of us have mastered the rare art of maintaining multiple personalities."[18]

Douglas Chismar, *liberal arts program director at Ringling College of Art and Design*

This chapter focuses on developing interpersonal skills, telephone and voice mail etiquette, teamwork proficiency, and meeting management skills. These are some of the soft skills employers seek in the hyperconnected competitive work environments of the digital age.

11-2 Communicating Face-to-Face on the Job

You have learned that e-mail is the preferred communication channel at work because it is faster, cheaper, and easier than telephone, mail, or fax. You also know that businesspeople have embraced instant messaging, texting, and social media. However, despite its popularity and acceptance, communication technology can't replace the richness or effectiveness of face-to-face communication if you wish to build or maintain a business relationship.[19] Imagine that you want to tell your boss how you solved a problem. Would you settle for a one-dimensional phone call, a text message, or an e-mail when you could step into her office and explain in person?

Face-to-face conversation has many advantages. It is the richest communication channel because you can use your voice and body language to make a point, convey warmth, and build rapport. You are less likely to be misunderstood because you can read feedback and make needed adjustments. In conflict resolution, you can reach a solution with fewer misunderstandings and cooperate to create greater levels of mutual benefit when communicating face-to-face.[20] Communicating in person remains the most effective of all communication channels, as you can see in Figure 11.2.

Figure 11.2 Media Richness and Communication Effectiveness

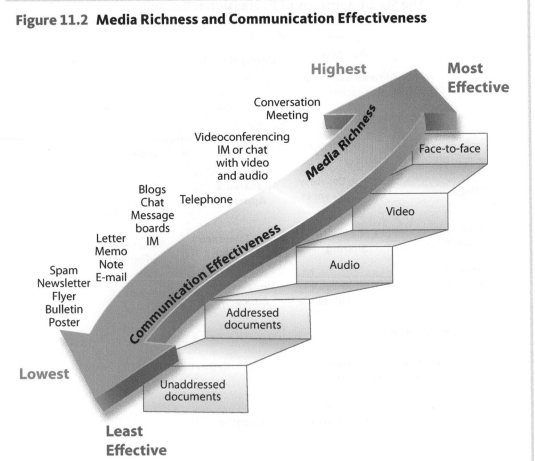

In this section you will explore professional interpersonal speaking techniques, starting with viewing your voice as a communication tool.

11-2a Using Your Voice as a Communication Tool

Studies suggest a strong correlation between voice and perceived authority and trust. Respondents typically favor lower-pitched voices in men and higher but not shrill female voices.[22] A voice carries so much nonverbal meaning that celebrities, actors, business executives, and others consult coaches and speech therapists to help them shake bad habits or avoid sounding less intelligent than they are. You too can pick up valuable tips for using your voice most effectively by learning how to control your pronunciation, voice quality, pitch, volume, rate, and emphasis.

Pronunciation. Proper pronunciation involves saying words correctly and clearly with the accepted sounds and accented syllables. You will have a distinct advantage in your job if you pronounce words correctly. How can you improve your pronunciation? The best ways are to listen carefully to educated people, to look words up in the dictionary, and to practice. Many online dictionaries provide audio files so you can hear words pronounced correctly.

Voice Quality. The quality of your voice sends a nonverbal message to listeners. It identifies your personality and your mood. Some voices sound enthusiastic and friendly, conveying the impression of an upbeat person who is happy to be with the listener. However, voices can also sound controlling, patronizing, slow-witted, angry, bored, or childish. This does not mean that the speaker necessarily has that attribute. It may mean that the speaker is merely carrying on a family tradition or pattern learned in childhood. To check your voice quality, record your voice and listen to it critically. Is it projecting a positive quality about you? Do you sound professional?

Young women in particular have been criticized for vocal fry, a creaky, raspy sound at the end of drawn-out sentences, but this speech habit occurs in men, too, and is generally perceived more favorably, suggesting gender bias. Negative perceptions of vocal fry appear to be generational.[23] If you want to impress an older recruiter, avoid this affectation.

Pitch. Effective speakers use a relaxed, controlled, well-pitched voice to attract listeners to their message. *Pitch* refers to sound vibration frequency; that is, the highness or lowness of a sound. Voices are most engaging when they rise and fall in conversational tones. Flat, monotone voices are considered boring and ineffectual.

Volume and Rate. The volume of your voice is the loudness or the intensity of sound. Just as you adjust the volume on your MP3 player or television set, you should adjust the volume of your speaking to the occasion and your listeners. *Rate* refers to the pace of your speech. If you speak too slowly, listeners can become bored and their attention can wander. If you speak too quickly, listeners may not be able to understand you. Most people normally talk at about 125 words a minute. Monitor the nonverbal signs of your listeners and adjust your volume and rate as needed.

Emphasis and Verbal Tics. By emphasizing or stressing certain words, you can change the meaning you are expressing. To make your message interesting and natural, use emphasis appropriately. Some speakers today are prone to *uptalk*. This is a habit of using a

How well you handle workplace conversations helps determine your career success.

Stockbyte/Getty Images

rising inflection at the end of a sentence resulting in a singsong pattern that makes statements sound like questions. Uptalk makes speakers seem weak and tentative. Their messages lack authority. On the job, managers wishing to sound confident and competent avoid uptalk. Moreover, employees don't realize that they are sabotaging their careers when they sprinkle their conversation with annoying fillers such as *like, you know, actually,* and *basically.*

11-2b Making Workplace Conversation Matter

Face-to-face conversation helps people work together harmoniously and feel that they are part of the larger organization. Workplace conversations may involve giving and taking instructions, providing feedback, exchanging ideas, brainstorming, participating in performance appraisals, or engaging in small talk about such things as families and sports. Following are several business etiquette guidelines that promote positive workplace conversations, both in the office and at work-related social functions.

Use Correct Names and Titles. Although the world seems increasingly informal, it is still wise to use titles and last names when addressing professional adults (*Ms. Grady, Mr. Schiano*). In some organizations senior staff members speak to junior employees on a first-name basis, but the reverse may not be encouraged. Probably the safest plan is to ask your supervisors how they want to be addressed. Customers and others outside the organization should always be addressed initially by title and last name. Wait for an invitation to use first names.

When you meet strangers, do you have trouble remembering their names? You can improve your memory considerably if you associate the person with an object, place, color, animal, job, adjective, or some other memory hook. For example, *technology pro Chiara, L.A. Steven, silver-haired Mr. Huber, baseball fan Greg, programmer Tori, traveler Ms. Rhee.* The person's name will also be more deeply imbedded in your memory if you use it immediately after being introduced, in subsequent conversation, and when you part.

Choose Appropriate Topics. In some workplace activities, such as social gatherings and interviews, you will be expected to engage in small talk. Stay away from controversial topics. Avoid politics, religion, and controversial current events that can trigger heated arguments. To initiate appropriate conversations, follow news sites such as CNN, NPR, the BBC, Google News, and major newspapers online. Subscribe to e-newsletters that deliver relevant news to you via e-mail. Listen to reputable radio and TV shows discussing current events. Try not to be defensive or annoyed if others present information that upsets you.

Watch out for dubious websites and be skeptical of news items on Facebook as too many have been shown to be planted, fake stories. Check several trustworthy publications or media outlets to evaluate the veracity of a news story. Be particularly wary of unverified Twitter posts.

Avoid Negative Remarks. Workplace conversations are not the place to complain about your colleagues, your friends, the organization, or your job. No one enjoys listening to whiners. What's more, your criticism of others may come back to haunt you. A snipe at your boss or a complaint about a coworker may reach him or her, sometimes embellished or distorted with meanings you did not intend. Be circumspect in all negative judgments. It goes without saying that workplace grievances should never be posted online.

Listen to Learn. In conversations with managers, colleagues, subordinates, and customers, train yourself to expect to learn something. Being attentive is not only instructive but also courteous. Being receptive and listening with an open mind means not

Active listening is an important, yet underused workplace skill.

Elena Elisseeva/Shutterstock.com

interrupting or prejudging. Let's say you wish to work at home for part of your workweek. You try to explain your idea to your boss, but he cuts you off, saying, *It is out of the question; we need you here every day.* Suppose instead he had said, *I have strong reservations about your telecommuting, but maybe you will change my mind,* and then settles in to listen to your presentation. In this case, even if your boss refuses your request, you will feel that your ideas were heard.

Give Sincere and Specific Praise. The Greek philosopher Xenophon once said, "The sweetest of all sounds is praise." Probably nothing promotes positive workplace relationships better than sincere and specific praise. Whether the compliments and appreciation are traveling upward to management, downward to workers, or horizontally to colleagues, everyone responds well to recognition. Organizations run more smoothly and morale is higher when people feel appreciated. In your workplace conversations, look for ways to recognize good work and good people. Try to be specific. Instead of *You did a great job in running that meeting,* say something more specific, such as *Your excellent leadership skills certainly kept that meeting short, focused, and productive.*

Act Professionally in Social Situations. You will likely attend many work-related social functions during your career, including dinners, picnics, holiday parties, and other events. It is important to remember that your actions at these events can help or harm your career. Dress appropriately, and avoid or limit alcohol consumption. Choose appropriate conversation topics, and make sure that your voice and mannerisms communicate that you are glad to be there.

11-2c Receiving Workplace Criticism Gracefully

Most of us hate giving criticism, but we dislike receiving it even more. However, giving and receiving criticism on the job is normal. The criticism may be given informally—for example, during a casual conversation with a supervisor or coworker. Sometimes the criticism is given formally—for example, during a performance evaluation. You need to accept and respond professionally when receiving criticism.

When being criticized, you may feel that you are being attacked. Your heart beats faster, your temperature shoots up, your face reddens, and you respond with the classic fight-or-flight reflex. You want to instantly retaliate or escape from the attacker. However, focusing on your feelings distracts you from hearing what is being said and prevents you from responding professionally. The following suggestions can help you respond positively to criticism so that you can benefit from it:

- **Listen without interrupting.** Even though you might want to protest, hear the speaker out.
- **Determine the speaker's intent.** Unskilled communicators may throw verbal bricks with unintended negative-sounding expressions. If you think the intent is positive, focus on what is being said rather than reacting to poorly chosen words.
- **Acknowledge what you are hearing.** Respond with a pause, a nod, or a neutral statement such as *I understand you have a concern.* This buys you time. Don't disagree, counterattack, or blame, which may escalate the situation and harden the speaker's position.
- **Paraphrase what was said.** In your own words, restate objectively what you are hearing.
- **Ask for more information if necessary.** Clarify what is being said. Stay focused on the main idea rather than interjecting side issues.

- **Agree—if the comments are accurate.** If an apology is in order, give it. Explain what you plan to do differently. If the criticism is on target, the sooner you agree, the more likely you will be to receive respect from the other person.

- **Disagree respectfully and constructively—if you feel the comments are unfair.** After hearing the criticism, you might say, *May I tell you my perspective?* Alternatively, you could say, *How can we improve this situation in a way you believe we can both accept?* If the other person continues to criticize, say, *I want to find a way to resolve your concern. When do you want to talk about it next?*

- **Look for a middle position.** Search for a middle position or a compromise. Be genial even if you don't like the person or the situation.

- **Learn from criticism.** Most work-related criticism is given with the best of intentions. You should welcome the opportunity to correct your mistakes and to learn from them. Responding positively to workplace criticism can help you improve your job performance. In the words of a career coach, if you make a mistake on the job, "own it and hone it."[24] Learn from it.

11-2d Providing Constructive Criticism on the Job

Today's workplace often involves team projects. As a team member, you will be called on to judge the work of others. In addition to working on teams, you can also expect to become a supervisor or manager one day. As such, you will need to evaluate subordinates. Good employees want and need timely, detailed observations about their work to reinforce what they do well and help them overcome weak spots. However, making that feedback constructive is not always easy. Depending on your situation, you may find the following suggestions helpful:

- **Mentally outline your conversation.** Think carefully about what you want to accomplish and what you will say. Find the right words and deliver them at the right time and in the right setting.

- **Generally, use face-to-face communication.** Most constructive criticism is best delivered in person. Personal feedback offers an opportunity for the listener to ask questions and give explanations. Occasionally, however, complex situations may require a different strategy. You might write out your opinions and deliver them by telephone or in writing. A written document enables you to organize your thoughts, include all the details, and be sure of keeping your cool. Remember, though, that written documents create permanent records—for better or worse.

- **Focus on improvement.** Instead of attacking, use language that offers alternative behavior. Use phrases such as *Next time, you could. ...*

- **Offer to help.** Criticism is accepted more readily if you volunteer to help eliminate or solve the problem.

- **Be specific.** Instead of a vague assertion such as *Your work is often late*, be more specific: *The specs on the Riverside job were due Thursday at 5 p.m., and you didn't hand them in until Friday.* Explain how the person's performance jeopardized the entire project.

- **Avoid broad generalizations.** Don't use words such as *should, never, always,* and other sweeping expressions because they may cause the listener to shut down and become defensive.

- **Discuss the behavior, not the person.** Instead of *You seem to think you can come to work anytime you want*, focus on the behavior: *Coming to work late means that we have to fill in with someone else until you arrive.*

- **Use the word *we* rather than *you*.** Saying *We need to meet project deadlines* is better than saying *You need to meet project deadlines.* Emphasize organizational expectations rather than personal ones. Avoid sounding accusatory.

- **Encourage two-way communication.** Even if well planned, criticism is hard to deliver. It may hurt the feelings of the employee. Consider ending your message like this: *It can be hard to hear this type of feedback. If you would like to share your thoughts, I'm listening.*

- **Avoid anger, sarcasm, and a raised voice.** Criticism is rarely constructive when tempers flare. Plan in advance what you will say and deliver it in low, controlled, and sincere tones.

- **Keep it private.** Offer praise in public; offer criticism in private. "Setting an example" through public criticism is never a wise management policy, as AOL CEO Tim Armstrong learned after brutally firing a worker in front of more than 1,000 Patch news network employees.

When giving or receiving criticism at work, stay calm. Plan what you will say. Keep criticism factual and deliver it in a low, controlled voice.

11-3 Following Professional Telephone and Voice Mail Etiquette

LEARNING OUTCOME 3

Practice professional telephone skills and polish your voice mail etiquette.

Presenting yourself well on the telephone is a skill that is still very important in today's workplace. Despite the heavy reliance on e-mail, in certain situations calling may be the most efficient channel of communication, whether mobile or on your office line. Business communication experts advise workers to pick up the phone when they have a lot of information to convey or when the topic is sensitive. In these cases a quick call is a lot more efficient than e-mailing back and forth.[25] As a business communicator, you can be more productive, efficient, and professional by following some simple suggestions. This section focuses on telephone etiquette and voice mail techniques.

11-3a Making Telephone Calls Professionally

Before making a telephone call, decide whether the intended call is really necessary. Could you find the information yourself? If you wait a while, will the problem resolve itself? Perhaps your message could be delivered more efficiently by some other means. Some companies have found that telephone calls are often less important than the work they interrupt. Alternatives to phone calls include instant messaging, texting, e-mail, memos, and calls to automated voice mail systems. If you must make a telephone call, consider using the following suggestions to make it productive:

- **Plan a mini-agenda.** Have you ever been embarrassed when you had to make a second telephone call because you forgot an important item the first time? Before calling, jot down notes regarding all the topics you need to discuss.

- **Use a three-point introduction.** When placing a call, immediately (a) name the person you are calling, (b) identify yourself and your affiliation, and (c) give a brief explanation of your reason for calling. For example: *May I speak to Larry Lopez? This is Hillary Dahl of Sebastian Enterprises, and I'm seeking information about a software program called ZoneAlarm Internet Security.* This kind of introduction enables the receiving individual to respond immediately without asking further questions.

- **Be brisk if you are rushed.** For business calls when your time is limited, avoid questions such as *How are you?* Instead, say, *Lisa, I knew you would be the only one who could answer these two questions for me.* Another efficient strategy is to set a contract with the caller: *Look, Lisa, I have only ten minutes, but I really wanted to get back to you.*

OFFICE INSIDER

"The truth is, while it certainly isn't rocket science, proper telephone etiquette in a work environment involves a bit more than the ability to utter a greeting. Since it may be your initial point of contact with a client, customer or even your employer, it is your opportunity to make a good first impression."[26]

Dawn Rosenberg McKay, *career planning professional*

- **Be cheerful and accurate.** Let your voice show the same kind of animation that you radiate when you greet people in person. Try to envision the individual answering the telephone. A smile can affect the tone of your voice, so smile at that person. Speak with an enthusiastic, attentive, and respectful tone. Moreover, be accurate about what you say. *Hang on a second; I will be right back* rarely is true. It is better to say, *It may take me two or three minutes to get that information.*

- **Be professional and courteous.** Remember that you are representing yourself and your company when you make phone calls. Use professional vocabulary and courteous language. Say *thank you* and *please* during your conversations. Don't eat, drink, or chew gum while talking on the phone. Articulate your words clearly. Avoid doing other work during the phone call so that you can focus entirely on the conversation.

- **End the call politely.** The responsibility for ending a call lies with the caller. This is sometimes difficult to do if the other person rambles on. You may need to use the following tactful cues: (a) *I have enjoyed talking with you;* (b) *I have learned what I needed to know, and now I can proceed with my work;* (c) *Thanks for your help;* (d) *I must go now, but may I call you again if I need . . .?;* or (e) *Should we talk again in a few weeks?*

- **Avoid telephone tag.** If you can't reach someone, ask when it would be best to call again. State that you will call at a specific time—and do it. If you ask a person to call you, give a time when you can be reached.

- **Leave complete voice mail messages.** Always enunciate clearly and speak slowly when leaving your telephone number or spelling your name. Provide a complete message, including your name, telephone number, and the time and date of your call. Briefly explain your purpose so that the receiver can be ready with the required information when returning your call.

11-3b Receiving Telephone Calls Professionally

With a little forethought, you can project a professional image and make your telephone a productive tool in your communication tool belt.[27] Developing good telephone manners and techniques, such as the following, will also reflect well on you and your organization.

- **Answer promptly and courteously.** Try to answer the phone on the first or second ring if possible. Smile as you pick up the phone.

- **Identify yourself immediately.** In answering your telephone or someone else's, provide your name, title or affiliation, and a greeting. For example, *Larry Lopez, Digital Imaging Corporation. How may I help you?* Force yourself to speak clearly and slowly. The caller may be unfamiliar with what you are saying and fail to recognize slurred syllables.

- **Be responsive and helpful.** If you are in a support role, be sympathetic to callers' needs. Instead of *I don't know,* try *That is a good question; let me investigate.* Instead of *We can't do that,* try *That is a tough one; let's see what we can do.* Avoid *No* at the beginning of a sentence. It sounds harsh because it suggests rejection.

- **Practice telephone confidentiality.** When answering calls for others, be courteous and helpful, but don't give out confidential information. It is better to say, *She is away from her desk* or *He is out of the office* than to report a colleague's exact whereabouts. Also be tight-lipped about sharing company information with strangers.

- **Take messages carefully.** Few things are as frustrating as receiving a potentially important phone message that is illegible. Repeat the spelling of names and verify telephone numbers. Write messages legibly and record their time and date.

- **Leave the line respectfully.** If you must put a call on hold, let the caller know and give an estimate of how long you expect the call to be on hold. Give the caller the option of holding. *Say, Would you prefer to hold, or would you like me to call you back?* If the caller is on hold for a long period of time, check back periodically.

- **Explain what you are doing when transferring calls.** Give a reason for transferring, and identify the extension to which you are directing the call in case the caller is disconnected.

11-3c Using Smartphones for Business

The smartphone has become an essential part of communication in the workplace. The number of U.S. cell phone users has by far outpaced the number of landline telephone users, and the number of people using mobile electronic devices and tablet computers keeps growing.[28] Approximately 92 percent of Americans now own a cell phone, 68 percent of U.S. adults have a smartphone,[29] and almost half of wireless customers live without landlines.[30]

Constant connectivity is posing new challenges in social settings and is perceived as distracting to group dynamics, a Pew study found.[31] However, people's views on acceptable cell phone use vary. More than three quarters don't object to using a cell phone while walking down the street, on public transport, and when waiting in line. Even in restaurants, smartphone use is acceptable to 38 percent. However, respondents strongly condemned cell phone use during meetings, in movie theaters, and in places of worship.

Because so many people depend on their mobile devices, it is important to understand proper use and etiquette. Most of us have experienced thoughtless and rude cell phone behavior. Researchers say that the rampant use of mobile electronic devices has increased workplace incivility. Most employees consider texting and compulsive e-mail checking while working and during meetings disruptive, even insulting. To avoid offending, smart business communicators practice cell phone etiquette, as outlined in Figure 11.3.

11-3d Making the Best Use of Voice Mail

Because telephone calls can be disruptive, most businesspeople are making extensive use of voice mail to screen incoming calls. Incoming information is delivered without interrupting potential receivers and without all the niceties that most two-way conversations require. Voice mail also eliminates telephone tag, inaccurate message taking, and time zone barriers. Both receivers and callers can use etiquette guidelines to make voice mail work most effectively for them.

On the Receiver's End. Your voice mail should project professionalism and provide an easy way for your callers to leave messages for you. Here are some voice mail etiquette tips:

- **Don't overuse voice mail.** Don't use voice mail to avoid taking phone calls. Individuals who screen all incoming calls cause irritation, resentment, and

Figure 11.3 Professional Cell Phone Use

Show courtesy

- Don't force others to hear your business.
- Don't make or receive calls in public places, such as post offices, banks, retail stores, trains, and buses.
- Don't allow your phone to ring in theaters, restaurants, museums, classrooms, and meetings.
- Apologize for occasional cell phone blunders.

Keep it down

- Speak in low, conversational tones. Cell phone microphones are sensitive, making it unnecessary to raise your voice.
- Choose a professional ringtone and set it on low or vibrate.

Step outside

- If a call is urgent, step outside to avoid being disruptive.
- Make full use of caller ID to screen incoming calls. Let voice mail take routine calls.

Drive now, talk and text later

- Talking while driving increases accidents almost fourfold, about the same as driving intoxicated.
- Texting while driving is even more dangerous. Don't do it!

needless follow-up calls. It is better to answer calls yourself than to let voice mail messages build up.

- **Prepare a professional, concise, friendly greeting.** Make your voice mail greeting sound warm and inviting, both in tone and content. Your greeting should be in your own voice, not a computer-generated voice. Identify yourself, thank the caller, and briefly explain that you are unavailable. Invite the caller to leave a message or, if appropriate, to call back. Here's a typical voice mail greeting: *Hi! This is Larry Lopez of Proteus Software, and I appreciate your call. I'm either working with customers or talking on another line at the moment. Please leave your name, number, and reason for calling so that I can be prepared when I return your call.* If you screen your calls as a time management technique, try this message: *I'm not near my phone right now, but I should be able to return calls after 3:30.*

- **Test your message.** Call your number and assess your message. Does it sound inviting? Sincere? Professional? Understandable? Are you pleased with your tone? If not, record your message again until it conveys the professional image you want.

- **Respond to messages promptly.** Check your messages regularly, and try to return all voice mail messages within one business day.

- **Plan for vacations and other extended absences.** If you will not be picking up voice mail messages for an extended period, let callers know how they can reach someone else if needed.

On the Caller's End. When leaving a voice mail message, follow these tips:

- **Be prepared to leave a message.** Before calling someone, be prepared for voice mail. Decide what you are going to say and what information you are going to include in your message. If necessary, write your message down before calling.

- **Leave a concise, thorough message.** When leaving a message, always identify yourself using your complete name and affiliation. Mention the date and time you called and a brief explanation of your reason for calling. Always leave a complete phone number, including the area code. Tell the receiver the best time to return your call. Don't ramble.

- **Use a professional and courteous tone.** When leaving a message, make sure that your tone is professional, enthusiastic, and respectful. Smile when leaving a message to add warmth to your voice.

- **Speak slowly and articulate.** Make sure that your receiver will be able to understand your message. Speak slowly and pronounce your words carefully, especially when providing your phone number. If you suspect a poor connection, repeat the number before saying goodbye. The receiver should be able to write information down without having to replay your message.

- **Be careful with confidential information.** Don't leave confidential or private information in a voice mail message. Remember that anyone could gain access to this information.

- **Don't make assumptions.** If you don't receive a call back within a day or two after leaving a message, don't get angry or frustrated. Assume that the message wasn't delivered or that it couldn't be understood. Call back and leave another message, or send the person an e-mail.

LEARNING OUTCOME 4

Understand the importance of teamwork in today's digital era workplace, and explain how you can contribute positively to team performance.

11-4 Adding Value to Professional Teams

As we discussed in Chapter 1, collaboration is the rule today, and an overwhelming majority of white-collar professionals (82 percent) need to partner with others to complete their work.[32] Research by design company Gensler shows that the 2,000 knowledge workers surveyed nationally spent on average about 20 percent of their time collaborating.[33] Workers collaborate not only at their desks but also informally in hallways and unassigned workspaces or in rooms equipped with the latest teleconferencing tools. Many connect remotely with their smart electronic devices. Major companies—for example, Google, Samsung, AT&T, Zappos, and ING Direct—have redesigned their workspaces to meet this growing need for collaboration.[34] Needless to say, solid soft skills rule in face-to-face as well as far-flung teams.

Teams can be effective in solving problems and in developing new products. Take, for example, the collaboration between NASA and private aerospace company SpaceX in developing the Red Dragon Mission to Mars. The two organizations couldn't be more different, yet they capitalize on their respective strengths. NASA is providing its technical expertise and testing facilities, while SpaceX, with its characteristic speed and efficiency, is responsible for Red Dragon design, hardware, and operations.[35]

11-4a Excelling in Teams

You will discover that the workplace is teeming with teams: diverse, dispersed, digital, and dynamic (4-D) teams.[36] You might find yourself a part of a work team, project team, customer support team, supplier team, design team, planning team, functional team, cross-functional team, or some other group. All of these teams are formed to accomplish specific goals.

It's no secret that one of the most important objectives of businesses is finding ways to do jobs better at less cost. This objective helps explain the popularity of teams, which are formed for the following reasons:

- **Better decisions.** Decisions are generally more accurate and effective because group and team members contribute different expertise and perspectives.
- **Faster responses.** When action is necessary to respond to competition or to solve a problem, small groups and teams can act rapidly.
- **Increased productivity.** Because they are often closer to the action and to the customer, team members can see opportunities for improving efficiency.
- **Greater buy-in.** Decisions arrived at jointly are usually better received because members are committed to the solution and are more willing to support it.
- **Less resistance to change.** People who have input into decisions are less hostile, aggressive, and resistant to change.
- **Improved employee morale.** Personal satisfaction and job morale increase when teams are successful.
- **Reduced risks.** Responsibility for a decision is diffused, thus carrying less risk for any individual.

Regardless of their specific purpose, teams normally go through predictable phases as they develop. The psychologist B. A. Tuckman identified four phases: *forming, storming, norming,* and *performing,* as Figure 11.4 illustrates.[38] Some groups move quickly from *forming* to *performing.* Other teams may never reach the final stage of *performing.* However, most struggle through disruptive, although ultimately constructive, team-building stages.

11-4b Collaborating in Virtual Teams

In addition to working side by side in close proximity with potential teammates, you can expect to collaborate with coworkers in other cities and even in other countries. Such collaborations are referred to as *virtual teams.* This is a group of people who, aided by information technology, must accomplish shared tasks largely without face-to-face contact across geographic boundaries, sometimes on different continents and across time zones.[39] Some research suggests that team members consider virtual communication less productive than face-to-face interaction; nearly half feel

Figure 11.4 Four Phases of Team Development in Decision Making

Forming	Storming	Norming	Performing
• Select members. • Become acquainted. • Build trust. • Form collaborative culture.	• Identify problems. • Collect and share information. • Establish decision criteria. • Prioritize goals.	• Discuss alternatives. • Evaluate outcomes. • Apply criteria. • Prioritize alternatives.	• Select alternative. • Analyze effects. • Implement plan. • Manage project.

confused and overwhelmed by collaboration technology. Other studies argue that well-managed dispersed teams can outperform teams that meet in person.[40]

Although Yahoo and Best Buy have reversed their acclaimed work-at-home policies, virtual teams are here to stay—for example, at IBM, SAP, and General Electric. The tech giants rely on virtual teams for synergy, training, and for managing workers across many time zones. IBM employs 200,000 people worldwide, SAP relies on 30,000 workers in 60 countries, and GE has a global workforce of 90,000.[41] Many well-known German companies with a global reach maintain headquarters in picturesque small German towns (think Volkswagen, Adidas, Hugo Boss, and software corporation SAP). Virtual technology enables them to connect with their facilities in locations around the globe, wherever needed talent may reside.[42] In the digital age, work is increasingly viewed as what you do rather than a place you go.

In some organizations, remote coworkers may be permanent employees from the same office or may be specialists called together for temporary projects. Regardless of the assignment, virtual teams can benefit from shared views, a mix of skills, and diversity.

11-4c Identifying Positive and Negative Team Behavior

How can you be a high-performing team member? The most effective groups have members who are willing to establish rules and abide by them. Effective team members are able to analyze tasks and define problems so that they can work toward solutions. Helpful team members strive to resolve differences and encourage a warm, supportive climate by praising and agreeing with others. When agreement is near, they move the group toward its goal by summarizing points of understanding. These and other positive traits are shown in Figure 11.5.

Not all groups, however, have members who contribute positively. Negative behavior is shown by those who constantly put down the ideas and suggestions of others. They may waste the group's time with unnecessary recounting of personal achievements or irrelevant topics. Also disturbing are team members who withdraw and refuse to be drawn out. To be a productive and welcome member of a group, be prepared to perform the positive tasks described in Figure 11.5. Avoid the negative behaviors.

11-4d Defining Successful Teams

The use of teams has been called the solution to many ills in the current workplace.[43] Someone even observed that as an acronym TEAM means Together, Everyone Achieves More.[44] However, teams that do not work well together can actually

Figure 11.5 Positive and Negative Group Behaviors

POSITIVE GROUP BEHAVIORS

+ Setting rules and abiding by them

+ Analyzing tasks and defining problems

+ Contributing information and ideas

+ Showing interest by listening actively

+ Encouraging members to participate

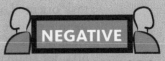

NEGATIVE GROUP BEHAVIORS

– Blocking the ideas of others

– Insulting and criticizing others

– Wasting the group's time

– Making improper jokes and comments

– Failing to stay on task

– Withdrawing, failing to participate

increase frustration, lower productivity, and create employee dissatisfaction. Experts who have studied team dynamics and decisions have discovered that effective teams share some or all of the following characteristics.

Stay Small and Embrace Diversity. Teams may range from 2 to 25 members, although 4 or 5 is an optimal number for many projects. Teams smaller than ten members tend to agree more easily on a common objective and form more cohesive units.[45] Larger groups have trouble interacting constructively, much less agreeing on actions.[46] Jeff Bezos, chairman and CEO of Amazon, reportedly said: "If you can't feed a team with two pizzas, the size of the team is too large."[47] For the most creative decisions, teams generally have male and female members who differ in age, ethnicity, social background, training, and experience. The key business advantage of diversity is the ability to view a project from multiple perspectives.[48] Many organizations are finding that diverse teams can produce innovative solutions with broader applications than homogeneous teams can.

Agree on a Purpose. An effective team begins with a purpose. Working from a general purpose to specific goals typically requires a huge investment of time and effort. Meaningful discussions, however, motivate team members to buy in to the project. When the state of Montana decided to curb its traffic fatalities and serious injuries, the Montana Department of Transportation formed a broad coalition consisting of local, state, and federal agencies as well as traffic safety advocacy groups. Various stakeholders (e.g., state agencies, insurance companies, local tribal leaders, and motorcycle safety representatives) joined in the effort to develop wide-ranging traffic safety programs. With input from all parties, a comprehensive highway safety plan, Vision Zero, was conceived that set targets and performance measures.[49]

Establish Procedures. The best teams develop procedures to guide them. They set up intermediate goals with deadlines. They assign roles and tasks, requiring all members to contribute equivalent amounts of real work. They decide how they will make decisions, whether by majority vote, consensus, or other methods. Procedures are continually evaluated to ensure movement toward the team's goals.

Confront Conflict. Poorly functioning teams avoid conflict, preferring sulking, gossiping, or backstabbing. A better plan is to acknowledge conflict and address the

OFFICE INSIDER

"The average worker still spends half of his or her time performing activities that require concentration. We need to strike a balance between providing spaces for collaboration and heads-down concentration. As technology advances and mobility—outside and inside the office—becomes the norm, virtual and face-to-face collaboration are both critically important."[50]

Jan Johnson, *vice president of design and workplace resources at Allsteel*

root of the problem openly using the six-step plan outlined in Figure 11.6. Although it may feel emotionally risky, direct confrontation saves time and enhances team commitment in the long run. To be constructive, however, confrontation must be task oriented, not person oriented. An open airing of differences, in which all team members have a chance to speak their minds, should center on the strengths and weaknesses of the various positions and ideas—not on personalities. After hearing all sides, team members must negotiate a fair settlement, no matter how long it takes.

Communicate Effectively. The best teams exchange information and contribute ideas freely in an informal environment often facilitated by technology. Team members speak and write clearly and concisely, avoiding generalities. They encourage feedback. Listeners become actively involved, read body language, and ask clarifying questions before responding. Tactful, constructive disagreement is encouraged. Although a team's task is taken seriously, successful teams are able to inject humor into their interactions.

Collaborate Rather Than Compete. Effective team members are genuinely interested in achieving team goals instead of receiving individual recognition. They contribute ideas and feedback unselfishly. They monitor team progress, including what is going right, what is going wrong, and what to do about it. They celebrate individual and team accomplishments.

Accept Ethical Responsibilities. Teams as a whole have ethical responsibilities to their members, to their larger organizations, and to society. Members have a number of specific responsibilities to each other. As a whole, teams have a responsibility to represent the organization's view and respect its privileged information. They should not discuss with outsiders any sensitive issues without permission. In addition, teams have a broader obligation to avoid advocating actions that would endanger members of society at large.

Share Leadership. Effective teams often have no formal leader. Instead, leadership rotates to those with the appropriate expertise as the team evolves and moves from one phase to another. Many teams operate under a democratic approach. This approach can achieve buy-in to team decisions, boost morale, and create fewer hurt feelings and less resentment. In times of crisis, however, a strong team member may need to step up as a leader.

The skills that make you a valuable and ethical team player will serve you well when you run or participate in professional meetings.

Figure 11.6 Six Steps for Dealing With Conflict

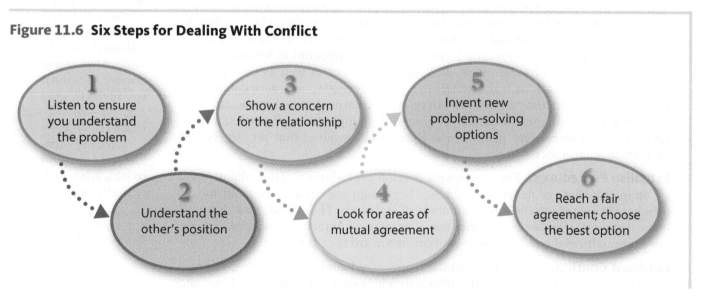

1. Listen to ensure you understand the problem
2. Understand the other's position
3. Show a concern for the relationship
4. Look for areas of mutual agreement
5. Invent new problem-solving options
6. Reach a fair agreement; choose the best option

Chapter 11: Professionalism at Work: Business Etiquette, Ethics, Teamwork, and Meetings

11-5 Planning and Participating in Face-to-Face and Virtual Meetings

LEARNING OUTCOME 5

Discuss effective practices and technologies for planning and participating in productive face-to-face meetings and virtual meetings.

As you prepare to join the workforce, expect to attend meetings—lots of them! Estimates suggest that workers on average spend four hours a week in meetings and consider more than half of that time as wasted.[51] Managers spend even more time in meetings. In one survey, managers considered over a third of meeting time unproductive and reported that two thirds of meetings fell short of their stated objectives.[52] Much to the dismay of managers, at Seagate Technology in Cupertino, California, some work groups were spending more than 20 hours a week in meetings.[53] However, if meetings are well run, workers actually desire more, not fewer, of them.[54]

Business meetings consist of three or more people who assemble to pool information, solicit feedback, clarify policy, seek consensus, and solve problems. However, as growing numbers of employees work at distant locations, meetings have changed. Workers cannot always meet face-to-face. To be able to exchange information effectively and efficiently, you will need to know how to plan and participate in face-to-face as well as *virtual meetings*.

Although meetings are disliked, they can be career-critical. Instead of treating them as thieves of your valuable time, try to see meetings as golden opportunities to demonstrate your leadership, communication, and problem-solving skills. To help you make the most of these opportunities, this section outlines best practices for running and contributing to meetings.

11-5a Preparing for the Meeting

A face-to-face meeting provides the most nonverbal cues and other signals that help us interpret the intended meaning of words. Therefore, an in-person meeting is the richest of available media. Yet meetings are also costly, draining the productivity of all participants. If you are in charge of a meeting, determine your purpose, decide how and where to meet, choose the participants, invite them using a digital calendar, and organize an agenda.

Determining the Purpose of the Meeting. No meeting should be called unless it is important, can't wait, and requires an exchange of ideas. In a global poll, 77 percent of respondents stated that they preferred face-to-face meetings for deal-making and mission-critical decisions; more than two thirds liked to brainstorm and discuss complex technical concepts in person.[55]

If people are merely being informed, it's best to send an e-mail, text message, or memo. Pick up the phone or leave a voice mail message, but don't call a costly meeting. To decide whether the purpose of the meeting is valid, consult the key people who will be attending. Ask them what outcomes they desire and how to achieve those goals. This consultation also sets a collaborative tone and encourages full participation.

Deciding How and Where to Meet. Once you are sure that a meeting is necessary, you must decide whether to meet face-to-face or virtually. If you decide to meet in person, reserve a conference room. If you decide to meet virtually, select the appropriate media and make any necessary arrangements for your voice conference, videoconference, or Web conference. These communication technologies are discussed in Chapter 1.

Selecting Meeting Participants. The purpose of the meeting determines the number of participants, as shown in Figure 11.7. If the meeting purpose is motivational, such as an awards ceremony for sales reps of cosmetics giant Avon or nutrition supplement seller Herbalife, then the number of participants is potentially unlimited. However, for decision making, consultants recommend limiting the session to four

OFFICE INSIDER

"In a co-located meeting, there are social norms: You don't get up and walk around the room, not paying attention. Virtual meetings are no different: You don't go on mute and leave the room to get something. In a physical meeting, you would never make a phone call and 'check out' from the meeting. So in a virtual meeting, you shouldn't press mute and respond to your emails, killing any potential for lively discussion, shared laughter and creativity."[56]

Keith Ferrazzi, *CEO of consulting and training company Ferrazzi Greenlight*

Figure 11.7 Meeting Purpose and Number of Participants

to seven participants.[57] Other meetings may require a greater circle of stakeholders and those who will implement the decision.

Let's consider Timberland's signature employee volunteer program. Company employees might meet with business partners and community members to decide how best to revitalize communities in need all over the world during Timberland's annual Serv-a-Palooza event.[58] Inviting key stakeholders who represent various interests, perspectives, and competencies ensures valuable input and, therefore, is more likely to lead to informed decisions.

Using Digital Calendars to Schedule Meetings. Finding a time when everyone can meet is often difficult. Fortunately, digital calendars now make the task quick and efficient. Popular programs and mobile apps are Google Calendar, Apple Calendar, and the business favorite, Outlook Calendar, shown in Figure 11.8. Online

While meetings rank high on employee lists of top time-killers at work, respected business leaders take action to never let a meeting go to waste. Amazon's Jeff Bezos places an empty chair at meetings to represent the customer's place in the room. Virgin Group founder Richard Branson stages meetings in nontraditional spaces—such as poolside or at a park—to foster creativity. Stanford management professor Bob Sutton holds stand-up meetings without chairs to keep gatherings brief and on point. Former Apple chief Steve Jobs ejected individuals from meetings to weed out unnecessary participants.[59] Most recently, some adventurous software companies have turned to invigorating and core-strengthening plank meetings. In these athletic daily scrum meetings, participants drop

to the floor and must remain in the plank position while speaking.[60] What other steps can managers take to make meetings more effective?

calendars and mobile apps enable users to make appointments, schedule meetings, and keep track of daily activities.

To schedule meetings, you enter a meeting request and add the names of attendees. You select a date, enter a start and end time, and list the meeting subject and location. Then the meeting request goes to each attendee. Later you check the attendee availability tab to see a list of all meeting attendees. As the meeting time approaches, the program automatically sends reminders to attendees. The free Web-based meeting scheduler and mobile app Doodle is growing in popularity because it helps users poll participants to determine the best date and time for a meeting.

Distributing an Agenda and Other Information. At least two days before a meeting, distribute an agenda of topics to be discussed. Also include any reports or materials that participants should read in advance. For continuing groups, you might also include a copy of the minutes of the previous meeting. To keep meetings productive, limit the number of agenda items. Remember, the narrower the focus, the greater the chances for success. A good agenda, as illustrated in Figure 11.9, covers the following information:

- Date and place of meeting
- Start time and end time

Figure 11.8 Using Calendar Programs

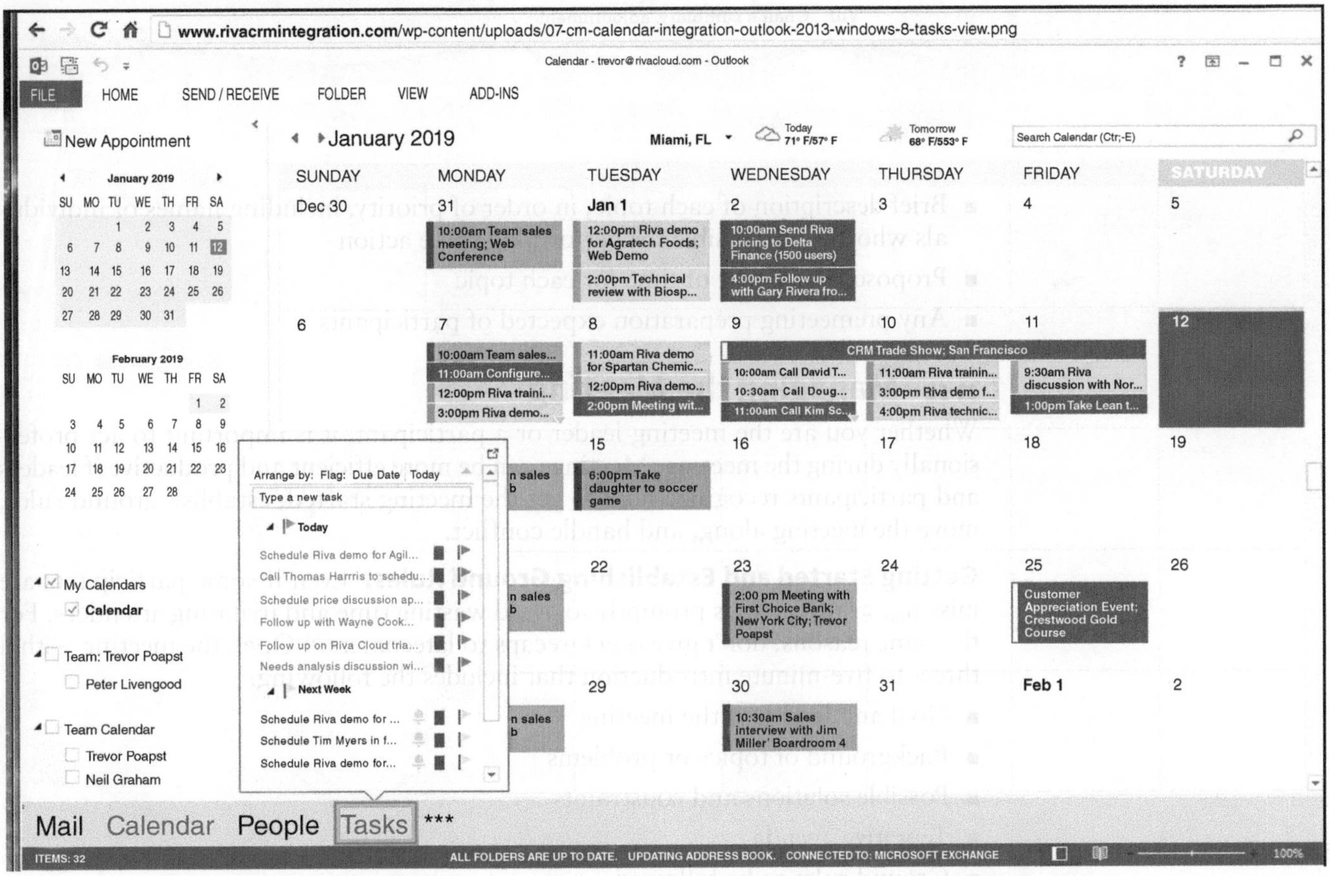

Calendar programs ease the frustration of scheduling meetings for busy people. The program allows you to check colleagues' calendars (if permission is given), locate a free time, schedule a meeting, send out an initial announcement, and follow up with reminders.

Figure 11.9 Typical Meeting Agenda

```
                              AGENDA
                    Quantum Travel International
                           Staff Meeting
                        September 4, 2019
                           10 to 11 a.m.
                         Conference Room

    I.   Call to order; roll call

    II.  Approval of agenda

    III. Approval of minutes from previous meeting

                                          Person        Proposed Time
    IV.  Committee reports
         A. Website update               Jared          5 minutes
         B. Tour packages                Lakisha         10 minutes

    V.   Old business
         A. Equipment maintenance        John            5 minutes
         B. Client escrow accounts       Alicia          5 minutes
         C. Internal newsletter          Adrienne        5 minutes

    VI.  New business
         A. New accounts                 Garth           5 minutes
         B. Pricing policy for Asian tours  Minh         15 minutes

    VII. Announcements

    VIII. Chair's summary, adjournment
```

- Brief description of each topic, in order of priority, including names of individuals who are responsible for performing some action
- Proposed allotment of time for each topic
- Any premeeting preparation expected of participants

11-5b Managing the Meeting

Whether you are the meeting leader or a participant, it is important to act professionally during the meeting. Meetings can be more efficient and productive if leaders and participants recognize how to get the meeting started, establish ground rules, move the meeting along, and handle conflict.

Getting Started and Establishing Ground Rules. Even if some participants are missing, start meetings promptly to avoid wasting time and irritating attendees. For the same reasons, don't give quick recaps to latecomers.[61] Open the meeting with a three- to five-minute introduction that includes the following:

- Goal and length of the meeting
- Background of topics or problems
- Possible solutions and constraints
- Tentative agenda
- Ground rules to be followed

Typical ground rules include communicating openly, being supportive, listening carefully, participating fully, confronting conflict frankly, silencing cell phones and other digital devices, and following the agenda. More formal groups follow parliamentary procedures based on Robert's Rules. The next step is to assign one participant to take minutes and one to act as a recorder. The recorder uses a computer and projector or stands at a flipchart or whiteboard to list the main ideas being discussed and agreements reached.

Moving the Meeting Along. An effective leader lets others talk and tries to involve all participants. If the group has one member who dominates, the leader might say, *Thanks, Gary, for that perspective, but please hold your next point while we hear how Rachel would respond to that.* To draw in reticent attendees, be positive, restate important points, and thank them for contributing. Ask people directly but kindly for input: *Do you have anything you wish to share?*

To avoid allowing digressions to sidetrack the group, try generating a parking lot list, a list of important but divergent issues that should be discussed later. Another way to handle digressions is to say, *Folks, we're drifting astray here. Please forgive me for pressing on, but let's return to the central issue of....* It is important to adhere to the agenda and the schedule. Equally important, when the group seems to have reached a consensus, is to summarize the group's position and see whether everyone agrees.

Handling Conflict in Meetings. As you learned earlier, conflict is natural and even desirable. However, it can also cause awkwardness and uneasiness. In meetings, conflict typically develops when people feel unheard or misunderstood. If two people clash, the best approach is to encourage each to make a complete case while group members give their full attention. Let each one question the other. Then, the leader should summarize what was said, and the participants should offer comments. The group may modify a recommendation or suggest alternatives before reaching consensus on a direction to follow.

11-5c Concluding the Meeting and Following Up

End the meeting at the agreed time or sooner. The leader should summarize all decisions, assigned tasks, and deadlines. It may be necessary to ask attendees to volunteer for completing action items. All participants should understand what was accomplished. One effective technique that encourages participation is round-robin, in which people take turns summarizing briefly their interpretations of what was decided and what happens next. Of course, this closure technique works best with smaller groups. The leader should conclude by asking the group to set a time for the next meeting. He or she should assure the group that a report will follow. Finally, the leader should thank participants for attending.

If minutes were taken, they should be distributed within a couple of days of the meeting.

Meeting management programs and mobile apps offer a structured template such as that shown in Figure 11.10, which includes brief meeting minutes, key points and decisions, and action items. The leader needs to ensure that decisions are executed. The leader may need to call participants to remind them of their assignments and also to solicit help if necessary.

11-5d Interacting Professionally in Virtual Meetings

Virtual meetings are real-time gatherings of dispersed participants who connect with communication technology. As travel costs rise and companies slash budgets, many organizations are cutting back on meetings that require travel.[63] Instead, people may meet in audioconferences using telephones or in videoconferences using the Internet. Steady improvements in telecommunications networks, software applications, and bandwidth continue to fuel the shift to virtual meetings. These meetings have many purposes, including training employees, making sales presentations, coordinating team activities, and talking to customers. Despite measurable savings, some researchers as well as users dispute the effectiveness of virtual meetings; however, at

Figure 11.10 E-Mail Meeting Minutes

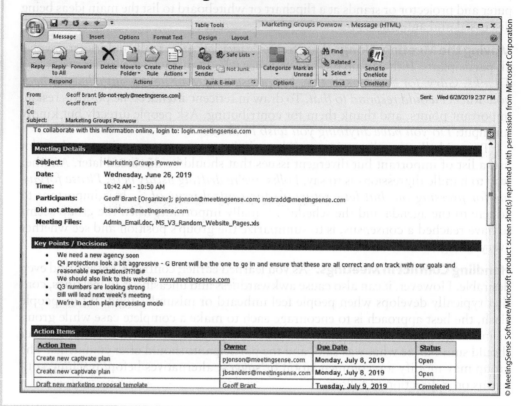

least two studies suggest that well-run virtual teams can be highly productive and outperform co-located teams.[64]

Although the same good meeting management techniques discussed for face-to-face meetings apply, additional skills and practices are important in virtual meetings. The following best practices recommended by experienced meeting facilitators will help you address premeeting issues such as technology glitches, scheduling across time zones, and language challenges.[65] Creating ground rules, anticipating limited media richness, managing turn-taking, and humanizing the interaction with remote members all achieve the best results during virtual meetings.

- **Select the most appropriate technology.** Decide whether audioconferencing or videoconferencing is needed. Choose the appropriate program or application.

- **Ensure that all participants are able to use the technology.** Coach attendees who may need help before the session begins.

- **Encourage participants to log in 15 minutes early.** Some programs require downloads and installations that can cause immense frustration if not done early.

- **Be aware of different time zones.** Use Coordinated Universal Time (UTC) to minimize confusion resulting from mismatched local times. Avoid spanning a lunch hour or holding someone overtime.

- **Rotate your meeting time to be fair to all dispersed group members.** Ensure that everyone shares the burden of an inconvenient time.[66]

- **Decide what language to use.** If the meeting language may be difficult for some participants, think about using simple expressions and repeating major ideas. Always follow up in writing.

- **Explain how questions may be asked and answered.** Many meeting programs allow participants to virtually raise their hands using an icon on the computer screen and to type in their questions.

- **Ensure that it is clear who is speaking in audioconferences.** Ask participants to always say their names before beginning to comment.
- **Remind the group to silence all electronic alerts and alarms.** Ask participants to mute ringers and buzzers and control background noise, or you may also hear dogs barking, telephones ringing, and toilets flushing.
- **Don't multitask.** Giving your full attention is critical. That includes texting and checking e-mail.
- **Anticipate the limitations of virtual technology.** Given the lack of nonverbal cues, be as precise as possible. Use simple language and summarize the discussion often. Confirm your understanding of the discussion. Project an upbeat, enthusiastic, and strong voice.
- **Manage turn-taking.** Ask questions of specific people. Invite each participant to speak for 30 seconds without interruption. Avoid asking vague questions such as *Does everyone agree?*
- **Humanize virtual meetings.** Build camaraderie and trust. Leave time for small talk to establish a warm environment. Build trust and interest by logging in early and greeting others as they join in.

Some companies use teleconferencing informally to stimulate bonding and spontaneous collaboration between distant locations. Evernote, the company that provides a popular app for notetaking and archiving, set up a virtual window between Mountain View, California, and its studio in Austin, Texas. A giant video screen connects the two offices in real time but not to facilitate meetings; rather, it invites workers simply to chat and exchange ideas.[67] Figure 11.11 shows how athletic gear company Sportster Marketing used Web conferencing to meet virtually and design a new sports watch.

Although many acknowledge that virtual meetings may not be as effective as face-to-face meetings,[68] virtual meetings are here to stay. Learning to plan and participate in them professionally will enhance your career as a business communicator.

Figure 11.11 Understanding Web Conferencing

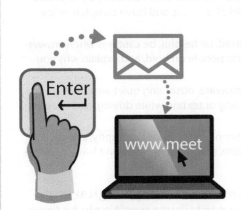

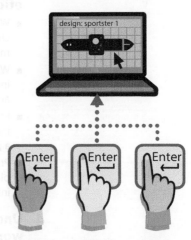

1. E-Mail Contact:
Alan T., president of Sportster Marketing, an athletic gear company in Seattle, WA, sends an email to Meghan R., chief designer at NexxtDesign in Venice, CA, to discuss a new sports watch. The e-mail includes meeting date and time and a link to launch the session.

2. Virtual Meeting:
When the Web conference begins, participants see live video of each other's faces on their screens. They look at photos of sports watches, share ideas, sketch designs on a shared "virtual whiteboard," and review contract terms.

3. Design Collaboration:
NexxtDesign artists and Sportster Marketing managers use peer-to-peer software that allows them to share spaces on each other's computers. The software enables them to take turns modifying the designs, and it also tracks all the changes.

Summary of Learning Outcomes

1 Build your credibility and gain a competitive advantage by developing professionalism, an ethical mind-set, and business etiquette skills.

- Professionalism, good business etiquette, developed soft skills, social intelligence, polish, and civility are desirable workplace behaviors that are complemented by a positive online presence.
- Employers most want employees who can prioritize their work, work in teams, and exhibit a positive attitude in addition to displaying good workplace manners and other interpersonal skills.
- Professionalism means having integrity and being ethical; experts believe that no sharp distinction between ethics and etiquette exists. We should always treat others with respect.
- Practicing business etiquette on the job and online can put you ahead of others who lack polish.

2 Use your voice as a communication tool, master face-to-face workplace interaction, foster positive relations on the job, and accept as well as provide constructive criticism gracefully.

- In-person communication is the richest communication channel; use your voice effectively by honing your pronunciation, voice quality, pitch, volume and rate, and emphasis.
- To excel in face-to-face conversations, use correct names and titles, choose appropriate topics, be positive, listen to learn, give sincere praise, and act professionally in social situations.
- When receiving criticism, avoid interrupting, paraphrase what you are hearing, agree if the criticism is accurate, disagree respectfully, look for compromise, and learn from criticism.
- When criticizing, plan your remarks, do it in person, focus on improvement, offer help, be specific, use the word *we*, encourage two-way communication, stay calm, and keep it private.

3 Practice professional telephone skills and polish your voice mail etiquette.

- When calling, follow an agenda, use a three-point introduction, be brisk, try to sound cheerful, be professional and courteous, avoid phone tag, and leave complete voice mail messages.
- When answering, be courteous, identify yourself, be helpful, be cautious when answering calls for others, be respectful when putting people on hold, and explain why you are transferring calls.
- Practice smartphone etiquette by being considerate, observing quiet areas, using your indoor voice, taking only urgent calls, not calling or texting while driving, and choosing a professional ringtone.
- Prepare a friendly voice mail greeting and respond to messages promptly; as a caller, plan your message, be concise, watch your tone, speak slowly, and don't leave sensitive information.

4 Understand the importance of teamwork in today's digital era workplace, and explain how you can contribute positively to team performance.

- Teams are popular because they lead to better decisions, faster responses, increased productivity, greater buy-in, less resistance, improved morale, and reduced risks.
- The four phases of team development are forming, storming, norming, and performing.
- Virtual teams are collaborations among remote coworkers connecting with technology.

- Positive group behaviors include establishing and following rules, resolving differences, being supportive, praising others, and summarizing points of understanding.
- Negative behaviors include having contempt for others, wasting the team's time, and withdrawing.
- Successful teams are small and diverse, agree on a purpose and procedures, confront conflict, communicate well, don't compete but collaborate, are ethical, and share leadership.

5 Discuss effective practices and technologies for planning and participating in productive face-to-face meetings and virtual meetings.

- Before a meeting businesspeople determine its purpose and location, choose participants, use a digital calendar, and distribute an agenda.
- Experienced meeting leaders move the meeting along and confront any conflict; they end the meeting on time, make sure everyone is heard, and distribute meeting minutes promptly.
- Virtual meetings save travel costs but require attention to communication technology and to the needs of dispersed participants regarding issues such as different time zones and language barriers.
- Virtual meetings demand specific procedures to handle questions, noise, lack of media richness, and turn-taking. Because they are impersonal, virtual meetings benefit from building camaraderie and trust.

Chapter Review

1. What is the difference between ethics and etiquette? (L.O. 1)

2. Define the five traits and skills listed in the chapter that demonstrate professionalism. (L.O. 1)

3. Explain the advantages of face-to-face conversation over other communication channels. (L.O. 2)

4. Name several business etiquette guidelines that promote positive workplace conversations, in the office and at work-related social functions. (L.O. 2)

5. How can you ensure that your telephone calls on the job are productive? Name at least six suggestions. (L.O. 3)

6. List at least three guidelines that courteous cell phone users follow to avoid offending others. (L.O. 3)

7. What are some of the reasons for the popularity of workplace teams? List at least five. (L.O. 4)

8. Name the four phases of team development as identified by psychologist B. A. Tuckman, and explain what happens in each stage. (L.O. 4)

9. What is the best approach to address conflict in meetings? (L.O. 5)

10. What techniques can make virtual meetings as effective as face-to-face meetings? (L.O. 5)

Critical Thinking

11. Employers try to screen for and encourage soft skills such as excellent communication, promptness, a positive attitude, good teamwork skills, and civility. On this difficult mission, they try novel approaches. A recruiter would intentionally drop a piece of trash by his office door just before an interview. He then would hire anyone who picked it up.[69] One gas station manager rewarded his workers by relieving them of bathroom cleaning duty if they started their shifts on time. Discuss these techniques. Do you believe they are effective? (L.O. 1, 4)

12. Think of typical workplace situations and how you might communicate in each. When would you seek an in-person conversation, pick up the phone, call a virtual meeting, or send an e-mail, IM, or text? (L.O. 1–5)

13. Try to recall situations in which you were criticized or dished out criticism yourself. Was the criticism constructive? Why or why not? How did you feel either as a giver or receiver of criticism? (L.O. 2)

14. Describe the advantages of face-to-face communication as opposed to interactions facilitated by technology such as telephones, e-mail, instant messaging, texting, the Web, social networking sites, and so on. When is face-to-face communication more effective? (L.O. 2, 3)

15. Career expert Andrea Kay stresses that knowing oneself and showing empathy are important components of the soft skills that make people employable: "Many, many jobs are lost and careers derailed because of the way people act with each other, respond to stress, or deal with a conflict. … If you don't understand how you come across, or get swept away in your emotions, or don't recognize how others feel, how can you approach a difficult conversation with sensitivity to the other person?"[70] Have you ever been surprised at how you came across to others or misread another person's feelings? (L.O. 1, 4, 5)

Activities and Cases

11.1 Workplace Conflict: Six-Step Procedure to the Rescue! (L.O. 1, 4, 5)

> Team

Although conflict is a normal part of every workplace, if unresolved, it can create hard feelings and reduce productivity.

YOUR TASK. Analyze the following scenarios. In teams, discuss each scenario and apply the six-step procedure for dealing with conflict outlined in Figure 11.6. Choose two of the scenarios to role-play, with two of your team members taking roles.

a. A warehouse manager and a maintenance manager frequently yell at each other, fuming as they clash over policies and procedures. The fighting has become so personal and intense that the two departments no longer are able to collaborate. The supervisor overseeing the feuding parties wants to fire both managers.
b. Baby boomers and Generation X employees working for a biomedical research facility repeatedly lock horns with the millennials on the staff. The lab workers from different generations don't view each other favorably. The boomer and Gen X cohorts consider the millennials lazy, criticizing their work ethic. The millennials view the older colleagues as inflexible and hostile toward change.
c. The author of a lengthy report refuses to collaborate with another colleague on future projects because she feels that the review of her document by the peer was superficial, short, and essentially useless. The report author is angry at the lack of attention her 25-page paper received.
d. Two management team members disagree on a new company social media policy. One wants to ban personal visits to Facebook and Twitter totally. The other thinks that an outright ban is impossible to implement and might raise the ire of employees. He is more concerned with limiting Internet misuse, including visits to online game, pornography, and shopping sites. The management team members agree that they need a social media policy, but they disagree on what to allow and what to prohibit.

11.2 Soft Skills: What Employers Want (L.O. 1)

> Communication Technology > Social Media > Team > Web

What soft skills do employers request when they list job openings in your field?

YOUR TASK. Individually or in teams, check the listings at an online job board. Visit Monster, CollegeRecruiter, CareerBuilder, or Indeed. Follow the instructions to search job categories and locations. Study many job listings in your field. Print or otherwise save the results of your search. How often do the ads mention communication, teamwork, and computer skills? What tasks do the ads mention? Discuss your findings with your team members. Then prepare a list of the most frequently requested soft skills. Your instructor may ask you to submit your findings and/or report to the class. If you are not satisfied with the job selection at any job board, choose ads posted on the websites of companies you admire or on LinkedIn.

11.3 Soft Skills: Identifying Personal Strengths (L.O. 1)

> Web

When hiring future workers, employers look for hard skills (those we learn, such as mastery of software applications or accountancy procedures) and soft skills. Soft skills are personal characteristics, strengths, and other assets.

Studies have divided soft skills into four categories:

- Thinking and problem solving
- Oral and written communication
- Personal qualities and work ethic
- Interpersonal and teamwork

YOUR TASK. Using the preceding categories to guide you, identify your own soft skills, paying attention to those you think a potential employer would value. Prepare lists of at least four items in each of the four categories. For example, as evidence of problem solving, you might list a specific workplace or student problem you recognized and solved. You will want to weave these words and phrases into cover letters and résumés, which are covered in Chapter 13.

11.4 Voice Quality: How Do I Sound? (L.O. 2)

> Team

Recording your voice gives you a chance to learn how you sound to others and provides an opportunity to use your voice more effectively. Don't be surprised if you fail to recognize your own voice or if it sounds strange to your ears.

YOUR TASK. Record yourself reading a news or business article.

a. If you think your voice sounds a bit high, practice speaking slightly lower.
b. If your voice is low or expressionless, practice speaking slightly louder and with more inflection.
c. Ask a colleague, teacher, or friend to provide feedback on your pronunciation, pitch, volume, rate, and professional tone.

11.5 Communication Channels: Which Media in Each Situation? (L.O. 2)

> Communication Technology > E-Mail > Social Media

YOUR TASK. First decide whether the following messages need to be communicated orally or in writing. After consulting the media richness diagram in Figure 11.2, consider how rich the medium must be in each communication situation to convey the message most appropriately and reliably. Your choices can include an e-mail, a letter, a report, texting, instant messaging, a telephone call, a live chat, teleconferencing, a face-to-face conversation, or a team meeting. Describe the advantages and disadvantages of each choice.

a. Working at 8 a.m. in your Miami office, you need to get in touch with your counterpart at your company's Seattle office and ask a few clarifying formatting questions about a report on which the two of you are collaborating.
b. Following a trade show visit, you are returning to company headquarters, where you must attend an important department meeting. It looks as though you will be at least 15 minutes late. What are your options?
c. Eric, the information technology vice president, must tell employees about a new company social media policy. He has two employees in mind who particularly need this information.
d. As soon as possible, you need to learn from Lori in Shipping and Receiving whether she and her colleagues can fulfill a large, time-sensitive customer order. If she cannot, you need her advice on where you can get it done.
e. As manager of your company's Human Resources Department, you must fire three employees in a company-wide initiative to reduce costs.
f. It isn't your fault, but an order for 500 custom T-shirts for a company-wide charity event ordered by a longtime customer is only partially ready. Roughly half of the T-shirts can be delivered. The customer is angry.

g. As chairman of the employee benefits committee, you have worked with your committee for two months evaluating several health plan options that meet new government standards. You are now ready to convey the recommendations of the committee to management.

11.6 Constructive Criticism: It's Part of the Job (L.O. 2)

No one likes to give it or receive it, but sometimes criticism is unavoidable, even desirable. Constructive criticism in the workplace is necessary when team members need feedback and managers must assess team effectiveness.

YOUR TASK. To remedy each of the following unprofessional actions, supply the appropriate solution following the guidelines provided in this chapter.

a. Manager Jasper has a hot temper. He exploded when Felix, one of his subordinates, came late to a staff meeting. Jasper told Felix that he hated his tardiness and that Felix was always late.
b. Hot-headed manager Jasper loudly confronted Stella in her cubicle within earshot of staff. Stella had requested time off as an important deadline was looming, and the project was already late.
c. Regional manager Alexa delivered a stern lecture to an underperforming sales rep who was clearly stunned and hurt.
d. Anne provided feedback to a dysfunctional team by spontaneously approaching team members in the hallway. Face-to-face with the argumentative team, she was at a loss for words and felt that she did not convey her points fully.
e. Supervisor Josh hates any kind of conflict and is tempted to deliver his negative feedback of a team member by e-mail.

11.7 Telephone Skills: Keeping It Professional (L.O. 3)

> Team

Acting out the roles of telephone caller and receiver is an effective technique for improving skills. To give you such practice, your instructor will divide the class into pairs.

YOUR TASK. For each scenario take a moment to read and rehearse your role silently. Then play the role with your partner. If time permits, repeat the scenarios, changing roles.

Partner 1

a. You are the personnel manager of Blu Cellular, Inc. Call Daria Alameda, office manager at Tactical IT Corporation. Inquire about a job applicant, Adeline Chung, who listed Ms. Alameda as a reference.
b. Call Ms. Alameda again the following day to inquire about the same job applicant, Adeline Chung. Ms. Alameda answers today, but she talks on and on, describing the applicant in great detail. Tactfully close the conversation.
c. You are now the receptionist for Nicolas Sarikakis, of Sarikakis Imports. Answer a call for Mr. Sarikakis, who is working in another office, at Ext. 2219, where he will accept calls.
d. You are now Nicolas Sarikakis, owner of Sarikakis Imports. Call your attorney, Jacqueline Goodman-Heine, about a legal problem. Leave a brief, incomplete message.
e. Call Ms. Goodman-Heine again. Leave a message that will prevent telephone tag.

Partner 2

a. You are the receptionist for Tactical IT Corporation. The caller asks for Daria Alameda, who is home sick today. You don't know when she will be able to return. Answer the call appropriately.
b. You are now Ms. Alameda, office manager. Describe Adeline Chung, an imaginary employee. Think of someone with whom you have worked. Include many details, such as her ability to work with others, her appearance, her skills at computing, her schooling, her ambition, and so forth.
c. You are now an administrative assistant for attorney Jacqueline Goodman-Heine. Call Nicolas Sarikakis to verify a meeting date Ms. Goodman-Heine has with Mr. Sarikakis. Use your own name in identifying yourself.
d. You are now the receptionist for attorney Jacqueline Goodman-Heine. Ms. Goodman-Heine is skiing in Vail and will return in two days, but she does not want her clients to know where she is. Take a message.
e. Take a message again.

11.8 Voice Mail: Recording a Greeting Like a Pro (L.O. 3)

> Communication Technology   E-Mail   Team   Web

To present a professional image, smart businesspeople carefully prepare their outgoing voice mail greetings and announcements. After all, they represent their companies and want to be perceived as polished and efficient. Before recording a greeting, most workers plan and perhaps even jot down what they will say. To be concise, the greeting should not run longer than 25 seconds.

YOUR TASK. Use the guidelines in this chapter to plan your greeting. Invent a job title and the name of your company. Indicate when and how callers can reach you. Individually or as a team, record a professional voice mail greeting using a smartphone or another digital recording device. If the instructor directs, share your recording by sending it via e-mail to a designated address for evaluation. Alternatively, team members may be asked to exchange their recorded greetings for a peer critique. If you own an iPhone, a newer iPod

Touch, or an iPad, download a free app such as Voice Memos that allows voice recordings. Android smartphone owners can likewise download free voice recorder apps. These mobile applications are easy to use, and when the recording is completed, you have the option of sharing it by e-mail, by Bluetooth, on Facebook, and so forth.

11.9 Voice Mail: Leaving a Professional Message (L.O. 3)

> Communication Technology   Web

Voice mail messages can be very effective communication tools as long as they are professional and make responding to them easy.

YOUR TASK. If your instructor allows, call his or her office number after hours or within a specified time frame. Plan what you will say; if needed, jot down a few notes. Leave a professional voice mail message as described in this chapter. Start by introducing yourself by name, then give your telephone number, and finally, leave a brief message about something you discussed in class, read in the chapter, or want the instructor to know about you. Speak slowly, loudly enough, and clearly, so your instructor won't need to replay your message.

11.10 Workplace Conflict: The Perils of Groupthink (L.O. 4)

> Team

"Nothing great is achieved without some conflict," says Enrique Conterno, senior vice president and president at Eli Lilly Diabetes. "Conflict sharpens the senses; it invites full engagement in solving important problems. However, you must create more light than heat when you engage in conflict. Heat degrades the substrate of innovation, while light catalyzes it."[71] You learned about *groupthink* in Chapter 1. It describes a behavior characterized by a lack of critical thinking and extreme conformity to the values of a group.

The absence of conflict is not always a good sign, researchers believe. They point to studies of work teams in hospitals, in which the failure to speak up can lead to disastrous medical errors. Or they analyze airline crashes that can result from a felt lack of "psychological safety" that may prevent even very competent people from speaking up. Researchers also study business misconduct by corporations whose employees knew of the wrongdoing but weren't comfortable enough to report it.[72] Often, groupthink is the culprit.

YOUR TASK. Do you agree with the preceding views on workplace conflict and groupthink? Look back at your teamwork experience and consider tensions that arose. How were they addressed and settled? Have you worked on teams that were conflict free? Were you ever afraid to speak up? Could negative situations have been salvaged by using the tips in this chapter? Discuss these and similar questions in small groups or in front of the class. If asked, provide a written assessment of your views on workplace conflict.

11.11 Meetings: Attacking Dysfunction (L.O. 5)

> E-Mail   Team

As you have learned, facilitating a productive meeting requires skills that may be critical to your career success.

YOUR TASK. Individually or as a team, describe how you would deal with the following examples of unproductive or dysfunctional behavior and other challenges in a team meeting that you are running. Either report your recommendations verbally, or, if your instructor directs, summarize your suggestions in an e-mail or memo.

a. Liam likes to make long-winded statements and often digresses to unrelated subjects.
b. Olivia keeps interrupting other speakers and dominates the discussion.
c. Ben and Oscar are hostile toward each other and clash over an agenda item.
d. Mia arrives 15 minutes late and noisily unpacks her briefcase.
e. Grace, Lydia, and Levi are reading e-mails and texting under the table.
f. Emily is quiet, although she is taking notes and seems to be following the discussion attentively.
g. Levi, a well-known office clown, is telling off-color jokes while others are discussing the business at hand.
h. The meeting time is up, but the group has not met the objective of the meeting.

11.12 Meetings: Stand Up to Keep Team Talk Short and Sweet (L.O. 5)

> Communication Technology   E-Mail   Team

Here is an idea to shorten tedious meetings: Ban sitting down! A growing number of tech companies hold mandatory morning meetings in which nonwork chatter is frowned upon and all participants must stand. Called *the huddle* in one company and *a daily scrum* in another, these regular stand-up meetings last no longer than 15 minutes. At one company, if someone starts rambling, an employee holds up a rubber rat. A Microsoft development team determines the next speaker by tossing around a rubber chicken called Ralph. Other gimmicks include passing around a 10-pound medicine ball to literally keep the meeting moving. At one company, latecomers must pay a small fine, run a lap around the office building, or sing a nursery rhyme such as "I'm a Little Teapot." Other methods to speed up the proceedings include holding meetings just before lunch or gathering in cold stairwells.[73]

The idea of stand-up meetings is spreading in the wake of Agile, a method in software development that involves compressing lengthy projects into short segments. This approach also includes speedy daily updates from colleagues about three things: what was accomplished since the previous meeting, what will be done today, and what stands in the way of finishing the job. It turns out that the practice of holding meetings standing up dates back to some military commanders in World War I. A researcher who conducted a study of stand-up meetings found that they were about a third shorter than sit-down meetings, and the quality of decision making did not suffer at all. A recent survey of more than 6,000 global tech workers found that 78 percent held daily stand-up meetings.[74]

YOUR TASK. As a team, brainstorm all possible applications of quick stand-up meetings. What types of businesses could benefit from such meetings? How would you ensure on-time arrival, participation and order during the meeting, and turn-taking? What type of sanctions would you impose for violations? If your instructor directs, write an e-mail to persuade your current or past boss to adopt stand-up meetings.

11.13 Virtual Meetings: Making Sure the Team Is on Board (L.O. 5)

> Communication Technology ❯ Team ❯ Web

Caroline Bodhi works at the headquarters for a large HMO that contracts with physician groups across the nation. Her position requires her to impose organizational objectives and systems on smaller groups that often resist such interference. Caroline recently needed to inform regional groups that the home office was instituting a systemwide change to hiring practices. To save costs, she set up a Web conference between her office in Durham, North Carolina, and others in Milwaukee, Wisconsin; Albuquerque, New Mexico; and Portland, Oregon. Caroline set the meeting for 10 a.m. Eastern Standard Time. At the designated date and hour, she found that the Portland team was not logged in and she had to delay the session. When the Portland team finally did log in, Caroline launched into her presentation. She explained the reasons behind the change in a PowerPoint presentation that contained complex data she had not distributed prior to the conference. Caroline heard cell phone ringtones and typing in the background as she spoke. Still, she pushed through her one-hour presentation without eliciting any feedback.

YOUR TASK. In teams, discuss ways Caroline might have improved the Web conference. Prepare a list of recommendations from your team.

11.14 Virtual Meetings: Connecting by Skype or FaceTime to Clarify an Order (L.O. 4, 5)

> Communication Technology ❯ Social Media ❯ Team ❯ Web

Paramount Fitness Corporation, a commercial strength equipment manufacturer in California, contracts with several distributors overseas who exclusively sell Paramount weight machines to gyms and fitness studios, not to the general public. The distributor in the UK, Rowan Been, has sent a confusing order by e-mail containing incorrect item numbers and product names as well as inconsistent quantities of items. Mr. Been doesn't respond to telephone calls or e-mail requests for clarification. You remember that you conversed with Mr. Been via Skype and notice to your delight that your distributor is online.

YOUR TASK. Using Skype or FaceTime, call a classmate designated to play Mr. Been and request clarification of the rather large order. Improvise the details of the order in a Skype or FaceTime call to your peer (with or without a camera) applying the tips for virtual meetings in this chapter. Alternatively, your instructor may introduce a short background fact sheet or script for each participant, guiding your conversation and defining your roles and the particulars of the order. To use Skype or FaceTime with or without a camera, select a laptop, computer lab desktop computer, smartphone, iPod Touch, or iPad. This exchange can occur in the classroom or computer lab where the image can be projected onto a screen. The person playing the remote partner should leave the room and connect from a quiet place outside. Fellow students and your instructor will evaluate your virtual meeting with Mr. Been.

11.15 Virtual Meetings: Visiting Online Office Hours (L.O. 2, 5)

> Communication Technology ❯ Social Media

In distance courses in particular, some instructors hold virtual office hours. When using course-management systems such as Blackboard and Moodle, your professors can create class chat rooms. At appointed times, you may join your instructor and your peers in the online chat room and ask questions, request clarification, or comment on the class and the teaching material. Some of your professors may offer video chat—for example, by Skype.

YOUR TASK. During virtual office hours, practice professional demeanor and courtesy. Your class is a workshop environment in which you are practicing appropriate workplace etiquette. Impress your instructor by following the guidelines in this chapter—for example, by offering a friendly, respectful greeting, introducing yourself, communicating clearly, writing correct prose, being an active participant in group meetings, providing and accepting constructive criticism, and exhibiting a positive can-do attitude. Plan your virtual visit as you would a professional phone conversation, also described in this chapter. Your instructor may give you informal feedback or decide to use a more formal assessment such as a performance appraisal.

Other Punctuation

Although this checkup concentrates on Sections 2.23–2.29 in the Grammar/Mechanics Handbook, you may also refer to other punctuation principles. In the space provided, write the letter of the correctly punctuated sentence. Also record the appropriate G/M section for the principle involved. When you finish, compare your responses with those provided at the bottom of the page. If your answers differ, study carefully the appropriate principles.

_____a_____ (2.26a)

EXAMPLE

(Emphasize.)

a. The biggest wine-producing states—California, Washington, and Oregon—are all located on the Pacific Coast.

b. The biggest wine-producing states (California, Washington, and Oregon) are all located on the Pacific Coast.

c. The biggest wine-producing states, California, Washington, and Oregon, are all located on the Pacific Coast.

_____ 1. (Emphasize.)

a. The scholarship committee has invited three recipients (Matt Martinez, Debbie Lee, and Traci Person) to speak at the awards ceremony.

b. The scholarship committee has invited three recipients—Matt Martinez, Debbie Lee, and Traci Person—to speak at the awards ceremony.

c. The scholarship committee has invited three recipients—Matt Martinez, Debbie Lee, and Traci Person, to speak at the awards ceremony.

_____ 2. a. Our June financial figures (see Appendix A) show a sharp increase in operating expenses.

b. Our June financial figures—see Appendix A—show a sharp increase in operating expenses.

c. Our June financial figures, see Appendix A, show a sharp increase in operating expenses.

_____ 3. a. I wondered whether the deadline was April 1 or April 15?

b. I wondered whether the deadline was April 1 or April 15.

c. I wondered, whether the deadline was April 1 or April 15?

_____ 4. a. Three of the best-paying U.S. cities for women: San Jose, Sunnyvale, and Santa Clara, are in Silicon Valley.

b. Three of the best-paying U.S. cities for women, San Jose, Sunnyvale, and Santa Clara are in Silicon Valley.

c. Three of the best-paying U.S. cities for women—San Jose, Sunnyvale, and Santa Clara—are in Silicon Valley.

_____ 5. a. "Why not invest," said Warren Buffet, "in companies you really like?"

b. "Why not invest, said Warren Buffet, "in companies you really like?"

c. "Why not invest, said Warren Buffet, in companies you really like?"

_____ 6. a. Have you read the "Forbes" article titled "Genetic Tests Create Pitfalls"?

b. Have you read the _Forbes_ article titled "Genetic Tests Create Pitfalls"?

c. Have you read the "Forbes" article titled _Genetic Tests Create Pitfalls?_

_____ 7. a. Did M. Diaz promise to come at 2 p.m.?

b. Did Ms. Diaz promise to come at 2 p.m.?

c. Did Ms. Diaz promise to come at 2 p.m.?

_____ 8. a. Wow! All sales reps made their goals.
b. Wow, all sales reps made their goals.
c. Wow. All sales reps made their goals!

_____ 9. a. The word extant means "still in existence."
b. The word "extant" means "still in existence."
c. The word *extant* means "still in existence."

_____ 10. a. Mr. Sutton said he had received BA and MS degrees, didn't he?
b. Mr. Sutton said he had received B.A. and M.S. degrees didn't he?
c. Mr Sutton said he had received BA and MS degrees, didn't he?

1. b (2.26a) **2. a** (2.26a) **3. b** (2.27) **4. c** (2.26a) **5. a** (2.26a) **6. b** (2.28a) **7. b** (2.23b, 2.28f) **8. a** (2.24, 2.23b) **9. c** (2.25) **10. a** (2.28d) (2.23b, 2.24)

Every chapter provides an editing exercise to fine-tune your grammar and mechanics skills. The following meeting minutes have errors in spelling, grammar, punctuation, number form, concise wording, and other writing faults. Study the guidelines in the Grammar/Mechanics Handbook (Appendix D), including the lists of Confusing Words and Frequently Misspelled Words.

YOUR TASK. Edit the following (a) by inserting corrections in your textbook or on a photocopy using the proofreading marks in Appendix C or (b) by downloading the message from **www.cengagebrain.com** and correcting at your computer.

Honolulu-Pacific Federal Interagency Board

Room 25, 310 Ala Moana Boulevard, Honolulu

February 4, 2019

Present: Debra Chinnapongse, Tweet Jackson, Irene Kishita, Barry Knaggs, Kevin Poepoe, and Ralph Mason

Absent: Alex Watanabe

The meeting was call to order by Chair Kevin Poepo at 9:02 a.m. in the morning. Minutes from the January 6th meeting was read and approve.

Old Business

Debra Chinnapongse discussed the cost of the annual awards luncheon that honors outstanding employees. The ticket price does not cover all the expenses incured. Major expenses include: awards, leis, and complementary lunches for the judges, VIP guests and volunteers. Honolulu-Pacific Federal Interagency Board can not continue to make up the difference between income from tickets and costs for the luncheon. Ms. Chinnapongse reported that it had come to her attention that other interagency boards relied on members contributions for their awards' programs.

MOTION: To send a letter to board members asking for there contributions to support the annual awards luncheon. (Chinapongse/Kishita). PASSED 6-0.

Reports

Barry Knaggs reported that the homeland defense committee sponsored a get acquainted meeting in November. More then eighty people from various agencys attended.

New Business

The chair announced a Planing Meeting to be held in March regarding revising the emergency dismissal plan. In other New Business, Ralph Mason recommended that the staff read an article titled Enhancing Nonprofit Resources that recently appeared in the Honolulu Star-Advertiser.

Next Meeting

The next meeting will be held in early Aprl at the Fleet and Industrial Supply Center, Pearl harbor. The meeting will include a tour of the Red Hill under ground fuel storage facility.

The meeting was adjourned at 10:25 am by Keven Poepoe.

Respectfully submitted,

Business Etiquette: Breaking the Smartphone Habit in Meetings

Businesspeople today often compulsively eyeball their smartphones and tablets to read e-mail, search Google, and check Facebook or Twitter during meetings. In fact, in a Robert Half survey of executives, 81 percent confessed to having committed more or less frequent smartphone etiquette violations during virtual meetings. At the same time, 76 percent stated that meeting participants who answered their e-mail or surfed the Internet would jeopardize their career prospects.[75] Workers tapping away at their smart devices may be a common sight, but the tide is turning. Increasingly, many professionals are tired of disruptions caused by electronic gadgets during meetings.

Etiquette consultants concur: "Electronic devices are like the smoking of the '90s," says Pamela Eyring, president of The Protocol School of Washington. "Companies are aggravated and losing productivity." Businesses hire her to enact formal policies and to teach workers "why it's not a good idea to be texting while your boss is speaking at the podium," Eyring says.[76] Nancy Flynn, executive director of the ePolicy Institute and author of *The Handbook of Social Media*, has this suggestion: "Require employees to turn off mobile devices during business-related meetings, seminars, conferences, luncheons and any other situation in which a ringing phone or tapping fingers are likely to disrupt proceedings or interrupt a speaker's or participant's train of thought."

Flynn notes that banning electronic devices in meetings is not just about interruptions: "You don't want employees shooting video via a smartphone during a meeting in which company secrets are discussed, then uploading the video to YouTube or sharing it with a competitor, reporter or other third party."[77] Organizations are only beginning to establish policies on smartphone use in meetings. Mat Ishbia, CEO at United Shore Financial Services LLC in Troy, Michigan, has banned all personal technology in his company's meetings to preempt distractions. After some grumbling, his staff now reaps the benefits of meetings that are a third shorter. "There is no distraction," Ishbia says, "The only thing to do is either write on a piece of paper in your notes or listen to the person."[78]

CAREER APPLICATION. Assume that you have been asked to develop a policy discussing the use of mobile electronic devices in meetings. Your boss can't decide whether to ask you to develop a short policy or a more rigorous one. Keep in mind that meeting participants could have legitimate reasons for using mobile electronic devices—for example, to take notes, look up calendar items, or fact-check a disputed point. How could this conflict between disruptive and valid uses of mobile devices in meetings be resolved?

YOUR TASK. As an individual or with a team, compose two documents: (a) a short statement that treats employees as grown-ups who can exercise intelligent judgment and (b) a more complete set of guidelines that spell out exactly what should and should not be done.

Business Presentations

ra2studio/Shutterstock.com

Learning Outcomes

After studying this chapter, you should be able to do the following:

1 Recognize various types of business presentations, appreciate the importance of speaking skills for your career, and discuss two important first steps in preparing for any talk.

2 Explain how to organize your business presentation most effectively, and know how to build audience rapport.

3 Understand contemporary visual aids and how to guard against PowerPoint pitfalls.

4 Create an impressive, error-free multimedia presentation that shows a firm grasp of basic visual design principles.

5 Specify delivery techniques for use before, during, and after a presentation to keep the audience engaged.

12-1 Creating Effective Business Presentations

Unlike life coach Tony Robbins, activist Martin Luther King Jr., or Microsoft cofounder and philanthropist Bill Gates, few of us will ever talk to an audience of millions—whether face-to-face or aided by technology. We won't be invited to give a TED talk, motivate multitudes, or introduce a spectacular new invention. At some point, however, all businesspeople have to inform others or sell an idea. Such informative and persuasive presentations are often conveyed in person and involve audiences of various sizes. If you are like most people, you have some apprehension when speaking in public. That's normal. Good speakers are made, not born. The good news is that you can conquer the fear of public speaking and hone your skills with instruction and practice.

12-1a Speaking Skills and Your Career

The savviest future businesspeople take advantage of opportunities in college to develop their speaking skills. Such skills often play an important role in a successful career. As you have seen in Chapters 1 and 11, soft skills such as speaking skills rank very high on recruiters' wish lists. In a PayScale survey, 39 percent of managers found new graduates lacking in public speaking; 46 percent would like to see better overall communication skills.[1] Speaking skills are useful at every career stage. You might, for example, have to make a sales pitch before customers, speak to a professional gathering, or describe your company's expansion plans to your banker.

When you are in the job market, remember that recruiters are eager to hire excellent speakers and communicators. According to an annual survey of career services professionals, 67 percent of the respondents named verbal communication as a key attribute they seek in an applicant; being well-spoken ranks among the top ten employability skills.[2]

This chapter prepares you to use speaking skills in making professional oral presentations, whether alone or as part of a team, whether face-to-face or virtually. Before we dive into the specifics of how to become an excellent presenter, the following section addresses the types of business presentations you may encounter in your career.

LEARNING OUTCOME 1

Recognize various types of business presentations, appreciate the importance of speaking skills for your career, and discuss two important first steps in preparing for any talk.

12-1b Understanding Presentation Types

A common part of a business professional's life is making presentations. Some presentations are informative, whereas others are persuasive. Some are face-to-face; others, virtual. Some are performed before big audiences, whereas others are given to smaller groups. Some presentations are elaborate; others are simple. Figure 12.1 shows a sampling of business presentations you may encounter in your career.

12-1c Knowing Your Purpose

Regardless of the type of presentation, you must prepare carefully to ensure that it is effective. The most important part of your preparation is deciding what you want to accomplish. Do you want to sell a health care program to a prospective client? Do you want to persuade management to increase the marketing budget? Whether your goal is to persuade or to inform, you must have a clear idea of where you are going. At the end of your presentation, what do you want your listeners to remember or do?

Figure 12.1 Types of Business Presentations

Briefing
- Overview or summary of an issue, proposal, or problem
- Delivery of information, discussion of questions, collection of feedback

Report
- Oral equivalent of business reports and proposals
- Informational or persuasive oral account, simple or elaborate

Podcast
- Online, prerecorded audio clip delivered over the Web
- Opportunity to launch products, introduce and train employees, and sell products and services

Virtual Presentation
- Collaboration facilitated by technology (telephone or Web)
- Real-time meeting online with remote colleagues

Webinar
- Web-based presentation, lecture, workshop, or seminar
- Digital transmission with or without video to train employees, interact with customers, and promote products

OFFICE INSIDER

"Poor presentation skills mean that leaders fail to inspire their teams, products fail to sell, entrepreneurs fail to attract funding, and careers fail to soar. That seems like a big price to pay for neglecting such a basic skill that anyone can improve upon."[3]

Carmine Gallo,
communication coach, keynote speaker, author

Abigail Williams, a loan officer at Main Street Trust, faced such questions as she planned a talk for a class in small business management. (You can see the outline for her talk in Figure 12.4) Abigail's former business professor had asked her to return to campus and give his students advice about obtaining loans to start new businesses. Because Abigail knew so much about this topic, she found it difficult to extract a specific purpose statement for her presentation. After much thought she narrowed her purpose to this: *To inform potential entrepreneurs about three important factors that loan officers consider before granting start-up loans to launch small businesses.* Her entire presentation focused on ensuring that the students understood and remembered three principal ideas.

12-1d Knowing Your Audience

As in any type of communication, a second key element in preparation is analyzing your audience, anticipating the reactions of audience members, and adjusting to their needs if necessary. Audiences may fall into four categories, as summarized in Figure 12.2. By anticipating your audience, you have a better idea of how to organize your presentation. A friendly audience, for example, will respond to humor and personal experiences. A hostile audience requires an even, controlled delivery style with objective data and expert opinion. Whatever type of audience you will face, remember to plan your presentation so that it focuses on audience benefits. People in your audience will want to know what's in it for them.

Other elements, such as the age, gender, education level, experience, and size of the audience, will affect your style and message. Analyze the following questions to determine your organizational pattern, delivery style, and supporting material:

Figure 12.2 Succeeding With Four Audience Types

Audience Members	Organizational Pattern	Delivery Style	Supporting Material
Friendly			
They like you and your topic.	Use any pattern. Try something new. Involve the audience.	Be warm, pleasant, and open. Use lots of eye contact and smiles.	Include humor, personal examples, and experiences.
Neutral			
They are calm, rational; their minds are made up, but they think they are objective.	Present both sides of the issue. Use pro/con or problem/solution patterns. Save time for audience questions.	Be controlled. Do nothing showy. Use confident, small gestures.	Use facts, statistics, expert opinion, and comparison and contrast. Avoid humor, personal stories, and flashy visuals.
Uninterested			
They have short attention spans; they may be there against their will.	Be brief—no more than three points. Avoid topical and pro/con patterns that seem lengthy to the audience.	Be dynamic and entertaining. Move around. Use large gestures.	Use humor, cartoons, colorful visuals, powerful quotations, and startling statistics.

> **Avoid** darkening the room, standing motionless, passing out handouts, using boring visuals, or expecting the audience to participate.

Hostile			
They want to take charge or to ridicule the speaker; they may be defensive, emotional.	Organize using a noncontroversial pattern, such as a topical, chronological, or geographical strategy.	Be calm and controlled. Speak evenly and slowly.	Include objective data and expert opinion. Avoid anecdotes and humor.

> **Avoid** a question-and-answer period, if possible; otherwise, use a moderator or accept only written questions.

- How will this topic appeal to this audience?
- How can I relate this information to my listeners' needs?
- How can I earn respect so that they accept my message?
- What would be most effective in making my point? Facts? Statistics? Personal experiences? Expert opinion? Humor? Cartoons? Graphic illustrations? Demonstrations? Case histories? Analogies?
- What measures must I take to ensure that this audience remembers my main points?

After considering these questions, you will be able to start organizing the content and planning the features that will help you build rapport with your audience.

12-2 Organizing Content to Connect With Audiences

LEARNING OUTCOME 2

Explain how to organize your business presentation most effectively, and know how to build audience rapport.

After determining your purpose and analyzing the audience, you are ready to collect information and organize it logically. Good organization and intentional repetition are the two most powerful keys to ensuring audience comprehension and retention. In fact, many speech experts recommend the following admittedly repetitious, but effective, plan:

Step 1: Tell them what you are going to tell them.
Step 2: Tell them.
Step 3: Tell them what you have told them.

Although it is redundant, this strategy works well because most people retain information best when they hear it repeatedly. Let's examine how to construct the three parts of an effective presentation: introduction, body, and conclusion.

12-2a Capturing Attention in the Introduction

How many times have you heard a speaker begin with, *It's a pleasure to be here.* Or, *Today I'm going to talk about. . . .* Boring openings such as these get speakers off to a dull start. Avoid such banalities by striving to accomplish three goals in the introduction to your presentation:

- Capture listeners' attention and get them involved.
- Identify yourself and establish your credibility.
- Preview your main points.

If you are able to appeal to listeners and involve them in your presentation right from the start, you are more likely to hold their attention until the finish. Consider some of the techniques you used to open sales letters: a question, a startling fact, a joke, a story, or a quotation. Some speakers achieve involvement by opening with a question or command that requires audience members to raise their hands or stand up. Additional techniques to gain and keep audience attention are presented in Figure 12.3.

To establish your credibility, you need to describe your position, knowledge, or experience—whatever qualifies you to speak. The way you dress, the self-confidence you display, and your direct eye contact can also build credibility. In addition, try to connect with your audience. Listeners respond particularly well to speakers who reveal something of themselves and identify with them. A consultant addressing office workers might reminisce about how he started as an administrative assistant; a CEO might tell a funny story in which the joke is on her. Use humor if you can pull it off (not everyone can); self-effacing humor may work best for you.

OFFICE INSIDER

"Engaging your audience can mean telling stories with which people can identify, using illustrations or exercises that engage all their senses, asking rhetorical questions, using 'you' rather than 'I' phrasing, polling the audience for their opinion, telling hero stories about audience members, and so forth."[4]

Dianna Booher, *communication consultant and author*

Figure 12.3 Gaining and Keeping Audience Attention

iStock.com/Izabela Habur

Experienced speakers know how to capture the attention of an audience and how to maintain that attention throughout a presentation. You can spruce up your presentations by trying these twelve proven techniques.

- **A promise.** Begin with a realistic promise that keeps the audience expectant (for example, *By the end of this presentation, you will know how you can increase your sales by 50 percent!*).

- **Drama.** Open by telling an emotionally moving story or by describing a serious problem that involves the audience. Throughout your talk include other dramatic elements, such as a long pause after a key statement. Change your vocal tone or pitch. Professionals use high-intensity emotions such as anger, joy, sadness, or excitement.

- **Eye contact.** As you begin, command attention by surveying the entire audience to take in all listeners. Give yourself two to five seconds to linger on individuals to avoid fleeting, unconvincing eye contact. Don't just sweep the room and the crowd.

- **Movement.** Leave the lectern area whenever possible. Walk around the conference table or down the aisles of the presentation room. Try to move toward your audience, especially at the beginning and end of your talk.

- **Questions.** Keep listeners active and involved with rhetorical questions. Ask for a show of hands to get each listener thinking. The response will also give you a quick gauge of audience attention.

- **Demonstrations.** Include a member of the audience in a demonstration (for example, *I'm going to show you exactly how to implement our four-step customer courtesy process, but I need a volunteer from the audience to help me*).

- **Samples/props.** If you are promoting a product, consider using items to toss out to the audience or to award as prizes to volunteer participants. You can also pass around product samples or promotional literature. Be careful, though, to maintain control.

- **Visuals.** Give your audience something to look at besides yourself. Use a variety of visual aids in a single session. Also consider writing the concerns expressed by your audience on a flipchart, a whiteboard, or a smart board as you go along.

- **Attire.** Enhance your credibility with your audience by dressing professionally for your presentation. Professional attire will help you look competent and qualified, making your audience more likely to listen and take you seriously.

- **Current events/statistics.** Mention a current event or statistic (the more startling, the better) that is relevant to your topic and to which the audience can relate.

- **A quote.** Quotations, especially those made by well known individuals, can be powerful attention-getting devices. The quotation should be pertinent to your topic, short, and interesting.

- **Self-interest.** Review your entire presentation to ensure that it meets the critical *What's-in-it-for-me* audience test. People are most interested in things that benefit them.

After capturing attention and establishing your credibility, you will want to preview the main points of your topic, perhaps with a visual aid.

Take a look at Abigail Williams's introduction, shown in Figure 12.4, to see how she integrated all the elements necessary for a good opening.

12-2b Organizing the Body of the Presentation

The most effective oral presentations focus on a few principal ideas. Therefore, the body of your short presentation (20 minutes or shorter) should include a limited number of main points—say, two to four. Develop each main point with adequate, but not excessive, explanation and details. Too many details can obscure the main message, so keep your presentation simple and logical. Remember, listeners have no pages to refer to should they become confused.

Figure 12.4 Outlining an Oral Presentation

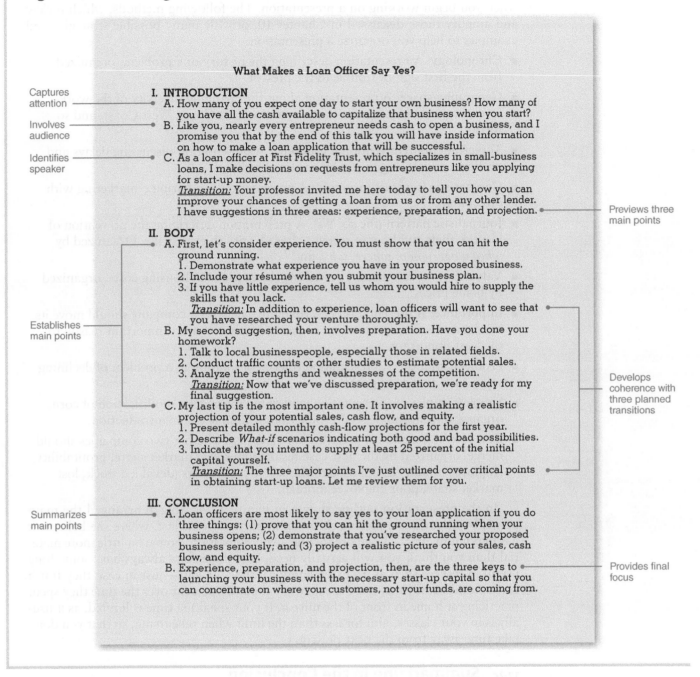

What Makes a Loan Officer Say Yes?

Captures attention ⎯⎯

Involves audience ⎯⎯

Identifies speaker ⎯⎯

I. INTRODUCTION
  A. How many of you expect one day to start your own business? How many of you have all the cash available to capitalize that business when you start?
  B. Like you, nearly every entrepreneur needs cash to open a business, and I promise you that by the end of this talk you will have inside information on how to make a loan application that will be successful.
  C. As a loan officer at First Fidelity Trust, which specializes in small-business loans, I make decisions on requests from entrepreneurs like you applying for start-up money.
     Transition: Your professor invited me here today to tell you how you can improve your chances of getting a loan from us or from any other lender. I have suggestions in three areas: experience, preparation, and projection.

Previews three main points

Establishes main points ⎯⎯

II. BODY
  A. First, let's consider experience. You must show that you can hit the ground running.
     1. Demonstrate what experience you have in your proposed business.
     2. Include your résumé when you submit your business plan.
     3. If you have little experience, tell us whom you would hire to supply the skills that you lack.
        Transition: In addition to experience, loan officers will want to see that you have researched your venture thoroughly.
  B. My second suggestion, then, involves preparation. Have you done your homework?
     1. Talk to local businesspeople, especially those in related fields.
     2. Conduct traffic counts or other studies to estimate potential sales.
     3. Analyze the strengths and weaknesses of the competition.
        Transition: Now that we've discussed preparation, we're ready for my final suggestion.
  C. My last tip is the most important one. It involves making a realistic projection of your potential sales, cash flow, and equity.
     1. Present detailed monthly cash-flow projections for the first year.
     2. Describe *What-if* scenarios indicating both good and bad possibilities.
     3. Indicate that you intend to supply at least 25 percent of the initial capital yourself.
        Transition: The three major points I've just outlined cover critical points in obtaining start-up loans. Let me review them for you.

Develops coherence with three planned transitions

Summarizes main points ⎯⎯

III. CONCLUSION
  A. Loan officers are most likely to say yes to your loan application if you do three things: (1) prove that you can hit the ground running when your business opens; (2) demonstrate that you've researched your proposed business seriously; and (3) project a realistic picture of your sales, cash flow, and equity.
  B. Experience, preparation, and projection, then, are the three keys to launching your business with the necessary start-up capital so that you can concentrate on where your customers, not your funds, are coming from.

Provides final focus

When Abigail Williams began planning her presentation, she realized immediately that she could talk for hours on her topic. She also knew that listeners are not good at separating major and minor points. Therefore, instead of drowning her listeners in information, she sorted out a few main ideas. In the banking industry, loan officers generally ask the following three questions of each budding entrepreneur: (a) Are you ready to hit the ground running in starting your business? (b) Have you done your homework? and (c) Have you made realistic projections of sales, cash flow, and equity investment? These questions would become her main points, but Abigail wanted to streamline them further so that her audience would be sure to remember them. She encapsulated the questions in three words: *experience, preparation,* and *projection.* As you can see in Figure 12.4, Abigail prepared a sentence outline showing these three main ideas. Each is supported by examples and explanations.

How to organize and sequence main ideas may not be immediately obvious when you begin working on a presentation. The following methods, which review and amplify those discussed in Chapter 10, provide many possible strategies and examples to help you organize a presentation:

- **Chronology:** A presentation describing the history of a problem, organized from the first sign of trouble to the present.
- **Geography/space:** A presentation about the changing diversity of the workforce, organized by regions in the country (East Coast, West Coast, and so forth).
- **Topic/function/conventional grouping:** A presentation discussing delays and on-time arrivals, organized by names of airlines.
- **Comparison/contrast (pro/con):** A presentation comparing e-marketing with direct mail.
- **Journalistic pattern (the six Ws):** A presentation describing the prevention of identity theft and how to recover after identity thieves strike. Organized by *who, what, when, where, why,* and *how.*
- **Value/size:** A presentation describing fluctuations in housing costs, organized by home prices.
- **Importance:** A presentation describing five reasons a company should move its headquarters to a specific city, organized from the most important reason to the least important.
- **Problem/solution:** A presentation offering a solution to a problem of declining sales, such as reducing staff.
- **Simple/complex:** A presentation explaining the genetic modification of corn, organized from simple seed production to complex gene introduction.
- **Best case/worst case:** A presentation analyzing whether two companies should merge, organized by the best-case results (improved market share, profitability, employee morale) as opposed to the worst-case results (devalued stock, lost market share, poor employee morale).

In the presentation outline shown in Figure 12.4, Abigail arranged the main points by importance, placing the most important point last, where she believes it has maximum effect. When organizing any presentation, prepare a little more material than you think you will actually need. Savvy speakers always have something useful in reserve such as an extra handout, slide, or idea—just in case they finish early. At the same time, most speakers go about 25 percent over the time they spent practicing at home in front of the mirror. If your speaking time is limited, as it usually is in your classes, aim for less than the limit when rehearsing, so that you don't take time away from the next presenters.

12-2c Summarizing in the Conclusion

Nervous speakers often rush to wrap up their presentations because they can't wait to flee the stage. However, listeners will remember the conclusion more than any other part of a speech. That's why you should spend some time making it as effective as you can. Strive to achieve three goals:

- Summarize the main themes of the presentation.
- Leave the audience with a specific and memorable take-away.
- Include a statement that allows you to exit the podium gracefully.

A conclusion is like a punch line and must stand out. Think of it as the high point of your presentation, a valuable kernel of information to take-away. The valuable kernel of information, or take-away, should tie in with the opening or present a forward-looking idea. Avoid merely rehashing, in the same words, what you said before, but ensure that you will leave the audience with very specific information or benefits and a positive impression of you and your company. The take-away is the value of the presentation to the audience and the benefit audience members believe they have received. The tension that you built in the early parts of the talk now culminates in the close. Compare these poor and improved conclusions:

> **Poor conclusion:** *Well, I guess that's about all I have to say. Thanks for your time.*
> **Improved:** *In bringing my presentation to a close, I will restate my major purpose. . . .*
> **Improved:** *In summary, my major purpose has been to. . . .*
> **Improved:** *In conclusion, let me review my three major points. They are. . . .*

Notice how Abigail Williams, in the conclusion shown in Figure 12.4, summarized her three main points and provided a final focus to listeners.

If you are making a recommendation, you might end as follows: *In conclusion, I recommend that we retain Matrixx Marketing to conduct a telemarketing campaign beginning September 1 at a cost of X dollars. To do so, I suggest that we (a) finance this campaign from our operations budget, (b) develop a persuasive message describing our new product, and (c) name Kayla Hannen to oversee the project.*

In your conclusion you could use an anecdote, an inspiring quotation, or a statement that ties in the opener and offers a new insight. Whatever you choose, be sure to include a closing thought that indicates you are finished.

12-2d Establishing Audience Rapport

Good speakers are adept at building audience rapport. They form a bond with the audience, often entertaining as well as informing. How do they do it? From observations of successful and unsuccessful speakers, we have learned that the good ones use a number of verbal and nonverbal techniques to connect with their audiences. Their helpful techniques include providing effective imagery, supplying verbal signposts, and using body language strategically.

Effective Imagery. You will lose your audience quickly if you fill your talk with abstractions, generalities, and dry facts. To enliven your presentation and enhance comprehension, try using some of the techniques presented in Figure 12.5. However, beware of exaggeration or distortion. Keep your imagery realistic and credible.

Verbal Signposts. Speakers must remember that listeners, unlike readers of a report, cannot control the rate of presentation or read through pages to review main points. As a result, listeners get lost easily. Knowledgeable speakers help the audience recognize the organization and main points in an oral message with verbal signposts. They keep listeners on track by including helpful previews, summaries, and transitions, such as these:

- **Previewing**

  The next segment of my talk presents three reasons for. . . .

  Let's now consider the causes of. . . .

- **Summarizing**

  Let me review with you the major problems I have just discussed.

  You see, then, that the most significant factors are. . . .

- **Switching directions**

  Thus far we have talked solely about. . .; now let's move to. . . .

  I have argued that . . . and . . ., but an alternate view holds that. . . .

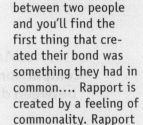

OFFICE INSIDER

"Take any relationship between two people and you'll find the first thing that created their bond was something they had in common.... Rapport is created by a feeling of commonality. Rapport is power."[5]

Tony Robbins, *entrepreneur, best-selling author, philanthropist*

Figure 12.5 Engaging the Audience With Effective Imagery

Metaphor **Comparison between dissimilar things without the words** *like* **or as**	**Worst- or Best- Case Scenario** **The worst or best that could happen**
• Our competitor's CEO is a snake when it comes to negotiating. • My desk is a garbage dump.	• If we don't back up now, a crash could wipe out all customer data. • If we fix the system now, we can expand our customer files and also increase sales.

Analogy **Comparison of similar traits between dissimilar things**	**Personal Anecdote** **A personal story**
• Product development is similar to conceiving, carrying, and delivering a baby. • Downsizing is comparable to an overweight person's regimen of dieting and exercising.	• Let me share a few personal blunders online and what I learned from my mistakes. • I always worried about my pets while I was away. That's when I decided to start a pet hotel.

Personalized Statistics **Statistics that affect the audience**	**Simile** **Comparison that includes the words** *like* **or** *as*
• Look around you. Only three out of five graduates will find a job right after graduation. • One typical meal at a fast food restaurant contains all the calories you need for an entire day.	• Our critics used our report like a drunk uses a lamppost—for support rather than illumination. • She's as happy as someone who just won the lottery.

You can further improve any oral presentation by including appropriate transitional expressions such as *first, second, next, then, therefore, moreover, on the other hand, on the contrary*, and *in conclusion*. These transitional expressions build coherence, lend emphasis, and tell listeners where you are headed. Notice in Abigail Williams's outline in Figure 12.4 the specific transitional elements designed to help listeners recognize each new principal point.

Nonverbal Messages. Although what you say is most important, the nonverbal messages you send can also have a powerful effect on how well your audience receives your message. How you look, how you move, and how you speak can make or break your presentation. The following suggestions focus on nonverbal tips to ensure that your verbal message resonates with your audience.

■ **Look terrific!** Like it or not, you will be judged by your appearance. For everything but small in-house presentations, be sure to dress professionally. The rule of thumb is that you should dress at least as well as the best-dressed person in the audience.

- **Animate your body.** Be enthusiastic and let your body show it. Stand with good posture to show confidence. Emphasize ideas to enhance points about size, number, and direction. Use a variety of gestures, but, if you want to look natural, don't plan them in advance.

- **Punctuate your words.** You can keep your audience interested by varying your tone, volume, pitch, and pace. Use pauses before and after important points. Allow the audience to take in your ideas.

- **Get out from behind the podium.** Avoid standing rigidly behind a podium. Movement makes you look natural and comfortable, unless you pace nervously. You might pick a few places in the room to walk to calmly. Even if you must stay close to your visual aids, make a point of leaving them occasionally so that the audience can see your whole body.

- **Vary your facial expression.** Begin with a smile, but change your expressions to correspond with the thoughts you are voicing. You can shake your head to show disagreement, roll your eyes to show disdain, look heavenward for guidance, or wrinkle your brow to show concern or dismay.

Whenever possible, beginning presenters should have an experienced speaker watch them and give them tips as they rehearse. Your instructor is an important coach who can provide you with invaluable feedback. In the absence of helpers, record yourself and watch your nonverbal behavior on camera. Are you doing what it takes to build rapport?

12-3 Understanding Contemporary Visual Aids

Before you make a business presentation, consider this wise proverb: *Tell me, I forget. Show me, I remember. Involve me, I understand.* Your goals as a speaker are to make listeners understand, remember, and act on your ideas. To get them interested and involved, include effective visual aids. Some experts claim that we acquire 85 percent of all our knowledge visually: "Professionals everywhere need to know about the incredible inefficiency of text-based information and the incredible effects of images," says developmental biologist John Medina.[7] Therefore, an oral presentation that incorporates visual aids is far more likely to be understood and retained than one lacking visual enhancement.

Good visual aids serve many purposes. They emphasize and clarify main points, thus improving comprehension and retention. They increase audience interest, and they make the presenter appear more professional, better prepared, and more persuasive. Well-designed visual aids illustrate and emphasize your message more effectively than words alone; therefore, they may help shorten a meeting or achieve your goal faster. Good visuals also serve to jog the memory of a speaker, thus improving self-confidence, poise, and delivery.

LEARNING OUTCOME 3
Understand contemporary visual aids and how to guard against PowerPoint pitfalls.

12-3a Types of Visual Aids

Speakers have many forms of media at their fingertips if they wish to enhance their presentations. Figure 12.6 describes the pros and cons of several visual aids, both high-tech and low-tech, that can guide you in selecting the best one for any speaking occasion. Two of the most popular visuals for business presentations are multimedia slides and handouts. Zoom presentations, an alternative to multimedia slides, are growing in popularity.

Multimedia Slides. With today's excellent software programs—such as Microsoft PowerPoint, Apple Keynote, Apache OpenOffice Impress, Google Slides, and Adobe Presenter—you can create or enhance dynamic, colorful presentations with your desktop, laptop, tablet, or smartphone. The output from these programs is generally

Figure 12.6 Pros and Cons of Visual Aid Options

Medium: High Tech	Pros	Cons
Multimedia slides	Create professional appearance with many color, art, graphic, and font options. Allow users to incorporate video, audio, and hyperlinks. Offer ease of use and transport via removable storage media, Web download, or e-mail attachment. Are inexpensive to update.	Present potential incompatibility issues. Require costly projection equipment and practice for smooth delivery. Tempt user to include razzle-dazzle features that may fail to add value. Can be too one-dimensional and linear.
Zoom presentations	Enable presenter to zoom in on and out of content to show the big picture or specific details in nonlinear, 3D quality. Provide attractive templates. Allow users to insert rich media. Offer an interactive, cinematic, and dynamic experience.	Require Internet access because they are cloud based. Don't allow editing of images. Offer limited font choices. Can be difficult to operate for some presenters used to individual slides; can make moving around the canvas challenging. Zooming can be distracting and even nauseating.
Video	Gives an accurate representation of the content; strongly indicates forethought and preparation.	Creates potential for compatibility issues related to computer video formats. Is generally expensive to create and update.

Medium: Low Tech		
Handouts	Encourage audience participation. Are easy to maintain and update. Enhance recall because audience keeps reference material.	Increase risk of unauthorized duplication of speaker's material. Can be difficult to transport. May cause speaker to lose audience's attention.
Flipcharts or whiteboards	Provide inexpensive option available at most sites. Enable users to (a) create, (b) modify or customize on the spot, (c) record comments from the audience, and (d) combine with more high-tech visuals in the same presentation.	Require graphics talent. Can be difficult for larger audiences to see. Can be cumbersome to transport. Easily wear with use.
Props	Offer a realistic reinforcement of message content. Increase audience participation with close observation.	Lead to extra work and expense in transporting and replacing worn objects. Are of limited use with larger audiences.

shown on a computer screen, a TV monitor, an LCD (liquid crystal display) panel, or a projection screen. With a little expertise and the right equipment, you can create multimedia presentations that include audio, videos, images, animation, and hyperlinks, as described shortly in the discussion of multimedia presentations. Multimedia slides can also be uploaded to a website or broadcast on the Web. At least two dozen apps, plug-ins, add-ons, and converters enhance or provide an alternative to PowerPoint.

Handouts. You can enrich and complement your presentations by distributing pictures, outlines, brochures, articles, charts, summaries, or other supplements. Speakers who use multimedia presentation software often prepare a set of their slides along with notes to hand out to viewers. To avoid distractions and to keep control, announce and discuss handouts during the presentation, but delay distributing them until after you finish.

Zoom Presentations. Many business presenters feel limited by multimedia slides, which tend to be linear. As a result, some communicators prefer more dynamic visual aids. Using software such as Prezi, a cloud-based presentation and storytelling tool, businesspeople can design 3D presentations. These 3D presentations allow the speaker to zoom in and out of images to help the audience understand and remember content, details, and relationships.[8] Zoom presentations allow presenters to communicate their ideas in a more exciting, creative way. Audience members also seem to appreciate the cinematic, interactive quality of these presentations. Figure 12.7 shows what a typical Prezi canvas looks like during the design process.

12-3b Moving Beyond PowerPoint Bullets

Electronic slideshows, created using PowerPoint in particular, are a staple of business presentations. However, overuse or misuse may be the downside of the ever-present PowerPoint slideshow. Over almost three decades of the software program's existence, millions of poorly created and badly delivered presentations have tarnished PowerPoint's reputation as an effective communication tool. Tools are helpful only when used properly.

In the last few years, several communication consultants have tried to show businesspeople how they can move beyond bullet points. The experts recommend creating slideshows that tell a story and send a powerful message with much less text and more images.[9] Presentation guru Garr Reynolds urges readers to unleash their creativity: "Do not rely on Microsoft or Apple or anyone else to dictate your choices. Most of all, do not let mere habit—and the habits of others—dictate your decisions on how you prepare and design and deliver your presentations."[11] However, before breaking with established rules and expectations, you first need to understand design basics.

Even much-touted alternatives to PowerPoint, such as Prezi, emaze, and Slide-Rocket, require some knowledge of the sound design principles covered in the next section. Figure 12.8 shows some of the tools that SlideRocket provides to create a visually rich presentation. The goal is to abandon boring bulleted lists.

Figure 12.7 Prezi Zoom Presentation

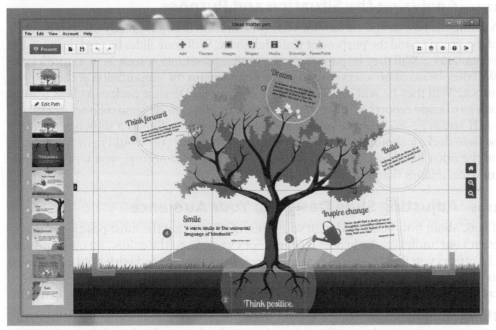

Source: http://prezi-a.akamaihd.net/presskit/Prezi%20Desktop/PreziDesktop_Windows.png

Prezi uses one canvas for a presentation rather than individual slides. Here is an example of the main canvas of a zoom presentation. Clicking on any section of this canvas will zoom in on detailed information. For example, if you click on the area around the tree roots, you will zoom in on a quote about thinking positively, as shown in the thumbnail images in the left pane.

Figure 12.8 SlideRocket Presentation

SlideRocket is a cloud-based presentation software. Like PowerPoint, it allows users to create slides, but it takes the emphasis off bullet points. Instead, SlideRocket offers numerous tools to help users create visually rich slides: stock photos, flash animation, 2D and 3D transitional effects, tables, and charts.

Source: http://www.sliderocket.com/product/

LEARNING OUTCOME 4
Create an impressive, error-free multimedia presentation that shows a firm grasp of basic visual design principles.

12-4 Preparing Engaging Multimedia Presentations

When operated by proficient designers and skillful presenters, PowerPoint, Keynote, or Prezi can add visual impact to any presentation. Of course, gaining expertise with a software program requires an investment of time and effort. You could take a course, or you could teach yourself through an online tutorial.

Some presenters prefer to create their visuals first and then develop the narrative around them. Others prepare their content first and then create the visual component. The risk associated with the first approach is that you may be tempted to spend too much time making your visuals look good and not enough time preparing your content. Remember that great-looking slides never compensate for thin content.

The following sections explain how to adjust your visuals to the situation and your audience. You will also receive how-to instructions for creating engaging and visually appealing PowerPoint, SlideRocket, or Prezi presentations.

12-4a Analyzing the Situation and Purpose

Making the best design choices for your presentation depends greatly on your analysis of the situation and the purpose of your slideshow. Will your slides be used during a live presentation? Will they be part of a self-running presentation such as in a store kiosk? Will they be saved on a server so that users can stream the presentation at their convenience? Will they be sent as a PowerPoint show or a PDF slide deck to a client instead of a hard-copy report? Will your presentation mainly run on smartphones or tablets?

If you are e-mailing the presentation or posting it online as a self-contained file or slide deck, it should feature more text than one that you would deliver orally. If, on the other hand, you are creating slides for a live presentation, you will likely rely more on images than on text.

12-4b Adjusting Slide Design to Your Audience

Think about how you can design your presentation to get the most positive response from your audience. Audiences respond, for example, to the colors, images, and special effects you use. Primary ideas are generally best conveyed with bold colors such as blue, green, and purple. Because the messages that colors convey can vary from culture to culture, presenters must choose colors and other design elements carefully.

The Meaning of Color. In the United States, blue is the color of credibility, tranquility, conservatism, and trust. Therefore, it is the background color of choice for many business presentations and social media sites. Green relates to interaction, growth, money, and stability. It can work well as a background or an accent color. Purple can also work as a background or accent color. It conveys spirituality, royalty, dreams, and humor.[12] As for text, adjust the color in such a way that it provides high contrast so it is readable. White or yellow, for example, usually works well on dark backgrounds.

Adapt the slide colors based on where you will give the presentation. Use light text on a dark background for presentations in darkened rooms. Use dark text on a light background for presentations in lighted rooms. Avoid using a dark font on a dark background, such as red text on a dark blue background. In the same way, avoid using a light font on a light background, such as white text on a pale blue background. Keep in mind that colors that look vibrant on your monitor may look washed out when projected onto a screen.

The Power of Images. Adapt the amount of text on your slide to how your audience will use the slides. As a general guideline, most graphic designers encourage the use of the *6-x-6 rule*: "Six bullets per screen, max; six words per bullet, max."[13] You may find, however, that breaking this rule is sometimes necessary, particularly when your users will be viewing the presentation on their own with no speaker assistance. For most purposes, though, strive to break free from bulleted lists whenever possible and minimize the use of text.

When using presentation software such as PowerPoint, try to avoid long, boring bulleted lists. You can alter layouts by repositioning, resizing, or changing the fonts for the placeholders in which your title, bulleted list, organization chart, video clip, photograph, or other elements appear. Figure 12.9 shows how to make your slides visually more appealing and memorable even with relatively small changes.

Notice that the bulleted items on the Before Revision slide in Figure 12.9 are not parallel. Some are redundant and unnecessarily long. The wording looks as if the author had been brainstorming or freewriting a first draft. The black font is increasingly harder to read on the blue gradient background color. On the After Revision slide, the former bullets have become short captions that accompany illustrations that add interest and highlight the message. You may use stock photos

OFFICE INSIDER

"Frequently in good presentations, photos serve well in a meta-phorical or conceptual sense, or to set a backdrop tone for what the audience is hearing from the presenter, and not necessarily to communicate actual content.... TED's most viewed talk of all time hasn't a single slide, and many of TED's most successful talks have a focus on what's said, not seen."[14]

Aaron Weyenberg, *creator of TED conference slides*

Figure 12.9 Revising and Enhancing Slides for Greater Impact

Before Revision

Reasons for Selling Online

- Your online business can grow globally.
- Customer convenience.
- You can conduct your business 24/7.
- No need for renting a retail store or hiring employees.
- Reduce inquiries by providing policies and a privacy statement.
- Customers can buy quickly and easily.

After Revision

Why You Should Sell Online

Grow business globally.   Offer convenience to customers.   Conduct business 24/7.

Save on rent and staff.   Create policies to reduce inquiries.

The slide on the left contains bullet points that are not parallel and that overlap in meaning. The second and sixth bullet points say the same thing. Moreover, some bullet points are too long. After revision, the slide on the right has a more convincing title illustrating the "you" view. The bullet points are shorter, and each begins with a verb for parallelism and an emphasis on action. The illustrations add interest.

that you can download from the Web for personal or school use without penalty, or consider taking your own digital pictures.

You can also use other PowerPoint features, such as SmartArt, to add variety and pizzazz to your slides. Converting pure text and bullet points to graphics, charts, and other images will keep your audiences interested and help them retain the information you are presenting.

The Impact of Special Effects. Just as you anticipate audience members' reactions to color and images, you can usually anticipate their reactions to special effects. Using animation and sound effects—flying objects, swirling text, clashing cymbals, and the like—only because they are available is not a good idea. Special effects distract your audience, drawing attention away from your main points. Add animation features only if doing so helps convey your message or adds interest to the content. When your audience members leave, they should be commenting on the ideas you conveyed—not on the wild swivels and sound effects. The zooming effect of Prezi presentations can add value to your presentation as long as it helps your audience understand connections and remember content. The motion should not make your listeners dizzy.

12-4c Building Your Business Presentation

After considering design principles and their effects, you are ready to start putting together your presentation. In this section you will learn how to organize and compose your presentation, which templates to choose, and how to edit, proofread, and evaluate your work.

Organizing Your Presentation. When you prepare your presentation, translate the major headings in your outline into titles for slides. Then build bullet points using short phrases. In Chapter 4 you learned to improve readability by using graphic highlighting techniques, including bullets, numbers, and headings. In preparing a PowerPoint, SlideRocket, or Prezi presentation, you will use those same techniques.

The slides (or canvas) you create to accompany your spoken ideas can be organized with visual elements that will help your audience understand and remember what you want to communicate. Let's say, for example, that you have three points in your presentation. You can create a blueprint slide that captures the three points in a visually appealing way, and then you can use that slide several times throughout your presentation. Near the beginning, the blueprint slide provides an overview of your points. Later, it provides transitions as you move from point to point. For transitions, you can direct your audience's attention by highlighting the next point you will be talking about. Finally, the blueprint slide can be used near the end to provide a review of your key points.

Composing Your Presentation. During the composition stage, many users fall into the trap of excessive formatting and programming. They fritter away precious time fine-tuning their slides or canvas and don't spend enough time on what they are going to say and how they will say it. To avoid this trap, set a limit for how much time you will spend making your slides or canvas visually appealing. Your time limit will be based on how many "bells and whistles" (a) your audience expects and (b) your content requires to make it understandable.

Not every point nor every thought requires a visual. In fact, it's smart to switch off the presentation occasionally and direct the focus to yourself. Darkening the screen while you discuss a point, tell a story, give an example, or involve the audience will add variety to your presentation.

Create a slide or canvas only if it accomplishes at least one of the following purposes:
- Generates interest in what you are saying and helps the audience follow your ideas
- Highlights points you want your audience to remember
- Introduces or reviews your key points
- Provides a transition from one major point to the next
- Illustrates and simplifies complex ideas

Consider perusing the Help articles built into your presentation software or purchasing one of many inexpensive guides to electronic slide presentations. Your presentations will be more appealing and you will save time if you know, for example, how to design with master slides and how to create your own templates.

Working With Templates. All presentation programs require you to (a) select or create a template that will serve as the background for your presentation and (b) make each slide by selecting a layout that best conveys your message. Novice and even advanced users often choose existing templates because they are designed by professionals who know how to combine harmonious colors, borders, bullet styles, and fonts for pleasing visual effects. If you prefer, you can alter existing templates so they better suit your needs. Adding a corporate logo, adjusting the color scheme to better match the colors used on your organization's website, or selecting a different font are just some of the ways you can customize existing templates. One big advantage of templates is that they get you started quickly.

Be careful, though, of what one expert has labeled "visual clichés."[15] Overused templates and clip art that come preinstalled with PowerPoint, SlideRocket, and Prezi can weary viewers who have seen them repeatedly in presentations. Instead of using a standard template, search for *PowerPoint template, SlideRocket template,* or *Prezi template* in your favorite search tool. You will see hundreds of templates available as free downloads. Unless your employer requires that presentations all have the same look, your audience will appreciate fresh templates that complement the purpose of your presentation and provide visual variety.

Revising and Proofreading Your Presentation. Use the PowerPoint slide sorter view to rearrange, insert, and delete slides during the revision process. You can use the Prezi editor to make any necessary changes to your canvas. This is the time to focus on making your presentation as clear and concise as possible. If you are listing items, be sure they all use parallel grammatical form. Figure 12.10 shows how to revise a PowerPoint slide to improve it for conciseness, parallelism, and other features. Study the design tips described in the first slide, and determine which suggestions their author did not follow. Then compare it with the revised slide.

Figure 12.10 Designing More Effective Slides

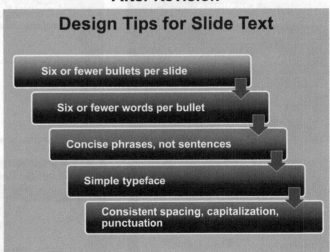

The slide on the left uses a difficult-to-read font style. In addition, the slide includes too many words per bullet and violates most of the slide-making rules it covers. After revision, the slide on the right provides a pleasing color combination, uses short bullet points in a readable font style, and creates an attractive list using PowerPoint SmartArt features.

As you are revising, check carefully to find spelling, grammar, punctuation, and other errors. Use the PowerPoint, SlideRocket, or Prezi spell-check feature, but don't rely on it solely. Careful proofing, preferably from a printed copy of the slideshow, is a must. Nothing is as embarrassing as projecting errors on a huge screen in front of an audience. Also, check for consistency in how you capitalize and punctuate points throughout the presentation.

Evaluating Your Presentation. Finally, critically evaluate your slideshow. Is your message presented in a visually appealing way? Have you tested your slides on the equipment and in the room you will be using during your presentation? Do the colors you selected work in this new setting? Are the fonts readable from the back of the room in terms of styles and sizes? Figure 12.11 shows examples of PowerPoint slides that incorporate what you have learned in this discussion.

The dark purple background and the matching hues in the slideshow shown in Figure 12.11 are standard choices for many business presentations. With an unobtrusive dark background, white fonts are a good option for maximum contrast and, hence, readability. The creator of the presentation varied the slide design to break the monotony of bulleted or numbered lists. Images and animated diagrams add interest and zing to the slides.

Some presenters allow their PowerPoint slides, SlideRocket slides, or Prezi canvases to steal their thunder. Advertising mogul David Ogilvy once observed, "Most people use PowerPoint like a drunk uses a lamppost—for support rather than for

Figure 12.11 PowerPoint Slides That Illustrate Multimedia Presentations

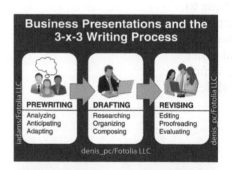
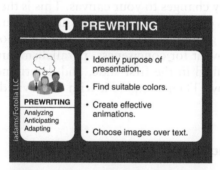

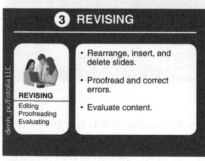

illumination."[16] Although multimedia presentations can supply terrific sizzle, they cannot replace the steak. In developing a presentation, don't expect your slides to carry the show. You can avoid being upstaged by not relying totally on your slides or canvas. Remember that you are still the main attraction!

12-4d Seven Steps to Making a Powerful Multimedia Presentation

We have now discussed many suggestions for making effective PowerPoint, SlideRocket, and Prezi presentations, but you may still be wondering how to put it all together. Figure 12.12 presents a step-by-step process for creating a powerful multimedia presentation.

Figure 12.12 Seven Steps to a Powerful Multimedia Presentation

1 Start with the text.

What do you want your audience to believe, do, or remember? Organize your ideas into an outline with major and minor points.

2 Select background and fonts.

Choose a template or create your own. Focus on consistent font styles, sizes, colors, and backgrounds. Try to use no more than two font styles in your presentation. The point size should be between 24 and 36, and title fonts should be larger than text font.

3 Choose images that help communicate your message.

Use relevant clip art, infographics, photographs, maps, or drawings to illustrate ideas. Microsoft Office Online is accessed in PowerPoint and contains thousands of clip art images and photographs, most of which are in the public domain and require no copyright permissions. Before using images from other sources, determine whether permission from the copyright holder is required.

4 Create graphics.

Use software tools to transform boring bulleted items into appealing graphics and charts. PowerPoint's SmartArt feature can be used to create organization charts, cycles and radials, time lines, pyramids, matrixes, and Venn diagrams. Use PowerPoint's Chart feature to develop various types of charts including line, pie, and bar charts. But don't overdo the graphics!

5 Add special effects.

To keep the audience focused, use animation and transition features to control when objects or text appear. With motion paths, 3D, and other animation options, you can move objects to various positions on the slide and zoom in and out of images and text on your canvas; or to minimize clutter, you can dim or remove them once they have served their purpose.

6 Create hyperlinks.

Make your presentation more interactive and intriguing by connecting to videos, spreadsheets, or websites.

7 Move your presentation online.

Make your presentation available by posting it to the Internet or an organization's intranet. Even if you are giving a face-to-face presentation, attendees appreciate these electronic handouts. The most complex option for moving your multimedia presentation to the Web involves a Web conference or broadcast. You can convert your presentations to PDF documents or send them via e-mail as files that open directly in PowerPoint or Prezi. SlideRocket presentations can be embedded in a website or blog to be viewed by anyone who visits the site.

LEARNING OUTCOME **5**

Specify delivery techniques for use before, during, and after a presentation to keep the audience engaged.

12-5 Polishing Your Delivery and Following Up

Once you have organized your presentation and prepared visuals, you are ready to practice delivering it. You will feel more confident and appear more professional if you know more about delivery methods and techniques to use before, during, and after your presentation.

12-5a Choosing a Delivery Method

Inexperienced speakers often hold on to myths about public speaking. They may believe that they must memorize an entire presentation or read from a manuscript to be successful. Let's debunk the myths and focus on effective delivery techniques.

Avoid Memorizing Your Presentation. Unless you are an experienced performer, you will sound robotic and unnatural if you try to recite your talk by heart. What's more, forgetting your place can be disastrous! That is why we don't recommend memorizing an entire oral presentation. However, memorizing significant parts—the introduction, the conclusion, and perhaps a meaningful quotation—can make your presentation dramatic and impressive.

Don't Read From Your Notes. Reading your business presentation to an audience from notes or a manuscript is boring, and listeners will quickly lose interest. Because reading suggests that you don't know your topic well, the audience loses confidence in your expertise. Reading also prevents you from maintaining eye contact. You can't see audience reactions; consequently, you can't benefit from feedback.

Deliver Your Presentation Extemporaneously. The best plan for delivering convincing business presentations, by far, is to speak *extemporaneously*, especially when you are displaying a multimedia presentation, such as a PowerPoint slideshow, Slide-Rocket slideshow, or Prezi canvas. Extemporaneous delivery means speaking freely, generally without notes, after preparing and rehearsing. You comment on the multimedia visuals you have prepared. Reading from notes or a manuscript in addition to a PowerPoint slideshow, SlideRocket slides, or a Prezi canvas will damage your credibility.

Know When Notes Are Appropriate. If you give a talk without multimedia technology, you may use note cards or an outline containing key sentences and major ideas, but beware of reading from a script. By preparing and then practicing with your notes, you can use them while also talking to your audience in a conversational manner.

WORKPLACE IN FOCUS

Many people fear public speaking. And while tips for overcoming performance anxiety often suggest calming down before a presentation, one Harvard researcher says that the cure for stage fright is not relaxing oneself, but recasting anxiety as excitement—and embracing it. According to a recent study by Alison Wood Brooks of Harvard Business School, individuals who convinced themselves that their nervousness was excitement prior to giving a speech performed better than those who attempted to relax.

Brooks argues that speakers can recast anxiety as excitement simply through active self-talk, such as saying aloud "I am excited" or "get excited." What other tips can speakers use to help overcome stage fright?[17]

Your notes should be neither entire paragraphs nor single words. Instead, they should contain a complete sentence or two to introduce each major idea. Below the topic sentence(s), outline subpoints and illustrations. Note cards will keep you on track and prompt your memory, but only if you have rehearsed the presentation thoroughly.

12-5b Before Your Presentation

Speaking in front of a group will be less daunting if you allow for adequate preparation, sufficient practice, and rehearsals. Being prepared and confident so you can interact with the audience, and being familiar with the equipment to limit surprises, will also enhance your peace of mind. Review the following tips for a smooth start.

Prepare Thoroughly. One of the most effective strategies for reducing stage fright is knowing your subject thoroughly. Research your topic diligently and prepare a careful sentence outline. One expert advises presenters to complete their Power-Point slides, SlideRocket slides, or Prezi canvases a week before the actual talk and rehearse several times each day before the presentation.[18] Those who try to wing it usually suffer the worst butterflies—and give the worst presentations. Figure 12.13 offers tips for combating the fear of public speaking.

Rehearse Repeatedly. When you rehearse, practice your entire presentation. In PowerPoint you may print out speaker's notes, an outline, or a handout featuring

Figure 12.13 Conquering Stage Fright

Ever get nervous before making a presentation? Everyone does! And it's not all in your head, either. When you face something threatening or challenging, your body reacts in what psychologists call the fight-or-flight response. This physical reflex provides your body with increased energy to deal with threatening situations. It also creates those sensations—dry mouth, sweaty hands, increased heartbeat, and stomach butterflies—that we associate with stage fright. The fight-or-flight response arouses your body for action—in this case, making a presentation.

Because everyone feels some form of apprehension before speaking, it's impossible to eliminate the physiological symptoms altogether. However, you can reduce their effects with the following techniques:

- **Breathe deeply.** Use deep breathing to ease your fight-or-flight symptoms. Inhale to a count of ten, hold this breath to a count of ten, and exhale to a count of ten. Concentrate on your counting and your breathing; both activities reduce your stress.

- **Convert your fear.** Don't view your sweaty palms and dry mouth as evidence of fear. Interpret them as symptoms of exuberance, excitement, and enthusiasm to share your ideas.

- **Know your topic and come prepared.** Feel confident about your topic. Select a topic that you know well and that is relevant to your audience. Prepare thoroughly and practice extensively.

- **Use positive self-talk.** Remind yourself that you know your topic and are prepared. Tell yourself that the audience is on your side—because it is! Moreover, most speakers appear to be more confident than they feel. Make this apparent confidence work for you.

- **Take a sip of water.** Drink some water to alleviate your dry mouth and constricted voice box, especially if you're talking for more than 15 minutes.

- **Shift the spotlight to your visuals.** At least some of the time the audience will be focusing on your slides, transparencies, handouts, or whatever you have prepared—and not totally on you.

- **Ignore any stumbles.** If you make a mistake, ignore the stumble and keep going. Don't apologize or confess your nervousness. The audience will forget any mistakes quickly.

- **Feel proud when you finish.** You will be surprised at how good you feel when you finish. Take pride in what you have accomplished, and your audience will reward you with applause and congratulations. Your body, of course, will call off the fight-or-flight response and return to normal!

miniature slides, which are excellent for practice. If you don't use an electronic slideshow, place your outline sentences on separate note cards. You may also wish to include transitional sentences to help you move to the next topic as you practice. Rehearse alone or before friends and family. Also consider making an audio or video recording of your rehearsals so you can evaluate your effectiveness.

Time Yourself. Most audiences tend to get restless during longer talks. Therefore, try to complete your presentation in 20 minutes or less. If you have a time limit, don't go over it. Set a simple kitchen timer during your rehearsal to keep track of time. Better yet, use the PowerPoint function Rehearse Timings in the Slide Show tab to measure the length of your talk as you practice. Other presentation software packages offer similar features.

Dress Professionally. Dressing professionally for a presentation will make you look more credible to your audience. You will also feel more confident. If you are not used to professional attire, practice wearing it so you appear comfortable during your presentation.

Check the Room and the Equipment. If you are using a computer, a projector, or sound equipment, be certain they are operational. Before you start, check the lighting, the electrical outlets, and the position of the viewing screen. Confirm that the places you plan to stand are not in the line of the projected image. Audience members don't appreciate having part of the slide displayed on your body. Ensure that the seating arrangement is appropriate to your needs. Make sure that all video or Web links are working and that you know how to operate all features the first time you try.

Greet Members of the Audience. Try to make contact with a few members of the audience when you enter the room, while you are waiting to be introduced, or when you walk to the podium. Your body language should convey friendliness, confidence, and enjoyment.

Practice Stress Reduction. If you feel tension and fear while you are waiting your turn to speak, use stress-reduction techniques, such as deep breathing. Additional techniques to help you conquer stage fright are presented in Figure 12.13.

No matter how much time you put into preshow setup and testing, you still have no guarantee that all will go smoothly. Therefore, always bring backups of your presentation. Transferring your presentation to a CD or a USB flash drive that could run from any available computer might prove useful. Likewise, copying your file to the cloud (e.g., Dropbox or Google Drive) or sending it to yourself as an e-mail attachment can be beneficial.

12-5c During Your Presentation

To stay in control during your talk, build credibility, and engage your audience, follow these time-tested guidelines for effective speaking:

Start With a Pause and Present Your First Sentence From Memory. When you first approach the audience, take a moment to make yourself comfortable. Establish your control of the situation. By memorizing your opening, you can immediately develop rapport with the audience through eye contact. You will also sound confident and knowledgeable.

Maintain Eye Contact. If the size of the audience overwhelms you, pick out two individuals on the right and two on the left. Talk directly to these people. Don't ignore listeners in the back of the room. Even when presenting to a large audience, try to make genuine, not fleeting eye contact with as many people as possible during your presentation.

Control Your Voice and Vocabulary. This means speaking in moderated tones but loudly enough to be heard. Eliminate verbal static, such as *ah, er, like, you know,* and *um.* Silence is preferable to meaningless fillers when you are thinking of your next idea.

Show Enthusiasm. If you are not excited about your topic, how can you expect your audience to be? Show passion for your topic through your tone, facial expressions, and gestures. Adding variety to your voice also helps to keep your audience alert and interested.

Skip the Apologies. Avoid weak openings, such as *I know you have heard this before, but we need to review it anyway.* Or: *I had trouble with my computer and the slides, so bear with me.* Unless the issue is blatant, such as not being able to load the presentation or make the projector work, apologies are counterproductive. Focus on your presentation.

Slow Down and Know When to Pause. Many novice speakers talk too rapidly, displaying their nervousness and making it very difficult for audience members to understand their ideas. Put the brakes on and listen to what you are saying. Pauses give the audience time to absorb an important point. Silence can be effective especially when you are transitioning from one point to another. Paraphrase and elaborate on what the listeners have seen. Don't read verbatim from the slides.

Move Naturally. If you have a lectern, don't hide behind it. Move about casually and naturally. Avoid fidgeting with your clothing, hair, or items in your pockets. Do not roll up your sleeves or put your hands in your pockets. Learn to use your body to express a point.

Control Visual Aids With Clickers, Pointers, and Blank Screens. Discuss and interpret each visual aid for the audience. Move aside as you describe it so people can see it fully. Learn to advance your slides remotely with a clicker. Use a laser pointer if necessary, but steady your hand if it is shaking. Dim the slideshow when not discussing the slides. In Slide Show view in PowerPoint, press *B* on the keyboard to blacken the screen or *W* to turn the screen white. In Prezi, remember to zoom back out when necessary.

Avoid Digressions. Stick to your outline and notes. Don't suddenly include clever little anecdotes or digressions that occur to you on the spot. If it is not part of your rehearsed material, leave it out so you can finish on time.

Summarize Your Main Points and Drive Home Your Message. Conclude your presentation by reiterating your main points or by emphasizing what you want the audience to think or do. Once you have announced your conclusion, proceed to it directly.

12-5d After Your Presentation

As you are concluding you presentation, handle questions and answers competently and provide handouts, if appropriate. Try the following techniques:

Distribute Handouts. If you prepared handouts with data the audience will not need during the presentation, pass them out when you finish to prevent any distraction during your talk.

Encourage Questions but Keep Control. If the situation permits a question-and-answer period, announce it at the beginning of your presentation. Then, when you finish, ask for questions. Set a time limit for questions and answers. If you don't know the answer to a question, don't make one up or panic. Instead, offer to find the answer within a day or two. If you make such a promise, be sure to follow through. Don't allow one individual to dominate the Q & A period. Keep the entire audience involved.

Repeat Questions. Although you may have heard the question, some audience members may not have. Begin each answer by repeating the question. This also gives you thinking time. Then, direct your answer to the entire audience.

Reinforce Your Main Points. You can use your answers to restate your primary ideas (*I'm glad you brought that up because it gives me a chance to elaborate on …*). In answering questions, avoid becoming defensive or debating the questioner.

OFFICE INSIDER

"Don't be afraid to show enthusiasm for your subject. 'I'm excited about being here today' says good things to an audience. It generally means that you are confident, you have something of value to say, and you are prepared to state your case clearly. Boredom is contagious."[19]

Dianna Booher, *communication consultant and author*

Avoid *Yes*, but Answers. The word *but* immediately cancels any preceding message. Try replacing it with *and*. For example, *Yes, X has been tried. And Y works even better because.* . . .

End With a Summary and Appreciation. To signal the end of the session before you take the last question, say something like *We have time for just one more question.* As you answer the last question, try to work it into a summary of your main points. Then, express appreciation to the audience for the opportunity to present.

Summary of Learning Outcomes

1 Recognize various types of business presentations, appreciate the importance of speaking skills for your career, and discuss two important first steps in preparing for any talk.

- Excellent presentation skills are sought by employers and will benefit you at any career stage.
- Presentation types include briefings, reports, podcasts, and webinars; they can be informative or persuasive, face-to-face or virtual, and complex or simple.
- Savvy speakers know what they want to accomplish and are able to adjust to friendly, neutral, uninterested, as well as hostile audiences.

2 Explain how to organize your business presentation most effectively, and know how to build audience rapport in a presentation.

- In the opening, capture the audience's attention, introduce yourself and establish your credibility, and preview your talk.
- Organize the body according to chronology, space, function, comparison/contrast, a journalistic pattern, value/size, importance, problem/solution, simple/complex, or best case/worst case.
- In the conclusion, summarize the main topics of your talk, leave the audience with a memorable take-away, and end with a statement that provides a graceful exit.
- Build rapport by using effective imagery, verbal signposts, and positive nonverbal messages.

3 Understand contemporary visual aids and how to guard against PowerPoint pitfalls.

- Your audience is more likely to retain your talk if you use well-prepared visual aids.
- Good visuals emphasize and clarify main points, increase audience interest, prove you are professional, illustrate your message better than words alone, and serve to jog your memory.
- Common types of visual aids are multimedia slides, zoom presentations, videos, handouts, flipcharts and whiteboards, as well as props.
- In good hands PowerPoint is helpful; aspire to using more images and less text.

4 Create an impressive, error-free multimedia presentation that shows a firm grasp of basic visual design principles.

- The purpose and the audience determine the slide design, which includes color, images, and special effects.
- Building a presentation involves organizing and composing slide content; avoiding overused templates; and revising, proofreading, and evaluating the final product.
- The seven steps to creating impressive multimedia slides are as follows: start with the text, select a template, choose images, create graphics, add special effects, create hyperlinks, and post online.

5 Specify delivery techniques for use before, during, and after a presentation to keep the audience engaged.

- When delivering a business presentation, don't memorize your talk or read from notes; rather, speak extemporaneously and use notes only when you're not using presentation software.
- Before your presentation prepare and rehearse, time yourself, dress professionally, check the room and equipment, greet members of the audience, and practice stress reduction.
- During the presentation deliver your first sentence from memory, maintain eye contact, control your voice, show enthusiasm, slow down, move naturally, use visual aids skillfully, and stay on topic.
- After the presentation distribute handouts, encourage and repeat questions, reinforce your main points, avoid *Yes, but* answers, and end with a summary and appreciation.

Chapter Review

1. How do speaking skills affect promotions and career success? (L.O. 1)

2. List and describe five types of presentations a business professional might make. (L.O. 1)

3. Which effective three-step organizational plan do many speech experts recommend, and why does it work well for oral presentations despite its redundancy? (L.O. 2)

4. What three goals should you accomplish in the introduction to your presentation? (L.O. 2)

5. Name at least eight techniques that can help you gain and keep audience attention. (L.O. 2)

6. List high-tech and low-tech visual aids that you can use when speaking to an audience. Which two are the most popular? (L.O. 3)

7. What is the 6-x-6 rule, and what might prompt a presentation slide creator to break it? (L.O. 4)

8. How can you learn more about an unfamiliar audience before creating your presentation? (L.O. 1, 2)

9. Which delivery method is best for persuasive business presentations? Explain why. (L.O. 5)

10. How can speakers overcome stage fright? Name at least six helpful techniques. (L.O. 5)

Critical Thinking

11. Why should even practiced speakers plan their presentations when addressing a business audience instead of just "winging it?"

12. Communication expert Dianna Booher claims that enthusiasm is infectious and "boredom is contagious."[20] What does this mean for you as a presenter? How can you avoid being a boring speaker? (L.O. 2, 4, 5)

13. Why do many communication consultants encourage businesspeople to move beyond bullet points? What do they recommend instead and why? (L.O. 3)

14. How can you prevent multimedia presentation software from stealing your thunder? (L.O. 4)

15. General Motors CEO Mary Barra inherited a mess when she ascended to the top post in her beleaguered company. Several GM car models had exhibited problems with their ignition switches, which turned off engines at highway speeds, causing 124 deaths and 275 injuries. As early as 2001, company insiders knew about the problem, but ultimately took no action. Even as the scandal broke, GM first underreported the casualties.[21] Mary Barra pulled no punches. In a town hall meeting, she unflinchingly addressed a global audience.[22] Applying lessons learned in this chapter, what would you advise chief executive Mary Barra to do when she communicates with the public about the scandal? What could Barra say to restore trust in the company? (L.O. 1–3)

Activities and Cases

12.1 Analyzing the Audience (L.O. 2, 4)

> Web

YOUR TASK. Select a recent issue of *The Wall Street Journal, Bloomberg Businessweek, The Economist, Money, Forbes, Fast Company,* or another business periodical approved by your instructor. Based on an analysis of your classmates, select an article that will appeal to them and that you can relate to their needs. Submit to your instructor a one-page summary that includes the following: (a) the author, article title, source, issue date, and page reference; (b) a one-paragraph article summary; (c) a description of why you believe the article will appeal to your classmates; and (d) a summary of how you can relate the article to their needs.

12.2 Examining Iconic Speeches (L.O. 1, 2, 5)

> Web

YOUR TASK. Search online for a speech by a significant businessperson or well-known political figure. Consider watching the following iconic political speeches, considered to be among the best in the twentieth century: Martin Luther King Jr.'s "I Have a Dream" speech, President Kennedy's inaugural address, and Franklin Delano Roosevelt's Pearl Harbor address.[23] If you prefer business tycoons dispensing advice, search for the best-known commencement speeches—for example, Steve Jobs' "Stay Hungry, Stay Foolish" Stanford address, Salman Khan's "Live Your Life Like It's Your Second Chance" speech, or Sheryl Sandberg's "Rocketship" commencement speech at Harvard. Transcripts of these and other well-known speeches are also available online.[24] Write a memo report or give a short presentation to your class critiquing the speech in terms of the following:

a. Effectiveness of the introduction, body, and conclusion

b. Evidence of effective overall organization

c. Use of verbal signposts to create coherence

d. Emphasis of two to four main points

e. Effectiveness of supporting facts (use of examples, statistics, quotations, and so forth)

f. Focus on audience benefits

g. Enthusiasm for the topic

h. Body language and personal mannerisms

12.3 Inviting a Professional Speaker (L.O. 1, 2, 4, 5)

> Communication Technology   Social Media   Team   Web

Have you ever wondered why famous business types, politicians, athletes, and other celebrities can command high speaking fees? How much are they really making per appearance, and what factors may justify their sometimes exorbitant fees? You may also wonder how a motivational speaker or corporate trainer might benefit you and your class or your campus community. Searching for and selecting an expert is easy with several commercial speakers bureaus vying for clients. All bureaus provide detailed speaker bios, areas of expertise, and fees. One even features video previews of its clients.

The preeminent agencies for booking talent are All American Speakers, BigSpeak Speakers Bureau, Speakerpedia, and Brooks International Speakers & Entertainment Bureau. Among the many All American Speakers leadership personalities are Mark Cuban, Barbara Corcoran, and Biz Stone. BigSpeak standouts are top chef Anthony Bourdain, cancer research advocate Dr. Susan Love, and distance swimmer Diana Nyad. Speakerpedia represents the likes of economist Nouriel Roubini, Jack Welch, Richard Branson, and Suze Orman. Brooks International features financier and philanthropist Mike Milken and TV commentator and personal finance expert Terry Savage, among others.

YOUR TASK. Imagine that you have a budget of up to $100,000 to hire a well-known public speaker. In teams or individually, select a business-related category of speaker by visiting one of the speakers bureaus online. For example, choose several prominent personal finance gurus (Suze Orman, Terry Savage, and others) or successful entrepreneurs and venture capitalists (Elon Musk, Richard Branson, Jack Welch). Other categories are motivational speakers, philanthropists, and famous economists. Study their bios for clues about their expertise and accomplishments.

Comparing at least three speakers, come up with a set of qualities that apparently make these individuals sought-after speakers. Consider how those qualities could enlighten you and your peers. To enrich your experience and enhance your knowledge, watch videos of your chosen speakers on YouTube or the TED website, if available. Check talent agencies, personal websites, and Facebook for further information. Write a memo report about your speaker group, or present your findings orally, with or without a slide presentation. If your instructor directs, recommend your favorite speaker and give reasons for your decision.

12.4 Following a Business Tycoon on Twitter (L.O. 1–5)

> Communication Technology   Social Media   Web

YOUR TASK. On Twitter, in the Search window on top of the page, enter the name of the businessperson whose tweets you wish to follow. Elon Musk, Richard Branson, Suze Orman, Guy Kawasaki, and other well-known businesspeople are avid Twitter users. Over the course of a few days, read the tweets of your favorite business mogul. After a while, you should be able to discern some trends and areas of interest. Note whether and how your subject responds to queries from followers. What are his or her favorite topics? Report your findings to the class, verbally with notes or using PowerPoint or Prezi. If you find particularly intriguing tweets and links, share them with the class.

12.5 Conquering the Fear of Public Speaking (L.O. 5)

Communication Technology   E-Mail   Social Media   Team

What scares you the most about making a presentation in front of your class? Being tongue-tied? Fearing all eyes on you? Messing up? Forgetting your ideas and looking unprofessional?

YOUR TASK. Discuss the previous questions as a class. Then, in groups of three or four, talk about ways to overcome these fears. Your instructor may ask you to write a memo, an e-mail, a discussion board contribution or social media post (individually or collectively) summarizing your suggestions. If your instructor prefers, you may break out of your small groups and report your best ideas to the entire class.

12.6 Anticipating Speaking in Your Field (L.O. 1)

Social Media   Team   Web

YOUR TASK. Interview one or two individuals in your professional field—in person or by e-mail or using social media (e.g., LinkedIn). How is oral communication important in this profession? Does the need for oral skills change as one advances? What suggestions can these people make to newcomers to the field for developing proficient oral communication skills? Discuss your findings with your class. Your instructor may ask you to complete your research as a team and prepare a written or oral report to be presented in class.

12.7 Creating an Outline for an Oral Presentation (L.O. 1, 2)

One of the hardest parts of preparing an oral presentation is developing the outline.

YOUR TASK. Select an oral presentation topic from the list in Activity 12.14, or suggest an original topic. Prepare an outline for your presentation using the following format:

Title
Purpose

                                               I. INTRODUCTION

State your name   A.

Gain attention and involve the audience   B.

Establish credibility   C.

Preview main points   D.

Transition

                                               II. BODY

Main point   A.
                                                 1.

Illustrate, clarify, contrast   2.
                                                 3.

Transition

Main point   B.
                                                 1.

Illustrate, clarify, contrast   2.
                                                 3.

Transition

Main point   C.
                                                 1.

Illustrate, clarify, contrast   2.
                                                 3.

Transition

                                           III. CONCLUSION

Summarize main points   A.

Provide final focus or take-away   B.

Encourage questions   C.

12.8 Examining a TED Talk (L.O. 1–5)

> **E-Mail** > **Social Media** > **Web**

To learn from the presentation skills of the best speakers today, visit the TED channel on YouTube or the TED website. Watch one or more of the 24,001 TED talks (motto: Ideas worth spreading) available online. Standing at over one billion views worldwide, the presentations cover topics from the fields of technology, entertainment, and design (TED).

YOUR TASK. If your instructor directs, select and watch one of the TED talks and outline it. You may also be asked to focus on the selected speaker's presentation techniques based on the guidelines you have studied in this chapter. Jot down your observations either as notes for a classroom discussion or to serve as a basis for an informative memo or e-mail. If directed by your instructor, compose a concise yet informative tweet directing Twitter users to your chosen TED talk and commenting on it.

12.9 Showcasing Your Job (L.O. 1–5)

> **Communication Technology**

What if you had to create a presentation for your classmates and instructor, or perhaps a potential recruiter, that describes the multiple tasks you perform at work? Could you do it in a five-minute PowerPoint, SlideRocket, or Prezi presentation?

Your instructors, for example, may wear many hats. Most academics (a) teach; (b) conduct research to publish; and (c) provide service to the department, college, university, and community. Can you see how those aspects of their profession lend themselves to an outline of primary slides (teaching, publishing, service) and second-level slides (instructing undergraduate and graduate classes, presenting workshops, and giving lectures under the teaching label)?

YOUR TASK. Now it's your turn to introduce the duties you perform (or performed) in a current or past job, volunteer activity, or internship in a brief, simple, yet well-designed PowerPoint or Prezi presentation. Your goal is to inform your audience of your job duties in a three- to five-minute talk. Use animation features and graphics where appropriate. Your instructor may show you a completed example of this project.

12.10 Honing a Perfect Elevator Pitch (L.O. 1, 2)

"Can you pass the elevator test?" asks presentation whiz Garr Reynolds in a new twist on the familiar scenario.[25] He suggests that this technique will help you sharpen your core message. In this exercise you need to pitch your idea in a few brief moments instead of the 20 minutes you had been granted with your vice president of product marketing. You arrive at her door for your appointment as she is leaving, coat and briefcase in hand. Something has come up. This meeting is a huge opportunity for you if you want to get the OK from the executive team. Could you sell your idea during the elevator ride and the walk to the parking lot? Reynolds asks. Although this scenario may never happen, you will possibly be asked to shorten a presentation, say, from an hour to 30 minutes or from 20 minutes to 5 minutes. Could you make your message tighter and clearer on the fly?

YOUR TASK. Take a business idea you may have, a familiar business topic you care about, or a promotion or raise you wish to request. Create an impromptu two- to five-minute speech making a good case for your core message. Even though you won't have much time to think about the details of your speech, you should be sufficiently familiar with the topic to boil it down and yet be persuasive.

12.11 Making Sense of *Fortune* Lists (L.O. 1, 2)

> **Web**

YOUR TASK. Using a research database, perform a search to learn how *Fortune* magazine determines which companies make its annual lists. Research the following lists. Then organize and present a five- to ten-minute informative talk to your class.

a. Fortune 500
b. Global 500
c. 100 Best Companies to Work For
d. World's Most Admired Companies

12.12 Presenting an Intriguing Business Topic (L.O. 1–3)

> Social Media > Web

YOUR TASK. Find an interesting business article, and verbally present it to the class with or without notes. Summarize the article and explain why you have chosen it and why you believe it's valuable. Another option is to select a short business-related video clip. First introduce the video and summarize it. Time permitting, show the video in class. Visit any business website—for example, *The Wall Street Journal, Forbes, or Bloomberg Businessweek*. If your instructor directs, compose a tweet recommending or commenting on your article or video clip. Of the available 140 characters, leave at least 10 for retweeting.

12.13 Advocating for a Cause (L.O. 1–5)

> Communication Technology > Social Media > Web

Do you care deeply about a particular nonprofit organization or cause? Perhaps you have donated to a cancer charity or volunteered for a local faith-based nonprofit. The Red Cross, Greenpeace, and the World Wildlife Fund (WWF) may be household names, but thousands of lesser-known nonprofit organizations are also trying to make the world a better place.

Professional fund-raiser and nonprofit service expert Sarah W. Mackey encourages volunteers-to-be to become ambassadors for their favorite organizations. Much like brand ambassadors, advocates for nonprofits should wear the nonprofit's logo, invite friends, tell their families, raise money, volunteer, and spread the word on social media, Mackey says.[26] Some nonprofits—for example, the California-based environmental group Heal the Bay—are proactive. They offer speakers bureau training to volunteers eager to reach out to their communities and raise awareness.[27] Ambassadors do good, become professional speakers, and acquire valuable skills to put on their résumés, a win-win-win!

YOUR TASK. Select your favorite charity. If you need help, find your charity or cause by visiting GuideStar, a nongovernmental watchdog that monitors nonprofits, or simply Google *list of nonprofits*. Learn as much as you can from your organization's website and from articles written about it. Also, vet your charity by checking it out on GuideStar. Then assemble your information into a logical outline, and create a persuasive oral presentation using presentation software. Your goal is not only to introduce the charity but also to inspire your peers to seek more information and to volunteer. **Tip:** Focus on the benefits, direct and indirect, of volunteering for this charity. Finally, if your instructor asks, practice writing tweets advocating for your organization and calling the public to action.

12.14 Selecting a Topic for an Oral Presentation (L.O. 1, 2, 5)

> Communication Technology > Web

YOUR TASK. Select a report topic from the following suggestions or from the expanded list of Report Topics at **www.cengagebrain.com** in the Book Resources folder. Prepare a five- to ten-minute oral presentation. Consider yourself an expert who has been called in to explain some aspect of the topic before a group of interested people. Because your time is limited, prepare a concise yet forceful presentation with effective visual aids.

a. What kind of incentives could your company offer to motivate employees to make healthier food choices and to exercise more?
b. How can businesses benefit from Facebook and Twitter? Cite examples in your chosen field.
c. Which is financially more beneficial to a business, leasing or buying copiers?
d. Tablet computers are eroding the market share previously held by laptops and netbooks. Which brands are businesses embracing and why? Which features are must-haves?
e. What kind of marketing works with students on college campuses? Word of mouth? Internet advertising? Free samples? How do students prefer to get information about goods and services?
f. How can consumers protect themselves from becoming victims of identity theft?
g. How can companies and nonprofits protect themselves from hackers?
h. How could an intercultural training program be initiated in your school?
i. Companies usually do not admit shortcomings. However, some admit previous failures and use them to strategic advantage. For example, Microsoft acknowledged the shortcomings of Windows 8, its redesigned operating system that users found confusing and annoying. Find three or more examples of companies admitting weaknesses, and draw conclusions from their strategies. Would you recommend this as a sound marketing strategy?
j. How can students and other citizens contribute to conserving gasoline and other fossil fuels to save money and help slow global climate change?
k. What is the career outlook in a field of your choice? Consider job growth, compensation, and benefits. What kind of academic or other experience is typically required in your field?

l. Find a recent "disruptive" (i.e., game-changing or groundbreaking) start-up and study its business model. What need does it fill? Is it about to change its industry significantly? What are its prospects? (For example, check out Uber, Lyft, Airbnb, or Coursera.)

m. What is telecommuting, and for what kinds of workers is it an appropriate work alternative?

n. What options (think aid, grants, and scholarships) do students have to finance their college tuition and fees as costs continue to rise?

o. What is the economic outlook for a given product, such as hybrid cars, laptop computers, digital cameras, fitness equipment, or a product of your choice?

p. What is Bitcoin and why are banks and law enforcement authorities concerned about it?

q. What franchise would offer the best investment opportunity for an entrepreneur in your area?

r. How should a job candidate prepare for a video interview via Skype or FaceTime?

s. What should a guide to proper cell phone use include?

t. Are internships worth the effort?

u. Why should a company have a written e-mail and social media policy?

v. Where should your organization hold its next convention?

w. What is the outlook for real estate (commercial or residential) investment in your area?

x. What do personal assistants for celebrities do, and how does one become a personal assistant? (Investigate the Association of Celebrity Personal Assistants.)

y. What kinds of gifts are appropriate for businesses to give clients and customers during the holiday season?

z. What rip-offs are on the Federal Trade Commission's List of Top 10 Consumer Scams, and how can consumers avoid falling for them?

12.15 Creating a Multimedia Presentation (no additional research required) (L.O. 1–5)

Communication Technology

You are a consultant and have been hired to improve the effectiveness of corporate trainers. These trainers frequently make presentations to employees on topics such as conflict management, teamwork, time management, problem solving, performance appraisals, and employment interviewing. Your goal is to teach these trainers how to make better presentations.

YOUR TASK. Create six visually appealing slides based on the following content, which will be spoken during your presentation titled Effective Employee Training. The comments shown here are only a portion of a longer presentation.

Trainers have two options when they make presentations. The first option is one-way communication in which the trainer basically dumps the information on the audience and leaves. The second option is a two-way approach that involves the audience. The benefits of the two-way approach are that it helps the trainer connect with the audience and reinforce key points, it increases audience retention rates, and it changes the pace and adds variety to the presentation. The two-way approach also encourages audience members to get to know each other. Because today's employees demand more than just a talking head, trainers must engage their audiences by involving them in a dialogue.

If you decide to interact with your audience, you need to choose an approach that suits your delivery style. Also, think about which options your audience would be likely to respond to most positively. Let's consider some interactivity approaches now. Realize, though, that these ideas are presented to help you get your creative juices flowing. After reading the list, think about situations in which these options might be effective. You could also brainstorm to come up with creative ideas to add to this list.

- Ask employees to guess at statistics before revealing them.
- Ask an employee to share examples or experiences.
- Ask a volunteer to help you demonstrate something.
- Ask the audience to complete a questionnaire or worksheet.
- Ask the audience to brainstorm or list things as fast as possible.
- Ask a variety of question types to achieve different purposes.
- Invite the audience to work through a process or examine an object.
- Survey the audience.
- Pause to let the audience members read something to themselves.
- Divide the audience into small groups to discuss an issue.

Capitalization

Review Sections 3.01–3.16 in the Grammar/Mechanics Handbook. In the space provided, write the letter of the sentence with correct capitalization. Also record the appropriate G/M section for the principle involved. When you finish, compare your responses with those provided at the bottom of the page. If your answers differ, review the appropriate principles.

__b__ (3.16, 3.05)   EXAMPLE   a. In the Fall Seth enrolled in history, Spanish, and Psychology.
b. In the fall Seth enrolled in history, Spanish, and psychology.
c. In the Fall Seth enrolled in History, Spanish, and Psychology.

_____   1. a. All united airlines passengers must exit the Plane at gate 16.
b. All United Airlines Passengers must exit the Plane at Gate 16.
c. All United Airlines passengers must exit the plane at Gate 16.

_____   2. a. The Economics Professor stated that tax rates for Japanese citizens were quite low.
b. The economics professor stated that tax rates for Japanese citizens were quite low.
c. The Economics professor stated that tax rates for Japanese citizens were quite low.

_____   3. a. During the spring she was interviewed for a position in the federal government.
b. During the spring she was interviewed for a position in the Federal Government.
c. During the Spring she was interviewed for a position in the federal government.

_____   4. a. Traveling North on Highway 10, my Aunt and Uncle had an accident last July.
b. Traveling north on Highway 10, my Aunt and Uncle had an accident Last July.
c. Traveling north on Highway 10, my aunt and uncle had an accident last July.

_____   5. a. The Chair of our Employee Benefits Committee convinced the Manager to serve.
b. The chair of our Employee Benefits Committee convinced the manager to serve.
c. The chair of our employee benefits committee convinced the manager to serve.

_____   6. a. At a Community College in the South, the most popular mobile apps are YouTube, Instagram, and Facebook.
b. At a community college in the South, the most popular mobile apps are YouTube, Instagram, and Facebook.
c. At a Community College in the south, the most popular mobile apps are youtube, instagram, and facebook.

_____   7. a. Did you see *The New York Times* article titled "Reebok to pay $25 million for toning shoe claims"?
b. Did you see *The new york times* article titled "Reebok to pay $25 million for toning shoe claims"?
c. Did you see *The New York Times* article titled "Reebok to Pay $25 Million for Toning Shoe Claims"?

_____   8. a. I bought the Dell Inspiron computer, but you may purchase any laptop you choose.
b. I bought the Dell Inspiron Computer, but you may purchase any Laptop you choose.
c. I bought the Dell Inspiron computer, but you may purchase any Laptop you choose.

_____ 9. a. In the Spring our Admissions Director plans to travel to venezuela, colombia, and ecuador to recruit new Students.

b. In the Spring our Admissions Director plans to travel to Venezuela, Colombia, and Ecuador to recruit new Students.

c. In the spring our admissions director plans to travel to Venezuela, Colombia, and Ecuador to recruit new students.

_____ 10. a. Please consult figure 3.2 in chapter 5 for U.S. census bureau figures regarding non-english-speaking residents.

b. Please consult Figure 3.2 in Chapter 5 for U.S. Census Bureau figures regarding non-English-speaking residents.

c. Please consult figure 3.2 in chapter 5 for U.S. Census Bureau figures regarding non-English-speaking residents.

1. c (3.04, 3.07) 2. b (3.01, 3.02) 3. a (3.16, 3.10) 4. c (3.08, 3.06g) 5. b (3.01, 3.08) 6. b (3.01, 3.08) 7. c (3.12) 8. a (3.11) 9. c (3.16, 3.06e, 3.01) 10. b (3.07, 3.04, 3.15)

Every chapter provides an editing exercise to fine-tune your grammar and mechanics skills. The following executive summary requires edits that address capitalization, punctuation, parallelism, concise wording, and other writing issues. Study the guidelines in the Grammar/Mechanics Handbook (Appendix D), including the lists of Confusing Words and Frequently Misspelled Words.

YOUR TASK. Edit the following (a) by inserting corrections in your textbook or on a photocopy using the proofreading marks in Appendix C or (b) by downloading the summary from **www.cengagebrain.com** and correcting at your computer.

EXECUTIVE SUMMARY
Purpose of Report

The purposes of this report are to: (1) Determine the Sun Coast University campus communitys awareness of the campus recycling program and (2) Recommend ways to increase participation. Sun Coasts recycling program was intended to respond to the increasing problem of waste disposal, to fulfill it's social responsibility as an educational institution and to meet demands of legislation that made it a requirement for individuals and organizations to recycle.

A Survey was conducted in an effort to learn about the campus communitys recycling habits and to make an assessment of the participation in the recycling program that is current. A total of 220 individuals responded to the Survey, but 27 Surveys could not be used. Since Sun coast universitys recycling program now include only aluminum, glass, paper and plastic, these were the only materials considered in this Study.

Recycling at Sun coast

Many Survey respondents recognized the importance of recycling, they stated that they do recycle aluminum, glass, paper and plastic on a regular basis either at home or at work. However most respondents displayed a low level of awareness of the on-campus program. At least half of the respondents were unfamiliar with the location of the bins around campus, therefore, they had not participated in the Recycling Program. Other responses indicated that the bins were not located in convenent locations.

Reccommendations for increasing recycling participation

To increase participation in the recycling Program, we recommend the following:

1. Relocate the Recycling Bins for greater visibility.

2. Development of incentive programs to gain the participation of on-campus groups.

3. Training student volunteers to give on-campus presentations that give an explanation of the need for Recycling, and the benefits of such a Program.

4. We should increase Advertising in regard to the program.

Effective and Professional Team Presentations

If you have been part of a team effort before, you know that such projects can be frustrating—particularly when some team members don't carry their weight or produce poor-quality work. Very often members struggle to resolve conflict. On the other hand, team projects can be harmonious and productive when members establish ground rules and follow these steps:

- **Prepare to work together.** First, you should (a) compare team members' schedules to set up the best meetings times, (b) plan regular face-to-face and virtual meetings, and (c) discuss how you will deal with team members who are not contributing to the project or are submitting shoddy work.

- **Plan the presentation.** Your team will need to agree on (a) the specific purpose of the presentation, (b) your audience, (c) the length of the presentation, (d) the types of visuals to include, and (e) the basic structure and content of the presentation.

- **Assign duties.** Once you decide what your presentation will cover, give each team member a written assignment that details his or her responsibilities, such as researching content, producing visuals, developing handouts, building transitions between segments, and showing up for team meetings and rehearsals.

- **Collect information.** To gather or generate information, teams can brainstorm together, conduct interviews, or search the Web. The team should set deadlines for collecting information and should discuss how to ensure the accuracy and currency of the information collected. Team members should exchange periodic progress reports on how their research is coming along.

- **Organize and develop the presentation.** Once your team has completed the research, start working on the presentation. Determine the organization of the presentation, compose a draft in writing, and prepare presentation slides and other visual aids. The team should meet often in person or online to discuss the presentation and to decide which members are responsible for delivering what parts of the presentation. Each member should build a transition to the next member's topic and strive for logical connections between segments.

- **Edit, rehearse, and evaluate.** Before you deliver the presentation, rehearse several times as a team. Make sure transitions from speaker to speaker are smooth. For example, a speaker might say, *Now that I have explained how to prepare for the meeting, Ashley is going to discuss how to get the meeting started.* Decide who will be responsible for advancing slides during the presentation (either on the computer or using a remote). Practice fielding questions if you plan to have a question-and-answer session. Decide how you are going to dress to look professional and competent. Run a spell-checker and proofread your presentation slides to ensure that the design, format, and vocabulary are consistent.

- **Deliver the presentation.** Show up on time for your presentation and wear appropriate attire. Deliver your part of the presentation professionally and enthusiastically. Remember that your audience is judging the team on its performance, not the individuals. Do what you can to make your team shine!

CAREER APPLICATION. Your boss named you to a team that is to produce an organizational social media communication strategy for your company. You know this assignment will end with an oral presentation to management. Your first reaction is dismay. You have been on teams before in the classroom, and you know how frustrating they can be. However, you want to give your best, and you resolve to contribute positively to this team effort.

YOUR TASK. In small groups or with the entire class, discuss effective collaboration. How can members contribute positively to teams? How should teams deal with members who aren't contributing or who have negative attitudes? What should team members do to ensure that the final presentation is professional and well coordinated? How can the team use technology to improve collaboration? If your instructor directs, summarize your findings in writing or in a brief presentation.

Employment Communication

6

Pla2na/Shutterstock.com

Monkey Business Images/Shutterstock.com

The Job Search, Résumés, and Cover Messages

D8nn/Shutterstock.com

Learning Outcomes

After studying this chapter, you should be able to do the following:

1 Begin a job search by recognizing emerging trends and technologies, exploring your interests, evaluating your qualifications, and investigating career opportunities.

2 Apply savvy search strategies by analyzing how job seekers find their jobs and how they use digital tools to explore the open job market.

3 Expand your job-search strategies by using both traditional and digital tools in pursuing the hidden job market.

4 Organize your qualifications and skills into effective résumé categories, and use that information to prepare a personalized LinkedIn profile.

5 Enhance your job search and résumé by taking advantage of digital tools.

6 Understand the value of cover messages and how to draft and submit a customized message to highlight your candidacy.

13-1 Job Searching in the Digital Age

Good news! For the eighth year in a row, college graduates can look forward to an uptick in hiring.[1] Whether you are actively looking for a position now or hope to do so later, becoming aware of job trends and requirements is important so that you can tailor your education to be successful when you enter the market. This chapter presents cutting-edge advice regarding job searching, résumé writing, and cover messages to give you an advantage in a labor market that is more competitive, more mobile, and more dependent on technology than ever before.

A successful job search today requires a blend of old and new job-hunting skills. Traditional techniques are still effective, but savvy job candidates must also be ready to act on emerging trends, some of which are presented in Figure 13.1. Job boards, social networks, and mobile technologies have all become indispensable tools in hunting for a job. Surprisingly, however, even in this digital age, the primary routes to hiring continue to be personal networking, referrals, and whom you know.

If you are fearful of entering a highly competitive job market, think of the many advantages you have. "Organizations are very interested in hiring young people because they have a lot of energy and are willing to do whatever it takes to get the job done," says one career specialist.[2] Think about your recent training, current skills, and enthusiasm. Remember, too, that you are less expensive to hire than older, experienced candidates. In addition, you have this book with the latest research, invaluable advice, and perfect model documents to guide you in your job search. Think positively!

Figure 13.1 Considering the Latest Trends in Job Searching and Résumés

Mobile technologies are on the rise.

Candidates use apps to apply for jobs, and recruiters use mobile devices to post jobs, contact candidates, and forward résumés to colleagues.

Networking— it's whom you know.

Recruiters say their best job candidates come from referrals. Now, more than ever, you need to be proactive in making professional connections.

Communication and interpersonal skills are in high demand.

Sales and marketing careers are booming, and these careers demand writing, speaking, and team skills.

Social media presence is a must.

Those who haven't developed a social media presence may be left in the dust.

It's all digital.

Today candidates e-mail their résumés, post them to Internet job boards, or publish them on their own Web pages.

Résumés must please scanners and skimmers.

Overwhelmed with candidates, recruiters hurriedly skim résumés preselected by scanning devices.

13-1a Using Technology to Aid Your Job Search

Technology is increasingly an integral part of the job-search process. Nearly every job hunter today has at least one mobile device, and the number of apps for these devices is overwhelming. You can download apps to plan your career, organize the job-search process, scour numerous job boards, receive immediate job alerts, and even arrange lunch dates to network and meet others in your field. Working from a smartphone, you can create, store, and send a résumé from the beach, from a train, or whenever a terrific opening pops up.

Organizations Bet on Technology. Beyond mobile devices, technology has greatly affected the way organizations announce jobs, select candidates, screen résumés, and conduct interviews. Big (and increasingly medium-sized) companies tend to use *applicant tracking systems* (ATS) to automatically post openings, select résumés, rank candidates, and generate interview requests. In this chapter you'll learn to craft your job search and résumé to take advantage of tracking systems and other technologies flooding the job-search market.

It's an Employers' Market. At the same time that a tsunami of technology is revolutionizing the job scene, other significant changes in the labor market will affect your job search and subsequent employment. In years past the emphasis was

LEARNING OUTCOME 1

Begin a job search by recognizing emerging trends and technologies, exploring your interests, evaluating your qualifications, and investigating career opportunities.

on what the applicant wanted. Today it's on what the employer wants.[3] Employers are most interested in how candidates will add value to their organizations. That's why today's most successful candidates customize their résumés to highlight their qualifications for each opening. In addition, career paths are no longer linear; most new-hires will not start in a job and steadily rise through the ranks. Jobs are more short-lived and people are constantly relearning and retraining.

The Résumé Is Not Dead. The résumé is still important, but it may not be the document that introduces the job seeker these days. Instead, the résumé may come only after the candidate has established a real-world relationship. What's more, chances are that your résumé and cover message will be read digitally rather than in print. However, although some attention-grabbing publications scream that the print résumé is dead, the truth is that every job hunter needs one. Whether offered online or in print, your résumé should be always available and current.

It's natural to think that the first step in finding a job is writing a résumé. However, that's a mistake. The job-search process actually begins long before you are ready to prepare your résumé. Regardless of the kind of employment you seek, you must invest time and effort in getting ready. Your best plan for landing the job of your dreams involves four steps as illustrated in Figure 13.2.

13-1b Launching Your Job Search With Self-Analysis

The first step in a job search is analyzing your interests and goals and evaluating your qualifications. This means looking inside yourself to explore what you like and dislike so that you can make good employment choices. For guidance in choosing a career that eventually proves to be satisfying, ask yourself the following questions:

- What are you passionate about? Can you turn this passion into a career?
- Do you enjoy working with people, data, or things?
- How important are salary, benefits, technology support, and job stimulation?
- Must you work in a specific city, geographical area, or climate?
- Are you looking for security, travel opportunities, money, power, or prestige?
- How would you describe the perfect job, boss, and coworkers?

Evaluating Your Qualifications. In addition to analyzing your interests and goals, take a good look at your qualifications. Remember that today's job market is not so much about what you want, but what the employer wants. What assets do you have to offer? Your responses to the following questions will target your thinking as well as

Figure 13.2 Four Steps of a Successful Job Search

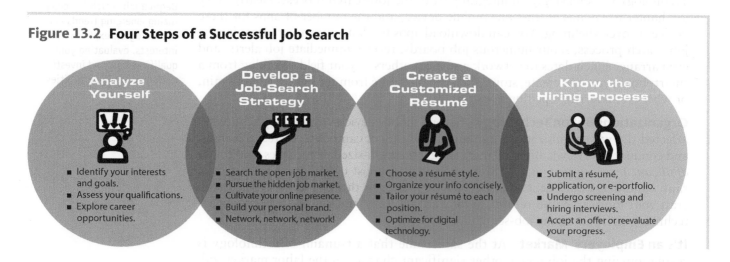

Analyze Yourself
- Identify your interests and goals.
- Assess your qualifications.
- Explore career opportunities.

Develop a Job-Search Strategy
- Search the open job market.
- Pursue the hidden job market.
- Cultivate your online presence.
- Build your personal brand.
- Network, network, network!

Create a Customized Résumé
- Choose a résumé style.
- Organize your info concisely.
- Tailor your résumé to each position.
- Optimize for digital technology.

Know the Hiring Process
- Submit a résumé, application, or e-portfolio.
- Undergo screening and hiring interviews.
- Accept an offer or reevaluate your progress.

prepare a foundation for your résumé. Always keep in mind, though, that employers seek more than empty assurances; they will want proof of your qualifications.

- What technology skills can you present? What specific software programs are you familiar with, what Internet expertise do you have, and what social media skills can you offer?

- Do you communicate well in speech and in writing? Are you proficient in another language? How can you verify these abilities?

- What other skills have you acquired in school, on the job, or through activities? How can you demonstrate these skills?

- Do you work well with people? Do you enjoy teamwork? What proof can you offer? Consider extracurricular activities, clubs, class projects, and jobs.

- Are you a leader, self-starter, or manager? What evidence can you provide? What leadership positions have you held?

- Do you learn quickly? Can you think critically? How can you demonstrate these characteristics?

13-1c Investigating Career Opportunities

The job picture in the United States is extraordinarily dynamic and flexible. On average, workers between ages eighteen and thirty-eight in the United States will have ten different employers over the course of their careers. The median job tenure of wage earners and salaried workers is 4.4 years with a single employer.[4] Although you may frequently change jobs in the future (especially before you reach age forty), you still need to train for a specific career. In exploring job opportunities, you will make the best decisions when you can match your interests and qualifications with the requirements and rewards of specific careers. Where can you find the best career data? Here are some suggestions:

- **Visit your campus career center.** Most campus career centers have literature, inventories, career-related software programs, and employment or internship databases that allow you to explore such fields as accounting, finance, office technology, information systems, and hotel management.

- **Search for apps and online help.** Many job-search sites—such as Indeed, Monster, and CareerBuilder—offer career-planning information and resources. One popular app is iPQ Career Planner, a free tool with a 52-question assessment test to zero in on your strengths and weaknesses.

- **Use your library.** Print and online resources in your library are especially helpful. Consult O*NET Occupational Information Network, Dictionary of Occupational Titles, Occupational Outlook Handbook, and Jobs Rated Almanac for information about job requirements, qualifications, salaries, and employment trends.

- **Take a summer job, internship, or part-time position in your field.** Nothing is better than trying out a career. Many companies offer internships and temporary or part-time jobs to begin training college students and to develop relationships with them.

- **Interview someone in your chosen field.** People are usually flattered when asked to describe their careers. Inquire about needed skills, required courses, financial and other rewards, benefits, working conditions, future trends, and entry requirements.

- **Volunteer with a nonprofit organization.** Many colleges and universities encourage service learning. In volunteering their services, students gain valuable experience, and nonprofits appreciate the expertise and fresh ideas that students bring.

- **Monitor the classified ads.** Early in your college career, begin monitoring want ads and the websites of companies in your career area. Check job availability, qualifications sought, duties, and salary ranges. Don't wait until you are about to graduate to explore the job market.

LEARNING OUTCOME 2

Apply savvy search strategies by analyzing how job seekers find their jobs and how they use digital tools to explore the open job market.

13-2 Developing a Job-Search Strategy Focused on the Open Job Market

Once you have analyzed what you want in a job and what you have to offer, you are ready to focus on a job-search strategy. You're probably most interested in how job seekers today are finding their jobs. What methods did they use? A study by staffing firm Jobvite, summarized in Figure 13.3, reveals how 1,404 human resources and recruiting professionals find the best talent. The high percentage of successful personal referrals (78 percent) and social media hiring (56 percent) suggests that your job hunt should focus laser sharp on networking in its various forms—maximizing personal and social media networking, followed by pursuing leads resulting from internships.[5] Although personal networking remains the No. 1 tool for finding a desirable position, technology plays a weighty role in the job search. Savvy job seekers employ both traditional as well as social and mobile job-search strategies. In response, organizations are optimizing the application process for mobile users.[6]

Don't forget your campus resources! A global survey found that 80 percent of employers (86 percent in the United States) consider on-campus interviews the most effective recruiting tool in finding qualified business school graduates.[7]

Both networking and online searching are essential tools in locating jobs, but where are those jobs? The *open job market* consists of jobs that are advertised or listed. The *hidden job market* consists of jobs that are never advertised or listed. Some analysts and authors claim that between 50 and 80 percent of all jobs are filled before they even make it to online job boards or advertisements.[8] Those openings are in the hidden job market, which we will explore shortly. First, let's start where most job seekers start—in the open job market.

13-2a Searching the Open Job Market

The open job market consists of positions that are advertised or listed publicly. Most job seekers start searching by using Google to look for positions in their field and within their commute areas. Sadly, searching online is a common, but not always rewarding, approach. Both recruiters and job seekers complain about online job boards, such as Monster and Indeed. Corporate recruiters say that the big job boards bring a flood of candidates, many unsuited for the listed jobs. Job candidates grumble that listings are frequently outdated and fail to produce leads.

Although the Internet may seem like a giant swamp that swallows résumés, job boards can provide valuable job-search information such as résumé, interviewing, and salary tips. Job boards also serve as a jumping-off point in most searches. They inform candidates about the kinds of jobs available and the skill sets required. Some professionals, however, believe that job boards may be

Figure 13.3 How Do Recruiters Find Their Best Talent?

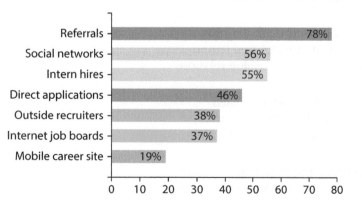

Referrals	78%
Social networks	56%
Intern hires	55%
Direct applications	46%
Outside recruiters	38%
Internet job boards	37%
Mobile career site	19%

Source: 2015 Jobvite Recruiter Nation Survey of 1,404 recruiters and HR professionals in various U.S. industries. Data total more than 100 percent because respondents could list more than one choice.

on their way out.[9] Social media sites have taken the recruitment world by storm, and savvy millennials and others are eagerly turning to LinkedIn, Facebook, and Twitter to search for jobs. Still, many job seekers will begin their search with job boards.

Exploring the Big Boards. As Figure 13.3 indicates, the number of jobs found through job boards is substantial. Four of the most popular job sites are useful for college students:

- **Indeed** is the No. 1 job site, offering millions of job listings aggregated from thousands of websites. It accounts for more hires than all the other job boards combined.

- **CareerBuilder** allows you to filter by several criteria such as location, degree required, and pay range.

- **Monster** permits you to upload your résumé and offers networking boards as well as a search alert service that sends you targeted posts.

- **CollegeGrad** describes itself as the "number one entry-level job site" for students and graduates. Applicants can search for entry-level jobs, internships, summer jobs, and jobs requiring one or more years of work experience.

Pursuing Company Leads. Probably the best way to find a job online is at a company's own website. Many companies post job openings only at their own sites to avoid being inundated by the hordes of applicants—many unqualified—responding to postings at online job boards. A company's website is the first place to go if you have a specific employer in mind. You might find vision and mission statements, a history of the organization, and names of key hiring managers. Possibly you will see a listing for a position that doesn't fit your qualifications. Even though you're not right for this job, you have discovered that the company is hiring. Don't be afraid to send a résumé and cover message expressing your desire to be considered for future jobs. Rather than seeking individual company sites, you might prefer to visit aggregator **LinkUp**. It shows constantly updated job listings from small, midsized, and large companies.

Checking Niche Sites. If you seek a job in a specialized field, look for a niche site, such as **Dice** for technology jobs, **Advance Healthcare Network** for jobs in the medical field, and **Accountemps** for temporary accounting positions. Niche websites also exist for job seekers with special backgrounds or needs, such as **GettingHired** for disabled workers and **Workforce50** for older workers. If you are looking for a short-term job, check out **CoolWorks**, which specializes in seasonal employment. If you yearn for a government job, try **USA Student Jobs**, a website for students and recent graduates interested in federal service.

Taking Advantage of Mobile Apps. Job seekers are eagerly embracing smartphone apps to gain an edge in the job search. With many of the following mobile apps, you can access and vet job openings as soon as they are listed—even when you are on the go.[10] Like its full website, the **Indeed Job Search** app lets you filter your search results based on your field, desired salary, and location. The app **Hidden Jobs** lists nearly 2 million unpublicized positions by tracking company job announcements so you don't have to. **Intro** is an app that connects you to people in your field or in your social media network. **JobAware** allows you to integrate all your Internet job-search activities including LinkedIn. **JobCompass** helps you narrow the search to your zip code. **LinkedUp Job Search Engine, Monster, Reach, Simply Hired, Snagajob,** and **Switch** all offer mobile links to job listings from a variety of sources.

Checking Newspapers, Career Fairs, and Other Sources. Despite the rush to mobile technology, some organizations still list openings in newspapers. Don't overlook this possibility, especially for local jobs. Plenty of jobs can also be found through career fairs and university and college alumni contacts.

When posting job-search information online, it's natural to want to put your best foot forward and openly share information that will get you a job. The challenge is to strike a balance between supplying enough information and protecting yourself. To avoid some of the risks involved, see the cautions described in Figure 13.4.

LEARNING OUTCOME 3

Expand your job-search strategies by using both traditional and digital tools in pursuing the hidden job market.

13-3 Unlocking the Hidden Job Market With Networking

Not all available positions are announced or advertised in the open job market. As mentioned earlier, between 50 and 80 percent of jobs are estimated to be in the hidden job market.[11] Companies prefer to avoid publicizing job announcements for a number of reasons. They don't welcome the deluge of unqualified candidates. What's more, companies dislike hiring unknown quantities. Career coach Donald Asher, author of *Cracking the Hidden Job Market*, sets this scene: Imagine you are a hiring manager facing hundreds of résumés on your desk and a coworker walks in with the résumé of someone she vouches for. Which résumé do you think hits the top of the stack?[12] Companies prefer known quantities.

The most successful job candidates seek to transform themselves from unknown into known quantities through networking. More jobs today are found through referrals and person-to-person contacts than through any other method. That's because people trust what they know. Therefore, your goal is to become known to a large network of people, and this means going beyond close friends.

13-3a Building a Personal Network

Because most candidates find jobs today through networking, be prepared to work diligently to build your personal networks. This effort involves meeting people and talking to them about your field or industry so that you can gain information and

Figure 13.4 Protecting Yourself When Posting at Online Job Boards

- **Use reputable, well-known sites** and never pay to post your résumé.

- **Don't divulge personal data** such as your date of birth, social security number, or home address. Use your city and state or region in place of your home address.

- **Set up a separate e-mail account** with a professional-sounding e-mail address for your job search.

- **Post privately** if possible. Doing so means that you can control who has access to your e-mail address and other information.

- **Keep careful records** of every site on which you posted. At the end of your job search, remove all posted résumés.

- **Don't include your references** or reveal their contact information without permission.

- **Don't respond to "blind" job postings** (those without company names or addresses). Unfortunately, scammers use online job boards to post fake job ads to gather your personal information.

locate job vacancies. Not only are many jobs never advertised, but some positions aren't even contemplated until the right person appears. One recent college graduate underwent three interviews for a position, but the company hired someone else. After being turned down, the grad explained why he thought he was perfect for this company but perhaps in a different role. Apparently, the hiring manager agreed and decided to create a new job (in social media) because of the skills, personality, and perseverance of this determined young grad. Traditional networking pays off, but it requires dedication. Here are three steps that will help you establish your own network:

Step 1. Develop a contacts list. Make a list of anyone who would be willing to talk with you about finding a job. Figure 13.5 suggests possibilities. Even if you haven't talked with people in years, reach out to them in person or online. Consider asking your campus career center for alumni willing to talk with students. Also dig into your social networking circles, which we will discuss shortly.

Step 2. Make contacts in person and online. Call the people on your list or connect online. To set up a meeting in person, say, *Hi, _____. I'm looking for a job and I wonder if you could help me out. When could I come over to talk about it?* During your visit be friendly, well organized, polite, and interested in what your contact has to say. Provide a copy of your résumé, and try to keep the conversation centered on your job search. Your goal is to get two or more referrals. In pinpointing your request, ask, *Do you know of anyone who might have an opening for a person with my skills?* If the person does not, ask, *Do you know of anyone else who might know of someone?*

Step 3. Follow up on your referrals. Call or contact the people on your list. You might say something like, *Hello. I'm Stacy Rivera, a friend of Jason Tilden. He suggested that I ask you for help. I'm looking for a position as a marketing trainee, and he thought you might be willing to spare a few minutes and steer me in the right direction.* Don't ask for a job. During your referral interview, ask how the individual got started in this line of work, what he or she likes best (or least) about the work, what career paths exist in the field, and what problems a newcomer must overcome. Most important, ask how a person with your background and skills might get started in the field. Send an informal thank-you note to anyone who helps you in your job search, and stay in touch with the most promising people. Ask whether you could stay in contact every three weeks or so during your job search.

Unfortunately, many new grads are reluctant to engage in traditional person-to-person networking because it feels pushy and it definitely requires much effort. They are much more comfortable with networking through social media sites.

Figure 13.5 **Whom to Contact in Networking**

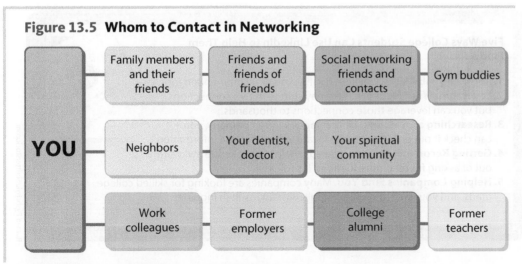

13-3b Prospecting for Jobs on Social Media

As digital technology continues to change our lives, job candidates have powerful tools at their disposal: social media networks. Social media have become critical in a job search. If you just send out your résumé blindly, not much will happen. However, if you have a referral, your chances of landing an interview multiply. The growth of social networks has opened up an additional path to developing those coveted referrals.

Networking on LinkedIn to Find a Job. If you are seriously looking for a job, it's extremely important that you list yourself on LinkedIn. This social media site dominates the world of job searching and recruiting. In a poll of 1,855 recruiting and staffing professionals, 95 percent said that they used LinkedIn as a recruiting tool.[13] It's truly the place to find and be found, especially for new graduates. It lists well over a million and a half student jobs and internships in addition to millions of full-time jobs.[14] Developing a credible presence on LinkedIn enables you to post information about yourself in one central place where it's available to potential employers, graduate schools, future colleagues, and people you will want to stay connected to. A LinkedIn page tells the working world that you are a professional, and it remains significant even after you obtain a position.

One of the best ways to use LinkedIn is to search for a company in which you are interested. Try to find company employees who are connected to other people you know. Then use that contact as a referral when you apply. You can also send an e-mail to everyone in your LinkedIn network asking for help or for people they could put you in touch with. Don't be afraid to ask an online contact for advice on getting started in a career and for suggestions to help a newcomer break into that career. Another excellent way to use a contact is to have that person look at your résumé and help you tweak it. Like Facebook, LinkedIn has status updates, and it's a good idea to update yours regularly so that your connections know what is happening in your career search and afterward.

LinkedIn can aid your job search in at least five ways, as shown in Figure 13.6. Because LinkedIn functions in many ways as a résumé, you will find tips for preparing your LinkedIn profile in the next pages.

Enlisting Other Social Networks in a Job Hunt. In addition to LinkedIn, job seekers can join Facebook, Twitter, and Google+ to find job opportunities, market themselves to companies, showcase their skills, highlight their experience, and possibly land that dream job. Because organizations may post open jobs to their Facebook

Figure 13.6 Harnessing the Power of LinkedIn

Five Ways College Students Can Use LinkedIn to Help Them Find a Job

1. **Receiving Job Alerts.** LinkedIn notifies you of recommended jobs.
2. **Leveraging Your Network.** You may start with two connections, but you can leverage those connections to thousands.
3. **Researching a Company.** Before applying to a company, you can check it out on LinkedIn and locate valuable inside information.
4. **Getting Recommendations.** LinkedIn helps you take the awkwardness out of asking for recommendations. It's so easy!
5. **Helping Companies Find You.** Many companies are looking for skilled college grads, and your strong profile on LinkedIn can result in inquiries.

Roman Pyshchyk/Shutterstock.com

Employers routinely refer to job applicants' social media sites to discover indiscretions. Perhaps less commonly known, however, is that Facebook is increasingly used as a tool to recruit employees. Savvy job seekers know to use the social networking platform to expand their professional connections, illustrate their social media know-how, and craft their profiles to accentuate work history. When using Facebook as part of a job search, candidates must be extremely careful to separate personal friends from professional contacts. The professional contacts list becomes a way for job seekers to reach out by posting industry-related content and personal work-related status updates. How can you build your personal brand on Facebook?[16]

Robin Beckham/BEEPstock/Alamy Stock Photo

or Twitter pages prior to advertising them elsewhere, you might gain a head start on submitting an application by following them on these sites.

If you have a Facebook account, examine your profile and decide what you want prospective employers to see—or not see. Look for digital dirt. Delete or hide any potentially embarrassing images or posts. Use privacy settings scrupulously, and create special lists for professional contacts. Facebook lets you view your profile as others may see you. Use that feature at least occasionally, and choose your friends wisely.

Employers often scrutinize the online presence of candidates on social media sites—Facebook, Instagram, and Twitter in particular—for evidence of applicants' credibility. In fact, one report revealed that nine out of ten recruiters use social media to search, keep tabs on, and vet candidates before the interview.[17] Make sure your social networking accounts represent you professionally. You can make it easy for your potential employer to learn more about you by including an informative bio in your Twitter or Facebook profile and link it to your LinkedIn profile. You can also make yourself more discoverable by posting thoughtful blog posts and tweets on topics related to your career goal.

13-3c Creating Your Personal Brand

A large part of your job-search strategy involves building a brand for yourself. You may be thinking, *Who me? A brand?* Yes, absolutely! Even college graduates should seriously consider branding because finding a job in a competitive market is tough. Before you get into the thick of the job hunt, focus on developing your brand so that you know what you want to emphasize.

Personal branding involves deciding what makes you special and desirable in the job market. What is your unique selling point? What special skill set makes you stand out among all job applicants? What would your instructors or employers say is your greatest strength? Think about your intended audience. What are you promoting about yourself?

Experts suggest that you create a tagline that describes what you do, who you are, and what's special about you. A nurse wrote this fetching tagline:

Tireless, caring Registered Nurse who helps pediatric cancer patients and their families feel at ease throughout treatment and recovery

If you prefer a shorter tagline for your business card, consider the sample taglines for new grads in Figure 13.7. It's OK to shed a little modesty and strut your stuff. However, do keep your tagline simple, short, and truthful so that it's easy to remember.

Once you have a tagline, prepare a professional-looking business card with your name and tagline. Include an easy-to-remember e-mail address such as *firstname .lastname@domain.com*. Consider using CardDrop, an app that creates a digital business card to connect with new contacts and help you be remembered.

Now that you have your tagline and business card, work on an elevator speech. This is a pitch that you can give in 60 seconds or less describing who you are and what you can offer. Tweak your speech for your audience, and practice until you can say it naturally. Here are suggestions to help you prepare your own authentic elevator speech depending on your situation:

Hi, my name is _____, and I am about to graduate from _____ with a degree in _____. I'm looking to _____ because I enjoy _____. Recently I _____ where I was able to develop skills such as _____. I'm most confident about my skills in _____. I'm inspired by the field (or position of) _____ because _____. Do you have any suggestions or advice on how I can _____?

Figure 13.7 Branding YOU

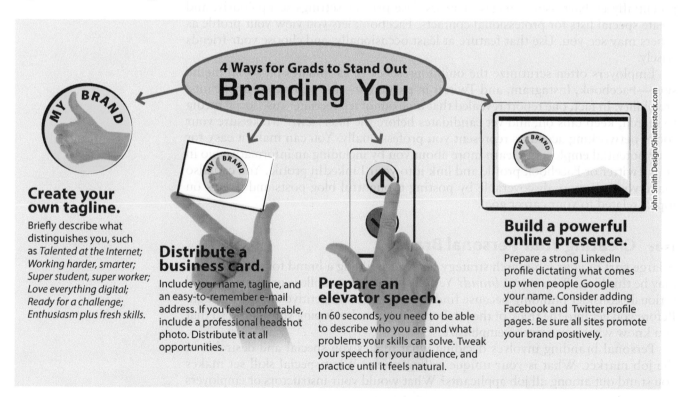

4 Ways for Grads to Stand Out
Branding You

MY BRAND

Create your own tagline.
Briefly describe what distinguishes you, such as *Talented at the Internet; Working harder, smarter; Super student, super worker; Love everything digital; Ready for a challenge; Enthusiasm plus fresh skills.*

Distribute a business card.
Include your name, tagline, and an easy-to-remember e-mail address. If you feel comfortable, include a professional headshot photo. Distribute it at all opportunities.

Prepare an elevator speech.
In 60 seconds, you need to be able to describe who you are and what problems your skills can solve. Tweak your speech for your audience, and practice until it feels natural.

Build a powerful online presence.
Prepare a strong LinkedIn profile dictating what comes up when people Google your name. Consider adding Facebook and Twitter profile pages. Be sure all sites promote your brand positively.

John Smith Design/Shutterstock.com

13-4 Customizing Your Résumé

In today's highly competitive job market, you must focus on what the employer needs. That's why you must customize your résumé for every position you seek. The competition is so stiff today that you cannot get by with a generic, one-size-fits-all résumé. Although you can start with a basic résumé, you should customize it to fit each company and position if you want it to stand out from the crowd. In short, your résumé is a branding tool, a marketing document.[18]

The Internet has made it so simple to apply for jobs that recruiters are swamped with applications. As a job seeker, you have between 5 and 20 seconds to catch the recruiter's eye—if your résumé is even read by a person. It may very well first encounter an applicant tracking system (ATS). This software helps businesses automatically post openings, screen résumés, rank candidates, and generate interview requests. These automated systems make writing your résumé doubly challenging. Although your goal is to satisfy a recruiter or hiring manager, that person may never see your résumé unless it is selected by the ATS. Because so many organizations are using ATS software today, this chapter provides you with the latest advice on how to get your résumé ranked highly—so that it will then proceed to the real human beings who will call you for an interview.

13-4a Choosing a Résumé Style

The first step in preparing a winning, customized résumé that appeals to both the human reader and the ATS screening device is to decide what style to use. Résumés usually fall into two categories: chronological and functional. This section presents basic information as well as insider tips on how to choose an appropriate résumé style, determine its length, and arrange its parts. You will also learn about adding a summary of qualifications, which many busy recruiters welcome. Models of the résumé styles discussed in the following sections are shown in our comprehensive Résumé Gallery.

What Is a Chronological Résumé? The most popular résumé format is the chronological format, shown in Figures 13.10, 13.11, and 13.12 in our Résumé Gallery. The chronological résumé lists work history job by job but in reverse order, starting with the most recent position. Recruiters favor the chronological format because they are familiar with it and because it quickly reveals a candidate's education and experience. The chronological style works well for candidates who have experience in their field of employment and for those who show steady career growth, but it is less helpful for people who have changed jobs frequently or who have gaps in their employment records. For college students and others who lack extensive experience, the functional résumé format may be preferable.

What Is a Functional Résumé? The functional résumé, shown in Figure 13.13, focuses on a candidate's skills rather than on past employment. Like a chronological résumé, a functional résumé begins with the candidate's name, contact information, job objective, and education. Instead of listing jobs, though, the functional résumé groups skills and accomplishments in special categories, such as Supervisory and Management Skills or Retailing and Marketing Experience. This résumé style highlights accomplishments and can de-emphasize a negative employment history.

People who have changed jobs frequently, who have gaps in their employment records, or who are entering an entirely different field may prefer the functional résumé. Recent graduates with little or no related employment experience often find the functional résumé useful. Older job seekers who want to downplay a long job history and job hunters who are afraid of appearing overqualified may also prefer the functional format. Be aware, though, that online job boards may insist on the chronological format. In addition, some recruiters are suspicious of functional résumés, thinking the candidate is hiding something.

13-4b How Long Should a Résumé Be?

Experts disagree on how long a résumé should be. Conventional wisdom has always held that recruiters prefer one-page résumés. However, recruiters who are serious about candidates often prefer the kind of details that can be provided in a two-page or longer résumé. What's more, with today's digital résumés, length is no longer restricted. The best advice is to make your résumé as long as needed to present your skills to recruiters and hiring managers. Individuals with more experience will naturally have longer résumés. Those with fewer than ten years of experience, those making a major career change, and those who have had only one or two employers will likely have one-page résumés. Those with ten years or more of related experience may have two-page résumés. Finally, some senior-level managers and executives with a lengthy history of major accomplishments might have résumés that are three pages or longer.[20]

13-4c Organizing Your Information Into Effective Résumé Categories

Although résumés have standard categories, their arrangement and content should be strategically planned. A customized résumé emphasizes skills and achievements aimed at a particular job or company. It shows a candidate's most important qualifications first, and it de-emphasizes weaknesses. In organizing your qualifications and information, try to create as few headings as possible; more than six looks cluttered. No two résumés are ever exactly alike, but most writers include all or some of these categories: Contact Information, Career Objective, Summary of Qualifications, Education, Experience, Capabilities and Skills, and Awards and Activities.

Contact Information. Your résumé, whether chronological or functional, should start with an uncluttered and simple main heading. The first line should always be your name; add your middle initial for an even more professional look. Format your name so that it stands out on the page. Following your name, list your contact information, including your mailing address, phone number, and e-mail address. Some candidates are omitting their street addresses to protect their privacy and for safety reasons. Your telephone should be one where you can receive messages. The outgoing message at this number should be in your voice, it should state your full name, and it should be concise and professional. If you include your cell phone number and are expecting an important call from a recruiter, pick up only when you are in a quiet environment and can concentrate.

For your e-mail address, be sure it sounds professional instead of something like *toosexy4you@gmail.com* or *sixpackguy@gmx.com*. Also be sure that you are using a personal e-mail address. Putting your work e-mail address on your résumé announces to prospective employers that you are consuming your current employer's resources to look for another job. If you have a LinkedIn profile or a website where an e-portfolio or samples of your work can be viewed, include the link in the main heading.

Career Objective. Although experts don't agree on whether to include an objective on a résumé, nearly all agree that if you do, it should be very specific. A well-written objective—customized for the job opening—makes sense, especially for new graduates with fresh training and relevant skills. Strive to include strategic keywords from the job listing because these will help tracking systems select your résumé. Focus on what you can contribute to the organization, not on what the organization can do for you.

> **Poor objective:** *To obtain a position with a well-established organization that will lead to a lasting relationship in the field of marketing.* (Sounds vague and self-serving.)

Improved objective: *To obtain a position that capitalizes on my recent training in business writing and marketing to boost customer contacts and expand brand penetration using my social media expertise.* (Names specific skills and includes nouns that might snag the attention of an applicant tracking system.)

Instead of an objective, one résumé expert recommends listing the job title of the position for which you are applying, including the words *Target Job Title* as shown here:

Target Job Title: Medical Administrative Assistant

Using a customized objective or a job title makes it clear that you have taken the time and made the effort to prepare your résumé for a specific position.[21] If you decide to omit a career objective, be sure to discuss your career goals in your cover message.

Summary of Qualifications. Some experts view the summary of qualifications (also called a *career summary, résumé summary,* or *profile statement*) as a very concise version of a cover message. They believe that it's more important than a career objective.[22] This summary should memorably tell the recruiter what you have to offer the employer and help you stand out from the crowd of applicants. Once a job is advertised, a hiring manager may get hundreds or even thousands of résumés. A summary ensures that a recruiter who is skimming résumés quickly will notice your most impressive qualifications. Additionally, because résumés today may be viewed on mobile devices, the summary spotlights your most compelling qualifications in a highly visible spot.

When formulating this statement, consider your experience in the field, your education, your unique skills, awards you have won, certifications you hold, and any other accomplishments. Strive to quantify your achievements wherever possible. In three to five bullet points, target the most important qualifications an employer will be looking for as described in the job listing. Focus on nouns that might be selected as keywords by an applicant tracking system. Examples appear in Figures 13.11 and 13.14.

Some recruitment advice falls outside the current consensus of job-search experts. Not a fan of terse bullet points, clichés, and ATS, recruiting pro Liz Ryan wants to see applicants' personality authentically shine through in their narratives. She urges résumé writers to sound human by using the first person pronoun *I* and to tell compelling "dragon-slaying stories" to illustrate their expertise.[24] This advice to come across as an authentic human being with compelling success stories is solid, but using first person *I* seems most suitable for a LinkedIn profile, not a traditional résumé.

Education. The next component in a chronological résumé is your education—if it is more noteworthy than your work experience. In this section you should include the name and location of schools, dates of attendance, major fields of study, and degrees received. By the way, once you have attended college, you should not list high school information on your résumé.

Your grade point average (GPA) and/or class ranking may be important to prospective employers. One way to enhance your GPA is to calculate it in your major courses only (for example, *3.6/4.0 in major*). It is not unethical so long as you clearly show that your GPA is in the major only. Looking to improve their hiring chances, some college graduates are now offering an unusual credential: their scores on the Graduate Record Examination. Large companies and those specializing in computer software and financial services reportedly were most interested in applicants' GRE scores.[25] Some organizations even consider SAT scores in their hiring process.[26]

OFFICE INSIDER

One expert values authenticity in the applications process above all else. She advises candidates to sound human, not robotic: "The Summary is the most important part of a Human-Voiced Résumé, because it frames your background and your next career steps for the hiring manager's benefit. Once your reader (your hiring manager) reads your Summary, he or she understands who you are and how you roll. Your job history follows the Summary and amplifies the frame you shared in the Summary."[23]

Liz Ryan, *founder and CEO, Human Workplace; author*

Under Education you might be tempted to list all the courses you took, but such a list makes for dull reading and consumes valuable space. Include a brief list of courses only if you can relate them to the position you seek. When relevant, include certificates earned, seminars attended, workshops completed, scholarships awarded, and honors earned. If your education is incomplete, include such statements as *BS degree expected 6/18* or *80 units completed in 120-unit program*. Title this section Education, Academic Preparation, or Professional Training. If you are preparing a functional résumé, you will probably put the Education section below your skills summary, as shown in Figure 13.13.

Work Experience or Employment History. When your work or volunteer expe-rience is significant and relevant to the position sought, this information should appear before your education. List your most recent employment first and work backward, including only those jobs that you think will help you win the targeted position. A job application form may demand a full employment history, but your résumé may be selective. Be aware, though, that time gaps in your employment history will probably be questioned in the interview. For each position show the following:

- Employer's name, city, and state
- Dates of employment (month and year)
- Most important job title
- Significant duties, activities, accomplishments, and promotions

Be sure to include relevant volunteer work. A survey conducted by LinkedIn revealed that 41 percent of LinkedIn hiring managers consider volunteer work expe-rience as respectable as paid work experience when evaluating candidates.[27]

Your employment achievements and job duties will be easier to read if you place them in bulleted lists. Rather than list every single thing you have done, customize your information so that it relates to the targeted job. Your bullet points should be concise but not complete sentences, and they usually do not include personal pro-nouns (*I, me, my*). Strive to be specific:

Poor: *Worked with customers*

Improved: *Developed superior customer service skills by successfully interact-ing with 40+ customers daily*

Whenever possible, quantify your achievements:

Poor: *Did equipment study and report*

Improved: *Conducted research and wrote final study analyzing equipment needs of 100 small businesses in Houston*

Poor: *Was successful in sales*

Improved: *Personally generated orders for sales of $90,000 annually*

In addition to technical skills, employers seek individuals with communication, management, and interpersonal capabilities. This means you will want to select work experiences and achievements that illustrate your initiative, dependability, responsibility, resourcefulness, flexibility, and leadership. Employers also want people who can work in teams.

Poor: *Worked effectively in teams*

Improved: *Enjoyed collaborating with five-member interdepartmental team in developing ten-page handbook for temporary workers*

Poor: *Joined in team effort on campus*

Improved: *Headed 16-member student government team that conducted most successful voter registration in campus history*

Statements describing your work experience should include many nouns relevant to the job you seek. These nouns may match keywords sought by the applicant tracking system. To appeal to human readers, your statements should also include action verbs, such as those in Figure 13.8. Starting each of your bullet points with an action verb helps ensure that your bulleted lists are parallel.

Capabilities and Skills. Recruiters want to know specifically what you can do for their companies. List your special skills, including many nouns that relate to the targeted position. Highlight your familiarity with the Internet, search engines, software programs, social media, office equipment, and communication technology tools. Use expressions such as *proficient in*, *competent in*, *experienced in*, and *ability to* as illustrated in the following:

Poor:	*Have payroll experience*
Improved:	*Proficient in preparing federal, state, and local payroll tax returns as well as franchise and personal property tax returns*
Poor:	*Trained in computer graphics*
Improved:	*Certified in graphic design including infographics through an intensive 350-hour classroom program*
Poor:	*Have writing skills*
Improved:	*Competent in writing, editing, and proofreading reports, tables, letters, memos, e-mails, manuscripts, and business forms*

You will also want to showcase exceptional aptitudes, such as working well under stress, learning computer programs quickly, and interacting with customers. If possible, provide details and evidence that back up your assertions. Include examples of your writing, speaking, management, organizational, interpersonal, and presentation skills—particularly those talents that are relevant to your targeted job. For recent graduates, this section can be used to give recruiters evidence of your potential and to highlight successful college projects.

Figure 13.8 Action Verbs for a Powerful Résumé

Communication Skills	Teamwork, Supervision Skills	Management, Leadership Skills	Research Skills	Clerical, Detail Skills	Creative Skills
clarified	advised	analyzed	assessed	activated	acted
collaborated	coordinated	authorized	collected	approved	conceptualized
explained	demonstrated	coordinated	critiqued	classified	designed
interpreted	developed	directed	diagnosed	edited	fashioned
integrated	evaluated	headed	formulated	generated	founded
persuaded	expedited	implemented	gathered	maintained	illustrated
promoted	facilitated	improved	interpreted	monitored	integrated
resolved	guided	increased	investigated	proofread	invented
summarized	motivated	organized	reviewed	recorded	originated
translated	set goals	scheduled	studied	streamlined	revitalized
wrote	trained	strengthened	systematized	updated	shaped

Awards, Honors, and Activities. If you have three or more awards or honors, highlight them by listing them under a separate heading. If not, put them in the Education or Work Experience section if appropriate. Include awards, scholarships (financial and other), fellowships, dean's list, honors, recognition, commendations, and certificates. Be sure to identify items clearly. Your reader may be unfamiliar, for example, with Greek organizations, honors, and awards; tell what they mean.

Poor:	*Recipient of Star award*
Improved:	*Recipient of Star award given by Pepperdine University to outstanding graduates who combine academic excellence and extracurricular activities*

It's also appropriate to include school, community, volunteer, and professional activities. Employers are interested in evidence that you are a well-rounded person. This section provides an opportunity to demonstrate leadership and interpersonal skills. Strive to use action statements.

Poor:	*Treasurer of business club*
Improved:	*Collected dues, kept financial records, and paid bills while serving as treasurer of 35-member business management club*

Personal Data. Résumés in the United States omit personal data, such as birth date, marital status, height, weight, national origin, health, disability, and religious affiliation. Such information doesn't relate to genuine occupational qualifications, and recruiters are legally barred from asking for such information. Some job seekers do, however, include hobbies or interests (such as skiing or photography) that might grab the recruiter's attention or serve as conversation starters. For example, let's say you learn that your hiring manager enjoys distance running. If you have run a marathon, you may want to mention it. Many executives practice tennis or golf, two sports highly suitable for networking. You could also indicate your willingness to travel or to relocate, since many companies will be interested.

Include References? Listing references directly on a résumé takes up valuable space. Moreover, references are not normally instrumental in securing an interview—few companies check them before the interview. Instead, recruiters prefer that you bring to the interview a list of individuals willing to discuss your qualifications. Therefore, you should prepare a separate list, such as that in Figure 13.9, when you begin your job search. Consider three to five individuals, such as instructors, your current employer or previous employers, colleagues or subordinates, and other professional contacts. Ask whether they would be willing to answer inquiries regarding your qualifications for employment. Be sure, however, to provide them with an opportunity to refuse. No reference is better than a negative one. Better yet, to avoid rejection and embarrassment, ask only those contacts who you are confident will give you a glowing endorsement.

Do not include personal or character references, such as friends, family, or neighbors, because recruiters rarely consult them. One final note: Most recruiters see little reason for including the statement *References furnished upon request.* It is unnecessary and takes up precious space.

13-4d Preparing a LinkedIn Résumé

Because it's usually the first place hiring managers and recruiters go to look for candidates online, be sure to prepare a LinkedIn profile/résumé. It takes a little effort, but it's well worth the investment. LinkedIn provides a template with standard

Figure 13.9 Sample Reference List

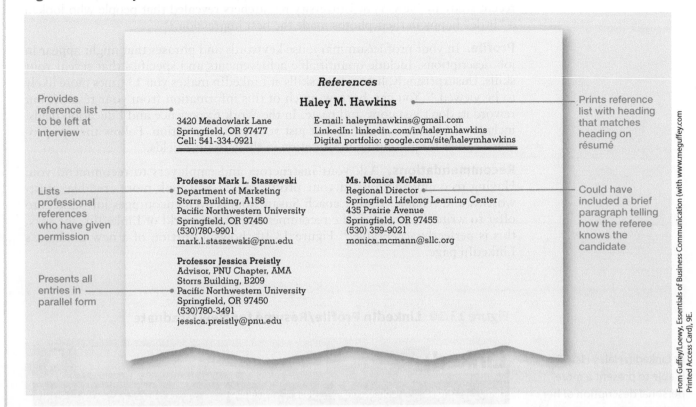

Provides reference list to be left at interview

Lists professional references who have given permission

Presents all entries in parallel form

References

Haley M. Hawkins

3420 Meadowlark Lane
Springfield, OR 97477
Cell: 541-334-0921

E-mail: haleymhawkins@gmail.com
LinkedIn: linkedin.com/in/haleymhawkins
Digital portfolio: google.com/site/haleymhawkins

Professor Mark L. Staszewski
Department of Marketing
Storrs Building, A158
Pacific Northwestern University
Springfield, OR 97450
(530)780-9901
mark.l.staszewski@pnu.edu

Professor Jessica Preistly
Advisor, PNU Chapter, AMA
Storrs Building, B209
Pacific Northwestern University
Springfield, OR 97450
(530)780-3491
jessica.preistly@pnu.edu

Ms. Monica McMann
Regional Director
Springfield Lifelong Learning Center
435 Prairie Avenue
Springfield, OR 97455
(530) 359-9021
monica.mcmann@sllc.org

Prints reference list with heading that matches heading on résumé

Could have included a brief paragraph telling how the referee knows the candidate

From Guffey/Loewy, Essentials of Business Communication (with www.meguffey.com Printed Access Card), 9E.

résumé categories in which you fill in your qualifications. Compared with a print résumé, LinkedIn has many advantages. You have ample space to expand the description of your skills and qualifications. Your LinkedIn page also allows you to be more conversational and personal than you can be within the confines of a restricted résumé. You can even use the pronoun *I* to tell your story more naturally and passionately.

Headline. To stand out, prepare an informative headline that appears below your name. It should include keywords in your field and a brief description of what you want, such as the following:

Marketing Grad and Social Media Branding Specialist Seeking Internship

Recent Grad With Billing and Coding Training in Medical Insurance Field

Seeking Recruiter/Human Resources Assistant Position in Health Services Field

Finance and Management Grad Looking for Position as Analyst Trainee

Some experts suggest that you write an even longer headline that takes full advantage of the 120-character LinkedIn space to sell yourself. Check out this recent grad's headline:

Communication Graduate Specializing in Millennials and Mobile Marketing Interested in Survey Research and Data Analysis

Because the headline is important, LinkedIn won't let you leave it blank. Use the headline to promote your most enticing expertise.

Photo. To increase your chance of being selected, definitely include a photo. Profiles with photos are known to score 14 times more views than those without. Your photo should be a head-and-shoulder shot in work-appropriate attire. Should you smile? A recent study by New York University researchers revealed that people who looked a "little" happy in their photos made the best impression.[29]

Profile. In your profile/summary, use keywords and phrases that might appear in job descriptions. Include quantifiable achievements and specifics that reveal your skills. Unsurprisingly, listing your skills at LinkedIn makes you 13 times more likely to be viewed.[30] You can borrow much of this information from your résumé, but reword it; don't just copy and paste. In the Work Experience and Education fields, include all of your experience, not just your current position. Follow the tips provided earlier for presenting information in these résumé fields.

Recommendations. Ask your instructors and employers to recommend you. Having recommendations in your profile makes you look more credible, trustworthy, and reliable. Career coach Susan Adams even encourages job seekers to offer to write the draft for the recommender; in the world of LinkedIn, she says, this is perfectly acceptable.[31] Figure 13.10 shows a portion of a new graduate's LinkedIn page.

Figure 13.10 LinkedIn Profile/Résumé for New Graduate

At LinkedIn Haley Hawkins is able to present a more personal description of her background, education, and experience than on her résumé. She includes a photo and a headline, "Honors graduate in e-marketing with social expertise." Her summary briefly describes her skills and experience, but one expert warns candidates not to cut corners on the summary statement. Describe what motivates you and use first-person pronouns, unlike what you would do on a résumé. LinkedIn gives you a chance to be more conversational than you can be in a résumé. You may be asked to present this same kind of personalized résumé information at job boards.

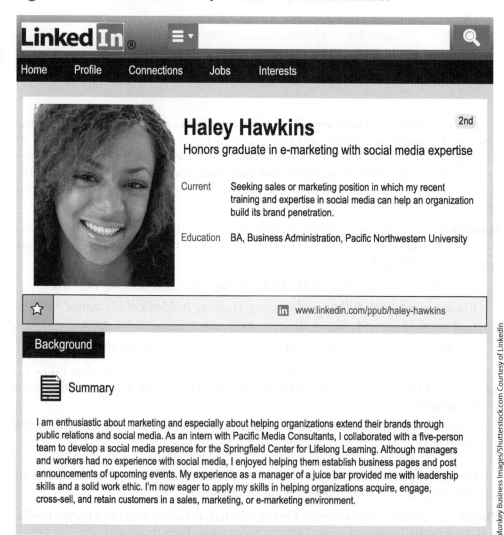

Monkey Business Images/Shutterstock.com Courtesy of LinkedIn

Figure 13.11 Chronological Résumé: Recent University Graduate With Limited Experience

Haley Hawkins used Microsoft Word to design a traditional chronological résumé that she plans to give to recruiters at campus job fairs or during interviews. The two-column formatting enables recruiters and hiring managers to immediately follow the chronology of her education and experience. This formatting is easy to create by using the Word table feature and removing the borders so that no lines show.

Haley includes an objective that is specific in describing what she seeks but broad enough to encompass many possible positions. Her summary of qualifications emphasizes the highlights of her experience and education. Because she has so little experience, she includes a brief list of related courses to indicate her areas of interest and training. Although she has limited paid experience that relates to the position she seeks, she is able to capitalize on her intern experience by featuring accomplishments and transferable skills.

Haley M. Hawkins

3420 Meadowlark Lane
Springfield, OR 97477
Cell: 541-334-0921

E-mail: haleymhawkins@gmail.com
LinkedIn: linkedin.com/in/haleymhawkins
Digital portfolio: google.com/site/haleymhawkins

OBJECTIVE
Position in sales, marketing, or e-marketing in which my marketing, communication, and social media expertise helps an organization expand its brand penetration.

SUMMARY OF QUALIFICATIONS
- Graduated with honors in e-marketing from Pacific Northwestern University
- Applied e-marketing training as a successful intern
- Experienced in posting to Twitter, Facebook, and YouTube
- Developed strong work ethic with part-time jobs that financed more than 50 percent of my education
- Honed leadership skills as vice president of award-winning chapter of American Marketing Association

EDUCATION AND RELATED COURSE WORK
BA in Business Administration, Pacific Northwestern University, Cum Laude   **May, 2019**
Major: Business Administration with e-marketing emphasis.
Minor: Organizational Communication
GPA: Major, 3.7; overall 3.5 (A = 4.0)

Marketing Research and Analysis   Marketing Communication
Social Relations in the Workplace   Professional Public Relations
Writing for the Web and Social Media   Organizational Behavior

PROFESSIONAL EXPERIENCE
Social Media Intern   09/2018–02/2019
Pacific Media Consultants, Springfield, Oregon
- Collaborated with 5-person team to develop social media presence for Center for LifeLong Learning
- Introduced clients to LinkedIn and established Facebook and Twitter accounts for LifeLong Learning staff
- Demonstrated how to boost social media presence with announcements and tweets of upcoming activities
- Prepared brochure, handouts, name tags, and press kit to promote one Saturday event
- Handled over 40 client calls with the account management team, ranging from project check-ins to inbound inquiries

Manager   06/2016–08/2018
Juice Zone, Eugene, Oregon
- Developed management skills in assuming all responsibilities in owners' absence including finances, scheduling, and oversight
- Supervised daily store operation and managed a team of 5 to 10 employees to ensure productivity and profitability

HONORS ACTIVITIES
Received Brooks Award as the outstanding graduate in marketing based on academic excellence and service

Figure 13.12 Chronological Résumé: Student Seeking Internship

Although Amy has had one internship, she is seeking another as she is about to graduate. To aid her search, she prepared a chronological résumé that emphasizes her education and related course work. She elected to omit her home address because she prefers that all communication take place digitally or by telephone. Instead of a career objective, she states exactly the internship position she seeks.

Notice that in her résumé Amy uses standard headings that would be easily recognized by an applicant tracking system. She decided not to start with a summary of qualifications because she has little to offer. Instead, she focused on her experience and related it to the position she seeks.

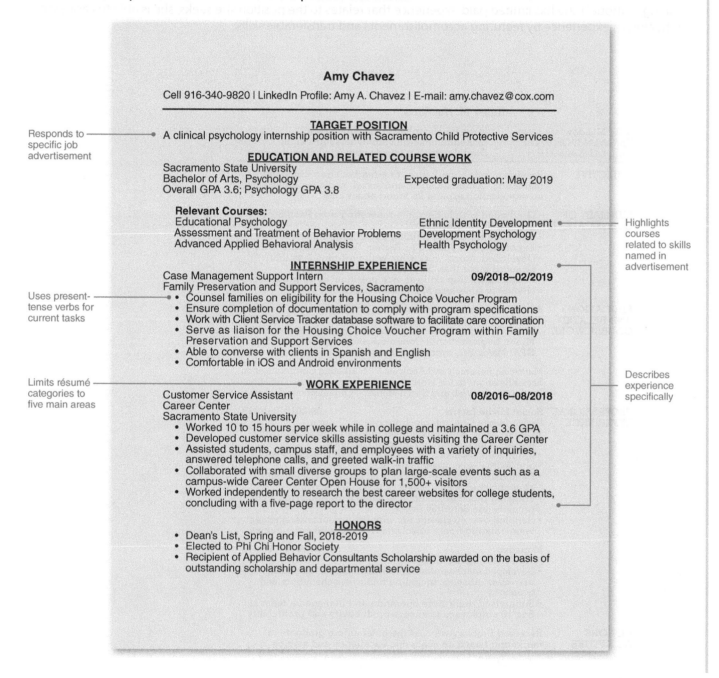

Responds to specific job advertisement

Uses present-tense verbs for current tasks

Limits résumé categories to five main areas

Highlights courses related to skills named in advertisement

Describes experience specifically

Amy Chavez

Cell 916-340-9820 | LinkedIn Profile: Amy A. Chavez | E-mail: amy.chavez@cox.com

TARGET POSITION
A clinical psychology internship position with Sacramento Child Protective Services

EDUCATION AND RELATED COURSE WORK
Sacramento State University
Bachelor of Arts, Psychology   Expected graduation: May 2019
Overall GPA 3.6; Psychology GPA 3.8

Relevant Courses:
Educational Psychology   Ethnic Identity Development
Assessment and Treatment of Behavior Problems   Development Psychology
Advanced Applied Behavioral Analysis   Health Psychology

INTERNSHIP EXPERIENCE
Case Management Support Intern   09/2018–02/2019
Family Preservation and Support Services, Sacramento
- Counsel families on eligibility for the Housing Choice Voucher Program
- Ensure completion of documentation to comply with program specifications
- Work with Client Service Tracker database software to facilitate care coordination
- Serve as liaison for the Housing Choice Voucher Program within Family Preservation and Support Services
- Able to converse with clients in Spanish and English
- Comfortable in iOS and Android environments

WORK EXPERIENCE
Customer Service Assistant   08/2016–08/2018
Career Center
Sacramento State University
- Worked 10 to 15 hours per week while in college and maintained a 3.6 GPA
- Developed customer service skills assisting guests visiting the Career Center
- Assisted students, campus staff, and employees with a variety of inquiries, answered telephone calls, and greeted walk-in traffic
- Collaborated with small diverse groups to plan large-scale events such as a campus-wide Career Center Open House for 1,500+ visitors
- Worked independently to research the best career websites for college students, concluding with a five-page report to the director

HONORS
- Dean's List, Spring and Fall, 2018-2019
- Elected to Phi Chi Honor Society
- Recipient of Applied Behavior Consultants Scholarship awarded on the basis of outstanding scholarship and departmental service

Figure 13.13 Functional Résumé: Recent College Graduate With Unrelated Part-Time Experience

Recent graduate Dallas Dayal chose this functional format to de-emphasize his meager work experience and emphasize his potential in sales and marketing. This version of his résumé is more generic than one targeted for a specific position. Nevertheless, it emphasizes his strong points with specific achievements and includes an employment section to satisfy recruiters. The functional format presents ability-focused topics. It illustrates what the job seeker can do for the employer instead of narrating a history of previous jobs. Although recruiters prefer chronological résumés, the functional format is a good choice for new graduates, career changers, and those with employment gaps.

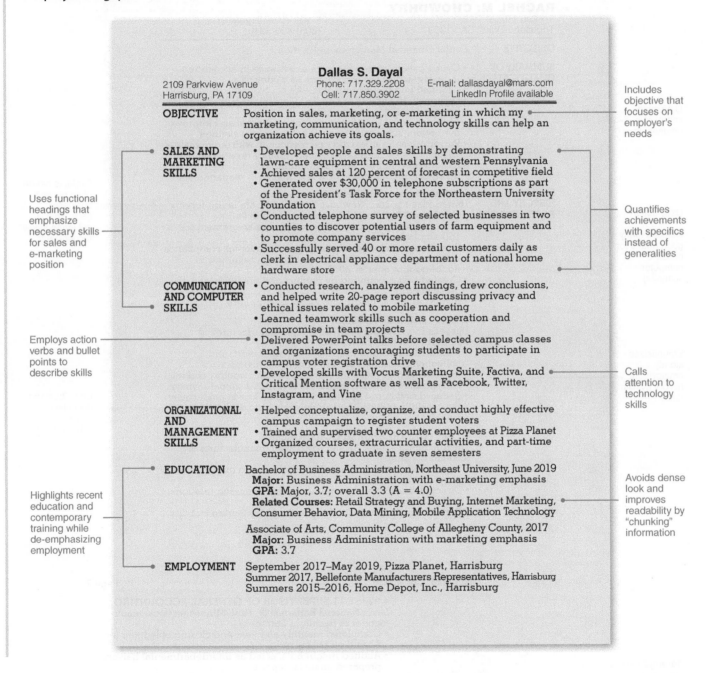

Dallas S. Dayal

2109 Parkview Avenue
Harrisburg, PA 17109

Phone: 717.329.2208
Cell: 717.850.3902

E-mail: dallasdayal@mars.com
LinkedIn Profile available

Includes objective that focuses on employer's needs

OBJECTIVE — Position in sales, marketing, or e-marketing in which my marketing, communication, and technology skills can help an organization achieve its goals.

Uses functional headings that emphasize necessary skills for sales and e-marketing position

SALES AND MARKETING SKILLS
- Developed people and sales skills by demonstrating lawn-care equipment in central and western Pennsylvania
- Achieved sales at 120 percent of forecast in competitive field
- Generated over $30,000 in telephone subscriptions as part of the President's Task Force for the Northeastern University Foundation
- Conducted telephone survey of selected businesses in two counties to discover potential users of farm equipment and to promote company services
- Successfully served 40 or more retail customers daily as clerk in electrical appliance department of national home hardware store

Quantifies achievements with specifics instead of generalities

COMMUNICATION AND COMPUTER SKILLS
- Conducted research, analyzed findings, drew conclusions, and helped write 20-page report discussing privacy and ethical issues related to mobile marketing
- Learned teamwork skills such as cooperation and compromise in team projects

Employs action verbs and bullet points to describe skills

- Delivered PowerPoint talks before selected campus classes and organizations encouraging students to participate in campus voter registration drive
- Developed skills with Vocus Marketing Suite, Factiva, and Critical Mention software as well as Facebook, Twitter, Instagram, and Vine

Calls attention to technology skills

ORGANIZATIONAL AND MANAGEMENT SKILLS
- Helped conceptualize, organize, and conduct highly effective campus campaign to register student voters
- Trained and supervised two counter employees at Pizza Planet
- Organized courses, extracurricular activities, and part-time employment to graduate in seven semesters

Highlights recent education and contemporary training while de-emphasizing employment

EDUCATION — Bachelor of Business Administration, Northeast University, June 2019
Major: Business Administration with e-marketing emphasis
GPA: Major, 3.7; overall 3.3 (A = 4.0)
Related Courses: Retail Strategy and Buying, Internet Marketing, Consumer Behavior, Data Mining, Mobile Application Technology

Associate of Arts, Community College of Allegheny County, 2017
Major: Business Administration with marketing emphasis
GPA: 3.7

Avoids dense look and improves readability by "chunking" information

EMPLOYMENT — September 2017–May 2019, Pizza Planet, Harrisburg
Summer 2017, Bellefonte Manufacturers Representatives, Harrisburg
Summers 2015–2016, Home Depot, Inc., Harrisburg

Figure 13.14 Chronological Résumé: University Graduate With Substantial Experience

Because Rachel has many years of experience and seeks executive-level employment, she highlighted her experience by placing it before her education. Her summary of qualifications highlighted her most impressive experience and skills. This chronological two-page résumé shows the steady progression of her career to executive positions, a movement that impresses and reassures recruiters.

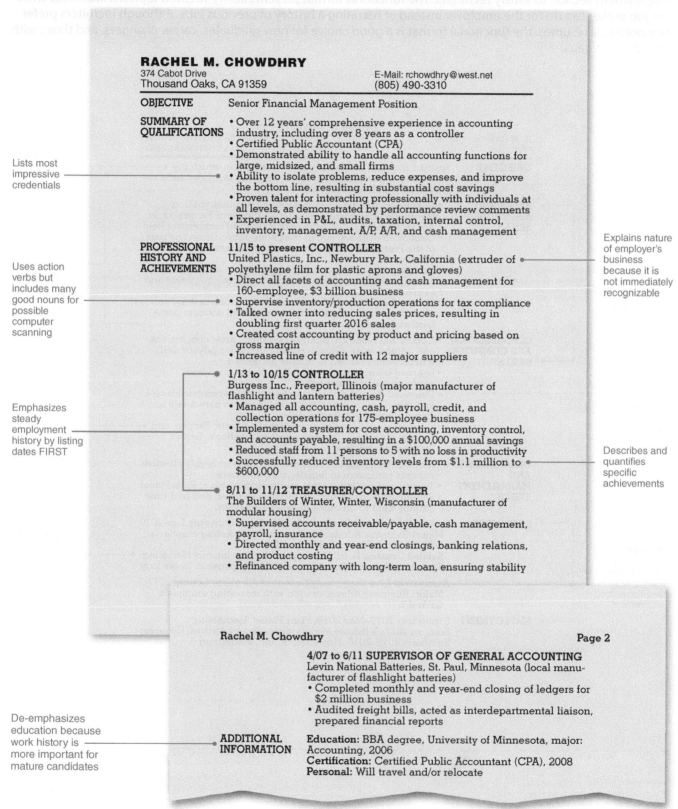

RACHEL M. CHOWDHRY
374 Cabot Drive
Thousand Oaks, CA 91359

E-Mail: rchowdhry@west.net
(805) 490-3310

OBJECTIVE Senior Financial Management Position

SUMMARY OF QUALIFICATIONS
- Over 12 years' comprehensive experience in accounting industry, including over 8 years as a controller
- Certified Public Accountant (CPA)
- Demonstrated ability to handle all accounting functions for large, midsized, and small firms
- Ability to isolate problems, reduce expenses, and improve the bottom line, resulting in substantial cost savings
- Proven talent for interacting professionally with individuals at all levels, as demonstrated by performance review comments
- Experienced in P&L, audits, taxation, internal control, inventory, management, A/P, A/R, and cash management

Lists most impressive credentials

PROFESSIONAL HISTORY AND ACHIEVEMENTS

11/15 to present CONTROLLER
United Plastics, Inc., Newbury Park, California (extruder of polyethylene film for plastic aprons and gloves)
- Direct all facets of accounting and cash management for 160-employee, $3 billion business
- Supervise inventory/production operations for tax compliance
- Talked owner into reducing sales prices, resulting in doubling first quarter 2016 sales
- Created cost accounting by product and pricing based on gross margin
- Increased line of credit with 12 major suppliers

Uses action verbs but includes many good nouns for possible computer scanning

Explains nature of employer's business because it is not immediately recognizable

1/13 to 10/15 CONTROLLER
Burgess Inc., Freeport, Illinois (major manufacturer of flashlight and lantern batteries)
- Managed all accounting, cash, payroll, credit, and collection operations for 175-employee business
- Implemented a system for cost accounting, inventory control, and accounts payable, resulting in a $100,000 annual savings
- Reduced staff from 11 persons to 5 with no loss in productivity
- Successfully reduced inventory levels from $1.1 million to $600,000

Emphasizes steady employment history by listing dates FIRST

Describes and quantifies specific achievements

8/11 to 11/12 TREASURER/CONTROLLER
The Builders of Winter, Winter, Wisconsin (manufacturer of modular housing)
- Supervised accounts receivable/payable, cash management, payroll, insurance
- Directed monthly and year-end closings, banking relations, and product costing
- Refinanced company with long-term loan, ensuring stability

Rachel M. Chowdhry   Page 2

4/07 to 6/11 SUPERVISOR OF GENERAL ACCOUNTING
Levin National Batteries, St. Paul, Minnesota (local manufacturer of flashlight batteries)
- Completed monthly and year-end closing of ledgers for $2 million business
- Audited freight bills, acted as interdepartmental liaison, prepared financial reports

De-emphasizes education because work history is more important for mature candidates

ADDITIONAL INFORMATION
Education: BBA degree, University of Minnesota, major: Accounting, 2006
Certification: Certified Public Accountant (CPA), 2008
Personal: Will travel and/or relocate

13-4e Polishing Your Résumé and Keeping It Honest

As you continue to work on your résumé, look for ways to improve it. For example, consider consolidating headings. By condensing your information into as few headings as possible, you will produce a clean, professional-looking document. Study other résumés for valuable formatting ideas. Ask yourself what graphic highlighting techniques you can use to improve readability: capitalization, underlining, indenting, and bulleting. Experiment with headings and styles to achieve a pleasing, easy-to-read message. Moreover, look for ways to eliminate wordiness. For example, instead of *Supervised two employees who worked at the counter,* try *Supervised two counter employees.* Review Chapter 4 for more tips on writing concisely.

A résumé is expected to showcase a candidate's strengths and minimize weaknesses. For this reason, recruiters expect a certain degree of self-promotion. Some résumé writers, however, step over the line that separates honest self-marketing from deceptive half-truths and flat-out lies. Distorting facts on a résumé is unethical; lying may be illegal. Most important, either practice can destroy a career. In the Communication Workshop at the end of this chapter, learn more about how to keep your résumé honest and about the consequences of fudging the facts.

13-4f Proofreading Your Résumé

After revising your résumé, you must proofread, proofread, and proofread again for spelling, grammar, mechanics, content, and format. Then have a knowledgeable friend or relative proofread it yet again. This is one document that must be perfect. Because the job market is so competitive, one typo, one misspelled word, or a single grammatical error could eliminate you from consideration.

By now you may be thinking that you'd like to hire someone to write your résumé. Don't! First, you know yourself better than anyone else could know you. Second, you will end up with either a generic or a one-time résumé. A generic résumé in today's highly competitive job market will lose out to a customized résumé nine times out of ten. Equally useless is a one-time résumé aimed at a single job. What if you don't get that job? Because you will need to revise your résumé many times as you seek a variety of jobs, be prepared to write (and rewrite) it yourself.

13-5 Using Digital Tools to Enhance Your Job Search

LEARNING OUTCOME 5

Enhance your job search and résumé by taking advantage of digital tools.

Just as electronic media have changed the way candidates seek jobs, these same digital tools are transforming the way employers select qualified candidates. As discussed earlier, the first reader of your résumé may very well be an applicant tracking system (ATS). As many as 90 percent of large companies and scores of smaller companies are now employing these systems. However, they are not without their critics. Job candidates find the application process frustrating and the technology subject to glitches. Even after repeatedly entering the required information into clunky online forms, they can't be sure that a human will ever review it.[33] Enterprises run the risk of missing out on talented candidates who don't fit the standardized screening criteria or find the experience too daunting.

So why are applicant tracking systems so popular with businesses? Thanks to technology, applying for jobs has become so effortless that organizations are flooded with résumés. Screening systems whittle down the applicant pool to just a handful of qualified applicants for the human hiring managers to review more closely. The sad truth for applicants, however, is that up to 75 percent of résumés don't make it past the ATS screening.[34]

13-5a Maximizing the Rank of Your Résumé

The higher your résumé ranks when it is evaluated by an applicant tracking system, the more likely it will be reviewed by a recruiter or hiring manager. In the past candidates tried to game the system by stuffing their résumés with keywords. Newer screening systems are not so easily fooled. Although keywords are important, "the system looks for relevance of the keyword to your work history and education," advises job-search authority Quint Careers.[35] In addition to including the right keywords in context, your résumé must qualify in other ways to be selected. The following techniques, in addition to those cited earlier, can boost the probability that your résumé will rank high enough to qualify for review by a human reader.

■ **Include specific keywords or keyword phrases.** Study carefully any advertisements and job descriptions for the position you want. Describe your experience, education, and qualifications in terms associated with the job advertisement or job description for this position. However, don't just plop a keyword into your résumé; use it in context to ensure ATS recognition (e.g., *collaborated within four-member team to create a pilot business plan*).

■ **Focus on nouns.** Although action verbs will make your résumé appeal to a recruiter, the ATS will often be looking for nouns in three categories: (a) a job title, position, or role (e.g., *accountant, Web developer, team leader*); (b) a technical skill or specialization (e.g., *JavaScript, e-newsletter editor*); and (c) a certification, a tool used, or specific experience (e.g., *Certified Financial Analyst, Chartered Financial Analyst*).

■ **Use variations of the job title.** Tracking systems may seek a slightly different job title from what you list. To be safe, include variations and abbreviations (e.g., *occupational therapist, certified occupational therapist,* or *COTA*). If you don't have experience in your targeted area, use the job title you seek in your objective.

■ **Concentrate on the Skills section.** A majority of keywords employers seek relate to specialized or technical skill requirements. Therefore, be sure the Skills section of your résumé is loaded with nouns that describe your skills and qualifications.

■ **Keep the formatting simple.** Stay away from logos, pictures, symbols, and shadings.

■ **Use conventional headings.** Include familiar headings such as *Skills, Qualifications,* and *Education.* ATS software may not recognize headings such as *Professional Engagement* or *Core Competencies.*

13-5b Showcasing Your Qualifications in a Career E-Portfolio

With the workplace becoming increasingly digital, you have yet another way to display your qualifications to prospective employers—the career e-portfolio. This is a collection of digital files that can be navigated with the help of menus and hyperlinks much like a personal website.

What Goes in a Career E-Portfolio? An e-portfolio provides viewers with a snapshot of your talents, accomplishments, and technical skills. In this digital age, your e-portfolio can become one of the top hits in an Internet search for your name.[36] It may include a copy of your career-specific résumé, reference letters, commendations for special achievements, awards, certificates, work samples, a complete list of your courses, thank-you letters, and other items that tout your accomplishments. An e-portfolio could also offer links to digital copies of your artwork, film projects, videos, blueprints, documents, photographs, multimedia files, and blog entries that might otherwise be difficult to share with potential employers.

Because e-portfolios offer a variety of resources in one place, they have many advantages, as seen in Figure 13.15. When they are posted on websites, they can be viewed at an employer's convenience. Let's say you are talking on the phone with an employer in another city who wants to see a copy of your résumé. You can simply refer the employer to the website where your résumé resides. E-portfolios can also be seen by many individuals in an organization without circulating a paper copy. However, the main reason for preparing an e-portfolio is that it permits you to show off your talents and qualifications more thoroughly than you can in a print résumé.

Some recruiters may be skeptical about e-portfolios because they fear that such presentations will take more time to view than paper-based résumés do. As a result, nontraditional job applications may end up at the bottom of the pile or be ignored. That's why some applicants submit a print résumé or e-mail a digital copy in addition to an e-portfolio.

How Are E-Portfolios Accessed? E-portfolios are generally accessed at websites, where they are available anytime to employers. If the websites are not password protected, however, you should remove personal information. Some colleges and universities host student e-portfolios. In addition, institutions may provide instruction and resources for scanning photos, digitizing images, and preparing graphics. E-portfolios may also be burned onto CDs and DVDs to be mailed to prospective employers.

13-5c Expanding Your Employment Chances With a Video Résumé

Still another way to expand your employment possibilities is with a video résumé. Video résumés enable job candidates to present their experience, qualifications, and interests in video form. This format has many benefits. It allows candidates to demonstrate their public speaking, interpersonal, and technical skills more impressively than they can in traditional print résumés. Both employers and applicants can save recruitment and travel costs by using video résumés. Instead of flying distant candidates to interviews, organizations can see them digitally.

Video résumés are becoming more prevalent with the popularity of YouTube, inexpensive webcams, and widespread broadband. With simple edits on a computer,

Figure 13.15 Making a Career E-Portfolio

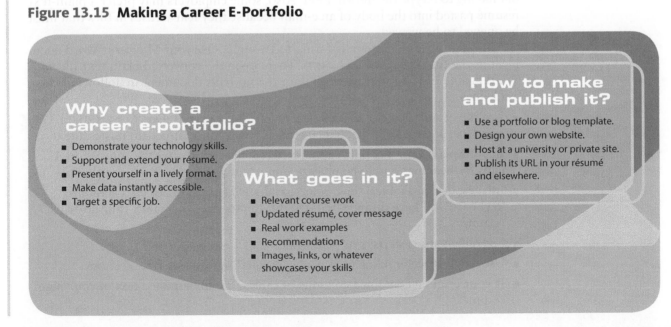

Why create a career e-portfolio?

- Demonstrate your technology skills.
- Support and extend your résumé.
- Present yourself in a lively format.
- Make data instantly accessible.
- Target a specific job.

What goes in it?

- Relevant course work
- Updated résumé, cover message
- Real work examples
- Recommendations
- Images, links, or whatever showcases your skills

How to make and publish it?

- Use a portfolio or blog template.
- Design your own website.
- Host at a university or private site.
- Publish its URL in your résumé and elsewhere.

you can customize a video message to a specific employer and tailor your résumé for a particular job opening. In making a video résumé, dress professionally in business attire, just as you would for an in-person interview. Keep your video to three minutes or less. Explain why you would be a good employee and what you can do for the company that hires you.

Before committing time and energy to a video résumé, decide whether it is appropriate for your career field. Such presentations make sense for online, media, social, and creative professions. Traditional organizations, however, may be less impressed. Done well, a video résumé might give you an edge. Done poorly, however, it could bounce you from contention.

13-5d How Many Résumés and What Format?

At this point you may be wondering how many résumés you should make, and what format they should follow. The good news is that you need only one basic résumé that you can customize for various job prospects, and you can save your Microsoft Word files in various formats.

Preparing a Basic Hard-Copy Résumé. The one basic résumé you should prepare in Word first is a traditional paper résumé to print and hand out. It should be attractively formatted to maximize readability. This hard-copy résumé is useful (a) during job interviews, (b) for person-to-person networking situations, (c) for recruiters at career fairs, and (d) when you are competing for a job that does not require an electronic submission.

The Résumé Gallery in this chapter provides ideas for simple layouts that are easily duplicated and adapted. You can also examine résumé templates for design and format ideas. Their inflexibility, however, may be frustrating as you try to force your skills and experience into a predetermined template sequence.

Creating a Plain-Text Résumé for Online and E-Mail Submission. After preparing a basic résumé for printing, you can save your Microsoft Word document as a plain-text résumé that is available to you when you fill out employers' application forms online. Many job-board sites and most government employers require job candidates to complete official application forms. Even if your résumé contains the same information, an application form is often required for legal and data processing as well as for employer convenience. A simple plain-text résumé enables you to copy and paste parts of the document into the cloud-based submission forms without having to retype the information. Also, some employers may prefer a plain-text résumé pasted into the body of an e-mail because they fear viruses in files that must be opened to be viewed.

To create a plain, minimally formatted résumé, save your Microsoft Word document as the file type *plain text* (*txt). Then, open the converted plain-text file with Word again, and continue to work with the no-frills document by following these guidelines:

- Use the default Courier font or select Helvetica or Arial. Don't revert to italics, boldface, and underlining, which could cause some scanners to misread text.

- In your plain-text file, only capital letters will remain after the conversion. Use caps for headings and to emphasize important words, but don't overdo the caps.

- Images, designs, tables, tabs, colors, and any characters not on a standard keyboard will have disappeared. Do not reintroduce them into your no-frills résumé.

- For bullets, use asterisks or plus signs.

- Use white space or a line of hyphens or equal signs to separate sections.

- If your original contained columns or tables, fix any jumbled text in your plain résumé.

- Information placed in a header or footer may appear at the bottom of the file after the conversion. Move your name and contact information to the top of the page.
- Paste a copy of your plain résumé into an e-mail message and send it to yourself to check its appearance and detect any formatting problems. Also e-mail it to a friend to try it out.

13-5e Submitting Your Résumé

The format you choose for submitting your résumé depends on what is required. If you are responding to a job advertisement, be certain to read the listing carefully to learn how the employer wants you to submit your résumé. Not following the prospective employer's instructions can eliminate you from consideration before your résumé is even reviewed. If you have any doubt about what format is desired, send an e-mail inquiry to a company representative, or call and ask. Most organizations request one of the following submission formats:

- **Word document.** Some organizations ask candidates to send their résumés and cover messages in hard copy by surface mail. Others request that résumés be submitted as Word documents attached to e-mail messages, despite the fear of viruses.
- **PDF document.** For safety reasons some employers prefer PDF (portable document format) files. A PDF résumé looks exactly like the original and cannot be altered easily. Converting your résumé from Word can be easily done by saving it as a PDF file, which preserves all formatting.
- **Plain-text document.** As discussed earlier, some employers may expect applicants to submit résumés and cover letters as plain-text documents. Such minimally formatted documents are also widely used for posting to online job boards or for sending by e-mail. Plain-text résumés may be embedded within or attached to plain-text e-mail messages.
- **Company database.** Larger organizations may prefer that you complete an online form with your résumé information. This enables them to plug your data into their formats for rapid searching and applicant tracking. You can cut and paste the information from your plain, minimally formatted résumé into the form. Some businesses may ask you to upload your résumé as a Word, PDF, or image file. To keep your formatting intact, opt for a PDF or image file.
- **Fax.** Despite advances such as scanning and printing to e-mail, fax transmission is not dead. Doctors, lawyers, some realtors, car dealers, and PR people for various reasons are holding on to the fading technology. Fans swear that faxing is simpler and more secure than printing, scanning, and e-mailing.[37] Because print quality is often poor, use the fax method only if requested or if a submission deadline is upon you. Then, follow up with your polished printed or digital résumé.

Because your résumé is probably the most important message you will ever write, you will revise it many times. With so much information in concentrated form and with so much riding on its outcome, your résumé demands careful polishing, proofreading, and critiquing.

13-6 Cover Messages—Do They Still Matter?

A cover message, also known as a *cover letter* or *letter of application*, has always been a graceful way of introducing your résumé. However, with the steady movement toward online recruiting and digitized applicant tracking systems, cover letters are losing significance for recruiters. A survey by Jobvite revealed that 63 percent of

LEARNING OUTCOME 6

Understand the value of cover messages and how to draft and submit a customized message to highlight your candidacy.

the 1,404 recruiter respondents thought that cover messages were unimportant.[38] Employment counselors, such as Jen H. Luckwaldt at PayScale, were quick to point out that Jobvite's core business is helping recruiters find candidates through social networks, thus possibly slanting the findings.[39]

Another survey of hiring professionals suggested that a whopping 90 percent ignored cover letters. Why? Recruiters are inundated with applications and have little time to read them.[40] Merely 20 percent of private-sector HR professionals (34 percent in government; a third in smaller organizations) told the Society of Human Resource Management that they would warn against omitting a cover message. However, this minority is adamant that good cover messages matter because they make applicants more personable and memorable.[41]

Although some recruiters may not value cover messages, they are still important to hiring managers. A well-written cover message can help a candidate stand out in a flood of applications. If you are required to apply via software that limits your input, how can you get your cover message and résumé to key decision makers? Use LinkedIn or the company website to learn the names of those involved with hiring, and send your résumé and cover letter directly to these individuals calling attention to your candidacy.

13-6a Writing Customized Cover Messages

Especially in today's competitive employment scene, you must make yourself stand out. Cover messages reveal to employers your ability to put together complete sentences and to sound intelligent. In addition, many employers still prefer that you e-mail a résumé and a cover letter because it's more convenient for them than going online.[43] A well-crafted personal cover message showcases your special talents without relying on a chronology of your education and employment.

Even the recruiting professionals who favor cover messages disagree about their length. Some prefer short messages with no more than two paragraphs embedded in an e-mail message. Other recruiters desire longer messages that supply more information, thus giving them a better opportunity to evaluate a candidate's qualifications and writing skills. These recruiters argue that hiring and training new employees is expensive and time consuming; therefore, they welcome extra data to guide them in making the best choice the first time. Follow your judgment in writing a brief or a longer cover message.

Regardless of its length, a cover message should have three primary parts: (a) an opening that captures attention, introduces the message, and identifies the position; (b) a body that sells the candidate and focuses on the employer's needs; and (c) a closing that requests an interview and motivates action. When putting your cover message together, remember that the biggest mistake job seekers make when writing cover messages is being too generic. You should, therefore, write a personalized, customized cover message for every position that interests you.

13-6b Gaining Attention in the Opening

Your cover message will be more appealing—and more likely to be read—if it begins by addressing the reader by name. Rather than sending your letter to the *Hiring Manager* or *Human Resources Department*, try to identify the name of the appropriate individual by studying the company's website. You could also call the human resources department and ask the name of the person in charge of hiring. Another possibility is using LinkedIn to find someone working in the same department as the position in the posted job. This person may know the name of the hiring manager. If you still cannot find the name of any person to address, you might replace the salutation of your letter with a descriptive subject line such as *Application for Marketing Specialist Position*.

How you open your cover message depends largely on whether the application is solicited or unsolicited. If an employment position has been announced and applicants are being solicited, you can use a direct approach. If you do not know whether a position is open and you are prospecting for a job, use an indirect approach. Whether direct or indirect, the opening should attract the attention of the reader. Strive for openings that are more imaginative than *Please consider this letter an application for the position of . . . or I would like to apply for. . . .*

Openings for Solicited Jobs. When applying for a job that has been announced, consider some of the following techniques to open your cover message:

- **Refer to the name of an employee in the company.** Remember that employers always hope to hire known quantities rather than complete strangers.

    Jacob Benoit, a member of your Customer Service Department, told me that Alliance Resources is seeking a customer service trainee. The enclosed summary of my qualifications demonstrates my preparation for this position.

    At the suggestion of Abigail Freed, in your Legal Services Department, I submit my qualifications for the position of staffing coordinator.

    Melanie Cervantes, placement director at Southwest University, told me that Dynamic Industries has an opening for a technical writer with knowledge of Web design and graphics.

- **Refer to the source of your information precisely.** If you are answering an advertisement, include the exact position advertised and the name and date of the publication. If you are responding to a position listed on an online job board, include the website name and the date the position was posted.

    From your company's website, I learned about your need for a sales representative for the Ohio, Indiana, and Illinois regions. I am very interested in this position and am confident that my education and experience are appropriate for the opening.

    My talent for interacting with people, coupled with more than five years of customer service experience, make me an ideal candidate for the director of customer relations position you advertised on the CareerJournal website on August 3.

- **Refer to the job title, and describe how your qualifications fit the requirements.** Hiring managers are looking for a match between an applicant's credentials and the job needs.

    Ceradyne Company's marketing assistant opening is an excellent match with my qualifications. As a recent graduate of Western University with a major in marketing, I offer solid academic credentials as well as industry experience gained from an internship at Flotek Industries.

    Will an honors graduate with a degree in recreation and two years of part-time experience organizing social activities for a convalescent hospital qualify for your position of activity director?

    Because of my specialized training in finance and accounting at Michigan State University, I am confident that I have the qualifications you described in your advertisement for a staff accountant trainee.

Openings for Unsolicited Jobs. If you are unsure whether a position actually exists, you might use a more persuasive opening. Because your goal is to convince the hiring manager to read on, try one of the following techniques:

- **Demonstrate an interest in and knowledge of the reader's business.** Show this person that you have done your research and that this organization is more than a mere name to you.

Because Signa HealthNet, Inc., is organizing a new information management team for its recently established group insurance division, could you use the services of a well-trained information systems graduate who seeks to become a professional systems analyst?

I read with great interest the article in Forbes *announcing the upcoming launch of US Bank. Congratulations on this new venture and its notable $50 million in loans precharter! The possibility of helping your bank grow is exciting, and I would like to explore a potential employment match that I am confident will be mutually beneficial.*

- **Show how your special talents and background will benefit the company.** Human resources managers need to be convinced that you can do something for them.

Figure 13.16 Solicited Cover Letter

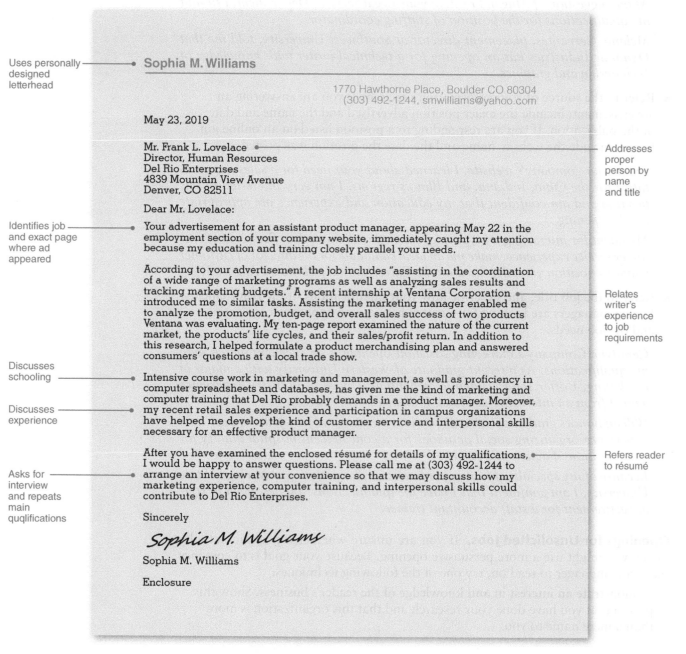

Uses personally designed letterhead →

Sophia M. Williams

1770 Hawthorne Place, Boulder CO 80304
(303) 492-1244, smwilliams@yahoo.com

May 23, 2019

Mr. Frank L. Lovelace ● → Addresses proper person by name and title
Director, Human Resources
Del Rio Enterprises
4839 Mountain View Avenue
Denver, CO 82511

Dear Mr. Lovelace:

Identifies job and exact page where ad appeared →
Your advertisement for an assistant product manager, appearing May 22 in the employment section of your company website, immediately caught my attention because my education and training closely parallel your needs.

According to your advertisement, the job includes "assisting in the coordination of a wide range of marketing programs as well as analyzing sales results and tracking marketing budgets." A recent internship at Ventana Corporation ● → Relates writer's experience to job requirements
introduced me to similar tasks. Assisting the marketing manager enabled me to analyze the promotion, budget, and overall sales success of two products Ventana was evaluating. My ten-page report examined the nature of the current market, the products' life cycles, and their sales/profit return. In addition to this research, I helped formulate a product merchandising plan and answered consumers' questions at a local trade show.

Discusses schooling →
Intensive course work in marketing and management, as well as proficiency in computer spreadsheets and databases, has given me the kind of marketing and computer training that Del Rio probably demands in a product manager. Moreover,
Discusses experience →
my recent retail sales experience and participation in campus organizations have helped me develop the kind of customer service and interpersonal skills necessary for an effective product manager.

After you have examined the enclosed résumé for details of my qualifications, ● → Refers reader to résumé
I would be happy to answer questions. Please call me at (303) 492-1244 to
Asks for interview and repeats main qualifications →
arrange an interview at your convenience so that we may discuss how my marketing experience, computer training, and interpersonal skills could contribute to Del Rio Enterprises.

Sincerely

Sophia M. Williams

Sophia M. Williams

Enclosure

Could your rapidly expanding publications division use the services of an editorial assistant who offers exceptional language skills, an honors degree from the University of Mississippi, and two years' experience in producing a campus literary publication?

In applying for an advertised job, Sophia Williams wrote the solicited cover letter shown in Figure 13.16. Notice that her opening identifies the position advertised on the company's website so that the reader knows exactly what advertisement Sophia means. Using features on her word processing program, Sophia designed her own letterhead that uses her name and looks like professionally printed letterhead paper.

More challenging are unsolicited cover messages, such as the letter of Jared Chen shown in Figure 13.17. Because he hopes to discover or create a job, his opening must grab the reader's attention immediately. To do that, he capitalizes on company

Figure 13.17 Unsolicited Cover Letter

Uses personal business style with return address above date

3580 Edgewater Drive
Lakewood, OH 44107
May 25, 2019

Mr. David D. Dangelo
Vice President, Operations
Sports Universe, Inc.
2210 Euclid Avenue
Cleveland, OH 44110

Dear Mr. Dangelo:

Shows resourcefulness and knowledge of company

Today's *Cleveland Plain Dealer Online* reports that your organization plans to expand its operations to include national distribution of sporting goods, and it occurs to me that you will be needing highly motivated, self-starting sales representatives and marketing managers. Here are three significant qualifications I have to offer:

Uses bulleted list to make letter easier to read

- Four years of formal training in business administration, including specialized courses in sports management, retailing, marketing promotion, and consumer behavior.

- Practical experience in demonstrating and selling consumer products, as well as successful experience in telemarketing.

- Excellent communication skills and a strong interest in most areas of sports, which helped me become a student sportscaster at Ohio State's The Fan, 97.1 FM sports radio station.

Keeps letter brief to retain reader's attention

Refers to enclosed résumé

May we talk about how I can put these qualifications, and others summarized in the enclosed résumé, to work for Sports Universe as it develops its national sales force? I'll call during the week of June 5 to discuss your company's expansion plans and the opportunity for an interview.

Takes initiative for follow-up

Sincerely,

Jared W. Chen

Jared W. Chen

Enclosure

information appearing in an online article. Jared purposely kept his cover letter short and to the point because he anticipated that a busy executive would be unwilling to read a long, detailed letter. Jared's unsolicited letter prospects for a job. Some job candidates feel that such letters may be even more productive than efforts to secure advertised jobs, because prospecting candidates face less competition and show initiative. Notice that Jared's letter uses a personal business letter format with his return address above the date.

13-6c Promoting Your Strengths in the Message Body

Once you have captured the attention of the reader and identified your purpose in the letter opening, you should use the body of the letter to plug your qualifications for this position. If you are responding to an advertisement, you will want to explain how your preparation and experience fulfill the stated requirements. If you are prospecting for a job, you may not know the exact requirements. Your employment research and knowledge of your field, however, should give you a reasonably good idea of what is expected for the position you seek.

It is important to stress reader benefits. In other words, you should describe your strong points in relation to the needs of the employer. Corporate HR expert and author Liz Ryan calls this pitch to help solve the recruiter's problems a *pain letter*.[44] She is suggesting that your cover letter credibly prove to the employer how hiring you would fulfill an unmet need that you may have identified in your research. In other words, you are the solution to a burning problem the company may have. Hiring officers want you to tell them what you can do for their organizations. This is more important than telling what courses you took in college or what duties you performed in your previous jobs.

Poor:	*I have completed courses in business communication, report writing, and technical writing.*
Improved:	*Courses in business communication, report writing, and technical writing have helped me develop the research and writing skills required of your technical writers.*

In the body of your letter, you may choose to discuss relevant personal traits. Employers are looking for candidates who, among other things, are team players, take responsibility, show initiative, and learn easily. Don't just list several personal traits, though; instead, include evidence that proves you possess these traits. Notice how in the following paragraph action verbs paint a picture of a promising candidate:

In addition to developing technical and academic skills at Florida Central University, I have gained interpersonal, leadership, and organizational skills. As vice president of the business students' organization, Gamma Alpha, I helped organize and supervise two successful fund-raising events. These activities involved conceptualizing the tasks, motivating others to help, scheduling work sessions, and coordinating the efforts of 35 diverse students. I enjoyed my success with these activities and look forward to applying my experience in your management trainee program.

Finally, in this section or the next, refer the reader to your résumé. Do so directly or as part of another statement.

Direct reference to résumé:	*Please refer to the attached résumé for additional information regarding my education, experience, and skills.*
Part of another statement:	*As you will notice from my enclosed résumé, I will graduate in June with a bachelor's degree in business administration.*

13-6d Motivating Action in the Closing

After presenting your case, you should conclude by asking confidently for an interview. Don't ask for the job. To do so would be presumptuous and naïve. In requesting an interview, you might suggest reader benefits or review your strongest points. Sound sincere and appreciative. Remember to make it easy for the reader to agree by supplying your telephone number and the best times to call you. In addition, keep in mind that some hiring officers prefer that you take the initiative to call them. Avoid expressions such as *I hope*, which weaken your closing. Here are possible endings:

Poor:	*I hope to hear from you soon.*
Improved:	*This brief description of my qualifications and the additional information on my résumé demonstrate my readiness to put my accounting skills to work for McLellan and Associates. Please call me at (405) 488-2291 before 10 a.m. or after 3 p.m. to arrange an interview.*
Poor:	*I look forward to a call from you.*
Improved:	*To add to your staff an industrious, well-trained administrative assistant with proven Internet and communication skills, call me at (350) 492-1433 to arrange an interview. I look forward to meeting with you to discuss further my qualifications.*
Poor:	*Thanks for looking over my qualifications.*
Improved:	*I look forward to the opportunity to discuss my qualifications for the financial analyst position more fully in an interview. You can reach me at (213) 458-4030.*

13-6e Sending Your Résumé and Cover Message

How you submit your résumé depends on the employer's instructions, which usually involve one of the following methods:

- Send a short e-mail with both your cover message and résumé attached.
- Send your cover in an e-mail and attach your résumé (plain text, Word document, or PDF).
- Submit both your cover message and résumé by pasting them into the body of an e-mail. Convert both to plain text with minimal formatting first, as described earlier.
- Send your cover message and résumé as printed Word documents by U.S. mail.

Serious job candidates take the time to prepare a professional cover message. If you are e-mailing your résumé, use the same cover message you would send by surface mail, but shorten it a bit, as illustrated in Figure 13.18. Just below your name, include your street address, e-mail address, and phone number.

13-6f Final Tips for Successful Cover Messages

As you revise your cover message, notice how many sentences begin with *I*. Although it is impossible to talk about yourself without using *I*, you can reduce "I" domination with a number of thoughtful techniques. Make activities and outcomes, and not yourself, the subjects of sentences. Sometimes you can avoid "I" domination by focusing on the "you" view. Another way to avoid starting sentences with *I* is to move phrases from within the sentence to the beginning.

Poor:	*I took classes in business communication and computer applications.*
Improved:	*Classes in business communication and computer applications prepared me to. . . . (Make activities the subject.)*

Figure 13.18 Partial E-Mail Cover Message

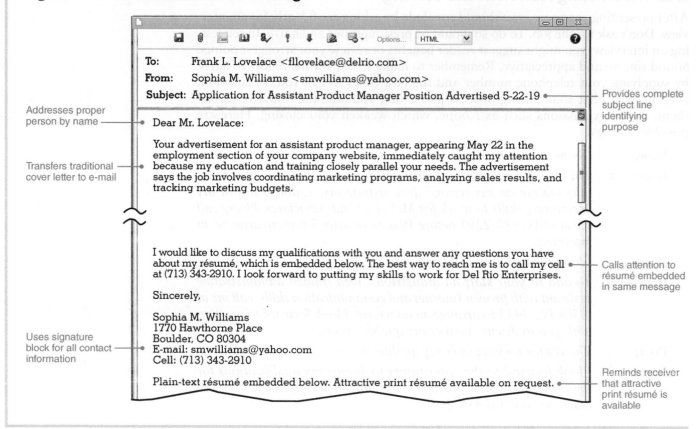

Addresses proper person by name ——

Transfers traditional cover letter to e-mail ——

Uses signature block for all contact information ——

Provides complete subject line identifying purpose

Calls attention to résumé embedded in same message

Reminds receiver that attractive print résumé is available

To: Frank L. Lovelace <fllovelace@delrio.com>
From: Sophia M. Williams <smwilliams@yahoo.com>
Subject: Application for Assistant Product Manager Position Advertised 5-22-19

Dear Mr. Lovelace:

Your advertisement for an assistant product manager, appearing May 22 in the employment section of your company website, immediately caught my attention because my education and training closely parallel your needs. The advertisement says the job involves coordinating marketing programs, analyzing sales results, and tracking marketing budgets.

I would like to discuss my qualifications with you and answer any questions you have about my résumé, which is embedded below. The best way to reach me is to call my cell at (713) 343-2910. I look forward to putting my skills to work for Del Rio Enterprises.

Sincerely,

Sophia M. Williams
1770 Hawthorne Place
Boulder, CO 80304
E-mail: smwilliams@yahoo.com
Cell: (713) 343-2910

Plain-text résumé embedded below. Attractive print résumé available on request.

Poor:	*I enjoyed helping customers, which taught me to. . . .*
Improved:	*Helping customers was a real pleasure and taught me to. . . .* (Make outcomes the subject.)
Poor:	*I am a hardworking team player who. . . .*
Improved:	*You are looking for a hardworking team player who. . . .* (Use the "you" view.)
Poor:	*I worked to support myself all through college, thus building. . . .*
Improved:	*All through college, I worked to support myself, thus building. . . .* (Move phrases to the beginning.)

However, strive for a comfortable style. In your effort to avoid sounding self-centered, don't write unnaturally.

Like your résumé, your cover message must look professional and suggest quality. This means using a traditional letter style, such as block format. Also, be sure to print it on the same quality paper as your résumé. As with your résumé, proofread it several times yourself; then have a friend read it for content and mechanics. Don't rely on spell-check to find all the errors. Like your résumé, your cover message must be perfect.

Summary of Learning Outcomes

1 Begin a job search by recognizing emerging trends and technologies, exploring your interests, evaluating your qualifications, and investigating career opportunities.

- Recognize that searching for a job in this digital age now includes such indispensable tools as job boards, social networks, and mobile technologies.
- Emphasis today is on what the employer wants, not what the candidate wants.
- Start the process by learning about yourself, your field of interest, and your qualifications. How do your skills match what employers seek?
- To investigate career opportunities, visit a campus career center, search for apps and online help, take a summer job, interview someone in your field, volunteer, or join professional organizations.
- Identify job availability, the skills and qualifications required, duties, and salaries.

2 Apply savvy search strategies by analyzing how job seekers find their jobs and how they use digital tools to explore the open job market.

- Research reveals that job seekers found their best jobs through personal networking, job boards, classified advertisements, recruiters, college fairs, and other connections.
- In searching the open job market—that is, jobs that are listed and advertised—study the big job boards, such as Indeed, CareerBuilder, Monster, and CollegeGrad.
- To find a job with a specific company, go directly to that company's website and check its openings and possibilities.
- For jobs in specialized fields, search some of the many niche sites, such as Dice for technology positions or CoolWorks for seasonal employment.
- Take advantage of mobile apps to access and vet job openings as soon as they are listed. Create and actively maintain a profile on LinkedIn.
- Protect yourself when using online job boards by posting privately, not revealing personal information, keeping careful records, and avoiding blind job postings.

3 Expand your job-search strategies by using both traditional and digital tools in pursuing the hidden job market.

- Estimates suggest that as many as 80 percent of jobs are in the hidden job market—that is, never advertised. Successful job candidates find jobs in the hidden job market through networking.
- An effective networking procedure involves (a) developing a contacts list, (b) reaching out to these contacts in person and online in search of referrals, and (c) following up on referrals.
- Because electronic media and digital tools continue to change our lives, savvy candidates use social media networks—especially LinkedIn—to extend their networking efforts.
- Invaluable in a job search, LinkedIn enables candidates to receive job alerts, leverage their networks, research companies, get recommendations, and help companies locate them online.
- Effective networking strategies include building a personal brand, preparing a professional business card with a tagline, composing a 60-second elevator speech that describes what you can offer, and developing a strong online presence.

4 Organize your qualifications and skills into effective résumé categories, and use that information to prepare a personalized LinkedIn profile.

- Because of intense competition, you must customize your résumés to appeal to an applicant tracking system (ATS) as well as to a human reader.

- Chronological résumés, which list work and education by dates, rank highest with recruiters. Functional résumés, which highlight skills instead of jobs, may be helpful for people with little experience, those changing careers, and those with negative employment histories.
- Arrange your skills and achievements to aim at a particular job or company.
- Study models to effectively arrange the résumé main heading and the optional career objective, summary of qualifications, education, work experience, capabilities, and awards and activities sections.
- The most effective résumés include action verbs to appeal to human readers and job-specific nouns that become keywords selected by applicant tracking systems.
- Prepare a LinkedIn page with a headline, photo, and profile, which includes information about your education, skills, and experience. Encourage your instructors and employers to post recommendations.
- Look for ways to strengthen your résumé by polishing, proofreading, and checking for honesty and accuracy.

5 **Enhance your job search and résumé by taking advantage of digital tools.**

- To maximize the rank of your résumé by an applicant tracking system, include specific keywords such as nouns that name job titles, technical skills, and tools used or specific experience.
- Consider preparing a career e-portfolio to showcase your qualifications. Feature your talents, accomplishments, and technical skills. These digital files may include examples of academic performance, photographs, multimedia files, and other items beyond what can be shown in a résumé.
- A video résumé enables you to present your experience, qualifications, and interests in video form.
- Start with a basic Word résumé that you can print or save in various formats. For example, you can make a plain-text résumé stripped of most formatting to cut and paste from instead of retyping text in online job applications, or to embed within plain-text e-mail messages.
- Decide whether to submit your résumé as a Word, plain-text, or PDF document. You may be asked to enter your information into company databases for applicant tracking.

6 **Understand the value of cover messages and how to draft and submit a customized message to highlight your candidacy.**

- Although applicant tracking systems may accept only a résumé, cover messages still play an important role in the job application process, especially to hiring managers.
- Cover messages help recruiters make decisions, and they enable candidates to set themselves apart from others.
- In the opening of a cover message, gain attention by addressing the receiver by name and identifying the job. You might also identify the person who referred you.
- In the body of the message, build interest by stressing your strengths in relation to the stated requirements. Explain what you can do for the targeted company.
- In the body or closing, refer to your résumé, request an interview, and make it easy for the receiver to respond.
- If you are submitting your cover message by e-mail, shorten it a bit and include your complete contact information in the signature block.

Chapter Review

1. In this digital age, list six of the latest trends in job searching and résumé writing. (L.O. 1)

2. When preparing to search for a job, what should you do before writing a résumé? (L.O. 1)

3. List seven ways you can explore career opportunities while still in college. (L.O. 1)

4. How do job seekers find their best jobs? (L.O. 2)

5. Although one may not actually find a job on the Internet, how can the big job boards be helpful to job hunters? (L.O. 2)

6. What is the hidden job market, and how can candidates find jobs in it? (L.O. 3)

7. In searching for a job, how can you build a personal brand, and why is it important to do so? (L.O. 3)

8. How do chronological and functional résumés differ, and what are the advantages and disadvantages of each? (L.O. 4)

9. What is an ATS, and how does it affect the way you prepare a résumé? (L.O. 5)

10. Why is it important to include a cover message with all résumés you send, even if you send them by e-mail? (L.O. 6)

Critical Thinking

11. The way candidates search for jobs and the way they are hired has changed dramatically in the digital age. Name some of the changes that have taken place. In your opinion, have the changes had a positive or a negative effect? Why? (L.O. 1)

12. Why do you think some businesses avoid advertising job openings? If jobs are unlisted, how can candidates locate them? (L.O. 3)

13. Some employment authors claim that the paper résumé is dead or dying. What's behind this assertion, and how should current job candidates respond? (L.O. 4)

14. Why might it be more effective to apply for unsolicited jobs than for advertised jobs? Discuss the advantages and disadvantages of messages that prospect for jobs. (L.O. 6)

15. Millennials are frequently criticized for job hopping, but some career experts believe that changing one's job every few years is now common and might even benefit a young worker's career. Are millennials getting a bad rap? How is changing jobs good or bad for your career? (L.O. 1–3)

Radical Rewrites

13.1 Radical Rewrite: Rescuing a Slapdash Résumé (L.O. 4)

The following poorly organized and poorly written résumé needs help to remedy its misspellings, typos, and inconsistent headings.

YOUR TASK. Analyze Elliana's sad résumé. List at least eight weaknesses. Your instructor may ask you to revise sections of this résumé before showing you an improved version.

Résumé of Elliana E. Estrada
1340 East Phillips Ave., Apt. D Littleton, CO 80126
Phone 455-5182 • E-Mail: Hotchilibabe@gmail.com

OBJECTIVE

I'm dying to land a first job in the "real world" with a big profitable company that will help me get ahead in the accounting field.

SKILLS

Word processing, Internet browsers (Explorer and Google), PowerPoint, Excel, type 40 wpm, databases, spreadsheets; great composure in stressful situations; 3 years as leader and supervisor and 4 years in customer service

EDUCATION

Arapahoe Community College, Littleton, Colorado. AA degree Fall 2017

Now I am pursuing a BA in Accounting at CSU-Pueblo, majoring in Accounting; my minor is Finance. My expected degree date is June 2019; I recieved a Certificate of Completion in Entry Level Accounting in December 2016.

I graduated East High School, Denver, CO in 2013.

Highlights:

- Named Line Manger of the Month at Target, 08/2014 and 09/2015
- Obtained a Certificate in Entry Level Accounting, June 2016

- Chair of Accounting Society, Spring and fall 2017
- Dean's Honor List, Fall 2018
- Financial advisor training completed through Primerica (May 2018)
- Webmaster for M.E.Ch.A, Spring 2019

Part-Time Employment

Financial Consultant, 2018 to present

I worked only part-time (January 2018-present) for Primerica Financial Services, Pueblo, CO to assist clients in refinancing a mortgage or consolidating a current mortgage loan and also to advice clients in assessing their need for life insurance.

Target, Littleton, CO. As line manager, from September 2012-March 2016, I supervised 22 cashiers and front-end associates. I helped to write schedules, disciplinary action notices, and performance appraisals. I also kept track of change drawer and money exchanges; occasionally was manager on duty for entire store.

Mr. K's Floral Design of Denver. I taught flower design from August, 2012 to September, 2013. I supervised 5 florists, made floral arrangements for big events like weddings, send them to customers, and restocked flowers.

List at least eight weaknesses.

13.2 Radical Rewrite: Inadequate Cover Letter (L.O. 6)

The following cover letter accompanies Elliana Estrada's résumé (**Radical Rewrite 13.1**). Like her résumé, the cover letter needs major revision.

YOUR TASK. Analyze Elliana's cover letter and list at least eight weaknesses. Your instructor may ask you to revise this letter before showing you an improved version.

To Whom It May Concern:

I saw your internship position yesterday and would like to apply right away. It would be so exiting to work for your esteemed firm! An internship would really give me much needed real-world experience and help my career.

I have all the qualifications you require in your add and more. I am a junior at Colorado State University-Pueblo and an Accounting major (with a minor in Finance). Accounting and Finance are my passion and I want to become a CPA and a financial advisor. I have taken Intermediate I and II and now work as a financial advisor with Primerica Financial Services in Pueblo. I should also tell you that I was at Target for four years. I learned alot, but my heart is in accounting and finance.

I am a team player, a born leader, motivated, reliable, and I show excellent composure in stressful situation, for example, when customers complain. I put myself through school and always carry at least 15 units while working part time.

You will probably agree that I am a good candidate for your internship position, which should start July 1. I feel that my motivation, passion, and strong people skills will serve your company well.

Sincerely,

List at least eight weaknesses.

Activities and Cases

13.3 Performing Self-Analysis Before the Job Search (L.O. 1)

E-Mail

YOUR TASK. In an e-mail or a memo addressed to your instructor, answer the questions in the section "Launching Your Job Search With Self-Analysis." Draw a conclusion from your answers. What kind of career, company, position, and location have emerged from your self-analysis?

13.4 Examining Your Job Credentials (L.O. 1, 4)

YOUR TASK. Prepare four worksheets that inventory your qualifications in these areas: employment; education; capabilities and skills; and awards, honors, and activities. Use active verbs when appropriate and specific nouns that describe job titles and skills.

a. **Employment.** Begin with your most recent job or internship. For each position list the following information: employer; job title; dates of employment; and three to five duties, activities, or accomplishments. Emphasize activities related to your job goal. Strive to quantify your achievements.

b. **Education.** List degrees, certificates, and training accomplishments. Include courses, seminars, and skills that are relevant to your job goal. Calculate your grade point average in your major.

c. **Capabilities and skills.** List all capabilities and skills that qualify you for the job you seek. Use words and phrases such as *skilled, competent, trained, experienced,* and *ability to.* Also list five or more qualities or interpersonal skills necessary for success in your field. Write action statements demonstrating that you possess some of these qualities. Empty assurances aren't good enough; try to show evidence (*Developed teamwork skills by working with a committee of eight to produce a . . .*).

d. **Awards, honors, and activities.** Explain any awards so that the reader will understand them. List campus, community, and professional activities that suggest you are a well-rounded individual or possess traits relevant to your target job.

13.5 Investigating Your Future Career (L.O. 1)

Communication Technology   **Web**

Many people know amazingly little about the work done in various occupations and the training requirements.

YOUR TASK. Use the online *Occupational Outlook Handbook* at **http://www.bls.gov/ooh**, prepared by the U.S. Department of Labor's Bureau of Labor Statistics (BLS), to learn more about an occupation of your choice. This is the nation's premier source for career information. The career profiles featured cover hundreds of occupations and describe what people in these occupations do, the work environment, how to get these jobs, how much they earn, and more. Each profile also includes BLS employment projections for the 2010–2020 decade.

Find the description of a position for which you could apply in two to five years. Learn about what workers do on the job, working conditions, training and education needed, earnings, and expected job prospects. Print or save the pages from the *Occupational Outlook Handbook* that describe employment in the area in which you are interested. If your instructor directs, attach these copies to the cover letter you will write in **Activity 13.10**, or post them to your course-management system (e.g., Blackboard or Moodle).

13.6 What Are You Worth? Finding Salary Information (L.O. 1)

> Web

What salary can you expect in your chosen career?

YOUR TASK. Visit **http://www.salary.com** and select an occupation based on the kind of employment you are seeking now or will be seeking after you graduate. Skip any advertisements that pop up. Follow the link labeled Personal and then click Salaries. Use your current geographic area or the location where you would like to work after graduation. What wages can you expect in this occupation? Click to learn more about this occupation. Take notes on three or four interesting bits of information you uncovered about this career. Save the wage information for easy access and sharing with fellow students, or bring a printout to class. Be prepared to discuss what you learned.

Alternatively, use **http://www.glassdoor.com**, a social network of company or industry insiders and current as well as past employees. The anonymous evaluations of businesses and their management on Glassdoor are candid. They provide a snapshot of companies' practices, culture, interview questions, actual salaries, CEO approval ratings, and other hard-to-find information. Glassdoor seems more comprehensive than Salary.com, even though its graphics are not as snazzy.

13.7 Seeking a Compatible Position (L.O. 1)

> Web

Where are the jobs? Even though you may not be in the market at the moment, become familiar with the kinds of available positions because job awareness should be an important part of your education.

YOUR TASK. Save or print a job advertisement or announcement from (a) a job board such as Indeed; (b) LinkedIn, Glassdoor, or a mobile app such as JobAware and JobCompass; (c) a company website; (d) a professional association listing; or (e) the classified section of a newspaper, online or in print. Select an advertisement or announcement describing the kind of employment you are seeking now or plan to seek when you graduate. Save this ad or announcement to attach to the résumé you will write in **Activity 13.9**.

13.8 Sharing a Résumé on the Internet (L.O. 2)

> E-Mail   Team   Web

Learn about the procedure for posting résumés on Internet job boards.

YOUR TASK. Prepare a list of the three most promising websites where you could post your résumé. In a class discussion or in an e-mail to your instructor, describe the procedure involved in posting a résumé and the advantages for each site.

13.9 Creating and Polishing Your Résumé (L.O. 4)

> Team

YOUR TASK. Using the data you developed in **Activity 13.4**, write your résumé. Aim it at the full-time job, part-time position, or internship that you located in **Activity 13.7**. Attach the job or internship listing to your résumé. Also prepare a list of references. Your instructor may assign a peer or small-group editing session. Revise your résumé until it is perfect.

13.10 Writing a Unique, Personable Cover Message (L.O. 6)

> E-Mail   Team   Web

YOUR TASK. Using the job listing you found for **Activity 13.7**, write a cover message introducing your résumé. Decide whether it should be a letter or an e-mail. Review the chapter discussion of cover messages. Hiring managers want your true self to shine through. Avoid canned phrases. Instead, try to work out how you wish to come across in your message. If your instructor directs, you may get help from your peers in editing and polishing your cover message. Again, revise until it is perfect.

13.11 Using LinkedIn in Your Job Search (L.O. 2)

> Social Media   Team   Web

LinkedIn is the acknowledged No. 1 site for job seekers and recruiters. It's free and easy to join. Even if you are not in the job market yet, becoming familiar with LinkedIn can open your eyes to the kinds of information that employers seek and also give you practice in filling in templates such as those that applicant tracking systems employ.

YOUR TASK. If you haven't done so already, set up a LinkedIn account and complete a profile. This consists of a template with categories to fill in. The easiest way to begin is to view a LinkedIn video taking you through the steps of creating a profile. Search for *LinkedIn Profile Checklist*. It discusses how to fill in information in categories such as the following:

- **Photo.** Have a friend or a professional take a photo that shows your head and shoulders. No selfies! Wear work-appropriate attire and a smile.
- **Headline.** Use a tagline to summarize your professional goals.
- **Summary.** Explain what motivates you, what you are skilled at, and where you want to go in the future.
- **Experience.** List the jobs you have held, and be sure to enter the information precisely in the template categories. You can even include photos and videos of your work.

You can fill in other categories such as Organizations, Honors, and Publications. After completing a profile, discuss your LinkedIn experience with classmates. If you already have an account set up, discuss how it operates and your opinion of its worth. How can LinkedIn help students now and in the future?

13.12 Enlisting Twitter in Your Job Search (L.O. 5)

> Social Media   Team   Web

Twitter résumés are a new twist on job hunting. While most job seekers struggle to contain their credentials on one page, others are tweeting their credentials in 140 characters or fewer! Here is an example from TheLadders.com:

> *RT #Susan Moline seeks a LEAD/SR QA ENG JOB http://bit.ly/1ThaW@TalentEvolution-http://bit.ly/QB5DC@TweetMyJobs.com #résumé #QA-Jobs-CA*

Are you scratching your head? Let's translate: (a) RT stands for retweet, allowing your Twitter followers to repeat this message to their followers. (b) The hashtag (#) always means *subject;* prefacing your name, it makes you easy to find. (c) The uppercase abbreviations indicate the job title, here *Lead Senior Quality Assurance Engineer.* (d) The first link is a tiny URL, a short Web address or alias provided free at TinyURL.com and by other URL-shrinking services. The first short link reveals the job seeker's Talent Evolution profile page; the second directs viewers to a job seeker profile created on TweetMyJobs.com. (e) The hashtags indicate the search terms used as seen here: name, quality assurance jobs in California, and the broad term *résumé.* When doing research from within Twitter, use the @ symbol with a specific Twitter user name or the # symbol for a subject search. Experts recommend that job seekers connect with and follow the businesses they favor. They can create a custom private list that will provide a timeline of tweets from just the listed companies and individuals.

YOUR TASK. As a team or individually, use Twitter's search bar to look for job openings. You can type in a location, the search term *hiring,* and seniority level such as *entry level* or *director.* You will see tweets about open positions in your area. Create a custom list to filter for your desired job-related tweets. Search Twitter for your desired open position. Report your results to your peers and instructor.

13.13 Preparing Professional E-Portfolios (L.O. 5)

> Communication Technology   E-Mail   Team   Web

Take a minute to conduct a Google search on your name. What comes up? Are you proud of what you see? If you want to change that information—and especially if you are in the job market—think about creating a career e-portfolio. Building such a portfolio has many benefits. It can give you an important digital tool to connect with a large audience. It can also help you expand your technology skills, confirm your strengths, recognize areas you need to develop, and establish goals for improvement. Many students are creating e-portfolios with the help of their schools.

YOUR TASK NO. 1. Before attempting to build your own career e-portfolio, take a look at those of other students. Use the Google search term *student career e-portfolio* to see lots of samples. Your instructor may assign you individually or as a team to visit specific digital portfolio sites and summarize your findings in a memo, an e-mail, or a brief oral presentation. You could focus on user and mobile friendliness, site design, page layout, links provided, software tools used, colors selected, or types of documents included.

YOUR TASK NO. 2. Next, examine websites that provide tutorials and tips on how to build career e-portfolios. One of the best sites can be found by searching for *career e-portfolios San Jose State University.* San Jose State has a platform aptly named Portfolium. Your instructor may have you individually or as a team write a memo or an e-mail summarizing tips on how to create an e-portfolio and choose the types of documents to include. Alternatively, your instructor may ask you to create your own career e-portfolio. Your college may even offer hosting. Inquire in your college of business or the career services department at your university.

Number Style

Review Sections 4.01–4.13 in the Grammar/Mechanics Handbook. Then study each of the following pairs. Assume that these expressions appear in the context of e-mails, letters, reports, or memos. Write *a* or *b* in the space provided to indicate the preferred number style and record the number of the G/M principle illustrated. When you finish, compare your responses with those at the bottom of this page. If your answers differ, study carefully the appropriate principles.

a   (4.01a)   **EXAMPLE**   a. two smartphones   b. 2 smartphones

_____   1. a. fifteen employees   b. 15 employees

_____   2. a. Fifth Avenue   b. 5th Avenue

_____   3. a. twenty-one new phone apps   b. 21 new phone apps

_____   4. a. June 1st   b. June 1

_____   5. a. thirty dollars   b. $30

_____   6. a. on the 15th of July   b. on the fifteenth of July

_____   7. a. at 4:00 p.m.   b. at 4 p.m.

_____   8. a. 3 200-page reports   b. three 200-page reports

_____   9. a. over fifty years ago   b. over 50 years ago

_____   10. a. 2,000,000 people   b. 2 million people

1. b (4.01a) **2.** a (4.05b) **3.** a (4.01a) **4.** b (4.03) **5.** b (4.03) **6.** a (4.02) **7.** b (4.04) **8.** b (4.07) **9.** b (4.08) **10.** b (4.10)

Every chapter provides an editing exercise to fine-tune your grammar and mechanics skills. The following résumé requires edits that address grammar, punctuation, capitalization, number form, and other writing issues. Study the guidelines in the Grammar/Mechanics Handbook (Appendix D), including the lists of Confusing Words and Frequently Misspelled Words.

YOUR TASK. Edit the following (a) by inserting corrections in your textbook or on a photocopy using the proofreading marks in Appendix C or (b) by downloading the message from **www.cengagebrain.com** and correcting at your computer.

Jennifer V. Holloway

3010 East 8th Avenue
Monroe, Mich. 48162

jholloway@cybermw.com

SUMMARY OF QUALIFICATIONS

- Over three years experience working in customer relations
- Partnered with Assistant Manager to create mass mailing by merging three thousand customers names and addresses in ad campaign
- Hold AA Degree in Administrative Assisting
- Proficient with MS Word, excel, powerpoint, and the internet

EXPERIENCE

Administrative Assistant, Monroe Mold and Machine Company, Munroe, Michigan June 2018 to present

- Answer phones, respond to e-mail and gather information for mold designers
- Key board and format proposals for various machine Platforms and Configurations
- Help company with correspondence to fulfill it's guarantee that a prototype mold can be produced in less than 1 week
- Worked with Assistant Manger to create large customer mailings; enter data in Excel

Shift Supervisor, Monroe Coffee Shop, Monroe, Michigan
May 2017 to May 2018

- Trained 3 new employees, opened and closed shop handled total sales
- Managed shop in the owners absence
- Builded satisfied customer relationships

Server, Hostess, Expeditor, Busser, Roadside Girll, Toledo, Ohio
April 2015 to April 2017

- Helped Owner expand menu from twenty to thirty-five items
- Develop procedures that reduce average customer wait time from sixteen to eight minutes

AWARDS AND ACHEIVEMENTS

- Deans List, Spring, 2018, Fall, 2017
- Awarded 2nd prize in advertise essay contest, 2017

EDUCATION

- AA degree, Munroe Community College, 2018
- Major: Office Administation and Technology
  GPA in major: 3.8 (4.0 = A)

Padding the Résumé: No Harm, No Foul?

Given today's competitive job market, it might be tempting to puff up your résumé. You certainly wouldn't be alone in telling fibs or outright whoppers. A recent CareerBuilder survey of 2,532 hiring and human resources managers revealed that 56 percent have caught a lie on a résumé.[45]

Candidates may embellish their skills or background information to qualify for a position, but it's a risky game. Background checks are much easier now with the Internet and professionals who specialize in sniffing out untruths. What's more, puffing up your qualifications may be unnecessary. The same CareerBuilder survey revealed that 42 percent of employers would consider a candidate who met only three out of five key qualifications for a job.[46]

After they have been hired, candidates may think they are safe—but organizations often continue the checking process. If hiring officials find a discrepancy in a GPA or prior experience and the error is an honest mistake, they meet with the new-hire to hear an explanation. If the discrepancy wasn't a mistake, they will likely fire the person immediately.

No job seeker wants to be in the unhappy position of explaining résumé errors or defending misrepresentation. Avoiding the following actions can keep you off the hot seat:

- **Enhancing education, grades, or honors.** Some job candidates claim degrees from colleges or universities when in fact they merely attended classes. Others increase their grade point averages or claim fictitious honors. Any such dishonest reporting is grounds for dismissal when discovered. In some states (e.g., Texas, New Jersey, and Kentucky), it's illegal to falsify or embellish one's degree or its origin. Criminal charges may result from résumé fraud.[47]
- **Inflating job titles and salaries.** Wishing to elevate their status, some applicants misrepresent their titles or increase their past salaries. For example, one technician called himself a programmer when he had actually programmed only one project for his boss. A mail clerk who assumed added responsibilities conferred upon herself the title of supervisor.
- **Puffing up accomplishments.** Job seekers may inflate their employment experience or achievements. One clerk, eager to make her photocopying duties sound more important, said that she assisted the *vice president in communicating and distributing employee directives*. Similarly, guard against taking sole credit for achievements that required many people. When recruiters suspect dubious claims on résumés, they nail applicants with specific—and often embarrassing—questions during their interviews.
- **Altering employment dates.** Some candidates extend the dates of employment to hide unimpressive jobs or positions they lost. Others try to hide periods of unemployment and illness. Although their employment histories have no gaps, their résumés are dishonest and represent potential booby traps.

CAREER APPLICATION. Delaney finally got an interview for the perfect job. The big problem, however, is that she padded her résumé a little by making the gaps in her job history a bit smaller. Oh, yes, and she increased her last job title from administrative assistant to project manager. After all, she was really doing a lot of his work. Now she's worried about the upcoming interview. She's considering coming clean and telling the truth. On the other hand, she wonders whether it is too late to submit an updated résumé and tell the interviewer that she noticed some errors. Of course, she could do nothing. A final possibility is withdrawing her application.

YOUR TASK. In groups, discuss Delaney's options. What would you advise her to do? Why?

Interviewing and Following Up

GI/Jamie Grill/GettyImages

Learning Outcomes

After studying this chapter, you should be able to do the following:

1 Understand the purposes, sequence, and types of job interviews, including screening, one-on-one, panel, group, sequential, and video interviews.

2 Know what to do *before* an interview, including ensuring professional phone techniques, researching the target company, rehearsing success stories, cleaning up digital dirt, and fighting fear.

3 Explain what to do *during* an interview, including controlling nonverbal messages and answering typical interview questions.

4 Describe what to do *after* an interview, including thanking the interviewer, contacting references, and writing follow-up messages.

5 Prepare additional employment documents such as applications, rejection follow-up messages, acceptance messages, and resignation letters.

14-1 Interviewing Effectively in Today's Competitive Job Market

Just as searching for a job has changed dramatically in this digital age, so has interviewing. The good news is that employers are hiring. Whether you are completing your education and searching for your first serious position or are in the workforce and striving to change jobs—a job interview can be life changing. Because employment is a major part of everyone's life, the job interview takes on enormous importance.

Most people consider job interviews extremely stressful, eliciting as much or more anxiety than making a speech or going on a first date. However, the more you learn about the process and the more prepared you are, the less stress you will feel. Moreover, a job interview is a two-way street. It is not just about being judged by the employer. You, the applicant, will be using the job interview to evaluate the employer. Do you really want to work for this organization?

To be successful in a highly competitive labor market, you must keep up with the latest trends and techniques that recruiters use to choose the very best candidates. Figure 14.1 illustrates six hot trends in interviewing today. To help you respond to these trends, this chapter presents the latest tips as well as other traditional techniques that will improve your interviewing skills and boost your confidence.

Yes, job interviews can be intimidating and stressful. However, you can expect to ace an interview when you know what's coming and prepare thoroughly. Preparation often determines who gets the job. First, though, you need to know the purposes of employment interviews, the typical sequence of events, and the types of interviews you might encounter in your job search.

LEARNING OUTCOME **1**

Understand the purposes, sequence, and types of job interviews, including screening, one-on-one, panel, group, sequential, and video interviews.

14-1a Purposes and Sequencing of Employment Interviews

An interview has several purposes for you as a job candidate. It is an opportunity to (a) convince the employer of your potential, (b) learn more about the job and the company, and (c) expand on the information in your résumé. This is the time for you to gather information to determine whether you would fit into the company culture. You should also be thinking about whether this job suits your career goals.

From the employer's perspective, the interview is an opportunity to (a) assess your abilities in relation to the requirements of the position; (b) discuss your training, experience, knowledge, and abilities in more detail; (c) see what drives and motivates you; and (d) decide whether you would fit into the organization.

The hiring process often follows a six-stage sequence, as illustrated in Figure 14.2. Following the application, interviews proceed from screening interviews to hiring interviews.

14-1b Screening Interviews

Screening interviews do just that—they screen candidates to eliminate those who fail to meet minimum requirements. Companies use screening interviews to save time and money by weeding out lesser qualified candidates before scheduling face-to-face or video interviews. Although initial screening interviews may be conducted during job fairs or on college campuses, they usually take place by telephone or video.

During an initial screening interview, the interviewer will probably ask you to provide details about the education and experience listed on your résumé; therefore, you must be prepared to promote your qualifications. If you do well on the initial interview, you may be invited to a secondary screening interview. This interview may be conducted

Figure 14.1 Latest Trends in Interviewing

Early-stage screening by technology
Telephone and webcam interviews early in the process weed out candidates who are underskilled or overpriced.

Longer, multiple interviews
Employers are taking nearly twice as long to hire people as they did several years ago.

On-the-spot interviewing
Savvy candidates keep PDFs of their résumés and credentials on their smartphones for quick viewing.

Psychometric and skills tests
Employers give psychological tests to reveal a candidate's strengths; they also require presentations and projects mimicking on-the-job tasks.

Behavioral and situational questions
Hot trends include requests that begin with "Tell me about a time when you. . . ." or questions that pose what-if situations about issues that could arise on the job.

Group interviews
Employers may interview many candidates together, or multiple hiring managers may interview one candidate individually.

Figure 14.2 Six Stages of the Hiring Process

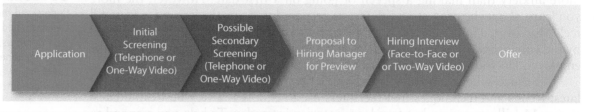

Application → Initial Screening (Telephone or One-Way Video) → Possible Secondary Screening (Telephone or One-Way Video) → Proposal to Hiring Manager for Preview → Hiring Interview (Face-to-Face or Two-Way Video) → Offer

by a human resources specialist with more specific questions relating to the open position. It could be a telephone or a video interview scheduled on Skype. The interviewer is trying to decide whether you are a strong enough candidate to be interviewed by a hiring manager.

14-1c Hiring/Placement Interviews

The most promising candidates selected from screening interviews are invited to hiring/placement interviews. Hiring managers want to learn whether candidates are motivated, qualified, and a good fit for the position. Their goal is to learn how the candidate would fit into their organization. Conducted in depth, hiring/placement interviews may take many forms.

One-on-One Interviews. In one-on-one interviews, which are the most common type, you can expect to sit down with a company representative and talk about the job and your qualifications. If the representative is the hiring manager, questions will be specific and job related. If the representative is from human resources, the questions will probably be more general.

Panel Interviews. Panel interviews are typically conducted by people who will be your supervisors and colleagues. Usually seated around a table, interviewers take turns asking questions. Panel interviews are advantageous because they save the company time and money, and they show you how the staff works together. If possible before these interviews, try to gather basic biographical information about each panel member. This information may be available on the company website or LinkedIn. When answering questions, maintain eye contact with the questioner as well as with the other interviewers.[1] Demonstrate active listening skills. Expect to repeat information you may have given in earlier interviews. Try to take paper-and-pen notes during the interview so that you can remember each person's questions and what was important to that individual. Don't take notes on a laptop or other digital device as interviewers may think you are checking incoming texts. Follow up with each interviewer on the panel.

Group Interviews. Group interviews occur when a company interviews several candidates for the same position at the same time. Some employers use this technique to evaluate leadership skills and communication styles. During a group interview, be yourself, listen well, be confident yet respectful, and look for an opportunity to lead without steamrolling your competitors.[2] Even if you are nervous, try to remain calm, take your time when responding, and express yourself clearly. The

Radius Images/Getty Images

Group interviews can be stressful and frustrating for interviewees. However, employers who use this tool believe that "cattle-call" interviews allow them to rank candidates quickly in the categories of teamwork, leadership, and stress management.

key during a group interview is to make yourself stand out from the other candidates in a positive way.[3]

Sequential Interviews. In a sequential interview, you meet individually with two or more interviewers one-on-one over the course of several hours or days. For example, you may meet with human resources representatives, your hiring manager, and potential future supervisors and colleagues in your division or department. You must listen carefully and respond positively to all interviewers. Promote your qualifications to each one; don't assume that any interviewer knows what was said in a previous interview. Keep your responses fresh, even when repeating yourself many times over. Subsequent interviews also tend to be more in depth than first interviews, which means that you need to be even more prepared and know even more about the company.

Video Interviews. Perhaps the hottest trend in interviewing is the rush to video interviews. One-way (asynchronous) video interviewing enables a candidate to respond to a list of prescripted questions prepared by the hiring organization. When convenient, the candidate creates a video recording of the answers. The interviewer can view the job seeker, but the job seeker cannot see the interviewer. One-way interviewing benefits employers by cutting the time needed to meet lots of candidates; it benefits candidates by enabling them to be interviewed at their leisure without traveling to distant locations. Candidates also can practice and perfect their responses by rerecording.

Two-way video interviewing is similar to regular face-to-face interviewing, but it is typically conducted through video chat. A key advantage of two-way interviewing is that it provides an interactive forum enabling hiring companies to better assess a candidate's communication skills, body language, and personality. Preparing for either a one-way or a two-way video interview is extremely important; check out Figure 14.3 for tips to help you succeed in video interviews.

Figure 14.3 Preparing for a Video Interview

Do your homework.	Plan your answers.	Check your tech.	Control your room.	Dress to impress.	Practice, practice, practice!	Be the best you can be.
Using the Internet, learn all you can about the company, its competitors, its products, and its goals.	For one-way interviews, prepare perfect responses to the questions. For two-way interviews, practice until you can look into the camera and answer flawlessly.	Know how the webcam and microphone work to ensure clear audio and video. Position the camera at eye level.	Place a light behind your computer to avoid shadows. Use an attractive and quiet room. Avoid distractions: barking dogs, crying children, flushing toilets, or ringing phones.	Be well groomed on camera as you would be in a face-to-face interview. Wear a suit when interviewing for a professional position. Avoid distracting prints, overly bright colors, and loud jewelry.	Know your answers well enough to be natural and comfortable in saying them, but avoid sounding mechanical. This requires lots and lots of practice.	Sit up straight. Look interested by leaning forward slightly. Don't let your eyes drop, suggesting you are reading from a script. Don't mumble or fidget. Focus on answers and stories that show why you are the best fit for the job.

No matter what interview structure you encounter, you will feel more comfortable if you know what to do before, during, and after the interview.

LEARNING OUTCOME 2

Know what to do *before* an interview, including ensuring professional phone techniques, researching the target company, rehearsing success stories, cleaning up digital dirt, and fighting fear.

OFFICE INSIDER

"Do your homework. We're impressed when candidates have taken the time to do some research and learn about us. Since you are here on this site, you obviously find value in this too. Take a look around and learn as much as you can. Being prepared will also minimize your anxiety."[4]

Deloitte, *advice for interviewees on the company's U.S. website*

14-2 Before the Interview

Once you have sent out at least one résumé or filled out at least one job application, consider yourself an active job seeker. Being active in the job market means that you should be prepared to be contacted by potential employers. As discussed earlier, employers often use screening interviews to narrow the list of candidates. If you do well in the screening interview, you will be invited to an in-person or video meeting.

14-2a Ensuring Professional Phone Techniques

Even with the popularity of e-mail, most employers contact job applicants by phone to set up interviews. Employers can judge how well applicants communicate by hearing their voices and expressions over the phone. Once you are actively looking for a job, anytime the phone rings, it could be a potential employer. Don't make the mistake of letting an unprofessional voice mail message or a lazy roommate or a sloppy cell phone manner ruin your chances. To make the best impression, try these tips:

- On your answering device or in your voice mail, make sure that your outgoing message is concise and professional, with no distracting background sounds. It should be in your own voice and include your full name for clarity. You can find more tips for leaving professional telephone messages in Chapter 11.

- Tell those who might answer your phone at home about your job search. Explain to them the importance of acting professionally and taking complete messages. Family members or roommates can affect the first impression an employer has of you.

- If you have children, prevent them from answering the phone during your job search. Children of all ages are not known for taking good messages!

- If you have put your cell phone number on your résumé, don't answer unless you are in a good location to carry on a conversation with an employer. It is hard to pay close attention while driving, even with hands-free equipment, or while eating in a noisy restaurant!

- Use voice mail to screen calls. By screening incoming calls, you can be totally in control when you return a prospective employer's call. Organize your materials and ready yourself psychologically for the conversation.

14-2b Making the First Conversation Impressive

Whether you answer the phone directly or return an employer's call, make sure you are prepared for the conversation. Remember that this is the first time the employer has heard your voice. How you conduct yourself on the phone will create a lasting impression. To make that first impression a positive one, follow these tips:

- Keep a list on your cell phone or near your landline of positions for which you have applied.

- Treat any call from an employer just like an interview. Use a professional tone and businesslike language. Be polite and enthusiastic, and sell your qualifications.

- If caught off guard by the call, ask whether you can call back in a few minutes. Take that time to organize your materials and yourself.

- Have your résumé available so that you can answer any questions that come up. Also have your list of references, a calendar, and a digital or paper notepad handy.

- Be prepared for a screening interview. As discussed earlier, the first phone call could very well be the actual screening interview.

- Take good notes during the phone conversation. Obtain accurate directions if necessary, and verify the spelling of your interviewer's name. If you will be interviewed by more than one person, get all of their names.

- If given a chance, ask for an interview on Tuesday at 10:30 a.m. This is considered the most opportune time. Avoid pre- or post-lunch meetings, the start of the day on Monday, and the end of the day on Friday.[5]

- Before you hang up, reconfirm the date and time of your interview. You could say something like *I look forward to meeting with you next Wednesday at 2 p.m.*

14-2c Researching the Target Company

Once you have scheduled an in-person or video interview, you need to start preparing for it. One of the most important steps in effective interviewing is gathering detailed information about a prospective employer. Never enter an interview cold. Recruiters are impressed by candidates who have done their homework.

Scouring the Internet for Important Company Data. Search the potential employer's website, news sources, trade journals, industry directories, and social media presence. Follow the official company Twitter feed, and read the tweets of the firm's top managers and other industry influencers. Unearth information about the job, the company, and the industry. Learn all you can about the company's history, mission and goals, size, geographic locations, and number of employees. Check out its customers, competitors, culture, management structure, reputation in the community, financial condition, strengths and weaknesses, and future plans, as well as the names of its leaders. A good place to start is the About Us section on an organization's website. In addition, look for company blogs. Blogs are excellent sources for company research. Finally, don't forget to google the interviewer.

Analyzing the Company's Advertising. Examine the company's ads in business publications online or in print, and don't neglect any hard-copy promotional materials, including sales and marketing brochures. One candidate, a marketing major, spent a great deal of time poring over brochures from an aerospace contractor. During his initial interview, he shocked and impressed the recruiter with his knowledge of the company's guidance systems. The candidate had, in fact, relieved the interviewer of his least-favorite task—explaining the company's complicated technology.

Digging for Inside Information. To unearth up-to-the minute information, network via LinkedIn, Facebook, and Twitter. Follow the company on Facebook and Twitter. Comment shrewdly on the organization's status updates and other posts. Beyond these sites, check out employee review websites such as Glassdoor to get the inside scoop on what it's like to work there.[7] LinkedIn has beefed up its job-search options and company information resources in its browser version (click the Jobs link) as well as in the LinkedIn smartphone app. Better yet, download the stand-alone LinkedIn Job Search app to track your job hunt, log potential openings, and discover whether you know someone who already works at the company.[8] Try to connect with someone who is currently employed—but not working in the immediate area where you wish to be hired. Be sure to seek out someone who is discreet.

 As you learn about a company, you may uncover information that convinces you that this is not the company for you. It is always better to learn about negatives early in the process. More likely, though, the information you collect will help you tailor your interview responses to the organization's needs. You know how flattered you feel when an employer knows about you and your background. That feeling works both ways. Employers are pleased when job candidates take an interest in them.

14-2d Rehearsing Success Stories

To feel confident and be able to sell your qualifications, prepare and practice success stories. These stories are specific examples of your educational and work-related experience that demonstrate your qualifications and achievements. Look over the job description and your résumé to determine what skills, training, personal characteristics, and experience you want to emphasize during the interview. Then prepare a success story for each one. Incorporate numbers, such as dollars saved or percentage of sales increase, whenever possible. Your success stories should be detailed but brief. Think of them as 30-second sound bites.

Practice telling your success stories until they fluently roll off your tongue and sound natural. Then in the interview be certain to find places to insert them. Tell stories about (a) dealing with a crisis, (b) handling a tough interpersonal situation, (c) successfully juggling many priorities, (d) changing course to deal with changed circumstances, (e) learning from a mistake, (f) working on a team, and (g) going above and beyond expectations.

14-2e Cleaning Up Digital Dirt

Potential employers definitely screen a candidate's online presence using Google and social media sites such as Facebook, Instagram, LinkedIn, and Twitter. A recent Career-Builder survey revealed that 49 percent of hiring managers who screen candidates via social networks said they had found information that caused them not to hire a candidate. What turned them off? The top reasons cited were (a) provocative or inappropriate photographs, videos, or information; (b) content about drinking or doing drugs; (c) discriminatory comments related to race, religion, and other protected categories; (d) criticism of previous employers or colleagues; and (e) poor communication skills.[9]

Teasing photographs and provocative comments about drinking, drug use, and sexual exploits make students look immature and unprofessional. Think about cleaning up your online presence by following these steps:

Who hasn't had an "oops" moment after pressing Send? Similarly, some social media users are still oblivious to privacy settings and post inappropriate content that can sabotage their career plans. Before searching for a job, candidates should clean up their digital act.

- **Remove questionable content.** Remove any incriminating, provocative, or distasteful photos, content, and links that could make you look unprofessional to potential employers.

- **Stay positive.** Don't complain about things in your professional or personal life online. Even negative reviews you have written on sites such as Amazon can turn employers off.

- **Be selective about who is on your list of friends.** You don't want to miss out on an opportunity because you seem to associate with negative, immature, or unprofessional people. Your best bet is to make your personal social networking pages private, but monitor your privacy settings because they often change.

- **Don't discuss your job search if you are still employed.** Employees can find themselves in trouble with their current employers by writing status updates or sending tweets about their job searches.

14-2f Dressing for, Traveling to, and Arriving at Your Interview

The big day has arrived! Ideally, you are fully prepared for your interview. Now you need to make sure everything goes smoothly. On the day of your interview, give yourself plenty of time to groom and dress.

Deciding What to Wear. What to wear may worry you because business attire today ranges from ultracasual to formal suits. The best plan is to ask your interviewer what is appropriate, advises career counselor Liz Ryan.[10] Ask this when the interview is arranged, and you will be greatly relieved. Here's what you definitely should not wear, according to a Monster.com expert: (a) ill-fitting clothes; (b) overly casual attire, such as jeans, tennis shoes, shorts, T-shirts, hats, flip-flops, and any item promoting messages or brands; (c) distracting items; (d) excessive accessories; or (e) something very different from what the interviewer suggested.[11]

Avoiding Being Rushed. Make sure you can arrive at the employer's office without being rushed. If something unexpected happens that will cause you to be late, such as an accident or bridge closure, call the interviewer right away to explain what is happening. Most interviewers will be understanding, and your call will show that you are responsible. On the way to the interview, don't smoke, don't eat anything messy or smelly, and don't load up on perfume or cologne. Arrive at the interview five to ten minutes early, but not earlier. If you are very early, wait in the car or in a café nearby. If possible, check your appearance before going in.

Being Polite and Pleasant. When you enter the office, be courteous and congenial to everyone. Remember that you are being judged not only by the interviewer but also by the receptionist and anyone else who sees you before and after the interview. They will notice how you sit, what you read, and how you look. Introduce yourself to the receptionist, and wait to be invited to sit. You may be asked to fill out a job application while you are waiting. You will find tips for doing this effectively later in this chapter.

Greeting the Interviewer and Making a Positive First Impression. Greet the interviewer confidently, and don't be afraid to initiate a handshake. Doing so exhibits professionalism and confidence. Extend your hand, look the interviewer directly in the eye, smile pleasantly, and say, *I'm pleased to meet you, Mr. Thomas. I am Constance Ferraro.* In this culture a firm, not crushing, handshake sends a nonverbal message of poise and assurance. After introductions, wait for the interviewer to offer you a chair. Make small talk with upbeat comments, such as *This is a beautiful headquarters* or *I'm very impressed with the facilities you have here.* Don't immediately begin rummaging in your briefcase for your résumé. Being at ease and unrushed suggest that you are self-confident.

14-2g Fighting Fear

Other than public speaking, employment interviews are the most dreaded events in people's lives. One survey revealed that job interviews are more stressful than going on a blind date, being pulled over by the police, or taking a final exam without studying.[12] One of the best ways to overcome fear is to know what happens in a typical interview. You can further reduce your fears by following these suggestions:

- **Practice interviewing.** Try to get as much interviewing practice as you can—especially with real companies. The more times you experience the interview situation, the less nervous you will be. However, don't schedule interviews unless you are genuinely interested in the organization. If offered, campus mock interviews also provide excellent practice, and the interviewers will offer tips for improvement.

- **Prepare thoroughly.** Research the company. Know how you will answer the most frequently asked questions. Be ready with success stories. Rehearse your closing statement. Knowing that you have done all you can to be ready for the interview is a tremendous fear preventive.

- **Understand the process.** Find out ahead of time how the interview will be structured. Will you be meeting with an individual, or will you be interviewed by a panel? Is this the first of a series of interviews? Don't be afraid to ask about these details before the interview so an unfamiliar situation won't catch you off guard.

- **Dress professionally.** If you have checked with the interviewer in advance and know that you are dressed properly, you will feel more confident. When in doubt, tend toward more conservative, professional attire.

- **Breathe deeply.** Take deep breaths, particularly if you feel anxious while waiting for the interviewer. Deep breathing makes you concentrate on something other than the interview and also provides much-needed oxygen.

- **Know that you are not alone.** Everyone feels some anxiety during a job interview. Interviewers expect some nervousness, and a skilled interviewer will try to put you at ease.

- **Remember that an interview is a two-way street.** The interviewer isn't the only one who is gleaning information. You have come to learn about the job and the company. In fact, during some parts of the interview, you will be in charge. This should give you courage.

LEARNING OUTCOME 3

Explain what to do *during* an interview, including controlling nonverbal messages and answering typical interview questions.

14-3 During the Interview

Throughout the interview you will be answering questions and asking your own questions. Your demeanor, body language, and other nonverbal cues will also be on display. The interviewer will be trying to learn more about you, and you should be learning more about the job and the organization. Although you may be asked some unique questions, many interviewers ask standard, time-proven questions, which means that you can prepare your answers ahead of time. You can also prepare by learning techniques to control those inevitable butterflies in the tummy.

14-3a Sending Positive Nonverbal Messages and Acting Professionally

You have already sent nonverbal cues to your interviewer by arriving on time, being courteous, dressing professionally, and greeting the receptionist confidently. You will continue to send nonverbal messages throughout the interview. Remember that what comes out of your mouth and what is written on your résumé are not the only messages an interviewer receives from you. Nonverbal messages also create powerful impressions on people. You can send positive nonverbal messages during face-to-face and online interviews by following these tips:

- **Control your body movements.** Keep your hands, arms, and elbows to yourself. Don't lean on a desk. Keep your feet on the floor. Don't cross your arms in front of you. Keep your hands out of your pockets.

- **Exhibit good posture.** Sit erect, leaning forward slightly. Don't slouch in your chair; at the same time, don't look too stiff and uncomfortable. Good posture demonstrates confidence and interest.

- **Practice appropriate eye contact.** A direct eye gaze, at least in North America, suggests interest and trustworthiness. If you are being interviewed by a panel, remember to maintain eye contact with all interviewers.

- **Use gestures effectively.** Nod to show agreement and interest. Gestures should be used as needed, but not overused.

- **Smile enough to convey a positive attitude.** Have a friend give you honest feedback on whether you generally smile too much or not enough.

- **Listen attentively.** Show the interviewer you are interested and attentive by listening carefully to questions. This will also help you answer questions appropriately. Do not interrupt any speaker.

- **Turn off your electronic devices.** Avoid the embarrassment of having your smartphone ring, or even as much as buzz, during an interview. Turn off your electronic devices completely; don't just switch them to vibrate.

- **Don't chew gum.** Chewing gum during an interview is distracting and unprofessional.

- **Sound enthusiastic and interested—but sincere.** The tone of your voice has an enormous effect on the words you say. Avoid sounding bored, frustrated, or sarcastic during an interview. Employers want employees who are enthusiastic and interested.

- **Avoid empty words.** Filling your answers with verbal fillers such as *um*, *uh*, *like*, and *basically* communicates that you are not prepared. Also avoid annoying distractions such as clearing your throat repeatedly or sighing deeply.

- **Be confident, but not cocky.** Most recruiters want candidates who are self-assured but not too casual or even arrogant. Let your body language, posture, dress, and vocal tone prove your confidence. Speak at a normal volume and enunciate words clearly without mumbling.

alexmillos/Shutterstock.com

Recruiters may apply the airport test.

Naturally, hiring managers make subjective decisions based on intuition, but they need to ferret out pleasant people who fit in. To that end, some recruiters apply the airport test to candidates, asking themselves the following: Would I want to be stuck in the airport for 12 hours with this person if my flight were delayed?[13]

14-3b Preparing to Answer Interview Questions

One way you can compensate for lack of experience is to have carefully prepared and well-rehearsed responses to typical interview questions. In addition, the way you answer questions can be almost as important as what you say. Use the interviewer's name and title from time to time when you answer. *Yes, Ms. Luna, I would be pleased to tell you about. . . .* People like to hear their own names, but don't overuse this technique. Avoid answering questions with a simple *yes* or *no*; elaborate on your answers to better promote yourself and your assets. Keep your answers positive; don't criticize anything or anyone.

During the interview don't be afraid to clarify vague questions. Some interviewers are inexperienced and ill at ease in the role. You may even have to ask your own question to understand what was asked: *By _____, do you mean _____?* Consider closing out some of your responses with *Does that answer your question, Mr. Cruz?* or *Would you like me to elaborate on any particular experience?*

Always aim your answers at the key characteristics interviewers seek: expertise, competence, motivation, interpersonal skills, decision-making skills, enthusiasm for the company and the job, and a pleasing personality. Remember to stay focused on your strengths. Don't reveal weaknesses, even if you think they make you look human. You won't be hired for your weaknesses, only for your strengths.

As you respond, be sure to use good English and enunciate clearly. Avoid slurred words such as *gonna* and *din't*, as well as slangy expressions such as *yeah, like,* and *ya know.* As you practice answering expected interview questions, it is always a good idea to make an audio or video recording. Is your speech filled with verbal static?

You can't expect to be perfect in an employment interview. No one is. However, you can avert sure disaster by avoiding certain topics and behaviors such as those described in Figures 14.4 and 14.5.

The following sections present questions that may be asked during employment interviews. To get you thinking about how to respond, we have provided an answer for, or a discussion of, one or more of the questions in each group. As you read the remaining questions in each group, think about how you could respond most effectively. For additional questions, contact your campus career center, or consult one

OFFICE INSIDER

"Practice interviewing out loud with mentors, adult fans, or even in the mirror. Most students have not done many (if any) job interviews—and definitely not when under pressure. It's important to hear the words you intend to speak, including the tone, emphasis, inflections and facial impressions, so that you don't blow it when it really counts. It's rare to get a second chance."[14]

Andy Chan, *vice president for Personal & Career Development, Wake Forest University*

Figure 14.4 Ten Interview Actions to Avoid

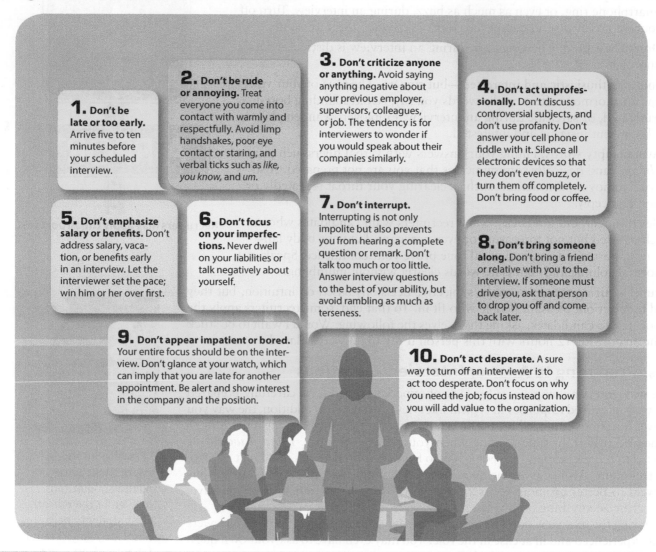

1. Don't be late or too early. Arrive five to ten minutes before your scheduled interview.

2. Don't be rude or annoying. Treat everyone you come into contact with warmly and respectfully. Avoid limp handshakes, poor eye contact or staring, and verbal ticks such as *like*, *you know*, and *um*.

3. Don't criticize anyone or anything. Avoid saying anything negative about your previous employer, supervisors, colleagues, or job. The tendency is for interviewers to wonder if you would speak about their companies similarly.

4. Don't act unprofessionally. Don't discuss controversial subjects, and don't use profanity. Don't answer your cell phone or fiddle with it. Silence all electronic devices so that they don't even buzz, or turn them off completely. Don't bring food or coffee.

5. Don't emphasize salary or benefits. Don't address salary, vacation, or benefits early in an interview. Let the interviewer set the pace; win him or her over first.

6. Don't focus on your imperfections. Never dwell on your liabilities or talk negatively about yourself.

7. Don't interrupt. Interrupting is not only impolite but also prevents you from hearing a complete question or remark. Don't talk too much or too little. Answer interview questions to the best of your ability, but avoid rambling as much as terseness.

8. Don't bring someone along. Don't bring a friend or relative with you to the interview. If someone must drive you, ask that person to drop you off and come back later.

9. Don't appear impatient or bored. Your entire focus should be on the interview. Don't glance at your watch, which can imply that you are late for another appointment. Be alert and show interest in the company and the position.

10. Don't act desperate. A sure way to turn off an interviewer is to act too desperate. Don't focus on why you need the job; focus instead on how you will add value to the organization.

---

of the career websites discussed in Chapter 13. If you rehearse success stories and anticipate interview questions, you will steer clear of the most common interview pitfalls shown in Figure 14.5.

14-3c Questions to Get Acquainted

After opening introductions, recruiters generally try to start the interview with personal questions designed to put you at ease. They are also striving to gain an overview to see whether you will fit into the organization's culture. When answering these questions, keep the employer's needs in mind and try to incorporate your success stories.

1. Tell me about yourself.
   Experts agree that you must keep this answer short (one to two minutes tops) but on target. Use this chance to promote yourself. Stick to educational, professional, or business-related strengths; avoid personal or humorous references. Be ready with at least three success stories illustrating characteristics important to this job. Demonstrate responsibility you have been given; describe how you contributed as a team player. Try practicing

Figure 14.5 How to Bomb a Job Interview

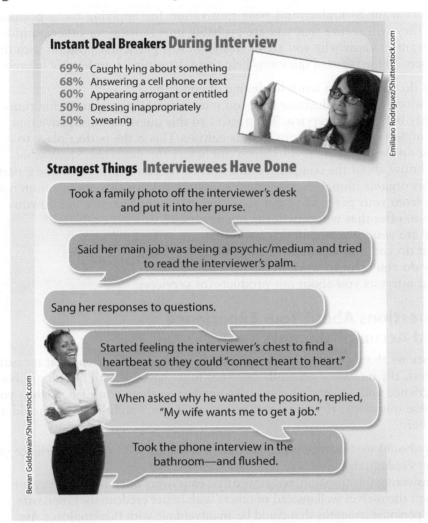

Instant Deal Breakers During Interview

- 69% Caught lying about something
- 68% Answering a cell phone or text
- 60% Appearing arrogant or entitled
- 50% Dressing inappropriately
- 50% Swearing

Emiliano Rodriguez/Shutterstock.com

Strangest Things Interviewees Have Done

Took a family photo off the interviewer's desk and put it into her purse.

Said her main job was being a psychic/medium and tried to read the interviewer's palm.

Sang her responses to questions.

Started feeling the interviewer's chest to find a heartbeat so they could "connect heart to heart."

When asked why he wanted the position, replied, "My wife wants me to get a job."

Took the phone interview in the bathroom—and flushed.

Bevan Goldswain/Shutterstock.com

Source: Based on CareerBuilder survey of more than 2,400 hiring managers. Retrieved from http://www.careerbuilder.com/share/aboutus/pressreleasesdetail.aspx?id=pr614&sd=1%2F12%2F2011&ed=12%2F31%2F2011

this formula: *I have completed a _____ degree with a major in _____. Recently I worked for _____ as a _____. Before that I worked for _____ as a _____. My strengths are _____ (interpersonal) and _____ (technical).* Rehearse your response in 30-second segments devoted to your education, work experience, qualifications, and skills.

2. What are your greatest strengths?
Reread your résumé and cover letter to review what you want to promote. Stress your strengths that are related to the position, such as *I am well organized, thorough, and attentive to detail.* Tell success stories and give examples that illustrate these qualities: *My supervisor says that my research is exceptionally thorough. For example, I recently worked on a research project in which I. . . .*

3. Do you prefer to work by yourself or with others? Why?
This question can be tricky. Provide a middle-of-the-road answer that not only suggests your interpersonal qualities but also reflects an ability to make independent decisions and work without supervision.

4. What was your major in college, and why did you choose it?

5. What are some things you do in your spare time?

14-3d Questions to Gauge Your Interest

Interviewers want to understand your motivation for applying for a position. Although they will realize that you are probably interviewing for other positions, they still want to know why you are interested in this particular position with this organization. These types of questions help them determine your level of interest.

1. Why do you want to work for [name of company]?
   Questions like this illustrate why you must research an organization thoroughly before the interview. The answer to this question must prove that you understand the company and its culture. This is the perfect place to bring up the company research you did before the interview. Show what you know about the company, and discuss why you want to become a part of this organization. Describe your desire to work for this organization not only from your perspective but also from its point of view. What do you have to offer that will benefit the organization?
2. Why are you interested in this position?
3. What do you know about our company?
4. Why do you want to work in the _____ industry?
5. What interests you about our products (or services)?

14-3e Questions About Your Experience and Accomplishments

After questions about your background and education and questions that measure your interest, the interview generally becomes more specific with questions about your experience and accomplishments. Remember to show confidence when you answer these questions. If you are not confident in your abilities, why should an employer be?

1. Why should we hire you when we have applicants with more experience or better credentials?
   In answering this question, remember that employers often hire people who present themselves well instead of others with better credentials. Emphasize your personal strengths that could be an advantage with this employer. Are you a hard worker? How can you demonstrate it? Have you had recent training? Some people have had more years of experience but actually have less knowledge because they have done the same thing over and over. Stress your experience using the latest methods and equipment. Be sure to mention your computer training and Internet savvy. Emphasize that you are open to new ideas and learn quickly. Above all, show that you are confident in your abilities.
2. Describe the most rewarding experience of your career so far.
3. How have your education and professional experiences prepared you for this position?
4. What were your major accomplishments in each of your past jobs?
5. What was a typical workday like?
6. What job functions did you enjoy most? Least? Why?
7. Tell me about your computer skills.
8. Who was the toughest boss you ever worked for and why?
9. What were your major achievements in college?
10. Why did you leave your last position? OR: Why are you leaving your current position?

14-3f Questions About the Future

Questions that look into the future tend to stump some candidates, especially those who have not prepared adequately. Employers ask these questions to see whether you are goal oriented and to determine whether your goals are realistic.

1. Where do you expect to be five (or ten) years from now?
   Formulate a realistic plan with respect to your present age and situation. The important thing is to be prepared for this question. It is a sure kiss of death to respond that you would like to have the interviewer's job! Instead, show an interest in the current job and in making a contribution to the organization. Talk about the levels of responsibility you would like to achieve. One employment counselor suggests showing ambition but not committing to a specific job title. Suggest that you hope to have learned enough to have progressed to a position in which you will continue to grow. Keep your answer focused on educational and professional goals, not personal goals.
2. If you got this position, what would you do to be sure you fit in?
3. This is a large (or small) organization. Do you think you would like that environment?
4. Do you plan to continue your education?
5. What do you predict for the future of the _____ industry?
6. How do you think you can contribute to this company?
7. What would you most like to accomplish if you get this position?
8. How do you keep current with what is happening in your profession?

14-3g Challenging Questions

The following questions may make you uncomfortable, but the important thing to remember is to answer truthfully without dwelling on your weaknesses. As quickly as possible, convert any negative response into a discussion of your strengths.

1. What is your greatest weakness?
   It is amazing how many candidates knock themselves out of the competition by answering this question poorly. Actually, you have many choices. You can present a strength as a weakness (*Some people complain that I'm a workaholic or too attentive to details*). However, hiring managers have heard that cliché too often. Instead, mention a corrected weakness (*Because I was terrified of making presentations, I took a college course and also joined a speakers' club*). You could cite an unrelated skill (*I really need to brush up on my Spanish*). You could cite a learning objective (*One of my long-term goals is to learn more about coding and programming*). Another possibility is to reaffirm your qualifications (*I have no weaknesses that affect my ability to do this job*).
2. What type of people do you have no patience for?
   Avoid letting yourself fall into the trap of sounding overly critical. One possible response is, *I have always gotten along well with others. But I confess that I can be irritated by complainers who don't accept responsibility.*
3. If you could live your life over, what would you change and why?
4. How would your former (or current) supervisor describe you as an employee?
5. What do you want the most from your job?
6. What is your grade point average, and does it accurately reflect your abilities?
7. Have you ever used drugs?
8. Who in your life has influenced you the most and why?
9. What are you reading right now?
10. Describe your ideal work environment.
11. Is the customer always right?
12. How do you define success?

14-3h Questions About Salary

Nearly all salaries are negotiable, depending on your qualifications. Knowing the typical salary range for the target position is very important in this negotiation. The recruiter can tell you the salary ranges—but you will have to ask. If you have had little experience, you will probably be offered a salary somewhere between the low point and the midpoint in the range. With more experience, you can negotiate for a higher figure. A word of caution, though. One personnel manager warns that candidates who emphasize money are suspect because they may leave if offered a few thousand dollars more elsewhere. See the Communication Workshop at the end of this chapter for dos and don'ts in negotiating a starting salary. Here are typical salary-related questions:

1. What salary are you looking for?
   One way to handle salary questions is to ask politely to defer the discussion until it is clear that a job will be offered to you (*I'm sure when the time comes, we will be able to work out a fair compensation package. Right now, I'd rather focus on whether we have a match*). If salary comes up and you are not sure whether the job is being offered to you, it's time to be blunt. Ask, "Are you making me a job offer?" Another possible response to a salary question is to reply candidly that you can't know what to ask until you know more about the position and the company. If you continue to be pressed for a dollar figure, give a salary range with an annual dollar amount. Be sure to do research before the interview so that you know what similar jobs are paying in your geographic region. As an expert negotiator said, "In business as in life, you don't get what you deserve, you get what you negotiate."[15] See the Communication Workshop for more tips on discussing salary.
2. How much are you presently earning?
3. How much do you think you are worth?
4. How much money do you expect to earn within the next ten years?
5. Are you willing to take a pay cut from your current (or previous) job?

Efforts currently underway could make questions about salary history in interviews illegal nationwide. Massachusetts is the first state to bar employers from asking about candidates' previous compensation. Proponents of the new law want to close the wage gap between men and women and to ensure that low-income earners don't remain stuck in lower-paying jobs.[16] Until this issue is decided, expect questions about your past compensation.

14-3i Situational Questions

Questions related to situations help employers test your thought processes and logical thinking. When using situational questions, interviewers describe a hypothetical situation and ask how you would handle it. Situational questions differ based on the type of position for which you are interviewing. Knowledge of the position and the company culture will help you respond favorably to these questions. Even if the situation sounds negative, keep your response positive. Here are a few examples with possible responses to the first two:

1. How would you respond if your fellow team members strongly resisted a proposal you made in a meeting?
   You might explain the rationale behind your proposal with specific examples of the benefits that the recommendation could bring to the team. If the team continues to oppose your proposal, you should let it go and move on.
2. What would you do if you knew that your boss gave your team data that was totally wrong?
   Let's say, for example, that in a team meeting your boss provided data that had not been updated, and you recognized the error immediately. Before responding, you should confirm that your figures are correct. Then you might tactfully share the correct data in a private conversation with your boss. You could suggest that the error was an oversight perhaps caused by figures that were released after an initial report, and say that you know

that your boss would want to base the team project on accurate data. You would not correct your boss in front of the team, and you would try to understand how the mistake was made.

3. Your supervisor has just told you that she is dissatisfied with your work, but you think it is acceptable. How would you resolve the conflict?

4. Your supervisor has told you to do something a certain way, and you think you know a far better way to complete the task. What would you do?

5. Assume that you are hired for this position. You soon learn that one of the staff is extremely resentful because she applied for your position and was turned down. As a result, she is being unhelpful and obstructive. How would you handle the situation?

6. A colleague has told you in confidence that she suspects another colleague of stealing. What would your actions be?

7. You have noticed that communication between upper management and first-level employees is eroding. How would you address this problem?

14-3j Behavioral Questions

Instead of traditional interview questions, you may be asked to tell stories. The interviewer may say, *Describe a time when . . .* or *Tell me about a time when. . . .* To respond effectively, learn to use the storytelling, or STAR, technique, as illustrated in Figure 14.6. Ask yourself, what the Situation or Task was, what Action you took, and what the Results were.[17] Practice using this method to recall specific examples of your skills and accomplishments. To be fully prepared, develop a coherent and articulate STAR narrative for every bullet point on your résumé. When answering behavioral questions, describe only educational and work-related situations or tasks, and try to keep them as current as possible.

1. Tell me about a time when you solved a difficult problem.
   Tell a concise story explaining the situation or task, what you did, and the result. For example, *When I was at Ace Products, we continually had a problem of excessive back orders. After analyzing the situation, I discovered that orders went through many unnecessary steps. I suggested that we eliminate much paperwork. As a result, we reduced back orders by 30 percent.* Go on to emphasize what you learned and how you can apply that learning to this job. Practice your success stories in advance so you will be ready.

Figure 14.6 Using the STAR Technique to Answer Behavioral Interview Questions

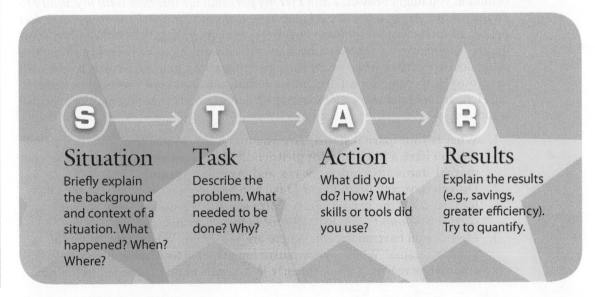

S	T	A	R
Situation	Task	Action	Results
Briefly explain the background and context of a situation. What happened? When? Where?	Describe the problem. What needed to be done? Why?	What did you do? How? What skills or tools did you use?	Explain the results (e.g., savings, greater efficiency). Try to quantify.

2. Describe a situation in which you were able to use persuasion to convince someone to see things your way.

The recruiter is interested in your leadership and teamwork skills. You might respond as follows: *I have learned to appreciate the fact that the way you present an idea is just as important as the idea itself. When trying to influence people, I put myself in their shoes and find some way to frame my idea from their perspective. I remember when I. . . .*

3. Describe a time when you had to analyze information and make a recommendation.
4. Describe a time that you worked successfully as part of a team.
5. Tell me about a time that you dealt with confidential information.
6. Give me an example of a time when you were under stress to meet a deadline.
7. Tell me about a time when you had to go above and beyond the call of duty to get a job done.
8. Tell me about a time you were able to deal with another person successfully even though that individual did not like you personally (or vice versa).
9. Give me an example of when you showed initiative and took the lead.
10. Tell me about a recent situation in which you had to deal with an upset customer or coworker.

14-3k Illegal and Inappropriate Questions

U.S. federal law states that "it is illegal to discriminate against someone (applicant or employee) because of that person's race, color, religion, sex (including gender identity, sexual orientation, and pregnancy), national origin, age (forty and older), disability or genetic information."[18] Therefore, it is inappropriate for interviewers to ask any question related to these areas. These questions become illegal, though, only when a court of law determines that the employer is asking them with the intent to discriminate.[19]

Many illegal interview questions are asked innocently by inexperienced interviewers. A recent survey revealed that 20 percent of interviewers admitted that they had unknowingly asked an illegal question.[20] Some interviewers are only trying to be friendly when they inquire about your personal life or family. Regardless of the intent, how should you react? If you find the question harmless and if you want the job, go ahead and answer it. If you think that answering it would damage your chance to be hired, try to deflect the question tactfully with a response such as *Could you tell me how my marital status relates to the responsibilities of this position?* or, *I prefer to keep my personal and professional lives separate.*

If you are uncomfortable answering a question, try to determine the reason behind it; you might answer, *I don't let my personal life interfere with my ability to do my job,* or, *Are you concerned with my availability to work overtime?* Another option, of course, is to respond to any inappropriate or illegal question by confronting the interviewer and threatening a lawsuit or refusing to answer. However, you could not expect to be hired under these circumstances. In any case, you might wish to reconsider working for an organization that sanctions such procedures.

Here are selected inappropriate and illegal questions that you may or may not want to answer[21]:

1. What is your marital status? Are you married? Do you live with anyone? Do you have a boyfriend (or girlfriend)? (However, employers can ask your marital status after hiring for tax and insurance forms.)
2. Do you have any disabilities? Have you had any recent illnesses? (But it is legal to ask if the person can perform specific job duties, such as *Can you carry a 50-pound sack up a 10-foot ladder five times daily?*)
3. I notice you have an accent. Where are you from? What is the origin of your last name? What is your native language? (However, it is legal to ask what languages you speak fluently if language ability is related to the job.)

4. Have you ever filed a workers' compensation claim or been injured on the job?
5. Have you ever had a drinking problem or been addicted to drugs? (But it is legal to ask if a person uses illegal drugs.)
6. Have you ever been arrested? (But it is legal to ask, *Have you ever been convicted of _____?* when the crime is related to the job.)
7. How old are you? What is your date of birth? When did you graduate from high school? (But it is legal to ask, *Are you 16 [or 18 or 21] years old or older?* depending on the age requirements for the position.)
8. Of what country are you a citizen? Are you a U.S. citizen? Where were you born? (But it is legal to ask, *Are you authorized to work in the United States?*)
9. What is your maiden name? (But it is legal to ask, *What is your full name?* or, *Have you worked under another name?*)
10. Do you have any religious beliefs that would prevent you from working weekends or holidays? (An employer can, however, ask you if you are available to work weekends and holidays or otherwise within the company's required schedule.)
11. Do you have children? Do you plan to have children? Do you have adequate child-care arrangements? (However, employers can ask for dependent information for tax and insurance purposes after you are hired. Also, they can ask if you would be able to travel or work overtime on occasion.)
12. How much do you weigh? How tall are you? (However, employers can ask you about your height and weight if minimum standards are necessary to safely perform a job.)
13. Are you in debt?
14. Do you drink socially or smoke?

14-3l Asking Your Own Questions

Usually, near the end of the interview, you will be asked whether you have any questions. The worst thing you can do is say *no*, which suggests that you are not interested in the position. Instead, ask questions that will help you gain information and will impress the interviewer with your thoughtfulness and interest in the position. Remember that this interview is a two-way street. You must be happy with the prospect of working for this organization. You want a position that matches your skills and personality. Use this opportunity to learn whether this job is right for you. Be aware that you don't have to wait for the interviewer to ask you for questions. You can ask your own questions throughout the interview to learn more about the company and position. Here are some questions you might ask:

1. What will my duties be (if not already discussed)?
2. Tell me what it is like working here in terms of the people, management practices, workloads, expected performance, and rewards.
3. What training programs are available from this organization? What specific training will be given for this position?
4. Who would be my immediate supervisor?
5. What is the organizational structure, and where does this position fit in?
6. Is travel required in this position?
7. How and by whom will my job performance be evaluated?
8. Assuming my work is excellent, where do you see me in five years?
9. How long do employees generally stay with this organization?
10. What are the major challenges for a person in this position?
11. What do you see in the future of this organization?
12. May I have a tour of the facilities?

13. This job seems to be exactly what I'd really like to do. Do we have a fit here?
14. What is the next step in the hiring process?
15. When do you expect to make a decision?

Do not ask about salary or benefits, especially during the first interview. It is best to let the interviewer bring those topics up first.

14-3m Ending Positively

After you have asked your questions, the interviewer will signal the end of the interview, usually by standing up or by expressing appreciation that you came. If not addressed earlier, you should at this time find out what action will follow. Career coach Don Georgevich recommends asking the interviewer when a decision will be made and whether you may follow up. "Interviewers always say yes," he reports, "and now you have permission to call them. In fact, they will expect your call."[22] This is not the time to be shy. Too many candidates leave the interview without knowing their status or when they will hear from the recruiter.

Before you leave, summarize your strongest qualifications, show your enthusiasm for obtaining this position, and thank the interviewer for a constructive interview and for considering you for the position. Ask the interviewer for a business card, which will provide the information you need to write a thank-you message.

Shake the interviewer's hand with confidence, and acknowledge anyone else you see on the way out. Be sure to thank the receptionist. Departing gracefully and enthusiastically will leave a lasting impression on those responsible for making the final hiring decision.

LEARNING OUTCOME 4

Describe what to do *after* an interview, including thanking the interviewer, contacting references, and writing follow-up messages.

14-4 After the Interview

After leaving the interview, immediately make notes of what was said in case you are called back for a second interview. Write down key points that were discussed, the names of people you spoke with, and other details of the interview. Ask yourself what went really well and what you could improve. Note your strengths and weaknesses during the interview so you can work to improve in future interviews.

14-4a Sending a Thank-You Message

After a job interview, always send a thank-you message. Why? This courtesy sets you apart from other applicants, many of whom will not bother. In addition, more than one in five hiring managers say they are less likely to hire a candidate who doesn't follow up an interview with a message; 86 percent say failing to send a timely thank-you note indicates an interviewee's lack of follow-through.[23] Your message also reminds the interviewer of your visit and shows your good manners and genuine enthusiasm for the job.

Generally, you have three options for your message: a handwritten note card, a typed letter printed on bond paper, or an e-mail. No texts. Handwritten cards are always impressive. They stand out because they are becoming rare.[24] However, 89 percent of the managers in one survey said that sending a thank-you e-mail was altogether acceptable. Your preparation and knowledge of the company culture will help you determine whether a traditional thank-you message sent by U.S. mail or an e-mail is more appropriate. Some experts even recommend sending both![25] If you choose e-mail, make sure that you use professional language, standard capitalization, and proper punctuation. Promptness is essential when following up. Send your thank-you note within a few hours but no later than 24 hours after the interview. This is where snail mail falls short and may work against you.[26]

In your thank-you message, refer to the date of the interview, the exact job title for which you were interviewed, and specific topics discussed. Try to mention something you liked about the interview such as *Job interviews can be stressful, but you made me feel comfortable, and I am grateful for that.* Avoid worn-out phrases, such as *Thank you for taking the time to interview me.* Be careful, too, about overusing *I*, especially to begin sentences. Most important, show that you really want the job and that you are qualified for it. Notice how the letter in Figure 14.7 conveys enthusiasm and confidence.

If you have been interviewed by more than one person, send a separate personalized thank-you message to each interviewer.

14-4b Contacting Your References

Once you have thanked your interviewer, it is time to alert your references that they may be contacted by the employer. You might also have to request a letter of recommendation to be sent to the employer by a certain date. As discussed in Chapter 13, you should have already asked permission to use these individuals as references, and you should have supplied them with a copy of your résumé and information about the types of positions you are seeking.

To provide the best possible recommendation, your references need information. What position have you applied for with what company? What should they stress to the prospective employer? Let's say you are applying for a specific job that requires a letter of recommendation. Professor Patel has already agreed to be a reference for you. To get the best letter of recommendation from Professor Patel, help her out. Write an e-mail or letter telling her about the position, its requirements, and the recommendation deadline. Include copies of your résumé, college transcript, and, if applicable, the job posting or ad with detailed information about the opening. You might remind her of a positive experience with you that she could use in the recommendation. Remember that recommenders need evidence to support generalizations. Give them appropriate ammunition, as the student has done in the following request:

Dear Professor Patel:

Recently, I interviewed for the position of administrative assistant in the Human Resources Department of Host International. Because you kindly agreed to help me, I am now asking you to write a letter of recommendation to Host.

The position calls for good organizational, interpersonal, and writing skills, as well as computer experience. To help you review my skills and training, I enclose my résumé. As you may recall, I earned an A in your business communication class last fall; and you commended my long report for its clarity and organization.

Please send your letter to Mr. Marquis Jones at Host International before July 1 in the enclosed stamped, addressed envelope. I'm grateful for your support and promise to let you know the results of my job search.

Sincerely,

14-4c Following Up

If you don't hear from the interviewer within five days, or at the specified time, consider following up. Of course, if you have remembered to ask the interviewer when a decision is expected and whether you may follow up, you are all set. Otherwise, the standard advice to job candidates is to contact the interviewer with a follow-up e-mail or phone call.

An e-mail to find out how the decision process is going may be your best bet because such a message is less intrusive than a phone call. An e-mail message also gives the interviewer time to look up your status information, leaves a written record,

In a reference request letter, tell immediately why you are writing. Identify the target position and company.

Specify the job requirements to help the recommender know what to stress.

Provide a stamped, addressed envelope.

Figure 14.7 Interview Follow-Up Message

Todd D. Delgado

95 Grasslands Road, Valhalla, NY 10595
(914) 769-5002, toddddelgado@gmail.com

Uses customized letterhead but could have merely typed street and city address above dateline

June 1, 2019

Ms. Tiffany Escalante
iDesign Marketing & Media
1055 Westchester Avenue
White Plains, NY 10604

Dear Ms. Escalante:

Mentions the interview date and specific job title

Talking with you Wednesday, May 31, about the graphic designer position in White Plains was both informative and interesting.

Personalizes the message by referring to topics discussed in the interview

Thanks for describing the position in such detail and for introducing me to Ms. Dangelo, the senior designer. Her current project designing an annual report in four colors sounds fascinating as well as quite challenging.

Highlights specific skills for the job

Now that I've learned in greater detail the specific tasks of your graphic designers, I'm more than ever convinced that my computer and creative skills can make a genuine contribution to your graphic productions. My training in design and layout using PhotoShop and InDesign ensures that I could be immediately productive on your staff.

Shows good manners, appreciation, and perseverance—traits that recruiters value

Reminds reader of interpersonal skills as well as enthusiasm and eagerness for this job

You will find me an enthusiastic and hardworking member of any team effort. As you requested, I'm enclosing additional samples of my work. I'm eager to join the graphics staff at your White Plains headquarters, and I look forward to hearing from you soon.

Sincerely,

Todd D. Delgado

Todd D. Delgado
Enclosures

and eliminates annoying phone tag.[28] The following follow-up e-mail message would impress the interviewer:

Inquire courteously; don't sound angry or desperate.

> *Dear Ms. Wu:*
>
> *I enjoyed my interview with you last Wednesday for the graphic designer position. You should know that I'm very interested in this opportunity with iDesign Marketing & Media. Because you mentioned that you might have an answer this week, I'm eager to know how your decision process is coming along. I look forward to hearing from you.*
>
> *Sincerely,*

If you follow up by phone, say something like, *I'm calling to find out the status of your search for the _____ position.* Or you could say, *I'm wondering what else I can do to convince you that I'm the right person for this job.* It's important to sound professional and courteous. Sounding desperate, angry, or frustrated that you have not been contacted can ruin your chances.

Depending on the response you get to your first follow-up request, you may have to follow up additional times. Keep in mind, though, that some employers won't tell you about their hiring decision unless you are the one hired. Don't harass the interviewer, and don't force a decision. If you don't hear back from an employer within several weeks after following up, it is best to assume that you didn't get the job, and you should continue your job search.

14-5 Preparing Additional Employment Documents

Although the résumé and cover letter are your major tasks, other important documents and messages are often required during the job-search process. You may need to complete an employment application form and write follow-up messages. You might also have to write a letter of resignation when leaving a job. Because each of these tasks reveals something about you and your communication skills, you will want to put your best foot forward. These documents often subtly influence company officials to offer a job.

14-5a Application Form

Some organizations require job candidates to fill out job application forms instead of, or in addition to, submitting résumés. This practice permits them to gather and store standardized data about each applicant. Whether the application is on paper or online, follow the directions carefully and provide accurate information. The following suggestions can help you be prepared:

- Carry a card or notes saved on your mobile device summarizing vital statistics not included on your résumé. If you are asked to fill out an application form in an employer's office, you will need a handy reference to the following data: graduation dates; beginning and ending dates of all employment; salary history; full names, titles, and present work addresses of former supervisors; full addresses and phone numbers of current and previous employers; and full names, occupational titles, business addresses, and telephone numbers of people who have agreed to serve as references.
- Look over all the questions before starting.
- If filling out a paper form, write neatly using blue or black ink. Many career counselors recommend printing your responses; cursive handwriting can be difficult to read.
- Answer all questions honestly. Write *Not applicable* or *N/A* if appropriate. Don't leave any sections blank.
- Use accurate spelling, grammar, capitalization, and punctuation.
- If asked for the position desired, give a specific job title or type of position. Don't say, *Anything* or *Open.* These answers make you look unfocused; moreover, they make it difficult for employers to know what you are qualified for or interested in.
- Be prepared for a salary question. Unless you know what comparable employees are earning in the company, the best strategy is to suggest a salary range or to write *Negotiable* or *Open.* See the Communication Workshop at the end of this chapter for tips on dealing with money matters while interviewing.

LEARNING OUTCOME 5

Prepare additional employment documents such as applications, rejection follow-up messages, acceptance messages, and resignation letters.

- Be ready to explain the reasons for leaving previous positions. Use positive or neutral phrases such as Relocation, *Seasonal*, *To accept a position with more responsibility*, *Temporary position*, *To continue education*, or *Career change*. Avoid words and phrases such as *Fired, Quit, Didn't get along with supervisor*, or *Pregnant*.
- Look over the application before submitting to make sure it is complete and that you have followed all instructions.

If asked to input data into fields on an electronic application, have a flash drive ready or access your cloud drive to retrieve digital records that you can carefully copy and paste into windows on electronic forms.

14-5b Application or Résumé Follow-Up Message

If your résumé or application generates no response within a reasonable time, you may decide to send a short follow-up e-mail or letter such as the following. Doing so (a) jogs the memory of the personnel officer, (b) demonstrates your serious interest, and (c) allows you to emphasize your qualifications or to add new information.

Dear Ms. Gutierrez:

> *Open by reminding the reader of your interest.*

Please know that I am still interested in becoming an administrative support specialist with Quad, Inc.

> *Review your strengths or add new qualifications.*

Since submitting an application [or résumé] in May, I have completed my degree and have been employed as a summer replacement for office workers in several downtown offices. This experience has honed my communication and team-work skills. It has also introduced me to a wide range of office procedures.

> *Close positively; avoid accusations that make the reader defensive.*

Please keep my application in your active file and let me know when my formal training, technical skills, and practical experience can go to work for you.

Sincerely,

14-5c Rejection Follow-Up Message

If you didn't get the job and you think it was perfect for you, don't give up. Employment specialists encourage applicants to respond to a rejection. The candidate who was offered the position may decline, or other positions may open up. In a rejection follow-up e-mail or letter, it is OK to admit that you are disappointed. Be sure to add, however, that you are still interested and will contact the company again in a month in case a job opens up. Then follow through for a couple of months—but don't overdo it. You should be professional and persistent, not annoying. Here is an example of an effective rejection follow-up message:

Dear Mr. O'Leary:

> *Subordinate your disappointment to your appreciation at being notified promptly and courteously.*

Although disappointed that someone else was selected for your accounting position, I appreciate your promptness and courtesy in notifying me.

> *Emphasize your continuing interest.*

Because I am confident that you would benefit from my technical and inter-personal skills in your fast-paced environment, please consider keeping my résumé in your active file. My desire to become a productive member of your Transamerica staff remains strong.

Our interview on _____ was very enjoyable, and I especially appreciate the time you and Ms. Goldstein spent describing your company's expansion into international markets. To enhance my qualifications, I have enrolled in a course in international accounting at CSU.

Refer to specifics of your interview.

Should you have an opening for which I am qualified, you may reach me at (818) 719-3901. In the meantime, I will call you in a month to discuss employment possibilities.

Take the initiative; tell when you will call for an update.

Sincerely,

14-5d Job Acceptance or Rejection Message

When all your hard work pays off, you will be offered the position you want. Although you will likely accept the position over the phone, it is a good idea to follow up with an acceptance e-mail or letter to confirm the details and to formalize the acceptance. Your acceptance message might look like this:

Dear Ms. Reed:

It was a pleasure talking with you earlier today. As I mentioned, I am delighted to accept the position of project manager with Innovative Creations, Inc., in your Seattle office. I look forward to becoming part of the IC team and starting work on a variety of exciting and innovative projects.

Confirm your acceptance of the position with enthusiasm.

As we agreed, my starting salary will be $52,000, with a full benefits package including health and life insurance, retirement plan, and two weeks of vacation per year.

Review salary and benefits details.

I look forward to starting my position with Innovative Creations on September 16, 2019. Before that date I will send you the completed tax and insurance forms you need. Thanks again for everything, Ms. Reed.

Include the specific starting date.

Sincerely,

If you must turn down a job offer, show your professionalism by writing a sincere letter. This letter should thank the employer for the job offer and explain briefly that you are turning it down. Taking the time to extend this courtesy could help you in the future if this employer has a position you really want. Here's an example of a job rejection letter:

Dear Mr. Rosen:

Thank you very much for offering me the position of sales representative with Bendall Pharmaceuticals. It was a difficult decision to make, but I have accepted a position with another company.

Thank the employer for the job offer and decline the offer without giving specifics.

I appreciate your taking the time to interview me, and I wish Bendall Pharmaceuticals much success in the future.

Express gratitude and best wishes for the future.

Sincerely,

Confirm the exact date of resignation. Remind the employer of your contributions.

Offer assistance to prepare for your departure.

Offer thanks and end with a forward-looking statement.

14-5e Resignation Letter

After you have been in a position for a period of time, you may find it necessary to leave. Perhaps you have been offered a better position, or maybe you have decided to return to school full-time. Whatever the reason, you should leave your position gracefully and tactfully. Although you will likely discuss your resignation in person with your supervisor, it is a good idea to document your resignation by writing a formal letter. Some resignation letters are brief, whereas others contain great detail. Remember that many resignation letters are placed in personnel files; therefore, you should format and write yours using the professional business letter–writing techniques you learned earlier. Here is an example of a basic letter of resignation:

Dear Ms. Byrne:

This letter serves as formal notice of my resignation from Allied Corporation, effective Friday, August 16. I have enjoyed serving as your project manager for the past two years, and I am grateful for everything I have learned during my employment with Allied.

Please let me know what I can do over the next two weeks to help you prepare for my departure. I would be happy to help with finding and training my replacement.

Thanks again for providing such a positive employment experience. I will long remember my time here.

Sincerely,

Although the employee who wrote the preceding resignation letter gave the standard two-week notice, you may find that a longer notice is necessary. The higher your position and the greater your responsibility, the longer the notice you give your employer should be. You should, however, always give some notice as a courtesy.

Writing job acceptance, job rejection, and resignation letters requires effort. That effort, however, is worth it because you are building bridges that may carry you to even better jobs in the future.

Summary of Learning Outcomes

1 Understand the purposes, sequence, and types of job interviews, including screening, one-on-one, panel, group, sequential, and video interviews.

- Current trends in interviewing include (a) early-stage screening by technology; (b) longer, multiple interviews; (c) on-the-spot interviewing; (d) psychometric and skills tests; (e) behavioral and situational questions; and (f) group interviews.
- As a job candidate, you have the following purposes in an interview: (a) convince the employer of your potential, (b) learn more about the job and the company, and (c) expand on the information in your résumé.
- From the employer's perspective, the interview is an opportunity to (a) assess your abilities in relation to the requirements of the position; (b) discuss your training, experience,

knowledge, and abilities in more detail; (c) see what drives and motivates you; and (d) decide whether you would fit into the organization.

- Screening interviews, conducted by telephone or video, seek to eliminate less qualified candidates.
- Hiring/placement interviews may be one-on-one, panel, group, sequential, or video.

2 Know what to do *before* an interview, including ensuring professional phone techniques, researching the target company, rehearsing success stories, cleaning up digital dirt, and fighting fear.

- Prepare for telephone screening interviews by ensuring professional answering techniques and screening incoming calls.
- Make the first conversation impressive by using professional, businesslike language, and having your résumé, a calendar, and a list of references handy.
- Research the target company by scouring the Internet and the company's advertising to learn about its products, history, mission, goals, size, geographic locations, employees, customers, competitors, culture, management structure, reputation in the community, finances, strengths, weaknesses, and future plans.
- Strive to locate inside information through social media.
- Rehearse 30-second success stories that demonstrate your qualifications and achievements.
- Check your online presence and strive to clean up any digital dirt.
- Decide what to wear to the interview by asking the interviewer what is appropriate.
- To reduce fear before an interview, remind yourself that you are thoroughly prepared and that interviewing is a two-way street.

3 Explain what to do *during* an interview, including controlling nonverbal messages and answering typical interview questions.

- During your interview send positive nonverbal messages by controlling body movements, showing good posture, maintaining eye contact, using gestures effectively, and smiling enough to convey a positive, professional attitude.
- Listen attentively, turn off your cell phone or other electronic devices, don't chew gum, and sound enthusiastic and sincere.
- Be prepared to respond to traditional inquiries such as *Tell me about yourself*.
- Practice answering typical questions such as why you want to work for the organization, why you should be hired, how your education and experience have prepared you for the position, where you expect to be in five or ten years, what your greatest weaknesses are, and how much money you expect to earn.
- Be ready for situational questions that ask you to respond to hypothetical situations. Expect behavioral questions that begin with *Tell me about a time when you. . . .*
- Think about how you would respond to illegal or inappropriate questions, as well as questions you would ask about the job.
- End the interview positively by summarizing your strongest qualifications, showing enthusiasm for obtaining the position, thanking the interviewer, asking what the next step is, and requesting permission to follow up.

4 Describe what to do *after* an interview, including thanking the interviewer, contacting references, and writing follow-up messages.

- After leaving the interview, immediately make notes of the key points discussed.
- Note your strengths and weaknesses during the interview so that you can work to improve in future interviews.
- Write a thank-you letter, card, or e-mail including the date of the interview, the exact job title for which you were interviewed, specific topics discussed, and gratitude for the interview.

- Alert your references that they may be contacted.
- If you don't hear from the interviewer when expected, call or send an e-mail to follow up. Sound professional, not desperate, angry, or frustrated.

5 Prepare additional employment documents such as applications, rejection follow-up messages, acceptance messages, and resignation letters.

- When filling out an application form, look over all the questions before starting.
- If asked for a salary figure, provide a salary range or write *Negotiable* or *Open*.
- If you don't get the job, consider writing a letter that expresses your disappointment but also your desire to be contacted in case a job opens up.
- If you are offered a job, write a letter that confirms the details and formalizes your acceptance.
- When refusing a position, write a sincere letter turning down the job offer.
- Upon resigning from a position, write a letter that confirms the date of resignation, offers assistance to prepare for your departure, and expresses thanks.

Chapter Review

1. How can you lower the stakes and reduce the amount of stress you might potentially experience while anticipating a job interview? (L.O. 1)

2. Briefly describe the types of hiring/placement interviews you may encounter. (L.O. 1)

3. How can you make the first telephone conversation with an employer impressive? (L.O. 2)

4. What are success stories, and how can you use them? (L.O. 2)

5. Should candidates be candid with interviewers when asked about their weaknesses? (L.O. 3)

6. What are situational and behavioral interview questions, and how can you craft responses that will make a favorable impression on the interviewer? (L.O. 3)

7. List the steps you should take immediately following your job interview. (L.O. 4)

8. Why should you always send a thank-you message after a job interview, and what are your options for making your note impressive? (L.O. 4)

9. If you receive a job offer, why is it important to write an acceptance message, and what should it include? (L.O. 5)

10. Is it a good idea to follow up after a job rejection? Why or why not? (L.O. 5)

Critical Thinking

11. Online psychometric and skills tests with multiple-choice questions have become a hot trend in recruiting today. Employers may ask not only how applicants would handle tricky situations, but also how happy they are or how much they have stolen from their previous employer. The multiple-choice format poses a dilemma for applicants because they don't know whether to be truthful or say what the employer might want to hear. Is this practice fair? What are some advantages and disadvantages of this practice? (L.O. 1, 2)

12. Like criminal background checks and drug tests, social media background checks have become commonplace in today's recruiting. What are the pros and cons of conducting such checks as a primary or sole means of screening applicants? (L.O. 1, 2)

13. Why is it a smart strategy to thank an interviewer, to follow up, and even to send a rejection follow-up message? Are any risks associated with this strategy? (L.O. 4, 5)

14. If you are asked an illegal interview question, why is it important to first assess the intentions of the interviewer? (L.O. 3)

15. As businesses increasingly emphasize workplace ethics, you may be asked in an interview to tell about a time when you were challenged ethically. One workplace compliance officer advised candidates not to respond that you have never faced an ethical challenge. "You want a candidate," he said, "who avoids misconduct, not someone who lies and says they've never done anything wrong."[31] Do you agree? (L.O. 1, 3)

Radical Rewrites

Note: Radical Rewrites are provided at **www.cengagebrain.com** for you to download and revise. Your instructor may show a suggested solution.

14.1 Radical Rewrite: Camille's Poor Interview Follow-Up Letter (L.O. 4)

> Team

Camille Montano has the right idea in sending a follow-up message after her interview for an accounting position in Denver. However, her message could be more effective.

YOUR TASK. Based on what you have learned in this chapter, in teams or in a class discussion, list at least five weaknesses. Look for problems with punctuation, wordiness, proofreading, capitalization, sentence structure, and other writing techniques you have studied.

1340 East Phillips Avenue
Apartment D
Littleton, CO 80126
June 17, 2019

Ms. Michelle Genovese
High Country Accounting
2810 East Sixth Avenue
Denver, CO 80218-3453

Dear Ms. Genovese:

It was altogether extremely enjoyable to talk with you about the open position at High Country Accounting. The position as you presented it seems to be a excellent match for my training and skills. The creative approach to Account Management that you described, confirmed my desire to work in a imaginative firm such as High County Accounting.

I would bring to the position strong organizational skills, and I have the ability to encourage others to work cooperatively within the department. My training in analysis and application of accounting data and financial reporting; as well as my experience as a financial consultant in the mortgage industry would enable me to help with the backlog of client projects that you mentioned.

I certainly understand your departments need for strong support in the administrative area. I am definitely attentive to details and my organizational skills will help to free you to deal with more pressing issues in the management area. I neglected to emphasize during our very interesting interview that I also have a minor in finance despite the fact that it was on my résumé.

Thanks for taking the time to interview me, and explain the goals of your agency along with the dutys of this position. As I am sure you noticed during the interview I am very interested in working for High Country Accounting because I need to get a job to start paying off my student loans, and look forward to hearing from you about this position. In the event that you might possibly need additional information from me or facts about me, all you need to do is shoot me an e-mail.

Sincerely,

Camille Montano

Camille Montano

List at least five weaknesses.

Activities and Cases

14.2 Surviving Cattle-Call Interviews (L.O. 1)

> Social Media > Web

Group interviews are not for the fainthearted, and opinions on the practice are mixed. "Cattle-call" interviews can be stressful, shocking, even demeaning, some participants feel. One interviewee for an executive-level public relations position described being herded into a room with 200 other applicants where interviewers started bellowing questions at participants. Employers who like this tool say that cattle-call interviews are fair and efficient because they allow the quick ranking of candidates in categories such as teamwork, leadership, and stress management.

YOUR TASK. To deepen your understanding of group interviews, search the Web for articles and blogs using the keywords *group job interviews* or *cattle-call interviews*. Job-search advice sites offer tips on coping with the anxiety of group interviewing. Collect the advice and report your insights in class or in a written document as determined by your instructor.

14.3 What Social Media Info Helps or Hurts Your Job Prospects? (L.O. 1, 2)

> E-Mail > Social Media > Team > Web

Hiring managers are increasingly searching social media sites to research job candidates. A recent CareerBuilder survey revealed that most hiring managers aren't intentionally looking for digital dirt. Six in ten employers say they are merely looking for information about candidates "that supports their qualifications for the job."[32]

Surprisingly, it may not be what they find but what is missing that matters. More than four in ten hiring managers say "they are less likely to interview job candidates if they are unable to find information about that person online." Hiring managers who did find social media information online revealed that the following items turned them off:

Social Media Behavior Hurting Job Seekers

Provocative or inappropriate photographs, videos, or information	46 percent
Information about candidate drinking or using drugs	43 percent
Discriminatory comments related to race, religion, gender, etc.	33 percent
Complaints about previous company or fellow employees	31 percent
Poor communication skills	29 percent

Conversely, social media behavior that impresses recruiters includes the following: candidate's background information supported job qualifications (44 percent), candidate's site conveyed a professional image (44 percent), candidate's personality came across as a good fit with company culture (43 percent), candidate was well-rounded and showed a wide range of interests (40 percent), and candidate had great communication skills (36 percent).

YOUR TASK. Conduct a social media audit in your course. Armed with the knowledge acquired in this chapter and the information in this activity, critically evaluate fellow students' social media sites such as Facebook, Instagram, Google+, Twitter, and LinkedIn. In pairs or larger groups, look for positive attributes as well as negative qualities that may repel hiring managers. Report your findings orally or compile them in an e-mail or memo. If you identify negative behavior, discuss remedies such as how to remove offensive material.

14.4 Putting Social Media to Work to Investigate Jobs (L.O. 2)

> Social Media > Web

Blogs and social media sites such as Facebook, Twitter, and LinkedIn are becoming important tools in the job-search process. By accessing blogs, company Facebook profiles, LinkedIn pages, and Twitter feeds, job seekers can locate much insider information about a company's culture and day-to-day activities.

YOUR TASK. Using the Web, locate a blog that is maintained by an employee of a company where you would like to work. Monitor the blog for at least a week. Also, access the company's Facebook and Instagram pages, check its LinkedIn presence, and monitor any Twitter feeds for at least a week. Prepare a short report summarizing what you learned about the company through reading the blog postings, status updates, and tweets. Include a statement of whether this information would be valuable during your job search.

14.5 Preparing for Interviews and Researching Salary Data With Glassdoor (L.O. 1, 2)

> E-Mail > Social Media > Web

Most likely you are familiar with LinkedIn, the social network devoted to all things career. Perhaps you already have a LinkedIn profile and downloaded its job-search mobile app. However, did you know that Glassdoor is another superb source of job-search information, postings, and reviews? In anonymous posts, Glassdoor dishes on company reviews, salary comparisons, CEO approval ratings, interviews, and more. If you want authentic insider data about job interviews and other invaluable information, check out Glassdoor.

Let's say you want to know what LinkedIn is like as an employer and how happy applicants are with LinkedIn's interview process. You would search for information about the company by its name and could refine your search by targeting a specific job title and location. You would see that at 4.3, the career network has a fairly high rating overall and that its CEO Jeff Weiner has achieved a stellar 97 percent approval rating.

YOUR TASK. At the Glassdoor site, search for your dream employer. You can select from industries or search for companies by name. Examine the reviews and the interview modalities. How happy are interviewees and current workers with their employers? Share your results with the class, and, if asked, report your findings in a document—a memo, e-mail, or informal report.

14.6 Yes, You Can Interview People in Fewer Than 140 Characters! (L.O. 1, 3)

> Social Media > Team > Web

Digital marketing strategist, angel investor, and best-selling author Jay Baer published an e-book, *The Best of Twitter 20* that presents 22 Twitter interviews (twitterviews) he conducted with social media luminaries. The experts, to whom Baer posed 20 questions in no more than 140 characters within approximately 90 minutes, include Joseph Jaffe, Gary Vaynerchuk, Spike Jones, and Amber Naslund.

YOUR TASK. Search for a phrase such as *Baer and The Twitter 20*. Visit Baer's blog Convince & Convert, download the free e-book, or read it online. You can also access the individual links on Baer's website, taking you directly to the social media expert of your choice. Study the twitterviews. Then, if your instructor directs, team up for a role-play, in which one student acts as the interviewer and the other plays the interviewee. The roles can be switched after a while. Prepare at least five concise career-related questions that you will convert into tweets. In turn, your counterpart will tweet back his or her answers. If you don't want to use a live Twitter feed, type up your tweets in a word processing program that will allow you to count characters. You can model your list of tweets on Baer's transcript format.

14.7 Building Interview Skills With Worksheets (L.O. 2, 3)

Successful interviews require diligent preparation and repeated practice. To be well prepared, you need to know what skills are required for your targeted position. In addition to computer and communication skills, employers generally want to know whether you work well with a team, accept responsibility, solve problems, work efficiently, meet deadlines, show leadership, save time and money, and work hard.

YOUR TASK. Consider a position for which you are eligible now or one for which you will be eligible when you complete your education. Identify the skills and traits necessary for this position. If you prepared a résumé in Chapter 13, be sure that it addresses these targeted areas. Now prepare interview worksheets listing at least ten technical and other skills or traits you think a recruiter will want to discuss in an interview for your targeted position.

14.8 Telling Success Stories (L.O. 3)

You can best showcase your talents if you are ready with your own success stories that illustrate how you have developed the skills or traits required for your targeted position.

YOUR TASK. Using the worksheets you created in **Activity 14.7**, prepare success stories that highlight the required skills or traits. Select three to five stories to develop into answers to potential interview questions. For example, here is a typical question: *How does your background relate to the position we have open?* A possible response: *As you know, I have just completed an intensive training program in _____. In addition, I have over three years of part-time work experience in a variety of business settings. In one position I was selected to manage a small business in the absence of the owner. I developed responsibility and customer service skills in filling orders efficiently, resolving shipping problems, and monitoring key accounts. I also inventoried and organized products worth over $200,000. When the owner returned from a vacation to Florida, I was commended for increasing sales and received a bonus in recognition of my efforts.* People relate to and remember stories. Try to shape your answers into memorable stories.

14.9 Digging for Digital Dirt: Keeping a Low Profile Online (L.O. 2)

> Social Media   Web

Before embarking on your job hunt, you should find out what employers might find if they searched your personal life in cyberspace, specifically on Facebook, Instagram, Twitter, and so forth. Running your name through Google and other search engines, particularly enclosed in quotation marks to lower the number of hits, is usually the first step. To learn even more, try some of the people-search sites such as 123people, Snitch.name, and PeekYou. They collect information from a number of search engines, websites, and social networks.

YOUR TASK. Use Google, 123people, and another search tool to explore the Internet for your full name, enclosed in quotation marks. In Google, don't forget to run an *Images* search at **http://www.google.com/images** to find any photos of questionable taste. If your instructor requests, share your insights with the class—not the salacious details, but general observations—or write a short memo summarizing the results.

14.10 Talent Assessments: Reviewing Job Scenarios (L.O. 1, 2)

> Web

What do Macy's, PetSmart, Radio Shack, Walmart, and Burger King have in common? They use preemployment testing to identify applicants who will fit into the organization. Unlike classical aptitude tests that began in the military, today's online multiple-choice tests assess integrity, collegiality, and soft skills in general.

To give you a flavor of these talent assessments, here are three typical scenarios:

1. *You have learned that eye contact is important in communication. How much eye contact should you have when conversing with someone in a professional environment?*	2. *You are attending an important meeting with colleagues who are more senior than you are. How much should you speak at the meeting?*	3. *You just found out that people at work are spreading a bad rumor about you that is untrue. How would you respond?*
A At all times. You want to make sure the person knows you are paying attention.	A You should look very interested but not speak at all unless they request it.	A Tell everybody that it is not true. You need to clear your name.
B About 60–70 percent of the time	B You should speak only when the topic is in your area of expertise.	B Don't react to it at all. It'll blow over eventually.
C Every now and then. You don't want to make the other person uncomfortable.	C You should try to talk as much as possible to show your knowledge.	C Find out who started it so you talk to them to make sure that they will never do it again.
D About half the time	D You should speak in the beginning of the meeting and every now and then.	D Talk to others about another coworker's rumor so people will forget about yours.

YOUR TASK. Answer the questions; then compare your answers with those of your classmates. Discuss the scenarios. What specific skills or attributes might each question be designed to measure? Do you think such questions are effective? What might be the best way to respond to the scenarios? Your instructor may share the correct answers with you. If your instructor directs, search the Web for more talent assessment questions. Alternatively, your instructor might ask you to create your own workplace (or college) scenarios to help you assess an applicant's soft skills. As a class you could compare questions/scenarios and quiz each other.

14.11 Getting Ready for Interview Wear (L.O. 2, 3)

> Web

As you prepare for your interview by learning about the company and the industry, don't forget a key component of interview success: creating a favorable first impression by wearing appropriate business attire. Job seekers often have nebulous ideas about proper interview wear. Some wardrobe mishaps include choosing a conservative power suit but accessorizing it with beat-up casual shoes or a shabby bag. Grooming glitches include dandruff on dark suit fabric, dirty fingernails, and mothball odor. Women sometimes wrongly assume that any black clothing items are acceptable, even if they are too tight, revealing, sheer, or made of low-end fabrics. Most image consultants agree that workplace wardrobe falls into three main categories: business formal, business casual, and casual. Only business formal is considered proper interview apparel.

YOUR TASK. To prepare for your big day, search the Web for descriptions and images of *business formal*. You may research *business casual* and *casual* styles, but for an interview, always dress on the side of caution—conservatively. Compare prices and look for suit sales to buy one or two attractive interview outfits. Share your findings (notes, images, and price range for suits, solid shoes, and accessories) with the class and your instructor.

14.12 Rehearsing Interview Questions (L.O. 2, 3)

> Team

Practice makes perfect in interviewing. The more often you rehearse responses to typical interview questions, the closer you are to getting the job.

YOUR TASK. Select three questions from each of these question categories discussed in this chapter: questions to get acquainted, questions to gauge your interest, questions about your experience and accomplishments, questions about the future, and challenging questions. Write your answers to each set of questions. Try to incorporate skills and traits required for the targeted position, and include success stories where appropriate. Polish these answers and your delivery technique by practicing in front of a mirror or by making an audio or video recording. Your instructor may choose this assignment as a group activity in class.

14.13 Anticipating Situational Interview Questions (L.O. 2, 3)

> Team   Web

Situational interview questions can vary widely from position to position. You should know enough about a position to understand some of the typical situations you would encounter regularly.

YOUR TASK. Use your favorite search tool to locate typical descriptions of a position in which you are interested. Based on these descriptions, develop a list of six to eight typical situations someone in this position would face; then write situational interview questions for each of these scenarios. In pairs, role-play interviewer and interviewee, alternating with each question.

14.14 Examining Behavioral Interview Questions (L.O. 2, 3)

> Team   Web

Behavioral interview questions are increasingly popular, and you will need a little practice before you can answer them easily.

YOUR TASK. Use your favorite search tool to locate lists of behavioral questions on the Internet. Select five skill areas such as communication, teamwork, and decision making. For each skill area, find three behavioral questions that you think would be effective in an interview. In pairs, role-play interviewer and interviewee, alternating with each question. You goal is to answer effectively in one or two minutes. Remember to use the STAR method when answering.

14.15 Creating a Digital or Paper Interview Cheat Sheet (L.O. 2, 3)

> Team

Even the best-rehearsed applicants sometimes forget to ask the questions they prepared, or they fail to stress their major accomplishments in job interviews. Sometimes applicants are so rattled they even forget the interviewer's name. To help you keep your wits during an interview, make a cheat sheet—either paper or digital—that summarizes key facts, answers, and questions. Review it before the interview and again as the interview is ending to be sure you have covered everything that is critical.

YOUR TASK. Prepare a cheat sheet with the following information:
Day and time of interview:
Meeting with [name(s) of interviewer(s), title, company, city, state, zip, telephone, cell, fax, video, e-mail]:
Major accomplishments (four to six):

Management or work style (four to six):
Things you need to know about me (three or four items):
Reason I left my last job:
Answers to difficult questions (four or five answers):
Questions to ask interviewer:
Things I can do for you:

14.16 Tackling Inappropriate and Illegal Interview Questions (L.O. 3)

Although some questions are considered inappropriate and potentially illegal by the government, many interviewers ask them anyway—whether intentionally or unknowingly. Being prepared is important.

YOUR TASK. Assume you are being interviewed at one of the top companies on your list of potential employers. The interviewing committee consists of a human resources manager and the supervising manager of the department in which you would work. At various times during the interview, the supervising manager asks questions that make you feel uncomfortable. For example, he asks whether you are married. You know this question is inappropriate, but you see no harm in answering it. Then, however, he asks how old you are. Because you started college early and graduated in three and a half years, you are worried that you may not be considered mature enough for this position. However, you have most of the other qualifications required, and you are convinced you could succeed on the job. How should you answer this question?

14.17 Turning Tables: Interviewing the Interviewer (L.O. 3)

When it is your turn to ask questions during the interview process, be ready.

YOUR TASK. Decide on three to five questions that you would like to ask during an interview. Write them down and practice asking them so that you sound confident and sincere.

14.18 Role-Playing Mock Interviews (L.O. 3)

> Team

One of the best ways to understand interview dynamics and to develop confidence is to role-play the parts of interviewer and candidate in a mock interview.

YOUR TASK. Choose a partner for this activity. Each partner makes a list of two interview questions for each of the eight interview question categories presented in this chapter. In team sessions you and your partner role-play an actual interview. One acts as interviewer; the other is the candidate. Prior to the interview, the candidate tells the interviewer the job he or she is applying for and the name of the company. For the interview, the interviewer and candidate should dress appropriately and sit in chairs facing each other. The interviewer greets the candidate and makes the candidate comfortable. The candidate gives the interviewer a copy of his or her résumé. The interviewer asks three (or more depending on your instructor's time schedule) questions from the candidate's list. The interviewer may also ask follow-up questions, if appropriate. When finished, the interviewer ends the meeting graciously. After one interview, partners reverse roles and repeat.

14.19 YouTube: Picking Up Interview Skills (L.O. 3)

> Web

The adage *Practice makes perfect* is especially true for interviewing. The more you confront your fears in mock or real interviews, the calmer and more confident you will be when your dream job is on the line. Short of undergoing your own interview, you can also learn from observation. YouTube and other video sites offer countless video clips showing examples of excellent, and poor, interviewing techniques.

YOUR TASK. Visit YouTube or search the Internet for interview videos. Select a clip that you find particularly entertaining or informative. Watch it multiple times and jot down your observations. Then summarize the scenario in a paragraph or two. Provide examples of interview strategies that worked and those that didn't, applying the information you learned in this chapter. If required, share your insights about the video with the class.

14.20 Interviewing Over Meals: Table Manners on Display (L.O. 3)

> Team   Web

Although they are less likely for entry-level candidates, interviews over business meals are a popular means to size up the social skills of a job seeker, especially in second and subsequent interviews. Candidates coveting jobs with a lot of face-to-face contact with the public may be subjected to the ultimate test: table manners. Interviews are nerve-racking and intimidating enough, but imagine having to juggle silverware, wrangle potentially messy food, and keep your clothing stain free—all this while listening carefully to what is being said around the table and giving thoughtful, confident answers.

YOUR TASK. Researching tips can help you avoid the most common pitfalls associated with interviews over meals. Use your favorite search engine and try queries such as *interview dining tips, interviewing over meals,* and so forth. Consider the credibility of your sources. Are they authorities on the subject? Compile a list of tips and jot down your sources. Share the list with your peers. If your instructor directs, discuss the categories of advice provided. Then, as a class assemble a comprehensive list of the most common interview tips.

14.21 Thanking the Interviewer (L.O. 4)

> Team

You have just completed an exciting employment interview, and you want the interviewer to remember you favorably.

YOUR TASK. Write a follow-up thank-you letter to Ronald T. Ranson, Human Resources Development, Electronic Data Sources, 1328 Peachtree Plaza, Atlanta, GA 30314 (or a company of your choice). Make up any details needed.

14.22 Following Up After Submitting Your Résumé (L.O. 4)

> E-Mail

A month has passed since you sent your résumé and cover letter in response to a job advertisement. You are still interested in the position and would like to find out whether you still have a chance.

YOUR TASK. Write a follow-up e-mail or letter to an employer of your choice that does not offend the reader or damage your chances of employment.

14.23 Refusing to Take *No* for an Answer (L.O. 5)

After an excellent interview with Electronic Data Sources (or a company of your choice), you are disappointed to learn that someone else was hired. However, you really want to work for EDS.

YOUR TASK. Write a follow-up message to Ronald T. Ranson, Human Resources Development, Electronic Data Sources, 1328 Peachtree Plaza, Atlanta, GA 30314 (or a company of your choice). Indicate that you are disappointed but still interested.

14.24 Saying *Yes* to a Stellar Job Offer (L.O. 5)

> E-Mail

Your dream has come true: you have just been offered an excellent position. Although you accepted the position on the phone, you want to send a formal acceptance e-mail or letter.

YOUR TASK. Write a job acceptance message to an employer of your choice. Include the specific job title, your starting date, and details about your compensation package. Make up any necessary details.

14.25 Demonstrating Your Growing Value to the Organization (L.O. 1, 4, 5)

Your boss has paid your tuition for this course. As you complete the course, he or she asks you for a letter about your experience in the course.

YOUR TASK. Write a letter to your boss in a real or imaginary organization explaining how this course made you more valuable to the organization.

Grammar/Mechanics Checkup 14

Total Review

This exercise reviews all of the guidelines in the Grammar/Mechanics Handbook as well as the lists of Confusing Words and Frequently Misspelled Words. Choose the correct option. When you finish, compare your responses with those at the bottom of the page.

c _____

EXAMPLE
a. The board have voted to give all employee's retroactive pay rises.
b. The Board has voted to give all employees' retroactive pay raises.
c. The board has voted to give all employees retroactive pay raises.

_____ 1. a. In the fall each of the companies plans to increase its hiring.
b. In the Fall each of the companys plan to increase it's hiring.
c. In the fall each of the companys plan to increase its hiring.

_____ 2. a. Our Accounting Department processed expense claims for Ryan and I, but Ryans was lost.
b. Our Accounting Department processed expense claims for Ryan and me, but Ryan's was lost.
c. Our accounting department processed expense claims for Ryan and me, but Ryan's was lost.

_____ 3. a. The Marketing Manager assigned Jennifer and I the best 2 new sales territorys.
b. The marketing manager assigned Jennifer and me the best two new sales territories.
c. The marketing manager assigned Jennifer and I the best two new sales territorys.

_____ 4. a. 3 types of similar storms of the tropics are: cyclones, typhoons and hurricanes.
b. Three types of similar storms' of the tropics are: cyclones, typhoons and hurricanes.
c. Three types of similar storms of the tropics are cyclones, typhoons, and hurricanes.

_____ 5. a. It's too early to determine whether we'll make a profit before September 15.
b. Its to early to determine whether we'll make a profit before September 15.
c. It's too early to determine whether we'll make a profit before September 15th.

_____ 6. a. If I was her, I would pay off the principal of the loan immediatly.
b. If I were her, I would pay off the principal of the loan immediately.
c. If I was her I would pay off the principle of the loan immediately.

_____ 7. a. German shoppers generally bring there own bags for grocery; therefore they were unaccustomed to Walmarts bagging techniques.
b. German shoppers generally bring their own bags for grocerys, therefore, they were unaccustomed to Walmarts bagging techniques.
c. German shoppers generally bring their own bags for groceries; therefore, they were unaccustomed to Walmart's bagging techniques.

_____ 8. a. About 1/2 of Pizza Huts 8,000 outlets will make deliverys, the others focuses on walk-in customers.
b. About one-half of Pizza Hut's 8,000 outlets will make deliveries; the others focus on walk-in customers.
c. About one-half of Pizza Hut's eight thousand outlets will make deliverys, the others focus on walk in customers.

_____ 9. a. If the Manager had seen the senders invoice, she would have payed it quickly.
b. If the manager had saw the sender's invoice, she would have payed it quick.
c. If the manager had seen the sender's invoice, she would have paid it quickly.

_____ 10. a. The company's insurance carrier inquired whether at this point in our contract it could change significant terms.
b. The company's insurance carrier inquired whether, at this point in our contract, it could change significant terms?
c. The companys insurance carrier inquired whether at this point in our contract, it could change significant terms?

1.a 2.b 3.b 4.c 5.a 6.b 7.c 8.b 9.c 10.a

Every chapter provides an editing exercise to fine-tune your grammar and mechanics skills. The following interview follow-up message requires edits that address grammar, punctuation, capitalization, number style, concise wording, and other writing issues. Study the principles in the Grammar/Mechanics Handbook (Appendix D), including the lists of Confusing Words and Frequently Misspelled Words.

YOUR TASK. Edit the following (a) by inserting corrections in your textbook or on a photocopy using the proofreading marks in Appendix C or (b) by downloading the message from **www.cengagebrain.com** and correcting at your computer.

2871 Milburn Avenue
Toledo, OH 43610
May 30, 2019

Mr. Kipp Frymoyer
Madison Avenue Associates
1802 Madison Avenue
Toledo, OH 43604

Dear Mr. Frymoyer

It was extremely enjoyable to talk with you on Wenesday about the Assistant Account Manager position at Madison Avenue Associate. The position, as you presented it seems to be an excelent match for my training and skills. The creative approach to Account Management that you described, confirmed my desire to work in a imaginative firm such as Madison Avenue Associates.

In addition to an enthusiastic attitude I would bring to the position strong communication skills, and the ability to encourage others to work cooperatively within the department. My Graphic Arts training and experience will help me work with staff artists, and provide a understanding of the visual aspects of you work.

I certainly understand your departments need for strong support in the administrative area. My attention to detail and my organizational skills will help to free you to deal with more pressing issues in the management area. Despite the fact that it was on my résumé I neglected to emphasize during our interview that I worked for 2 summers as a temporary office worker. This experience helped me to develop administrative support and clerical skills as well as to understand the every day demands of a busy office.

Thanks for taking the time to interview me, and explain the goals of your agency along with the dutys of this position. As I mentioned during the interview I am very interested in working for Madison Avenue Associate, and look forward to hearing from you about this position. In the event that you might possibly need additional information from me or facts about me, all you need to do is shoot me an e-mail at jsteiger@buckeye.com.

Sincerely,

Jessica Steiger

Jessica Steiger

Money Talk: Negotiating a Salary

Recent graduates generally don't have much bargaining power when pursuing entry-level positions. However, it does not hurt to try if you bring some special expertise or experience to the table.[33] Also, a positive job outlook seems to be boosting compensation for today's college graduates.[34] To discuss compensation effectively, though, you must be prepared for salary questions, and you should know what you are worth. You also need to know basic negotiation strategies. Alas, negotiating doesn't come naturally to Americans. "Most people in our country are not used to bargaining," says salary expert Matthew Deluca. "But if you don't bargain, you are not going to get all you should."[35] The following negotiating rules, recommended by career experts, can guide you to a better beginning salary.[36]

Rule No. 1: Avoid discussing salary for as long as possible in the interview process.

The longer you delay salary discussion, the more time you will have to convince the employer that you are worth what you are asking for. Ideally, you should try to avoid discussing salary until you know for sure that the interviewing company is making a job offer. The best time for you to negotiate your salary is between the time you are offered the position and the time you accept it. Wait for the employer to bring salary up first. If salary comes up and you are not sure whether the job is being offered to you, it is time to be blunt. Here are some things you could say:

Are you making me a job offer?

What is your salary range for positions with similar requirements?

I'm very interested in the position, and my salary would be negotiable.

Tell me what you have in mind for the salary range.

Rule No. 2: Know in advance the probable salary range for similar jobs in similar organizations in your region.

Many job-search websites provide salary information. One of the best sources for salary and other candid insider information is Glassdoor. It allows you to search by region, so you know what similar jobs are paying in your area. The important thing here is to think in terms of a wide salary range. Let's say you are hoping to start at between $50,000 and $55,000. To an interviewer, you might say, *I was looking for a salary in the low to mid fifties.* This technique is called bracketing. In addition, stating your salary range in an annual dollar amount sounds more professional than asking for an hourly wage. Be sure to consider such things as geographic location, employer size, industry standards, the state of the economy, and other factors to make sure that the range you come up with is realistic.

Rule No. 3: When negotiating, focus on what you are worth, not on what you need.

Throughout the interview and negotiation process, focus continually on your strengths. Make sure the employer knows everything of value that you will bring to the organization. You have to prove that you are worth what you are asking for. Employers pay salaries based on what you will accomplish on the job and contribute to the organization. When discussing your salary, focus on how the company will benefit from these contributions. Don't bring personal issues into the negotiation process. No employer will be willing to pay you more because you have bills to pay, mouths to feed, or debt to settle.

Rule No. 4: Never say *no* to a job before it is offered.

Why would anyone refuse a job offer before it is made? It happens all the time. Let's say you were hoping for a salary of $60,000. The interviewer tells you that the salary scheduled for this job is $55,000. You respond, *Oh, that is out of the question!* Before you were offered the job, you have, in effect, refused it. Instead, wait for the job offer; then start negotiating your salary.

Rule No. 5: Ask for a higher salary first, and consider benefits.

Within reason, always try to ask for a higher salary first. This will leave room for this amount to decrease during negotiations until it is closer to your original expectations. Remember to consider the entire compensation package when negotiating.[37] You may be willing to accept a lower salary if benefits such as insurance, flexible hours, time off, and retirement are attractive.

Rule No. 6: Be ready to bargain if offered a low starting salary.

Companies are often willing to pay more for someone who interviews well and fits their culture. If the company seems right to you and you are pleased with the sound of the open position but you have been offered a low salary, say, *That is somewhat lower than I had hoped, but this position does sound exciting. If I were to consider this, what sorts of things could I do to quickly become more valuable to this organization?* Also discuss such factors as bonuses based on performance or a shorter review period. You could say something like, *Thanks for the offer. The position is very much what I want in many ways, and I am delighted at your interest. If I start at this salary, may I be reviewed within six months with the goal of raising the salary to _____?*

Another possibility is to ask for more time to think about the low offer. Tell the interviewer that this is an important decision and you need some time to consider the offer. The next day you can call and say, *I am flattered by your offer, but I cannot accept because the salary is lower than I would like. Perhaps you could reconsider your offer or keep me in mind for future openings.*

Rule No. 7: Be honest.

Be honest throughout the entire negotiation process. Don't inflate the salaries of your previous positions to try to get more money. Don't tell an employer that you have received other job offers unless it is true. These lies can be grounds for being fired later on.

Rule No. 8: Get the final offer in writing.

Once you have agreed on a salary and compensation package, get the offer in writing. You should also follow up with a position acceptance message—letter or e-mail—as discussed earlier in the chapter.

CAREER APPLICATION. You have just passed the screening interview and have been asked to come in for a personal interview with the human resources representative and the hiring manager of a company where you are very eager to work. Although you are delighted with the company, you have promised yourself that you will not accept any position that pays less than $55,000 to start.

YOUR TASK. With a partner, role-play the positions of interviewer and interviewee. The interviewer sets the scene by discussing preliminaries and offers a salary of $50,000. The interviewee responds to preliminary questions and to the salary offer. Then, reverse roles and repeat the scenario.

Document Format Guide

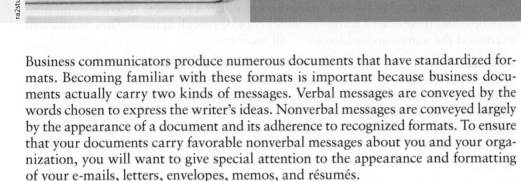

Business communicators produce numerous documents that have standardized formats. Becoming familiar with these formats is important because business documents actually carry two kinds of messages. Verbal messages are conveyed by the words chosen to express the writer's ideas. Nonverbal messages are conveyed largely by the appearance of a document and its adherence to recognized formats. To ensure that your documents carry favorable nonverbal messages about you and your organization, you will want to give special attention to the appearance and formatting of your e-mails, letters, envelopes, memos, and résumés.

E-Mail Messages

E-mail is an appropriate channel for short messages. Usually, e-mails do not replace business letters or memos that are lengthy, require permanent records, or transmit confidential or sensitive information. This section describes formats and usage. The following suggestions, illustrated in Figure A.1, may guide you in setting up the parts

Figure A.1 Typical E-Mail

To: Sara Staiger <sstaiger@carrier.com>
From: Alicia Shinoyama<ashinoyama@carrier.com>
Subject: Responding to Your Request to Add Dependents — Includes descriptive subject line

Hello, Sara, — Provides salutation to reflect friendliness and to mark the beginning of the message

Yes, you may add new dependents to your health plan coverage. Because you are a regular, active employee, you are eligible to add unmarried dependent children (biological, adopted, step, and foster) under age 26 if they are full-time students. You may also be eligible to enroll your domestic partner as your dependent, as part of a pilot program.

Uses single-spacing within paragraphs and double-spacing between paragraphs

For all new dependents, you must submit a completed Verification of Dependent Eligibility Form. You must also submit a photocopy of a document that verifies their eligibility. An acceptable verification document for a spouse is a photocopy of your marriage certificate. For children, submit a photocopy of a birth certificate, adoption certificate, or guardianship certificate. Please call the Health Benefits Unit at Ext. 2558 for more information or to ask for an application.

Alicia Shinoyama
Coordinator, Health Benefits
E-mail: ashinoyama@carrier.com — Closes with name and full contact information to ensure identification
Office: (719) 443-7791, Ext. 2558
Cell: (719) 381-3443

of any e-mail. Always check, however, with your organization to ensure that you follow its practices.

To Line. Include the receiver's e-mail address after *To*. If the receiver's address is recorded in your address book, you just have to click it. Be sure to enter all addresses very carefully since one mistyped letter prevents delivery.

From Line. Most mail programs automatically include your name and e-mail address after *From*.

Cc and Bcc. Insert the e-mail address of anyone who is to receive a copy of the message. *Cc* stands for carbon copy or courtesy copy. Don't be tempted, though, to send needless copies just because it is easy. *Bcc* stands for blind carbon copy. Some writers use *bcc* to send a copy of the message without the addressee's knowledge. Writers also use the *bcc* line for mailing lists. When a message is sent to a number of people and their e-mail addresses should not be revealed, the *bcc* line works well to conceal the names and addresses of all receivers.

Subject. Identify the subject of the e-mail with a brief but descriptive summary of the topic. Be sure to include enough information to be clear and compelling. Capitalize the initial letters of main words. Main words are all words except (a) the articles *a*, *an*, and *the*; (b) prepositions containing two or three letters (such as *at*, *to*, *on*, *by*, *for*); (c) the word *to* in an infinitive (*to work*, *to write*); and (d) the word *as*—unless any of these words are the first or last word in the subject line.

Salutation. Include a brief greeting, if you like. Some writers use a salutation such as *Dear Erica* followed by a comma or a colon. Others are more informal with *Hi, Erica*; *Hello, Erica*; *Good morning*; or *Greetings*.

Message. Ideally, cover just one topic in your message, and try to keep your total message under three screens in length. Single-space and be sure to use both upper- and lowercase letters. Double-space between paragraphs.

Closing. If you choose to conclude an e-mail with a closing, you might use *Cheers*, *Thanks*, *Best wishes*, or *Warm regards*, followed by your name and complete contact information. Some people omit their e-mail address because they think it is provided automatically. However, programs and routers do not always transmit the address. Except for messages to colleagues, always include your contact information in the closing.

Attachment. Use the attachment window or button to select the name of any file you wish to send with your e-mail. You can also attach a Web page to your message.

Business Letters

Business communicators write business letters primarily to correspond with people outside the organization. Letters may go to customers, vendors, other businesses, and the government. The following information will help you format your letters following conventional guidelines.

Conventional Letter Placement, Margins, and Line Spacing. Following are guidelines for formatting conventional business letters:

- For a clean look, choose a sans serif font such as Arial, Calibri, Tahoma, or Verdana. For a more traditional look, choose a serif font such as Times New Roman. Use a 10-point, 11-point, or 12-point size.
- Use a 2-inch top margin for the first page of a letter printed on letterhead stationery. This will place the date on line 13. Use a 1-inch top margin for second and succeeding pages.

- Justify only the left margin. Set the line spacing to single.
- Choose side margins according to the length of your letter. Set 1.5-inch margins for short letters (under 200 words) and 1-inch margins for longer letters (200 or more words).
- Leave from 2 to 10 blank lines following the date to balance the message on the page. You can make this adjustment after keying your message.

Formatting Letters With Microsoft Word. If you are working with Microsoft Word, the default margins are set at 1 inch and the default font is set at 11-point Calibri. The default setting for line spacing is 1.15, and the paragraph default is 10 points of blank space following each paragraph or each tap of the Enter key. Many letter writers find this extra space excessive, especially after parts of the letter that are normally single-spaced. The model documents in this book show conventional single-spacing with 1 blank line between paragraphs. To format your documents with conventional spacing and yet retain a clean look, we recommend that you change the Microsoft defaults to the following: Arial or Calibri font set for 11 points, line spacing at 1.0, and spacing before and after paragraphs at 0.

Spacing and Punctuation. In the distant past, typists left 2 spaces after end punctuation (periods, question marks, and so forth). This practice was necessary, it was thought, because typewriters did not have proportional spacing and sentences were easier to read when 2 spaces separated them. Professional typesetters, however, never followed this practice because they used proportional spacing, and readability was not a problem. Influenced by the look of typeset publications, most writers now leave only 1 space after end punctuation. As a practical matter, however, it is not wrong to use 2 spaces, if done consistently.

Business Letter Parts

Professional-looking business letters are arranged in a conventional sequence with standard parts. Following is a discussion of how to use these letter parts properly. Figure A.2 illustrates the parts of a block style letter.

Letterhead. Most business organizations use 8½ × 11-inch paper printed with a letterhead displaying their official name, street address, Web address, e-mail address, and telephone and fax numbers. The letterhead may also include a logo and an advertising message.

Dateline. If you are preparing a letter on letterhead paper, place the date 1 blank line below the last line of the letterhead or 2 inches from the top edge of the paper (line 13). If you are using plain paper, place the date immediately below your return address. Because the date goes on line 13, start the return address an appropriate number of lines above it. The most common dateline format is as follows: *June 9, 2019.* Don't add *rd, nd,* or *st* when writing the date. For European or military correspondence, use the following dateline format: *9 June 2019.* Notice that no commas are used.

Addressee and Delivery Notations. Delivery notations such as *VIA U.S. MAIL, E-MAIL, FAX TRANSMISSION, FEDEX, MESSENGER DELIVERY, CONFIDENTIAL,* and *CERTIFIED MAIL* are typed in all capital letters between the dateline and the inside address.

Inside Address. Type the inside address—that is, the address of the organization or person receiving the letter—single-spaced, starting at the left margin. The number of lines between the dateline and the inside address depends on the size of the letter body, the type size (point or pitch size), and the length of the typing lines. Generally, 1 to 9 blank lines are appropriate.

Figure A.2 Block and Modified Block Letter Styles

Letterhead

Island Graphics
893 Dillingham Boulevard
Honolulu, HI 96817-8817
(808) 493-2310
http://www.islandgraphics.com

▼ Dateline is 2 inches from the top or 1 blank line below letterhead

Dateline — September 13, 2019

▼ 1 to 9 blank lines

Inside address —
Mr. T. M. Wilson, President
Visual Concept Enterprises
1901 Kaumualii Highway
Lihue, HI 96766

▼ 1 blank line

Salutation — Dear Mr. Wilson:

▼ 1 blank line

Subject line — Subject: Block Letter Style

▼ 1 blank line

This letter illustrates block letter style, about which you asked. All typed lines begin at the left margin. The date is usually placed 2 inches from the top edge of the paper or one blank line below the last line of the letterhead, whichever position is lower.

Body —
This letter also shows mixed punctuation. A colon follows the salutation, and a comma follows the complimentary close. Open punctuation requires no colon after the salutation and no comma following the close; however, open punctuation is seldom seen today.

If a subject line is included, it appears one blank line below the salutation. The word *Subject* is optional. Most readers will recognize a statement in this position as the subject without an identifying label. The complimentary close appears one blank line below the end of the last paragraph.

▼ 1 blank line

Complimentary close — Sincerely,

▼ 3 blank lines

Mark H. Wong

Signature block —
Mark H. Wong
Graphic Designer

▼ 1 blank line

Reference initials — MHW:pil

**Modified block style,
Mixed punctuation**

In the modified block style letter shown at the left, the date is centered or aligned with the complimentary close and signature block, which start at the center. Mixed punctuation includes a colon after the salutation and a comma after the complimentary close, as shown above and at the left.

Be careful to duplicate the exact wording and spelling of the recipient's name and address on your documents. Usually, you can copy this information from the letterhead of the correspondence you are answering. If, for example, you are responding to *Jackson & Perkins Company*, do not address your letter to *Jackson and Perkins Corp.*

Always be sure to include a courtesy title such as *Mr., Ms., Mrs., Dr.,* or *Professor* before a person's name in the inside address—for both the letter and the envelope. Although many women in business today favor *Ms.,* you should use whatever title the addressee prefers.

Generally spell out *Avenue, Street,* and *Company* unless they appear as abbreviations in the printed letterhead of the document being answered.

Attention Line. An attention line allows you to send your message officially to an organization but to direct it to a specific individual, officer, or department. However, if you know an individual's complete name, it is always better to use it as the first line of the inside address and avoid an attention line. Placing an attention line first in the address block enables you to paste it directly onto the envelope:

Attention Marketing Director
The MultiMedia Company
931 Calkins Avenue
Rochester, NY 14301

Salutation. For most letter styles, place the letter greeting, or salutation, 1 blank line below the last line of the inside address or the attention line (if used). If the letter is addressed to an individual, use that person's courtesy title and last name (*Dear Ms. Davis*). Even if you are on a first-name basis (*Dear Kim*), be sure to add a colon (not a comma or a semicolon) after the salutation. Do not use an individual's full name in the salutation (not *Dear Ms. Kim Davis*) unless you are unsure of gender (*Dear Leslie Davis*).

It's always best to address messages to people. If, however, a message is addressed to an organization, consider these salutations: an organization of men (*Gentlemen*), an organization of women (*Ladies*), an organization of men and women (*Ladies and Gentlemen*). If a message is addressed to an undetermined individual, consider these salutations: a woman (*Dear Madam*), a man (*Dear Sir*), a title (*Dear Customer Service Representative*).

Subject and Reference Lines. Although experts suggest placing the subject line 1 blank line below the salutation, many businesses actually place it above the salutation. Use whatever style your organization prefers. Reference lines often show policy or file numbers; they generally appear 1 blank line above the salutation. Use initial capital letters for the main words or all capital letters.

Body. Most business letters and memorandums are single-spaced, with double-spacing between paragraphs. Very short messages may be double-spaced with indented paragraphs.

Complimentary Close. Typed 1 blank line below the last line of the letter, the complimentary close may be formal (*Very truly yours*) or informal (*Sincerely* or *Cordially*).

Signature Block. In most letter styles, the writer's typed name and optional identification appear 3 or 4 blank lines below the complimentary close. The combination of name, title, and organization information should be arranged to achieve a balanced look. The name and title may appear on the same line or on separate lines, depending on the length of each. Use commas to separate categories within the same line, but not to conclude a line.

Sincerely yours,   Cordially yours,

Jeremy M. Wood   *Casandra Baker-Murillo*

Jeremy M. Wood, Manager   Casandra Baker-Murillo
Technical Sales and Services   Executive Vice President

Some organizations include their names in the signature block. In such cases the organization name appears in all caps 1 blank line below the complimentary close, as shown here:

Cordially,

LIPTON COMPUTER SERVICES

Shelina A. Simpson

Shelina A. Simpson
Executive Assistant

Reference Initials. If used, the initials of the typist and writer are typed 1 blank line below the writer's name and title. Generally, the writer's initials are capitalized and the typist's are lowercased, but this format varies.

Enclosure Notation.   When an enclosure or attachment accompanies a document, a notation to that effect appears 1 blank line below the reference initials. This notation reminds the typist to insert the enclosure in the envelope, and it reminds the recipient to look for the enclosure or attachment. The notation may be spelled out (*Enclosure, Attachment*), or it may be abbreviated (*Enc., Att.*). It may indicate the number of enclosures or attachments, and it may also identify a specific enclosure (*Enclosure: Form 1099*).

Copy Notation.   If you make copies of correspondence for other individuals, you may use *cc* to indicate courtesy copy, *pc* to indicate photocopy, or merely *c* for any kind of copy. A colon following the initial(s) is optional.

Second-Page Heading.   When a letter extends beyond one page, use plain paper of the same quality and color as the first page. Identify the second and succeeding pages with a heading consisting of the name of the addressee, the page number, and the date. Use the following format or the one shown in Figure A.3:

Ms. Sara Hendricks   2   May 3, 2019

Both headings appear 6 blank lines (1 inch) from the top edge of the paper followed by 2 blank lines to separate them from the continuing text. Avoid using a second page if you have only 1 line or the complimentary close and signature block to fill that page.

Plain-Paper Return Address.   If you prepare a personal or business letter on plain paper, place your address immediately above the date. Do not include your name; you will type (and sign) your name at the end of your letter. If your return address

Figure A.3 Second-Page Heading

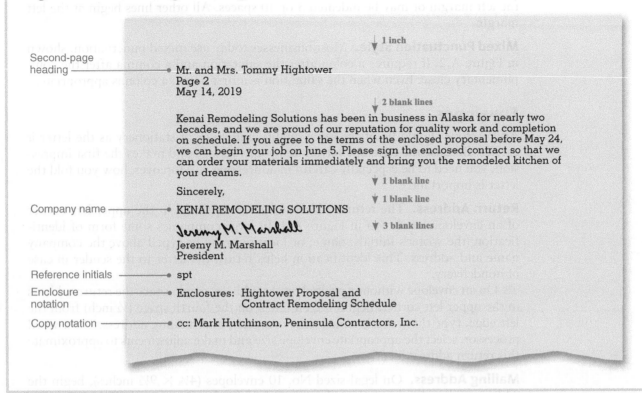

Second-page heading →

Mr. and Mrs. Tommy Hightower
Page 2
May 14, 2019

↓ 1 inch

↓ 2 blank lines

Kenai Remodeling Solutions has been in business in Alaska for nearly two decades, and we are proud of our reputation for quality work and completion on schedule. If you agree to the terms of the enclosed proposal before May 24, we can begin your job on June 5. Please sign the enclosed contract so that we can order your materials immediately and bring you the remodeled kitchen of your dreams.

Sincerely,

↓ 1 blank line

↓ 1 blank line

Company name →

KENAI REMODELING SOLUTIONS

↓ 3 blank lines

Jeremy M. Marshall
Jeremy M. Marshall
President

Reference initials → spt

Enclosure notation → Enclosures: Hightower Proposal and
                                    Contract Remodeling Schedule

Copy notation → cc: Mark Hutchinson, Peninsula Contractors, Inc.

contains 2 lines, begin typing so that the date appears 2 inches from the top. Avoid abbreviations except for a two-letter state or province abbreviation.

580 East Leffels Street
Springfield, OH 45501
December 14, 2019

Ms. Ellen Siemens
Escrow Department
TransOhio First Federal
1220 Wooster Boulevard
Columbus, OH 43218-2900

Dear Ms. Siemens:

For letters in the block style, type the return address at the left margin. For modified block style letters, start the return address at the center to align with the complimentary close.

Letter and Punctuation Styles

Most business letters today are prepared in either block or modified block style, and they generally use mixed punctuation.

Block Style. In the block style, shown in Figure A.2, all lines begin at the left margin. This style is a favorite because it is easy to format.

Modified Block Style. The modified block style differs from the block style in that the date and closing lines appear in the center, as shown at the bottom of Figure A.2. The date may be (a) centered, (b) begun at the center of the page (to align with the closing lines), or (c) backspaced from the right margin. The signature block—including the complimentary close, writer's name and title, or organization identification—begins at the center. The first line of each paragraph may begin at the left margin or may be indented 5 or 10 spaces. All other lines begin at the left margin.

Mixed Punctuation Style. Most businesses today use mixed punctuation, shown in Figure A.2. It requires a colon after the salutation and a comma after the complimentary close. Even when the salutation is a first name, a colon is appropriate.

Envelopes

An envelope should be of the same quality and color of stationery as the letter it carries. Because the envelope introduces your message and makes the first impression, you need to be especially careful in addressing it. Moreover, how you fold the letter is important.

Return Address. The return address is usually printed in the upper left corner of an envelope, as shown in Figure A.4. In large companies some form of identification (the writer's initials, name, or location) may be typed above the company name and address. This identification helps return the letter to the sender in case of nondelivery.

On an envelope without a printed return address, single-space the return address in the upper left corner. Beginning on line 3 on the fourth space (½ inch) from the left edge, type the writer's name, title, company, and mailing address. On a word processor, select the appropriate envelope size and make adjustments to approximate this return address location.

Mailing Address. On legal-sized No. 10 envelopes (4⅛ × 9½ inches), begin the address on line 13 about 4¼ inches from the left edge, as shown in Figure A.4. For small envelopes (3⅝ × 6½ inches), begin typing on line 12 about 2½ inches from

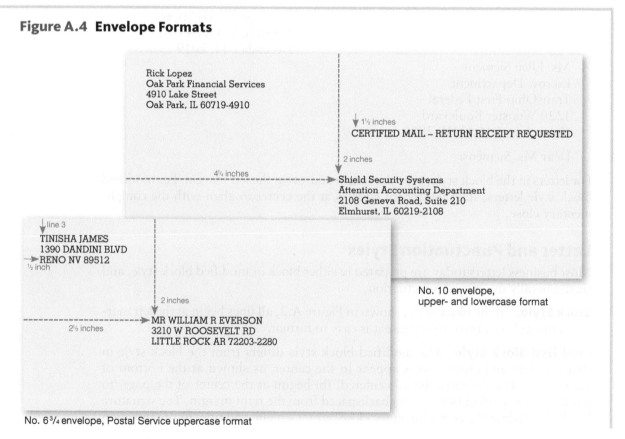

Figure A.4 Envelope Formats

Rick Lopez
Oak Park Financial Services
4910 Lake Street
Oak Park, IL 60719-4910

↓ 1½ inches
CERTIFIED MAIL – RETURN RECEIPT REQUESTED

2 inches

4¼ inches

Shield Security Systems
Attention Accounting Department
2108 Geneva Road, Suite 210
Elmhurst, IL 60219-2108

No. 10 envelope,
upper- and lowercase format

↓ line 3
TINISHA JAMES
1390 DANDINI BLVD
RENO NV 89512
½ inch

2 inches

2½ inches

MR WILLIAM R EVERSON
3210 W ROOSEVELT RD
LITTLE ROCK AR 72203-2280

No. 6¾ envelope, Postal Service uppercase format

the left edge. On a word processor, select the correct envelope size and check to be sure your address falls in the desired location.

The U.S. Postal Service recommends that addresses be typed in all caps without any punctuation. This Postal Service style, shown in the small envelope in Figure A.4, was originally developed to facilitate scanning by optical character readers. Today's OCRs, however, are so sophisticated that they scan uppercase and lowercase letters easily. Many companies today do not follow the Postal Service format because they prefer to use the same format for the envelope as for the inside address. If the same format is used, writers can take advantage of word processing programs to copy

Figure A.5 Abbreviations of States, Territories, and Provinces

State or Territory	Two-Letter Abbreviation	State or Territory	Two-Letter Abbreviation
Alabama	AL	North Carolina	NC
Alaska	AK	North Dakota	ND
Arizona	AZ	Ohio	OH
Arkansas	AR	Oklahoma	OK
California	CA	Oregon	OR
Canal Zone	CZ	Pennsylvania	PA
Colorado	CO	Puerto Rico	PR
Connecticut	CT	Rhode Island	RI
Delaware	DE	South Carolina	SC
District of Columbia	DC	South Dakota	SD
Florida	FL	Tennessee	TN
Georgia	GA	Texas	TX
Guam	GU	Utah	UT
Hawaii	HI	Vermont	VT
Idaho	ID	Virgin Islands	VI
Illinois	IL	Virginia	VA
Indiana	IN	Washington	WA
Iowa	IA	West Virginia	WV
Kansas	KS	Wisconsin	WI
Kentucky	KY	Wyoming	WY
Louisiana	LA	**Canadian Province**	
Maine	ME	Alberta	AB
Maryland	MD	British Columbia	BC
Massachusetts	MA	Labrador	LB
Michigan	MI	Manitoba	MB
Minnesota	MN	New Brunswick	NB
Mississippi	MS	Newfoundland	NF
Missouri	MO	Northwest Territories	NT
Montana	MT	Nova Scotia	NS
Nebraska	NE	Ontario	ON
Nevada	NV	Prince Edward Island	PE
New Hampshire	NH	Quebec	PQ
New Jersey	NJ	Saskatchewan	SK
New Mexico	NM	Yukon Territory	YT
New York	NY		

the inside address to the envelope, thus saving keystrokes and reducing errors. Having the same format on both the inside address and the envelope also looks more professional and consistent. For those reasons you may choose to use the familiar uppercase and lowercase combination format. But you will want to check with your organization to learn its preference.

In addressing your envelopes for delivery in the United States or in Canada, use the two-letter state and province abbreviations shown in Figure A.5. Notice that these abbreviations are in capital letters without periods.

Folding. The way a letter is folded and inserted into an envelope sends additional nonverbal messages about a writer's professionalism and carefulness. Most businesspeople follow the procedures shown here, which produce the least number of creases to distract readers.

For large No. 10 envelopes, begin with the letter face up. Fold slightly less than one third of the sheet toward the top, as shown in the following diagram. Then fold down the top third to within ⅓ inch of the bottom fold. Insert the letter into the envelope with the last fold toward the bottom of the envelope.

For small No. 6¾ envelopes, begin by folding the bottom up to within ⅓ inch of the top edge. Then fold the right third over to the left. Fold the left third to within ⅓ inch of the last fold. Insert the last fold into the envelope first.

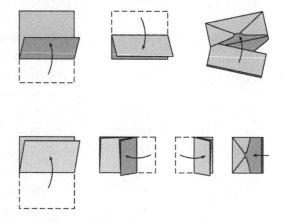

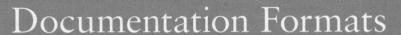

Documentation Formats

everything possible/Shutterstock.com

For many reasons business writers are careful to properly document report data. Citing sources strengthens a writer's argument, as you learned in Chapter 10, while also shielding the writer from charges of plagiarism. Moreover, good references help readers pursue further research. As a business writer, you can expect to routinely borrow ideas and words to show that your ideas are in sync with the rest of the business world, to gain support from business leaders, or simply to save time in developing your ideas. To be ethical, however, you must show clearly what you borrowed and from whom.

Source notes tell where you found your information. For quotations, paraphrases, graphs, drawings, or online images you have borrowed, you need to cite the original authors' names, full titles, and the dates and facts of publication. The purpose of source notes, which appear at the end of your report, is to direct your readers to the complete references. Many systems of documentation are used by businesses, but they all have one goal: to provide clear, consistent documentation.

Rarely, business writers use content notes, which are identified with a raised number at the end of the quotation. At the bottom of the page, the number is repeated with a remark, clarification, or background information.

During your business career, you may use a variety of documentation systems. The two most common systems in the academic world are those of the American Psychological Association (APA) and the Modern Language Association (MLA). Each organization has its own style for text references and bibliographic lists. This textbook uses a modified MLA style. However, business organizations may use their own documentation systems.

Before starting any research project, whether for a class or in a business, inquire about the preferred documentation style. For school assignments ask about specifics. For example, should you include URLs and dates of retrieval for Web sources? For workplace assignments ask to see a previous report either in hard-copy version or as an e-mail attachment.

In your business and class writing, you will usually provide a brief citation in parentheses that refers readers to the complete reference that appears in a references or works-cited section at the end of your document. Following is a summary of APA and MLA formats with examples.

American Psychological Association Format

First used primarily in the social and physical sciences, the APA documentation format uses the author-date method of citation. This method, with its emphasis on current information, is especially appropriate for business. Within the text, the date of publication of the referenced work appears immediately after the author's name (Rivera, 2016), as illustrated in the brief APA example in Figure B.1. At the end of the report, all references appear alphabetically on a page labeled "References." The APA format does not require a date of retrieval for online sources, but you should check with your instructor or supervisor about the preferred format for your class or organization. For more information about the APA format, see the *Publication Manual of the American Psychological Association*, Sixth Edition (Washington, DC: American Psychological Association, 2009).

APA In-Text Format. Within your text, document each text, figure, or personal source with a short description in parentheses. Following are selected guidelines summarizing the important elements of APA style:

- For a direct quotation, include the last name of the author(s), if available, and the year of publication; for example, *(Meadows, 2016, p. 32)*. If no author is shown in the text or on a website, use a shortened title or a heading that can be easily located on the References page; for example, *(History, n.d.)*.

- If you mention the author in the text, do not use the name again in the parenthetical reference. Just cite the date; for example, *According to Meadows (2016)*.

Figure B.1 Portions of APA Text Page and References

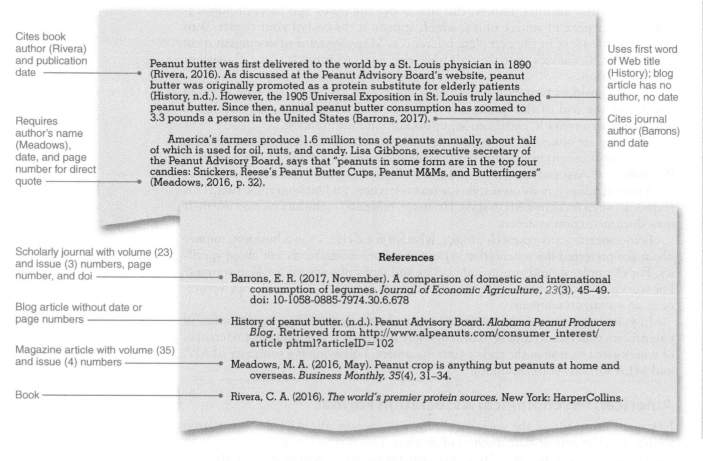

Cites book author (Rivera) and publication date

Requires author's name (Meadows), date, and page number for direct quote

Peanut butter was first delivered to the world by a St. Louis physician in 1890 (Rivera, 2016). As discussed at the Peanut Advisory Board's website, peanut butter was originally promoted as a protein substitute for elderly patients (History, n.d.). However, the 1905 Universal Exposition in St. Louis truly launched peanut butter. Since then, annual peanut butter consumption has zoomed to 3.3 pounds a person in the United States (Barrons, 2017).

America's farmers produce 1.6 million tons of peanuts annually, about half of which is used for oil, nuts, and candy. Lisa Gibbons, executive secretary of the Peanut Advisory Board, says that "peanuts in some form are in the top four candies: Snickers, Reese's Peanut Butter Cups, Peanut M&Ms, and Butterfingers" (Meadows, 2016, p. 32).

Uses first word of Web title (History); blog article has no author, no date

Cites journal author (Barrons) and date

Scholarly journal with volume (23) and issue (3) numbers, page number, and doi

Blog article without date or page numbers

Magazine article with volume (35) and issue (4) numbers

Book

References

Barrons, E. R. (2017, November). A comparison of domestic and international consumption of legumes. *Journal of Economic Agriculture, 23*(3), 45–49. doi: 10-1058-0885-7974.30.6.678

History of peanut butter. (n.d.). Peanut Advisory Board. *Alabama Peanut Producers Blog*. Retrieved from http://www.alpeanuts.com/consumer_interest/ article phtml?articleID=102

Meadows, M. A. (2016, May). Peanut crop is anything but peanuts at home and overseas. *Business Monthly, 35*(4), 31–34.

Rivera, C. A. (2016). *The world's premier protein sources.* New York: HarperCollins.

- Search for website dates on the home page or at the bottom of Web pages. If no date is available for a source, use *n.d.*

APA Reference Format. As with all documentation methods, APA has specific capitalization, punctuation, and sequencing rules, some of which are summarized here:

- Include the last name of the author(s) followed by initials. APA is gender neutral, so first and middle names are not spelled out; for example, *(Aten, K.)*.
- Show the date of publication in parentheses immediately after the author's name. A magazine citation will also include the month and day in the parentheses.
- Use sentence-style capitalization for all titles except journal article titles. Do not use quotation marks.
- Italicize titles of magazines, newspapers, books, and journals.
- Include the digital object identifier (DOI) when available for online periodicals. If no DOI is available, include the home page URL unless the source is difficult to retrieve without the entire URL.
- Break a URL or DOI only before a mark of punctuation such as a slash.

If the website content may change, as in a wiki, include a retrieval date; for example, *Retrieved 7 July 2017 from* http://www.encyclopediaofmath.org/index.php /MainPage. Please note, however, that many instructors require that all Web references be identified by their URLs.

To better understand the format of a scholarly journal article in the References section, see Figure B.2.

For an expanded list of APA documentation format examples, see Figure B.3.

Modern Language Association Format

Writers in the humanities and the liberal arts frequently use the Modern Language Association (MLA) documentation format, illustrated briefly in Figure B.4. In parentheses close to the textual reference, include the author's name and page cited *(Rivera 25)*. At the end of your writing on a page titled "Works Cited," list all the sources alphabetically. Some writers include all of the sources consulted. Include the URLs for Web references. For more information, consult the *MLA Handbook*, Eighth Edition (New York: The Modern Language Association of America, 2016).

Figure B.2 Anatomy of an APA Journal Article

Figure B.3 APA Sample References

Reference

Print magazine or newspaper article → Bachman, A. (2016, April 17). Smart investing tips. *Small Business Weekly*. pp. 10–12.

Bell, R. L., & Martin, J. S. (2014) *Managerial communication*. New York: Business Expert Press. ← Book

Video → Butman, J. (2013, May 29). *Becoming an idea entrepreneur*. Harvard Business Review (Producer). (Video). Retrieved from https://hbr.org/video/2363618060001/becoming-an-idea-entrepreneur

C. H. Robinson. (2015). *2015 Annual Report*. Retrieved from http://investor.crobinson.com/phoenix.zhtml?c=97366&p=irol-reportsannual ← Annual report

Blog → Cohen, H. (2015, May 4). How to succeed with earned media: 34 case studies. Media PR (Blog). Retrieved from http://heidicohen.com/earned-media-examples

Cox, A. T., & Followill, R. (2012). The equitable financing of growth: A proportionate share methodology for calculating individual development impact fees. *The Engineering Economist: A Journal Devoted to the Problems of Capital Investment, 57*(3), 141–156. doi:10.1080/0013791X.2012.702195 ← Print journal with volume (57) and issue (3) numbers as well as DOI

Online magazine with URL → Davidson, A. (2015, May 5). What Hollywood can teach us about the future of work. *New York Times Magazine*. Retrieved from http://www.nytimes.com/2015/05/10/magazine/what-hollywood-can-teach-us-about-the-future-of-work.html?ref=business

Dunams, A. (2014, February 21). *All in: Elevating your leadership game*. (Audio podcast). Retrieved from http://www.aliciadunams.com/bestselling-author-alicia-dunams-all-in-evaluating-your-leadership-game-podcast-series-makes-itunes-new-and-noteworthy ← Podcast

Online article, no author → How to start a business online. (2015). *Entrepreneur*. Retrieved from http://www.entrepreneur.com/article/17524

Heuristic. (n.d.). In *Merriam-Webster's online dictionary* (11th ed.). Retrieved from http://www.m-w/dictionary/heuristic ← Online reference work, no author or editor

Online journal → Ola, J. C., & Proffitt, D. (2015). The stock market response to CEO changes: Does gender matter? *International Journal of Business and Management, 10*(5). Retrieved from http://www.ccsenet.org/journal/index.php/ijbm/article/view/45287

Riley, N. S. (2015, May 1). Birds, bees and bureaucracies. (Review of the book *Too Hot to Handle*, by Jonathan Zimmerman). *The Wall Street Journal*, p. A11. ← Book review

Note: Although APA style prescribes double-spacing for the references page, we show single-spacing to conserve space and to represent preferred business usage.

MLA In-Text Format. Following any borrowed material in your text, provide a short parenthetical description. Here are selected guidelines summarizing important elements of MLA style:

■ For a direct quotation, enclose in parentheses the last name of the author(s), if available, and the page number without a comma *(Rivera 25)*. If a website has no author, use a shortened title of the page or a heading that is easily found on the works-cited page *(History)*.

Figure B.4 Portions of MLA Text Page and Works Cited

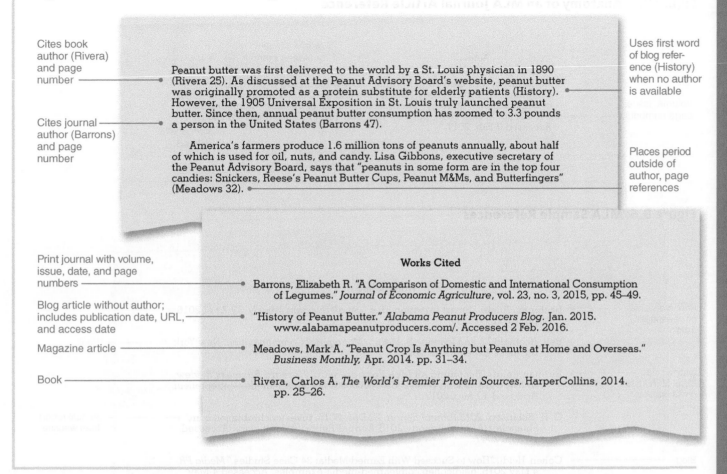

Cites book author (Rivera) and page number

Cites journal author (Barrons) and page number

Uses first word of blog reference (History) when no author is available

Places period outside of author, page references

Peanut butter was first delivered to the world by a St. Louis physician in 1890 (Rivera 25). As discussed at the Peanut Advisory Board's website, peanut butter was originally promoted as a protein substitute for elderly patients (History). However, the 1905 Universal Exposition in St. Louis truly launched peanut butter. Since then, annual peanut butter consumption has zoomed to 3.3 pounds a person in the United States (Barrons 47).

America's farmers produce 1.6 million tons of peanuts annually, about half of which is used for oil, nuts, and candy. Lisa Gibbons, executive secretary of the Peanut Advisory Board, says that "peanuts in some form are in the top four candies: Snickers, Reese's Peanut Butter Cups, Peanut M&Ms, and Butterfingers" (Meadows 32).

Print journal with volume, issue, date, and page numbers

Blog article without author; includes publication date, URL, and access date

Magazine article

Book

Works Cited

Barrons, Elizabeth R. "A Comparison of Domestic and International Consumption of Legumes." *Journal of Economic Agriculture*, vol. 23, no. 3, 2015, pp. 45–49.

"History of Peanut Butter." *Alabama Peanut Producers Blog.* Jan. 2015. www.alabamapeanutproducers.com/. Accessed 2 Feb. 2016.

Meadows, Mark A. "Peanut Crop Is Anything but Peanuts at Home and Overseas." *Business Monthly,* Apr. 2014. pp. 31–34.

Rivera, Carlos A. *The World's Premier Protein Sources.* HarperCollins, 2014. pp. 25–26.

- If you mention the author in the text, do not use the name again in parentheses, as *According to Rivera (27).*

MLA Works-Cited Format. In a section called "Works Cited," list all references alphabetically by author or, if no author is available, by title. As with all documentation methods, MLA has specific capitalization and sequencing rules. Some of the most significant rules are summarized here:

- Include the author's last name first, followed by the first name and initial, as (*Rivera, Charles A.*).
- Enclose in quotation marks the titles of articles, essays, stories, chapters of books, pages in websites, articles in blogs, individual episodes of television and radio broadcasts, and short musical compositions.
- Italicize the titles of books, journals, websites, magazines, and newspapers.
- Include the URL for online references, unless your instructor or organization prefers to omit URLs.
- Do not identify the medium (such as *Web, Print,* and *Video*) as required in the previous *MLA Handbook.*

To better understand the anatomy of the format of an MLA scholarly journal article reference, see Figure B.5. For an expanded list of contemporary MLA documentation format examples, see Figure B.6.

Figure B.5 Anatomy of an MLA Journal Article Reference

Authors

Article title in quotation marks

Volume, issue, page numbers

Aten, Kathryn, and Gail Fann Thomas. "Crowdsourcing Strategizing: Communication Technology Affordances and the Communicative Constitution of Organizational Strategy." *International Journal of Business Communication*, vol. 53, no. 2, Apr. 2016, pp. 148–180. doi: 10.1177/2329488415627269. Accessed 3 Feb. 2017.

Journal title in italics

Access date

Date of publication

Digital object identifier (doi)

Figure B.6 MLA Sample References

Works Cited

Print magazine or newspaper article

Bachman, Alicia. "Smart Investing Tips." *Small Business Weekly.* 17 April 2016, pp. 10–12.

Bell, Reginald L., and Jeanette S. Martin. *Managerial Communication.* New York: Business Expert Press, 2014.

Book

Online video
Note: MLA style omits *http://* in URLs

Butman, John. "Becoming an Idea Entrepreneur." *Harvard Business Review*, 29 May 2013, hbr.org/video/23636180600001/becoming-an-idea-entrepreneur. Accessed 19 Aug. 2017.

C. H. Robinson. *2015 Annual Report.* 22 Dec. 2015, investor.chrobinson.com/ Financials/Annual-Reports/2015-Annual-Report/default.aspx. Accessed 12 Sep. 2017.

Annual report from website

Blog

Cohen, Heidi. "How to Succeed With Earned Media: 34 Case Studies." *Media PR,* 4 May 2015, heidicohen.com/earned-media-examples. Accessed 4 May 2015.

Cox, Arthur T., and Robert Followill. "The Equitable Financing of Growth: A Proportionate Share Methodology for Calculating Individual Development Impact Fees." *The Engineering Economist: A Journal Devoted to the Problems of Capital Investment,* vol. 57, no. 3 (2012), pp. 141–156. Accessed 6 Jan. 2013.

Print journal with volume (57) and issue (3) numbers

Online magazine

Davidson, Adam. "What Hollywood Can Teach Us About the Future of Work." 5 May 2015, www.nytimes.com/2015/05/10/magazine/what-hollywood-can-teach-us-about-the-future-of-work.html?_r=0. Accessed 9 July 2015.

Dunams, Alicia. "All In: Elevating Your Leadership Game." 21 Feb. 2014, www.stitcher.com/podcast/alicia-dunams/all-in-podcast-with-alicia-dunams. Accessed 4 Feb. 2016.

Podcast

Online article, no author

"How to Start a Business Online." *Entrepreneur,* 2015, www-entrepreneur.com/ article/17524. Accessed 23 May 2017.

Hunter, Douglas. "Re: CEOs' exorbitant salaries." Received by Hector Sotomeyor, 23 June 2017.

E-mail message

Online journal with volume (10) and issue (5) numbers as well as doi

Ola, J. Christian, and Dennis Proffitt. "The Stock Market Response to CEO Changes: Does Gender Matter?" *International Journal of Business and Management,* vol. 10, no. 5, 2015, www.ccsenet.org/journal/index.php/ijbm/article/view/45287 Accessed 10 Apr. 2017. doi: http://dx.doi.org/10.5539/ijbm.v10n5p1

Riley, Naomi Schaefer. "Birds, Bees and Bureaucracies." *The Wall Street Journal.* Review of *Too Hot to Handle,* by Jonathan Zimmerman. 1 May 2015, p. 11.

Book review

Note: Access dates for online references are optional. Check with your instructor or organization about whether to cite URLs and dates of access.

Correction Symbols and Proofreading Marks

In marking your papers, your instructor may use the following symbols or abbreviations to indicate writing weaknesses. Studying these symbols and suggestions will help you understand your instructor's remarks. Knowing this information can also help you evaluate and improve your own e-mails, memos, letters, reports, and other writing. These symbols are keyed to the Grammar/Mechanics Handbook and to the text.

Adj	Hyphenate two or more adjectives that are joined to create a compound modifier before a noun. See G/M 1.17e.
Adv	Use adverbs, not adjectives, to describe or limit the action. See G/M 1.17d.
Apos	Use apostrophes to show possession. See G/M 2.20–2.22.
Assgn	Follow the assignment instructions.
Awk	Recast to avoid awkward expression.
Bias	Use inclusive, bias-free language. See Chapter 2.
Cap	Use capitalization appropriately. See G/M 3.01–3.16.
CmConj	Use a comma before the coordinating conjunction in a compound sentence. See G/M 2.05.
CmDate	Use commas appropriately in dates, addresses, geographical names, degrees, and long numbers. See G/M 2.04.
CmIn	Use commas to set off internal sentence interrupters. See G/M 2.06c.
CmIntr	Use commas to separate introductory clauses and certain phrases from independent clauses. See G/M 2.06.
CmSer	Use commas to separate three or more items (words, phrases, or short clauses) in a series. See G/M 2.01.
Coh	Improve coherence between ideas. Repeat key ideas, use pronouns, or use transitional expressions. See Chapter 3.
Cl	Improve the clarity of ideas or expression so that the point is better understood.
CS	Avoid comma-splice sentences, Do not use a comma to splice (join) two independent clauses. See Chapter 3.

CmUn	Avoid unnecessary commas. See G/M 2.15.
:	Use a colon after a complete thought that introduces a list of items. Use a colon in business letter salutations and to introduce long quotations. See G/M 2.17–2.19.
DM	Avoid dangling modifiers by placing modifiers close to the words they describe or limit. See Chapter 3.
Dash	Use a dash to set off parenthetical elements, to emphasize sentence interruptions, or to separate an introductory list from a summarizing statement. See G/M 2.26.
Direct	Use the direct strategy by emphasizing the main idea. See Chapter 3.
Filler	Avoid fillers such *as there are* or long lead-ins such as *this is to inform you that*. See Chapter 4.
Format	Choose an appropriate format for this document.
Frag	Avoid fragments by expressing ideas in complete sentences. A fragment is a broken-off part of a sentence. See Chapter 3.
MM	Avoid misplaced modifiers by placing modifiers close to the words they describe or limit. See Chapter 3.
Num	Use number or word form appropriately. See G/M 4.01–4.13.
Ob	Avoid stating the obvious.
Org	Improve organization by grouping similar ideas.
Par	Express ideas in parallel form. See Chapter 3.
Paren	Use parentheses to set off nonessential sentence elements such as explanations, directions, questions, or references. See G/M 2.27.
Period	Use one period to end a statement, command, indirect question, or polite request. See G/M 2.23.
Pos	Express an idea positively rather than negatively. See Chapter 2.
PosPro	Use possessive-case pronouns to show ownership. See G/M 1.07 and 1.08d.
Pro	Use nominative-case pronouns as subjects of verbs and as subject complements. Use objective-case pronouns as objects of prepositions and verbs. See G/M 1.07 and 1.08.
ProAgr	Make pronouns agree in number and gender with the words to which they refer (their antecedents). See G/M 1.09.
ProVag	Be sure that pronouns such as *it, which, this*, and *that* refer to clear antecedents.
?	Use a question mark after a direct question and after statements with questions appended. See G/M 2.24.
Quo	Use quotation marks to enclose the exact words of a speaker or writer; to distinguish words used in a special sense; or to enclose titles of articles, chapters, or other short works. See G/M 2.28.
Redun	Avoid expressions that repeat meaning or include unnecessary words. See Chapter 4.

RunOn	Avoid run-on (fused) sentences. A sentence with two independent clauses must be joined by a coordinating conjunctions (*and, or, nor, but*) or by a semicolon (;). See Chapter 3.
Self	Use *self*-ending pronouns only when they refer to previously mentioned nouns or pronouns. See G/M 1.08h.
;	Use a semicolon to join closely related independent clauses. A semicolon is also an option to join separate items in a series when one or more of the items contain internal commas. See G/M 2.16.
Shift	Avoid a confusing shift in verb tense, mood, or voice. See G/M 1.15c.
Sp	Check misspelled word(s).
Trans	Use an appropriate transition. See Chapter 3 and Chapter 12.
Tone	Use a conversational, positive, and courteous tone that promotes goodwill. See Chapter 2.
You	Focus on developing the "you" view. See Chapter 2.
VbAgr	Make verbs agree with subjects. See G/M 1.10.
VbMood	Use the subjunctive mood to express hypothetical (untrue) ideas. See G/M 1.12.
VbTnse	Use present-tense, past-tense, and part-participle forms correctly. See G/M 1.13.
VbVce	Use active- and passive-voice verbs appropriately. See G/M 1.11.
WC	Focus on precise word choice. See Chapter 4.
Wordy	Avoid wordiness including flabby expressions, long lead-ins, unnecessary *there is/are* fillers, redundancies, and trite business phrases. See Chapter 4.

Figure C.1 Proofreading Marks

Proofreading Marks

Proofreading Mark	Draft Copy	Final Copy
⪤ Align horizontally	TO: Rick Munoz	TO: Rick Munoz
‖ Align vertically	166.32 132.45	166.32 132.45
☰ Capitalize	Coca-cola	Coca-Cola
	sending a pdf file	sending a PDF file
◡ Close up space	meeting at 3 p.m.	meeting at 3 p.m.
⏋⏉ Center	Recommendations	Recommendations
ℱ Delete	in my final judgement	in my judgment
∨ Insert apostrophe	our companys product	our company's product
∧ Insert comma	you will of course	you will, of course,
⩘ Insert hyphen	tax free income	tax-free income
⊙ Insert period	Ms Holly Hines	Ms. Holly Hines
∨ Insert quotation mark	shareholders receive a bonus.	shareholders receive a "bonus."
# Insert space	wordprocessing program	word processing program
/ Lowercase (remove capitals)	the Vice President	the vice president
	HUMAN RESOURCES	Human Resources
⊏ Move to left	I. Labor costs	I. Labor costs
⊐ Move to right	A. Findings of study	A. Findings of study
○ Spell out	aimed at 2 depts	aimed at two departments
¶ Start new paragraph	Keep the screen height of your computer at eye level.	Keep the screen height of your computer at eye level.
⋯ Stet (don't delete)	officials talked openly	officials talked openly
∽ Transpose	accounts recievable	accounts receivable
bf Use boldface	Conclusions	**Conclusions**
ital Use italics	The Perfect Résumé	*The Perfect Résumé*

Bogdan Sonjachnyj/Shutterstock.com

D

Grammar/Mechanics Handbook

Introduction

If you are like most readers studying this book, you want to upgrade your skills and enter the workplace quickly. For that reason, we provide a condensed review of basic grammar and mechanics written just for you. This Grammar/Mechanics Handbook offers a rapid systematic review with these resources:

- **Grammar/Mechanics Diagnostic Pretest.** The 65-point pretest helps you assess your strengths and weaknesses. Your instructor will check your answers in class or give you an answer key.

- **Grammar/Mechanics Summary Profile.** The G/M Profile reveals your strengths as well as pinpoints specific areas in which you need remedial instructions or study.

- **Grammar/Mechanics Review.** After taking the diagnostic pretest, you can study the rules in the Grammar/Mechanics Review, which contains many checkup exercises to enable you to try out and reinforce your knowledge.

Grammar/Mechanics Diagnostic Pretest

Guffey/Loewy, Essentials of Business Communication   **Name** _____

This diagnostic pretest is intended to reveal your strengths and weaknesses in using the following:

plural nouns	commas	number style
pronouns	semicolons, colons	confusing words, spelling
verbs	apostrophes	sentence structure
adjectives, adverbs	capitalization	

The pretest is organized into sections corresponding to the preceding categories. Most of these topics are covered in the Grammar/Mechanics Handbook, although sentence structure is presented in the textbook. When you finish, check your answers with your instructor and fill out the Grammar/Mechanics Summary Evaluation at the end of the test.

A. Plural Nouns

In sections A through F, each sentence is either correct or has one error related to the category under which it is listed. If a sentence is correct, write *C*. If it has an error, underline the error and write the correct form in the space provided.

> **EXAMPLE:** Several businesses hired specialists to write patchs that updated their computer software

_____ patches

Appendix D: Grammar/Mechanics Handbook

_____ 1. Three of the <u>attornies</u> for the defendants were from other cities.

_____ 2. Recent graduates discussed the pros and cons of attending colleges or <u>universitys</u>.

_____ 3. The Miller family had a sign painted for their house saying "The <u>Miller's</u>."

_____ 4. Neither the Sheas nor the <u>Lopez's</u> knew about the changes in beneficiaries.

_____ 5. All administrative assistants were asked to work the next four <u>Saturday's</u>.

B. Pronouns—1

_____ 6. My boss and <u>myself</u> are willing to send copies to whoever needs them.

_____ 7. Some of the work for Alexis and <u>I</u> had to be reassigned to Hunter and him.

_____ 8. Although <u>it's</u> motor was damaged, the car started immediately for the mechanic and me.

_____ 9. Just between you and <u>I</u>, do you know who the new manager will be?

_____ 10. Each of the online superstores offered <u>their</u> coupons on mobile devices.

C. Pronouns—2

_____ 11. Was that great idea <u>your's</u>?

_____ 12. If you were <u>me</u>, whom would you nominate?

_____ 13. When I return the call, for whom should I ask?

_____ 14. Everyone agrees that <u>us</u> employees deserve a raise.

_____ 15. It's too early to tell whether Facebook will change <u>it's</u> user terms again.

D. Verbs—1

_____ 16. Each of our representatives <u>are</u> aware of the problems involved.

_____ 17. A description of the property, together with several other legal documents, <u>were</u> submitted by my attorney.

_____ 18. What <u>does</u> integrity, reliability, and integrity have in common?

_____ 19. Neither of the two contracts <u>were</u> approved by our client.

_____ 20. Our product team <u>have</u> implemented a new quality control plan.

E. Verbs—2

_____ 21. If I <u>was</u> the company owner, I certainly would have made changes.

_____ 22. We might have <u>chose</u> a different property if we had known about the lien.

_____ 23. Susan and Haden have <u>went</u> to their friend's house for a holiday dinner.

_____ 24. Blogs have <u>became</u> an important marketing tool for many companies.

_____ 25. That partially completed building has <u>set</u> there untouched for a year.

F. Adjectives, Adverbs

_____ 26. San Francisco is <u>more close</u> to Hawaii than Los Angeles is.

_____ 27. This is the <u>worse</u> coffee I have ever tasted.

_____ 28. Arianna felt <u>badly</u> that she couldn't attend the out-of-town meeting.

Appendix D: Grammar/Mechanics Handbook

29. The cookies smelled <u>deliciously</u> when they first came out of the oven. _____

30. The recently elected official benefited from his <u>coast to coast</u> campaign. _____

G. Commas

For each of the following sentences, insert any necessary commas. Count the number of commas you add. Write that number in the space provided. All punctuation must be correct to receive credit. If a sentence requires no punctuation, write 0.

> **EXAMPLE:** However, because of developments in theory and computer applications, management is become more of a science. _____2_____

31. For example management determines how assignments responsibilities and territories are delegated to employees. _____

32. Sam placed his online bid at 7:48 p.m. which was two minutes before the auction closed. _____

33. The construction of the U.S. interstate highway system began in 1956 and has given birth to many new industries. _____

34. Dominic Irving who is the product manager for DragonTech left a message for you _____

35. Although tired employees preferred the evening not the morning in-service training programs. _____

H. Semicolons, Commas, and Colons

For each of the following sentences, insert any necessary semicolons, commas, or colons. Count the number of marks you add. Write that number in the space provided. All punctuation must be correct to receive credit. If a sentence requires no punctuation, write 0.

36. Madison Santos turned in her report however she did not indicate the time period it covered. _____

37. As suggested by the report we must first secure adequate funding then we may consider expansion. _____

38. When you begin to research a report consider these sources of information databases articles and websites. _____

39. Interest payments on bonds are tax deductible dividend payments however are not. _____

40. Three countries with the highest literacy rates in the world are Cuba Georgia and Latvia. _____

I. Apostrophes

Write the correct letter in the space provided.

41. In just two _____ time, _____ salary nearly doubled. _____
    a. year's, Lisa's
    b. years', Lisas
    c. years', Lisa's

42. At the spring meeting of all _____, the issue of executive _____ came up. _____
    a. stockholders, salaries
    b. stockholders', salaries'
    c. stockholder's, salary's

43. _____ unlikely that the company's building and _____ contents were insured. _____
    a. It's, it's
    b. It's, its
    c. Its, its

44. This _____ sales figures were definitely better than last _____.
    a. year's, year's
    b year's, year
    c. year's, years

45. One _____ testimony convinced all jury _____ to convict.
    a. witnesses, members
    b. witness's, members
    c. witness's, members'

J. Capitalization

46. The loss of _____ jobs in the _____ is a topic that can provoke heated debate.
    a. Manufacturing, Northeast
    b. manufacturing, northeast
    c. manufacturing, Northeast

47. I gave my _____ the most popular Sony _____ as a Christmas gift last year.
    a. Mother, Smartphone
    b. mother, smartphone
    c. Mother, smartphone

48. Our _____ hurried to _____ to catch her flight to Chicago.
    a. Sales Manager, Gate 12
    b. sales manager, Gate 12
    c. Sales Manager, gate 12

49. The most popular snacks eaten during the _____ are _____.
    a. Super Bowl, chicken wings and pizza
    b. super bowl, chicken wings and pizza
    c. Super Bowl, Chicken Wings and Pizza

50. Martin Cooper, a _____ at Motorola, created the first true _____.
    a. General Manager, cell phone
    b. general manager, cell phone
    c. General manager, Cell Phone

K. Number Style

51. By purchasing her new car before _____, Isabella saved nearly _____.
    a. September 1st, five hundred dollars
    b. September 1, 500 dollars
    c. September 1, $500

52. The conference call is scheduled for _____ at _____.
    a. May 15, eleven a.m.
    b. May 15, 11 a.m.
    c. May 15th, 11 a.m. in the morning

53. _____ candidates are campaigning for the _____ open council seats.
    a. Eleven, four
    b. Eleven, 4
    c. 11, four

54. It's estimated that _____ people use Facebook from a mobile device.
    a. 2,500,000
    b. 2.5 million
    c. 2 million 5 hundred thousand

55. The Sony Ultra smartphone provides _____ of talk time, and its screen is _____ sharper than others.   _____
    a. 14 hours, 47 percent
    b. fourteen hours, 47%
    c. fourteen hours, forty-seven percent

L. Confusing Words, Spelling

56. _____ of computer users wonder whether it's _____ to leave their computers on overnight.   _____
    a. Allot, alright
    b. A lot, all right
    c. Allot, all right

57. If you have _____ signed in, it's _____ to do so again.   _____
    a. already, unnecessary
    b. all ready, unnecessary
    c. already, uneccessary

58. We would prefer to _____ this agreement rather _____ the previous one.   _____
    a. except, than
    b. accept, then
    c. accept, than

59. Stacy was _____ to take the counselor's _____ about scheduling her classes.   _____
    a. advised, advice
    b. adviced, advise
    c. adviced, advice

60. The _____ reason for the Google investigation was concern over the _____ that might be established.   _____
    a. principle, presedent
    b. principal, precedent
    c. principle, precident

M. Sentence Structure

For each of the following options, write the letter of the correct sentence in the space provided.

61. a. I'm not looking for the perfect job, I just want to get started.   _____
    b. I'm not looking for the perfect job; I just want to get started.
    c. I'm not looking for the perfect job I just want to get started.

62. a. Although we cannot predict the skills future jobs will require. We do know they will require brainpower and education.   _____
    b. Send an e-mail to all committee members, tell them our next meeting will be Friday.
    c. The message was meant to inform, but it merely confused everyone instead.

63. a. During a recession many candidates vie for fewer jobs. Which is why communication and technology skills are extremely important.   _____
    b. Being on time is important in North America, in other countries it is less important.
    c. Ethical companies experience less litigation, and they are the target of less government regulation.

64. a. Job applicants generally face two kinds of interviews: screening interviews and hiring interviews.   _____
    b. Thirty-year mortgage rates rose slightly this year. Since many banks are still offering rates lower than 5 percent.
    c. Don't make resolutions, create a step-by-step plan for working toward your goals.

65. a. Even with the popularity of e-mail. Most employers contact job applicants by phone to set up interviews.
    b. The résumé is still important; however, it may not be the document that introduces the job seeker today.
    c. Today what's important is not what the job applicant wants, it's what the employer wants.

Grammar/Mechanics Pretest Summary Evaluation

Place a check mark to indicate the number of correct answers you had in each category.

NUMBER CORRECT		5	4	3	2	1
1–5	Plural Nouns	_____	_____	_____	_____	_____
6–10	Pronouns—1	_____	_____	_____	_____	_____
11–15	Pronouns—2	_____	_____	_____	_____	_____
16–20	Verbs—1	_____	_____	_____	_____	_____
21–25	Verbs—2	_____	_____	_____	_____	_____
26–30	Adjectives, Adverbs	_____	_____	_____	_____	_____
31–35	Commas	_____	_____	_____	_____	_____
36–40	Semicolons, Commas, Colons	_____	_____	_____	_____	_____
41–45	Apostrophes	_____	_____	_____	_____	_____
46–50	Capitalization	_____	_____	_____	_____	_____
51–55	Number Style	_____	_____	_____	_____	_____
56–60	Confusing Words, Spelling	_____	_____	_____	_____	_____
61–65	Sentence Structure	_____	_____	_____	_____	_____

Scale: 5 = You have excellent skills; 4 = You need a light review; 3 = You need a careful review; 2 = You need to study the rules seriously; 1 = You need serious study and follow-up reinforcement.

Grammar/Mechanics Review

Parts of Speech (1.01)

1.01 Functions. English has eight parts of speech. Knowing the functions of the parts of speech helps writers better understand how words are used and how sentences are formed.

a. **Nouns** name persons, places, things, qualities, concepts, and activities (e.g., *Kevin, Phoenix, computer, joy, work, banking*).
b. **Pronouns** substitute for nouns (e.g., *he, she, it, they*).
c. **Verbs** show the action of a subject or join the subject to words that describe it (e.g., *walk, heard, is, was jumping*).
d. **Adjectives** describe or limit nouns and pronouns and often answer the questions *what kind? how many?* and *which one?* (e.g., *red* car, *ten* items, *good* manager).
e. **Adverbs** describe or limit verbs, adjectives, or other adverbs and frequently answer the questions *when? how? where?* or *to what extent?* (e.g., *tomorrow, rapidly, here, very*).

f. **Prepositions** join nouns or pronouns to other words in sentences (e.g., desk *in* the office, ticket *for* me, letter *to* you).

g. **Conjunctions** connect words or groups of words (e.g., you *and* I, Mark *or* Jill).

h. **Interjections** express strong feelings (e.g., *Wow! Oh!*).

Nouns (1.02–1.06)

Nouns name persons, places, things, qualities, concepts, and activities. Nouns may be grouped into a number of categories.

1.02 Concrete and Abstract.
Concrete nouns name specific objects that can be seen, heard, felt, tasted, or smelled. Examples of concrete nouns are *telephone*, *dollar*, *Cadillac*, and *tangerine*. Abstract nouns name generalized ideas such as qualities or concepts that are not easily pictured. *Emotion*, *power*, and *tension* are typical examples of abstract nouns.

Business writing is most effective when concrete words predominate. It is clearer to write *We need 16-pound copy paper* than to write *We need office supplies.*

1.03 Proper and Common.
Proper nouns name specific persons, places, or things and are always capitalized (*General Electric, Baltimore, Jennifer*). All other nouns are common nouns and begin with lowercase letters (*company, city, student*). Rules for capitalization are presented in Sections 3.01–3.16.

1.04 Singular and Plural.
Singular nouns name one item; plural nouns name more than one. From a practical view, writers seldom have difficulty with singular nouns. They may need help, however, with the formation and spelling of plural nouns.

1.05 Guidelines for Forming Noun Plurals.

a. Add *s* to most nouns (*chair, chairs; mortgage, mortgages; Monday, Mondays*).

b. Add *es* to nouns ending in *s, x, z, ch,* or *sh* (*bench, benches; boss, bosses; box, boxes; Lopez, Lopezes*).

c. Change the spelling in irregular noun plurals (*man, men; foot, feet; mouse, mice; child, children*).

d. Add *s* to nouns that end in *y* when *y* is preceded by a vowel (*attorney, attorneys; valley, valleys; journey, journeys*).

e. Drop the *y* and add *ies* to nouns ending in *y* when *y* is preceded by a consonant (*company, companies; city, cities; secretary, secretaries*).

f. Add *s* to the principal word in most compound expressions (*editors in chief, fathers-in-law, bills of lading, runners-up*).

g. Add *s* to most numerals, letters of the alphabet, words referred to as words, degrees, and abbreviations (*5s, 2000s, Bs, ands, CPAs, qts.*).

h. Add *'s* only to clarify letters of the alphabet that might be misread, such as *A's, I's, M's,* and *U's* and *i's, p's,* and *q's.* An expression like *c.o.d.s* requires no apostrophe because it would not easily be misread.

1.06 Collective.
Nouns such as *staff, faculty, committee, group,* and *herd* refer to a collection of people, animals, or objects. Collective nouns may be considered singular or plural depending on their action. See Section 1.10i for a discussion of collective nouns and their agreement with verbs.

Review Exercise A—Nouns

Choose the correct option. Then compare your responses with the key at the end of the book.

1. Several (a) attorneys, (b) attornies, (c) attorney's protested the judge's decision. _____

2. Please write to the (a) Davis's, (b) Davises, (c) Davis about the missing contract. _____

3. How many (a) company, (b) companies have ethics guidelines? _____

4. Four of the wooden (a) benches, (b) benchs must be repaired.

5. The stock market is experiencing abnormal (a) ups and downs, (b) up's and down's.

6. This office is usually quiet on (a) Sundays, (b) Sunday's.

7. Several news (a) dispatchs, (b) dispatches described the earthquake devastation.

8. Two major (a) country's, (b) countrys, (c) countries will participate in arms negotiations.

9. Some young children have difficulty writing their (a) bs and ds, (b) b's and d's.

10. The last shipment should have included two (a) bill of sales, (b) bills of sale.

11. Most (a) MBA's, (b) MBAs have taken courses in ethics.

12. The four (a) sister-in-laws, (b) sister-in-law's, (c) sisters-in-law get together for lunch every month.

13. Our organization is prepared to deal with foreign (a) currencies, (b) currencys.

14. Photographers no longer need an assortment of camera (a) lens, (b) lenses, (c) len's.

15. The two (a) boards of directors, (b) board of directors, (c) board's of directors met together.

Pronouns (1.07–1.09)

Pronouns substitute for nouns. They are classified by case.

1.07 Case. Pronouns function in three cases, as shown in the following chart.

Nominative Case	Objective Case	Possessive Case
(Used for subjects of verbs and subject complements)	(Used for objects of prepositions and objects of verbs)	(Used to show possession)
I	me	my, mine
we	us	our, ours
you	you	your, yours
he	him	his
she	her	her, hers
it	it	its
they	them	their, theirs
who, whoever	whom, whomever	whose

1.08 Guidelines for Selecting Pronoun Case.

a. Pronouns that serve as subjects of verbs must be in the nominative case:

   He and *I* (not *Him* and *me*) decided to apply for the jobs.

b. Pronouns that follow linking verbs (such as *am, is, are, was, were, be, being, been*) and rename the words to which they refer must be in the nominative case:

   It must have been *she* (not *her*) who placed the order. (The nominative-case pronoun *she* follows the linking verb *been* and renames its antecedent.)

   If it was *he* (not *him*) who called, I have his number. (The nominative-case pronoun *he* follows the linking verb *was* and renames its antecedent.)

c. Pronouns that serve as objects of verbs or objects of prepositions must be in the objective case:

   Mr. Andrews asked *them* to complete the proposal. (The pronoun *them* is the object of the verb *asked*.)

Appendix D: Grammar/Mechanics Handbook

All computer printouts are sent to *him*. (The pronoun *him* is the object of the preposition *to*.)

Just between you and *me*, profits are falling. (The pronoun *me* is one of the objects of the preposition *between*.)

d. Pronouns that show ownership must be in the possessive case. Possessive pronouns (such as *hers*, *yours*, *ours*, *theirs*, and *its*) require no apostrophes:

I bought a cheap cell phone, but *yours* (not *your's*) is expensive.

All parts of the machine, including *its* (not *it's*) motor, were examined.

The house and *its* (not *it's*) contents will be auctioned.

Don't confuse possessive pronouns and contractions. Contractions are shortened forms of subject-verb phrases (such as *it's* for *it is*, *there's* for *there is*, and *they're* for *they are*).

e. When a pronoun appears in combination with a noun or another pronoun, ignore the extra noun or pronoun and its conjunction. In this way pronoun case becomes more obvious:

The manager promoted Jeff and *me* (not *I*). (Ignore *Jeff and*.)

f. In statements of comparison, mentally finish the comparative by adding the implied missing words:

Next year I hope to earn as much as *she*. (The verb *earns* is implied here: … *as much as she earns*.)

g. Pronouns must be in the same case as the words they replace or rename. When pronouns are used with appositives, ignore the appositive:

A new contract was signed by *us* (not *we*) employees. (Temporarily ignore the appositive *employees* in selecting the pronoun.)

We (not *us*) citizens have formed our own organization. (Temporarily ignore the appositive *citizens* in selecting the pronoun.)

h. Pronouns ending in *self* should be used only when they refer to previously mentioned nouns or pronouns:

The CEO *himself* answered the telephone.

Robert and *I* (not *myself*) are in charge of the campaign.

i. Use objective-case pronouns as objects of the prepositions *between*, *but*, *like* and *except*:

Everyone but John and him (not *he*) qualified for the bonus.

Employees like Miss Gillis and *her* (not *she*) are hard to replace.

j. Use *who* or *whoever* for nominative-case constructions and *whom* or *whomever* for objective-case constructions. In making the correct choice, it's sometimes helpful to substitute *he* for *who* or *whoever* and *him* for *whom* or *whomever*:

For *whom* was this book ordered? (*This book was ordered for him/whom?*)

Who did you say would drop by? (*Who/He … would drop by?*)

Deliver the package to whoever opens the door. (In this sentence the clause *whoever* opens the *door* functions as the object of the preposition *to*. Within the clause itself, *whoever* is the subject of the verb *opens*. Again, substitution of *he* might be helpful: *He/Whoever opens the door*.)

1.09 Guidelines for Making Pronouns Agree With Their Antecedents.

Pronouns must agree with the words to which they refer (their antecedents) in gender and in number.

a. Use masculine pronouns to refer to masculine antecedents, feminine pronouns to refer to feminine antecedents, and neuter pronouns to refer to antecedents without gender:

The man opened *his* office door. (Masculine gender applies.)

A woman sat at *her* desk. (Feminine gender applies.)

This computer and *its* programs fit our needs. (Neuter gender applies.)

b. Use singular pronouns to refer to singular antecedents:

> Common-gender pronouns (such as *him* or *his*) traditionally have been used when the gender of the antecedent is unknown. Sensitive writers today, however, prefer to recast such constructions to avoid gender-biased pronouns. Study these examples for bias-free pronouns. See Chapter 2 for additional discussion of bias-free language.

>> Each student must submit *a* report on Monday.

>> All students must submit *their* reports on Monday.

>> Each student must submit *his or her* report on Monday. (This alternative is least acceptable since it is wordy and calls attention to itself.)

c. Use singular pronouns to refer to singular indefinite subjects and plural pronouns for plural indefinite subjects. Words such as *anyone, something,* and *anybody* are considered indefinite because they refer to no specific person or object. Some indefinite pronouns are always singular; others are always plural.

> Somebody in the group of touring women left *her* (not *their*) purse in the museum.

	Always Singular		**Always Plural**
anybody	either	nobody	both
anyone	everyone	no one	few
anything	everything	somebody	many
each	neither	someone	several

> Either of the companies has the right to exercise *its* (not *their*) option to sell stock.

d. Use singular pronouns to refer to collective nouns and organization names:

> The engineering staff is moving *its* (not *their*) facilities on Friday. (The singular pronoun *its* agrees with the collective noun *staff* because the members of *staff* function as a single unit.)

> Jones, Cohen, & Chavez, Inc., *has* (not *have*) canceled *its* (not *their*) contract with us. (The singular pronoun *its* agrees with *Jones, Cohen, & Chavez, Inc.,* because the members of the organization are operating as a single unit.)

e. Use a plural pronoun to refer to two antecedents joined by *and*, whether the antecedents are singular or plural:

> Our company president and our vice president will be submitting *their* expenses shortly.

f. Ignore intervening phrases—introduced by expressions such as *together with, as well as,* and *in addition to*—that separate a pronoun from its antecedent:

> One of our managers, along with several salespeople, is planning *his* retirement. (If you wish to emphasize both subjects equally, join them with *and*: One of our managers *and* several salespeople are planning *their* retirements.)

g. When antecedents are joined by *or* or *nor*, make the pronoun agree with the antecedent closest to it:

> Neither Jackie nor Kim wanted *her* (not *their*) desk moved.

Review Exercise B—Pronouns

Choose the correct option. Then compare your responses with the key at the end of the book.

1. Send e-mail copies of the policy to the project manager or (a) me, (b) myself.

2. Our blog was written by Jeremy and (a) I, (b) me, (c) myself before the news broke.

3. (a) Who, (b) Whom did you say the e-mail was addressed to? _____

4. The Employee Benefits Committee can be justly proud of (a) its, (b) their achievements. _____

5. Apparently one of the female applicants forgot to sign (a) her, (b) their application. _____

6. Just between you and (a) I, (b) me, (c) myself, I'm sure that Rachel will be named manager. _____

7. (a) Us, (b) We employees have been given an opportunity to earn stock benefits. _____

8. Both the printer and (a) its, (b) it's cover are missing. _____

9. Many inquiries were addressed specifically to Jeff and (a) I, (b) me, (c) myself. _____

10. We are certain that (a) our's, (b) ours will be the best entry in the contest. _____

11. The cheetah is the only cat in the world that cannot retract (a) its, (b) it's claws. _____

12. Please submit your expense claim to Max or (a) I, (b) me, (c) myself before June 1. _____

13. Deliver the package to (a) whoever, (b) whomever opens the door. _____

14. (a) Each student, (b) All students must complete their portfolios to pass the course. _____

15. Did you say that (a) your, (b) you're going to apply for the Facebook job? _____

Verbs (1.10–1.15)

Verbs show the action of a subject or join the subject to words that describe it.

1.10 Guidelines for Agreement With Subjects.

One of the most troublesome areas in English is subject-verb agreement. Consider the following guidelines for making verbs agree with subjects.

a. A singular subject requires a singular verb:

> The stock market *opens* at 10 a.m. (The singular verb *opens* agrees with the singular subject *market*.)

> He *doesn't* (not *don't*) work on Saturday.

b. A plural subject requires a plural verb:

> On the packing slip several items *seem* (not *seems*) to be missing.

c. A verb agrees with its subject regardless of prepositional phrases that may intervene:

> This list of management objectives is extensive. (The singular verb *is* agrees with the singular subject *list*.)

> Every one of the letters *shows* (not *show*) proper form.

d. A verb agrees with its subject regardless of intervening phrases introduced by *as well as, in addition to, such as, including, together with*, and similar expressions:

> An important memo, together with several contracts, *is* missing. (The singular verb *is* agrees with the singular subject *memo*.)

> The president, as well as several other top-level executives, *approves* of our proposal. (The singular verb *approves* agrees with the subject *president*.)

e. A verb agrees with its subject regardless of the location of the subject:

> Here is one of the contracts about which you asked. (The verb *is* agrees with its subject *one*, even though it precedes *one*. The adverb *here* cannot function as a subject.)

> There *are* many problems yet to be resolved. (The verb *are* agrees with the subject *problems*. The word *there* does not function as a subject.)

In the next office *are* several printers. (In this inverted sentence, the verb *are* must agree with the subject *printers*.)

   f. Subjects joined by *and* require a plural verb:

Analyzing the reader and organizing a strategy *are* the first steps in message writing. (The plural verb *are* agrees with the two subjects, *analyzing* and *organizing*.)

The tone and the wording of the message *were* persuasive. (The plural verb *were* agrees with the two subjects, *tone* and *wording*.)

   g. Subjects joined by *or* or *nor* may require singular or plural verbs. Make the verb agree with the closer subject:

Neither the memo nor the report *is* ready. (The singular verb *is* agrees with *report*, the closer of the two subjects.)

   h. The following indefinite pronouns are singular and require singular verbs: *anyone, anybody, anything, each, either, every, everyone, everybody, everything, many a, neither, nobody, nothing, someone, somebody,* and *something*:

Either of the alternatives that you present *is* acceptable. (The verb *is* agrees with the singular subject *either*.)

   i. Collective nouns may take singular or plural verbs, depending on whether the members of the group are operating as a unit or individually:

Our management team *is* united in its goal.

The faculty *are* sharply divided on the tuition issue. (Although acceptable, this sentence sounds better recast: The faculty *members* are sharply divided on the tuition issue.)

   j. Organization names and titles of publications, although they may appear to be plural, are singular and require singular verbs.

Clark, Anderson, and Horne, Inc., *has* (not *have*) hired a marketing consultant.

Thousands of Investment Tips is (not *are*) again on the best-seller list.

1.11 Voice. Voice is that property of verbs that shows whether the subject of the verb acts or is acted upon. Active-voice verbs direct action from the subject toward the object of the verb. Passive-voice verbs direct action toward the subject.

Active voice:	Our employees *send* many e-mail messages.
Passive voice:	Many e-mail messages *are sent* by our employees.

Business writers generally prefer active-voice verbs because they are specific and forceful. However, passive-voice constructions can help a writer be tactful. Chapter 3 presents strategies for effective use of active- and passive-voice verbs.

1.12 Mood. Three verb moods express the attitude or thought of the speaker or writer toward a subject: (a) the indicative mood expresses a fact; (b) the imperative mood expresses a command; and (c) the subjunctive mood expresses a doubt, a conjecture, or a suggestion.

Indicative:	I *am looking* for a job.
Imperative:	*Begin* your job search with the want ads.
Subjunctive:	I wish I *were* working.

Only the subjunctive mood creates problems for most speakers and writers. The most common use of subjunctive mood occurs in clauses including *if* or *wish*. In such clauses substitute the subjunctive verb *were* for the indicative verb *was*:

If he *were* (not *was*) in my position, he would understand.

Mr. Simon acts as if he *were* (not *was*) the boss.

We wish we *were* (not *was*) able to ship your order.

The subjunctive mood can maintain goodwill while conveying negative information. The sentence *We wish we were able to ship your order* sounds more pleasing to a customer than *We cannot ship your order*. However, for all practical purposes, both sentences convey the same negative message.

1.13 Tense. Verbs show the time of an action by their tense. Speakers and writers can use six tenses to show the time of sentence action; for example:

Present tense:	I *work;* he *works.*
Past tense:	I *worked;* she *worked.*
Future tense:	I *will work;* he *will work.*
Present perfect tense:	I *have worked;* he *has worked.*
Past perfect tense:	I *had worked;* she *had worked.*
Future perfect tense:	I *will have worked;* he *will have worked.*

1.14 Guidelines for Verb Tense.

a. Use present tense for statements that, although introduced by past-tense verbs, continue to be true:

> What did you say his name *is*? (Use the present tense *is* if his name has not changed.)

b. Avoid unnecessary shifts in verb tenses:

> The manager *saw* (not *sees*) a great deal of work yet to be completed and *remained* to do it herself.

Although unnecessary shifts in verb tense are to be avoided, not all the verbs within one sentence have to be in the same tense; for example:

> She *said* (past tense) that she *likes* (present tense) to work late.

1.15 Irregular Verbs. Irregular verbs cause difficulty for some writers and speakers. Unlike regular verbs, irregular verbs do not form the past tense and past participle by adding *-ed* to the present form. Here is a partial list of selected troublesome irregular verbs. Consult a dictionary if you are in doubt about a verb form.

Troublesome Irregular Verbs

Present	Past	Past Participle *(always use helping verbs)*
begin	began	begun
break	broke	broken
choose	chose	chosen
come	came	come
drink	drank	drunk
go	went	gone
lay (to place)	laid	laid
lie (to rest)	lay	lain
ring	rang	rung
see	saw	seen
write	wrote	written

a. Use only past-tense verbs to express past tense. Notice that no helping verbs are used to indicate simple past tense:

> The auditors *went* (not *have went*) over our books carefully.

> He *came* (not *come*) to see us yesterday.

b. Use past-participle forms for actions completed before the present time. Notice that past-participle forms require helping verbs:

Steve *had gone* (not *had went*) before we called. (The past-participle *gone* is used with the helping verb *had*.)

c. Avoid inconsistent shifts in subject, voice, and mood. Pay particular attention to this problem area because undesirable shifts are often characteristic of student writing.

Inconsistent:	When Mrs. Taswell read the report, the error was found. (The first clause is in the active voice; the second, passive.)
Improved:	When Mrs. Taswell read the report, she found the error. (Both clauses are in the active voice.)
Inconsistent:	The clerk should first conduct an inventory. Then supplies should be requisitioned. (The first sentence is in the active voice; the second, passive.)
Improved:	The clerk should first conduct an inventory. Then the clerk should requisition supplies. (Both sentences are in the active voice.)
Inconsistent:	All workers must wear security badges, and you must also sign a daily time card. (This sentence contains an inconsistent shift in subject from *all workers* in the first clause to you in the second clause.)
Improved:	All workers must wear security badges, and they must also sign a daily time card.
Inconsistent:	Begin the transaction by opening an account; then you enter the customer's name. (This sentence contains an inconsistent shift from the imperative mood in the first clause to the indicative mood in the second clause.)
Improved:	Begin the transaction by opening an account; then enter the customer's name. (Both clauses are now in the imperative mood.)

Review Exercise C—Verbs 1

Choose the correct option. Then compare your responses with the key at the end of the book.

1. Improved communication technologies and increased global competition (a) is, (b) are changing the world of business.

2. Our directory of customer names and addresses (a) was, (b) were out-of-date.

3. Yesterday Ms. Mendez (a) choose (b) chose a new office on the second floor.

4. If you had (a) saw, (b) seen the rough draft, you would better appreciate the final copy.

5. Specific training as well as ample experience (a) is, (b) are important for that position.

6. One of the reasons that sales have declined in recent years (a) is, (b) are the lack of effective social media advertising.

7. Either of the proposed laws (a) is, (b) are going to affect our business negatively.

8. Our management team and our attorney (a) is, (b) are researching the privacy issue.

9. If you had (a) wrote, (b) written us earlier, we could have authorized the change.

10. Blogs have (a) became, (b) become an important marketing tool for many businesses.

11. If I (a) was, (b) were you, I would ask for a raise.

12. Merger statutes (a) require, (b) requires that a failing company accept bids from several companies before merging with one.

13. How long has the contract been (a) laying, (b) lying on your desk?

14. Have you (a) broke, (b) broken the news of the merger yet to the employees?

15. His cell phone had (a) rung, (b) rang so often during the meeting that he had to leave.

Review Exercise D—Verbs 2

In the following sentence pairs, choose the one that illustrates consistency in the use of subject, voice, and mood. Then compare your responses with the key at the end of the book.

1. a. You need more than a knowledge of technology; one also must be able to interact well with people.
   b. You need more than a knowledge of technology; you also must be able to interact well with people.

2. a. Ricardo and Pete were eager to continue, but Steven wanted to quit.
   b. Ricardo and Pete were eager to continue, but Steven wants to quit.

3. a. The salesperson should consult the price list; then you can give an accurate quote to a customer.
   b. The salesperson should consult the price list; then the salesperson can give an accurate quote to a customer.

4. a. Read all the instructions first; then you install the printer program.
   b. Read all the instructions first, and then install the printer program.

5. a. She was an enthusiastic manager who always had a smile for everyone.
   b. She was an enthusiastic manager who always has a smile for everyone.

Adjectives and Adverbs (1.16–1.17)

Adjectives describe or limit nouns and pronouns. They often answer the questions *what kind? how many?* or *which one?* Adverbs describe or limit verbs, adjectives, or other adverbs. They often answer the questions *when? how? where?* or *to what extent?*

1.16 Forms. Most adjectives and adverbs have three forms, or degrees: positive, comparative, and superlative.

	Positive	Comparative	Superlative
Adjective:	clear	clearer	clearest
Adverb:	clearly	more clearly	most clearly

Some adjectives and adverbs have irregular forms.

	Positive	Comparative	Superlative
Adjective:	good	better	best
	bad	worse	worst
Adverb:	well	better	best

Adjectives and adverbs composed of two or more syllables are usually compared by the use of *more* and *most;* for example:

> The Payroll Department is *more efficient* than the Shipping Department.
> Payroll is the *most efficient* department in our organization.

1.17 Guidelines for Use.

a. Use the comparative degree of the adjective or adverb to compare two persons or things; use the superlative degree to compare three or more:

> Of the two plans, which is *better* (not *best*)?

> Of all the plans, we like this one *best* (not *better*).

b. Do not create a double comparative or superlative by using -er with *more* or -est with *most*:

> His explanation couldn't have been *clearer* (not *more clearer*).

c. A linking verb (*is, are, look, seem, feel, sound, appear*, and so forth) may introduce a word that describes the verb's subject. In this case be certain to use an adjective, not an adverb:

The characters on the monitor look *bright* (not *brightly*). (Use the adjective *bright* because it follows the linking verb *look* and modifies the noun *characters*.)

The company's letter made the customer feel *bad* (not *badly*). (The adjective *bad* follows the linking verb *feel* and describes the noun *customer*.)

d. Use adverbs, not adjectives, to describe or limit the action of verbs:

She business is running *smoothly* (not *smooth*). (Use the adverb *smoothly* to describe the action of the verb *running*. *Smoothly* tells how the business is running.)

Don't take his remark *personally* (not *personal*). (The adverb *personally* describes the action of the verb *take*.)

Serena said she did *well* (not *good*) on the test. (Use the adverb *well* to tell how she did.)

e. Two or more adjectives that are joined to create a compound modifier before a noun should be hyphenated:

The *four-year-old* child was tired.

Our agency is planning a *coast-to-coast* campaign.

Hyphenate a compound modifier following a noun only if your dictionary shows the hyphen(s):

Our speaker is very *well-known*. (Include the hyphen because most dictionaries do.)

The tired *child* was four years old. (Omit the hyphens because the expression follows the word it describes, *child*, and because dictionaries do not indicate hyphens.)

f. Keep adjectives and adverbs close to the words they modify:

She asked for *a cup of hot coffee* (not *a hot cup of coffee*).

Patty *had only two days* of vacation left (not *only had two days*).

Students may sit *in the first five rows* (not *in five first rows*).

He *has saved almost* enough money for the trip (not *has almost saved*).

g. Don't confuse *there* with the possessive pronoun *their* or the contraction *they're*:

Put the documents *there*. (The adverb *there* means "at that place or at that point.")

There are two reasons for the change. (The pronoun *there* is used as function word to introduce a sentence or a clause.)

We already have *their* specifications. (The possessive pronoun *their* shows ownership.)

They're coming to inspect today. (The contraction *they're* is a shortened form of *they are*.)

Review Exercise E—Adjectives and Adverbs

Choose the correct option. Then compare your responses with the key at the end of the book.

1. If we had been more (a) careful, (b) carefuler, the box might not have broken.

2. To avoid a (a) face to face, (b) face-to-face confrontation, she sent an e-mail.

3. Darren completed the employment test (a) satisfactorily, (b) satisfactory.

4. What exactly does (a) there, (b) their, (c) they're company want us to do?

5. We all felt (a) bad, (b) badly when our team lost the competition.

6. The time passed (a) quicker, (b) more quickly than we expected.

7. We now offer a (a) money back, (b) money-back guarantee.

8. Today's financial news is (a) worse, (b) worst than yesterday's.

9. You must check the document (a) page by page, (b) page-by-page.

10. Please don't take his comments (a) personal, (b) personally.

11. Of the two proposals, this one is (a) more, (b) most persuasive.

12. Please wait right over (a) there, (b) their, (c) they're until the interviewer is ready.

13. If she does (a) good, (b) well in the interview, Melanie will be hired.

14. San Francisco is (a) more close, (b) closer to Hawaii than Los Angeles is.

15. When giving your presentation, try to speak (a) natural, (b) naturally.

Prepositions (1.18)

Prepositions are connecting words that join nouns or pronouns to other words in a sentence. The words *about, at, from, in,* and *to* are examples of prepositions.

1.18 Guidelines for Use.

a. Include necessary prepositions:

>   What type *of* software do you need (not *what type software*)?

>   I graduated *from* high school two years ago (not *I graduated high school*).

b. Omit unnecessary prepositions:

>   Where is the meeting? (Not *Where is the meeting at?*)

>   Both printers work well. (Not *Both of the printers.*)

>   Where are you going? (Not *Where are you going to?*)

c. Avoid the overuse of prepositional phrases.

Weak:	We have received your application for credit at our branch in the Fresno area.
Improved:	We have received your Fresno credit application.

d. Repeat the preposition before the second of two related elements especially when the second element is distant from the first:

>   Applicants use the résumé effectively by summarizing their most important experiences and *by* relating their education to the jobs sought.

e. Include the second preposition when two different prepositions modify a single object:

>   George's appreciation *of* and aptitude *for* computers led to a promising career.

Conjunctions (1.19)

Conjunctions connect words, phrases, and clauses. They act as signals, indicating when a thought is being added, contrasted, or altered. Coordinate conjunctions (such as *and, or, but*) and other words that act as connectors (such as *however, therefore, when, as*) tell the reader or listener in what direction a thought is heading. They are like road signs signaling what's ahead.

1.19 Guidelines for Use.

a. Use coordinating conjunctions to connect only sentence elements that are parallel or balanced.

Weak:	His report was correct and written in a concise manner.
Improved:	His report was correct and concise.
Weak:	Management has the capacity to increase fraud, or reduction can be achieved through the policies it adopts.
Improved:	Management has the capacity to increase or reduce fraud through the policies it adopts.

b. Do not use the word *like* as a conjunction:

>   It seems *as if* (not *like*) this day will never end.

c. Avoid using *when* or *where* inappropriately. A common writing fault occurs in sentences with clauses introduced by *is when* and *is where*. Written English ordinarily requires a noun (or a group of words functioning as a noun) following the linking verb *is*. Instead of acting as conjunctions in these constructions, the words *where* and *when* function as adverbs, creating faulty grammatical equations (adverbs cannot complete equations set up by linking verbs). To avoid the problem, revise the sentence, eliminating *is when* or *is where*.

Weak:	A bullish market is when prices are rising in the stock market.
Improved:	A bullish market is created when prices are rising in the stock market.
Weak:	A flowchart is when you make a diagram showing the step-by-step progression of a procedure.
Improved:	A flowchart is a diagram showing the step-by-step progression of a procedure.
Weak:	A podcast is where a prerecorded audio program is posted to a website.
Improved:	A podcast is a prerecorded audio program posted to a website.

A similar faulty construction occurs in the expression *I hate when*. English requires nouns, noun clauses, or pronouns to act as objects of verbs, not adverbs.

Weak:	I hate when we're asked to work overtime.
Improved:	I hate it when we're asked to work overtime.
Improved:	I hate being asked to work overtime.

d. Don't confuse the adverb *then* with the conjunction *than*. *Then* means "at that time"; *than* indicates the second element in a comparison:

We would rather remodel *than* (not *then*) move.

First, the equipment is turned on; *then* (not *than*) the program is loaded.

Review Exercise F—Prepositions and Conjunctions

Choose the sentence that is expressed more effectively. Then compare your responses with the key at the end of the book.

1. a. The chief forgot to tell everyone where today's meeting is.
   b. The chief forgot to tell everyone where today's meeting is at.

2. a. Derek Garcia graduated college last June.
   b. Derek Garcia graduated from college last June.

3. a. I hate when my cell loses its charge.
   b. I hate it when my cell loses its charge.

4. a. Business messages should be concise, correct, and clear.
   b. Business messages should be concise, correct, and written clearly.

5. a. We expect to finish up the work soon.
   b. We expect to finish the work soon.

6. a. At the beginning of the program in the fall of the year at the central office, we experienced staffing difficulties.
   b. When the program began last fall, the central office experienced staffing difficulties.

7. a. This course is much more time consuming than I expected.
   b. This course is much more time consuming then I expected.

8. a. An ombudsman is an individual hired by management to investigate and resolve employee complaints.
   b. An ombudsman is when management hires an individual to investigate and resolve employee complaints.

9. a. We need computer operators who can load software, monitor networks, and files must be duplicated.
   b. We need computer operators who can load software, monitor networks, and duplicate files.

10. a. I'm uncertain where to take this document to.
    b. I'm uncertain where to take this document.

11. a. What style of typeface should we use for the social media brochure?
    b. What style typeface should we use for the social media brochure?

12. a. Software tags our photos, recommends products to buy online, and offers ads based on our interests.
    b. Software tags our photos, recommends products to buy online, and ads are also offered based on our interests.

13. a. Is the newly hired manager any more efficient then the previous one?
    b. Is the newly hired manager any more efficient than the previous one?

14. a. Where should I send the application form to?
    b. Where should I send the application form?

15. a. Net income is when all expenses are subtracted from total revenue.
    b. Net income results when all expenses are subtracted from total revenue.

Punctuation Review

Commas 1 (2.01–2.04)

2.01 Series. Commas are used to separate three or more equal elements (words, phrases, or short clauses) in a series. To ensure separation of the last two elements, careful writers always use a comma before the conjunction in a series:

> Business letters usually contain a dateline, address, salutation, body, and closing. (This series contains words.)

> The job of an ombudsman is to examine employee complaints, resolve disagreements between management and employees, and ensure fair treatment. (This series contains phrases.)

> Trainees complete basic keyboarding tasks, technicians revise complex documents, and editors proofread completed projects. (This series contains short clauses.)

2.02 Direct Address. Commas are used to set off the names of individuals being addressed:

> Your inquiry, *Mrs. Johnson*, has been referred to me.

> We genuinely hope that we may serve you, *Mr. Lee.*

2.03 Parenthetical Expressions. Skilled writers use parenthetical words, phrases, and clauses to guide the reader from one thought to the next. When these expressions interrupt the flow of a sentence and are unnecessary for its grammatical completeness, they should be set off with commas. Examples of commonly used parenthetical expressions follow:

all things considered	however	needless to say
as a matter of fact	in addition	nevertheless
as a result	incidentally	no doubt
as a rule	in fact	of course
at the same time	in my opinion	on the contrary
consequently	in the first place	on the other hand
for example	in the meantime	therefore
furthermore	moreover	under the circumstances

> *As a matter of fact*, I wrote to you just yesterday. (Phrase used at the beginning of a sentence.)

We will, *in the meantime,* send you a replacement order. (Phrase used in the middle of a sentence.)

Your satisfaction is our first concern, *needless to say.* (Phrase used at the end of a sentence.)

Do not use commas if the expression is necessary for the completeness of the sentence:

Kimberly *had no* doubt that she would finish the report. (Omit commas because the expression is necessary for the completeness of the sentence.)

2.04 Dates, Addresses, and Geographical Items.
When dates, addresses, and geographical items contain more than one element, the second and succeeding elements are normally set off by commas.

a. Dates:

The conference was held February 2 at our home office. (No comma is needed for one element.)
The conference was held February 2, 2019, at our home office. (Two commas set off the second element.)
The conference was held Tuesday, February 2, 2019, at our home office. (Commas set off the second and third elements.)
In February 2019 the conference was held. (This alternate style omitting commas is acceptable if only the month and year are written.)

b. Addresses:

The letter addressed to Mr. Jim W. Ellman, 600 Via Novella, Agoura, CA 91306, should be sent today. (Commas are used between all elements except the state and zip code, which in this special instance act as a single unit.)

c. Geographical items:

She moved from Toledo, Ohio, to Champaign, Illinois. (Commas set off the state unless it appears at the end of the sentence, in which case only one comma is used.)

In separating cities from states and days from years, many writers remember the initial comma but forget the final one, as in the examples that follow:

The package from Austin, Texas{,} was lost.

We opened June 1, 2010{,} and have grown steadily since.

Review Exercise G—Commas 1

Choose the correctly punctuated item. Then compare your responses with the key at the end of the book.

1. a. Your refund, Mr. Takada, was issued yesterday.
    b. Your refund, Mr. Takada was issued yesterday.

2. a. The safety hazard, on the contrary can be reduced if workers wear rubber gloves.
    b. The safety hazard, on the contrary, can be reduced if workers wear rubber gloves.

3. a. Every accredited TV newscaster, radio broadcaster, and blogger had access to the media room.
    b. Every accredited TV newscaster, radio broadcaster and blogger had access to the media room.

4. a. MegaTech's main offices are located in Boulder, Colorado and Seattle, Washington.
    b. MegaTech's main offices are located in Boulder, Colorado, and Seattle, Washington.

5. a. His book explains how to choose appropriate legal protection for ideas, trade secrets, copyrights, and patents.
    b. His book explains how to choose appropriate legal protection for ideas, trade secrets, copyrights and patents.

6. a. You may however prefer to correspond directly with the manufacturer in Hong Kong.
    b. You may, however, prefer to correspond directly with the manufacturer in Hong Kong.

7. a. Are there any alternatives, in addition to those that we have already considered?
    b. Are there any alternatives in addition to those that we have already considered?

8. a. The rally is scheduled for Monday, January 12, in the football stadium.
   b. The rally is scheduled for Monday, January 12 in the football stadium.

9. a. Kevin agreed to unlock the office open the mail and check all the equipment in my absence.
   b. Kevin agreed to unlock the office, open the mail, and check all the equipment in my absence.

10. a. In the meantime thank you for whatever assistance you are able to furnish.
    b. In the meantime, thank you for whatever assistance you are able to furnish.

11. a. As a rule we do not provide complimentary tickets.
    b. As a rule, we do not provide complimentary tickets.

12. a. I wonder, Professor Mizrahi, whether you could send my recommendation as soon as possible.
    b. I wonder, Professor Mizrahi whether you could send my recommendation as soon as possible.

13. a. Most people by the way, do not like the idea of passengers using cell phones while flying on planes.
    b. Most people, by the way, do not like the idea of passengers using cell phones while flying on planes.

14. a. Wal-Mart opened its first store in Shanghai on July 28, 2005 in the Pudong area.
    b. Wal-Mart opened its first store in Shanghai on July 28, 2005, in the Pudong area.

15. a. Wireless technology allows you to respond to customers' requests, change sales forecasts, and manage suppliers while you are away from the office.
    b. Wireless technology allows you to respond to customers' requests, change sales forecasts and manage suppliers while you are away from the office.

Commas 2 (2.05–2.09)

2.05 Independent Clauses. An independent clause is a group of words that has a subject and a verb and that could stand as a complete sentence. When two such clauses are joined by *and, or, nor,* or *but,* use a comma before the conjunction:

> We can ship your merchandise July 12, but we must have your payment first.

> Net income before taxes is calculated, and this total is then combined with income from operations.

Notice that each independent clause in the preceding two examples could stand alone as a complete sentence. Do not use a comma unless each group of words is a complete thought (that is, has its own subject and verb).

> Our CPA calculates net income before taxes *and* then combines that figure with income from operations. (No comma is needed because no subject follows *and.*)

2.06 Dependent Clauses. Dependent clauses do not make sense by themselves; for their meaning they depend on independent clauses.

a. **Introductory clauses.** When a dependent clause precedes an independent clause, it is followed by a comma. Such clauses are often introduced by *when, if,* and *as:*

> *When your request came,* we responded immediately.

> *As I mentioned earlier,* Mrs. James is the manager.

b. **Terminal clauses.** If a dependent clause falls at the end of a sentence, use a comma only if the dependent clause is an afterthought:

> We have rescheduled the meeting for October 23, *if this date meets with your approval.* (Comma used because dependent clause is an afterthought.)

> We responded immediately *when we received your request.* (No comma is needed.)

c. **Essential versus nonessential clauses**. If a dependent clause provides information that is unneeded for the grammatical completeness of a sentence, use commas to set it off. In determining whether such a clause is essential or nonessential, ask yourself whether the reader needs the information contained in the clause to identify the word it explains:

> Our district sales manager, *who just returned from a trip to the Southwest District*, prepared this report. (This construction assumes that there is only one district sales manager. Because the sales manager is clearly identified, the dependent clause is not essential and requires commas.)

> The salesperson *who just returned from a trip to the Southwest District* prepared this report. (The dependent clause in this sentence is necessary to identify which salesperson prepared the report. Therefore, use no commas.)

> The position of assistant sales manager, *which we discussed with you last week*, is still open. (Careful writers use *which* to introduce nonessential clauses. Commas are also necessary.)

> The position *that we discussed with you last week* is still open. (Careful writers use *that* to introduce essential clauses. No commas are used.)

2.07 Phrases. A phrase is a group of related words that lacks both a subject and a verb. A phrase that precedes a main clause is followed by a comma if the phrase contains a verb form or has four or more words:

> *Beginning November 1*, Worldwide Savings will offer two new combination checking/savings plans. (A comma follows this introductory phrase because the phrase contains the verb form *beginning*.)

> *To promote our plan*, we will conduct an extensive social media advertising campaign. (A comma follows this introductory phrase because the phrase contains the verb form *to promote*.)

> *In a period of only one year*, we were able to improve our market share by 30 percent. (A comma follows the introductory phrase—actually two prepositional phrases—because its total length exceeds four words.)

> *In 2019* our organization installed a multiuser system that could transfer programs easily. (No comma needed after the short introductory phrase.)

2.08 Two or More Adjectives. Use a comma to separate two or more adjectives that equally describe a noun. A good way to test the need for a comma is this: Mentally insert the word *and* between the adjectives. If the resulting phrase sounds natural, a comma is used to show the omission of *and*:

> We're looking for a *versatile, error-free* operating system. (Use a comma to separate *versatile* and *error-free* because they independently describe *operating system*. *And* has been omitted.)

> Our *experienced, courteous* staff is ready to serve you. (Use a comma to separate *experienced* and *courteous* because they independently describe *staff*. *And* has been omitted.)

> It was difficult to refuse the *sincere young* telephone caller. (No commas are needed between *sincere* and *young* because *and* has not been omitted.)

2.09 Appositives. Words that rename or explain preceding nouns or pronouns are called *appositives*. An appositive that provides information not essential to the identification of the word it describes should be set off by commas:

> James Wilson, *the project director for Sperling's*, worked with our architect. (The appositive, *the project director for Sperling's*, adds nonessential information. Commas set it off.)

Review Exercise H—Commas 2

Choose the correctly punctuated item. Then compare your responses with the key at the end of the book.

1. a. A corporation must register in the state in which it does business and it must operate within the laws of that state.
   b. A corporation must register in the state in which it does business, and it must operate within the laws of that state.

2. a. The manager made a point-by-point explanation of the distribution dilemma and then presented his plan to solve the problem.
   b. The manager made a point-by-point explanation of the distribution dilemma, and then presented his plan to solve the problem.

3. a. If you study the cost analysis, you will see that our company offers the best system at the lowest price.
   b. If you study the cost analysis you will see that our company offers the best system at the lowest price.

4. a. Molly Epperson who amassed the greatest number of sales points, won a bonus trip to Hawaii.
   b. Molly Epperson, who amassed the greatest number of sales points, won a bonus trip to Hawaii.

5. a. The salesperson who amasses the greatest number of sales points will win a bonus trip to Hawaii.
   b. The salesperson who amasses the greatest number of sales points, will win a bonus trip to Hawaii.

6. a. When you return the completed form, we will be able to process your application.
   b. When you return the completed form we will be able to process your application.

7. a. For the benefit of employees recently hired, we are offering a two-hour orientation.
   b. For the benefit of employees recently hired we are offering a two-hour orientation.

8. a. Some of the problems you outline in your recent e-mail, could be rectified through more stringent purchasing procedures.
   b. Some of the problems you outline in your recent e-mail could be rectified through more stringent purchasing procedures.

9. a. Scott Cook is a dedicated hardworking employee for our team and our company.
   b. Scott Cook is a dedicated, hardworking employee for our team and our company.

10. a. Stacy Wilson, our newly promoted office manager, has made a number of worthwhile suggestions.
    b. Stacy Wilson, our newly promoted office manager has made a number of worthwhile suggestions.

11. a. If your computer seems to be working more slowly lately you may be the victim of malware.
    b. If your computer seems to be working more slowly lately, you may be the victim of malware.

12. a. The work in this office is strictly confidential, as I am sure you are well aware.
    b. The work in this office is strictly confidential as I am sure you are well aware.

13. a. We expect honest thorough answers during the interview process.
    b. We expect honest, thorough answers during the interview process.

14. a. We hope that the new year will be prosperous for you, and that we may have many more opportunities to serve you.
    b. We hope that the new year will be prosperous for you and that we may have many more opportunities to serve you.

15. a. When you send an e-mail message, remember that it may be forwarded to others.
    b. When you send an e-mail message remember that it may be forwarded to others.

Commas 3 (2.10–2.15)

2.10 Degrees and Abbreviations. Degrees following individuals' names are set off by commas. Abbreviations such as *Jr.* and *Sr.* are also set off by commas unless the individual referred to prefers to omit the commas:

Anne G. Turner, *MBA*, joined the firm.

Michael Migliano, *Jr.*, and Michael Migliano, *Sr.*, work as a team.

Anthony A. Gensler *Jr.* wrote the report. (The individual referred to prefers to omit commas.)

The abbreviations *Inc.* and *Ltd.* are set off by commas only if a company's legal name has a comma just before this kind of abbreviation. To determine a company's practice, consult its stationery or a directory listing:

Firestone and Blythe, *Inc.*, is based in Canada. (Notice that two commas are used.)

Computers *Inc.* is extending its franchise system. (The company's legal name does not include a comma before *Inc.*)

2.11 Omitted Words. A comma is used to show the omission of words that are understood:

On Monday we received 15 applications; on Friday, only 3. (Comma shows the omission of *we received*.)

2.12 Contrasting Statements. Commas are used to set off contrasting or opposing expressions. These expressions are often introduced by such words as *not, never, but*, and *yet*:

The president suggested cutbacks, *not* layoffs, to ease the crisis.

Our budget for the year is reduced, *yet* adequate.

The greater the effort, the greater the reward.

If increased emphasis is desired, use dashes instead of commas, as in *Only the sum of $100—not $1,000—was paid on this account.*

2.13 Clarity. Commas are used to separate words repeated for emphasis. Commas are also used to separate words that may be misread if not separated:

The building is a long, long way from completion.

Whatever is, is right.

No matter what, you know we support you.

2.14 Quotations and Appended Questions.

a. A comma is used to separate a short quotation from the rest of a sentence. If the quotation is divided into two parts, two commas are used:

The manager asked, "Shouldn't the managers control the specialists?"

"Perhaps the specialists," replied Tim, "have unique information."

b. A comma is used to separate a question appended (added) to a statement:

You will confirm the shipment, won't you?

2.15 Comma Overuse. Do not use commas needlessly. For example, commas should not be inserted merely because you might drop your voice if you were speaking the sentence:

One of the reasons for expanding our East Coast operations is{,} that we anticipate increased sales in that area. (Do not insert a needless comma before a clause.)

I am looking for an article titled{,} "State-of-the-Art Communications." (Do not insert a needless comma after the word *titled*.)

Customers may purchase many food and nonfood items in convenience stores *such as*{,} 7-Eleven and Stop-N-Go. (Do not insert a needless comma after *such as*.)

We have{,} at this time{,} an adequate supply of parts. (Do not insert needless commas around prepositional phrases.)

Review Exercise I—Commas 3

Choose the correctly punctuated item. Then compare your responses with the key at the end of the book.

1. a. We expected Anna Cortez, not Tyler Rosen, to conduct the audit.
    b. We expected Anna Cortez, not Tyler Rosen to conduct the audit.

2. a. Brian said, "We simply must have a bigger budget to start this project."
    b. Brian said "We simply must have a bigger budget to start this project."

3. a. You returned the merchandise last month didn't you?
    b. You returned the merchandise last month, didn't you?

4. a. In short employees will now be expected to contribute more to their retirement funds.
    b. In short, employees will now be expected to contribute more to their retirement funds.

5. a. Randall Clark, Esq., and Jonathon Georges, MBA, joined the firm.
    b. Randall Clark, Esq. and Jonathon Georges, MBA joined the firm.

6. a. "America is now entering, said Dr. Williams, the Age of Information."
    b. "America is now entering," said Dr. Williams, "the Age of Information."

7. a. We are very fortunate to have, at our disposal, the services of experts.
    b. We are very fortunate to have at our disposal the services of experts.

8. a. In August customers opened at least 50 new accounts; in September, only about 20.
    b. In August customers opened at least 50 new accounts; in September only about 20.

9. a. Our company will expand into surprising new areas such as, women's apparel and fast food.
    b. Our company will expand into surprising new areas such as women's apparel and fast food.

10. a. No matter what you can count on us for support.
    b. No matter what, you can count on us for support.

11. a. During employment interviews it's good to be confident, not arrogant.
    b. During employment interviews it's good to be confident not arrogant.

12. a. "A résumé is a balance sheet without any liabilities", said personnel specialist Robert Half.
    b. "A résumé is a balance sheet without any liabilities," said personnel specialist Robert Half.

13. a. Most employees arrive to work at 7 a.m.; the rest at 8 a.m.
    b. Most employees arrive to work at 7 a.m.; the rest, at 8 a.m.

14. a. The octogenarians had known each other for a long, long time.
    b. The octogenarians had known each other for a long long time.

15. a. The candidate complained that, for no reason at all, he had been eliminated from the list.
    b. The candidate complained that for no reason at all he had been eliminated from the list.

Semicolons (2.16)

2.16 Independent Clauses, Series, Introductory Expressions.

a. **Independent clauses with conjunctive adverbs.** Use a semicolon before a conjunctive adverb that separates two independent clauses. Some of the most common conjunctive adverbs are *therefore, consequently, however,* and *moreover:*

Business messages should sound conversational; *therefore*, writers often use familiar words and contractions.

The bank closes its doors at 5 p.m.; *however*, the ATM is open 24 hours a day.

Notice that the word following a semicolon is *not* capitalized (unless, of course, that word is a proper noun).

b. **Independent clauses without conjunctive adverbs**. Use a semicolon to separate closely related independent clauses when no conjunctive adverb is used:

Bond interest payments are tax deductible; dividend payments are not.

Ambient lighting fills the room; task lighting illuminates each workstation.

Use a semicolon in *compound* sentences, not in *complex* sentences:

After one week the paper feeder jammed; we tried different kinds of paper. (Use a semicolon in a compound sentence.)

After one week the paper feeder jammed, although we tried different kinds of paper. (Use a comma in a complex sentence. Do not use a semicolon after *jammed*.)

The semicolon is very effective for joining two closely related thoughts. Don't use it, however, unless the ideas are truly related.

c. **Series with internal commas**. Use semicolons to separate items in a series when one or more of the items contains internal commas:

Delegates from Miami, Florida; Freeport, Mississippi; and Chatsworth, California, attended the conference.

The speakers were Kevin Lang, manager, Riko Enterprises; Henry Holtz, vice president, Trendex, Inc.; and Margaret Woo, personnel director, West Coast Productions.

d. **Introductory expressions**. Use a semicolon when an introductory expression such as *namely*, *for instance*, *that is*, or *for example* introduces a list following an independent clause:

Switching to computerized billing are several local companies; namely, Ryson Electronics, Miller Vending Services, and Black Home Heating.

The author of a report should consider many sources; for example, books, periodicals, databases, and newspapers.

Colons (2.17–2.19)

2.17 Listed Items.

a. **With colon**. Use a colon after a complete thought that introduces a formal list of items. A formal list is often preceded by such words and phrases as *these*, *thus*, *the following*, and *as follows*. A colon is also used when words and phrases like these are implied but not stated:

Additional costs in selling a house involve *the following*: title examination fee, title insurance costs, and closing fee. (Use a colon when a complete thought introduces a formal list.)

Collective bargaining focuses on several key issues: cost-of-living adjustments, fringe benefits, job security, and work hours. (The introduction of the list is implied in the preceding clause.)

b. **Without colon**. Do not use a colon when the list immediately follows a *to be* verb or a preposition:

The employees who should receive the preliminary plan are James Sears, Monica Spears, and Rose Lopez. (No colon is used after the verb *are*.)

We expect to consider equipment for Accounting, Legal Services, and Payroll. (No colon is used after the preposition *for*.)

2.18 Quotations. Use a colon to introduce long one-sentence quotations and quotations of two or more sentences:

> Our consultant said: "This system can support up to 32 users. It can be used for decision support, computer-aided design, and software development operations at the same time."

2.19 Salutations. Use a colon after the salutation of a business letter:

Gentlemen: Dear Mrs. Seaman: Dear Jamie:

Review Exercise J—Semicolons and Colons

Choose the correctly punctuated item. Then compare your responses with the key at the end of the book.

1. a. Technological advances make most videos viewable on small screens, consequently, mobile phone makers and carriers are rolling out new services and phones.
   b. Technological advances make most videos viewable on small screens; consequently, mobile phone makers and carriers are rolling out new services and phones.

2. a. Our branch in Oakview specializes in industrial real estate; our branch in Canoga Park concentrates on residential real estate.
   b. Our branch in Oakview specializes in industrial real estate, our branch in Canoga Park concentrates on residential real estate.

3. a. The sport model of the pickup truck is available in these colors; Olympic red, metallic silver, and Aztec gold.
   b. The sport model of the pickup truck is available in these colors: Olympic red, metallic silver, and Aztec gold.

4. a. We intend to send personal invitations to all prospective buyers, however, we have not yet decided just how to do this.
   b. We intend to send personal invitations to all prospective buyers; however, we have not yet decided just how to do this.

5. a. Many of our potential customers are in Southern California; therefore, our promotional effort will be strongest in that area.
   b. Many of our potential customers are in Southern California, therefore, our promotional effort will be strongest in that area.

6. a. Three dates have been reserved for initial interviews, January 15, February 1, and February 12.
   b. Three dates have been reserved for initial interviews: January 15, February 1, and February 12.

7. a. If you apply for an Advantage Express card today, we will waive the annual fee: moreover, you will earn 10,000 bonus miles.
   b. If you apply for an Advantage Express card today, we will waive the annual fee; moreover, you will earn 10,000 bonus miles.

8. a. The convention committee is considering Portland, Oregon; New Orleans, Louisiana; and Phoenix, Arizona.
   b. The convention committee is considering Portland, Oregon, New Orleans, Louisiana, and Phoenix, Arizona.

9. a. Several large companies allow employees access to their personnel files, namely, General Electric, Eastman Enterprises, and Infodata.
   b. Several large companies allow employees access to their personnel files; namely, General Electric, Eastman Enterprises, and Infodata.

10. a. Michelle first asked about salary, next she inquired about benefits.
    b. Michelle first asked about salary; next she inquired about benefits.

11. a. E-business is a risky undertaking, online companies seem to disappear as quickly as they appear.
    b. E-business is a risky undertaking; online companies seem to disappear as quickly as they appear.

12. a. Five of the worst passwords are your first name, your last name, the Enter key, Password, and the name of a sports team.
    b. Five of the worst passwords are: your first name, your last name, the Enter key, Password, and the name of a sports team.

13. a. Smart kitchens are now offered in new homes, for example, some homes come with ovens that can cook food on demand via a cell phone.
    b. Smart kitchens are now offered in new homes; for example, some homes come with ovens that can cook food on demand via a cell phone.

14. a. New York was chosen as the city where people would most like to live and work; San Diego came in second.
    b. New York was chosen as the city where people would most like to live and work, San Diego came in second.

15. a. The computer virus scheduled to hit April 1 was called: "Conflicker."
    b. The computer virus scheduled to hit April 1 was called "Conflicker."

Apostrophes (2.20–2.22)

2.20 Basic Rule. The apostrophe is used to show ownership, origin, authorship, or measurement.

Ownership:	We are looking for *Brian's keys*.
Origin:	At the *president's suggestion*, we doubled the order.
Authorship:	The *accountant's annual report* was questioned.
Measurement:	In *two years' time* we expect to reach our goal.

a. **Ownership words not ending in s.** To place the apostrophe correctly, you must first determine whether the ownership word ends in an *s* sound. If it does not, add an apostrophe and an *s* to the ownership word. The following examples show ownership words that do not end in an s sound:

the employee's file	(the file of a single employee)
a member's address	(the address of a single member)
a year's time	(the time of a single year)
a month's notice	(notice of a single month)
the company's building	(the building of a single company)

b. **Ownership words ending in s.** If the ownership word does end in an s sound, usually add only an apostrophe:

several employees' files	(files of several employees)
ten members' addresses	(addresses of ten members)
five years' time	(time of five years)
several months' notice	(notice of several months)
many companies' buildings	(buildings of many companies)

A few singular nouns that end in *s* are pronounced with an extra syllable when they become possessive. To these words, add '*s*.

my boss's desk   the waitress's table   the actress's costume

Use no apostrophe if a noun is merely plural, not possessive:

All the sales representatives, as well as the assistants and managers, had their names and telephone numbers listed in the directory.

2.21 Names Ending in s or an s sound. The possessive form of names ending in *s* or an *s* sound follows the same guidelines as for common nouns. If an extra syllable can be pronounced without difficulty, add *'s*. If the extra syllable is hard to pronounce, end with an apostrophe only.

Add apostrophe and s	Add apostrophe only
Russ's computer	New Orleans' cuisine
Bill Gates's business	Los Angeles' freeways
Mrs. Jones's home	the Morrises' family
Mr. Lopez's desk	the Lopezes' pool

Individual preferences in pronunciation may cause variation in a few cases. For example, some people may prefer not to pronounce an extra *s* in examples such as *Bill Gates' business*. However, the possessive form of plural names is consistent: *the Joneses' home, the Burgesses' children, the Bushes' car*. Notice that the article *the* is a clue in determining whether a name is singular or plural.

2.22 Gerunds. Use *'s* to make a noun possessive when it precedes a gerund, a verb form used as a noun:

> Mr. Smith's smoking prompted a new office policy. (*Mr. Smith* is possessive because it modifies the gerund *smoking*.)
>
> It was Betsy's careful proofreading that revealed the discrepancy.

Review Exercise K—Apostrophes

Correct any apostrophe errors in the following sentences. In the space provided for each item, write your correction. If a sentence is correct, write C. When you finish, compare your responses with the key at the end of the book.

1. In five years time, Lisa hopes to make her social media business very profitable.

2. The assistants have offices on the lower floors, but Ms. Lords office is on the third floor.

3. All the employees personnel folders must be updated.

4. The Sanchezes daughter lived in Florida for two years.

5. A patent protects an inventors invention for 17 years.

6. Both companies headquarters will be moved within the next six months.

7. The package of electronics parts arrived safely despite two weeks delay.

8. Many nurses believe that nurses notes are not admissible evidence in court.

9. It was Mr. Sanborns signing of the contract that made us happy.

10. Any of the auditors are authorized to conduct an independent action; however, only the CEO can change the councils directives.

11. All new depositors at our three bank branches qualify for free checking accounts.

12. Thousands of customers account information was stolen by hackers.

13. The United States' Treasury promotes economic growth and stability.

14. In just four years time, Jessica hoped to have her college loans repaid.

15. Many chefs prefer to work with organic products.

Other Punctuation (2.23–2.29)

2.23 Periods.

a. **Ends of sentences**. Use a period at the end of a statement, command, indirect question, or polite request. Although a polite request may have the same structure as a question, it ends with a period:

Corporate legal departments demand precise skills from staff members. (End a statement with a period.)

Get the latest data by reading current periodicals. (End a command with a period.)

Mr. Rand wondered whether we had sent any follow-up literature. (End an indirect question with a period.)

Would you please reexamine my account and determine the current balance. (A polite request suggests an action rather than a verbal response.)

b. **Abbreviations and initials**. Use periods after initials and after many abbreviations.

R. M. Johnson	c.o.d.	Ms.
p.m.	a.m.	Mr.
Inc.	i.e.	Mrs.

The latest trend is to omit periods in degrees and professional designations: BA, PhD, MD, RN, DDS. Use just one period when an abbreviation falls at the end of a sentence:

Guests began arriving at 5:30 p.m.

2.24 Question Marks. Direct questions are followed by question marks:

Did you send your proposal to Datatronix, Inc.?

Statements with questions added are punctuated with question marks:

We have completed the proposal, haven't we?

2.25 Exclamation Points. Use an exclamation point after a word, phrase, or clause expressing strong emotion. In business writing, however, exclamation points should be used sparingly:

Incredible! Every terminal is down.

2.26 Dashes. The dash (constructed at a keyboard by striking the hyphen key twice in succession) is a legitimate and effective mark of punctuation when used according to accepted conventions. As a connecting punctuation mark, however, the dash loses effectiveness when overused.

a. **Parenthetical elements**. Within a sentence a parenthetical element is usually set off by commas. If, however, the parenthetical element itself contains internal commas, use dashes (or parentheses) to set it off:

Three top salespeople—Tom Judkins, Tim Templeton, and Mary Yashimoto—received bonuses.

b. **Sentence interruptions**. Use a dash to show an interruption or abrupt change of thought:

News of the dramatic merger—no one believed it at first—shook the financial world.

Ship the materials Monday—no, we must have them sooner.

Sentences with abrupt changes of thought or with appended afterthoughts can usually be improved through rewriting.

c. **Summarizing statements**. Use a dash (not a colon) to separate an introductory list from a summarizing statement:

Sorting, merging, and computing—these are tasks that our data processing programs must perform.

2.27 Parentheses. One means of setting off nonessential sentence elements involves the use of parentheses. Nonessential sentence elements may be punctuated in one of three ways: (a) with commas, to make the lightest possible break in the normal flow of a sentence; (b) with dashes, to emphasize the enclosed material; and (c) with parentheses, to de-emphasize the enclosed material. Parentheses are frequently used to punctuate sentences with interpolated directions, explanations, questions, and references:

The cost analysis (which appears on page 8 of the report) indicates that the copy machine should be leased.

Units are lightweight (approximately 13 oz.) and come with a leather case and operating instructions.

The latest laser printer (have you heard about it?) will be demonstrated for us next week.

A parenthetical sentence that is not embedded within another sentence should be capitalized and punctuated with end punctuation:

The Model 20 has stronger construction. (You may order a Model 20 brochure by circling 304 on the reader service card.)

2.28 Quotation Marks.

a. **Direct quotations**. Use double quotation marks to enclose the exact words of a speaker or writer:

"Keep in mind," Mrs. Frank said, "that you must justify the cost of networking our office."

The boss said that automation was inevitable. (No quotation marks are needed because the exact words are not quoted.)

b. **Quotations within quotations**. Use single quotation marks (apostrophes on the keyboard) to enclose quoted passages within quoted passages:

In her speech Mrs. Deckman remarked, "I believe it was the poet Robert Frost who said, 'All the fun's in how you say a thing.'"

c. **Short expressions**. Slang, words used in a special sense, and words following *stamped* or *marked* are often enclosed within quotation marks:

Jeffrey described the damaged shipment as "gross." (Quotation marks enclose slang.)

Students often have trouble spelling the word "separate." (Quotation marks enclose words used in a special sense.)

Jobs were divided into two categories: most stressful and least stressful. The jobs in the "most stressful" list involved high risk or responsibility. (Quotation marks enclose words used in a special sense.)

The envelope marked "Confidential" was put aside. (Quotation marks enclose words following *marked*.)

In the four preceding sentences, the words enclosed within quotation marks can be set in italics, if italics are available.

d. **Definitions**. Double quotation marks are used to enclose definitions. The word or expression being defined should be underscored or set in italics:

The term *penetration pricing* is defined as "the practice of introducing a product to the market at a low price."

e. **Titles**. Use double quotation marks to enclose titles of literary and artistic works, such as magazine and newspaper articles, chapters of books, movies, television shows, poems, lectures, and songs. Names of major publications—such as books, magazines, pamphlets, and newspapers—are set in italics (underscored).

Particularly helpful was the chapter in Smith's *Effective Writing Techniques* titled "Right Brain, Write On!"

In the *Los Angeles Times* appeared John's article, "E-Mail Blunders"; however, we could not locate it online.

f. **Additional considerations**. In this country periods and commas are always placed inside closing quotation marks. Semicolons and colons, on the other hand, are always placed outside quotation marks:

Mrs. James said, "I could not find the article titled 'Cell Phone Etiquette.'"

The president asked for "absolute security": All written messages were to be destroyed.

Question marks and exclamation points may go inside or outside closing quotation marks, as determined by the form of the quotation:

Sales Manager Martin said, "Who placed the order?" (The quotation is a question.)

When did the sales manager say, "Who placed the order?" (Both the incorporating sentence and the quotation are questions.)

Did the sales manager say, "Ryan placed the order"? (The incorporating sentence asks a question; the quotation does not.)

"In the future," shouted Bob, "ask me first!" (The quotation is an exclamation.)

2.29 Brackets. Within quotations, brackets are used by the quoting writer to enclose his or her own inserted remarks. Such remarks may be corrective, illustrative, or explanatory:

Mrs. Cardillo said, "OSHA [Occupational Safety and Health Administration] has been one of the most widely criticized agencies of the federal government."

Review Exercise L—Other Punctuation

Choose the correctly punctuated item. Then compare your responses with the key at the end of the book.

1. a. Many customers wondered whether the store would be open the day after its fire.
   b. Many customers wondered whether the store would be open the day after its fire?

2. a. Was it Oprah Winfrey who said that the best jobs are those we'd do even if we didn't get paid.
   b. Was it Oprah Winfrey who said that "the best jobs are those we'd do even if we didn't get paid."
   c. Was it Oprah Winfrey who said that the best jobs are those we'd do even if we didn't get paid?

3. a. The expression *de facto* means "exercising power as if legally constituted."
   b. The expression "de facto" means "exercising power as if legally constituted."
   c. The expression de facto means exercising power as if legally constituted.

4. a. Was it the president who said, "This, too, will pass?"
   b. Was it the president who said, "This, too, will pass"?

5. a. Amazing! All sales reps have made their targets!
   b. Amazing. All sales reps have made their targets.

6. a. Your interview is scheduled to start at 3:45 p.m..
   b. Your interview is scheduled to start at 3:45 p.m.
   c. Your interview is scheduled to start at 3.45 p.m.

7. a. The CEO of Philip Morris said "We're being socially responsible in a rather controversial industry".
   b. The CEO of Philip Morris said, "We're being socially responsible in a rather controversial industry."

8. a. "In the future," shouted the manager, "ask me first!"
   b. "In the future, shouted the manager, ask me first."

9. a. Our operating budget for last year—see Appendix A, exceeded all expectations.
   b. Our operating budget for last year (see Appendix A) exceeded all expectations.

10. a. The article published in her blog was titled How to Ace That Job Interview.
    b. The article published in her blog was titled "How to Ace That Job Interview."

11. a. Max wondered whether he had accumulated enough units for his AA degree.
    b. Max wondered whether he had accumulated enough units for his AA degree?

12. a. You did change your PIN as the bank requested, didn't you?
    b. You did change your PIN, as the bank requested, didn't you.

13. a. Garth said he was "stoked" about his upcoming vacation to Mexico.
    b. Garth said, he was stoked about his upcoming vacation to Mexico.

14. a. Maria scored a perfect 800 (can you believe it) on the GMAT exam?
    b. Maria scored a perfect 800 (Can you believe it?) on the GMAT exam.

15. a. Currently our basic operating costs: rent, utilities, and wages—are 10 percent higher than last year.
    b. Currently our basic operating costs (rent, utilities, and wages) are 10 percent higher than last year.

Style and Usage

Capitalization (3.01–3.16)

Capitalization is used to distinguish important words. However, writers are not free to capitalize all words they consider important. Rules or guidelines governing capitalization style have been established through custom and use. Mastering these guidelines will make your writing more readable and more comprehensible.

3.01 Proper Nouns. Capitalize proper nouns, including the *specific* names of persons, places, schools, streets, parks, buildings, holidays, months, agreements, websites, software programs, apps, games, historical periods, and so forth. Do not capitalize common nouns that make only *general* references.

Proper nouns	Common nouns
Instagram, Flixster, WorldMate	popular mobile apps
Mexico, Canada	U.S. trading partners
El Camino College	a community college
Sam Houston Park	a park in the city
Phoenix Room, Statler Inn	a meeting room in the hotel
Memorial Day, New Year's Day	two holidays
Google, Facebook, Wikipedia	popular websites
George Washington Bridge	a bridge
Consumer Product Safety Act	a law to protect consumers
PowerPoint, Photoshop, Excel	software programs
Will Rogers World Airport	a municipal airport
January, February, March	months of the year

3.02 Proper Adjectives. Capitalize most adjectives that are derived from proper nouns:

Greek symbol	British thermal unit
Roman numeral	Freudian slip
Xerox copy	Hispanic markets

Do not capitalize the few adjectives that, although originally derived from proper nouns, have become common adjectives through usage. Consult your dictionary when in doubt:

manila folder	diesel engine
venetian blinds	china dishes

3.03 Geographic Locations. Capitalize the names of *specific* places such as continents, countries, states, mountains, valleys, lakes, rivers, oceans, and geographic regions:

New York City	Great Salt Lake
Allegheny Mountains	Pacific Ocean

San Fernando Valley	Delaware Bay
the East Coast	the Pacific Northwest

3.04 Organization Names. Capitalize the principal words in the names of all business, civic, educational, governmental, labor, military, philanthropic, political, professional, religious, and social organizations:

Genentech	Board of Directors, Midwest Bank
The Wall Street Journal*	San Antonio Museum of Art
New York Stock Exchange	Securities and Exchange Commission
United Way	National Association of Letter Carriers
Commission to Restore the Statue of Liberty	Association of Information Systems Professionals

3.05 Academic Courses and Degrees. Capitalize particular academic degrees and course titles. Do not capitalize general academic degrees and subject areas:

Professor Bernadette Ordian, *PhD*, will teach *Accounting* 221 next fall.

Mrs. Snyder, who holds *bachelor's* and *master's degrees*, teaches *marketing* classes.

Cole enrolled in classes in *history*, *business English*, and *management*.

3.06 Personal and Business Titles.

a. Capitalize personal and business titles when they precede names:

Vice President Ames	Uncle Edward
Board Chairman Frazier	Councilman Herbert
Governor G. W. Thurmond	Sales Manager Klein
Professor McLean	Dr. Samuel Washington

b. Capitalize titles in addresses, salutations, and closing lines:

Mr. Juan deSanto	Very truly yours,
Director of Purchasing	
Space Systems, Inc.	Clara J. Smith
Boxborough, MA 01719	Supervisor, Marketing

c. Generally, do not capitalize titles of high government rank or religious office when they stand alone or follow a person's name in running text:

The president conferred with the joint chiefs of staff and many senators.

Meeting with the chief justice of the Supreme Court were the senator from Ohio and the mayor of Cleveland.

Only the cardinal from Chicago had an audience with the pope.

d. Do not capitalize most common titles following names:

The speech was delivered by Robert Lynch, *president*, Academic Publishing. Lois Herndon, *chief executive officer*, introduced him.

e. Do not capitalize common titles appearing alone:

Please speak to the *supervisor* or to the *office manager*.

Neither the *president* nor the *vice president* could attend.

**Note:* Capitalize *the* only when it is part of the official name of an organization, as printed on the organization's stationery.

However, when the title of an official appears in that organization's minutes, bylaws, or other official document, it may be capitalized.

f. Do not capitalize titles when they are followed by appositives naming specific individuals:

We must consult our *director of research*, Ronald E. West, before responding.

g. Do not capitalize family titles used with possessive pronouns:

my mother	your father
our aunt	his cousin

h. Capitalize titles of close relatives used without pronouns:

Both *Mother* and *Father* must sign the contract.

3.07 Numbered and Lettered Items.
Capitalize nouns followed by numbers or letters (except in page, paragraph, line, and verse references):

Flight 34, Gate 12	Plan No. 2
Volume I, Part 3	Warehouse 33-A
Invoice No. 55489	Figure 8.3
Model A5673	Serial No. C22865404-2
State Highway 10	page 6, line 5

3.08 Points of the Compass.
Capitalize *north, south, east, west*, and their derivatives when they represent *specific* geographical regions. Do not capitalize the points of the compass when they are used in directions or in general references:

Specific regions	General references
from the South	heading north on the highway
living in the Midwest	west of the city
Easterners, Southerners	western Nevada, southern Indiana
going to the Middle East	the northern part of the United States
from the East Coast	the east side of the street

3.09 Departments, Divisions, and Committees.
Capitalize the names of departments, divisions, or committees within your own organization. Outside your organization capitalize only *specific* department, division, or committee names:

The inquiry was addressed to the *Legal Department in our Consumer Products Division*.

John was appointed to the *Employee Benefits Committee*.

Send your rèsumè to their *human resources division*.

A *planning committee* will be named shortly.

3.10 Governmental Terms.
Do not capitalize the words *federal, government, nation*, or *state* unless they are part of a specific title:

Unless *federal* support can be secured, the *state* project will be abandoned.

The *Federal Deposit Insurance Corporation* protects depositors from bank failure.

3.11 Product Names.
Capitalize product names only when they refer to trademarked items. Except in advertising, common names following manufacturers' names are not capitalized:

Magic Marker	Dell computer
Kleenex tissues	Swingline stapler

Q-tip swab	ChapStick lip balm
Levi 501 jeans	Excel spreadsheet
DuPont Teflon	Canon camera

3.12 Literary Titles. Capitalize the principal words in the titles of books, magazines, newspapers, articles, movies, plays, songs, poems, and reports. Do not capitalize articles (*a, an, the*), short conjunctions (*and, but, or, nor*), and prepositions of fewer than four letters (in, to, by, for) unless they begin or end the title:

Jackson's *What Job Is for You?* (Capitalize book titles.)

Gant's "Software for the Executive Suite" (Capitalize principal words in article titles.)

"Performance Standards to Go By" (Capitalize article titles.)

"The Improvement of Fuel Economy With Alternative Fuels" (Capitalize report titles.)

3.13 Beginning Words. In addition to capitalizing the first word of a complete sentence, capitalize the first word in a quoted sentence, independent phrase, item in an enumerated list, and formal rule or principle following a colon:

The business manager said, "*All* purchases must have requisitions." (Capitalize first word in a quoted sentence.)

Yes, if you agree. (Capitalize the first word in an independent phrase.)

Some of the duties of the position are as follows:

1. *Editing* and formatting Word files
2. *Arranging* video and teleconferences
3. *Verifying* records, reports, and applications (Capitalize first words in a vertical enumerated list.)

One rule has been established through the company: *No* smoking is allowed in open offices. (Capitalize a rule following a colon.)

3.14 Celestial Bodies. Capitalize the names of celestial bodies such as *Mars, Saturn*, and *Neptune*. Do not capitalize the terms *earth, sun*, or *moon* unless they appear in a context with other celestial bodies:

Where on *earth* did you find that manual typewriter?

Venus and *Mars* are the closest planets to *Earth*.

3.15 Ethnic References. Capitalize terms that refer to a particular culture, language, or race:

Asian	Hebrew
Caucasian	Indian
Latino	Japanese
Persian	Judeo-Christian

3.16 Seasons. Do not capitalize seasons:

In the *fall* it appeared that *winter* and *spring* sales would increase.

Review Exercise M—Capitalization

Choose the sentence with correct capitalization. Then compare your responses with the key at the end of the book.

1. a. My Uncle and I used PowerPoint to make a simple video featured on YouTube.
   b. My uncle and I used PowerPoint to make a simple video featured on YouTube.

2. a. The president and the vice president of Techtronics flew to the East Coast.
   b. The President and the Vice President of Techtronics flew to the East Coast.

Appendix D: Grammar/Mechanics Handbook

3. a. Your reservations are for flight 32 on American Airlines leaving from gate 14.
   b. Your reservations are for Flight 32 on American Airlines leaving from Gate 14.

4. a. After crossing the Sunshine Skyway bridge, we drove South to the Beach.
   b. After crossing the Sunshine Skyway Bridge, we drove south to the beach.

5. a. Dylan was enrolled in History, Spanish, Business Communication, and Physical Education courses.
   b. Dylan was enrolled in history, Spanish, business communication, and physical education courses.

6. a. Where in the world can we find better workers than robots?
   b. Where in the World can we find better workers than Robots?

7. a. The conference will be held in the empire room of the red lion motor inn.
   b. The conference will be held in the Empire Room of the Red Lion Motor Inn.

8. a. Zeke ordered a special keyboard for his Apple computer that has Greek symbols for engineering equations.
   b. Zeke ordered a special keyboard for his Apple Computer that has Greek symbols for Engineering equations.

9. a. Last spring it appeared that sales would pick up in the summer and fall months.
   b. Last Spring it appeared that sales would pick up in the Summer and Fall months.

10. a. Without Federal funds, our State cannot rebuild its infrastructure.
    b. Without federal funds, our state cannot rebuild its infrastructure.

11. a. The Boston Marathon is an annual Sporting Event hosted by the City of Boston on Patriots' Day.
    b. The Boston marathon is an annual sporting event hosted by the city of Boston on Patriots' day.
    c. The Boston Marathon is an annual sporting event hosted by the city of Boston on Patriots' Day.

12. a. A federal judge in San Francisco ruled that businesses must make their websites accessible to the blind.
    b. A Federal judge in San Francisco ruled that businesses must make their Websites accessible to the blind.

13. a. My Uncle Eduardo recently purchased a Ford Escape for his trip to the west coast this summer.
    b. My uncle Eduardo recently purchased a Ford Escape for his trip to the west coast this Summer.
    c. My Uncle Eduardo recently purchased a Ford Escape for his trip to the West Coast this summer.

14. a. Martin Cooper, a General Manager at Motorola, created the first true Cell Phone.
    b. Martin Cooper, a general manager at Motorola, created the first true cell phone.

15. a. The fishing industry in the Pacific Northwest is reeling from the impact of government regulations.
    b. The Fishing Industry in the Pacific Northwest is reeling from the impact of Government regulations.

Number Style (4.01–4.13)

Usage and custom determine whether numbers are expressed in the form of figures (e.g., *5, 9*) or in the form of words (e.g., *five, nine*). Numbers expressed as figures are shorter and more easily understood, yet numbers expressed as words are necessary in certain instances. The following guidelines are observed in expressing numbers in written sentences. Numbers that appear on business forms—such as invoices, monthly statements, and purchase orders—are always expressed as figures.

4.01 General Rules.

a. The numbers *one* through *ten* are generally written as words. Numbers above *ten* are written as figures:

> The bank had a total of *nine* branch offices in *three* suburbs.
>
> All *58* employees received benefits in the *three* categories shown.
>
> A shipment of *45,000* lightbulbs was sent from *two* warehouses.

b. Numbers that begin sentences are written as words. If a number beginning a sentence involves more than two words, however, the sentence should be revised so that the number does not fall at the beginning.

> *Fifteen* color options are available in our latest smartphone lineup.
>
> A total of *156* companies participated in the promotion (not *One hundred fifty-six companies participated in the promotion*).

4.02 Money.
Sums of money $1 or greater are expressed as figures. If a sum is a whole dollar amount, omit the decimal and zeros (whether or not the amount appears in a sentence with additional fractional dollar amounts):

> We budgeted *$300* for a digital camera, but the actual cost was *$370.96*.
>
> On the invoice were items for *$6.10*, *$8*, *$33.95*, and *$75*.

Sums less than $1 are written as figures that are followed by the word *cents*:
By shopping carefully, we can save *15 cents* per unit.

4.03 Dates.
In dates, numbers that appear after the name of the month are written as cardinal figures (*1, 2, 3,* etc.). Those that stand alone or appear before the name of a month are written as ordinal figures (*1st, 2nd, 3rd,* etc.):

> The Personnel Practices Committee will meet *May 7*.
>
> On the *5th* day of February and again on the *25th*, we placed orders.

In domestic business documents, dates generally take the following form: *January 4, 2015*. An alternative form, used primarily in military and foreign correspondence, begins with the day of the month and omits the comma: *4 January 2015*.

4.04 Clock Time.
Figures are used when clock time is expressed with *a.m.* or *p.m.* Omit the colon and zeros in referring to whole hours. When exact clock time is expressed with the contraction o'clock, either figures or words may be used:

> Mail deliveries are made at *11 a.m.* and *3:30 p.m.*
>
> At *four* (or *4*) *o'clock* employees begin to leave.

4.05 Addresses and Telephone Numbers.

a. Except for the number *one*, house numbers are expressed in figures:

> 540 Elm Street   17802 Washington Avenue
> One Colorado Boulevard   2 Highland Street

b. Street names containing numbers *ten* or lower are written entirely as words. For street names involving numbers greater than *ten*, figures are used:

> 330 Third Street   3440 Seventh Avenue
> 6945 East 32nd Avenue   4903 West 23rd Street

c. Telephone numbers are expressed with figures. When used, the area code is placed in parentheses preceding the telephone number:

Please call us at *(818) 347-0551* to place an order.

Mr. Sims asked you to call *(619) 554-8923*, Ext. 245, after 10 a.m.

4.06 Related Numbers.
Numbers are related when they refer to similar items in a category within the same reference. All related numbers should be expressed as the largest number is expressed. Thus if the largest number is greater than *ten*, all the numbers should be expressed in figures:

Only *5* of the original *25* applicants completed the processing. (Related numbers require figures.)

The two plans affected *34* employees working in *three* sites. (Unrelated numbers use figures and words.)

Exxon Oil operated *86* rigs, of which *6* were rented. (Related numbers require figures.)

The company hired *three* accountants, *one* customer-service representative, and *nine* sales representatives. (Related numbers under *ten* use words.)

4.07 Consecutive Numbers.
When two numbers appear consecutively and both modify a following noun, generally express the first number in words and the second in figures. If, however, the first number cannot be expressed in one or two words, place it in figures also (*120 70-cent* stamps). Do not use commas to separate the figures.

Historians divided the era into *four 25-year* periods. (Use word form for the first number and figure form for the second.)

We ordered *ten 30-page* color brochures. (Use word form for the first number and figure form for the second.)

Did the manager request *150 100-watt* bulbs? (Use figure form for the first number since it would require more than two words.)

4.08 Periods of Time.
Seconds, minutes, days, weeks, months, and years are treated as any other general number. Numbers above *ten* are written in figure form. Numbers below *ten* are written in word form unless they represent a business concept such as a discount rate, interest rate, or warranty period:

This business was incorporated over *50* years ago. (Use figures for a number above *ten*.)

It took *three* hours to write this short report. (Use words for a number under *ten*.)

The warranty period is limited to *2* years. (Use figures for a business term.)

4.09 Ages.
Ages are generally expressed in word form unless the age appears immediately after a name or is expressed in exact years and months:

At the age of *twenty-one*, Elizabeth inherited the business.

Wanda Tharp, *37*, was named acting president.

At the age of *4 years and 7 months*, the child was adopted.

4.10 Round Numbers.
Round numbers are approximations. They may be expressed in word or figure form, although figure form is shorter and easier to comprehend:

About *600* (or *six hundred*) stock options were sold.

It is estimated that *1,000* (or *one thousand*) people will attend.

For ease of reading, round numbers in the millions or billions should be expressed with a combination of figures and words:

Facebook estimates that it has *1.98 billion* users.

More than *163 million* viewers watched last year's Super Bowl game.

4.11 Weights and Measurements.
Weights and measurements are expressed with figures:

> The new deposit slip measures *2* by *6 inches*.

> Her new suitcase weighed only *2 pounds 4 ounces*.

> Toledo is *60 miles* from Detroit.

4.12 Fractions.
Simple fractions are expressed as words. Complex fractions may be written either as figures or as a combination of figures and words:

> Over *two thirds* of the stockholders have already voted.

> This microcomputer will execute the command in *1 millionth* of a second. (A combination of words and numbers is easier to comprehend.)

> She purchased a *one-fifth* share in the business.*

4.13 Percentages and Decimals.
Percentages are expressed with figures that are followed by the word *percent*. The percent sign (%) is used only on business forms or in statistical presentations:

> We had hoped for a *7 percent* interest rate, but we received a loan at *8 percent*.

> Over *50 percent* of the residents supported the plan.

Decimals are expressed with figures. If a decimal expression does not contain a whole number (an integer) and does not begin with a zero, a zero should be placed before the decimal point:

> The actuarial charts show that *1.74* out of *1,000* people will die in any given year.

> Inspector Norris found the setting to be *.005* inch off. (Decimal begins with a zero and does not require a zero before the decimal point.)

> Considerable savings will accrue if the unit production cost is reduced *0.1* percent. (A zero is placed before a decimal that neither contains a whole number nor begins with a zero.)

Quick Chart—Expression of Numbers

Use Words	Use Figures
Numbers *ten* and under	Numbers *11* and over
Numbers at beginning of sentence	Money
Ages	Dates
Fractions	Addresses and telephone numbers
	Weights and measurements
	Percentages and decimals

Review Exercise N—Number Style

Choose the option that is correctly expressed. Then compare your responses with the key at the end of the book.

1. She had (a) 2, (b) two laptops.

2. The store is on (a) Fifth, (b) 5th Avenue.

3. Our meeting is on (a) November ninth, (b) November 9, (c) November 9th.

4. That gift cost (a) forty dollars, (b) $40, (c) $40 dollars.

---

*Note: Fractions used as adjectives require hyphens.

5. The meeting starts at (a) 2 p.m., (b) 2:00 p.m., (c) 2 o'clock p.m.

6. One holiday football bowl game had (a) two, (b) 2 million viewers.

7. This appliance comes with a (a) 60-day, (b) sixty-day warranty.

8. The rug measures (a) four by six, (b) 4 by 6 feet.

9. It happened at least (a) 15, (b) fifteen years ago.

10. Your loan carried a (a) ten, (b) 10 percent interest rate.

11. Only (a) three, (b) 3 of the 25 e-mail messages were undeliverable.

12. The hotel has (a) 45, (b) forty-five rooms with views.

13. Domino's offered (a) 5 dollars, (b) $5, (c) $5 dollars off on every large pizza.

14. The shipment finally arrived at (a) 9 o'clock, (b) 9:00 in the evening, (c) 9 p.m.

15. The warranty period is limited to (a) 1 year, (b) one year.

Confusing Words

accede:	to agree or consent	*credible:*	believable
accept:	to receive	*creditable:*	good enough for praise or esteem; reliable
adverse:	opposing; antagonistic		
averse:	disinclined	*desert:*	arid land; to abandon
advice:	suggestion, opinion	*dessert:*	sweet food
advise:	to counsel or recommend	*device:*	invention or mechanism
affect:	to influence	*devise:*	to design or arrange
all ready:	prepared	*disburse:*	to pay out
all right:	satisfactory	*disperse:*	to scatter widely
already:	by this time	*effect:*	(n) outcome, result; (v) to bring about, to create
alright:	unacceptable variant spelling		
		elicit:	to draw out
altar:	structure for worship	*ensure:*	to make certain
alter:	to change	*envelop:*	(v) to wrap, surround, or conceal
appraise:	to estimate		
apprise:	to inform	*envelope:*	(n) a container for a written message
ascent:	(n) rising or going up		
assent:	(v) to agree or consent	*every day:*	each single day
assure:	to promise	*everyday:*	ordinary
capital:	(n) city that is seat of government; wealth of an individual; (adj) chief	*exceed:*	over a limit
		except:	to exclude; (prep) but
		farther:	a greater distance
		formally:	in a formal manner
capitol:	building that houses state or national lawmakers	*formerly:*	in the past
		further:	additional
cereal:	breakfast food	*grate:*	(n) a frame of crossed bars blocking a passage; (v) to reduce to small particles; to cause irritation
cite:	to quote; to summon		
coarse:	rough texture		
complement:	that which completes		
compliment:	(n) praise, flattery; (v) to praise or flatter	*great:*	(adj) large; numerous; eminent or distinguished
conscience:	regard for fairness	*hole:*	an opening
conscious:	aware	*illicit:*	unlawful
council:	governing body	*imply:*	to suggest indirectly
counsel:	(n) advice, attorney; (v) to give advice	*infer:*	to reach a conclusion
		insure:	to protect from loss
course:	a route; part of a meal; a unit of learning	*lean:*	(v) to rest against; (adj) not fat

liable:	legally responsible	principal:	(n) capital sum; school official; (adj) chief
libel:	damaging written statement	principle:	rule of action
lien:	(n) a legal right or claim to property	proceed:	to continue
		serial:	arranged in sequence
loose:	not fastened	sight:	a view; to see
lose:	to misplace	site:	location
miner:	person working in a mine	stationary:	immovable
minor:	a lesser item; person under age	stationery:	writing material
		than:	conjunction showing comparison
patience:	calm perseverance		
patients:	people receiving medical treatment	their:	possessive form of *they*
		then:	adverb meaning "at that time"
personal:	private, individual		
personnel:	employees	there:	at that place or point
plaintiff:	(n) one who initiates a lawsuit	they're:	contraction of *they are*
		to:	a preposition; the sign of the infinitive
plaintive:	(adj) expressive of suffering or woe		
		too:	an adverb meaning "also" or "to an excessive extent"
populace:	(n) the masses; population of a place		
		two:	a number
populous:	(adj) densely populated	waiver:	abandonment of a claim
precede:	to go before	waver:	to shake or fluctuate
precedence:	priority	whole:	complete
precedents:	events used as an example		

160 Frequently Misspelled Words

absence	column	development	February
accommodate	committee	disappoint	fiscal
achieve	congratulate	dissatisfied	foreign
acknowledgment	conscience	division	forty
across	conscious	efficient	fourth
adequate	consistent	embarrass	friend
advisable	consecutive	emphasis	genuine
analyze	consensus	emphasize	government
annually	control	employee	grammar
appointment	convenient	envelope	grateful
argument	correspondence	equipped	guarantee
automatically	courteous	especially	harass
bankruptcy	criticize	evidently	height
becoming	decision	exaggerate	hoping
beneficial	deductible	excellent	immediate
budget	defendant	exempt	incidentally
business	definitely	existence	incredible
calendar	dependent	extraordinary	independent
canceled	describe	familiar	indispensable
catalog	desirable	fascinate	interrupt
changeable	destroy	feasible	irrelevant

itinerary	offered	quantity	supervisor
judgment	omission	questionnaire	surprise
knowledge	omitted	receipt	tenant
legitimate	opportunity	receive	therefore
library	opposite	recognize	thorough
license	ordinarily	recommendation	though
maintenance	paid	referred	through
manageable	pamphlet	regarding	truly
manufacturer	permanent	remittance	undoubtedly
mileage	permitted	representative	unnecessarily
miscellaneous	pleasant	restaurant	usable
mortgage	practical	schedule	usage
necessary	prevalent	secretary	using
nevertheless	privilege	separate	usually
ninety	probably	similar	valuable
ninth	procedure	sincerely	volume
noticeable	profited	software	weekday
occasionally	prominent	succeed	writing
occurred	qualify	sufficient	yield

Key to Grammar/Mechanics Handbook Review Exercises

Review Exercise A—Nouns

1. a (attorneys) **2.** b (Davises) **3.** b (companies)
4. a (benches) **5.** a (ups and downs) **6.** a (Sundays)
7. b (dispatches) **8.** c (countries) **9.** b (b's and d's)
10. b (bills of sale) **11.** b (MBAs) **12.** c (sisters-in-law)
13. a (currencies) **14.** b (lenses) **15.** a (boards of directors)

Review Exercise B— Pronouns

1. a (me) **2.** b (me) **3.** b (Whom) **4.** a (its) **5.** a (her)
6. b (me) **7.** b (We) **8.** a (its) **9.** b (me) **10.** b (ours)
11. a (its) **12.** b (me) **13.** a (whoever) **14.** b (All students) **15.** b (you're)

Review Exercise C—Verbs 1

1. b (are) **2.** a (was) **3.** b (chose) **4.** b (seen)
5. a (is) **6.** a (is) **7.** a (is) **8.** b (are) **9.** b (written)
10. b (become) **11.** b (were) **12.** a (require)
13. b (lying) **14.** b (broken) **15.** a (rung)

Review Exercise D—Verbs 2

1. b **2.** a **3.** b **4.** b **5.** a

Review Exercise E—Adjectives and Adverbs

1. a (careful) **2.** b (face-to-face) **3.** a (satisfactorily)
4. b (their) **5.** a (bad) **6.** b (more quickly)
7. b (money-back) **8.** a (worse) **9.** a (page by page) **10.** b (personally) **11.** a (more) **12.** a (there)
13. b (well) **14.** b (closer) **15.** b (naturally)

Review Exercise F— Prepositions and Conjunctions

1. a **2.** b **3.** b **4.** a **5.** b **6.** b **7.** a **8.** a **9.** b **10.** b
11. a **12.** a **13.** b **14.** b **15.** b

Review Exercise G—Commas 1

1. a **2.** b **3.** a **4.** b **5.** a **6.** b **7.** b **8.** a **9.** b **10.** b
11. b **12.** a **13.** a **14.** b **15.** a

Review Exercise H—Commas 2

1. b 2. a 3. a 4. b 5. a 6. a 7. a 8. b 9. b 10. a 11. b 12. a 13. b 14. b 15. a

Review Exercise I—Commas 3

1. a 2. a 3. b 4. b 5. a 6. b 7. b 8. a 9. b 10. b 11. a 12. b 13. b 14. a 15. b

Review Exercise J—Semicolons and Colons

1. b 2. a 3. b 4. b 5. a 6. b 7. b 8. a 9. b 10. b 11. b 12. a 13. b 14. a 15. b

Review Exercise K—Apostrophes

1. years' 2. Lord's 3. employees' 4. Sanchezes' 5. inventor's 6. companies' 7. weeks' 8. nurses' notes 9. Sanborn's 10. council's 11. C 12. customers' 13. States 14. years' 15. C

Review Exercise L—Other Punctuation

1. a 2. c 3. a 4. b 5. a 6. b 7. b 8. a 9. b 10. b 11. a 12. a 13. a 14. b 15. b

Review Exercise M—Capitalization

1. b 2. a 3. b 4. b 5. b 6. a 7. b 8. a 9. a 10. b 11. c 12. a 13. c 14. b 15. a

Review Exercise N—Number Style

1. b (two) 2. a (Fifth) 3. b (November 9) 4. b ($40) 5. a (2 p.m.) 6. b (2) 7. a (60-day) 8. b (4 by 6) 9. a (15) 10. b (10) 11. b (3) 12. a (45) 13. b ($5) 14. c (9 p.m.) 15. a (1 year)

Notes

Chapter 1

1. National Association of Colleges and Employers (NACE). (2016, December 7). The attributes employers seek on a candidate's resume. Job Outlook 2017. Retrieved from http://www.naceweb.org/talent-acquisition/candidate-selection/the-attributes-employers-seek-on-a-candidates-resume; Hart Research Associates/Association of American Colleges & Universities. (2015, January 20). Falling short? College learning and career success. Retrieved from https://www.aacu.org/leap/public-opinion-research/2015-survey-results; Gray, K., & Koncz, A. (2014, November 18). The skills/qualities employers want in new college graduate hires. National Association of Colleges and Employers (NACE). Retrieved from https://www.naceweb.org/about-us/press/class-2015-skills-qualities-employers-want.aspx; Graduate Management Admission Council (GMAC). 2014 Corporate recruiters survey report, p. 19. Retrieved from http://www.gmac.com/market-intelligence-and-research/research-library/employment-outlook/2014-corporate-recruiters.aspx; Groysberg, B. (2014, March 18). The seven skills you need to thrive in the C-suite. Harvard Business Review. Retrieved from https://hbr.org/2014/03/the-seven-skills-you-need-to-thrive-in-the-c-suite

2. National Association of Colleges and Employers. (2016, December 16). Job outlook: Hiring for U.S. jobs expected to be flat. Retrieved from http://www.naceweb.org/job-market/trends-and-predictions/job-outlook-hiring-for-us-jobs-expected-to-be-flat

3. O'Rourke, J. (2013). Managerial communication (5th ed.). Upper Saddle River, NJ: Prentice Hall.

4. Canavor, N. (2012). Business writing in the digital age. Los Angeles: Sage, p. 4.

5. Alber, R. (2013). Deeper learning: Defining twenty-first century literacy. Edutopia. Retrieved from https://www.edutopia.org/blog/twenty-first-century-literacy-deeper-learning-rebecca-alber; Watanabe-Crockett, L. (2016). The critical 21st-century skills every student needs and why. Global Digital Citizen Foundation. Retrieved from https://globaldigitalcitizen.org/21st-century-skills-every-student-needs; Canavor, N. (2012). Business writing in the digital age. Los Angeles: Sage, pp. 1–3.

6. Davidson, K. (2016, August 30). The "soft skills" employers are looking for. The Wall Street Journal. Retrieved from http://blogs.wsj.com/economics/2016/08/30/the-soft-skills-employers-are-looking-for; Hart Research Associates/Association of American Colleges & Universities. (2015, January 20). Falling short? College learning and career success. Retrieved from https://www.aacu.org/leap/public-opinion-research/2015-survey-results

7. Watanabe-Crockett, L. (2016). The critical 21st-century skills every student needs and why. Global Digital Citizen Foundation. Retrieved from https://globaldigitalcitizen.org/21st-century-skills-every-student-needs

8. Kehaulani Goo, S. (2015, February 19). The skills Americans say kids need to succeed in life. Pew Research Center. Retrieved from http://www.pewresearch.org/fact-tank/2015/02/19/skills-for-success/#comments

9. Gallo, C. (2015, July 7). Richard Branson: "Communication is the most important skills any leader can possess." Forbes. Retrieved from http://www.forbes.com/sites/carminegallo/2015/07/07/richard-branson-communication-is-the-most-important-skill-any-leader-can-possess/#1ffa39a94ff2

10. Greenfield, R. (2016, December 7). Forget robots—people skills are the future of American jobs. Bloomberg. Retrieved from https://www.bloomberg.com/news/articles/2016-12-07/forget-robots-jobs-requiring-people-skills-are-the-future-of-american-labor; Deming, D. J. (2016, August). The growing importance of social skills in the labor market. Harvard University and National Bureau of Economic Relations (NBER). Retrieved from http://scholar.harvard.edu/files/ddeming/files/deming_socialskills_aug16.pdf

11. White, M. C. (2013, November 10). The real reason new college grads can't get hired. Time. Retrieved from http://business.time.com/2013/11/10/the-real-reason-new-college-grads-cant-get-hired

12. MacPhail, T. (2015, July 23). The importance of writing skills in tech-related fields. Vitae. Retrieved from https://chroniclevitae.com/news/1073-the-importance-of-writing-skills-in-tech-related-fields

13. 2016 workforce-skills preparedness report. (2016). PayScale. Retrieved from http://www.payscale.com/data-packages/job-skills

14. Davidson, K. (2016, August 30). The "soft skills" employers are looking for. The Wall Street Journal. Retrieved from http://blogs.wsj.com/economics/2016/08/30/the-soft-skills-employers-are-looking-for; National Association of Colleges and Employers (NACE). (2016, December 7). The attributes employers seek on a candidate's resume. Job Outlook 2017. Retrieved from http://www.naceweb.org/talent-acquisition/candidate-selection/the-attributes-employers-seek-on-a-candidates-resume

15. Madell, R. (2015, June 15). The 3 biggest social media snafus that can cost you the job. U.S. News & World Report. Retrieved from http://money.usnews.com/money/blogs/outside-voices-careers/2015/06/15/the-3-biggest-social-media-snafus-that-can-cost-you-the-job; Wong, V. (2013, June 27). Hey job applicants, time to stop the social-media sabotage. Bloomberg. Retrieved from www.businessweek.com/articles/2013-06-27/for-job-applicants-social-media-sabotage-is-still-getting-worse#r=read

16. Torres, N. (2015, August 26). Research: Technology is only making social skills more important. Harvard Business Review. Retrieved from https://hbr.org/2015/08/research-technology-is-only-making-social-skills-more-important

17. Satell, G. (2015, February 6). Why communication is today's most important skills. Forbes. Retrieved from http://www.forbes.com/sites/gregsatell/2015/02/06/why-communication-is-todays-most-important-skill/#42c84d563638

18. Graduate Management Admission Council (GMAC). (2014, August 7). Employers want communication skills in new hires. Retrieved from http://www.mba.com/us/the-gmat-blog-hub/the-official-gmat-blog/2014/aug/employers-want-communication-skills-in-new-hires.aspx

19. Ibid.

20. Davidson, K. (2016, August 30). Employers find "soft skills" like critical thinking in short supply. The Wall Street Journal. Retrieved from http://www.wsj.com/articles/employers-find-soft-skills-like-critical-thinking-in-short-supply-1472549400; Waller, N. (2016, October 25). Hunting for soft skills, companies scoop up English majors. The Wall Street Journal. Retrieved from http://www.wsj.com/articles/hunting-for-soft-skills-companies-scoop-up-english-majors-1477404061; Davidson, K. (2016, August 30). The "soft skills" employers are looking for. The Wall Street Journal. Retrieved from blogs.wsj.com/economics/2016/08/30/the-soft-skills-employers-are-looking-for

21. 2016 workforce-skills preparedness report. (2016). PayScale. Retrieved from http://www.payscale.com/data-packages/job-skills

22. Graduate Management Admission Council (GMAC). (2014, August 7). Employers want communication skills in new hires. Retrieved from http://www.mba.com/us/the-gmat-blog-hub/the-official-gmat-blog/2014/aug/employers-want-communication-skills-in-new-hires.aspx

23. Davidson, K. (2016, August 30). Employers find "soft skills" like critical thinking in short supply. The Wall Street Journal. Retrieved from http://www.wsj.com/articles/employers-find-soft-skills-like-critical-thinking-in-short-supply-1472549400

24. Yang, D. (2016, May 24). Who are you calling soft? The value of soft skills in a tech-obsessed economy. The Huffington Post. Retrieved from http://www.huffingtonpost.com/dennis-yang/who-are-you-calling-soft-_b_10110082.html

25. Cook, L. (2015, August 17). Seriously, go to college. U.S. News & World Report. Retrieved from http://www.usnews.com/news/blogs/data-mine/2015/08/17/study-benefits-of-a-college-degree-are-historically-high; Rampell, C. (2013, February 19). College premium: Better pay, better prospects. Economix Blogs, New York Times. Retrieved from http://economix.blogs.nytimes.com/2013/02/19/college-premium-better-pay-better-prospects/?_r=0

26. Shah, N. (2013, April 2). College grads earn nearly three times more than high school dropouts. WSJ Blogs. Retrieved from http://blogs.wsj.com/economics/2013/04/02/college-grads-earn-nearly-three-times-more-than-high-school-dropouts

27. Davidson, K. (2016, October 4). Soft skills give workers a big edge. It's time to start focusing on them in school, report says. *The Wall Street Journal*. Retrieved from http://blogs.wsj.com/economics/2016/10/04/soft-skills-give-workers-a-big-edge-its-time-to-start-focusing-on-them-in-school-report-says

28. Holland, K. (2008, September 28). The anywhere, anytime office. *The New York Times*, p. 14 BU14.

29. Tugend, A. (2014, March 7). It's unclearly defined, but telecommuting is fast on the rise. *The New York Times*. Retrieved from https://www.nytimes.com/2014/03/08/your-money/when-working-in-your-pajamas-is-more-productive.html

30. Silverman, R. E., & Sidel, R. (2012, April 17). Warming up to the officeless office. *The Wall Street Journal*. Retrieved from http://online.wsj.com/article/SB10001424052702304818404577349783161465976.html; Holland, K. (2008, September 28). The anywhere, anytime office. *The New York Times*, p. 14 BU14.

31. Edmondson, A. C. (2012, April). Teamwork on the fly. *Harvard Business Review*. Retrieved from http://hbr.org/2012/04/teamwork-on-the-fly/ar/1

32. Branson, R. (2015, May 11). My top 10 quotes on communication. Retrieved from https://www.virgin.com/richard-branson/my-top-10-quotes-on-communication

33. Washington, V. (n.d.). The high cost of poor listening. *Deskdemon*. Retrieved from http://us.deskdemon.com/pages/us/career/poor-listening

34. Accountemps/Robert Half. (2014, July 30). Boost your active listening skills with these tips. https://www.roberthalf.com/accountemps/blog/soft-skills-spotlight-active-listening

35. Bucero, A. (2006, July). Listen and learn. *PM Network*. Retrieved from http://search.ebscohost.com

36. Watzlawick, P., Beavin Bavelas, J., & Jackson, D. D. (2011). *Pragmatics of human communication: A study of interactional patterns, pathologies and paradoxes*. New York: W. W. Norton, p. 30.

37. Birdwhistell, R. (1970). *Kinesics and context*. Philadelphia: University of Pennsylvania Press.

38. Burton, V. (2016). *Successful women speak differently: 9 habits that build confidence, courage, and influence*. Eugene, OR: Harvest House Publishers, p. 65.

39. Hall, E. T. (1966). *The hidden dimension*. Garden City, NY: Doubleday, pp. 107–122.

40. Anderson Peters, K. (2014, July 14). Leadership presence: How to best present yourself in any situation. Robert Half Finance & Accounting. Retrieved from https://www.roberthalf.com/finance/blog/leadership-presence-how-to-best-present-yourself-in-any-situation

41. Kinsey Goman, C. (2016). Body language tips for women who mean business. American Marketing Association. Retrieved from http://www.amanet.org/training/articles/Body-Language-Tips-for-Women-Who-Mean-Business.aspx

42. Statistic Brain. (2016, August 13). Tattoo statistics. Retrieved from http://www.statisticbrain.com/tattoo-statistics; Singer, A. (2016, February 26). Tattoos in the workplace: The research Forbes was too lazy to do. *The Huffington Post*. Retrieved from http://www.huffingtonpost.com/annie-singer/tattoos-in-the-workplace-_b_9321408.html; Mishra, A., & Mishra, S. (2015, April). Attitude of professionals and students toward professional dress code, tattoos and body piercing in the corporate world. *International Journal of Innovative Research & Development*, 4(4), 324–331. Retrieved from http://www.ijird.com/index.php/ijird/article/view/69975/54946

43. Davis, T., Ward, D. A., & Woodland, D. (2010). Cross-cultural and international business communication—verbal. *National Business Education Association Yearbook: Cross-Cultural and International Business Education*, p. 3; Hall, E. T., & Hall, M. R. (2000). Key concepts: Underlying structures of culture. In: M. H. Albrecht (Ed.), *International HRM: Managing diversity in the workplace*. Hoboken, NJ: Wiley-Blackwell, pp. 200–202; Hall, E. T., & Hall, M. R. (1990). *Understanding cultural differences*. Yarmouth, ME: Intercultural Press, pp. 183–184.

44. Chaney, L. H., & Martin, J. S. (2011). *Intercultural business communication* (5th ed.). Upper Saddle River, NJ: Prentice Hall, p. 93.

45. Beamer, L., & Varner, I. (2011). *Intercultural communication in the global workplace* (5th ed.). Boston: McGraw-Hill Irwin, p. 143.

46. Chen, M.-J., & Miller, D. (2010, November). West meets East: Toward an ambicultural approach to management. *Academy of Management Perspectives*, 24(4), 19ff. Retrieved from http://search.ebscohost.com;

Sheer, V. C., & Chen, L. (2003, January). Successful Sino-Western business negotiation: Participants' accounts of national and professional cultures. *The Journal of Business Communication*, 40(1), 62.

47. Vargas, J. H., & Kemmelmeier, M. (2013). Ethnicity and contemporary American culture: A meta-analytic investigation of horizontal-vertical individualism-collectivism. *Journal of Cross-Cultural Psychology*, 44(2), 208–209. Retrieved from http://wolfweb.unr.edu/homepage/markusk/Vargas&Kemmelmeier2013JCCP.pdf; Coon, H. M., & Kemmelmeier, M. (2001, May). Cultural orientations in the United States. *Journal of Cross-Cultural Psychology*, 32(3), 359. Retrieved from http://gsappweb.rutgers.edu/cstudents/readings/Summer/Summer/Kelly_Diversity/Coon%202001%20individualism%20and%20collectivism.pdf; Gallois, C., & Callan, V. (1997). *Communication and culture*. New York: Wiley, p. 24.

48. Beamer, L., & Varner, I. (2011). *Intercultural communication in the global workplace* (5th ed.). Boston: McGraw-Hill Irwin, p. 312–316.

49. Sweetman, K. (2012, April 10). In Asia, power gets in the way. *Harvard Business Review*. Retrieved from https://hbr.org/2012/04/in-asia-power-gets-in-the-way

50. Copeland, L., & Griggs, L. (1991). *Going international*. New York: Penguin, p. 94. See also Beamer, L., & Varner, I. (2011). *Intercultural communication in the global workplace* (5th ed.). Boston: McGraw-Hill Irwin, p. 340.

51. Beamer, L., & Varner, I. (2011). *Intercultural communication in the global workplace* (5th ed.). Boston: McGraw-Hill Irwin, p. 350; Copeland, L., & Griggs, L. (1991). *Going international*. New York: Penguin, p. 12.

52. Klass, P. (2012, January 9). Seeing social media more as portal than as pitfall. *The New York Times*. Retrieved from http://www.nytimes.com/2012/01/10/health/views/seeing-social-media-as-adolescent-portal-more-than-pitfall.html

53. Limbu, M., & Gurung, B. (2013). *Emerging pedagogies in the networked knowledge society: Practices integrating social media and globalization*. Hershey, PA: IGI Global, p. 72.

54. Howell Major, C. (2015). *Teaching online: A guide to theory, research, and practice*. Baltimore: Johns Hopkins University Press, p. 187; Aragon, S. R. (2003, Winter). Creating social presence in online environments. *New Directions for Adult and Continuing Education*, 100, 59.

55. Carter, J. F. (2010, October 14). Why Twitter influences cross-cultural engagement. Mashable Social Media. Retrieved from http://mashable.com/2010/10/14/twitter-cross-cultural

56. McGrath, C. (2009, August 5). Five lessons learned about cross-cultural social networking. ThoughtFarmer. Retrieved from http://www.thoughtfarmer.com/blog/2009/08/05/5-lessons-cross-cultural-social-networking/#comments

57. Cultural sensitivities & regional differences in comms. Team Lewis. Retrieved from http://www.holmesreport.com/sponsored/article/cultural-sensitivities-regional-differences-in-comms

58. The new rules of global comms. (n.d.). [White paper]. Team Lewis, p. 5. Retrieved from http://www.holmesreport.com/sponsored/article/cultural-sensitivities-regional-differences-in-comms

59. Meeuf, K. (2014, December). Regional use of social networking tools. Software Engineering Institute, Carnegie Mellon University. Retrieved from http://repository.cmu.edu/cgi/viewcontent.cgi?article=1818&context=sei; Kunz, B. (2012, April 19). Facebook, Google must adapt as users embrace "unsocial" networks. *Bloomberg Businessweek*. Retrieved from http://www.businessweek.com

60. Delaney, R. (2014, October). Volontourism will boost your career. *Consulting—Specifying Engineer*. Retrieved from http://search.proquest.com/docview/1566688473?accountid=9840

61. Blumberg, A. (2015, April 21). In the Middle East, Muslims and Jews work in unison to care for the environment. *The Huffington Post*. Retrieved from http://www.huffingtonpost.com/2015/04/21/arava-institute-muslim-jewish-dialogue_n_7105274.html

62. Colby, S. L., & Ortman, J. M. (2015, March). Projections of the size and composition of the U.S. population: 2014 to 2060. United States Census Bureau. Retrieved from http://www.census.gov/content/dam/Census/library/publications/2015/demo/p25-1143.pdf

63. Xavier, J. (2014, March 31). Diversity defines our global economy. Do you speak the language? *Entrepreneur*. Retrieved from https://www.entrepreneur.com/article/232652

64. Boykiv, Y. (2015, June 3). How to build and sustain a diverse team. Fast Company. Retrieved from http://www.fastcompany.com/3046829/hit-the-ground-running/how-to-build-and-sustain-a-diverse-team

65. Phillips, K. W. (2014, October 1). How diversity makes us smarter. *Scientific American*. Retrieved from http://www.scientificamerican.com/article/how-diversity-makes-us-smarter

66. Boykiv, Y. (2015, June 3). How to build and sustain a diverse team. Fast Company. Retrieved from http://www.fastcompany.com/3046829/hit-the-ground-running/how-to-build-and-sustain-a-diverse-team

67. Roth, M. (2013, March 31). Conformity is the enemy: From groupthink to diversity. *The Huffington Post*. Retrieved from http://www.huffington-post.com/michael-roth/conformity-is-the-enemy_b_2987991.html

68. White, M. D. (2002). *A short course in international marketing blunders*. Novato, CA: World Trade Press, p. 46.

69. What's the universal hand sign for "I goofed"? (1996, December 16). *Santa Barbara News-Press*, p. D2.

70. Our diverse global community makes Airbnb possible. (n.d.). Retrieved from https://www.airbnb.com/diversity

71. *#ENTRYLEVELtweet: Taking Your Career From Classroom to Cubicle*. (2010). Silicon Valley: Thinkhaha ebook; Huhman, H. (n.d.). Networking 360: Coming full circle with networking. Careerealism. Retrieved from http://www.careerealism.com/networking-360-coming-full-circle-networking

72. Jobvite. (2014). 2014 Social recruiting survey. Jobvite. Retrieved from https://www.jobvite.com/wp-content/uploads/2014/10/Jobvite_SocialRecruiting_Survey2014.pdf

73. Garriott, O. (2015, February 6). 10 LinkedIn tips for students and new grads. LinkedIn Pulse. Retrieved from https://www.linkedin.com/pulse/10-tips-students-new-grads-linkedin-omar-garriott

Chapter 2

1. Silverman, D. (2009, February 10). Why is business writing so bad? *Harvard Business Review*. Retrieved from https://hbr.org/2009/02/why-is-business-writing-so-bad

2. Clark, B. (2006, April 19). The two most important words in blogging. *Copyblogger*. Retrieved from http://www.copyblogger.com/the-two-most-important-words-in-blogging

3. Arnold, V. (1986, August). Benjamin Franklin on writing well. *Personnel Journal*, p. 17.

4. Bacon, M. (1988, April). Quoted in Business writing: One-on-one speaks best to the masses. *Training*, p. 95.

5. Google. (2012, January 30). Personal communication with Mary Ellen Guffey.

6. Workplace in Focus based on Brooks, C. (2016, July 8). Do emojis have a place in work communications? *Business News Daily*. Retrieved from http://www.businessnewsdaily.com/9219-emojis-at-work.html

7. Blake, G. (2002, November 4). Insurers need to upgrade their employees' writing skills. *National Underwriter Life & Health Financial Services Edition*, 106(44), 35.

8. Be positive. (2009, March). *Communication Briefings*, p. 5. Adapted from Brandi, J. Winning at customer retention. Retrieved from www.customercarecoach.com

9. Gaertner-Johnston, L. (2012, July 3). The problem with "not a problem." *Business Writing Blog*. Retrieved from http://www.businesswritingblog.com/business_writing/2012/07/the-problem-with-not-a-problem-.html

10. Shimabukuro, J. (2006, December 11). Quoted in Wash. state sees results from "plain talk" initiative. *USA Today*, p. 18A.

Chapter 3

1. Tucci, J. M. (2004, September 1). Quoted in the National Writing Project. Writing: A ticket to work . . . or a ticket out. Retrieved from http://www.nwp.org/cs/public/print/resource/2154

2. Based on Kolowich, L. (2015, September 6). 7 brainstorming tricks to inspire brilliant ideas. *Hubspot.com*. Retrieved from https://blog.hubspot.com/marketing/brainstorm-productive; also based on Cirino, E. (2015, November 17). 5 tips for a productive brainstorming session. *USAToday.com*. Retrieved from http://college.usatoday.com/2015/11/17/brainstorming-session

3. Rindegard, J. (1999, November 22). Use clear writing to show you mean business. *InfoWorld*, p. 78.

4. Wiens, K. (2012, July 20). I won't hire people who use poor grammar. Here's why. *Harvard Business Review Blog*. Retrieved from https://hbr.org/2012/07/i-wont-hire-people-who-use-poo

5. Johnson, L. G. (2011, January 12). Avoid this simple 'comma splice' error. Retrieved from http://www.businesswritingblog.com/business_writing/2011/01/avoid-this-simple-comma-splice-error.html

6. Goddard, R. W. (1989, April). Communication: Use language effectively. *Personnel Journal*, 32.

7. A message to our fans. (2016, March 17). *SeaWorld cares*. Retrieved from https://seaworldcares.com/2016/03/A-Message-To-Our-Fans

8. Kim, L. (2015, February 2). Avoid this one punctuation habit that will destroy your credibility. *The Huffington Post*. Retrieved from http://www.huffingtonpost.com/larry-kim/avoid-this-one-punctuatio_b_10110546.html

9. O'Conner, P. T. (1996). *Woe is I*. New York: Putnam.

10. PayScale. (2016, May 17). Leveling up: How to win in the skills economy. [Press release]. Retrieved from http://www.payscale.com/about/press-releases/payscale-and-future-workplace-release%202016-workforce-skills-preparedness-report

11. Bernoff, J. (2016, September 6). Bad writing is destroying your company's productivity. *Harvard Business Review*. Retrieved from https://hbr.org/2016/09/bad-writing-is-destroying-your-companys-productivity

12. Booher, D. (2007). *The voice of authority*. New York: McGraw-Hill, p. 93.

Chapter 4

1. Powell, E. (2003, November/December). Ten tips for better business writing. *Office Solutions*, 20(6), 36.

2. Zinsser, W. (1998). *On writing well*. New York: Harper & Row.

3. Shankman, P. (2011, May 23). Why I will never, ever hire a "social media expert." *Business Insider*. Retrieved from http://www.businessinsider.com/why-i-will-never-ever-hire-a-social-media-expert-2011-5

4. Fogarty, M. (2010). Quoted in Coster, H. Ten tips for better business writing. *Forbes*. Retrieved from http://www.forbes.com/2010/05/03/better-business-writing-leadership-careers-tips.html

5. Bernoff, J. (2016, September 6). Bad writing is destroying your company's productivity. *Harvard Business Review*. Retrieved from https://hbr.org/2016/09/bad-writing-is-destroying-your-companys-productivity

6. McClusky, B. Quoted in Gausepohl, S. (2016, July 11). These 10 buzzwords are annoying your employees. *Business News Daily*. Retrieved from http://www.businessnewsdaily.com/3657-business-buzzwords.html

7. Sword, H. (2012, July 25). Zombie nouns. *3 Quarks Daily*. Retrieved from http://www.3quarksdaily.com/3quarksdaily/2012/07/zombie-nouns.html

8. Levitt, A. (2011, April 2). A word to Wall Street: "Plain English," please. *The Wall Street Journal*. Retrieved from http://www.wsj.com/articles/SB10001424052748704471904576231002037599510

9. The trouble with email. (2015, September 13). *Business Today*. Retrieved from http://businesstodaync.com/the-trouble-with-email

Chapter 5

1. Goas, T. (2015, April 29). Why you should care about email design. *Medium*. Retrieved from https://medium.com/email-design/why-you-should-care-about-email-design-3d4686639763#.dpr2vqscu

2. The Radicati Group. (2016, March). Email market, 2016–2020. Retrieved from http://www.radicati.com/wp/wp-content/uploads/2016/01/US-Email-Statistics-Report-2016-2020-Executive-Summary.pdf

3. Madrigal, A. C. (2014, August 14). Email is still the best thing on the Internet. *The Atlantic*. Retrieved from http://www.theatlantic.com/technology/archive/2014/08/why-email-will-never-die/375973

4. Feintzeig, R. (2014, June 17). A company without email? Not so fast. *The Wall Street Journal*. Retrieved from http://www.wsj.com/articles/a-company-without-email-not-so-fast-1403048134

5. Dean, J. (2016, October 25). Slack CEO Stewart Butterfield on the future of communication. *The Wall Street Journal*. Retrieved from http://www.wsj.com/articles/slack-ceo-stewart-butterfield-on-the-future-of-communication-1477405213; Pavlus, J. (2015, June 15). How email became the most reviled communication experience ever. *Fast Company*. Retrieved from https://www.fastcodesign.com/3047273/how-email-became-the-most-reviled-communication-experience-ever

6. van Rijn, J. (2016, February). The ultimate mobile email stats overview. *eMailmonday*. Retrieved from http://www.emailmonday.com/mobile-email-usage-statistics; O'Dell, J. (2014, January 22). 65% of all email gets opened first on a mobile device—and that's great news for marketers. *Venturebeat*. Retrieved from http://venturebeat.com/2014/01/22/65-of-all-email-gets-opened-first-on-a-mobile-device-and-thats-great-news-for-marketers

7. Smith, A. (2015, April 1). U.S. smartphone use in 2015. Pew Research Center. Retrieved from http://www.pewinternet.org/2015/04/01/us-smartphone-use-in-2015

8. Feintzeig, R. (2014, June 17). A company without email? Not so fast. *The Wall Street Journal*. Retrieved from http://www.wsj.com/articles/a-company-without-email-not-so-fast-1403048134

9. Bernoff, J. (2016). The state of business writing. The WOBS writing survey. Retrieved from http://tinyurl.com/hrmt87p

10. Lamb, S. E. (2015). *Writing well for business success*. New York: St. Martin's Griffin, p. 138.

11. Middleton, D. (2011, March 3). Students struggle for words. *The Wall Street Journal*, Executive ed. Retrieved from http://online.wsj.com/article/SB10001424052748703409904576174651780110970.html

12. Tschabitscher, H. (2016, September 25). How many emails are sent every day. *Lifewire*. Retrieved from https://www.lifewire.com/how-many-emails-are-sent-every-day-1171210; Gill, B. (2013, June). Vision statement: E-mail: Not dead, evolving. *Harvard Business Review*. Retrieved from http://hbr.org/2013/06/e-mail-not-dead-evolving

13. Lafrance, A. (2015, November 12). Is email evil? *The Atlantic*. Retrieved from http://www.theatlantic.com/technology/archive/2015/11/kill-email-die-email/415419

14. The Radicati Group. (2016, March). Email market, 2016–2020. Retrieved from http://www.radicati.com/wp/wp-content/uploads/2016/01/US-Email-Statistics-Report-2016-2020-Executive-Summary.pdf

15. O'Conner, K. (2016, July 25). Email is forever. *Houston Chronicle*. Retrieved from http://www.chron.com/life/article/Email-is-forever-8408295.php#photo-10577331

16. Boston, W., Campo-Flores, A., & Viswanatha, A. (2017, January 9). FBI arrests Volkswagen executive in emissions scandal. *The Wall Street Journal*. Retrieved from http://www.wsj.com/articles/fbi-arrests-volkswagen-executive-1483971808

17. Vance, A. (2014, December 4). The eight most expensive e-mail snafus in corporate history. *Bloomberg Business*. Retrieved from https://www.bloomberg.com/news/articles/2014-12-04/e-mail-the-eight-most-expensive-snafus-in-corporate-history

18. Brandeisky, K. (2016, July 22). 5 things you didn't know about using personal email at work. *Money*. Retrieved from http://time.com/money/3729939/work-personal-email-hillary-clinton-byod

19. O'Conner, K. (2016, July 25). Email is forever. *Houston Chronicle*. Retrieved from http://www.chron.com/life/article/Email-is-forever-8408295.php#photo-10577331

20. Brandeisky, K. (2016, July 22). 5 things you didn't know about using personal email at work. *Money*. Retrieved from http://time.com/money/3729939/work-personal-email-hillary-clinton-byod

21. Bernoff, J. (2016, September 20). 10 writing tips to make your emails less terrible. *Fortune*. Retrieved from http://fortune.com/2016/09/20/email-writing-tips; Tugend, A. (2012, April 21). What to think about before you hit "Send." *The New York Times*, p. B5.

22. Lamb, S. E. (2015). *Writing well for business success*. New York: St. Martin's Griffin, p. 139.

23. Kupritz, V. W., & Cowell, E. (2011). Productive management communication: Online and face-to-face. *Journal of Business Communication, 48*(1), 70–71.

24. Jaffe, E. (2014, October 9). Why it's so hard to detect emotion in emails and texts. *Fast Company Co.Design*. Retrieved from https://www.fastcodesign.com/3036748/evidence/why-its-so-hard-to-detect-emotion-in-emails-and-texts

25. Terk, N. (2012, January 18). E-mail education: Global headaches and universal best practices. Retrieved from http://www.newswiretoday.com/news/104276

26. Anderson, M. (2016, January 29). More Americans using smartphones for getting directions, streaming TV. Pew Research Center. Retrieved from http://www.pewresearch.org/fact-tank/2016/01/29/us-smartphone-use; Anderson, M. (2015, October 29). The demographics of device ownership. Pew Research Center. Retrieved from http://www.pewinternet.org/2015/10/29/the-demographics-of-device-ownership

27. d'Anselme, F. (2016, May 25). From ZeroEmail over social collaboration to wellbeing at work. LinkedIn. Retrieved from https://www.linkedin.com/pulse/from-zeroemail-over-social-collaboration-wellbeing-work-d-anselme; Matlack, C. (2015, October 8). One company tries life without (much) e-mail. *Bloomberg Business*. Retrieved from http://www.bloomberg.com/news/articles/2015-10-08/one-company-tries-life-without-much-e-mail

28. The Radicati Group. (2015, November 15). Instant messaging statistics report, 2015–2019. Retrieved from http://www.radicati.com/wp/wp-content/uploads/2015/02/Instant_Messaging_Statistics_Report_2015-2019_Executive_Summary.pdf

29. Baldwin, H. (2014, February 17). Instant messaging is going corporate. *Forbes*. Retrieved from http://www.forbes.com/sites/howardbaldwin/2014/02/17/instant-messaging-is-going-corporate

30. Pazos, P., Chung, J. M., & Micari, M. (2013). Instant messaging as a task-support tool in information technology organizations. *Journal of Business Communication, 50*(1), 78.

31. Bloch, M. (n.d.). Instant messaging and live chat etiquette tips. *Taming the Beast*. Retrieved from http://www.tamingthebeast.net/articles6/messaging-chat-etiquette.htm

32. Bit, K. (2014, June 9). Cohen's Point72 bans instant messaging for some managers. *Bloomberg Business*. Retrieved from https://www.bloomberg.com/news/articles/2014-06-09/cohen-s-point72-bans-instant-messaging-for-some-managers; Finnegan, M. (2013, December 6). JPMorgan plans instant messaging ban for traders. *Computerworld UK*. Retrieved from http://www.computerworlduk.com/news/it-business/jp-morgan-plans-instant-messaging-ban-for-traders-3493907

33. Flynn, N. (2012, March). *The social media handbook: Rules, policies, and best practices to successfully manage your organization's social media presence, posts, and potential*. San Francisco: Pfeiffer/Wiley, p. 20.

34. Marino, K. (2012, June 22). DWI: Driving while intexticated. [Infographic]. OnlineSchools.com. Retrieved from http://www.onlineschools.com/in-focus/driving-while-intexticated

35. Driving while intexticated: The new DWI. (2014). Retrieved from http://vehiclemd.com/driving-while-intexticated-the-new-dwi

36. Malito, A. (2015, November 19). Here's the price advisers pay for ignoring boring email archives. *Investment News*. Retrieved from http://www.investmentnews.com/article/20151119/FREE/151119923/heres-the-price-advisers-payfor-ignoring-boring-email-archives

37. Sidel, R. (2015, December 21). Hackers exploit staffers at banks. *The Wall Street Journal*, p. C1.

38. Flynn, N. (2012, March). *The social media handbook: Rules, policies, and best practices to successfully manage your organization's social media presence, posts, and potential*. San Francisco: Pfeiffer/Wiley.

39. Ali, A. (2009, October 6). Wikis: Where work gets done. IT Business Edge. Retrieved from http://www.itbusinessedge.com/cm/blogs/ali/wikis-where-work-gets-done/?cs=36409

40. The Emily Post Institute. (2017). Texting at the dinner table. Retrieved from http://emilypost.com/advice/texting-at-the-dinner-table; The Emily Post Institute. (2017). Texting manners. Retrieved from http://emilypost.com/advice/texting-manners

41. Vogt, N. (2016, June). Podcasting: Fact sheet. Pew Research Center. Retrieved from http://www.journalism.org/2016/06/15/podcasting-fact-sheet

42. Clark, D. (2014, October 28). How to launch a successful podcast – fast. *Forbes*. Retrieved from http://www.forbes.com/sites/dorieclark/2014/10/28/how-to-launch-a-successful-podcast-fast; Casel, B. (2011, March 25). 7 tips for launching a successful podcast. *Mashable*. Retrieved from http://mashable.com/2011/03/25/podcasting-tips

43. Miron, E., Palmor, A., Ravid, G., Sharon, A., Tikotsky, A., & Zirkel, Y. (2016). Principles and good practices for using wikis within organizations. In R. Chugh (Ed.), *Harnessing social media as a knowledge management tool*. Hershey, PA: IGI Global, p. 152; Behringer, N., & Sassenberg, K. (2015). Introducing social media for knowledge management: Determinants of employees' intentions to adopt new tools. *Computers in Human Behavior, 48*, 290–296. Retrieved from http://www.sciencedirect.com; Jackson, P., & Klobas, J. (2012). Deciding to use an enterprise wiki: The role of social institutions and scripts. *Knowledge Management Research & Practice, 11*, 323–333. doi:10.1057/kmrp.2012.20

44. Brichni, M., Mandran, N., Gzara, L., Dupuy-Chessa, S., & Rozier, D. (2014). Wiki for knowledge sharing, a user-centered evaluation approach: A case study at STMicroelectronics. *Journal of Knowledge Management, 18*(6), 1232–1217. Retrieved from http://www.emeraldinsight.com; Majchrzak, A., Wagner, C., & Yates, D. (2006). Corporate wiki users: Results of a survey. *CiteSeer*. Retrieved from http://citeseerx.ist.psu.edu/viewdoc/summary?doi=10.1.1.97.407

45. The five main uses of wikis based on Nations, D. (2009). The business wiki: Wiki in the workplace. About.com: Web Trends. Retrieved from http://webtrends.about.com/od/wiki/a/business-wiki.htm

46. Augustine, A. (2016, September 16). 5 wiki tools for building online communities. *Lifewire*. Retrieved from https://www.lifewire.com/wiki-tools-for-building-online-communities-771661

47. Barnes, N. G., & Griswold, J. (2016). Use of popular tools remains constant as use of Instagram expands quickly among the 2016 Fortune 500. Center for Marketing Research, University of Massachusetts Dartmouth. Retrieved from http://www.umassd.edu/cmr/socialmediaresearch/2016fortune500

48. Houlahan, A. (2015, September 28). The importance of blogging for your brand. Retrieved from https://www.adamhoulahan.com

49. Murphy, J. (2015, October 5). General Mills announces recall of certain boxes of Cheerios and Honey Nut Cheerios. *Taste of General Mills*. Retrieved from http://blog.generalmills.com/2015/10/general-mills-announces-recall-of-certain-boxes-of-cheerios-and-honey-nut-cheerios

50. Barnes, N. G., Lescault, A. M., & Holmes, G. (2015, November). The 2015 Fortune 500 and social media: Instagram gains, blogs lose. The Conference Board. Retrieved from https://www.conference-board.org/topics/publicationdetail.cfm?publicationid=7113&topicid=30&subtopicid=220

51. Based on Meister, J. (2015, March 30). Future of work: Using gamification for human resources. *Forbes*. Retrieved from http://www.forbes.com/sites/jeannemeister/2015/03/30/future-of-work-using-gamification-for-human-resources/#59327f5332ba

52. Lindstrom, M. (2012, July 3). How many lives does a brand have? *Fast Company*. Retrieved from http://www.fastcompany.com/1841927/buyology-martin-lindstrom-lives-of-brands-china-marketing

53. Brogan, C. (2012, July 13). Become a dream feeder. Retrieved from http://www.chrisbrogan.com/dreamfeeder

54. Devaney, T., & Stein, T. (2012, December 20). 9 things businesses shouldn't do on social media. *Forbes*. Retrieved from http://www.forbes.com/sites/capitalonespark/2012/12/20/9-things-businesses-shouldnt-do-on-social-media/#2fa7afa03bdc

55. Cairns, B. (2012, January 24). Blog comment. Retrieved from https://guykawasaki.com/how-to-increase-your-likability

56. Society for Human Resource Management. (2016, January 7). SHRM survey findings: Using social media for talent acquisition—recruitment and screening. Retrieved from https://www.shrm.org/hr-today/trends-and-forecasting/research-and-surveys/Documents/SHRM-Social-Media-Recruiting-Screening-2015.pdf

57. Statista. (2016, November 24). U. S. social media marketing—statistics & facts. Retrieved from https://www.statista.com/topics/1538/social-media-marketing

58. Purcell, K., & Rainie, L. (2014, December 30). Technology's impact on workers. Pew Research Center. Retrieved from http://www.pewinternet.org/2014/12/30/technologys-impact-on-workers

59. Pew Research Center. (2017, January 12). Social media fact sheet. Retrieved from www.pewinternet.org/fact-sheet/social-media

60. Greenwood, S., Perrin, A., & Duggan, M. (2016, November 11). Social media update 2016. Retrieved from http://www.pewinternet.org/2016/11/11/social-media-update-2016

61. Barnes, N. G., & Griswold, J. (2016). Use of popular tools remains constant as use of Instagram expands quickly among the 2016 Fortune 500. UMass Dartmouth. Retrieved from http://www.umassd.edu/cmr/socialmediaresearch/2015fortune500

62. Schaefer, M. (2014, February 11). IBM CEO Ginni Rometty points to social strategy with a twist. Retrieved from http://www.businessesgrow.com/2014/02/11/ginni-rometty

63. Li, C. (2015, April 7). Why no one uses the corporate social network. *Harvard Business Review*. Retrieved from https://hbr.org/2015/04/why-no-one-uses-the-corporate-social-network

64. Cardon, P. (2015). Enterprise social networks (Internal social media platforms). *NBEA 2015 Yearbook: Recent and Projected Technology Trends Affecting Business Education*, p. 37. Retrieved from http://www.mcssl.com/store/nbeaonlinebookstore/catalog/product/cbed6162e42c47619d0af3f6f83bc420

65. Lavenda, D. (2014, February 6). How Red Robin transformed its business with Yammer. *Fast Company*. Retrieved from https://www.fastcompany.com/3025396/work-smart/how-red-robin-burgers-got-yummier-with-yammer

66. Li, C. (2015, April 7). Why no one uses the corporate social network. *Harvard Business Review*. Retrieved from https://hbr.org/2015/04/why-no-one-uses-the-corporate-social-network

67. Burlingame, T. (2017, January 12). Pitch your best potato chip flavor idea for Lay's "Do Us a Flavor" contest. *Snack Chat*. Retrieved from http://www.fritolay.com/blog/blog-post/snack-chat/2017/01/12/pitch-your-best-potato-chip-flavor-idea-for-lay-s-do-us-a-flavor-contest.htm

68. Ciccatelli, A. (2014, April 14). The reality of managing social media risk in business. *Inside Counsel*. Retrieved from http://www.insidecounsel.com/2014/04/24/the-reality-of-managing-social-media-risk-in-busin?slreturn=1484534563

69. Belbey, J. (2015, May 21). Protect your firm from the 12 risks of social media. *Forbes*. Retrieved from http://www.forbes.com/sites/joannabelbey/2015/05/21/protect-your-firm-from-the-13-risks-of-social-media/#35c977715439

70. Proskauer Rose LLP. (2014). Social media in the workplace around the world 3.0. 2013/14 survey, p. 2. Retrieved from http://www.proskauer.com/files/uploads/social-media-in-the-workplace-2014.pdf

71. Flynn, N. (2012, March). *The social media handbook: Rules, policies, and best practices to successfully manage your organization's social media presence, posts, and potential.* San Francisco: Pfeiffer/Wiley, p. 80.

72. Pozin, I. (2014, July 12). Productivity vs. distraction: Should you block social media at work? *TNW News*. Retrieved from http://thenextweb.com/entrepreneur/2014/07/12/productivity-vs-distraction-block-social-media-work; Wright, A. D. (2012, February 3). Social media policies slowly catch on worldwide. *Society for Human Resource Management*. Retrieved from http://www.shrm.org/hrdisciplines/global/Articles/Pages/WorldwidePolicies.aspx

73. Huspeni, A. (2016, May 13). The major security risks small business face and how to defend against them. *Entrepreneur*. Retrieved from https://www.entrepreneur.com/article/275737

74. Pozin, I. (2014, July 12). Productivity vs. distraction: Should you block social media at work? *TNW News*. Retrieved from http://thenextweb.com/entrepreneur/2014/07/12/productivity-vs-distraction-block-social-media-work; Wright, A. D. (2012, February 3). Social media policies slowly catch on worldwide. Society for Human Resource Management. Retrieved from http://www.shrm.org/hrdisciplines/global/Articles/Pages/WorldwidePolicies.aspx

75. De Querol, R. (2016, January 25). Zygmunt Bauman: "Social media are a trap." *El País*. Retrieved from http://elpais.com/elpais/2016/01/19/inenglish/1453208692_424660.html

76. Leighton, H. (2017, January 18). Oklahoma State University students in hot water following controversial Martin Luther King Jr. post. *Houston Chronicle*. Retrieved from http://www.chron.com/national/article/Oklahoma-State-University-students-in-hot-water-10866508.php; Sternitzky-Di Napoli, D. (2016, November 15). Texas students expelled from Abilene Christian University for posting in blackface for Snapchat. *Houston Chronicle*. Retrieved from http://www.chron.com/news/houston-texas/article/Texas-students-expelled-from-Abilene-Christian-10615138.php#photo-11809428

77. Hutchins, B. (2015, April 20). Why you should never use Instagram bots to get more likes & followers. Business2Community. Retrieved from http://www.business2community.com/instagram/never-use-instagram-bots-get-likes-followers-01209425#mcsgkeHSeWJx6Y1S.97; Tynan, D. (2012, May 25). How companies buy Facebook friends, likes, and buzz. ITWorld.com. Retrieved from http://www.techhive.com/article/256240/how_companies_buy_facebook_friends_likes_and_buzz.html

78. Based on Heathfield, S. M. (2016, August 16). What are paid holidays in the U.S.? *The Balance*. Retrieved from https://www.thebalance.com/what-are-paid-holidays-in-the-u-s-1918150; Heathfield, S. M. (2016, August 29). Should your company offer a floating holiday? *The Balance*. Retrieved from https://www.thebalance.com/should-your-company-offer-a-floating-holiday-1917984

79. Swann, P. (2014). *Cases in public relations management: The rise of social media and activism* (2nd ed.). New York: Routledge.

80. Griner, D. (2017, January 3). Wendy's put a troll on ice with 2017's best tweet so far. *Adweek*. Retrieved from http://www.adweek.com/creativity/wendys-put-troll-ice-2017s-best-tweet-so-far-175334

81. Hutchinson, M. (2015, August 13). Are you prepared? Gartner predicts 90% of companies will soon use social customer care. *Salesforce*. Retrieved from https://www.salesforce.com/blog/2015/08/gartner-provides-insights-social-media.html

82. Evans, G. (2015, July 28). Why social customer care is HP's fastest growing service channel. *Salesforce*. Retrieved from https://www.salesforce.com/blog/2015/07/hp-social-media-marketing-strategy.html

83. Shanbhag, A. (2016, March 2). What happens when you quit social media? I found out. *Makeuseof*. Retrieved from http://www.makeuseof.com/tag/what-happens-when-you-quit-social-media-i-found-out;

Gaddis, B. (2016, February 9). Here's what happened when I quit social media. *The Huffington Post*. Retrieved from http://www.huffingtonpost.com/bailey-gaddis/heres-what-happened-when-i-quit-social-media_b_9152744.html; Hempel, J. (2015, August 2). I'm quitting social media to learn what I actually like. *Wired*. Retrieved from https://www.wired.com/2015/08/im-quitting-social-media-learn-actually-like; Sparkes, M. (2013, April 11). Twitter and Facebook "addicts" suffer withdrawal symptoms. *The Telegraph*. Retrieved from http://www.telegraph.co.uk/technology/social-media/9986950/Twitter-and-Facebook-addicts-suffer-withdrawal-symptoms.html

84. Moeller, S. D. (2010). 24 hours: Unplugged. Retrieved from http://withoutmedia.wordpress.com; The Associated Press. (2009, September 6). Center tries to treat Web addicts. *The New York Times*. Retrieved from http://www.nytimes.com

85. Irvine, M. (2009, July 12). Young workers push employers for wider Web access. *USA Today*. Retrieved from http://www.usatoday.com/tech/webguide/internetlife/2009-07-13-blocked-internet_N.htm; DeLisser, E. (1999, September 27). One-click commerce: What people do now to goof off at work. *The Wall Street Journal*. Retrieved from http://www.kenmaier.com/wsj19990927.htm

86. Lewis Maltby quoted in Passy, M. (2014, October 22). Should companies monitor their employees' social media? *The Wall Street Journal*. Retrieved from https://www.wsj.com/articles/should-companies-monitor-their-employees-social-media-1399648685

87. Hyman, J. (2016, June 29). Your employees are using social media at work; deal with it. *Workforce*. Retrieved from http://www.workforce.com/2016/06/29/your-employees-are-using-social-media-at-work-deal-with-it

88. Ford, J. (2009, November 9). Think twice about shopping online from work. Marketwatch.com. Retrieved from http://www.marketwatch.com/story/think-twice-about-shopping-online-from-work-2009-11-29; The 2007 electronic monitoring and surveillance survey. (2008, February 29). GPS Daily. Retrieved from http://www.gpsdaily.com

89. Woods, A. (2015, August 28). Social media, HR and progressive policy. *HRVoice*. Retrieved from http://www.hrvoice.org/social-media-hr-and-progressive-policy

Chapter 6

1. Internet usage statistics: The Internet big picture. (2016, June 30). Internet World Stats. Retrieved from http://www.internetworldstats.com/stats.htm

2. Based on Emily Post Institute. (n.d.). Effective business letters. Retrieved from http://www.emilypost.com/on-the-job/clients-customers-vendors-or-contractors/784-effective-business-letters

3. Perkins, B. (2016, January 13). Are we clear? Writing well can be key to your career. *Computerworld*. Retrieved from http://www.computerworld.com/article/3022061/it-management/are-we-clear-writing-well-can-be-key-to-your-career.html

4. Diamond, M. L. (2015, January 9). Viral power: Social media can kill a business. *USA Today*. Retrieved from http://www.usatoday.com/story/money/business/main-street/2015/01/09/social-media-business/21496637

5. Oracle Social Cloud. (n.d.). Social's shift to service. [White paper]. Retrieved from http://www.oracle.com/us/products/shift-to-service-2949449.pdf

6. Hyken, S. (2016, October 8). Six ways to avoid social media customer service failure. *Forbes*. Retrieved from http://www.forbes.com/sites/shephyken/2016/10/08/six-ways-to-avoid-social-media-customer-service-failure/#7635f0384628

7. Morrison, K. (2015, November 15). Nordstrom & Macy's among top 10 retailers on social media. *Adweek*. Retrieved from http://www.adweek.com/digital/nordstrom-macys-among-top-10-retailers-on-social-media

8. Oracle Social Cloud. (n.d.). Social's shift to service. [White paper]. Retrieved from http://www.oracle.com/us/products/shift-to-service-2949449.pdf

9. Bernstein, E. (2015, August 10). Don't hit send: Angry emails just make you angrier. *The Wall Street Journal*. Retrieved from https://www.wsj.com/articles/dont-hit-send-angry-emails-just-make-you-angrier-1439227360

10. Johnston Taylor, S. (2014, December 30). The best ways to file a consumer complaint. *U.S. News & World Report*. Retrieved from http://money.usnews.com/money/personal-finance/articles/2014/12/30/the-best-ways-to-file-a-consumer-complaint; Pilon, M. (2009, August 5). How to complain about a company. *The Wall Street Journal*. Retrieved from http://blogs.wsj.com/wallet/2009/08/05/how-to-complain-about-a-company; Torabi, F. (2011, July 28). Bad customer service? 3 smarter ways to complain. CBS News. Retrieved from http://www.cbsnews.com/8301-505144_162-41542345/bad-customer-service-3-smarter-ways-to-complain

11. White, M. C. (2015, October 19). Lost bags, at 140 characters, and airlines respond. *The New York Times*. Retrieved from https://www.nytimes.com/2015/10/20/business/lost-bags-at-140-characters-and-airlines-respond.html?_r=0

12. Ibid.

13. Peterson, H. (2014, July 2). Findlay waitress fired for Facebook post about tipping. WTOL 11. Retrieved from http://www.wtol.com/story/25918895/findlay-waitress-fired-for-facebook-post-about-tipping?hpt=us_bn9

14. Pet sitting business bites back after getting bad Yelp review. (2016, February 19). CBS News. Retrieved from http://www.cbsnews.com/news/yelp-negative-online-review-texas-couple-sued-jeremy-stoppelman

15. Campbell, C. (2015, February 15). 7 tips for listening—and responding—to your customers. *Inc*. Retrieved from http://www.inc.com/chris-campbell/7-tips-to-use-customer-reviews-to-your-advantage.html

16. Smith, B. (2015, January 23). In business, love means having to say you're sorry. LinkedIn. Retrieved from https://www.linkedin.com/pulse/business-love-means-having-say-youre-sorry-brad-smith

17. States with apology laws. (n.d.). Sorry works! Retrieved from http://www.sorryworks.net/apology-laws-cms-143; Ho, B., & Liu, E. (2010, October). Does sorry work? The impact of apology laws on medical malpractice. Social Science Research Network. Retrieved from http://dx.doi.org/10.2139/ssrn.1744225; Quinley, K. (2008, May). Apology programs. *Claims*, pp. 14–16. Retrieved from http://search.ebscohost.com. See also Runnels, M. (2009, Winter). Apologies all around: Advocating federal protection for the full apology in civil cases. *San Diego Law Review, 46*(1), 137–160. Retrieved from http://search.ebscohost.com

18. Arends, B. (2014, December 2). When apologizing makes no sense. *Fortune*. Retrieved from http://fortune.com/2014/12/02/apologies-public-relations-crisis

19. Davidow, M. (2003, February). Organizational responses to customer complaints: What works and what doesn't. *Journal of Service Research, 5*(3), 225. Retrieved from http://journals.sagepub.com/doi/abs/10.1177/1094670502238917

20. Keltner, D. (2016, May 22). The power of saying thank you. *The Guardian*. Retrieved from https://www.theguardian.com/lifeandstyle/2016/may/22/the-power-of-saying-thank-you-the-power-paradox-daniel-keltner

21. Baer, J. (2015, June 24). How asking for help can turn haters into brand advocates. *Inc*. Retrieved from http://www.inc.com/jay-baer/how-asking-for-help-can-turn-haters-into-brand-advocates.html; Ho, M. (2014, September 29). How to deal with negative Facebook comments on your brand's page. *Adweek: Social Times*. Retrieved from http://www.adweek.com/digital/how-to-deal-with-negative-facebook-comments

22. The Emily Post Institute. (2017). Advice: Sympathy notes and letters. Retrieved from http://emilypost.com/advice/sympathy-notes-and-letters; Heathfield, S. M. (2016, December 28). How to write a sympathy letter. *The Balance*. Retrieved from https://www.thebalance.com/how-to-write-a-sympathy-letter-1919093

23. Roesler, P. (2016, December 15). New law would void "non-disparagement" clauses that silence online reviews. Web Marketing Pros. Retrieved from http://www.webmarketingpros.com/blog/new-law-would-void-non-disparagement-clauses-that-silence-online-reviews

24. Based on Buddy Media. (2010). How do I respond to that? The definitive guide to Facebook publishing & moderation. Retrieved from https://christinastallings.files.wordpress.com/2011/01/definitive-guide-buddy-media-white-paper.pdf

25. Partially based on Gillette, F. (2010, July 19–25). Twitter, twitter, little stars. *Bloomberg Businessweek*, pp. 64–67.

26. 10 things you should know about Yelp. (2016, December). Retrieved from http://www.yelp.com/about

27. Adapted from Conaway, R. N., & Fernandez, T. L. (2000, March). Ethical preferences among business leaders: Implications for business schools. *Business Communication Quarterly, 63*(1), 23–31.

Chapter 7

1. Creelman, V. (2012). The case for "living" models. *Business Communication Quarterly, 75*(2), 181.

2. Veltsos, J. (2012). An analysis of data breach notifications as negative news. *Business Communication Quarterly, 75*(2), 198. doi: 10.1177/1080569912443081

3. Canavor, N. (2012). *Business writing in the digital age.* Thousand Oaks, CA: Sage, p. 62.

4. Joyce, C. (2012, November). The impact of direct and indirect communication. International Ombudsman Association. Retrieved from https://www.ombudsassociation.org/Resources/IOA-Publications/The-Independent-Voice/November-2012/The-Impact-of-Direct-and-Indirect-Communication.aspx

5. Bousis, G. Quoted in Young Entrepreneur Council. (2014, October 1). 9 (polite) ways to reject a customer. *Inc.* Retrieved from http://www.inc.com/young-entrepreneur-council/9-polite-ways-to-reject-a-customer.html

6. Kashtan, M. (2013, May 20). Saying "no" without saying "no": How to say "no" to someone so they know they still matter to us. *Psychology Today.* Retrieved from https://www.psychologytoday.com/blog/acquired-spontaneity/201305/saying-no-without-saying-no

7. Green Coffee Bean extract marketer to refund customers. (2015, January 27). Truth in Advertising. Retrieved from https://www.truthinadvertising.org/green-coffee-bean-extract-marketer-refund-customers; Oz watch: TV host pulls curtain on phony endorsements. (2013, May 31). Truth in Advertising. Retrieved from https://www.truthinadvertising.org/oz-watch-tv-host-pulls-curtain-on-phony-endorsements

8. Cited in Hollis, L. (2014, February 27). Sorry seems to be the hardest word. *Management Today UK.* Retrieved from http://www.managementtoday.co.uk/news/1281578/sorry-seems-hardest-word

9. Schweitzer, M. E. (2006, December). Wise negotiators know when to say "I'm sorry." *Negotiation, 4.* Retrieved from http://search.ebscohost.com

10. ten Brinke, L., & Adams, G. S. (2015). Saving face? When emotion displays during public apologies mitigate damage to organizational performance. *Organizational Behavior and Human Decision Processes, 133.* doi:10.1016/j.obhdp.2015.05.003. Retrieved from http://search.proquest.com

11. Grossman, D. (2013, August 21). Hit or miss'ive: AOL CEO Tim Armstrong's apology to employees is pathetic. Retrieved from http://www.yourthoughtpartner.com/blog/bid/69882/AOL-CEO-Tim-Armstrong-s-Apology-to-Employees-is-Pathetic; see also Post, P. (2013, August 15). AOL CEO's impulsive action leads to public apology. Job Doc. Retrieved from http://www.boston.com/jobs/news/jobdoc/2013/08/how_not_to_fire_a_employee.html

12. Amazon Web Services. (2017, March 2). Summary of the Amazon S3 service disruption in the Northern Virginia (US-EAST-1) region. Amazon. Retrieved from https://aws.amazon.com/message/41926; Stevens, L. (2017, March 2). Amazon finds the cause of its AWS outage: A typo. *The Wall Street Journal.* Retrieved from https://www.wsj.com/articles/amazon-finds-the-cause-of-its-aws-outage-a-typo-1488490506

13. Cited in Parmar, B. (2015, January 8). Corporate empathy is not an oxymoron. *Harvard Business Review.* Retrieved from https://hbr.org/2015/01/corporate-empathy-is-not-an-oxymoron

14. Warmbier, F. (2014, December 8). Walking away from a customer who demands a discount. *The New York Times.* Retrieved from https://boss.blogs.nytimes.com/2014/12/08/walking-away-from-a-customer-who-demands-a-discount/?_r=0

15. Glinton, S. (2016, January 11). "We didn't lie," Volkswagen CEO says of emission scandal. NPR. Retrieved from http://www.npr.org/sections/the-two-way/2016/01/11/462682378/we-didn't-lie-volkswagen-ceo-says-of-emissions-scandal

16. Zimmerman, E. (2012, April 7). Accentuating the positive to angry customers. *The New York Times.* Retrieved from http://www.nytimes.com

17. Zimmerman, E. (2012, April 7). Accentuating the positive to angry customers. *The New York Times.* Retrieved from http://www.nytimes.com; Mowatt, J. (2002, February). Breaking bad news to customers. *Agency Sales,* p. 30; Dorn, E. M. (1999, March). Case method instruction in the business writing classroom. *Business Communication Quarterly, 62*(1), 51–52.

18. Houlihan, M. (2012, September 21). Oops, my bad! 5 ways your business can improve by admitting to mistakes. *Entrepreneur.* Retrieved from https://www.entrepreneur.com/article/224491

19. Guliani, B. K. (2016, February 15). Twitter's greater revenue is due to its faster responses. Digital Vidya Blog. Retrieved from http://www.digitalvidya.com/blog/twitters-greater-revenue-is-due-to-its-faster-responses; Kapner, S. (2012, October 5). Citi won't sleep on customer tweets. *The Wall Street Journal,* p. 1.

20. Forbes, M. (1999). How to write a business letter. In K. Harty (Ed.), *Strategies for business and technical writing.* Boston: Allyn and Bacon, p. 108.

21. Robertson, K. (2004, April). Saying no: How to deliver bad news to a customer. KR Consulting. Retrieved from http://www.krconsulting.com/saying-no-how-to-deliver-bad-news-to-a-customer

22. Griffin Padgett, D. R., Cheng, S. S., & Parekh, V. (2013). The quest for transparency and accountability: Communicating responsibly to stakeholders in crises. *Asian Social Science, 9*(9). doi:10.5539/ass.v9n9p31; Browning, M. (2003, November 24). Work dilemma: Delivering bad news a good way. *Government Computer News,* p. 41; Mowatt, J. (2002, February). Breaking bad news to customers. *Agency Sales,* p. 30.

23. Engels, J. (2007, July). Delivering difficult messages. *Journal of Accountancy, 204*(1), 50–52. Retrieved from http://search.ebscohost.com; see also Lewis, B. (1999, September 13). To be an effective leader, you need to perfect the art of delivering bad news. *InfoWorld,* p. 124. Retrieved from http://books.google.com

24. Cited in Weeks, L. (2008, December 8). Read the blog: You're fired. National Public Radio. Retrieved from http://www.npr.org/templates/story/story.php?storyId=97945811

25. Bies, R. J. (2013, January). The delivery of bad news in organizations. *Journal of Management, 39*(1), 136–162. doi: 10.1177/0149206312461053

26. Based on Burbank, L. (2007, June 8). Personal items can be swept away between flights. *USA Today,* p. 3D.

Chapter 8

1. White, E. (2008, May 19). Art of persuasion becomes key. *The Wall Street Journal.* Retrieved from http://online.wsj.com/article/SB121115784262002373.html; McIntosh, P., & Luecke, R. A. (2011). *Increase your influence at work.* New York: American Management Association, p. 4.

2. Johnson, S. (2014, September 29). New research sheds light on daily ad exposures. *SJ Insights.* Retrieved from https://sjinsights.net/2014/09/29/new-research-sheds-light-on-daily-ad-exposures; Jones, J. P. (2004). *Fables, fashions, and facts about advertising: A study of 28 enduring myths.* Thousand Oaks, CA: Sage Publications (Kindle Edition), Chapter 2.

3. Fogg, B. J. (2008). Mass interpersonal persuasion: An early view of a new phenomenon. In: Proceedings. Third International Conference on Persuasive Technology 2008. Berlin, Germany: Springer.

4. Discussion based on Perloff, R. M. (2013). *The dynamics of persuasion: Communication and attitudes in the twenty-first century* (5th ed.). New York: Routledge.

5. Johnson, S. (2014, September 29). New research sheds light on daily ad exposures. *SJ Insights.* Retrieved from https://sjinsights.net/2014/09/29/new-research-sheds-light-on-daily-ad-exposures

6. Wike, R., Poushter, J., & Zainulbhai, H. (2016, June 28). America's international image. Pew Research Center. Retrieved from http://www.pewglobal.org/2016/06/28/americas-international-image

7. Adalian, J. (2015, December 2). The most popular U.S. TV shows in 18 countries around the world. Vulture. Retrieved from http://www.vulture.com/2015/12/most-popular-us-tv-shows-around-the-world.html?mid=facebook_nymag

8. Canavor, N. (2012). *Business writing in the digital age.* Thousand Oaks, CA: Sage, p. 169.

9. Perloff, R. M. (2013). *The dynamics of persuasion: Communication and attitudes in the twenty-first century* (5th ed.). New York: Routledge, p. 9.

10. Cialdini, R. B. (2009). *Influence: The psychology of persuasion.* New York: HarperCollins, p. xiv.

11. Rowell, D. M. (2008, January 4). How to create and structure a winning complaint: Being positive and fair gets you more. *The Travel Insider.* Retrieved from http://thetravelinsider.info/info/howtocomplain2.htm

12. Harwell, D. (2015, August 24). Starbucks' CEO sent this bizarre memo telling baristas to be nicer because of the stock turmoil. *The Washington Post.* Retrieved from https://www.washingtonpost.com/news/business/wp/2015/08/24/starbucks-chief-sent-a-bizarre-memo-telling-baristas-to-be-nicer-because-of-the-stock-market

13. Feloni, R. (2016, January 14). Zappos CEO Tony Hsieh explains why 18% of employees quit during the company's radical management experiment. *Business Insider.* Retrieved from http://www.businessinsider.com/zappos-ceo-tony-hsieh-on-holacracy-transition-2016-1; Silverman, R. E. (2015, May 20). At Zappos, banishing the bosses brings confusion. *The Wall Street Journal.* Retrieved from http://www.wsj.com/articles/at-zappos-banishing-the-bosses-brings-confusion-1432175402

14. Brandon, J. (2014, December 12). 20 leadership experts share their best leadership tip. *Inc.* Retrieved from http://www.inc.com/john-brandon/20-leadership-experts-share-their-best-leadership-tip.html

15. McIntosh, P., & Luecke, R. A. (2011). *Increase your influence at work.* New York: AMACOM, p. 2.

16. Gupta-Sunderji, M. (2014, July 22). The art of persuasion. *HRVoice.* Retrieved from http://www.hrvoice.org/the-art-of-persuasion

17. Taute, M. (2015, January 19). Disney creative director Will Gay: How to sell your ideas. The Creative Group, Robert Half. Retrieved from https://www.roberthalf.com/creativegroup/blog/disney-creative-director-will-gay-how-to-sell-your-ideas; Pollock, T. (2003, June). How to sell an idea. *SuperVision,* p. 15. Retrieved from http://search.proquest.com

18. Dooley, R. (2015, February 24). Neuromarketing: Pseudoscience no more. *Forbes.* Retrieved from https://www.forbes.com/sites/roger-dooley/2015/02/24/neuromarketing-temple/#365af8f9de94; Millward Brown. (2009). Using neuroscience to understand the role of direct mail, p. 2. Retrieved from http://www.millwardbrown.com/Insights/CaseStudies/NeuroscienceDirectMail.aspx

19. Compton, J. (2015, March 4). Direct mail goes digital. Direct Marketing. Retrieved from http://www.dmnews.com/direct-mail/direct-mail-goes-digital/article/400201; Direct mail statistics show B2B mailings are still effective. (2011, March 8). *Minuteman Press.* Retrieved from www.deerpark.minutemanpress.com/resources/infotips/direct-mail-statistics.html; Hartong, B. (2011, March). Revitalize your direct mail strategy. *Customer Interaction Solutions,* p. 10. Retrieved from http://proquest.umi.com

20. Frey, D. (2011, April 7). 8 reasons why direct mail is so powerful. Facebook. Retrieved from http://www.facebook.com/note.php?note_id=10150167591671657&comments

21. Ward, S. (2016, January 4). The B2B marketing mix: Direct mail campaigns. Pardot. Retrieved from http://www.pardot.com/blog/the-b2b-marketing-mix-direct-mail-campaigns; Macleod, I. (2013, October). Infographic: Consumers more likely to deal with direct mail immediately compared to email. The Drum. Retrieved from http://www.thedrum.com/news/2013/10/23/infographic-consumers-more-likely-deal-direct-mail-immediately-compared-email; DMA releases 2010 response rate trend report. (2010, June 15). Target Marketing. Retrieved from www.targetmarketingmag.com/article/dma-releases-report-direct-mail-email-paid-search-internet-display-drtv-response-rates/all/

22. Digital ad spending to surpass TV next year. (2016, March 8). *eMarketer.* Retrieved from https://www.emarketer.com/Article/Digital-Ad-Spending-Surpass-TV-Next-Year/1013671; Conlon, G. (2016, February 1). 2016 will be a growth year in marketing spending. DMN. Retrieved from http://www.dmnews.com/marketing-strategy/2016-will-be-a-growth-year-in-marketing-spending/article/469545

23. VanBoskirk, S. (2017, January 26). US digital marketing spend will near $120 billion by 2021. *Forbes.* Retrieved from https://www.forbes.com/sites/forrester/2017/01/26/us-digital-marketing-spend-will-near-120-billion-by-2021/#746b0ed9278b

24. Tinz, M. (2015, August 4). 4 ways to integrate direct mail into your digital marketing landscape. *Entrepreneur.* Retrieved from https://www.entrepreneur.com/article/249119

25. DMA Research. (April 2015). Statistical fact book. Retrieved from http://www.pfl.com/images/Statistical-Fact-Book-2015.pdf

26. Jensen, A. (2016, July 27). 25 direct mail statistics for 2016. Compu-Mail. Retrieved from http://compu-mail.com/blog/2016/07/27/25-direct-mail-statistics-for-2016

27. Ziglar, Z. (2003). *Ziglar on selling: The ultimate handbook for the complete sales professional.* Nashville, TN: Thomas Nelson, p. 173; Lowenstein, M. (2007, September 24). Make both an emotional and rational appeal to your customers: Inside-out and outside-in commitment and advocacy. CustomerThink.net. Retrieved from http://www.customerthink.com/article/make_emotional_rational_appeal_customers

28. Jensen, A. (2016, July 27). 25 direct mail statistics for 2016. Compu-Mail. Retrieved from http://compu-mail.com/blog/2016/07/27/25-direct-mail-statistics-for-2016; Haskel, D. (2015, April 14). 2015 DMA response rate report: Direct mail outperforms all digital channels combined by nearly 600%. IWCO Direct. Retrieved from http://www.iwco.com/blog/2015/04/14/dma-response-rate-report-and-direct-mail

29. Abramovich, G. (2012, March 13). P&G's new approach to digital. Digiday. Retrieved from http://digiday.com/brands/pgs-new-approach-to-digital

30. Email vastly preferred by consumers for brand communications. (2016, March 30). MarketingCharts. Retrieved from http://www.marketingcharts.com/online/email-vastly-preferred-by-consumers-for-brand-communications-66661

31. Colwyn, S. (2015, January 15). State of the art digital marketing 2015. Smart Insights. Retrieved from http://www.smartinsights.com/managing-digitalmarketing/marketing-innovation/state-of-digital-marketing/attachment/stateoftheartdigitalmarketingsmartinsights

32. Arno, C. (2015, February 9). How companies can engage with email marketing. TotalRetail. Retrieved from http://www.mytotalretail.com/article/how-companies-can-engage-with-email-marketing/3

33. Haskel, D. (2015, April 14). 2015 DMA response rate report: Direct mail outperforms all digital channels combined by nearly 600%. IWCO Direct. Retrieved from http://www.iwco.com/blog/2015/04/14/dma-response-rate-report-and-direct-mail

34. Patel, S. (2016, January 4). 5 easy ways to build more business relationships as an entrepreneur. Entrepreneur. Retrieved from https://www.entrepreneur.com/article/254465; *Harvard Business Review on reinventing your marketing.* (2011, May 7). Boston: Harvard Business Press Books.

35. Dvorak, J. C. (2015, October 21). Write an Amazon review, go to jail. *PC Magazine.* Retrieved from http://www.pcmag.com/article2/0,2817,2493493,00.asp

36. Domonoske, C. (2016, January 13). You, too, can dress like "El Chapo." NPR. Retrieved from http://www.npr.org/sections/thetwoway/2016/01/13/462901056/you-too-can-dresslike-el-chapo

37. Nicks, D. (2016, January 12). El Chapo's shirts are flying off the shelves. *Money.* Retrieved from http://time.com/money/4177540/el-chaposhirts-barabas; Masunaga, S. (2016, January 27). As seen on "El Chapo": There's a mad rush for this L.A. clothing company's shirts. *The Los Angeles Times.* Retrieved from http://www.latimes.com/business/la-fi-el-chapo-shirtmaker-20160127-story.html

38. Scenario based on Federal Trade Commission. (n.d.). FTC fact sheet: It looks good . . . but is it true? Retrieved from http://www.consumer.ftc.gov/sites/default/files/games/off-site/youarehere/pages/pdf/FTC-Ad-Marketing_Looks-Good.pdf

39. Weeks, J. (2015, October 30). Dietary supplements: Is regulation of the industry too lax? *CQ Researcher.* Retrieved from http://library.cqpress.com/cqresearcher/document.php?id=cqresrre2015103000; Wagner, L. (2015, November 17). Justice Department announces criminal charges against dietary supplement firms. NPR. Retrieved from http://www.npr.org/sections/thetwoway/2015/11/17/456396714/justice-department-announces-criminalcharges-against-dietary-supplement-firms

40. Robbins, R. (2016, January 5). Lumosity will pay $2 million to settle "deceptive" brain training claims. *Business Insider.* Retrieved from http://www.businessinsider.com/lumosity-pays-ftc-2-million-brain-training-claims-2016-1

41. Anand, S. (2012, June 19). George Clooney and Julia Roberts sue for unauthorized use of their names and images. *Advertising Law Blog.* Retrieved from http://www.lfirm.com/blog/2012/06/george-clooney-and-julia-roberts-sue-for-unauthorized-use-of-their-names-and-images.shtml

42. Duke, A. (2014, April 10). Katherine Heigl files $6 million suit against drugstore chain over tweet. CNN. Retrieved from http://www.cnn.com/2014/04/10/showbiz/katherine-heigl-duane-reade-lawsuit/index.html

43. Video released by Pershing Square Capital Management exposes senior distributors admitting that Herbalife uses a "level of inauthenticity," leading to "eventual deception." (2014, December 17). *The Associated Press.* Retrieved from http://www.readingeagle.com/ap/article/video-released-by-pershing-square-capital-management-exposes-senior-distributors-admitting-that-herbalife-uses-a-level-of-inauthenticity-leading-to-eventual-deception

44. Federal Trade Commission. (2012, May 16). Skechers will pay $40 million to settle FTC charges that it deceived consumers with ads for "toning shoes." Retrieved from https://www.ftc.gov/news-events/press-releases/2012/05/skechers-will-pay-40-million-settle-ftc-charges-it-deceived

45. Kerr, J. C. (2012, May 16). FTC: Skechers deceived customers with shoe ads. *U.S. News & World Report.* Retrieved from https://www.usnews.com/

news/us/articles/2012/05/16/feds-skechers-deceived-consumers-with-shoe-ads

46. Streitfeld, D. (2012, January 26). For $2 a star, an online retailer gets 5-star reviews. *The New York Times*. Retrieved from http://www.nytimes.com/2012/01/27/technology/for-2-a-star-a-retailer-gets-5-star-reviews.html

47. Streitfeld, D. (2012, August 25). The best book reviews money can buy. *The New York Times*. Retrieved from http://www.nytimes.com/2012/08/26/business/book-reviewers-for-hire-meet-a-demand-for-online-raves.html?pagewanted=all

48. Warner, D. (2015, April 10). The legal lowdown on fake or paid reviews. *Tech.Co*. Retrieved from http://tech.co/legal-lowdown-fake-paid-reviews-2015-04

Chapter 9

1. Sweet, K. (2017). Writing in third person in APA style. *The Pen and the Pad*. Retrieved from http://penandthepad.com/writing-third-person-apa-style-2056.html

2. Based on Survey Monkey (2017). Customers love SurveyMonkey. Retrieved from https://www.surveymonkey.com/mp/customers

3. Garner, B. (2013). *The HBR guide to better business writing*. Brighton, MA: Harvard Business Review Press.

Chapter 10

1. Troyner, R. (2014, November 20). Raleigh chooses design firm for Fire Station 6. *Triangle Business Journal*. Retrieved from http://www.bizjournals.com/triangle/morning_call/2014/11/raleigh-chooses-design-firm-for-fire-station-6.html

2. Piecewicz, M. (1999, January 12). Hewlett-Packard proposal manager. Personal communication with Mary Ellen Guffey.

3. Greenwood, G., & Greenwood, J. (2008). SBIR proposal writing basics: Resumes must be written well. Greenwood Consulting Group. Retrieved from http://www.g-jgreenwood.com/sbir_proposal_writing_basics91.htm

4. Texas A&M Transportation Institute. (2013, April 13). Voice-to-text apps offer no driving safety benefit; as with manual texting, reaction times double. Retrieved from https://tti.tamu.edu/2013/04/23/voice-to-text-apps-offer-no-driving-safety-benefit-as-with-manual-texting-reaction-times-double

5. Thomson, D. (2014, October 2). 10 research tips for finding answers online. *Ted Blog*. Retrieved from http://blog.ted.com/10-research-tips-for-finding-answers-that-elude-you

6. Goldsmith, B. (2002, June). The awesome power of asking the right questions. *OfficeSolutions*, 52; Bracey, G. W. (2001, November). Research-question authority. *Phi Delta Kappan*, 191.

7. Stuart, E. (2016, January 19). ASU professor resigns amid plagiarism accusations. *Phoenix New Times*. Retrieved from http://www.phoenixnewtimes.com/news/asu-professor-resigns-amid-plagiarism-accusations-7980419; Iyengar, R. (2015, November 25). 200 South Korean professors charged in massive plagiarism scam. *Time*. Retrieved from http://time.com/4126853/south-korea-professors-books-plagiarism-authors-publishers; McCabe, F. (2014, December 2). UNLV fires professor accused of "serial plagiarism." *Review Journal*. Retrieved from https://www.reviewjournal.com/news/education/unlv-fires-professor-accused-of-serial-plagiarism

8. Writing Tutorial Services, Indiana University. (2014, April 7). Plagiarism: What it is and how to recognize and avoid it. Retrieved from http://www.indiana.edu/~wts/pamphlets/plagiarism.shtml

9. Sharf, S. (2017, February 10). America's fastest-growing cities 2017. Retrieved from https://www.forbes.com/sites/samanthasharf/2017/02/10/americas-fastest-growing-cities-2017/#4ab074efc312

10. Saylor, M. (2012). *The mobile wave: How mobile intelligence will change everything*. New York: Vanguard Press, p. ix.

11. Office of Civic Engagement & Service. (n.d.). Definition of service learning. Fayetteville State University. Retrieved from http://www.uncfsu.edu/civic-engagement/service-learning/definition-of-service-learning

12. Park, A. (2011, January 6). Study linking vaccines to autism is "fraudulent." *Time*. Retrieved from http://healthland.time.com/2011/01/06/study-linking-vaccines-to-autism-is-fraudulent

13. Haberman, C. (2015, February 1). A discredited vaccine study's continuing impact on public health. *The New York Times*. Retrieved from http://www.nytimes.com/2015/02/02/us/a-discredited-vaccine-studys-continuing-impact-on-public-health.html

14. Perry, S. (2015, April 7). "Plagiarism, fraud, and predatory publishing" are polluting science, says bioethicist Arthur Caplan. *MinnPost*. Retrieved from https://www.minnpost.com/second-opinion/2015/04/plagiarism-fraud-and-predatory-publishing-are-polluting-science-says-bioethic

15. Iyengar, R. (2015, November 25). 200 South Korean professors charged in massive plagiarism scam. *Time*. Retrieved from http://time.com/4126853/south-korea-professors-books-plagiarism-authors-publishers

16. Edelstein, S. (2016, April 27). Now, finally, the Germans are getting scared of Tesla? Green Car Reports. Retrieved from http://www.greencarreports.com/news/1103623_now-finally-the-germans-are-getting-scared-of-tesla

17. Tufte, E. (1990). *Envisioning information*. Cheshire, CT: Graphics Press, p. 34.

18. Reena, J. (2006, October 16). Enough with the shoot-'em-ups. *Businessweek*, p. 92.

Chapter 11

1. McEwen, B. C. (2010). Cross-cultural and international career exploration and employability skills. *National Business Education Association Yearbook 2010: Cross-Cultural and International Business Education*, 48, 142.

2. Wells, A. (2017, January 9). The cost of workplace incivility. *Insurance Journal*. Retrieved from http://www.insurancejournal.com/magazines/editorsnote/2017/01/09/438162.htm; Porath, C. (2015, June 19). No time to be nice at work. *The New York Times*. Retrieved from https://www.nytimes.com/2015/06/21/opinion/sunday/is-your-boss-mean.html

3. Porath, C. (2014, November 19). Half of employees don't feel respected by their bosses. *Harvard Business Review*. Retrieved from https://hbr.org/2014/11/half-of-employees-dont-feel-respected-by-their-bosses

4. Porath, C. (2016, November 23). Civility at work helps everyone get ahead. *The Wall Street Journal*. Retrieved from https://www.wsj.com/articles/civility-at-work-helps-everyone-get-ahead-1479917555

5. Porath, C., MacInnis, D., & Folkes, V. (2011, April 17). It's unfair: Why customers who merely observe an uncivil employee abandon the company. *Journal of Service Research, 14*(3). doi: 10.1177/1094670511404393. Retrieved from http://jsr.sagepub.com/content/early/2011/04/15/1094670511404393

6. Porath, C. (2016, November 23). Civility at work helps everyone get ahead. *The Wall Street Journal*. Retrieved from https://www.wsj.com/articles/civility-at-work-helps-everyone-get-ahead-1479917555

7. Forni, P. M. (n.d.). Dr. Forni's civility web site. Johns Hopkins University. Retrieved from http://krieger.jhu.edu/civility/background.html

8. Davetian, B. (n.d.) The Civility Institute. Retrieved from http://www.civilityinstitute.com

9. Zwilling, M. (2015, August 7). 6 keys to a positive online presence and reputation. *Entrepreneur*. Retrieved from https://www.entrepreneur.com/article/249053

10. Johnson, D. (1988–2006). Dine like a diplomat. Seminar Script. The Protocol School of Washington, Columbia, South Carolina.

11. Asghar, R. (2014, May 27). Dining etiquette: The business meal as a test of character. *Forbes*. Retrieved from https://www.forbes.com/sites/robasghar/2014/05/27/dining-etiquette-the-business-meal-as-a-test-of-character/#1ad70245dd49

12. Albrecht, K. (2006). *Social intelligence: The new science of success*. San Francisco: Pfeiffer, p. 3.

13. Schawbel, D. (2013, September 4). The soft skills managers want. *Bloomberg Businessweek*. Retrieved from http://www.businessweek.com/articles/2013-09-04/the-soft-skills-managers-want

14. Grasz, J. (2014, April 10). Overwhelming majority of companies say soft skills are just as important as hard skills, according to a new CareerBuilder survey. CareerBuilder. Retrieved from http://www.careerbuilder.com/share/aboutus/pressreleasesdetail.aspx?sd=4/10/2014&id=pr817&ed=12/31/2014

15. Porath, C. (2015, June 19). No time to be nice at work. *The New York Times*. Retrieved from https://www.nytimes.com/2015/06/21/opinion/sunday/is-your-boss-mean.html

16. Ibid.

17. Hughes, T. (2008). Being a professional. Wordconstructions. Retrieved from http://www.wordconstructions.com/articles/business/professional.html; Grove, C., & Hallowell, W. (2002). The seven balancing acts of professional behavior in the United States: A cultural values perspective. Grovewell. Retrieved from http://www.grovewell.com/pub-usa-professional.html

18. Chismar, D. (2001). Vice and virtue in everyday (business) life. *Journal of Business Ethics, 29*, 169–176. doi: 10.1023/A:1006467631038

19. DeMers, J. (2015, January 29). Communication in 2015: Text, voice, video or in-person? *Inc.* Retrieved from http://www.inc.com/jayson-demers/communication-in-2015-text-voice-video-or-in-person.html; Plantronics. (2011). How we work: Communication trends of business professionals. [White paper]. Retrieved from http://www.idgconnect.com/view_abstract/25441/how-we-work-communication-trends-business-professionals

20. Mediation techniques for conflict resolution: Using online mediation. (2017, February 20). Harvard Law School Program on Negotiation. Retrieved from http://www.pon.harvard.edu/daily/mediation/dispute-resolution-using-online-mediation; Brenner, R. (2007, October 17). Virtual conflict. *Point Lookout*, Chaco Canyon Consulting. Retrieved from http://www.chacocanyon.com/pointlookout/071017.shtml; Drolet, A. L., & Morris, M. W. (2000, January). Rapport in conflict resolution: Accounting for how face-to-face contact fosters mutual cooperation in mixed-motive conflicts. *Journal of Experimental Social Psychology*, p. 26.

21. Vanderkam, L. (2015, September 30). The science of when you need in-person communication. *Fast Company*. Retrieved from https://www.fastcompany.com/3051518/the-science-of-when-you-need-in-person-communication

22. Borkowska, B. (2011). Female voice frequency in the context of dominance and attractiveness perception. *Animal Behaviour, 82*(1), 55–59; Niculescu, A., van Dijk, B., Nijholt, A., Haizhou, L., & See, S. (2013, March 31). Making social robots more attractive: The effects of voice pitch, humor and empathy. *International Journal of Social Robotics, 5*(2), 171–191; Derrick, D. C., & Elkins, A. C. (2012, November 30). The sound of trust: Voice as a measurement of trust during interactions with embodied conversational agents. *Group Decision and Negotiation, 22*(5), 897–913.

23. Grose, J. (2015, July 23). From upspeak to vocal fry: Are we "policing" young women's voices? Fresh Air. NPR. Retrieved from http://www.npr.org/2015/07/23/425608745/from-upspeak-to-vocal-fry-are-we-policing-young-womens-voices

24. Smith, J. (2013, December 20). How to use your 2013 mistakes to build a better 2014 at work. *Forbes*. Retrieved from http://www.forbes.com/sites/jacquelynsmith/2013/12/20/how-to-use-your-2013-mistakes-to-build-a-better-2014

25. Decker, K., & Decker, B. (2015, July 30). What email, IM, and the phone are each good for. *Harvard Business Review*. Retrieved from https://hbr.org/2015/07/what-email-im-and-the-phone-are-each-good-for

26. Rosenberg McKay, D. (2016, June 20). You had me at hello: Getting to know proper telephone etiquette. *The Balance*. Retrieved from https://www.thebalance.com/work-telephone-etiquette-526089

27. Plantronics. (2011). How we work: Communication trends of business professionals. [White paper]. Retrieved from http://www.idgconnect.com/view_abstract/25441/how-we-work-communication-trends-business-professionals

28. Anderson, M. (2015, October 29). Technology device ownership: 2015. Pew Research Center. Retrieved from http://www.pewinternet.org/2015/10/29/technology-device-ownership-2015

29. Ibid.

30. Keeter, S., & McGeeney, K. (2015, January 7). Pew Research will call more cellphones in 2015. Pew Research Center. Retrieved from http://www.pewresearch.org/fact-tank/2015/01/07/pew-research-will-call-more-cellphones-in-2015

31. Rainie, L., & Zickuhr, K. (2015, August 26). Americans' views on mobile etiquette. Pew Research Center. Retrieved from http://www.pewinternet.org/2015/08/26/americans-views-on-mobile-etiquette

32. Lechner, A. (2012, April 18). Better teamwork through better workplace design. *Harvard Business Review*. Retrieved from https://hbr.org/2012/04/better-teamwork-through-office

33. Gensler. (2013). 2013 U.S. workplace survey/key findings. Retrieved from https://www.gensler.com/uploads/documents/2013_US_Workplace_Survey_07_15_2013.pdf

34. Waber, B., Mangolfi, J., & Lindsay, G. (2014, October). Workspaces that move people. *Harvard Business Review*. Retrieved from https://hbr.org/2014/10/workspaces-that-move-people; Spreitzer, G., Bacevice, P., & Garrett, L. (2015, September). Why people thrive in coworking spaces. *Harvard Business Review*. Retrieved from https://hbr.org/2015/05/why-people-thrive-in-coworking-spaces; Ritz, J. (2016, January 9). See how this 1930s building in Hollywood is transformed into the workplace of the future. *Los Angeles Times*. Retrieved from http://www.latimes.com/home/la-hm-neuehouse-20160109-story.html

35. NASA collaboration with SpaceX's Red Dragon Mission. (2016, July 11). House Committee on Science, Space, and Technology. Retrieved form https://www.nasa.gov/sites/default/files/atoms/files/jreuter_reddragon_july_2016tagged_0.pdf

36. Haas, M., & Mortensen, M. (2016, June). The secrets of great teamwork. *Harvard Business Review*. Retrieved from https://hbr.org/2016/06/the-secrets-of-great-teamwork

37. Lakey, D. M. (2007). *The board building cycle: Nine steps to finding, recruiting, and engaging nonprofit board members*. 2nd ed. Washington, DC: BoardSource, p. 10.

38. Discussion of Tuckman's model based on Robbins, H. A., & Finley, M. (2000). *The new why teams don't work*. San Francisco: Berrett-Koehler, Chapter 29.

39. Zofi, Y. S. (2012). *A manager's guide to virtual teams*. New York: American Management Association, p. 1.

40. Ferrazzi, K. (2014, December). Getting virtual teams right. *Harvard Business Review*. Retrieved from https://hbr.org/2014/12/getting-virtual-teams-right

41. DeRosa, D. (2015, February 26). 3 companies with high-performing virtual teams. OnPoint Consulting. Retrieved from http://www.onpointconsultingllc.com/blog/3-companies-with-high-performing-virtual-teams

42. Geiger, F. (2014, December 22). Germany's big firms pay price for small-town ties. *The Wall Street Journal*. Retrieved from http://www.wsj.com/articles/germanys-big-firms-pay-price-for-small-town-ties-1419305459

43. The value of teamwork in the workplace. (2017). Robert Half. Retrieved from https://www.roberthalf.com/employers/hiring-advice/employee-retention/teamwork/the-value-of-teamwork-in-the-workplace; Mattson, D. (2015, February 19). 6 benefits of teamwork in the workplace. Sandler Training. Retrieved from https://www.sandler.com/blog/6-benefits-of-teamwork-in-the-workplace; Rey, J. (2010, June). Team building. *Inc., 32*(5), 68–71.

44. Ruffin, B. (2006, January). T.E.A.M. work: Technologists, educators, and media specialists collaborating. *Library Media Connection, 24*(4), 49. Retrieved from http://search.ebscohost.com

45. Ferrazzi, K. (2013, December 18). To make virtual teams succeed, pick the right players. HBR Blog Network. Retrieved from http://blogs.hbr.org/2013/12/to-make-virtual-teams-succeed-pick-the-right-players; Holtzman, Y., & Anderberg, J. (2011). Diversify your teams and collaborate: Because great minds don't think alike. *The Journal of Management Development, 30*(1), 79. doi: 10.1108/02621711111098389; Katzenbach, J., & Smith, D. (1994). *Wisdom of teams*. New York: HarperBusiness, p. 45.

46. Pratt, E. L. (2010). Virtual teams in very small classes. In R. Ubell (Ed.), *Virtual teamwork: Mastering the art and practice of online learning and corporate collaboration*. Hoboken, NJ: Wiley, pp. 93–94; Katzenbach, J. R., & Smith, K. (1994). *The wisdom of teams*. New York: HarperBusiness, p. 45.

47. Pratt, E. L. (2010). Virtual teams in very small classes. In R. Ubell (Ed.), *Virtual teamwork: Mastering the art and practice of online learning and corporate collaboration*. Hoboken, NJ: Wiley, p. 93.

48. Haas, M., & Mortensen, M. (2016, June). The secrets of great teamwork. *Harvard Business Review*. Retrieved from https://hbr.org/2016/06/the-secrets-of-great-teamwork

49. Montana Department of Transportation. (2016, June 27). Success through partnerships: Montana, Section 402. Highway safety plan for federal fiscal year 2017. Retrieved from https://www.mdt.mt.gov/publications/docs/brochures/safety/safety_plan.pdf

50. Johnson, J. (2016). Collaboration next: Planning for the way we work now and into the future. Insight to the Point, Allsteel. Retrieved from http://www.allsteeloffice.com/SynergyDocuments/WPA_Insight_Collaboration-Next.pdf

51. Feloni, R. (2015, December 19). 7 reasons why your work meetings are a waste of time—and how to fix them. *Business Insider UK*. Retrieved from http://uk.businessinsider.com/why-your-work-meetings-are-a-waste-of-time-2015-12?r=US&IR=T/#they-have-no-purpose-or-structure-1; Shellenbarger, S. (2015, July 7). Don't be the office schedule-wrecker. *The Wall Street Journal*. Retrieved from https://www.wsj.com/articles/dont-be-the-office-schedule-wrecker-1436290208; Wasted time in meetings costs the UK economy

51. £26 billion. (2012, May 20). Business Matters. Retrieved from http://www.bmmagazine.co.uk/in-business/wasted-time-in-meetings-costs-the-uk-economy-26-billion

52. Ferrazzi, K. (2014, December). Getting virtual teams right. *Harvard Business Review*. Retrieved from https://hbr.org/2014/12/getting-virtual-teams-right; Rogelberg, S. G., Shanock, L. R., & Scott, C. W. (2012). Wasted time and money in meetings: Increasing return on investment. *Small Group Research*, 43(2), 237. doi: 10.1177/1046496411429170

53. Shellenbarger, S. (2014, December 2). Stop wasting everyone's time. *The Wall Street Journal*. Retrieved from https://www.wsj.com/articles/how-to-stop-wasting-colleagues-time-1417562658

54. Rogelberg, S. G., Shanock, L. R., & Scott, C. W. (2012). Wasted time and money in meetings: Increasing return on investment. *Small Group Research*, 43(2), 237. doi: 10.1177/1046496411429170

55. Plantronics. (2011). How we work: Communication trends of business professionals. [White paper]. Retrieved from http://www.idgconnect.com/view_abstract/25441/how-we-work-communication-trends-business-professionals

56. Ferrazzi, K. (2015, Marcy 27). How to run a great virtual meeting. *Harvard Business Review*. Retrieved from https://hbr.org/2015/03/how-to-run-a-great-virtual-meeting

57. Shellenbarger, S. (2016, December 20). A manifesto to end boring meetings. *The Wall Street Journal*. Retrieved from https://www.wsj.com/articles/a-manifesto-to-end-boring-meetings-1482249683

58. Timberland's Serv-a-Palooza impacts communities worldwide. (2017). Retrieved from https://www.timberland.com/responsibility/stories/serv-a-palooza-impacts-communities-worldwide.html

59. Codrea-Rado, A. (2013, June 19). How Jeff Bezos, Richard Branson, and other business chiefs hold ruthlessly effective meetings. Quartz/Yahoo Finance. Retrieved from http://finance.yahoo.com/news/jeff-bezos-richard-branson-other-172057696.html

60. Nagarajan, J. (2016, April 17). Daily plank meeting—Going agile (literally). LinkedIn. Retrieved from https://www.linkedin.com/pulse/daily-plank-meeting-going-agile-literally-jeyaraj-nagarajan

61. Shellenbarger, S. (2015, July 7). Don't be the office schedule-wrecker. *The Wall Street Journal*. Retrieved from https://www.wsj.com/articles/dont-be-the-office-schedule-wrecker-1436290208

62. Bates, S. (2011). Running a meeting: Ten rookie mistakes and how to avoid them. Society of Actuaries. Retrieved from https://www.soa.org/library/newsletters/the-independent-consultant/2008/may/ind-2008-iss19-bates.aspx

63. Ferrazzi, K. (2014, December). Getting virtual teams right. *Harvard Business Review*. Retrieved from https://hbr.org/2014/12/getting-virtual-teams-right; Lohr, S. (2008, July 22). As travel costs rise, more meetings go virtual. *The New York Times*. Retrieved from http://www.nytimes.com

64. Ferrazzi, K. (2014, December). Getting virtual teams right. *Harvard Business Review*. Retrieved from https://hbr.org/2014/12/getting-virtual-teams-right

65. Schlegel, J. (2012). Running effective meetings: Types of meetings. Salary.com. Retrieved from http://www.salary.com/running-effective-meetings-6; Cohen, M. A., Rogelberg, S. G., Allen, J. A., & Luong, A. (2011). Meeting design characteristics and attendee perceptions of staff/team meeting quality. *Group Dynamics: Theory, Research, and Practice*, 15(1), 100–101; Schindler, E. (2008, February 15). Running an effective teleconference or virtual meeting. *CIO*. Retrieved from www.cio.com. See also Brenowitz, R. S. (2004, May). Virtual meeting etiquette. Article 601, *Innovative Leader*. Retrieved from http://www.winstonbrill.com

66. Watkins, M. D. (2013, June 27). Making virtual teams work: Ten basic principles. *Harvard Business Review*. Retrieved from https://hbr.org/2013/06/making-virtual-teams-work-ten

67. Bryant, A. (2012, April 7). The phones are out, but the robot is in. *International New York Times*. Retrieved from https://mobile.nytimes.com/2012/04/08/business/phil-libin-of-evernote-on-its-unusual-corporate-culture.html

68. Fox, J. T. (2014, October 8). Why virtual conferences will not replace face-to-face meetings. *International Meetings Review*. Retrieved from http://www.internationalmeetingsreview.com/research-education/why-virtual-conferences-will-not-replace-face-face-meetings-100145

69. Davidson, K. (2016, September 8). Soft skills in short supply? Says one reader: "Give up on the snowflakes. *The Wall Street Journal*. Retrieved from http://blogs.wsj.com/economics/2016/09/08/soft-skills-in-short-supply-says-one-reader-give-up-on-the-snowflakes

70. Graves, J. A. (2013, January 15). 25 career mistakes to banish for 2013. *U.S. News & World Report*. Retrieved from http://money.usnews.com/money/careers/slideshows/25-career-mistakes-to-banish-for-2013

71. Thompson, D.S., Butkus, G., Coquitt, A., & Boudreau, J. (2016, December 23). The right kind of conflict leads to better products. *Harvard Business Review*. Retrieved from https://hbr.org/2016/12/the-right-kind-of-conflict-leads-to-better-products

72. Ibid.

73. Silverman, R. E. (2012, February 2). No more angling for the best seat; more meetings are stand-up jobs. *The Wall Street Journal*. Retrieved from http://www.wsj.com/articles/SB10001424052970204652904577193460472598378

74. Ibid.

75. Robert Half. (2011). Business etiquette: New rules for a digital age, pp. 16, 23. Retrieved from http://www.roberthalf.com/business-etiquette

76. O'Brien Coffey, J. (2011, September). How to manage smartphones at meetings. *Executive Travel Magazine*. Retrieved from http://www.executivetravelmagazine.com/articles/how-to-manage-smartphones-at-meetings

77. Ibid.

78. Feintzeig, R. (2016, June 7). Putting meetings in "airplane mode." *The Wall Street Journal*. Retrieved from https://www.wsj.com/articles/putting-meetings-in-airplane-mode-1465358460

Chapter 12

1. Leveling up: How to win in the skills economy. (2016). PayScale. Retrieved from http://www.payscale.com/data-packages/job-skills

2. Job outlook 2015 survey. (2014, November 12). National Association of Colleges and Employers. Retrieved from http://www.umuc.edu/documents/upload/nace-job-outlook-2015.pdf

3. Gallo, C. (2014, September 25). New survey: 70% say presentation skills are critical for career success. *Forbes*. Retrieved from https://www.forbes.com/sites/carminegallo/2014/09/25/new-survey-70-percent-say-presentation-skills-critical-for-career-success/#5bc1495f8890

4. Booher, D. (n.d.). 5 tips for executives who become public speakers. Booher Research Institute. Retrieved from http://www.booherresearch.com/5-tips-executives-become-public-speakers

5. Robbins, T. (2017). Building powerful relationships with matching and mirroring. Robbins Research International. Retrieved from https://www.tonyrobbins.com/training/building-powerful-relationships-matching-mirroring

6. Smaone, V. (2015, June 24). The importance of using visual aids in a presentation. LinkedIn. Retrieved from https://www.linkedin.com/pulse/importance-using-visual-aids-presentation-vtm-smaone

7. Dr. John J. Medina as quoted in Reynolds, G. (2013). *Presentation Zen design* (2nd ed.). Berkeley, CA: New Riders, p. 97.

8. The basics. (2016). Prezi. Retrieved from http://prezi.com/the-basics

9. Atkinson, C. (2011). *Beyond bullet points* (3rd ed.). Redmond, WA: Microsoft Press.

10. Howder, R. (n.d.). About Prezi. Retrieved from http://prezi.com/about

11. Reynolds, G. (2008). *Presentation Zen*. Berkeley, CA: New Riders, p. 220. See also Reynolds, G. (2010). *Presentation Zen design*. Berkeley, CA: New Riders.

12. Booher, D. (2003). *Speak with confidence: Powerful presentations that inform, inspire, and persuade*. New York: McGraw-Hill Professional, p. 126. See also Paradi, D. (2009). Choosing colors for your presentation slides. Indezine. Retrieved from http://www.indezine.com/ideas/prescolors.html

13. Bates, S. (2005). *Speak like a CEO: Secrets for commanding attention and getting results*. New York: McGraw-Hill Professional, p. 113.

14. Wakefield, J. (2015, December 18). How to avoid "death by PowerPoint." *BBC News*. Retrieved from http://www.bbc.com/news/technology-35038429

15. Sommerville, J. (n.d.). The seven deadly sins of PowerPoint presentations. About.com: Entrepreneurs. Retrieved from http://entrepreneurs.about.com/cs/marketing/a/7sinsofppt.htm

16. Hedges, K. (2014, November 14). Six ways to avoid death by PowerPoint. *Forbes*. Retrieved from https://www.forbes.com/sites/work-in-progress/2014/11/14/six-ways-to-avoid-death-by-powerpoint/#44f8530864d4

17. Based on Berry, S. (2014, February 3). Suffer stage fright? Why you should get excited. *The Sydney Morning Herald*. Retrieved from http://www.smh.com.au/lifestyle/life/suffer-stage-fright-why-you-should-get-excited-20140203-31ww4.html

18. Graves, P. R., & Kupsh, J. (2011, January 21). *Presentation design and delivery*. Bloomington, IN: Xlibris, p. 10.

19. Booher, D. (2003). *Speak with confidence*. New York: McGraw-Hill, p. 9.

20. Ibid.

21. Korosec, K. (2015, August 24). Ten times more deaths linked to faulty switch than GM first reported. *Fortune*. Retrieved from http://fortune.com/2015/08/24/feinberg-gm-faulty-ignition-switch

22. Text, video of GM CEO Mary Barra on switch report. *USA Today*. Retrieved from https://www.usatoday.com/story/money/cars/2014/06/05/gm-ceo-mary-barra-speech-switch-recall-report/10012715

23. Search YouTube or search the top 100 speeches at American Rhetoric: http://www.americanrhetoric.com/top100speechesall.html

24. Nisen, M., & Guey, L. (2013, May 15). 23 of the best pieces of advice ever given to graduates. *Business Insider*. Retrieved from http://www.businessinsider.com/best-commencement-speeches-of-all-time-2013-5

25. Reynolds, G. (2008). *Presentation Zen*. Berkeley, CA: New Riders, pp. 64ff.

26. Mackey, S. W. (2012, November 4). Step up: Be an ambassador. Retrieved from http://sarahwmackey.com/2012/11/04/step-up-be-an-ambassador

27. How will you take part? (n.d.). Heal the bay. Retrieved from https://healthebay.org/take-part

Chapter 13

1. Gee, K. (2017, April 25). Where college seniors are falling short. *The Wall Street Journal*. Retrieved from https://www.wsj.com/articles/where-college-seniors-are-falling-short-1493118000; Gellman, L. (2016, April 26). Job outlook brightens for new college grads. *The Wall Street Journal*, p. B6; Russolillo, S. (2016, March 4). Is it a jobs report made for millennials? *The Wall Street Journal*, p. C1. Lidgett, A. (2015, October 8). More jobs for new grads? Employers want to hire 15 percent more college graduates in 2015–16 academic year: Report. *International Business Times*. Retrieved from http://www.ibtimes.com/more-jobs-new-grads-employers-want-hire-15-percent-more-college-graduates-2015-16-2132711

2. Chan, A. Quoted in Purdy, C. (n.d.). 10 job search mistakes of new college grads. Monster. Retrieved from http://career-advice.monster.com/job-search/getting-started/ten-jobsearch-mistakes-of-new-college-grads/article.aspx

3. Waldman, J. (2014, February 26). 10 things you need to know about today's job search. *Work It Daily*. Retrieved from https://www.workitdaily.com/todays-job-search

4. Bureau of Labor Statistics. (2015, March). National longitudinal surveys: Number of jobs held in a lifetime. Bureau of Labor Statistics. Retrieved from http://www.bls.gov/nls/nlsfaqs.htm#anch41; Bureau of Labor Statistics. (2014, September 18). Economic news release: Employee tenure summary. Bureau of Labor Statistics. Retrieved from http://www.bls.gov/news.release/tenure.nr0.htm; Kimmit, R. M. (2007, January 23). Why job churn is good. *The Washington Post*, p. A17. Retrieved from http://www.washingtonpost.com/wp-dyn/content/article/2007/01/22/AR2007012201089.html

5. 2015 Recruiter nation survey. (2015). Jobvite. Retrieved from https://www.jobvite.com/wp-content/uploads/2015/09/jobvite_recruiter_nation_2015.pdf

6. SHRM survey findings: Using social media for talent acquisition—Recruitment and screening. (2015). Society for Human Resource Management. Retrieved from https://www.shrm.org/hr-today/trends-and-forecasting/research-and-surveys/Documents/SHRM-Social-Media-Recruiting-Screening-2015.pdf

7. 2015 Corporate recruiters survey report. (2015). Graduate Management Admission Council. Retrieved from http://www.gmac.com/market-intelligence-and-research/gmac-surveys/corporate-recruiters.aspx

8. Laumeister, G. (2015, June 2). The hidden job market and what to do about it. DailyWorth. Retrieved from https://www.dailyworth.com/posts/3611-the-hidden-job-market-and-what-to-do-about-it-laumeister. See also Collamer, N. (2013, August 12). 6 ways to crack the 'hidden' job market. *Forbes*. Retrieved from http://www.forbes.com/sites/nextavenue/2013/08/12/6-ways-to-crack-the-hidden-job-market/#3c9bbc1c5e99

9. Stewart, R. (2015, November 25). 4 reasons why job boards are still a useful tool for employers. TalentCulture. Retrieved from http://www.talentculture.com/4-reasons-why-job-boards-are-still-a-useful-tool-for-employers

10. Fallon, N. (2016, December 26). 15 best job search apps. *Business News Daily*. Retrieved from http://www.businessnewsdaily.com/5992-best-job-search-apps.html

11. Doyle, A. (2016, March 24). What is the hidden job market? *The Balance*. Retrieved from https://www.thebalance.com/what-is-the-hidden-job-market-2062004; Collamer, N. (2013, August 12). 6 ways to crack the 'hidden' job market. *Forbes*. Retrieved from http://www.forbes.com/sites/nextavenue/2013/08/12/6-ways-to-crack-the-hidden-job-market/#1491d5c95e99; Mathison, D., & Finney, M. I. (2009). *Unlock the hidden job market: 6 steps to a successful job search when times are tough*. Upper Saddle River, NJ: Pearson Education, FI Press.

12. Richardson, V. (2011, March 16). Five ways inside the "hidden job market." Retrieved from http://www.dailyfinance.com/2011/03/16/five-ways-inside-the-hidden-job-market

13. Campbell, R. (2014, August 19). Why I do all my recruiting through LinkedIn. *The New York Times*. Retrieved from https://boss.blogs.nytimes.com/2014/08/19/why-i-do-all-of-my-recruiting-through-linkedin/?_r=0; 2014 Social Recruiting Survey. (2014). Jobvite. Retrieved from https://www.jobvite.com/wp-content/uploads/2014/10/Jobvite_SocialRecruiting_Survey2014.pdf

14. Garriott, O. (2015, February 6). 10 LinkedIn tips for students and new grads. LinkedIn Pulse. Retrieved from https://www.linkedin.com/pulse/10-tips-students-new-grads-linkedin-omar-garriott

15. Adams, S. (2012, March 27). Make LinkedIn help you find a job. Retrieved from http://www.forbes.com/sites/susanadams/2012/04/27/make-linkedin-help-you-find-a-job-2

16. Sundberg, J. (2016, February 8.) The rise of Facebook recruitment. *Link Humans*. Retrieved from http://linkhumans.com/blog/rise-facebook-recruitment

17. 2014 Jobvite Social Recruiting Survey. (2014). Jobvite. Retrieved from https://www.jobvite.com/wp-content/uploads/2014/10/Jobvite_SocialRecruiting_Survey2014.pdf

18. Gallo, A. (2014, December 19). How to write a résumé that stands out. *Harvard Business Review*. Retrieved from https://hbr.org/2014/12/how-to-write-a-resume-that-stands-out

19. Burdan, S. Quoted in Vaas, L. (n.d.). Customize your résumé for that plum job. *Ladders*. Retrieved from http://info.theladders.com/career-advice/customize-resume-for-plum-job

20. Doyle, A. (2017, April 5). How many pages should a resume be? *The Balance*. Retrieved from https://www.thebalance.com/how-many-pages-should-a-resume-be-2063305; Ryan, L. (2016, May 2). How long should my resume be? And 15 other resume tips. *Forbes*. Retrieved from https://www.forbes.com/sites/lizryan/2016/05/02/how-long-should-my-resume-be-and-15-other-resume-tips/2/#67ee223f3c48

21. Joyce, S. P. (2014, April 8). How to quickly and easily customize your résumé for each opportunity. Work Coach Café. Retrieved from http://www.workcoachcafe.com/2014/04/08/customize-your-resume

22. Doyle, A. (2016, October 21). Resume profile vs. resume objective. *The Balance*. Retrieved from https://www.thebalance.com/resume-profile-vs-resume-objective-2063185

23. Ryan, L. (2014, June 26). How to write a human-voiced resume. LinkedIn. Retrieved from https://www.linkedin.com/pulse/20140626010712-52594-how-to-write-a-human-voiced-resume

24. Ryan, L. (2014, June 26). How to write a human-voiced resume. LinkedIn. Retrieved from https://www.linkedin.com/pulse/20140626010712-52594-how-to-write-a-human-voiced-resume

25. Berrett, D. (2013, January 25). My GRE score says I'm smart. Hire me. *The Chronicle of Higher Education*, A4.

26. Korn, M. (2014, March 25). Job hunting? Dig up those old SAT scores. *The Wall Street Journal*. Retrieved from https://www.wsj.com/articles/job-hunting-dig-up-those-old-sat-scores-1393374186

27. LinkedIn for Volunteers. (n.d.). Use your skills to make a positive impact. Retrieved from https://volunteer.linkedin.com

28. Matuson, R. C. (n.d.). Recession-proof your résumé. HCareers. Retrieved from http://www.hcareers.com/us/resourcecenter/tabid/306/articleid/522/default.aspx

29. Hehman, E., Flake, J. K., & Freeman, J. B. (2015). Static and dynamic facial cues differentially affect the consistency of social evaluations. *Personality and Social Psychology Bulletin*, 1–12. doi: 10.1177/0146167215591495

30. Fisher, C. (2015, January 21). Brand YOU year: How to brand yourself without sounding like everyone else. LinkedIn Official Blog. Retrieved from http://blog.linkedin.com/2015/01/21/brand-you-year-how-to-brand-yourself-without-sounding-like-everyone-else

31. Adams, S. (2015, April 23). Seven ways to make LinkedIn help you find a job. *Forbes*. Retrieved from http://www.forbes.com/sites/susanadams/2015/04/23/seven-ways-to-make-linkedin-help-you-find-a-job/#15325a752079

32. Kreps, L. (2015, June 25). The legal risks of lying on your résumé. Shake Law.com. Retrieved from http://www.shakelaw.com/blog/lying-on-your-resume

33. Florentine, S. (2016, February 1). Why your ATS may be killing your recruiting efforts. *CIO*. Retrieved from http://www.cio.com/article/3028111/hiring/why-your-ats-may-be-killing-your-recruiting-efforts.html

34. Skillings, P. (2015, March 1). How to get the applicant tracking system to pick your résumé. Big Interview Blog. Retrieved from http://biginterview.com/blog/2015/03/applicant-tracking-system.html

35. Applicant tracking systems 101 for job-seekers: Understanding the ATS technology that dominates online job search. (n.d.). Quintessential Careers. Retrieved from http://www.quintcareers.com/understanding-applicant-tracking-systems

36. National Association of Colleges and Employers. (2015, April 1). Tips for helping students create an effective career eportfolio. Retrieved from http://www.naceweb.org/s04012015/students-create-career-eportfolio.aspx

37. Melendez, S. (2015, February 10). Why fax won't die. *Fast Company*. Retrieved from https://www.fastcompany.com/3042157/why-fax-wont-die; Null, C. (2014, January 13). Why the fax still lives (and how to kill it). *PC World*. Retrieved from http://www.pcworld.com/article/2083980/why-the-fax-still-lives-and-how-to-kill-it.html

38. The Jobvite recruiter national survey 2015. (2015, July). Jobvite. Retrieved from https://www.jobvite.com/wp-content/uploads/2015/09/jobvite_recruiter_nation_2015.pdf

39. Luckwaldt, J. H. (2015, September 28). Cover letters probably don't matter, but you still need one. PayScale. Retrieved from http://www.payscale.com/career-news/2015/09/cover-letters-probably-dont-matter-but-you-still-need-one#pageTop

40. Greenfield, R. (2016, September 28). The cover letter refuses to die. *Bloomberg*. Retrieved from https://www.bloomberg.com/news/articles/2016-09-28/the-cover-letter-refuses-to-die

41. Résumés, cover letters and interviews. (2014, April 28). Society for Human Resource Management. Retrieved from https://www.shrm.org/hr-today/trends-and-forecasting/research-and-surveys/pages/resume-cover-letter.aspx

42. Luckwaldt, J. H. (2015, September 28). Cover letters probably don't matter, but you still need one. PayScale. Retrieved from http://www.payscale.com/career-news/2015/09/cover-letters-probably-dont-matter-but-you-still-need-one#pageTop

43. Cavazos, N. (2014, April 15). Do cover letters matter? ZipRecruiter. Retrieved from https://www.ziprecruiter.com/blog/do-cover-letters-still-matter

44. Ryan, L. (2015, March 1). How to write your first pain letter. *Forbes*. Retrieved from https://www.forbes.com/sites/lizryan/2015/03/01/how-to-write-your-first-pain-letter/#c716de925465

45. Employers reveal biggest résumé blunders in annual CareerBuilder survey. (2015, December 31). CareerBuilder. Retrieved from http://www.careerbuilder.com/share/aboutus/pressreleasesdetail.aspx?sd=8/13/2015&id=pr909&ed=12/31/2015

46. Ibid.

47. Kreps, L. (2015, June 25). The legal risks of lying on your résumé. Shake Law.com. Retrieved from http://www.shakelaw.com/blog/lying-on-your-resume

Chapter 14

1. Quast, L. (2014, May 19). Job seekers: 7 tips for a successful panel interview. *Forbes*. Retrieved from https://www.forbes.com/sites/lisaquast/2014/05/19/job-seekers-7-tips-for-a-successful-panel-interview/#608914386089

2. Doyle, A. (2017, January 6). Group interview questions and interviewing tips. *The Balance*. Retrieved from https://www.thebalance.com/group-interview-questions-and-interviewing-tips-2061157

3. Cobert, A. (2017). Standing out from the crowd: How to nail a group interview. *The Muse*. Retrieved from https://www.themuse.com/advice/standing-out-from-the-crowd-how-to-nail-a-group-interview

4. Deloitte. (2017). Interview tips: From preparation to follow-up we offer seven tips to ensure a strong interview. Retrieved from https://www2.deloitte.com/us/en/pages/careers/articles/about-deloitte-careers-interview-tips.html

5. Smith, J. (2016, November 9). The perfect time to schedule your job interview. *Business Insider*. Retrieved from http://www.businessinsider.com/best-time-to-schedule-your-job-interview-2016-11

6. McIntosh, B. (2013, April 30). How to ace an interview with job success stories. Retrieved from http://www.biospace.com/News/how-to-ace-an-interview-with-job-success-stories/294802

7. Huhman, H. (2014, August 29). 7 things to research before any job interview. Glassdoor. https://www.glassdoor.com/blog/7-research-job-interview

8. Lunden, I. (2014, June 19). LinkedIn launches its first standalone job search app, privacy guaranteed. *TechCrunch*. Retrieved from https://techcrunch.com/2014/06/19/linkedin-launches-its-first-standalone-job-search-app

9. CareerBuilder. (2016, April 28). Number of employers using social media to screen candidates has increased 500 percent over the last decade. Retrieved from www.careerbuilder.com/share/aboutus/pressreleasesdetail.aspx?ed=12%2F31%2F2016&id=pr945&sd=4%2F28%2F2016

10. Ryan, L. (2015, March 21). What to wear to a job interview. *Forbes*. Retrieved from https://www.forbes.com/sites/lizryan/2015/03/21/what-to-wear-to-a-job-interview/#17449d294ad3

11. Conlan, C. (2014, April 15). The 6 worst things to wear in a job interview. *The Orange County Register*. Retrieved from http://www.ocregister.com/2014/04/15/the-6-worst-things-to-wear-to-a-job-interview

12. Active listening for interview success: How your ears can help you land the job. (2008, August 13). BioSpace. Retrieved from http://www.biospace.com/News/active-listening-for-interview-success-how-your/106881

13. Korkki, P. (2009, September 13). Subtle cues can tell an interviewer "pick me." *The New York Times*. Retrieved from http://www.nytimes.com

14. Chan, A. (2013, June 14). Top 10 interview tips for new college graduates. *The Huffington Post*. Retrieved from http://www.huffingtonpost.com/andy-chan/new-graduates-interview-tips_b_3443514.html

15. Karrass, C. L. (n.d.). *In business as in life, you don't get what you deserve, you get what you negotiate*. Beverly Hills, CA: Stanford St. Press.

16. Cowley, S. (2016, August 2). Illegal in Massachusetts: Asking your salary in a job interview. *The New York Times*. Retrieved from https://www.nytimes.com/2016/08/03/business/dealbook/wage-gap-massachusetts-law-salary-history.html?_r=0

17. Tyrell-Smith, T. (2011, January 25). Tell a story that will get you hired. *Money/U.S. News & World Report*. Retrieved from http://money.usnews.com/money/blogs/outside-voices-careers/2011/01/25/tell-a-story-that-will-get-you-hired

18. U.S. Equal Employment Opportunity Commission. (n.d.). Prohibited employment policies/practices. Retrieved from https://www.eeoc.gov/laws/practices

19. Lucas, S. (2012, February 29). When illegal interview questions are legal. CBS Moneywatch. Retrieved from http://www.cbsnews.com/news/when-illegal-interview-questions-are-legal

20. Grasz, J. (2015, April 9). 1 in 5 employers has unknowingly asked an illegal interview question. CareerBuilder. Retrieved from http://www.careerbuilder.com/share/aboutus/pressreleasesdetail.aspx?sd=4%2F9%2F2015&id=pr877&ed=12%2F31%2F2015

21. Common interview questions: What can you ask? (n.d.). Monster. Retrieved from https://hiring.monster.com/hr/hr-best-practices/small-business/conducting-an-interview/common-interview-questions.aspx; Grasz, J. (2015, April 9). 1 in 5 employers has unknowingly asked an illegal interview question. CareerBuilder. Retrieved from http://www.careerbuilder.com/share/aboutus/pressreleasesdetail.aspx?sd=4%2F9%2F2015&id=pr877&ed=12%2F31%2F2015

22. Georgevich, D. (2016, June 10). Career coach. Personal communication with Mary Ellen Guffey.

23. Stahl, A. (2015, December 5). How to ace the post-interview thank you note. *Forbes*. Retrieved from https://www.forbes.com/sites/ashleystahl/2015/12/05/how-to-ace-the-post-interview-thank-you-note/#22db46964108

24. Belli, G. (2017, January). Should we still be sending thank-you notes after interviews? PayScale. Retrieved from http://www.payscale.com/

career-news/2017/01/still-sending-thank-notes-interviews; Green, A. (2015, September 8). 21 things hiring managers wish you knew. *Business Insider.* Retrieved from http://www.businessinsider .com/21-things-hiring-managers-wish-you-knew-2015-9

25. Ryan, L. (2016, February 22). Send the perfect post-interview thank you note. *Forbes.* Retrieved from https://www.forbes.com/sites/lizryan/ 2016/02/22/send-the-perfect-post-interview-thank-you-note/ #62a5232b6d3c

26. Newman, R. (2016, May 30). Should you send a thank you note after an interview? ALWAYS. *The Huffington Post.* Retrieved from http:// www.huffingtonpost.com/entry/should-you-send-a-thank-you-note-after-an-interview_us_574c907fe4b0009f3d8494f2; Manning, K. (2016, March 4). Here's what to write in your thank-you note after a job interview. *Fast Company.* Retrieved from https://www.fastcompany .com/3057431/heres-what-to-write-in-your-thank-you-note-after-a-job-interview; Stahl, A. (2015, December 5). How to ace the post-interview thank you note. *Forbes.* Retrieved from https://www.forbes.com/sites/ ashleystahl/2015/12/05/how-to-ace-the-post-interview-thank-you-note/#22db46964108

27. Manning, K. (2016, March 4). Here's what to write in your thank-you note after a job interview. *Fast Company.* Retrieved from https:// www.fastcompany.com/3057431/heres-what-to-write-in-your-thank-you-note-after-a-job-interview

28. Owens, Y. (n.d.). 3 rules for following up with a recruiter. *The Muse.* Retrieved from https://www.themuse.com/advice/3-rules-for-following-up-with-a-recruiter

29. Smith, J. (2016, November 8). Here's exactly how many times you should follow up after a job interview. *Business Insider.* Retrieved from http:// www.businessinsider.com/how-to-follow-up-after-job-interview-2016-11

30. Ford, S. (2012, March 7). The 10 biggest mistakes when leaving your job. Retrieved from https://oiglobalpartners.com/the-10-biggest-mistakes-when-leaving-your-job

31. DeZube, D. (n.d.). How to interview to uncover a candidate's ethical standards. Monster. Retrieved from https://hiring.monster.com/hr/ hr-best-practices/recruiting-hiring-advice/interviewing-candidates/ interview-questions-to-ask-candidates.aspx

32. Number of employers using social media to screen candidates has increased 500 percent over the last decade. (2016, April 28). CareerBuilder. Retrieved from http://www.careerbuilder.com/share/ aboutus/pressreleasesdetail.aspx?ed=12%2F31%2F2016&id=pr945&sd =4%2F28%2F2016

33. Vogt, P. (n. d.). Entry-level salary (probably) isn't as negotiable as you think. Monster. Retrieved from http://career-advice.monster.com/ salary-benefits/negotiation-tips/entry-level-salary-negotiable/article .aspx

34. Lee, J. (2017, May 12). Average starting salaries for new grads is on the rise. *Inc.* Retrieved from https://www.inc.com/jenna-lee/about-to-graduate-your-starting-salary-may-be-something-to-smile-about. html; Camera, L. (2016, October 5). Hiring, starting salaries on the rise for college graduates. *U.S. News & World Report.* Retrieved from https://www.usnews.com/news/articles/2016-10-05/ hiring-starting-salaries-on-the-rise-for-college-graduates

35. DeZube, D. (n.d.). Ten questions to ask when negotiating a salary. Monster. Retrieved from https://www.monster.com/career-advice/ article/10-salary-negotiation-questions

36. Reshwan, R. (2016, June 6). 3 strategies for salary negotiations. *U.S. News & World Report.* Retrieved from http://money.usnews.com/money/ blogs/outside-voices-careers/articles/2016-06-06/3-strategies-for-salary-negotiations; Lankford, K. (n.d.). Step-by-step guide to negotiating a great salary. Monster. Retrieved from https:// www.monster.com/career-advice/article/salary-negotiation-guide; Malhotra, D. (2014, April). 15 rules for negotiating a job offer. *Harvard Business Review.* Retrieved from http://hbr.org/2014/04/15-rules-for-negotiating-a-job-offer/ar/3; Hansen, R. S. (n.d.). Job offer too low? Use these key salary negotiation techniques to write a counter proposal letter. Quintessential Careers. Retrieved from http://www. quintcareers.com/salary_counter_proposal.html; Hansen, R. S. (n.d.). Salary negotiation do's and don'ts for job-seekers. Quintessential Careers. Retrieved from http://www.quintcareers.com/salary-dos-donts.html

37. Hamilton, K. (2017, January). The careful art of negotiating your first salary. PayScale. Retrieved from http://www.payscale.com/ salary-negotiation-guide/the-art-of-negotiating-your-first-job-offer

Index

Italic page numbers indicate illustrative information in figures.

NUMBERS

3-x-3 writing process, 38, 76
  drafting, 39, *40, 41*
  pacing, 40
  planning, *41*
  prewriting, 39, *40, 41*
  revising, 40, *40, 41*, 63, 87
6-x-6 rule, 375

A

abbreviations
  avoid, 6, 22, 46, 124
  in business letters, A-5, A-6, A-7, A-9
  of job titles, 422
  period use with, D-30
  plural forms of, D-7
  of states, territories, and provinces,
    A-9, A-10
  in Twitter, 440
ABI/INFORM (ProQuest), 295
  search result page, *296*
abstract or executive summary, 286, *286*
academic courses and degrees,
    capitalization of, D-34
acceptance message, job, 467, 470, 482
accountability, 10
acronyms, 22
action invitation, in audience
    engagement, D-34
action items, *99*
action requests, *40, 99*, 120
  in claim messages, *159*, 160, 171
  in direct claims, 160
  in e-mail messages, *4*
  in feasibility reports, 270, *272*
  in persuasive claim e-mail, *225*
  persuasive message flowing
    upward, *227*
  in persuasive messages, 237
  rejecting, 197
  in request messages, 153–154
adaptation, 44
adapting the message, 41
adapting to audience
  bias-free language, 49–50
  developing "you" view, 36, 44–45, 52
  preferring plain language and familiar
    words, 50
  sounding conversational but
    professional, 45–46
addressee notations, business letters, A-3
addresses
  in block letter style, A-4, A-7

in business letters, 151, *152*, A-3, *A-4,*
    A-5, A-6, D-19
  capitalization of, D-34
  comma use with, C-1, D-20
  on cover letter, 429, 430, 431
  on envelope, A-8–A-9, A-10
  formatting of, 257
  of former supervisors, 465
  on interview follow-up message, 464
  local styles and conventions in, 21
  number use in, D-38
  on résumé, 410, 418
adjectives, 332
  capitalization of, 258, D-33
  comma use with, D-22, D-23–D-24
  comparative, D-15
  excessive use of, 90, 91
  forms, D-15
  function of, D-6
  guidelines for use, D-15–D-16
  hyphenation of, C-1
  positive, D-15
  proper, D-33
  superlative, D-15
  vivid, 95
adjustment messages, 150, 163–166,
    170, *171*
  explaining compliance and
    apologizing, 165
  writing, *163*
Adobe Presenter, 371
advanced search feature, 296
adverbs, 68, 69
  capitalization of, 258
  comparative, D-15
  excessive use of, 90
  forms, D-15
  function of, D-6
  guidelines for use, D-15–D-16
  positive, D-15
  in redundancy, 90, 91
  superlative, D-15
advertisements, *92*
  analyzing target company's, 449
age-biased language, *50*
ages, number use in, D-39
AIDA (attention, interest, desire, action)
    strategy, 229, 233, 236, 237
  for sales messages, *230*
Amazon, *329*
  meetings at, *344*
ambiguity, in intercultural
    communication, 21
American Psychological Association
    (APA), 310, 313, 318

American Psychological Association
    (APA) format, B-1–B-3
  direct quotation, B-2
  journal article reference, anatomy
    of, *B-3*
  justification/recommendation report,
    270–271
  references, B-3, *B-4*
  in-text format, B-2
  text page and references, portions
    of, *B-2*
APA. *See* American Psychological
    Association (APA)
Apache OpenOffice Impress, 371
apologies, 192–193, *195*
  in adjustment messages, 165
apostrophes, C-1
  basic rules for use, D-28–D-29
  in plurals, 49
appearance, 15
  of business documents, 14, *15*
  of business space, 15
  personal, 14, 15
appendixes, 311
  as back matter component, 310, 313
  in business reports, *291*
  in proposals, *286*, 312
Apple, *344*
Apple Calendar, 344
Apple Keynote, 371
Apple Watch, *8*
applicant tracking system (ATS), 399, 409,
    411, 421, 422, 433
applications
  follow-up messages, 466
  forms, 465–466, 470
  sharing, *9*
appositives, comma use with, D-22
Ask (Internet search tool), 296
assumptions, 23
ATS. *See* applicant tracking system (ATS)
attention, in audience engagement, *235*
attention line, in business letters, A-5
audience, 364–365
  analysis and report organization, *254*
  analyzing, 364
  benefits, 44, *223*
  connecting with, 365–371
  engagement, *235*, 365–366, *366, 370*
  profiling, *42*
  rapport, 369–371, 384
  response, *67*
  types, *364*
authority, 224
awkward expressions, C-1

B

back matter, 310–311
bad news, 66
  announcing to employees, *204, 205*
  announcing to employees and the public, 204–205
  announcing using direct strategy, *189*
  cushioning, 195–196
  delivering, *191*, 206
  delivering in person, 201–202
  delivering sensitively, *191*
  delivering within organizations, 207
  follow-up message, *200*
  indirect strategy for delivering, *190*
  managing within organizations, 201–206
  in refusing requests, *197*, 203
  See also negative messages; negative news
bar charts, 304, *305*
  in business reports, *303*
behavioral questions, in job interviews, 459–460
Bezos, Jeff, *344*
bias-free language, 49, *49, 50*, C-1
  in business messages, *52*
big ideas, in request messages, 153
Bing, 296
block style, in business letters, A-7
bloggers, *93*
blogging, 127–131
  best practices, 130–131
  by businesses, 128–130
blogs, *9, 43*
  best practices, 135
  corporate, 128
  writing, *131*
body
  of adjustment messages, *163*
  in AIDA strategy, *230*
  of blogs, 130
  of direct response letter, *152*
  of e-mail messages, 117
  of formal reports, 309–310
  of instruction messages, *157*
  of persuasive requests, *222*
  of response messages, *155*
body art, *14*
body language, 12
  monitoring of, 15
Booher, Dianna, 65
brackets, quotation mark use in, D-32
brainstorming, *64*
Branson, Richard, *344*
briefs, *363*
brochures, 228
buffers
  in delivering bad news, *190, 191, 204, 205*
  in e-mail denying a claim, *202*
  opening indirect messages with, 191–192

  in refusing typical requests and claims, *197*
  in refusing workplace requests, *203*
Buffet, Warren, 13
business cards, 408
business communication, effect of culture on, *16*
business documents, eye appeal of, 14
business etiquette skills, 327, 350
  developing, 326–330
business letters, *A-4*
  body of, A-5
  for delivering messages outside an organization, 151
  folding of, A-10
  font, A-2
  formatting of, 151–152
  formatting with Microsoft Word, A-3
  letter style, A-7
  margins, A-2–A-3
  parts of, A-3
  for positive and neutral messages, 170
  punctuation, A-3, A-7
  spacing, A-3
  for transmitting requests and replies, 153
business messages, 38
  analyzing the purpose, 41
  audience benefit focus, 44
  focus, *44*
  professionalism, *46*
  profiling the audience, *42*
  sounding conversational but professional, 45, 46
  tailoring to the audience, 42
  tone, *46*
  using direct strategy, 66
business phrases, trite, 92
business presentations, 376–379
  after, 383–384
  creating, 362–365
  delivery techniques, 385
  organizing body of, 366–368
  polishing and following up, 380–384
  preparing and rehearsing for, 381–382
  types of, 384
  See also multimedia presentations; oral presentations
business proposals
  external, 286–287
  formal, *286*, 312, 313
  informal, *286*, 288, 312
  internal, 286–287
  preparation of, 285–291
business protocol, 326
business reports
  collecting information for, 261–262
  components of, *291*, 308–312
  determining the problem and purpose, 259–261
  formal, *292, 293, 294*, 311–312, *311*

  formatting of, 256
  functions of, 253
  gathering and analyzing survey data for, *262*
  heading levels, *256*
  informal, *291*
  organization of, 254–255, 263, 291–294
  preparation of, 252–256, 291–294
Business Source Premier (EBSCO), 295
business writing, 51
businesslike language, *94*
buzzwords, *93*, 94

C

calendar programs
  for scheduling meetings, *345*
  See also Apple Calendar; digital calendars
calls to action
  blogs, 131
  in customer direct request e-mail, *154*
capitalization, *99*, C-1, D-33–D36
  to aid comprehension, 97
  in e-mail messages, *119*
  of headings, *260*
  of numbers, D-35
Carbonite, *8*
career opportunities, investigating, 401–402
CareerBuilder, 401, 433
Carter, Stephen L., 328
celestial bodies, capitalization of, D-36
cell phones. *See* telephone
challenging questions, in job interviews, 457
channel, communication, 43
  for announcing bad news, 204
  in business messages, *51–52*
  lean or rich, *43*
charts
  bar, *303*, 304, *305*
  flip, *372*
  flow, *302, 306*
  line, *303, 305*
  organizational, *303*, 307
  pie, *303, 306*
  segmented line, *305*
chat, *9*, 45
Chatter, 132
Chicago Manual of Style (CMS), 303, 313
Chismar, Douglas, 328
citation formats, 303
civility, 326, 327
claim justification, in persuasive claim e-mail, *225*
clarity, 88, *92*, C-1
  in business messages, *52*, 102
  comma use for, D-24
  in communicating negative news, 187
  enhancing, 47, 92–95